The Politics
of Ancient Israel

LIBRARY OF ANCIENT ISRAEL

Douglas A. Knight, *General Editor*

Sage, Priest, Prophet: Religious and Intellectual Leadership in Ancient Israel
Joseph Blenkinsopp

Oral World and Written Word: Ancient Israelite Literature
Susan Niditch

Scribes and Schools: The Canonization of the Hebrew Scriptures
Philip R. Davies

The Israelites in History and Tradition
Niels Peter Lemche

Reconstructing the Society of Ancient Israel
Paula M. McNutt

The Religion of Ancient Israel
Patrick D. Miller

The Politics
of Ancient Israel

NORMAN K. GOTTWALD

WESTMINSTER JOHN KNOX PRESS
LOUISVILLE, KENTUCKY

Scripture quotations are the translations of the author from the original languages.

Book design by Publishers' WorkGroup
Cover design by Kim Wohlenhaus

First edition
Published by Westminster John Knox Press
Louisville, Kentucky

This book is printed on acid-free paper that meets the American National Standards Institute Z39.48 standard. ∞

PRINTED IN THE UNITED STATES OF AMERICA
01 02 03 04 05 06 07 08 09 10 — 10 9 8 7 6 5 4 3 2 1

Library of Congress Cataloging-in-Publication Data

Gottwald, Norman K. (Norman Karol), 1926–
    The politics of ancient Israel / Norman K. Gottwald.
      p. cm.
    Includes bibliographical references (p.) and index.
    ISBN 0-664-21977-2
    1. Jews—Politics and government—To 70 A.D. 2. Jews—Civilization—To 70 A.D. 3. Bible. O.T.—Criticism, interpretation, etc. 4. Politics in the Bible. 5. Religion and state—Biblical teaching. I. Title.
DS111.2.G68 2000
320.933—dc21

00-043428

OZYMANDIAS

I met a traveller from an antique land,
Who said:— "Two vast and trunkless legs of stone
Stand in the desert. Near them, on the sand,
Half-sunk, a shattered visage lies, whose frown
And wrinkled lip, and sneer of cold command,
Tell that its sculptor well those passions read
Which yet survive, stamped on these lifeless things,
The hand that mocked them and the heart that fed:
And on the pedestal these words appear:
'My name is Ozymandias, king of kings:
Look on my works, ye Mighty, and despair!'
Nothing beside remains. Round the decay
Of that colossal wreck, boundless and bare
The lone and level sands stretch far away."

—Percy Bysshe Shelley, 1817

Contents

Foreword

xi

Acknowledgments

xiii

Abbreviations

xv

1. **Introducing Ancient Israelite Politics
   as an Interpretive Minefield**

   1

   Problematic Historical Sources

   1

   Ancient Near Eastern Political Context

   2

   Privileging Israel's Religion

   3

   Possible Histories

   4

   What Politics Leaves Out

   4

   Whose Politics?

   5

2. **Conceptualizing Politics: Beyond and Within Ancient Israel**

   7

   Politics as an Activity and as a Subject of Inquiry

   7

   Traditional Approaches to Israelite Politics

   12

   The Biblical Mapping of Israelite Politics

   15

   A Trajectory through Three Political Horizons

   15

   A Political Trajectory United, Divided, and Truncated

   16

   "Israel" and "Judah" as Ambiguous Historical Agents

   17

   A Political Trajectory Based on Problematic
      but Instructive Sources

   22

   Israelite and Ancient Near Eastern Political Pathways

   25

   Criticism, Imagination, and Ideology in Political Inquiry

   27

3. **Israelite Politics According to the Hebrew Bible** 32
   Politics in the Hebrew Bible: "Handle with Care" 32
   Israel's Decentralized Politics 35
      The Progenitors of Israel 36
      Israel from Egypt to Canaan 37
      Israel Settling in the Land 39
   Israel's Centralized Politics 45
      Israel under One State Regime 45
      Israel under Two State Regimes 52
      Characteristics of Israel's Centralized Politics in Biblical Texts 71
         Political History Depicted in Confusing Montage 71
         One People in Two Polities 74
         Gaining and Keeping Political Power 75
         Polemical Versions of State Religion 78
         Shifting and Declining Diplomatic and Military Fortunes 87
         Building Projects as Monuments to State Power 90
         Funding the State Apparatus 92
         Administering the State Apparatus 94
   Israel's Colonial Politics 96
      Neo-Babylonian Political Hegemony 97
      Persian Political Hegemony 100
      Hellenistic Political Hegemony 106
      Characteristics of Israel's Colonial Politics in Biblical Texts 108

4. **The Ancient Near Eastern Matrix of Israelite Politics** 113
   The Emergence of the State in the Ancient Near East 113
   Ancient Near Eastern Political Trajectories:
      Structures and Strategies 120
      Mesopotamia from 3000 to 1550 B.C.E. 121
      Egypt from 3000 to 1550 B.C.E. 127
      Mesopotamia, Anatolia, and Syro-Palestine from
         1500 to 538 B.C.E. 132
      Egypt from 1500 to 538 B.C.E. 138
      Mesopotamia, Egypt, Anatolia, Iran, and Macedonia
         from 538 to 63 B.C.E. 140
   Summary Assessment of Ancient Near Eastern Politics 144
      Primacy of State Power 144
      Maintenance of State Power 145
      State Economy 145
      State Administration 145

State Ideology   146
State Fragility   147
States as Aspiring Empires   147
Ephemeral States amid Ongoing Cultures   148
Multilingual Diplomacy and Multilingual States   149
Judah and Israel as Ancient Near Eastern States   150
    The Temporal Scale   150
    The Spatial Scale   150
    The Independence-Dependence Scale   150
    The Geopolitical Scale   151
    Political Division and Diminished State Power   152
    State Transmission and Cultivation of Prestate Traditions   152
    Small-Scale Tributary Monarchies   153
    The Dubious Claim of Participatory Government   153
    The Struggle for Dynastic Continuity   154
    The State and Judicial Institutions   155
    States Transformed into Religiocultural Enclaves   155
    The State and Religious Ideology   156

5. **Critically Imagining the Politics of Ancient Israel**   **158**
Israel's Decentralized Politics   158
Whence the Prestate Traditions?   159
    Actual Prestate Origins   159
    Early State Origins   159
    Late State Origins   159
    Colonial Origins   160
Why Were Prestate Traditions Preserved?   160
How Credible Are the Preserved Prestate Traditions?   162
Israel's Politics Centralized in a Single State   172
Why the Move to Statehood?   172
How Did the State Secure Its Hold?   176
Was Tenth-Century Israel an Actual State?   181
Israel's Politics Centralized in Two Rival States   185
Israelite and Judahite Archaeological Data   186
    Material Remains   186
    Texts and Inscriptions   190
Non-Israelite Texts and Inscriptions   192
Synthesis of Biblical and Extrabiblical Data on the Monarchy   198
    Modest Political Centralization   198
    A Larger, More Multicultural and Cosmopolitan Northern State   199

A Smaller, More Monocultural and Insular Southern State   200
Two States Struggling under Imperial Pressure   200
State Involvement in Foreign Trade   201
State Involvement in the Domestic Economy   202
The State and Literacy   203
Comparability of Israel and Judah to Other
    Ancient Near Eastern States   204
The Political Agenda of Israel and Judah   210
    Foreign Affairs and the Political Agenda of Israel and Judah 212
        Relations between Israel and Judah   212
        Relations with Neighboring States   216
        Relations with the Great Powers   222
    Domestic Affairs and the Political Agenda of Israel and Judah 227
        Relations within the Political Center   227
        Relations between the Political Center and Its Primary
            Beneficiaries   229
        Relations between the Political Center and the
            General Populace   231
Israel's Colonial Politics   235
    Extrabiblical Data: Material and Textual Evidence   236
    From Centered Autonomous Politics to Dispersed
        Dependent Politics   238
    The Political and Transpolitical Matrix of the Hebrew Bible 240
    Hasmonean "Exceptionalism"   242
    Was There a Distinctive Ancient Israelite Polity?   243

6. Epilogue   246
    Summing Up Ancient Israelite Politics   246
    The Legacy of Ancient Israelite Politics   249

Notes   253

Bibliography   321

Index of Biblical Passages and Ancient Sources   349

Index of Authors   354

Index of Subjects   359

Foreword

The historical and literary questions preoccupying biblical scholars since the Enlightenment have focused primarily on events and leaders in ancient Israel, the practices and beliefs of Yahwistic religion, and the oral and written stages in the development of the people's literature. Considering how little was known about Israel, and indeed the whole ancient Near East, just three centuries ago, the gains achieved to date have been extraordinary, due in no small part to the unanticipated discovery by archaeologists of innumerable texts and artifacts.

Recent years have witnessed a new turn in biblical studies, occasioned largely by a growing lack of confidence in the "assured results" of past generations of scholars. At the same time, an increased openness to the methods and issues of other disciplines such as anthropology, sociology, linguistics, and literary criticism has allowed new questions to be posed regarding the old materials. Social history, a well-established area within the field of historical studies, has proven especially fruitful as a means of analyzing specific segments of the society. Instead of concentrating predominantly on national events, leading individuals, political institutions, and "high culture," social historians attend to broader and more basic issues such as social organization, conditions in cities and villages, life stages, environmental contexts, power distribution according to class and status, and social stability and instability. To inquire into such matters regarding ancient Israel shifts the focus away from those with power and the events they instigated and onto the everyday realities and social subtleties experienced by the vast majority of the population. Such exploration has now gained new force with the application of various forms of ideological criticism and other methods designed to ferret out the political, economic, and social interests concealed in the sources.

This series represents a collaborative effort to investigate several specific topics—societal structure, politics, economics, religion, literature, material culture, law, intellectual leadership, ethnic identity, social marginalization, the international context, and canon formation—each in terms of its social dimensions and processes within ancient Israel. Some of these subjects have not been explored in depth until now; others are familiar areas currently in need of reexamination. While the sociohistorical approach provides the general perspective for most volumes of the series, each author has the latitude to determine the most appropriate means for dealing with the topic at hand. Individually and collectively, the volumes aim to expand our vision of the culture and society of ancient Israel and thereby generate new appreciation for its impact on subsequent history.

In the present volume, Norman Gottwald's treatment of the politics of ancient Israel moves well beyond the usual focus on the centralization of power to a fresh appraisal informed by current thinking on social structures and interactions. His approach—a "critically imaginative construal of ancient Israelite politics," as he calls it—is to cast the net broadly over the expanse of political activity in the country, trying to catch indications of the wielding of power at all stages and levels of Israelite society. Such a strategy is warranted because the biblical text represents the point of view of centralized authority, primarily from a relatively late period, and tends not to disclose the ideological interests at its core. Gottwald begins his perceptive study with a sketch of Israelite political history as recounted in the biblical literature. Then, mindful of the subtle nature of political power as it intertwines with the economic, social, and religious strands of the people's lives, he details the situations prevailing during the various periods of, first, the prestate communitarian culture; second, the state structures in the monarchies of both North and South; and finally, the colonial environment under imperial control. In contrast to the biblical portrayal, Gottwald argues that politics is not confined to the public realm of national affairs, but rather that power is widely diffused, always present to some degree in the local settings of family and village and, under the kings, shared with clients, bureaucrats, and cultic, commercial, and military figures. Despite some scholars' claims about Israel's distinctive character, his analysis of Israelite statehood in the context of its ancient Near Eastern neighbors reveals considerable similarity among them in their strategies and capacities to wield power. He also concludes that, contrary to the impression given by the Hebrew Bible, Yahwistic religion influenced the culture but was unable to maintain control over the politics of the country. Gottwald's sensitive analysis of the elusive yet far-reaching subject of politics thus leads to a new appreciation of its complexities in ancient Israel, including its role in virtually all aspects of life and thought.

Douglas A. Knight
General Editor

Acknowledgments

The possibility of conceiving this book as a departure from customary political histories of ancient Israel rests solidly on the foundation of recent exploding advances in the several methodological branches of biblical studies and ancient Near Eastern studies, as well as on similar ground-breaking approaches in archaeology, historiography, and the social sciences, especially in anthropology and political theory. Interdisciplinarity is no longer a longed-for goal but a practical possibility and an operative modality for increasing numbers of biblical scholars. My indebtedness to workers in all these disciplines, far too numerous to name, is extensively documented in the notes and bibliography.

Over the entire course of this project, my editor, Douglas A. Knight, has been constant in his encouragement and unfailing in his response to the questions with which I have peppered him from time to time. His comments on the unrevised draft have been unerringly helpful. Jack M. Sasson, who is as well informed about ancient Near Eastern studies as any biblical scholar, has offered copious comments on chapter 4 that have aided me in catching outright errors, in taking account of recent advances in the field, and in enriching my bibliographic sources. I am much in his debt. To Christine Dungan I owe special thanks for her painstaking preparation of the bibliography and index, which has enabled publication to proceed on a timely course.

Norman K. Gottwald
Berkeley, California
May 2000

Abbreviations

AASOR	Annual of the American Schools of Oriental Research
AB	Anchor Bible
ABD	*Anchor Bible Dictionary*. Edited by D. N. Freedman. 6 vols. New York, 1992.
AGJU	Arbeiten zur Geschichte des antiken Judentums und des Urchristentums
ANET	*Ancient Near Eastern Texts Relating to the Old Testament*. Edited by J. B. Pritchard. 3d ed. Princeton, 1969.
ASTI	Annual of the Swedish Theological Institute
BA	*Biblical Archaeologist*
BAR	*Biblical Archaeology Review*
BARead	*Biblical Archaeologist Reader*
BASOR	*Bulletin of the American Schools of Oriental Research*
BibInt	*Biblical Interpretation*
BJS	Brown Judaic Studies
BN	*Biblische Notizen*
BTB	*Biblical Theology Bulletin*
BWA(N)T	Beiträge zur Wissenschaft vom Alten (und Neuen) Testament
BZAW	Beihefte zur Zeitschrift für die alttestamentliche Wissenschaft
CAH	*Cambridge Ancient History*
CANE	*Civilizations of the Ancient Near East*. Edited by J. Sasson. 4 vols. New York, 1995.
CBQ	*Catholic Biblical Quarterly*
ConBOT	Coniectanea biblica: Old Testament Series
CurBS	*Currents in Research: Biblical Studies*
ErIsr	*Eretz-Israel*
FAT	Forschungen zum Alten Testament
FOTL	Forms of the Old Testament Literature
HSM	Harvard Semitic Monographs
HUCA	*Hebrew Union College Annual*

ICC	International Critical Commentary
IDB	*The Interpreter's Dictionary of the Bible.* Edited by G. A. Buttrick. 4 vols. Nashville, 1962.
IEJ	*Israel Exploration Journal*
IESS	*International Encyclopedia of the Social Sciences.* Edited by D. L. Sills. New York, 1968.
IOS	*Israel Oriental Society*
JAAR	*Journal of the American Academy of Religion*
JAOS	*Journal of the American Oriental Society*
JBL	*Journal of Biblical Literature*
JCS	*Journal of Cuneiform Studies*
JESHO	*Journal of the Economic and Social History of the Orient*
JHNES	Johns Hopkins Near Eastern Studies
JNES	*Journal of Near Eastern Studies*
JSOT	*Journal for the Study of the Old Testament*
JSOTSup	Journal for the Study of the Old Testament: Supplement Series
JSS	*Journal of Semitic Studies*
JTSA	*Journal of Theology for Southern Africa*
OBT	Overtures to Biblical Theology
OLA	Orientalia lovaniensia analecta
Or	*Orientalia* (NS)
OTL	Old Testament Library
RB	*Revue biblique*
RelSRev	*Religious Studies Review*
RSO	*Revista degli studi orientali*
SAAS	State Archives of Assyria Studies
SAOC	Studies in Ancient Oriental Civilizations
SBLMS	Society of Biblical Literature Monograph Series
SBLSBS	Society of Biblical Literature Sources for Biblical Study
SBLWAW	Society of Biblical Literature Writings from the Ancient World
SemeiaSt	Semeia Studies
SHANE	Studies in the History of the Ancient Near East
SJOT	*Scandinavian Journal of the Old Testament*
SWBA	Social World of Biblical Antiquity
TDNT	*Theological Dictionary of the New Testament.* Edited by G. Kittel and G. Friedrich. Translated by G. W. Bromiley. 10 vols. Grand Rapids, 1964–76.
TDOT	*Theological Dictionary of the Old Testament.* Edited by G. J. Botterweck and H. Ringgren. Translated by J. T. Willis, G. W. Bromiley, and D. E. Green. 8 vols. to date. Grand Rapids, 1974–.

VT	*Vetus Testamentum*
VTSup	Supplements to Vetus Testamentum
WBC	Word Biblical Commentary
ZAW	*Zeitschrift für die alttestamentliche Wissenschaft*

Chapter 1

Introducing Ancient Israelite Politics as an Interpretive Minefield

In traditional critical biblical scholarship, treatment of the politics of ancient Israel has consisted principally of writing the political history of Israel in a straightforward and largely unproblematic manner, drawing primarily on the Hebrew Bible, supplemented and corrected at points by archaeology and ancient Near Eastern texts. To be sure, there are recognized problems of gaps in the sources, contradictory versions of events, and presumed distortions here and there in the historical record. In the main, however, critical historians have been inclined to trust the biblical record in its overall depiction of events and in most of its details, with confidence that what was omitted in that record can be dependably supplied from external information or from well-reasoned hypotheses, and that this correction and supplementation can be done without upsetting the basic biblical framework. Many historians of ancient Israel continue to hold this optimistic view, and are even encouraged in it by the conviction that the accumulating archaeological evidence validates the overall biblical account. An examination of existing political histories of ancient Israel reveals a rather modest spectrum of differences in the reconstructions they offer based on the fundamental outline of the biblical traditions. If this approach is adopted, our political discourse about ancient Israel will consist of a point-by-point assessment and evaluation of the veracity of biblical traditions and will adhere closely to the paradigms provided by the Hebrew Bible.

PROBLEMATIC HISTORICAL SOURCES

Today, however, we stand in the midst of grave reservations about the reliability of the biblical texts for reconstructing history in any assured form. These caveats arise from two intersecting lines of thought. One caution follows from the perceived lateness of the final compilation of the Hebrew Bible, which in the eyes of many scholars throws into severe doubt the tenability of the information related about earlier historical periods. The events reported (narrated time) and the setting of those reporting (narrators' time) are perceived to be so far removed from one another, often by many centuries, that the very capacity of late traditionists to reconstruct earlier history is thrown into doubt. The second caution overlaps with and reinforces the first, namely, that the late compositors of the Hebrew Bible were so preoccupied with and limited by the horizons of their commitment to fashion a new "Israelite-Jewish" community following the destruction of the states of Israel and Judah, that their ideological perspective altogether cancels out any interest on their part in reporting the actual history of Israel before the collapse of those states.

On this view of our sources, when the factors of late composition of the traditions and their ideological alienation from Israel's preceding history are taken together, it is concluded that we simply cannot rely on the Hebrew Bible to tell us anything substantial about the history of Israel prior to the fifth-fourth centuries B.C.E. In short, the determinative writers/editors of the Hebrew Bible had little or no reliable information about earlier times and, in any case, were primarily interested to shape or invent images and accounts of the past that served their immediate interests in rebuilding Israelite/Jewish identity on a new foundation. If this approach is adopted, our political discourse about ancient Israel will proceed under grave suspicion about the biblical records and will seek some basis for assessing the politics of ancient Israel that does not fundamentally rely on a late, jaundiced account. Whether there exist sufficient resources outside of the Hebrew Bible to compensate for the fragile biblical resources is itself highly problematic. As a consequence, our dilemma as historians is that without a large measure of reliance on the Hebrew Bible, the politics of ancient Israel may remain undecipherable.

ANCIENT NEAR EASTERN POLITICAL CONTEXT

Unfortunately, in the midst of this deep dispute about the historicity of the Hebrew Bible, there has been a decline of interest in situating the politics of ancient Israel within the wider world of ancient Near Eastern politics. Even the most radical critics do not deny that there were monarchies in Israel and Judah, even as they dispute the events that preceded them, how early they were formed, how accurately they are represented in the Hebrew Bible, as well as the level of development they reached before they were cut short by larger powers. While disputing the internal development of Israelite politics, neither the more traditional nor the more radical historians of ancient Israel have thought much about Israelite politics in a comparative Near Eastern framework. To be sure, they have looked at the reported interactions of the Israelite states with other states and they have explored the possible institutional borrowings of Israel in fashioning its own political structures. But the larger issue of Israel's participation in a wider and pervasive political culture has not been addressed in necessary depth. Were the Israelite states more or less the same as other ancient Near Eastern states, or were they different in fundamental respects? When we address the politics of ancient Israel, is that domain a familiar instance of generic ancient Near Eastern politics, or is Israelite politics a phenomenon apart? What can be said about the interplay of generic and specific features in Israel's politics?

PRIVILEGING ISRAEL'S RELIGION

Bedeviling our inquiry is the bearing of Israelite religion on all inquiries into ancient Israel. The Hebrew Bible emphatically privileges religion as the primary factor in the history of Israel. The religious criteria invoked in the biblical traditions to assess the politics are claimed as decisive. The subsequent canonical appropriation of the Hebrew Bible by Judaism and Christianity has served to elevate that same set of criteria to a normative status, even for critical historians. When we evaluate the politics of ancient Israel, we are inevitably evaluating its religious component as reported by the Hebrew Bible. To question the politics is necessarily to question the religion. In the past, critical historians did not view the religion of Israel as a serious obstacle to discerning its political history, since they felt confident of making a judicious critical separation between the successive phases of Israelite religion, on the one hand, and between Israelite religion and contemporary religious views influenced by the Hebrew Bible, on the other hand. More radical historians contend, however, that the religious privileging of the Hebrew Bible is an abiding legacy that has insinuated itself so pervasively into all historical inquiry about ancient Israel that we remain under the spell of a sacred aura surrounding the very subject of biblical Israel.

In terms of our inquiry into the politics of ancient Israel, the issue might be put as follows: because the Hebrew Bible claims to record the achievement of a monotheism that is accepted as authoritative by Judaism and Christianity, are we to read the politics of ancient Israel in terms of that normative monotheism? Many historians aver that they do not so read, since they allow that the religion of Israel developed only slowly into the sort of monotheism generally accepted today. More skeptical historians insist, however, that we continue to read not only the religion of ancient Israel, but also its political life, as though they seamlessly formed a sacred realm of nascent or triumphant monotheism, severed in the last analysis from its wider secular matrix.

POSSIBLE HISTORIES

Alongside these issues arising from within the debate over the historicity of the biblical traditions, there are perspectives emanating from the fields of historiography, the philosophy of history, the social sciences, and literary and cultural criticism that are beginning to engage the attention of biblical scholars. These concerns have to do with the nature of history as an envisioned past and the role of observers who offer imaginative scenarios of that past. There is a lively sense of the textuality of all history and of the inevitably constructed nature of every reading of the past. The notion that we possess some unquestioned objective referent of "real events" against which the textual testimonies about the past can be definitively judged is presently either abandoned or sharply qualified. The result is not to forgo historical reconstructions but to offer them with greater self-awareness as to their hypothetical character, and to acknowledge that multiple readings of past history are in principle as tenable as multiple readings of present history. It is fairly easy to recognize that ancient commentators offered "metaphoric" or "mythic" constructions of the past to ground their understanding of the communities in which they lived. What has not been so evident is that we contemporary historians, with all our improved historiographic methods, make similar "metaphorical leaps" when it comes to the way we shape our readings of the past. We have more refined methods of research and fuller data, and are likely to be aware of greater complexity in past events than our forebears, but we too make overarching construals of the meaning of the past that are not simply the result of adding up many events and processes. We make synthetic judgments, attribute meaning and significance to the past, and proceed to appropriate our insights about the past as wisdom for the present. Furthermore, every such historiographic project can be disputed in sum or in part by yet another project relying more or less on the same body of evidence seen from a differing perspective.

WHAT POLITICS LEAVES OUT

Besides this sense of the fragility and indeterminacy of all readings of history, there is a renewed sense that what has passed for history, especially political history, is only a part of the human story. Much is omitted from the accounts of political regimes, or is only indirectly expressed or implied. These omissions have to do in part with the conditions that contributed to the exercise of political power by particular persons and groups and the conditions that contributed to the loss of that power. These omissions have also to do with how the subjects of political power have viewed the power exerted over them and how they have cooperated with or resisted that power, as well as the concrete effects that political power has had on their daily lives. New forms of historical and anthropological inquiry are raising these questions as absolutely vital to a proper understanding of politics as one network among others in the total field of social and cultural interaction. At the same time, many literary critics are coming to recognize that texts are not self-contained entities isolated from the social and political world in which they are produced, and that the most innocent of ostensibly "non-political" writings may speak tellingly of power relations in society. Political power is mediated, both internalized and resisted, through symbolic constructs that are thoroughly textual. Thus, what counts as evidence of "politics" may not easily be circumscribed by a single definition, and certainly not by one that refers only to the official actions of formal political bodies and their leaders.

WHOSE POLITICS?

Both in the realization that every telling of history is a fresh construal and that the political past embraces more than any single telling is capable of grasping, "ideology" has become a seminal term in historiographic discussions. Ideology presents two faces to historians. One of them opens out toward relativism, even solipsism, with the possible implication that all renderings of history are equally arbitrary and incommensurable. The other opens out toward modesty and self-awareness in offering our versions of history, challenging us to great care in our reading of evidence and daring us to be willing to revise our readings as we engage in discourse with counter-readings. In any case, it is futile to overlook that the way we historians understand the present is a major factor in how we read the past and that adjudication of past meanings is possible only in discourse and not by fiat. This sobering reality, that "subjective" historical readings are only negotiable in "intersubjective" discourse, implies that alternative or competing readings of history inevitably chasten and inform one another, such that any momentarily "majority" reading carries with it the caveats and reservations posed by its dialogue partners. Moreover, although a dominant reading of history may appear self-evident, a careful examination of its claims will expose traces of self-contradiction, arbitrariness, and insufficiency. While any particular reading of history, political or otherwise, may be relatively powerful in its coherence and adequacy in answer to certain questions of current importance, no reading is ever final. This is because the questions to be asked of history are inexhaustible and because the possible ways of answering them with some plausibility are equally inexhaustible. Granted that fiction and historiography display many genre differences, what Carlos Fuentes has said of the protean character of the novel genre is also applicable to construals of history: "The novel is a question that cannot be contained by a single answer, because it is social and society is plural. The novel is an answer that always says: 'the world is unfinished and cannot be contained by a single question'" (cited in the *New York Times Book Review,* Feb. 16, 1986). Because the world of the contemporary historian is perplexingly "unfinished," the world of ancient Israelite politics is also defiantly "unfinished." All this is to say that the present critically imaginative reading of Israelite politics, cogent as it may appear in its author's eyes, is necessarily open-ended and, in the last analysis, simply stands as one among a throng of alternative readings.

Conceptualizing Politics:
Beyond and Within Ancient Israel

POLITICS AS AN ACTIVITY AND AS A SUBJECT OF INQUIRY

The subject of politics is approached in so many ways and with such diverse conclusions that it is advisable to begin this study with a clarification of its presuppositions and methodological pathways. Seldom have studies of Israelite politics taken the trouble to lay out systematically their understanding of politics as a general field of discourse. The consequence is that we are left to infer why observers of Israel's past have pictured its politics in one way or another, both in terms of what counts as politics and in what relation politics stands to the other aspects of corporate life.

Power is the ability to marshal and apply resources toward strategic ends "exercised not only against the inertia of things, but against the *resistance of opposing wills*."[1] In the present inquiry, politics will be viewed as the public exercise of power, coupled with the legitimation of its use, within a given social and territorial space. In our traditional accounts of the human past over the last five thousand years, the most familiar and dominant form of political power is the institution of the state. Nevertheless, the state is not the only instantiation of public power, an observation that is of particular relevance to the full sweep of Israelite political history. Political power is practiced and legitimated through an institutional network that claims and enforces its authority in specified jurisdictions of the corporate life. Political power has to do with the mastery of natural and human resources for the achievement of goals that involve or affect an entire populace. Politics, however, is not simply coextensive with, nor does it exhaust, all the sources of power in a society. Typically, political power coordinates and channels, or represses and neutralizes, other forms of social power toward its own ends. Critical to any investigation of politics is the exploration of how the realm of political power is related to the other spheres of communal power at each juncture of a people's history.

Political power networks thrive in sustained interaction with economic, social, military, and ideological power networks. Additional candidates for the status of power networks are technology, culture, and religion. For the purposes of this study, technology is subsumed under the economic and military networks, while culture and religion are subsumed under social and ideological networks.[2] Political power is significantly intertwined with the exercise of power in these other networks. On the one hand, these corporate sources of power serve to limit political power and to shape the forms political power will take. On the other hand, the extrapolitical power sources have the capacity to enhance political power and to facilitate innovative actions in the political sphere.

Broadly considered, political power is of two kinds. The incipient political power network may be decentralized and embedded in the other networks to such an extent that its agents are subject to reprimand or recall by the community, or, alternatively, they are unable to prevent dissenting members of the community from withdrawing from their jurisdiction. This is the situation in societies that lack state institutions.[3] On the other hand, the political power network may be centralized and autonomous to the extent that it can perpetuate its authority and power without reliable recourse to revision, recall, or escape by the governed except through extraordinary institutional disruptions. This is the situation in societies that have developed state institutions. While there is no generally agreed upon definition of the state, the dividing line between embedded and autonomous political organization is widely recognized.[4]

To be sure, as will be abundantly clear in this examination of ancient Israelite politics, there is great difference of opinion as to whether or not particular known societies exhibited state polities. This uncertainty follows in part because of differing criteria for statehood, but it also stems from the social reality that movement from prestate to state political organization is frequently incremental and even largely "hidden" from the awareness of social actors, in both its mechanisms and its implications, until it has become an accomplished and not easily reversible fact.

Succinctly put, the nonstate political sector has limited *coordinating* powers, while the state political network has far-reaching *commanding* powers. As the sine qua non of statist politics, this capacity to coordinate by means of command is well expressed in the following formulation:

> Although one could multiply the ways in which human activities become "political," the main point lies in the "relating" function performed by political institutions. Through the decisions taken and enforced by public officials, scattered activities are brought together, endowed with a new coherence, and their future course shaped

> according to "public" considerations. In this way political institutions . . .
> serve to define, so to speak, "political space" or the locus wherein the
> tensional forces of society are related.[5]

What defines the state is its emphatic claim to exercise a monopoly of power over "the tensional forces of society" by enforcing its will within its stated jurisdiction, but the actual effectiveness of the state in enforcing that claim is dependent on many inhibiting and enabling circumstances. To be sure, the state also claims that this monopoly of power serves the general welfare of its subjects, but the extent to which that claim to legitimacy is acknowledged and internalized by the subject populace is one of the variable factors in the viability and longevity of states.

The formal study of politics is focused centrally on the political power network that exercises the highest authority over the broadest jurisdiction. This sovereign network is characteristically the state, whose structures and functions may be misperceived as the sum and substance of politics. In this study, a broader view of politics is taken in two respects.

First, in acknowledging that societies without specialized governmental organs also practice politics, we recognize that the members of those societies marshal communal energies and structures to negotiate diverse interests and resolve conflicts that overrule the desires of any single member or group. In such stateless societies political power is at play through social institutions and leadership roles that do not possess a monopoly of force but depend variously on prestige, custom, consensus, negotiation, feuding, arbitration, and honor/shame sanctions to sustain the polity. This means in principle that politics, in the sense of striving to have particular needs and interests protected or served by the community at large, is pursued with varying explicitness and intensity throughout all social spheres. In short, the absence of a differentiated political network does not mean the absence of politics, but rather the dispersal and diffusion of politics into the existing economic, social, cultural, and ideological networks.[6]

Second, in polities with differentiated state institutions, where political power is centralized, political power struggles do not cease in the other networks. The state seldom has the interest, or indeed the means, to intervene in all those lower-level political activities, since they are too numerous to monitor them all closely, and, in any event, from the state's perspective most substate politics may be trivial, or at least nonthreatening, to its overarching sovereignty. Even in those instances where the state feels impelled to be involved, it does not always have the power to control the terms and outcomes of political skirmishes in the economic, social, cultural, and ideological spheres. One route to the collapse of a political regime is by way of a gathering combination and amplification of many lesser political tensions and conflicts that eventuate in a palace or army coup, or in a broader rebellion, or precipitate the dissolution of the state altogether.[7]

Insofar as possible, the politics of any particular society must be traced in its interconnections with all the other public power networks. To treat politics in deliberate or naive isolation from the other corporate power networks yields a partial and superficial understanding. In practice, this means that it is not enough to give a descriptive profile of political offices held and functions performed, nor is it sufficient to trace a narrowly formulated history of political institutions and practices. In studying decentralized politics in political anthropology, for instance, this is readily recognized, because politics is so embedded in and intertwined with other societal institutions that no political profile or history may be possible that is not already a more general social or cultural history.[8] To some observers, however, state politics gives the deceptive impression of being a self-contained system. While it is unquestionably true that the state exhibits an autonomous political apparatus, it is simply unable to function without the assistance or compliance of the other power networks in its realm. As a result, both the accomplishments and failures of states are fundamentally conditioned by how they interface with those extrapolitical power networks and are consequently able or unable to marshal economic, social, military, and ideological resources for their distinctive projects.

Any particular political order, such as ancient Israel's, can be roughly characterized according to one or another typology of political forms and, on that basis, can be compared with other polities anywhere in time or space that are perceived to exhibit similar characteristics. It is often helpful to know what sorts of features one is likely to encounter in a particular polity in the light of information from what appear to be structurally related polities.[9] There are, however, at least two limitations to a comparativist approach. First, the ideal types of political order are admitted abstractions, heuristically valuable to be sure, but nonetheless abstractions. They are probative constructs based on certain generalizable patterns perceived to be operative in large numbers of specific cases. Their utility in classifying forms of political power is only a springboard to the analytic task of characterizing the particularities of each polity under consideration. Thus, political typologies assist us in laying out the range of political options that have been pursued by societies, but they are no more than a rough-hewn starting point for characterizing particular polities. Second, the typologies of political order are notably ahistorical. To the extent that they are rendered temporal, they tend to invoke a process of evolutionary development in which the less advanced political types give way to more advanced types in a virtually preordained movement toward greater complexity and enhanced power, often conceived unreflectively as social or moral "progress." However, this evolutionary assumption is itself a theoretical construct that does not unerringly accord with the history of politics in which the accumulation of political power has been uneven in its temporal pace and in its geographical distribution. Some particular polities have not "evolved" into greater complexity, while others have "devolved" to less complex forms. Nor is the social or moral superiority of one political type over another self-evident. Every polity must be examined in its particular historical location in terms of prevailing sociocultural, intellectual, and moral conditions. The pertinent historical location to be determined embraces the past political experience on which the polity draws, the interactive configuration of all the sources of domestic power, and the relations with foreign polities.

In sum, a proper study of any polity cannot be pursued by straightforward deduction from a typology of political forms or from a social evolutionary scheme. The "types" do not give us prescriptively the actual detail we seek but rather suggest the sorts of detail we may expect to find, but which in fact may or may not be present in any given instance, while the evolutionary "stages" of political development posit a trajectory that is grossly hypothetical, able to do no more than alert us to the possibility of transitional developments in any given polity. The patterns of formal and evolutionary typologies are much too blunt and schematic to give us access to the nuance and interplay of known historical polities.[10] Moreover, neither type of analysis directly addresses or settles the question of how well particular historical polities have served their constituents or whether a particular political type can be said to be in the best interests of humankind. Only political philosophy and ethics, rooted in claims about the fundamental needs of human beings, can formulate such judgments.

On the other hand, in saying that polities must be historically located, this study does not endorse the notion that all we have to do is lay out seriatim a host of data about a polity, whether chronologically or functionally, with the assumption that once they are catalogued, the data will become self-explanatory. To the contrary, what the present approach has in mind is a twofold perspective on the data: a local-historical time perspective and a world-historical time perspective. To attend to *local-historical time* means to investigate the specific ways the political network interacts with other domestic power networks and with foreign polities to produce political consequences for the society as a whole. To invoke *world-historical time* means to place the particularities of each local political experience in the context of preceding, contemporary, and subsequent political dynamics within the geopolitical domain deemed relevant to illuminating the local politics under consideration.[11]

In charting a dialectical course between local- and world-historical times, we may expect to identify certain patterns that emerge over spans of time and place, but they will be seen as historically emergent patterns. They will not be premised on assumptions about the unfolding essence of political types, but upon discernment of what has happened when all the sources of public power interact in the political arena to produce certain results in polities anchored differentially in time and space. This double focus of local- and world-historical time is necessary when comparing polities, but it is also an advisable perspective when investigating single polities such as ancient Israel.

It is, therefore, evident that this approach is broadly comparative in orientation, since it operates to correlate the political experience of many societies as a resource for understanding any one polity under examination. The critical point, however, is that these political experiences are correlated with reference to the varied conjunctions of historical circumstances as they operate from case to case rather than in terms of abstract typological and evolutionary categories that obscure the twists and turns of specific political histories. It is evident that an accumulation of social power, and of political power in particular, is noticeable over the course of human history, made possible by advances in technology, means of communication, and social organization. Nonetheless, human history has not followed a course of unbroken enhancement of political power, and it is not a history that can be affirmed as inevitable except by a theoretical gesture that is constantly embarrassed by the unanticipated convolutions of history.[12] What we are seeking in conjuring any portion of the political experience of humankind is neither a jumble of discrete data nor a one-size-fits-all grand theory, but a discernment of the sorts of conjunctions of factors that tend to recur from polity to polity, without dismissing the stubborn eccentricities of particular histories.

TRADITIONAL APPROACHES TO ISRAELITE POLITICS

It seems fair to say that the examination of ancient Israelite politics, in spite of prolific efforts, has been disappointingly superficial and incomplete.[13] Apart from the notorious problem of limited sources of information, the inquiry has been severely hampered by unexamined conceptions of politics as consisting of the structures and acts of states without sufficient anchorage to the social surround in which the formal politics were set. For example, the office of the king and the composition of the royal bureaucracy have been repeatedly examined, as have been the fortunes of the states of Israel and Judah vis-à-vis other states. The governmental institutions and offices of other ancient Near Eastern states have been scrutinized as possible models on which Israel and Judah drew in forming their state administrations. Many of these studies have been enriched by incorporating material and inscriptional remains that greatly increase our knowledge of the world of politics at the time. There is no doubt that these intensive delimited studies, comparing particular Israelite and ancient Near Eastern political institutions, constitute a large and necessary part of the project of understanding ancient Israelite politics.

The deficiency of these undertakings is that all too often they have proceeded in a narrowly descriptive manner that does not take the further step of exploring the connections between the explicitly political institutions and the other aspects of corporate life. Little attention has been paid to the interplay between politics and other sources of social power, and the interest in the connection between other ancient Near Eastern polities and Israel's way of pursuing politics has for the most part been selectively focused on institutional parallels and possible borrowings by Israel or on specific interstate diplomatic exchanges and military confrontations, particularly those referred to in biblical texts. There has been far less interest in pursuing a wider analysis of the enabling impulses and the limiting constraints operative within state polities in that ancient world. Moreover, because the main source of information about Israelite politics has been the Hebrew Bible, religion has been accorded an exaggerated and uncritical role as the prime mover in shaping Israelite politics.

Contributing to the weakness of prevailing studies of ancient Israelite politics is an inhibiting "empiricist" or "positivist" conception of what constitutes historical knowledge. Because the Hebrew Bible presents spotty political information composed or compiled at an indeterminate, and probably considerable, temporal remove from the events it describes, it has been tempting either to sketch a political portrait of ancient Israel restricted to the supposed "hard facts," or, confident that the religious authority of the text warrants great trust in its historical information, to credit most of its political information with solid facticity. These "secular" and "religious" positivisms are equally unsatisfactory. Neither of them takes account of the specific texture of "biblical historiography" (or "history-like" tradition) that defies and baffles modern categories of fiction and nonfiction.[14] Biblical reportage about the past is misrepresented when treated primarily as a repository of allegedly factual data that are to be voted valid or invalid on a point-by-point basis, on the one hand, or accepted at face value, on the other hand. This strongly positivist bent in representing ancient Israelite politics is deeply complicated by the long accretion of Jewish and Christian views about biblical authority and about the relation between religion and politics as they are articulated in biblical traditions.

To overcome this excessive historical "factualism," whether in its skeptical or credulous versions, requires an altered stance toward "doing history" that is sensitive to the reciprocal interplay between historical reconstruction and the literary imagination of its sources as articulated in a diversity of genres. A more generous view of the value of biblical sources for understanding the politics within and behind the text must be accompanied by a clear distinction between the religion and politics of ancient Israel and the religious and political experiences and outlooks of subsequent Jewish and Christian traditions and their spillover into secular political discourse. This is not to deny the palpable lines of connection between the biblical traditions and later appropriations of those traditions, nor is it to claim naively that a contemporary student of ancient Israel's politics can break free of later assumptions about biblical religion and politics simply by an act of will. It is rather to say that the biblical horizons, themselves already multiple, and the later diverging interpretive horizons have become so thoroughly mixed, conflated, and even homogenized, that a strenuous effort must be made to clear a space for those ancient Israelite politics to assume a particular shape that may or may not be accordant with how they have come to be viewed in mainstream Jewish, Christian, and Western secular political discourse.[15] The present study will raise critical questions and offer some perspectives and proposals for releasing ancient Israelite politics from the stranglehold of historical and religious positivism.

The most fruitful course for recovering the ancient Israelite political scene is to situate the offices and functions of Israel's political institutions in the historical vortex of corporate life where all the contending and cooperating networks of power met in varying patterns of collaboration, competition, and conflict. In particular, this means that the course of Israel's political life must be investigated without the premature closures of interpretation imposed by the moral and religious judgments of biblical writers and modern interpreters whose viewpoints, while they must be carefully considered, dare not be uncritically canonized as the final word on the subject. That being said, however, the religion of ancient Israel cannot be elided from an investigation of its politics, since all the political traditions in the Hebrew Bible are colored or framed by the ideologies of the traditionists. Moreover, it can be predicated with certainty that ancient Israel, like all other polities in its world, exhibited a religious component in its politics. The extent to which the nexus of politics and religion in ancient Israel corresponded to or diverged from biblical reports is a matter to be investigated. The point is that no particular biblical voice and no particular modern assessment should be allowed to swamp the discourse about Israel's politics without challenge and interrogation. Discourse about ancient Israelite politics must necessarily be at least a many-sided conversation among diverse biblical, ancient extrabiblical, and contemporary voices both scholarly and lay. A still wider conversation, beyond the scope of this study, would include biblical commentators over the centuries and political theorists and practitioners who have been informed in some measure by the biblical traditions.

THE BIBLICAL MAPPING OF ISRAELITE POLITICS

When we approach ancient Israel from the twofold perspective of local historical time and world historical time, certain features of its reported political experience suggest the strategies to be followed in this inquiry.

A Trajectory through Three Political Horizons

Probably the single most pervasive feature of the biblical political map is its insistent periodization of the Israelite political experience. The history of ancient Israel as recounted in its foundational document, the Hebrew Bible, stretches across three zones or horizons of political organization.

1. *First Horizon.* In its beginnings, Israel practiced a form of decentralized politics embedded and diffused throughout its social institutions (approximately 1250–1000 B.C.E.).

2. *Second Horizon.* In its midlife, Israel adopted centralized autonomous politics in a double sense: it developed specialized state institutions with a monopoly of domestic power that was also autonomous over against other states, even though its unitary polity split apart and the exercise of local power was radically curtailed by the intrusion of foreign states prior to the eventual loss of political independence (1000–586 B.C.E.).

3. *Third Horizon.* In its reconstituted life after the loss of statehood, Israel was forcibly subjected to a colonial form of centralized politics dictated by foreign sovereignties within which a native Israelite/Judahite hierarchy was empowered to act in local matters subject to the limits imposed

by imperial powers, broken only by an eighty-year span of independence in late Hellenistic times (586–63 B.C.E.).

A Political Trajectory United, Divided, and Truncated

It is crucial to observe that, according to the Hebrew Bible, the entire Israelite people did not journey together on the same trajectory of political transformation. For the last two-thirds of this political journey, Israelites followed two independent pathways. All Israel is said to have been involved in the initial decentralized stage and to have remained united in the first phase of statehood. Thereafter, however, the people split into two independent states. Both these states were eventually destroyed, the one after 200 years and the other after 350 years, whereupon their former subjects passed into colonial servitude. However, whereas the experiences of both state branches are recounted in the Hebrew Bible, the history of the northern branch is abruptly cut off when its state collapses in 722 B.C.E. The Hebrew Bible no longer considers the northerners to be legitimate members of Israel, either insisting that they would have to join southern Judah on its own terms (as in Chronicles) or refusing northern overtures altogether (as in Ezra–Nehemiah). The rationale given is that these northerners have so departed from the rule of the Davidic dynasty and have become so intermixed with other peoples that they have ceased to bear an Israelite identity. Consequently, since the biblical traditions trace the history of two separate polities stemming from an originally unified people, and then cease to treat the survivors of one of those polities as a segment of Israel, we are plunged into critical questions about the completeness and adequacy of this truncated and partisan representation of ancient Israelite politics.

In the first instance, we see clearly that the vantage point from which the whole history is recounted is that of the colonial Judahite community. Although much is said about the northern Israelites as long as they formed an independent state, a northern colonial Israelite voice is entirely absent from the traditions with the telling exception of the request of northern leaders to have a part in rebuilding the Jerusalem temple under Persian auspices (Ezra 4:1–2). Although this overture was rebuffed by the Judahite leaders (Ezra 4:3; cf. Neh. 2:20), it clearly implies that the northern survivors continued to identify themselves as genuinely Israelite, a perception amply supported by the ongoing Samarian community of Yahweh adherents. On the other hand, the dispute over rebuilding the temple does not obscure what appears to have been the major concern of the northern leaders and their counterparts in other provinces bordering Judah, namely, to prevent rebuilding of the walls of Jerusalem, strongly suggesting that their primary quarrel with Judah was fundamentally geopolitical (Ezra 4:6–23; Neh. 2:17–20; 4:1–9).

This exclusion of northern Israelites from the ongoing narrative underscores both the dissension among Israelites in drawing the boundaries of their community and the stark reality that in the end we have only the voice of one branch of self-identified Israelites concerning these conflicts. The Hebrew Bible describes this breach in Israel largely in religious terms, but the political grounds of the schism can be inferred from the way the biblical traditions recount the fortunes of northern statehood and the way in which Samarians, who constituted one community of colonial northerners, seem to have maintained strained relations with Judahite Yahwists until the final breach between the two communities in the second century B.C.E.

Second, if the last third of Israel's political journey is presented in so biased a way, we are led to wonder about the alleged unity of the people in the period before the split into two kingdoms. The biblical traditions presuppose a religious foundation for the unity of tribal Israel and the so-called "united" kingdom of Saul, David, and Solomon. The subsequent breach is explained by a religious declension on the part of the north, aided and abetted by Solomon's religious infidelities. But if this presumed religious unity is not to be taken for granted in preexilic Israel, what basis would remain for tribal and early monarchic Israel to have conceived of themselves as one people? Can we find more general cultural and social grounds for an early sense of community among these people to which religion and politics could have made further contributions, both reinforcing unity and generating conflict and division? The multiple and shifting identities of "Israel" within the biblical traditions deeply complicate our inquiry, but it appears that the unsettling problematic of Israelite identity was central to the stormy course of its political history.[16]

"Israel" and "Judah" as Ambiguous Historical Agents

One measure of the ambivalence about the identity of the people who are the subjects of the Hebrew Bible is found in the primary terms used to describe them. These terms are "Israel/Israelite(s)" and "Judah/Judahite(s)." These two sets of terms have some identifiable core meanings that distinguish them from one another; however, over the course of the reported history, additional meanings accrue to these terms, and their employment in particular textual contexts sometimes entails subtle shifts in semantic reference.[17] An overview of these variable usages will help to demonstrate the complex interrelation of cultural, political, and religious factors at play when "Israel" and "Judah" are conceptualized in biblical narratives as historical agents.

Israel is the encompassing name both for a tribally organized *people* who are said to share common culture and religion, and for the *area* they occupy in the central highlands of Palestine. In addition to its regular use in the Hebrew Bible to indicate this stateless society, it also appears in one Egyptian text.[18] Somewhat curiously, given the people's close tie to Yahweh, the name Israel is compounded with El, the more general Semitic term for deity, and carries the probable meaning of "El reigns" or "El is supreme."[19] This suggests that all or a major part of Israel once worshiped El before Yahweh was adopted as the community's primary deity.[20] By contrast, Judah is the name of only one of the member tribes of Israel. The relationship between Israel and Judah is personified in a father-son metaphor. The forefather Jacob, whose name is changed to Israel, becomes the progenitor of all the tribes, including Judah (Gen. 29:1–30:24; 32:22–32; 35:16–18). There are, however, indications that Judah did not join the other tribes of Israel until just before the state was formed, and perhaps not before the time of David.[21]

Under Saul, Israel becomes a kingdom, which may or may not have included Judah. David first becomes king of Judah and subsequently is accepted as king by the remainder of the tribes. The expanded kingdom of David, now composed of all the tribes, bears the name of Israel to denote a dynastic state rather than a confederation of tribes, although the latter connotation may be carried in some occurrences of the name and on occasion a double entendre may be intended, that is, Israel as a state composed of tribes and/or as a confederation of tribes that has become a state. When the kingdom divides after the death of Solomon, the northern tribes that had been the heart of the prestate society, and thus the matrix in which the term Israel first arose, adopt the name of Israel for their newly formed state. The continuing Davidic state in the south, composed solely of Judah and Benjamin, acquires the name of its principal member, Judah. This surprising adoption by the northern kingdom of the very name of the state it had rebelled against is understandable in that the northern tribes felt themselves to be the rightful inheritors of the old tribal confederacy of Israel whose norms they regarded as greatly abused in Solomon's "pseudo-Israel." The choice of the Davidic kingdom to call itself Judah appears to follow from the political reality that in the first stage of David's kingship he had ruled only over Judah, and it was to the same limited territorial scope that the rule of his dynasty reverted with the loss of the other tribes except for Benjamin. Possibly the choice of names for the two kingdoms may indicate that the term "Israel" was not so freighted with decisive religious meaning at the time as to preclude the southern kingdom from finding its Yahwist religious identity fully expressed by the terms "Judah" or "House of David."

Throughout the history of the two kingdoms, the northern and southern states are consistently called Israel and Judah respectively. However, the term Israel continues to be freighted with a wider cultural, and especially religious, meaning. It stands as a semantic marker for the community of Yahweh worshipers, and there is every indication that both kingdoms were officially devoted to the cult of Yahweh, albeit in differing manifestations, even when other deities were acknowledged. Various groups within the political entities Israel and Judah disputed over which of the two kingdoms, and which rulers within them, best preserved the old tribal heritage of "Israel," conceived as a sociocultural and religious legacy. The narrators of the book of Kings believe that the kingdom of Judah was the truest embodiment of sacral "Israel," but interestingly they also have a measure of praise for the preservation of Yahweh worship in the state of Israel, and they condemn many kings of Judah for their infidelity.[22] Chronicles, while dismissive of northern kings and strongly committed to the sole legitimacy of the Jerusalem cult, allows that sacral Israel is at least potentially present among those northerners willing to return to the Judahite fold.[23]

This notion that Israel was not simply coterminous with any single political entity has been variously described as the concept of greater Israel, wider Israel, larger Israel, or inclusive Israel. All of these descriptors are defensible, but the present study will avoid the label "greater Israel," since that term is frequently used to refer to the notion of a maximal Israelite empire extending from the border of Egypt to the Euphrates River, which finds expression in several biblical texts, presumably based on a Davidic-Solomonic geopolitical template (Gen. 15:18; Ex. 23:31; Deut. 1:7; 11:24; Josh. 1:4). The more inclusive Israel that haunts the biblical texts is the notion of a community of true worshipers of Yahweh. Although problematically equated with any particular political regime, this "imagined community" is not at all a disembodied "spiritual" community but a tangible social reality that entails "political" expression in the sense of actual embodiment of communally determined goals and values in its corporate life.[24]

With the fall of the state of Israel, a pronounced shift in the Israel/Judah semantics occurs. The populace of the northern kingdom, shorn of its leadership by deportation and intermixed with peoples from other parts of the Assyrian empire, is understandably no longer called Israel in a political sense, since the kingdom of Israel had perished. More portentous for subsequent developments, the survivors of the state of Israel are not spoken of by the biblical writers as members of inclusive Israel. Influential voices in the state of Judah assert the notion of Judah as the sole carrier of the religiocultural heritage of Israel. We are not told of the fate of the northerners once many of them have been deported and the rest have been incorporated into an Assyrian province. It is assumed that their culture and religion are so bastardized that they are no longer recognizable participants in inclusive Israel. In a sense, without renaming the kingdom of Judah as the kingdom of Israel, the southerners reclaim the heritage for which inclusive "Israel" stands, in part by incorporating into their own traditions narratives, prophecies, and songs that originated in the north. In Judahite eyes, northern "Samarians" (2 Kings 17:29) are an amalgam of the former subjects of the fallen state of Israel and foreign colonists introduced by the Assyrians whose superficial worship of Yahweh was intermixed with and thoroughly corrupted by polytheistic cults.[25]

For those Judahites who viewed themselves as the sole authentic members of an Israel committed to Yahweh, whose outlook shaped subsequent traditions, the eventual fall of the southern kingdom constituted a crisis. Judah as a state no longer existed, although Judah as a territory remained to become a Persian province to which a body of exiled expatriates returned in order to realize a purified communal expression of Israel. But this restored Judah, claiming to be in sole continuity with primal Israel, was no longer "inclusive" in the old sense. The resident or dispersed apostate northerners were judged to have forfeited their role in Israel as the community of Yahweh worshipers. Either, as in Ezra and Nehemiah, they were altogether inadmissible to the restored Judahite community, or, as in Chronicles, they could "re-enroll" individually as participants in Judahite "Israel" only by accepting the beliefs and practices that had come to be dominant in Judah. Since Chronicles issues this "invitation" in a historical retrospect of the kingdoms, it is not clear how the author envisions northern participation in Judahite worship now that both kingdoms have fallen, nor is it clear whether the Chronicler's more lenient attitude to northerners, putting them "on probation" as it were, precedes or follows the more stringent policies of Ezra and Nehemiah, or arose in direct challenge to the latter.

As to the actual course of events, there was an ongoing body of northerners who worshiped Yahweh and considered themselves "Israel," as is evident in their later cultivation of the Pentateuch as scripture and in their erection of a temple to Yahweh, and as is hinted at earlier by a troupe of northern pilgrims in mourning garb who journey toward Jerusalem to offer sacrifices on the destroyed temple site (Jer. 41:4–5). Moreover, it seems that, until the conclusive break between the Judahite Hasmonean kingdom and the Samarians toward the end of the second century B.C.E., uneasy relations were maintained between members of the two communities.[26]

If the restored Judahite leadership was increasingly "exclusive" in its conception of Israel in that it required strict religiocultural standards for Yahweh worship that excluded deviant believers both in Judah and Samaria, this "narrowing" of focus could not prevent an actual proliferation of Yahweh-worshiping communities throughout the ancient Near East in the so-called Diaspora. These far-flung communities, not directly "under the thumb" of restored Judah, developed loosely along lines that may have been as "irregular" in Judahite eyes as the practices of Samarian Yahwists.[27] In fact, in the Hebrew Bible fashioned by the restored Judahites, not only is the voice of the Samarian Yahwists absent, but also there is no biblical word from or about the scattered communites spun off from the Judahite Dispersion, with the exception of court legends in Daniel and Esther. What we know of these Diaspora communities comes from sources apart from the Hebrew Bible. The biblical focus is restrictively on Judah, and within Judah itself, as time passed, diverse forms of being Israelite developed, often in open conflict with one another. Only with the much later refinements of rabbinic Judaism was "order" established by means of mechanisms for resolving disputes in the various communities who laid claim to the Israelite heritage, and the present canon of the Hebrew Bible was forged, excluding many writings treasured by "Israelites" in both Palestine and the Diaspora.[28]

In the wake of the loss of statehood and the proliferation of communities claiming descent from Israel of the preexilic era, the terms "Israel" and "Judah" are conjoined after the exile in complex ways. "Israel" retains its encompassing reference to all valid Yahweh worshipers, amidst the many disputes over proper belief and practice, but it also acquires the extended meaning of a "fully realized Israel" yet to be established in the future and finding expression in a plethora of messianic and apocalyptic hopes.[29] Meanwhile, the term "Judah," having migrated in its geopolitical reference from tribe through kingdom to imperial province, takes on more and more religiocultural significance. Judah becomes the salient carrier and embodiment of the old Israelite heritage through the agency of the repatriated Yahwists who make large claims about the proper forms of faith and practice that have wide influence on Yahwists everywhere, though not enforceable control. As a result, the gentilic "Judahite," or "Judean" in its Hellenistic Greek rendering, expands from reference to people who live in Judah, or to features of their community, to include reference to Yahweh believers regardless of where they live in the ancient Near East or whether they have

ever had direct connections with Palestinian Judah. This expanded sense of
yĕhûdî / yĕhûdîm signifies a transition from the territorial and political aura
of "Judahite/Judahites" to the ecumenical religious aura of "Jew/Jews." The
terms "Judahite=Jew" and "Israelite" henceforth gradually became equally
valid names for worshipers of Yahweh wherever they lived in the ancient
world.[30] However, this twofold way of referring to Yahweh-worshiping
communities probably did not develop until late Hellenistic times.
Moreover, contrary to general opinion and the drift of most histories of
Israel, "Israel/ite," rather than "Judahite/Jew/Jewish," remained the preferred self-identifier of these communities until recent centuries.[31]

A Political Trajectory Based on Problematic but Instructive Sources

Although there is no doubt that the Hebrew Bible attests to ancient Israel's
transition from nonstate politics through statehood to colonial domination
by superior powers, it is evident that there are major questions about the
historical reliability of its traditional accounts. Since it is widely recognized
that the Hebrew Bible was completed, and some would say largely composed, in the era of colonial politics, it is understandable that doubts and
denials have arisen about its accuracy for reconstructing political institutions and events in precolonial times. Those who argue that virtually the
entirety of the Hebrew Bible was composed in the colonial period dismiss
any secure historical foundation for a nonstate or tribal period, and they are
inclined to deny the historical value of nearly all the state traditions except
for those few instances where documents from neighboring states make
mention of the kingdoms of Israel or Judah.[32] On this view, the tribal and
monarchic traditions are largely fictitious accounts intended to provide a
foundation charter for a religious community in colonial times. Given the
suspicions we have already expressed about the dominant ideology of the
biblical traditions, a healthy measure of caution toward the sources is
entirely reasonable.

Nonetheless, there are sound reasons for maintaining that an excessively
skeptical view of the biblical sources is unwarranted. Most historians of
ancient Israel readily agree that the finished form of the political traditions
of ancient Israel was arrived at only in colonial times, and that they are
thoroughly Judahite in their perspective and therefore strongly biased in
their historical judgments, but they find the notion that these traditions
were generated in their entirety, or even in the main, at so late a date to
be highly implausible. Their reasoning is twofold. From an internal point
of view, the political traditions preserved in the Hebrew Bible are so

diverse in their literary forms and so erratic, fragmentary, arcane, or even contradictory in the circumstantial details they relate that it is scarcely believable that they were created completely de novo.[33] Even when we grant that the postexilic Judahite community was striving to render a rationale for its existence based on a hoary past, it is difficult to imagine that those who fashioned this prodigious literary undertaking could have worked entirely, or even primarily, without written and/or oral sources. Moreover, from an external point of view, uneven and problematic as they are, the precolonial traditions fit broadly into historical horizons that are accordant with, and at points rendered highly plausible by, data from extrabiblical documents and archaeological excavations. It is virtually impossible to believe that authors or their informants, living hundreds of years later, could have concocted so much context-congruent information by a series of "lucky guesses."

The conjunction of these internal and external assessments of the traditions appears to rule out the possibility that writers centuries removed from the periods they recount could have been so prescient as to invent a story that fits as well as it does into what we otherwise know of those periods. And if it was indeed "cut from whole cloth," why is this narrative such a mishmash of literary forms and so grossly uneven in the kind of attention it gives to segments of the earlier history? Can all that jarring, half-digested literary and historical material really be explained by late colonial inventiveness, or is not much of it best explained by the particular interests and perspectives of earlier sources on which the final authors or compilers drew, even as they gave the old materials their own slant? It stretches credulity to think that any writer living after the exile would have carried in his head a chronologized list of the kings of Israel and Judah, or inventories of royal officials, or knowledge of the details of interstate politics from prior decades and centuries. If we grant, as we surely must, that such information was drawn from prior sources, whether oral or written, there is no reason to doubt that many other of the less "factual" traditions derived from preceding sources.

To claim the high likelihood of such prior sources is of course only the beginning of the task, since to assert that the finally composed traditions used earlier sources, some of them from the periods they describe, does not at all settle the question of the reliability of those sources. Or, more correctly put, it does not settle the kind of reliability they may have. It is only to say that these traditions must neither be dismissed out of hand nor "swallowed hook, line, and sinker." It is no more correct to accept a tradition prima facie as reliable because it appears to derive from the period it describes than it is to reject a tradition out of hand because it apparently has been preserved in a much later source. Given the textual realities, our task of penetrating the political experience of ancient Israel is contingent on a host of complex judgments about the value of the sources on a text-by-text basis.[34] Whether these traditions are early or late, they are now joined together arbitrarily, and thus disconcertingly, from the historian's point of view. Their multiple voices, diverse in form and content, often fragmentary and sometimes clashing, do not resolve into smooth historiography. Rather, they invite any number of historiographic constructs, which poses the stark necessity of evaluating and integrating the testimony of the sources in some larger picture shaped by the historian's analytic judgment and critical imagination.

Some of that critical process of evaluating and integrating sources will be concerned with specific items of information of the sort that constitute conventional political history. Does the writer have this or that fact right? Of equal importance in constructing an integrated account of Israelite politics will be to determine exactly what it is that writings of this sort, which are neither fiction nor nonfiction in terms of modern literary categories, either intended to convey or actually do convey, whatever their intentions. Is it solely a question of strict historical facts, or can traditions with factual confusions, exaggerations, and fabrications elucidate the political ethos of an earlier era? Or to put it otherwise, in what relation do such hybrid, catchall anthologies stand to the lived experience of the societies and polities from which their earlier sources derived? How much of their reliability falls in the realm of space-time historical accuracy and how much of their reliability consists in testifying to a sociopolitical dynamic in which major factors at work and central issues at stake in the past are rightly remembered even as details are dropped, invented, or misconstrued? And can these witnesses and traces from a vanished past be distinguished from the wishful imaginings of the final traditionists, as well as from the whimsical preferences of contemporary interpreters? Presently there is no broad consensus on these epistemological and methodological issues, nor is any likely to emerge in the foreseeable future.

The position adopted in this study follows from the above assessment of the sources. When the Hebrew Bible states that Israel lived through tribal, monarchic, and colonial periods, it is taken to be correct in that claim.[35] However, it must be conceded that our knowledge about the details of this political journey is incomplete and often fragile. For example, our certitude about the structural and historical lineaments of the second stage of statehood is much stronger, and about the third stage of colonial subjection somewhat stronger, than our certitude about the initial decentralized stage, primarily because both of the latter phases rest on multiple sources of evidence beyond those that can be mustered for the prestate phase. This difference in certitude derives from the largely preliterate status of Israel prior to statehood, and from prestate Israel's correspondent "invisibility" to state powers, with the exception of its mention in one Egyptian record. The autonomous political structures and economic transactions that generated the bulk of written records in early state societies were not present in Israel's decentralized beginnings.[36] Nonetheless, we do possess considerable written traces, meager as they are in solid information, of that first stage of Israel's life before it became a state.

Above all, the memory of a tribal Israel must be accepted as formally believable, whatever we make of the reported details, because of the very nature of state formation. This is so because states do not rise within a demographic and cultural wasteland, even though state origin myths are likely to stress the bleakness and chaos of life before the state-imposed order prevailed. State regimes do not rule over an undifferentiated aggregation of individuals without previous shared experiences and values, but have as their foundation a population with prior social coherencies of some sort, even when the populace is heterogeneous and their social structures and traditions are diverse and conflicted. It runs against the grain of social historical and anthropological evidence to imagine that Saul or David created the sociocultural entity "Israel" when they formed a state institution by that same name. In saying this, we are not narrowly focusing on when and how the term "Israel" was first used. Our point is that the populace that assented or capitulated to state rule, whatever name it bore, had a prior organized social existence with embedded political functions. Debate about whether this early tribal polity called itself "Israel" does not change the reality of a basic sociocultural continuity between the populace before it was ruled by a state and that same populace when it became subject to a state. To be sure, this is not to make any claims about the homogeneity of the prestate populace of the Israelite state, about its social and religious organization, or about its self-awareness as a people distinguished from other peoples.[37]

Israelite and Ancient Near Eastern Political Pathways

The transitions we have identified in Israel's passage through the three horizons of decentralized politics, autonomous state politics,. and colonial politics have left such clear markers in ancient Israelite traditions that Israel's political experience invites serious comparison with the fortunes of other ancient Near Eastern polities. The Hebrew Bible is constructed on the premise that one particular population lodged in Palestine at the beginning of the Iron Age retained its identity over centuries of time even as it altered its forms of community and modes of self-representation in the course of its rocky journey through three horizons of political experience. This claim to a persevering Israelite identity amidst extensive change opens up a complex of issues, among them being how it was that ancient Near Eastern societies moved from nonstate to state politics and on to imperial politics wherein strong polities enforced their dominion over weaker polities, and, in particular, what sorts of enduring cultural and religious identities persisted amid the vagaries of politics.

Viewed in ancient Near Eastern context, Israel's political experience is likely to have been roughly parallel to the fortunes of other ancient Near Eastern polities, so much so that Israelite and extra-Israelite politics may be able to illuminate one another in significant ways. It can at least be said with certainty that Israel was not unique among ancient Near Eastern states in undergoing political transformations that stood in dialectical tension with their cultural infrastructures. Although political gains and losses, together with economic transactions, constitute the major content of the surviving records, the persistence throughout the ancient Near East of "apolitical" literary genres that reflect a social and cultural life overreaching particular political regimes argues for a vibrant communal life that drew upon nonpolitical sources and was undeterred by the fortunes of politics. What is unique about ancient Israel is the knowledge we have of it in the highly self-conscious sedimentation of its intertwined political and cultural vicissitudes deposited in the Hebrew Bible. In other words, Israelite traditions captured aspects of a political history that may have been analogous to the tortuous journey of other ancient Near Eastern peoples who did not write of their experiences in this extended self-reflective manner but who did produce documents that disclose enough about the coexistence and interplay between political power and cultural creativity to bear fruitful comparison with Israel's political life.

It is not customary to think of ancient Israel in such a comprehensive ancient Near Eastern developmental framework, to the point of considering it as one instance of a number of polities that bear a decided family resemblance. To the contrary, as we have noted, most of the comparisons drawn between Israel and other states have been focused on delimited political institutions and practices, either to clarify their workings in Israel or to explore the non-Israelite political phenomena as possible models replicated by Israel viewed as a relative newcomer to ancient Near Eastern history. Normally, such comparisons have not extended to asking how Israel's entire political trajectory compares with the trajectories of other states in its vicinity, let alone in the wider ancient Near East. Whenever this threshold of macro comparison is approached, the inquiry is customarily aborted in one of two directions: either it is said that the biblical traditions are too incoherent and unreliable to reconstruct a plausible ancient Israelite political trajectory, or the biblical traditions are taken at near face value, and it is claimed that Israelite politics, like its religion, is so unique that it cannot be compared as a meaningful totality with other polities in its environment.

Given either of these judgments, all that is left is to compare particular political details that yield fragmentary results in the one case or serve as an apologia for the utter distinctiveness of Israel in the other case. To construct and ground a viable comparative framework it is necessary to bring together Israelite *local-historical time* and the ancient Near Eastern slice of *world-historical time* in dynamic interface, so that both the politics of ancient Israel and the politics of its neighbors may be more precisely delineated in their similarities and differences.

To draw together an account of the trajectory of ancient Near Eastern politics is a daunting task, if only because large stretches of that political history are no better documented than are Israelite politics, and sometimes not as well. Yet enough is known from Mesopotamian, Anatolian, Syro-Palestinian, and Egyptian sources to construct a tenable profile of the growth and accumulation of political power as its "leading edge" moved among different polities in the region.[38] Within this orientation, Israel's local historical experience can be viewed from a broader political perspective than is possible when debating one or another, or even a succession, of biblical texts that touch on politics. By aspiring to such a large-scale perspective, we may acquire a better picture of the political resources available to Israel, as well as a clearer sense of the political constraints that set the parameters within which Israel made its political choices.[39] At the same time, we may be able to get a more balanced assessment of the way that all the other power networks interacted with political power in ancient Israel. This broader contextualization of our study may also elucidate the role that religion played in Israel's politics, allowing us to evaluate the cogency of the paramount position that the biblical tradition insistently assigns to religious factors and impulses in shaping Israelite political behavior.

CRITICISM, IMAGINATION,
AND IDEOLOGY IN POLITICAL INQUIRY

Finally, we must articulate what is entailed when we grapple with ancient Israelite politics as an intellectual and political project accountable to contemporary audiences, and specifically to the readers of this book. Because the biblical sources are of varying date and historical value, and because they are shot through with strong moral and religious value judgments and profoundly shaped by the entrenched interests of the traditionists, it is clearly unenlightening to present ancient Israelite politics in the form of a narrative summary or restatement of the biblical traditions, even if that restatement is accompanied by harmonization of conflicting elements and inserted conjectures to fill narrative gaps.[40] To have intellectual and moral integrity, the critical imagination of the investigator must "start from scratch" by evoking and enacting an integral historical performance, much as a director reconstitutes the text of a drama.[41] This reenactment of the past will be controlled by as much factual precision as critical judgment appears to warrant, but its primary goal, amid the sorting out and patterning of the data, is to envision and conjure up the interplay of human interests and strivings at work in the political arena.

Consequently, to be a critical investigator means not to embrace or to dismiss peremptorily the face-value claims of the biblical sources, but rather to evaluate those claims as admittedly enmeshed in the political interests and strivings not only of the political actors depicted but also of the traditionists who depict them. The biblical traditionists are not simply describing someone else's politics but they are implicitly or explicitly enacting their own politics in the very telling. All political action is fraught with self-interest in one way or another, and all reports of political action are "value-added" reports. So concluding that we have established certain historical facts about ancient Israelite politics does not mean that those reasonably attested facts ever stood apart from a matrix of contending interests and divergent value judgments. We become necessarily observant of how the interests and values of narrators are displayed in the "facts" they relate, the "facts" they fail to relate, and the webs of meaning they weave around the "facts." In offering a critical imaginative reenactment of the past dependent on such sources, we are proposing answers to questions about our sources that can never be answered in the abstract. Do the interests and values that appear to animate the narrators allow both a fair account of the deeds of the political actors under review and at least some faithfulness to the interests and values that moved the political actors they depict? Or are the narrators blocked by ideological investments that, wittingly or unwittingly, cloud and distort the telling so egregiously that we can learn little or nothing of the past from their imaginative reenactments of history?

We can never give impregnable historical judgments, but we nonetheless must and do make relative judgments, many having the aura of high probability, and some even having the feel of near certitude. One reason they remain relative judgments is that they are inescapably shadowed by the self-interests, ambiguities, equivocations, and fallibilities both of the sources and the historians rendering the judgments. Above all, however, as we are reminded by "new historians," they remain relative judgments because they are not random, isolated assessments but occur as aspects of a particular imaginative "scenario," one among many possible ways of reading the same bundle of events. The discipline of history is "an ongoing tension between stories that have been told and stories that might be told. In this sense, it is more useful to think of history as an ethical and political practice than as an epistemology with a clear ontological status."[42] The scope of incontestable factuality in our critical and imaginative judgments is often smaller than we are prone to realize. Moreover, what for the moment seems evident and incontestable is often the least interesting and challenging part of historical reconstruction. The "contestable" is typically the "growing edge" where new historical insights spring forth. And, although the discipline of history as such provides no single "epistemology with a clear ontological status," every historical work reveals an epistemology that, for that historian if for no one else, has binding ontological force in shaping the particular historical reenactment at hand.[43]

The final complication in a critical imaginative reconstruction of ancient Israelite politics is that the critical investigator is no more free of interests and values than were the traditionists and political actors in ancient Israel. Our interests and values will inevitably affect what we study, how we shape our inquiry, what we count as evidence, what we understand to be the major forces and tendencies at work, and how we judge what we study to be related to matters of importance in our own lives and in our own world. So we have the reality of *politically imbued investigators* making use of *politically imbued traditionists* to learn about *politically imbued agents* in ancient Israel.[44] For those who consider this a counsel of despair in which all "objectivity" is doomed, it is very tempting to deny and suppress one's own interests and values as a critical investigator and to proceed as though one's judgments are value-free, at least on all interpretive points that matter.

By far the more productive recourse, however, is to realize that by "owning up" to our ideological investments, we critical investigators are actually more likely to be constructively "critical" than if we suppress our investments as unworthy "biases."[45] Being more self-conscious, we are freer to acknowledge when the interests and values we encounter in historical actors and their traditionists are presumably similar to or different from our own, even to the point of admiration or abhorrence, and in that very recognition to be obligated to honor the "otherness" of the historical actors. Especially common is the complaint that critical investigators are prone to fashioning their historical subjects in their own image, conceiving them to be prototypes or forerunners of contemporary personality types, social movements, political tendencies, or philosophical/religious perspectives they favor.

This problem of "preunderstanding" or "precommitment" on the part of the historian takes a particular form in biblical studies. Since Jews and Christians regard the Hebrew Bible as a source of religious authority, naive or deliberate retrojection of the Jewish and Christian present into the Israelite past is a recurrent temptation. The only remedy for this sort of disfigurement of the historical past by overlaying it with projections of present preoccupations is constant self-criticism by the investigator and openness to dialogue among investigators of all persuasions. Where the line falls in each instance between identifying authentic past realities and foisting the present on the past will always be an inescapable matter of debate.

So far, the relevant interests and values of the present investigator have not been explicitly divulged, although many of them have doubtless been indirectly disclosed. In most historical studies, the author's interests and values that are not immediately connected to the inquiry are not openly stated, and it is certainly not considered de rigueur to do so. To complete the full round of his methodology, however, it is necessary for the present author to disclose the personal interests and values that in his view are most likely to have a bearing on this study of ancient Israelite politics. The following ideological commitments of the author are proposed as of potential relevance to this study.[46]

This author views politics as an inevitable dimension of life, since there is always a matrix of cooperative and competitive motives, interests, and goals in any human group that must be negotiated in the shaping of public life. In short, he favors the fullest possible participatory politics. Moreover, he is a democratic socialist, since in his view there can be no adequate political democracy without economic democracy. He believes that a greater equalization of power and wealth is the single most important step that societies need to take in order to create a better human world. He values people over property, and social justice over law and order, although he is by no means scornful of property and law and order, insofar as they have an indispensable role to play in securing and enhancing an equitable society. He is a free-church christian, consciously using the lower-case *c* to renounce any sense of Christian religious superiority or imperialist designs. He rejects religious authoritarianism and, while sensing a religious dimension to be part of the human condition, he is frankly uncertain whether religious power in all its embodiments has brought more good or more harm to the world. He is resistant to political privilege based on religious or ethnic identity and favors a sharp separation of church and state, and for this reason regards Jewish, Christian, Islamic, and Hindu political nationalisms, and any other religiously framed political nationalism, as harmful to human community. At the same time, it is his conviction that all religious identities, individual or communal, are to be honored and accorded full human and political rights.

The author of this study further believes that some of his interests and values are resonant with interests and values expressed in ancient Israel, allowing for the great disparity between Israel's location in world-historical time and his own. On the other hand, there are many interests and values in ancient Israel toward which he is unsympathetic, insofar as they might be regarded as exemplary for the contemporary world. As a student of the past, he believes that the best way to clarify and advance those interests and values he espouses is to be as objective as possible in freely acknowledging interests and values in the past that are "alien" to or "incommensurable" with his own. More specifically, the present writer is convinced that in order to be faithful to his own ideological interests and values he must not consciously intrude them into his critical imaginative reconstructions of the past, in the precise sense that he dare not willfully or naively attribute his beliefs to ancient Israelites.

I am keenly aware that to state my commitments so explicitly, with little elaboration or nuance, may appear unseemly or banal. They are articulated nonetheless so as to include me in my role as historical "investigator" within the larger political reality that frames this historical inquiry, not only to inform others, but to remind myself that I have a stake in ancient Israel's politics to the extent that the legacy of those politics continues to impact the world in which I am an avowed political participant. Insofar as the political dimension of world-historical time continues to unfold and is ardently contested, all descriptions and assessments of the politics of ancient Israel remain intriguingly and contentiously open-ended, including the one articulated in this study.

CHAPTER 3

Israelite Politics According to the Hebrew Bible

POLITICS IN THE HEBREW BIBLE: "HANDLE WITH CARE"

This chapter will trace the Israelite political trajectory from a decentralized polity through statehood to colonial dependence as articulated in the biblical narrative traditions. The method will be exegetical and descriptive, hewing closely to the scope and detail of the political data in the narratives of Genesis through Kings, Chronicles, Ezra–Nehemiah, and the prophetic books, supplemented now and then by the political information found in nonnarrative biblical genres. For the moment, every effort will be made to prescind from a sustained historical-critical analysis of these biblical reports. In chapter 5, I shall take up a more deliberate critical assessment of the historical worth of the identified political data. The point in this strategy is to avoid premature critical conclusions before the full panorama of the textual claims about Israelite politics has been disclosed. In an attempt to be purposefully "noncritical" in this phase of the inquiry, I have chosen to follow the sequence of the narrative traditions as they are ordered in the Hebrew Bible.

Obviously, this procedure does not at all deny that a significant measure of critical judgment is entailed both in deciding which of the biblical data about ancient Israel are political in content or import and in the manner in which the biblical "political panorama" is presented. It is simply to say that the specific methods and criteria of literary and historical criticism will be muted until a descriptive profile of the biblical data is completed. With few exceptions, "historical-critical" comments and assessments deemed advisable will be consigned to notes or to brief asides in the text. In short, throughout this overview of Israelite politics I will be exercising the discrimination of any perceptive reader in noting omissions and apparently contradictory elements in the traditions.

One important criterion that I follow in assembling political data requires an "up-front" explanation. In deciding about the appropriate political subject matter, my review of the data will discriminate between discourse and metadiscourse. I will intentionally "bracket out" the moral and religious judgments that both enfold and punctuate the narratives with an "authorial" voice instructing readers about the "goodness" or the "badness" of the politics, and at times making readers privy to the deity's innermost judgments about Israelite politics. This may seem a futile task, since it is obvious that an ultimately religious perspective frames and overdetermines the whole body of traditions. The proposed bracketing maneuver is necessary, however, in order to allow the political phenomena to stand forth in their own right without "the rush to judgment" that the biblical writers and contemporary interpreters often engage in. It goes without saying that no two readers will altogether agree on where to draw the line between discourse and metadiscourse, between what is germane to the narrated events and what is germane to the narrator's assessment of the events.

The religious metadiscourse in the accounts of Israelite politics shapes a master narrative whose interpretive key is loyalty or disloyalty to Yahweh, the God of Israel. The rhetoric that articulates the loyalty/disloyalty options is stereotypical and abstract in the sense that the same judgmental jargon is applied to many rulers and regimes, frequently in the absence of detailed or nuanced charges specific to their situations. Moreover, these sweeping assumptions about religious loyalty/disloyalty often find little or no point of connection with the political narratives themselves; in fact, at times the political narratives are in outright contradiction to the religious interpretation put on them.

A flagrant example is the unrelenting claim of the metadiscourse on the divided kingdoms that, once it was built by Solomon, no valid worship of Yahweh could take place apart from the Jerusalem temple, thereby stigmatizing all worship conducted outside the capital city, both in the northern kingdom and at Judahite sites, as apostate or idolatrous. This assessment may reflect what some southerners thought of northern religion at the time, but it flies in the face of abundant evidence that northerners themselves regarded their worship of Yahweh to be completely valid, as exemplified by the ardent northern prophets Elijah and Elisha who worshiped on their own turf without the least awareness of any obligation toward the Jerusalem cult and without any attack on the official Yahweh cult of the northern kingdom. Moreover, there is ample reason to believe that the condemned worship at "high places," both in Israel and Judah, was an established and permitted part of the cult of Yahweh throughout the monarchic era. Indeed, this blanket condemnation of northern worship calls into question why the narrator would want to relate the history of a kingdom viewed as utterly apostate, and also highlights the contradiction between the total dismissal of northern religion on principle and the stories that report unimpugned Yahweh worship among many northerners.

A partial answer to this quandary may lie in the narrator's report that the secession of the north was after all "the will of Yahweh" in punishment for Solomon's idolatry (1 Kings 11:9–13, 29–39; 12:5, 24). This of course has the effect of turning the punishment of Solomon into an undeserved punishment of the northern tribes, but this inequity is never confronted by the narrator. Interestingly, Chronicles, which does *not* tell the story of the apostate northern kingdom, further omits the narratives in Kings about Solomon's idolatry and the granting of the northern kingdom to Jeroboam by the agency of the prophet Ahijah of Shiloh. These omissions leave the brief references to Ahijah and to Yahweh's intent to divide the kingdom, which the Chronicler repeats from the Kings account of the assembly at Shechem, utterly bereft of antecedent or context (2 Chron. 10:15 // 1 Kings 12:5, and 2 Chron. 11:4 // 1 Kings 12:24). It is obvious that both Kings and Chronicles are ambivalent toward the northern kingdom, both in what they say in their metadiscourse and in what they choose to tell readers about persons and events in the north.

Accordingly, this chapter will focus on the apparent religious beliefs and practices of political actors during the historical periods being described, while leaving aside those religious beliefs, practices, and interpretations of events that give strong indication of having been imposed from an extraneous perspective by the narrator. In other words, wherever it seems probable that religion was an integral aspect of the reported political activities, it will be described as an ingredient of the political matrix. Otherwise, the religious metadiscourse will be bracketed or alluded to very sparingly, especially where its taken-for-granted outlook blocks or obscures a concrete understanding of the political dynamics in particular contexts. For example, the biblical accounts of the judges and kings of Israel frequently describe one form of Israelite disloyalty to Yahweh as worship of the god Baal or other alien deities. When this formulaic claim is attached to a king whose reported deeds say nothing more detailed about such alien worship, there is no reason to include the claim as part of the political history. However, when it is said that Gideon replaced a Baal altar with a Yahweh altar (Judg. 6:24–32) and that Ahab built a temple for Baal in Samaria (1 Kings 16:33), later destroyed by Jehu (2 Kings 10:18–28), these data are treatable as part of the political record, even if we eventually draw conclusions about their meaning that differ from the interpretation of the narrator. To be sure, the line between generalizing religious rhetoric and actual religious beliefs and practices is not easily drawn in all cases. Later in our inquiry we will evaluate the religious metadiscourse in the biblical texts for its bearing on the scope and details of political information, as well as the interpretive "slant" it puts on political developments.

ISRAEL'S DECENTRALIZED POLITICS

In undertaking a phenomenological account of Israel's sociopolitical life prior to statehood as it is pictured in the Hebrew Bible, we encounter elusive descriptions that do not employ a consistent or precise vocabulary concerning communal structures and leadership roles. The later traditions about statehood speak of Israelite "kings" (*mĕlākîm* or *mōšĕlîm*) and "kingdoms" (*mamlākôt* or *mĕmšĕlôt*), and they employ the verbal construction "to rule over" (*limlōk 'al* or *limšōl 'al*) for the exercise of sovereign state authority and power, and the titles of various offices in the royal administration are specified. In marked contrast, for the earlier period there are no equivalent technical terms for the politically decentralized society. The texts speak of "Israel," "Israelites," "all Israel," or "the people," terms that lack political specificity. The most commonly encountered terms for a unit within the decentralized polity are usually translated "tribe" (*šēveṭ* or *maṭṭeh*, literally "staff"), and they are applied schematically to subsections of Israel regarded as formal coequals, even though there are obvious disproportions in the narrative space devoted to them. "Tribe" designates a geographical grouping that is internally structured by locale into clusters of villages and/or by clans or lineages in which preferential and protective kin relations are primary. Occasional reference is made to "the tribes of Israel." Frequently the community is referred to as a "congregation" (*'ēdâh*) or as an "assembly" (*qāhal*), but these terms describe the people collectively gathered for particular purposes rather than designate representative bodies or organs within a political system.[1]

Furthermore, whereas the founding act of statehood is reported, biblical traditions have no explicit account of the beginnings of an intertribal system that might have formed a larger sociopolitical entity composed of previously independent groups. The association of tribes is presupposed but its formation and constitution are never described. The tribes as subsections of prestate Israel are already adumbrated in Genesis (29:21–30:24; 35:16–20; 48:8–49:28) and they are presupposed among the Israelites in Egypt (Ex. 1:1–4; 6:14–25) and during their wilderness journeys (Numbers 1; 26). It may be conjectured that one or more of the enactments of "covenant" (*bĕrîth*) described in Exodus (24:1–11), Deuteronomy (26:16–19), and

Joshua (24:1–28) imply formal agreements among tribes or other social entities to constitute themselves a single organization for authorizing and coordinating certain social and political powers. That these "covenanting" accounts are accompanied by laws implies joint agreements concerning the administration of justice (Ex. 18:13–27; 23:1–3, 6–8). Since, however, the compacts are presented primarily as transactions between the people and deity, actual decentralized social and political structures and processes are largely unstated. Occasional sketches of aspects of sociopolitical structure are not anchored in a comprehensive description of social order (Ex. 18:13–27; Numbers 1; 26). The terms for leaders, such as "elder" (*zākēn*), "judge" (*šōphēṭ*), "prince, high official, army commander" (*śar*), "noble" (*nādîv*), "dignitary, chief" (*nāśî'*), "ruler" (*qāṣîn*), and "head, chief" (*rō'š*) are given virtually no context in sociopolitical organization and precious little description of their functions or duties beyond their particular actions in the narrative. In many cases they appear to be loose descriptors with no more precision than to designate communal "worthies" or "leaders." Their semantic fluidity is evident in the frequency with which they appear to be used interchangeably, a practice extending into subsequent periods of Israel's history.[2]

The Progenitors of Israel

In place of a founding community, Israel's origins are attributed to a single migratory family that proliferates into twelve tribes through population growth. The progenitors of Israel in Genesis 12—50 are described as heads of an extended family that spans four generations and whose total living membership did not exceed one hundred persons (Gen. 46:26–27). Kin relations through birth and marriage, plus affiliated servants, constitute the family. A single alternative tradition claims that Abraham, "the Hebrew," commanded 318 armed men, perhaps on the model of a band of free-booters or mercenary troops, who defeated a coalition of five kings from Mesopotamia and Anatolia who had invaded Palestine (Gen. 14:1–16). This family migrates on the fringes of Canaanite city-states and takes refuge from famine in Egypt. It occupies no permanent territory, although it has use rights to wells for watering its flocks and purchases land for burial purposes. In a politicized environment, the ancestral family interacts with the Palestinian city-states of Sodom, Salem (Jerusalem?), Gerar, Shechem, and Adullam, and even with the Egyptian pharaoh. When one of its members, Joseph, rises to a position of extraordinary political power, he does so as an officer in the Egyptian government. The relations of the ancestral family with surrounding polities are by turns peaceful and quarrelsome, and in one instance murderously violent (Genesis 34), but the family (or band, if we follow Genesis 14) does not in itself assume any political shape or make any sovereign political claims.

Nonetheless, in the overarching editorial discourse of Genesis the promise of eventually possessing the land of Canaan is issued by deity to each new generation of the family, and eventual Israelite statehood is foreshadowed "prophetically." Moreover, in the third generation, Jacob is given the byname of Israel (Gen. 32:22–32), his sons turn out to be the eponymous progenitors of the later tribes of Israel (Gen. 29:21–30:24; 35:16–20), and Jacob announces the future fortunes of his sons depicted as personified tribes (Gen. 48:8–49:28). In many respects, the accounts of these progenitors, their relations with one another and with surrounding peoples, are pointedly suggestive of the later history of the tribes and of the kingdoms of Israel and Judah.[3] The progenitors are later Israel in nuce.

Israel from Egypt to Canaan

There is a major demographic shift in the traditions from Jacob's descent into Egypt with fewer than one hundred family members to the subsequent enslavement of Israelites who have multiplied by the thousands. According to one extravagant reckoning they consist of more than 600,000 adult males, not counting priests (Num. 1:46; 26:51). They live together in workers' settlements and are allowed a measure of internal self-rule by elders, but are otherwise totally subservient to the Egyptians, who impress them into forced labor on government building projects. The division of the people into tribes is presupposed without explanation, although a less "organic" community is hinted at in references to "a mixed multitude" who left Egypt with them (Ex. 12:38) and "a rabble among them" who rebelled against Moses after their flight (Num. 11:4). In the wilderness between Egypt and Canaan, the community covenants with the deity Yahweh and agrees to organize itself around a body of laws divinely revealed to Moses (Exodus 19—24). The people as a whole (*hā'ām*) are also referred to as a "congregation" (*'ēdāh*) or an "assembly" (*qāhal*).

Moreover, for the first time in the narrative, Israelite priests appear, for whom extensive regulations and provisions are made, including a portable sanctuary, and their status and functions are sharply distinguished from the laity (Exodus 35—40; Leviticus and Numbers passim). The civil laws and religious laws governing the laity are far less complete, and many of them make sense only proleptically, since they assume settled agrarian existence, which Israel in the wilderness does not yet enjoy (Ex. 20:23–23:19; Leviticus 19—26; Deuteronomy 12—26).

Although a cohesive communal self-organization is posited for this body of wanderers, its structure and modes of operation are no more than vaguely alluded to. One of the laws mandates respect for a "dignitary/ruler" (*nāśî'*) of the people" (Ex. 22:28), possibly understood as one of the tribal or congregational heads (as in Num. 1:16 or Josh. 9:15, 18–19). In the wilderness, elders continue to appear as representatives of the people, and we also hear of capable men appointed as "officers" (*śārîm*) in a multitiered system for adjudicating disputes so that only the most difficult cases need be referred to Moses (Ex. 18:21). In a second recitation of the laws, Moses projects a juridical system to become effective once the wanderers have settled in the land. It provides for local "judges and officers" who are to refer disputed cases to a higher panel of priest (or priests) and a judge situated at a central site (Deut. 16:18–20; 18:8–13). Once again, these terms for leaders do not "flesh out" any precise social organizational design.[4]

Apart from repulsing an attack by Amalekites shortly after departing Egypt (Ex. 17:8–16), threatening contacts with other peoples are unreported until the Israelites pass from the wilderness of Sinai into Transjordan. The Midianite priest Jethro, Moses' father-in-law, advises Moses on administration of justice (Ex. 18:13–23), and a subsequent tradition relates that some Midianites accompanied Israel into Canaan (Judg. 1:16). In Transjordan, Israel encounters polities with royal rule and territorial claims, manages to avoid conflict with Edom, but is forced to fight and defeat Og and Sihon, heads of Amorite kingdoms (Num. 21:21–35). A threat from Moab in alliance with Midianites is averted when these enemies of Israel cannot get a favorable reading from a prophet-seer (Numbers 22—24). Later, Israel "takes vengeance" on the Midianites (Numbers 31:1–12), who are inexplicably represented as hostile to Israel, in contrast to the Jethro tradition of Midianite friendship. The source of Israel's weaponry and military organization is not commented on. While in Egyptian bondage, it is implied that Israelites were unarmed, but once escaped they have the military means to fend off attacks, overthrow hostile rulers, and acquire territories for settlement. Two military censuses by tribal divisions differ in that one gives only the names of tribal heads (Numbers 1), while the other gives only the names of subsections within each tribe (Numbers 26), but neither talks about weaponry or military organization per se.

All in all, the narratives and laws associated with Israel's movement from Egypt to the verge of Canaan depict a sizable company of people struggling to survive physically, engaging in warfare with peoples who block their way, and caught up in internal quarrels and conflicts. The tensions and conflicts running through the narratives concern provision of food and water, the best route to pursue through the desert and Transjordan, negotiation and battle with other peoples, struggles over leadership, and loyalty and obedience to the cult of Yahweh. Israel is not a polity with any present territorial claim, since it is only passing through the wilderness and Transjordan, and it entirely lacks a state hierarchy. Nonetheless, communal authority is embodied in Moses, who transmits the deity's designs for the community to the people, who are expected to obey whatever he commands.[5] The compliance of the people, however, is far from total or constant. So serious is the resistance to Moses, and to Yahweh's word through Moses, that the entire generation of wanderers who left Egypt, with the exception of Joshua and Caleb, is prevented from entering Canaan (Num. 14:20–38; Deut. 1:26–40). Even Moses and Aaron are excluded from entering the land because they "broke faith" with Yahweh by some act or attitude of insubordination that remains unclarified in the text (Num. 20:2–13; Deut. 3:23–29; 32:48–52; 34:1–8).

In sum, when the contents of the narratives and laws are scrutinized, they do not yield a coherent picture of how such a migrating community could have been organized and administered, both because there are gaps and contradictions in the traditions and because the laws are sparse on information about how they are to be administered and in many cases would have had no sphere of application until such time as the people were settled down. The Israel of these traditions is a strife-ridden religious community in transit, whose sociopolitical shape is nebulous and incidental to its religious status and its urgent quest for land.

Israel Settling in the Land

Upon entering Canaan, Joshua having replaced Moses as their leader, the Israelites continue the military campaigns begun in Transjordan. They capture Jericho and Ai (Joshua 6—8), and proceed to defeat coalitions of southern and northern Canaanite kings (Joshua 10—11). Some of the traditions claim virtual total conquest and annihilation of the rulers and inhabitants of Canaanite city-states (Josh. 11:16–12:24), whereas other traditions equivocate or give evidence that the conquest was not complete (Josh. 13:1–6a; 23; Judg. 1:1–3:6), that the conflicts were directed more against city-state rulers, armies, and bureaucrats than against all inhabitants of the land (Judges 4—5), and that, in fact, some Canaanites allied with or became a part of Israel.[6] Rahab and her family at Jericho (Joshua 2; 6:22–25), an unnamed man from Bethel and his family (Judg. 1:22–26), and four cities led by Gibeon (Joshua 9) are incorporated into Israel. These caveats about a total Israelite victory and occupation of the land are further strengthened by the traditions of Judges, at which point the portrayal of a united twelve-tribe Israel acting in concert breaks apart into descriptions of the regional gains, losses, and stalemates of individual tribes or groups of tribes.

The character of Israelite decentralized politics portrayed in the Joshua traditions continues with the same farrago of names for leaders and societal subunits exhibited in Exodus–Deuteronomy. "Officers" (*šōṭĕrîm*) carry Joshua's instructions throughout the camp (Josh. 1:10; 3:2), and in the assemblies of the people, after the conquest of Canaan is complete, they are joined by elders, judges, and heads (Josh. 23:2; 24:1). Elders appear, both alone (Josh. 8:10; 24:31) and yoked with officers and judges (Josh. 8:32), and military chiefs (*keṣînîm;* Josh. 10:24) are mentioned. "Dignitaries" (*nĕśî'îm*) are the congregational heads on the occasion of the covenant with the Gibeonites (Josh. 9:15, 18–19, 21). Priests are prominent as bearers and custodians of the ark (Joshua 3—6; 8:33), and Eleazar, priestly successor of Aaron, allots tribal lands in consort with "heads" of tribal families (Josh. 14:1; 19:51; 21:1), and these "heads" are equated with "dignitaries" (*ro'šîm=nĕśî'îm;* Josh. 22:14, 30). There are no explanations of how the jurisdictions of these leaders relate to one another within the community's total social organization.

The fullest articulation of social organization refers to levels within a tribe subdivided into lineages or clans and households (Josh. 7:16–18), but the political connections and implications of this scheme are unexpressed. In short, we are presented an agrarian people at arms, but we do not actually learn much about the details of their internal organization or what gives them unity, other than their religious affiliation. Joshua commands the people autocratically as did Moses, yet he is not a king, since his entitlement to lead is based on a commission by Moses and a pledge to keep the laws revealed through Moses (Joshua 1). And after the death of Joshua, he has no designated successor.

In the traditions of Judges, Ruth, and 1 Samuel, prior to the adoption of monarchy, two factors contribute to the recording of considerably more circumstantial detail than in the earlier traditions. One factor is that the Israelites are at last pictured as settled in the land; they are no longer wanderers, but resident farmers and herders. More importantly, the amorphous unity of "all Israel" is loosened to the extent that the actions of particular tribes in particular locales are recounted and some sense is given of the way that the tribes relate to one another. This more detailed reportage is mixed with traditions that still maintain an all-Israelite perspective, and the content of the narratives is primarily concerned with military defense rather than a broader spectrum of domestic affairs.

The differences between the Joshua and Judges traditions are immediately apparent in a succession of annalistic and anecdotal notations about the successes and failures of nine individual tribes in their efforts to gain footholds in various regions of the land (Judges 1). Only Judah and Simeon act in concert (Judg. 1:1–3, 17). While "House of Joseph" formally embraces Manasseh and Ephraim (Judg. 1:22–26), those two tribes are treated separately in the notes that follow (Judg. 1:27–29). Danite defeats in the western foothills are said to have been followed by the successes of the House of Joseph in the same region, but not as part of a coordinated campaign (Judg. 1:34–36). The fortunes of the tribes of Reuben and Gad are not given, since it appears that the nine tribes named are assumed to be fanning out from their base camp at Gilgal after they have crossed the Jordan together (Josh. 1:1; 2:1), and thus the Transjordanian territories of Reuben and Gad have already been secured (Numbers 32; Josh. 2:12–15). The tribe of Levi is omitted from consideration, since it is conceived as an extraterritorial body of priests who live in settlements assigned to them by the lay tribes (Josh. 21:1–42). This chain of notations in the opening chapter of Judges is said to refer to events "after the death of Joshua" (Judg. 1:1), but it covers areas of Canaan previously claimed as conquered under Joshua, and it returns the tribes to their entry point into Canaan as though the conquests under Joshua had never occurred (cf. Josh. 2:1; 3:1; 4:19; 9:6; 10:43 with Judg. 1:1, 16; 2:1).

With both Moses and Joshua deceased, the mantle of leadership falls on persons who are said "to judge" (*lišpōṭ*) Israel, but rarely are they directly called judges. A majority of the narratives about those who "judged" tell of their military victories at the head of tribal levies (Judg. 3:7–8:28; 10:6–12:6) or, in the case of Samson, as a solitary adventurer (Judges 13—16). However, Deborah, who stirs up Barak to muster an army against Canaanite kings, also "judges" by adjudicating cases brought to her in an open-air court (Judg. 4:4–5). Samuel "judges" Israel by holding court sessions during an annual circuit of towns in Benjamin (1 Sam. 7:15–17), and he is also pictured as "judging" Israel by presiding at a public fast day where he makes intercessory prayer and offers sacrifice for victory over invading Philistine forces (1 Sam. 7:5–11). Samuel's sons, whom he has appointed as judges in his old age, are condemned for bribery (1 Sam. 8:1–3), in contrast to their father's publically applauded probity (1 Sam. 12:1–5).

Six notables from various tribes, some of them with considerable possessions and one with an extensive intermarriage network, are said to have "judged" Israel in succession for stated periods of time, ranging from six to twenty-three years (Judg. 10:1–5; 12:7–13). Only Jephthah among the six named is accorded a narrative report, which pictures him as a military deliverer in Gilead who is offered the position of tribal head in return for his leadership in battle (Judg. 11:1–33; 12:7). Precisely what the narrator thought this "judging" of all Israel by six leaders entailed is not explained, either in the brief notes about them or elsewhere in the traditions. A complicating factor in the shifting uses of the word *lišpōṭ*="to judge" is that this term has a broad semantic range in Hebrew and in cognate languages, meaning variously "to rule/govern," "to judge/adjudicate," or "to vindicate/ deliver [in battle]," thus embracing administrative, judicial, and military functions.[7]

Alongside those said to "judge" Israel, there are numerous references to tribal officials, most of which already appeared in the traditions about Moses and Joshua, and, as in the former case, the terms are not standardized with reference to any comprehensive profile of leadership positions. The Song of Deborah contains terms for military leaders that are not duplicated in the reports of military organization under the later monarchy (Judges 5).[8] In the book of Judges, priests do not put in an appearance until two Levites appear as principals in stories at the end of the book (Judg. 17:7–18:31; 19:1–20:7), although only one of these priests performs cultic duties. Laity are free to preside at religious rites, but one story indicates considerable prestige if a household or a tribe can secure the services of a levitical priest (Judg. 17:7–13). Priests are more evident in the days of Samuel, bearing the ark into battle (1 Sam. 4:1–11), but lay sacrifice is maintained amid disputes with venal priests who seek to take more than a fair share of the sacrificial meat (1 Sam. 2:12–17).

In the Gideon traditions, a pronounced antipathy is expressed toward centralized politics embodied in kingship. After his victory over the Midianites, Gideon is invited by the exuberant Israelites "to rule over" them as founder of a dynasty, but he firmly rejects the proposal by stressing that only deity is entitled "to rule over" them. Instead, acting more the part of a "chief," he requests that the valuable trove of gold earrings captured from the Midianites be given to him, from which he makes a religious icon that he sets up in his hometown (Judg. 8:22–27). Abimelech, Gideon's son by a Shechemite concubine, cajoles and bribes the Shechemites to install him as king over a region that includes areas of Manasseh. Rebellion breaks out against him in Shechem, which he suppresses with great bloodshed, but he is killed while trying to put down a similar uprising in Thebez (Judges 9). The Abimelech narrative is punctuated by a satirical fable about kingship put in the mouth of the upstart king's brother (Judg. 9:7–15). The fable relates that when an assembly of trees sets out "to anoint a king over them," they invite the olive tree, the fig tree, and the vine "to sway over them," but each in turn emphatically refuses to desert its valued role as a producer of staple food and drink. In the end, the useless bramble agrees to be ruler of the trees, ludicrously inviting them "to take refuge in my shade," while also cautioning them that dried brambles are prone to trigger fires that can devour the loftiest trees. This biting mockery of kingship, picturesque and memorable, has the definite flavor of popular origin, in content if not in composition.

Elsewhere in Judges, enemy kings and their minions are scorned and satirized: Adonibezek, captured by Judah, has his thumbs and great toes cut off as retribution for his having done the same thing to seventy kings he captured (Judg. 1:5–7). Eglon of Moab is a fat and effete potentate who easily succumbs to the ruse by which Ehud assassinates him (Judg. 3:15–25). The mother of Sisera, together with her ladies-in-waiting, salivates over the captive maidens and embroidered dyed textiles they imagine he will bring back from his victory over Israel (Judg. 5:28–30). Gideon charges Zeba and Zalmunna, kings of Midian, with wantonly slaying his captured brothers (Judg. 8:18–19). Jephthah accuses the king of the Ammonites of falsifying the historical record when the latter alleges that he is only reclaiming territory that Israel had taken from Ammon (Judg. 11:12–28). The notable exception to this dire assessment of kingship is a terse editorial comment attached to two shocking stories at the end of Judges: "In those days, there was no king in Israel; every man did what right in his own eyes" (Judg. 17:6; 21:25, cf. 18:1; 19:1), obviously claiming that royal authority and power would have prevented such gross criminality and destructive divisiveness within the Israelite tribal association.

While there is no single coherent description of the social system of Israel within which its decentralized politics functioned, there are enough allusions to suggest certain parameters. Israel does not exhibit centralized politics: there is no king, other than the upstart Abimelech, who holds power for only three years over Shechem and an undefined part of Manasseh and appears to be less a "king" than a claimant to paramount chieftanship based on an abusive patron-client relationship. For long stretches of the traditions there is no autocrat comparable to Moses or Joshua to dominate the community by means of enforced religious norms or regulations, until Samuel emerges with flashes of authoritarianism that enable him to become a king-maker and a king-breaker. The several tribes are internally arranged along lineage or clan lines with the individual households linked to larger protective networks.[9] There are tribal leaders, generally called "elders," who deliberate over diplomatic and military decisions (Judg. 11:5–11; 21:16; 2 Sam. 3:17–18; 5:3). Judicial disputes and contractual matters are handled variously by village elders (Ruth 4:1–12), or by a judge who travels a circuit (1 Sam. 7:15–17), or by a person of high repute to whom people bring their claims for justice (Judg. 4:4–5). There is a priesthood, but it does not have a monopoly on sacrificial practice. It has been proposed that the segmented tribes of Israel were chiefdoms, but this is problematic because of the fractured leadership terminology we have described and because the chiefdom type in anthropological studies includes leaders with ascriptive powers based on kinship ties and leaders with achieved powers who exert paramount authority through subsidiary chiefs.[10]

Although individual tribes act on their own authority, there is communication among them and frequent cooperation between two or more tribes, especially for collective defense. In the battle against Sisera, six tribes join in the fray, and there is a strong enough expectation of mutual obligation that four tribes who did not participate are severely condemned (Judges 5). Judah, Simeon, and Levi are absent from this array of tribes, and Machir and Gilead replace the customary Manasseh and Gad. Elsewhere in lists of the tribes, stereotypically conceived as twelve in number, sometimes Levi and Joseph appear, and at other times Levi is omitted and Joseph is subdivided into Manasseh and Ephraim.[11] The expressed tensions and disputes among tribes, at times over prestige and honor in warfare and at other times over crimes of kidnapping or rape and murder, on occasion lead to fierce dissension or open warfare (Judg. 8:1–3; 12:1–6; 18:14–26; 20). The fullest account of such a dispute pictures a gathering of all the tribes to demand that the rapists and murderers of a priest's concubine be handed over for execution (Judg. 20:8–13). When the host tribe refuses to do so, the accusatory tribes attack and nearly annihilate the entire populace of the offending tribe (Judg. 20:8–48), after which they take extreme measures to secure the survival of the chastened tribe (Judges 21). This schematic account presupposes much stricter coordinated measures of social control among the tribes than appears elsewhere in the traditions for this period.[12]

Although the tribal traditions are rife with vignettes of social and political life sufficient to document decentralized politics at work within loosely coordinated economic, military, and ideological networks, there is no overall articulation of these networks in a larger "constitutional" design. In part this results from the varied foci and differing levels of concreteness and abstraction in the individual traditions, producing a disjunctive effect in the movement from one tradition to another, implying perhaps that later traditionists had little or no grasp of the macroorganization of society in earlier times. This ignorance of or indifference to the larger social organizational design probably also derives in considerable measure from the tradition's built-in assumption that Israel was already a twelve-tribe entity before it entered the land, and thus there appears to have been no felt need to describe its comprehensive structure under the new conditions of agrarian settlement.

ISRAEL'S CENTRALIZED POLITICS

The era of statehood is more fully and concretely described than either the preceding or the following phases of Israel's political life. A more connected narrative develops, reporting the circumstances giving rise to kingship, and thereafter identifying and commenting on each of the kings. Nevertheless, there is great unevenness in the scope and concreteness of the records. The first three rulers—Saul, David, and Solomon—are treated at considerable length, whereas the kings that follow are given far less attention. Both domestic affairs and relations with foreign powers are recounted, but the information is often terse and lacking in context, leaving many unresolved issues of interpretation. Considerable attention is devoted to cultic reforms focused on the Jerusalem temple. Minimal space is devoted to description of state organization, but in the case of a few reigns, the narrative provides details about bureaucratic structures and administrative practices.

There are two accounts of the course of statehood, one in Samuel–Kings, and a second in Chronicles.[13] As a whole, the former account is fuller on political affairs than the latter. Chronicles employs many, but not all, of the same traditions as Samuel–Kings, and it supplies additional traditions about Judah, while omitting the reigns of the northern kings except as they interact directly with Judahite regimes. Samuel–Kings devotes considerable attention to religious affairs and also has a substantial amount of religious metacommentary on the course of the kingdoms, while Chronicles focuses almost entirely on religious developments and is far more blatant in its religious interpretation of events. Prophets, whose writings are loosely dated to the reigns of kings, provide some insights into state politics, and Proverbs, which frequently alludes to kingship and matters of court etiquette, is also relevant to our subject. Some of the Psalms reveal aspects of state cultic practice and the ideology of kingship.

Israel under One State Regime

Israel is depicted as resorting to kingship at a time when it is severely threatened with subjection by the Philistines (1 Samuel 4—5; 7:5–14;

13:2–14:46), but the pressure toward more centralized politics also derives from complaints about the abusive conduct of priests and judges (1 Sam. 2:12–17; 8:1–2). While the primary focus is on a single leader who can effectively unite and command the military forces of Israel against an invader, there is also concern to eliminate corruption and greed in religious and judicial practice. But the rise of the state, as reported, does not follow a smooth course and is not an uncontested option. The traditions in 1 and 2 Samuel reflect a pronounced ambivalence toward kingship. The compelling attraction of a powerful and just ruler is offset by fear and suspicion that his rule will infringe on the local power networks, make heavy fiscal and labor demands on the populace, and possibly turn out in the end to be no permanent corrective to domestic corruption. Samuel, the last of the "judges," who is pictured by turns as prophet, priest, and judicial figure, embodies this widespread ambivalence toward kingship. In one version, he enthusiastically initiates the election of a king (1 Sam. 9:1–10:16; 11), but in another version he warns of the dire consequences of kingship and approves of the move to kingship with great reluctance (1 Sam. 8:4–22; 10:17–27; 12).

Saul is the first "king" (*melek*), but he is sometimes described more modestly as "chief" or "prince" (*nāgîd*). Saul is from a prosperous landed family in Benjamin, tall, handsome, and forceful, and an adept warrior, as is also his son Jonathan. In one version, Saul is the hand-picked choice of Samuel, and he is acclaimed king by the people after he demonstrates his military prowess against the Ammonites (1 Sam. 9:1–10:16; 11). In another version, after Samuel has severely castigated the people for wanting a king, Saul is chosen by lot in a public assembly and immediately declared king (1 Sam. 8:4–22; 10:17–24), whereupon Samuel enunciates and preserves in writing "the customary way of kingship" (*mišpāṭ hammĕlūkâh;* 1 Sam. 10:25), but nothing is indicated about the content of this document. Earlier, when Samuel cautioned against kingship prior to the choice of Saul, he told the people "the customary way of a king" (*mišpāṭ hammelek,* 1 Sam. 8:9–18) in laying heavy demands on his subjects. Since the written *mišpāṭ* follows the installation of Saul, it is probable that it is conceived as a regulative document, implying something like "the rights and duties of kingship," possibly bearing some relationship to instructions about the king in Deuteronomy 17:14–20.[14] Saul's "capital," or more properly his headquarters, is at his family estate in Gibeah of Benjamin. He commands a levy of Israelite troops supplementing his own tribal forces. There is no mention of appointed officials, except for Doeg ("chief of Saul's herdsmen," or more probably, "chief of Saul's runners=bodyguard," 1 Sam. 21:7), and no fiscal demands are made upon his subjects. Saul moves decisively against the Philistines, expelling them from the Israelite hill country where they had established "garrisons" or "checkpoints" in an effort to subject the Israelite highlanders to tribute (1 Sam. 13:1–14; 46, 52).

Trouble arises for Saul from two quarters: an alienated Samuel and an ascendant David. By initiating religious sacrifice on his own (1 Sam. 13:8–15), Saul angers Samuel, who soon withdraws his support from the king and confers leadership on David in a private meeting (1 Sam. 16:1–13). David, a young Judahite warrior, rises to great popularity because of his military skill, develops a fast friendship with Saul's son Jonathan, and is rewarded with marriage to one of Saul's daughters. Saul is pictured as developing a murderous jealousy toward David, who flees to the countryside and gathers around him a band of socially and economically disaffected followers (1 Sam. 22:1–2). Saul kills the priests of Nob because they have given aid to David, but he fails in several attempts to track down his fugitive nemesis (1 Sam. 21:1–9; 22:9–23; 23—24, 26). David and his renegade band eventually enter the service of one of the Philistine city-state rulers and, while purporting to be raiding Judahite settlements, attack other peoples and distribute booty to David's home tribe of Judah (1 Sam. 21:10–15; 27; 30). The Philistines mount a major campaign against Israel, and Saul and Jonathan die in a crushing defeat of the Israelite forces (1 Samuel 28—29; 31).

With the death of Saul, David goes up to Hebron and becomes king in Judah. Meanwhile, in the safety of Gilead, beyond the reach of the Philistines, Saul's son Ishbaal is made king of Israel under the dominance of Abner, commander of Saul's army (2 Sam. 2:1–11). When Ishbaal and Abner have a falling out, Abner conspires to shift the loyalty of the northern tribes to David in Judah. Abner is killed by Joab, close servant of David, and two captains in the northern army assassinate Ishbaal. The narrative summarizes this period with the remark, "There was a long war between the house of Saul and the house of David; David grew stronger and stronger, while the house of Saul became weaker and weaker" (2 Sam. 3:1).

Jonathan's son Mephibosheth=Meribaal, weak and crippled, offers no competition for the throne, leaving David as the sole contender for rule over the united tribes (2 Sam. 4:4; 9).[15] Already established as king of Judah, David enters into a compact (*bĕrîth*) at Hebron with the elders of the northern tribes, and possibly with the Judahite elders as well, to establish him as king over "all Israel" (2 Sam. 5:1–5).[16] Nothing is said about the terms or conditions of this authorization of David as king by the tribal representatives who had formerly given their allegiance to Saul. After ruling for seven and one-half years in Hebron, David seizes the previously non-Israelite city of Jerusalem and makes it his capital, thus shifting his center of power northward to a site close to the border between Judah and the northern tribes (2 Sam. 5:6–10). He builds a palace and takes a number of wives and concubines (2 Sam. 5:11–16).

The Philistines, who have previously regarded David as an ally, respond to the enlargement of his kingdom to include all Israel by attacking the newly founded state in full force, but they are roundly defeated in two battles and driven back into the coastal plain (2 Sam. 5:17–25; 8:1). Flushed with success, David undertakes a series of military campaigns in Transjordan, against Moab, Edom, and Ammon, and northward against Aramean kingdoms in Damascus, Hamath, and Zobah (2 Sam. 8:2–14; 10:1–11:1; 12:26–31). He is said to be uniformly victorious, subjecting them to dependence and taking booty and tribute.[17] The ark, a religious object which has served as a rallying point for the tribes from the time of Moses, is brought by David to Jerusalem with great fanfare (2 Samuel 6). Moreover, David has aspirations to build a temple to house the ark, but because of opposition by the prophet Nathan, he is able to do no more than purchase a site on which the temple will eventually be built (2 Samuel 7; 24:18–25).

The ensuing Davidic traditions give an extended colorful recital of the stormy relations within the house of David, on which hangs the issue of whom among David's several sons will succeed him on the throne. Amnon is killed by Absalom because he raped his half-sister Tamar (2 Samuel 13—14). Absalom, playing on the grievances of the populace over David's lax administration of justice, leads a revolt against his father, but is killed by Joab (2 Samuel 15—19). A revolt of the northern tribes, led by the Benjaminite Sheba, is suppressed by Joab (2 Sam. 20:1–22). In the end, Solomon, born of an adulterous relationship between David and Bathsheba, ascends to the throne in spite of a strong internal court faction favoring Adonijah (1 Kings 1—2).

Considering the expansiveness of the David narratives, surprisingly little is said about his administrative apparatus. Two lists of David's chief officers are given (2 Sam. 8:15–18; 20:23–26), which invite comparison, not only with one another, but also with a similar list of Solomon's state officials.[18] The two Davidic rosters agree on the following appointments:

> Joab, son of Zeruiah, commander of the army (*'al* [kōl]-*haṣṣāvâ*)
> Benaiah, son of Jehoiada, commander of the Cherethites ([*'al-*] *hakkĕrētî*=Cretans?) and Pelethites ([*'al-*]*happĕlētî*=Philistines?), presumably mercenary troops recruited as a bodyguard by

David on the basis of his previous service to the Philistine city of Gath

Jehoshaphat, son of Ahilud, herald or protocol officer ([ham]*mazkîr*)

Seraiah/Sheva, secretary or chief scribe (*sôphēr*)

Zadok and Abiathar, son of Ahimelech, priests (*kōhănîm*)

The lists differ in that one adds David's sons as priests (8:18), and the other adds Ira, the Jairite, as priest (20:26). Also, one of the lists supplies Adoram as the official in charge of forced labor (*'al-hammas*; 20:24). Solomon later banished Abiathar from the state priesthood and had Joab put to death. Apart from these lists, Ahithophel is called David's "counselor" (2 Sam. 15:12) and Hushai is described as "friend of the king" (2 Sam. 15:37; 16:16; 1 Chron. 27:33), possibly to be understood as an official post.[19]

There is no mention of David levying taxes on the Israelite populace; there is, however, a tradition about a census that David undertook, the results of which he apparently was unable to use for state purposes because of a pestilence that fell upon Israel (2 Sam. 24:1–17; 1 Chron. 21:21–27). In all probability this census is to be understood as an instrument for tax collection and military conscription.[20] Saul's legacy impinges on David to the extent that he makes provision for the former king's crippled grandson (2 Samuel 9), and he takes decisive action to expiate a breach of treaty with the Gibeonites that Saul had committed (2 Sam. 21:1–14).

In spite of the great favor with which David's rise to the throne is allegedly greeted, the traditions report two major rebellions against him: one arising within the royal household and the other stemming from followers of Saul. Absalom, aspiring to replace his father as king, comes close to succeeding but fails in the end because of his hesitation to press an initial military advantage. Sheba, a Benjaminite, articulating the northern sentiment that David's rule is grossly pro-Judahite at the expense of the other tribes, foments a revolt of the northern tribes that is crushed by David's army commander Joab. At the king's death, court factions back two different sons of David as his successor, and, in the seesaw struggle, Solomon wins out over Adonijah (1 Kings 1).

After ruthlessly eliminating those who opposed his succession (1 Kings 2), Solomon turns his energies to consolidating and enhancing the achievements of his father. He does not enlarge the kingdom of David but rather strives to defend its borders, multiply its economic resources and diplomatic connections, and provide the state with a sound ideological foundation. Defensively, he builds fortresses and store cities in support of a large chariot army, drawing heavily on forced labor from his subjects (1 Kings 5:13–18; 9:15–24; 10:26). Economically, he maximizes agricultural surplus (1 Kings 4:22–28; 5:11), levies imposts on Israelite merchants and tolls on transit trade through his kingdom (1 Kings 10:14), acquires horses and chariots from Anatolia and/or Egypt and sells some of them to north Syrian kings (1 Kings 10:28–29),[21] and opens up a lucrative trade in spices and other exotics with Sheba in south Arabia and points beyond (1 Kings 10:1–10, 13). Diplomatically, he establishes relations with Tyre, both to secure timber and to access the architectural and seafaring skills of that Phoenician maritime state (1 Kings 5:1–12; 9:26–28; 10:11–12, 22). Ideologically, he builds a royal temple to symbolize and cement the religious foundations of his rule (1 Kings 6:1–9:9).

Whereas we hear nothing about David's taxation of Israelites, Solomon divides his kingdom into twelve districts whose officials are responsible for provisioning the court on a monthly rotation (1 Kings 4:7–19, 22–28 [Heb. 5:6–13]). Although the geographic layout of these districts is very sketchily described, it appears that at least in some instances they cut across previous tribal territories, perhaps for reasons of economic rationality and possibly with the added intent of defusing tribal loyalties. The uncertain status of Judah in this redistricting is obscure (Judah is named only in the LXX of 1 Kings 4:19), since to include it creates thirteen districts rather than the twelve stated at the beginning of the list. Judah may be exempt from provisioning Solomon's court, or it may do so on a different basis.[22] Solomon makes systematic use of forced labor in his building projects. One text claims that he drafts men from all sectors of the kingdom (1 Kings 5:13–18 [Heb. 5:27–32]), but another insists that he exempts Israelites from the labor corvée while imposing it only on descendants of the pre-Israelite inhabitants of the land (1 Kings 9:15–22).[23] The portion of the labor force that works in Lebanon to secure and transport cedar and cypress timber is said to work on rotation, one month in Lebanon and one month at home. Since a majority of these drafted laborers are farmers and herders by occupation, the time away from fields and flocks must put a strain on domestic households and thus affect Solomon's tax base.

The roster of Solomon's high officials (*sārîm*) reads as follows (1 Kings 4:1–6):[24]

> Benaiah, son of Jehoiada, commander of the army [under David,
>   he was commander of the Cherethites and Pelethites, who
>   are not mentioned as a separate entity in Solomon's military
>   forces] (*'al-haṣṣāvâ*)

Jehoshaphat, son of Ahilud, herald or protocol officer (*ham-mazkîr*)

Elihoreph and Ahijah, sons of Shisha, secretaries or chief scribes (*sōphĕrîm*)

Azariah, son of Zadok, priest (*hakkōhên*)

Adoniram, son of Abda, overseer of forced labor (*'al-hammas*) [probably the same as Adoram, David's appointee in this position]

Azariah, son of Nathan, over the officers of the twelve districts (*'al-hannissāvîm*)

Zabud, son of Nathan, the king's friend (*rē'eh hammelek*)

Ahishar, chief steward of the palace and royal estates (*'al-habbāyit*)

Between the reigns of David and Solomon there is continuity in the high offices and their incumbents, but there are also changes and additions. The common offices are army commander, herald/protocol officer, secretary/ chief scribe, priest, and overseer of forced labor. The added Solomonic offices are overseer of the twelve district officers, the king's friend, and chief steward, and the one "dropped" office is commander of the Cretan and Philistine mercenaries, probably due to reorganization of the military. Serving under David and Solomon are Benaiah, in different roles, and Jehoshaphat and Adoram=Adoniram, in the same positions. Solomon's priest, Azariah, is the son of David's priest, Zadok, and it is likely that Elihoreph and Ahijah are sons of David's secretary, Seraiah/Shiva=Shisha (?). The Solomonic list is marred by several textual difficulties, and it is not certain how complete the lists of David's and Solomon's top officials actually are. Nonetheless, the addition of three officials by Solomon suggests greater administrative complexity and, in particular, an attempt at improved collection and management of kingdom resources. The order in which the officers are listed, headed by a single priest, suggests a shift from David's military emphasis to an elevation of cultic-ideological concerns as Solomon's highest priority.[25]

The claimed initial successes of Solomon are not sustainable beyond his lifetime. Trouble arises from two quarters, the one external and the other internal. Rebellious discontent in Edom is backed by Egypt (1 Kings 11:14–22), and Aram=Damascus breaks entirely free from Israelite rule (1 Kings 11:23–24), reducing the flow of foreign tribute and probably interfering with Solomon's lucrative income from transit trade in Transjordan. Eventually short on resources, Solomon surrenders territory to Tyre to rectify his trade imbalance with the Phoenician city-state (1 Kings 9:10–14). Even more seriously, Jeroboam, overseer of forced labor from the northern tribes, deserts ranks by fleeing to Egypt and returns at Solomon's death to lead a revolt of the northern tribes against Rehoboam, Solomon's son and successor (1 Kings 11:26–40; 12:1–16). Jeroboam is rewarded with investiture as the first monarch of the northern kingdom (1 Kings 12:20). The grievance of the northern tribes is that they have suffered greatly from the forced labor imposed by Solomon. The rupture of united Israel ensues when Solomon's successor, Rehoboam, refuses to offer relief from the onerous corvée. In a melee at Shechem, Adoram, his overseer of forced labor, is killed, and Rehoboam is forced to retreat ignominiously to Jerusalem.

Israel under Two State Regimes

The break between Judah and the northern tribes proved to be final. Once the schism occurred, neither state was able to conquer the other and achieve reunification, and a rapprochement between the two kingdoms under Ahab and Jehoshaphat did not long outlast their deaths. From the breakup of the Solomonic kingdom onward, we encounter a twofold referent for the term "Israel"; on the one hand it designates a polity, and on the other hand it designates a religiocultural community. In the parlance of state politics, "Israel" or "House of Israel" refers to the northern kingdom, in contrast to the southern kingdom of Judah or House of David. In the historical context at the time of the schism, both the cooptation of the name "Israel" by the northern kingdom and the southern kingdom's adherence to the name "Judah" as the core location of the Davidic dynasty are understandable. In the parlance of religious and cultural identity, however, as noted previously (see "'Israel' and 'Judah' as Ambiguous Historical Agents" in chap. 2), "Israel" continues to refer to the populace of both kingdoms insofar as they are conceived as sharing a heritage of Yahweh worship. Although the northern tribes are now lapsed or apostate Yahwists, they are still Judah's "kinsfolk, the people of Israel" (1 Kings 12:24), and Rehoboam is said to have "reigned over the people of Israel who lived in the cities of Judah" (1 Kings 12:17). Moreover, references to deity by Judahites, and in Judahite prayers, are invariably to "the God of Israel" and not to "the God of Judah." Even if somewhat begrudgingly, the narrator projects a larger, inclusive Israelite identity conceived as an "imagined community" that cuts across political boundaries.

In the eyes of the narrator, this larger shared Israelite identity, strained and fraught with contradictions, is not abrogated by the hostilities between the two states. There seems little reason to doubt that the narrator is harking back to actual affinities that joined the populace of the two kingdoms in close cultural and religious ties. This of course is not to claim that all the narrator's details and interpretations of those ties are necessarily accurate memories, for there is a tendency in Kings, heightened in Chronicles, to view the relation of Israel and Judah in a hyperreligious mode that stems from later historical contexts. We may well wonder, for example, if Judahites who retained "Israel/Israelite" as a term of religious self-reference would have referred to the northern kingdom as Israel, rather than more neutrally, and even derisively, as the House of Jeroboam or House of Omri, contrasted with their own House of David. As for the specific occurrences of the names, context usually makes it clear whether "Israel" or "Israelites" refers to the northern kingdom and its populace, as in the majority of cases, or to the larger religiocultural community, as expressed in the following: "So Israel departed to their tents. But Rehoboam reigned over the people of Israel who dwelt in the cities of Judah" (1 Kings 12:16b-17), but there are contexts where the referent of the signifier "Israel" is ambiguous and may intentionally be so framed.[26]

Instead of recounting the history of the two kingdoms seriatim, one after the other, or interweaving their fortunes to emphasize certain phases or aspects of the two histories, the architect of the book of Kings treats political developments in Israel and Judah in self-contained literary panels devoted to each of the rulers. The panels of varying length are framed by opening and closing regnal formulas. Moreover, the chronographer of Kings systematically "juggles" the sequence of these individual panels of northern and southern kings according to an ingenious synchronic scheme that has a modest but inexact parallel in ancient Near Eastern royal records.[27] During the period when the two kingdoms run parallel, the records of events are interwoven by switching back and forth according to the following pattern: beginning with Jeroboam I of Israel, after a king's reign is recounted in *either* of the two states, all rulers in the *other* state who came to power before his death are introduced and their reigns described. As soon as a king is reached whose death falls later than the last ruler already treated in Israel or Judah, the story line reverts to the next monarch in succession in the other state. The result is a "staggered" recital of the two-kingdom history, entailing some repetitions and a fair amount of chronological "backtracking," particularly when contemporary rulers in the two states are actors in the story. Into this synchronic framework are inserted terse annalistic reports of royal deeds and fuller accounts of diplomatic maneuvers, battles, political coups and purges, deeds of prophets, and religious reforms. Chronicles follows the same regnal formulas as Kings but lacks the latter's synchronisms, since it does not recount the history of the north per se, referring only to those kings of Israel who had direct relations with Judah.

The numbers supplied for the synchronisms and durations of royal reigns do not "add up" at a number of points, probably because of any of a number of factors affecting the computations: incorrect calculations by the chronographer or his sources, textual errors in transmission, and/or undisclosed fluctuations in calendar and manner of counting regnal years.[28] Indeed, chronological difficulties also attend the prior reigns of Saul, David, and Solomon. A textual lacuna means that we lack a report on the length of Saul's reign (1 Sam. 13:1), and the forty-year reigns assigned to David and Solomon may well be round numbers (1 Kings 2:1; 11:42). As a consequence, there is no consensus among the many scholars who have sought to reconcile the chronological data in Kings, nor can any be expected, short of new textual discoveries.[29] Depending on the particular chronological reconstruction proposed, the relative dates calculated from the biblical text are then assigned absolute dates on the basis of Assyrian and Neo-Babylonian astronomical observations that yield exact dates for the points where Israel and Judah are referred to in Mesopotamian documents.[30]

However, even though we can determine a number of absolute dates, such as Ahab's participation in the Battle of Qarqar in 853 B.C.E. and the fall of Samaria in 722 B.C.E., these extremely valuable synchronisms do not inform us how to sort and reconcile the relative dates in the biblical records.[31] For example, one of the variables probably operative in skewing the biblical chronology is the monarchic practice of coregency whereby a king ruled jointly for a time with his son and eventual successor.[32] Such a coregency is explicitly reported for Azariah and Jotham of Judah (2 Kings 15:5), necessitated by the illness of Azariah. Several other coregencies, both north and south, are commonly proposed in order to account for the discrepant chronological data. In the first place, we do not know how many coregencies occurred. More seriously, the "overlaps" in years when kings and coregents are hypothesized to have shared authority are computed in an entirely subjective fashion, based solely on the impulse to reconcile the biblical chronology. Such is also the case with proposals that premise a spring or a fall calendar, or alternating use of both, and likewise with schemes that elect to count the year of accession as the first year of a royal reign and those that exclude the accession year from the total years of a king's incumbency. To cap off the chronological puzzle, there are considerable differences in the numbers given in MT and in the LXX, the latter being no more reconcilable than those in the Hebrew text.

Further jousting with the tangled issues of royal chronology in this study is pointless, since there is no prospect of resolving them without further external evidence. The accompanying table of the rulers of Judah and Israel provides an approximate temporal framework for our discussion of particular kings and the one queen. The royal reigns in this list are spaced to render graphically the "synchronic logic" at work in the back-and-forth movement between the kingdoms that determines the sequence in which the rulers are presented. The table provides two sets of dates for each ruler according to the reconstructions of Edwin R. Thiele and Mordechai Cogan.[33] Placed side by side, their differing dates normally vary within a range of one to four years, with a maximum twelve-year variation in two instances, a spread in the dates that is typical of other reconstructions. The names of kings who founded dynasties are capitalized. Rulers who were assassinated are marked with an asterisk [*], and the coregencies posited by the chronologies adopted here are marked with a plus sign [+]. In all but one instance, Thiele and Cogan agree on which kings served as coregents, but they differ in the number of years they assign to these coregencies. The two names given to some kings are joined by an equal sign [=]. Two anomalous rulers, whose names are bracketed, lack a regnal formula: Athaliah because the narrator considers her reign illegitimate, and Tibni because he lost out to Omri in a protracted rivalry for the throne and thus was in the end merely a "would-be" king. A final feature of the table is a listing of the number of verses in Kings and Chronicles alloted to each ruler, showing the disproportionate allocations within each book and between them. References to kings of Israel in Chronicles are of course minimal since only northern kings who interacted with Judah receive mention.

Kings of Israel	Kings and Queen of Judah
JEROBOAM I 930–909 / 928–907 (103 / 36 vv.)	
	Rehoboam 930–913 / 928–911 (36 / 57 vv.)
	Abijam=Abijah 913–910 / 911–908 (8 / 23 vv.)
	Asa 910–869 / 908–867 (14 / 47 vv.)
Nadab* 909–908 / 907–906 (8 vv.)	
BAASHA 908–886 / 906–883 (8 / 6 vv.)	

Elah*
886–885 / 883–882
(9 vv.)

Zimri*
885 /882
(8 vv.)

[Tibni]
885–880 / 882–878
(2 vv.)

OMRI
885–874 / 882–871
(7 vv.)

Ahab
874–853 / 873–852
(209 including Elijah narratives / 34 vv.)

       Jehoshaphat
       872–848+ / 870–846+
       (43 / 99 vv.)

Ahaziah
853–852 / 852–851
(20 / 3 vv.)

Jehoram*
852–841 / 851–842
(182 including Elisha narratives / 4 vv.)

       Joram
       853–841+ / 851–843+
       (9 / 20 vv.)

       Ahaziah=Jehoahaz*
       841 / 843–842
       (11 / 9 vv.)

JEHU
841–814 / 842–814
(73 vv.)

       [Athaliah*]
       841–835 / 842–836
       (21 / 24 vv.)

       Joash=Jehoash*
       835–796 / 836–798
       (40 / 47 vv.)

Jehoahaz
814–798 / 817–800
(9 vv.)

Jehoash
798–782 / 800–784
(25 / 8 vv.)

       Amaziah*
       796–767 / 798–769
       (20 / 28 vv.)

Jeroboam II
793–753+ / 788–747+
(7 vv.)

       Azariah=Uzziah
       792–740+ / 785–733+
       (8 / 23 vv.)

Zechariah*
753 / 747
(5 vv.)

Shallum*
752 / 747
(4 vv.)

MENAHEM
752–742 / 747–737
(8 vv.)

Pekahiah*
742–740 / 737–735
(4 vv.)

Pekah*
740–732 / 735–732
(7 / 16 vv.)

Jotham
750–735+ / 759–743+
(7 / 9 vv.)

Ahaz=Jehoahaz I
735–715+ / 743–727+
(20 / 27 vv.)

Hoshea
732–723 / 732–724
(6 vv.)

Hezekiah
715–686 / 727–698
(95 / 117 vv.)

Manasseh
697–642+ / 698–642
(18 / 20 vv.)

Amon*
642–640 / 641–640
(8 / 5 vv.)

Josiah
640–609 / 639–609
(50 / 60 vv.)

Jehoahaz II=Shallum
609 / 609
(3 / 3 vv.)

Jehoiakim=Eliakim
609–598 / 608–598
(9 / 6 vv.)

Jehoiachin=(Je)coniah
598–597 / 598
(13 / 2 vv.)

Zedekiah=Mattaniah
597–586 / 596–586
(24 / 11 vv.)

Key to Table:
Name of king (or queen)
Dates of Thiele / Dates of Cogan
Number of biblical verses in Kings / Chronicles
   allotted to a ruler
Capitalized name indicates founder of a dynasty

*   Kings who were assassinated
\+   Includes years as a coregent
=   Kings given two names
[ ] Rulers without regnal formulas

Following the chronologies of Thiele and Cogan, a cursory overview shows that, although Judah outlasted Israel by 137/138 years, each state had the same number of rulers, twenty in each kingdom, if we include Tibni of Israel, who contested the crown with Omri for four years. Over the 332/334-year span of the kingdom of Judah, the average length of a monarch's reign was *seventeen* years, whereas over Israel's 207/204-year course the average length of a monarch's reign was only *ten* years. Also, the length of royal reigns varied widely in both kingdoms. In Israel, six kings ruled for four years or less, three of them for less than one year, while only *four* ruled for more than twenty years. In Judah, three kings ruled for two years or less, while *eight* ruled for more than twenty years. The higher frequency of assassinations in Israel than in Judah accounts in large measure for the brevity of many reigns in the north. Although wracked by political turmoil on many occasions, Judah adhered to a single dynasty in the line of David, with only one reported interruption. Nonetheless, there were two substantial dynasties in Israel (founded by Omri and Jehu), plus three aborted dynasties that barely lasted beyond the death of the founding ruler ("founded" by Jeroboam I, Baasha, and Menahem), as well as five kings who failed to place a successor on the throne. The reasons for the greater political stability of Judah compared to Israel, as well as the implications of this disparity for understanding the structure and history of the two states, will become clearer as our study proceeds.

A confusing feature of monarchic history is the number of identical names shared by different kings, as illustrated in the following synchronism: "In the thirty-seventh year of King Joash of Judah, Jehoash son of Jehoahaz began to reign over Israel in Samaria" (2 Kings 13:10). Two names are repeated in the northern kingdom: Jeroboam I and II, the latter doubtless named in honor of the founder of the state, and Pekahiah and Pekah, probably best explained by Pekah, the military officer who assassinated Pekahiah, usurping his predecessor's name in order to legitimate his coup.[34] In an Assyrian inscription, Ahaz is called Jehoahaz, which attests to two Jehoahaz rulers in Judah, in addition to a Jehoahaz in Israel. A number of shared names cut across the two states: Joram/Jehoram, Jehoahaz, Ahaziah, Joash/Jehoash, and Shallum. These are rather common Hebrew names, some with variant spellings; consequently, there is no reason to suspect a deliberate borrowing of names from one kingdom by the other. Interestingly, it has been proposed that the Joram/Jehoram rulers, whose reigns are coterminous at a time when the two kingdoms were in close alliance, may in fact have been one and the same person who occupied both thrones simultaneously.[35] In addition, a number of the Judahite kings are assigned two names, which have sometimes been interpreted as personal and regnal names respectively, but it is not known if rulers in either kingdom regularly acquired new names at their coronation. The change from Eliakim to Jehoiakim is uncertain evidence for regnal names as a customary practice, since the new name was imposed from without by pharaoh Neco and, in any case, only exchanged the "El" compound for a "Yah" compound attached to the same root (2 Kings 23:24).[36]

We shall now detail what the biblical traditions have to say about each of these rulers in terms of domestic and foreign developments before offering a characterization and provisional evaluation of the biblical data. Biblical sources are listed for each ruler, including prophetic texts that parallel Kings or provide additional narrative details. Information derived from Chronicles and prophetic books will be cited by chapter and verse; all other details come from Kings.

ISRAEL—930–908 / 928–906
　　JEROBOAM I: 1 Kings 11:26–14:20; 2 Chronicles 11:13–16; 13
　　NADAB: 1 Kings 15:25–32

The rift in the rule of the house of David over all Israel was instigated by the northern tribes who objected strenuously to the heavy corvée labor they had been compelled to perform on the building projects of Solomon. When Rehoboam refused concessions, Jeroboam, a former overseer of Solomon's labor battalions who had turned against his master, was made king by the assembly of northern tribes. Adoram, head over the hated corvée, was sent by Rehoboam to try to negotiate a last-minute peace, but he was abruptly killed by the rebellious northerners. Rehoboam was forced to retreat to Jerusalem, having lost by far the largest part of his kingdom. Jeroboam "built up" Shechem and Penuel as his places of residence, to which Tirzah was later added. To secure the political independence of Israel from Judah, he established shrines in the north and south of the kingdom at Dan and Bethel, with a priesthood and festival calendar distinct from the cult in Jerusalem, and he recognized the legitimacy of local shrines throughout the land. From all indications, the cult established by Jeroboam was a Yahweh-oriented alternative to the Jerusalem cult of Yahweh,[37] although it is roundly condemned as apostate by the narrator, and one tradition claims that Jeroboam deported to Judah Levites who had served Yahweh (2 Chron. 11:14). Late in his reign, in a battle with Abijam's Judahite forces, Jeroboam was defeated and lost border cities to Judah

(2 Chronicles 13). Nadab, Jeroboam's son, ruled only two years before he was assassinated by Baasha during an Israelite siege of the Philistine city of Gibbethon.

JUDAH—930–913 / 928–911
    REHOBOAM: 1 Kings 11:43–12:24; 14:21–31; 2 Chronicles 10—12

As ruler over a drastically reduced territory, Rehoboam strengthened his fortifications at several sites in Judah and Benjamin. Although he is said to have had thoughts of punitive action against the breakaway tribes, he did not attempt a major military campaign against them. In his fifth year, the Egyptian pharaoh Shishak carried out a devastating attack on Judah and plundered the Jerusalem temple and palace, as well as destroying fortified sites in Judah (2 Chron. 12:4), further weakening Rehoboam's position. Credited with eighteen wives, sixty concubines, twenty-eight sons, and sixty daughters, more than any other ruler after Solomon, Rehoboam assigned his sons to districts throughout Judah and groomed Abijah=Abijam as his successor (2 Chron. 11:18–23).

ISRAEL—908–885 / 906–882
    BAASHA: 1 Kings 15:33–16:7
    ELAH: 1 Kings 16:6, 8–10, 14

Baasha exterminated all members of Jeroboam's household who might endanger his rule. He fortified Ramah, a few miles north of Jerusalem, in an apparent attempt to interfere with trade and travel entering or exiting the Judahite capital. Asa, king of Judah, took drastic measures to foil Baasha's threatening action (see below). Elah, Baasha's son, reigned for two years, but while he was partying in his chief steward's house, he was killed by Zimri, commander of half of the royal chariot forces. All the members of Baasha's family were likewise killed. Zimri himself ruled a mere seven days before he met the same fate.

JUDAH—913–869 / 911–867
    ABIJAM=ABIJAH: 1 Kings 15:1–8; 2 Chronicles 13
    ASA: 1 Kings 15:9–24; 2 Chronicles 14—16

Abijam, with a short reign of three years, is said to have wrested some contested towns in Benjamin from Jeroboam's control after foiling an ambush by the Israelite forces (2 Chron. 13:13–20). Asa, his successor, increased fortifications, strengthened his army, and repelled an invasion by Zerah the Ethiopian at Mareshah in the Judahite foothills (2 Chron. 14:6–14). Later in his reign, severely challenged by Baasha's fortification of

Ramah, Asa turned for help to the Aramean kingdom of Damascus, ruled by Ben-hadad. Asa paid Ben-hadad a substantial amount of gold and silver to induce him to break off a treaty that the Aramean had made with Israel and to renew a treaty with Judah. Ben-hadad accepted the "bribe," attacked Israel, and subjected a large part of eastern upper Galilee to his control, forcing Baasha to withdraw from Ramah. This payment to Damascus was protested by some Judahites, against whom Asa retaliated sharply by imprisoning a prophet and "inflicting cruelties on some of the populace" (2 Chron. 16:7–10). Thereupon, Asa removed the stones and timbers from the Ramah fortifications and used them to build fortifications of his own at Geba and Mizpah. He is said to have carried out cultic reforms, including the expulsion of *haqqĕdēšîm* ("cult objects" or "male cult personnel" [?]; 1 Kings 15:12) from Judah and the dismissal of his mother Maacah from the position of "queen mother" because she had made an image for Asherah worship.

ISRAEL—885–841 / 882–842
   ZIMRI: 1 Kings 16:9–13, 15–20
   TIBNI: 1 Kings 16:21–22
   OMRI: 1 Kings 16:16–17, 21–26
   AHAB: 1 Kings 16:29–22:40, 51–53; 2 Chronicles 18:1–2
   AHAZIAH: 1 Kings 22:51–53; 2 Kings 1
   JEHORAM: 2 Kings 1:17; 3; 5:5–8; 6:8–8:6, 28–29; 9:14–26

Word of the murder of Elah by Zimri reached the Israelites who were besieging Gibbethon of the Philistines. The army immediately chose their commander, Omri, to be king. Omri marched up to Tirzah and seized the city. Seeing that his cause was lost, Zimri set fire to the palace and perished in the flames. At that point, Omri's entitlement to the crown was contested by Tibni, the populace being equally divided between them. It took four years for the faction supporting Omri to prevail. Midway in his reign, Omri bought a rural hillsite and erected there the fortified capital city of Samaria. He entered into treaty with Phoenician Tyre, sealing the bond between the two states with the marriage of Jezebel, the daughter of the Tyrian ruler Ethbaal, to his son Ahab. Either Omri or his son Ahab conquered Moab and imposed annual tribute. The prophet Micah, more than a century and a half later, refers to "the statutes/decrees (*ḥuqqôt*) of Omri" (Micah 6:16) in association with socioeconomic injustice, although it is unclear whether this is a literal or metaphorical allusion.

   Ahab continued to build in Samaria, including an ivory-paneled house for himself and a temple for Baal, the deity of his Tyrian wife (1 Kings 16:32; 22:39), and other cities were built or rebuilt, including Jericho (1 Kings

16:34; 22:39). As an aspect of rapprochement between Israel and Judah, Ahab gave his sister Athaliah in marriage to Jeshoshaphat's son Joram.[38] To enlarge the grounds of his secondary residence in Jezreel, Ahab attempted to purchase the vineyard of a freeholder, Naboth. When the latter refused, at Jezebel's instigation Ahab had his property confiscated on falsified charges of blasphemy and treason against Naboth (1 Kings 21). Rivalry between worshipers of Baal and Yahweh led to reciprocal killings of one another's prophets (1 Kings 18:3b-4, 7–14, 19, 22, 40; 19:1–3, 14). The effects of a prolonged famine are reflected in Ahab having to search throughout the land for springs and pasturage for the royal horses and mules (1 Kings 17:1; 18:1–6).

Ahab was heavily engaged in warfare with Aram-Damascus at whose hands Israel under Baasha had earlier suffered reversals. A siege of Samaria by Ben-hadad was broken (1 Kings 20:1–25), but Ben-hadad soon engaged Ahab in battle at Aphek in the Golan. Defeated a second time, the Aramean ruler sued for peace with an agreement to restore Israelite cities previously taken by him and to allow Ahab a trading concession in Damascus similar to one enjoyed in Samaria by a predecessor of Ben-hadad (1 Kings 20:26–34). Ahab's leniency toward the defeated king of Damascus elicits a sharp rebuke from an anonymous prophet who castigates the king of Israel for not killing Ben-hadad as an act of "ritual destruction" commanded by Yahweh (1 Kings 20:35–42), the same judgment that Samuel had leveled against Saul in sparing the Amalekite king Agag (1 Samuel 15). The motif of obligatory ritual murder of captives recurs in the laws and narratives of Deuteronomy through Kings.[39] The ritual murder of all captives taken in Canaan, together with the destruction of all their possessions, and the ritual murder of only the male captives from extra-Canaanite cities, is pro-grammatically commanded in Deuteronomy (20:10–18). This command is carried out erratically in the conquests reported in the book of Joshua. All in all, it appears that the obligation to destroy all captives and booty was honored more in the breach then in the observance.

Pressing his advantage against Damascus, Ahab enlists Jehoshaphat in a joint Israelite-Judahite attack on Ramoth-Gilead but loses his life in the failed battle (1 Kings 22:1–37). The death of Ahab, which had been fore-cast by no less than three prophets (1 Kings 20:42; 21:20–24; 22:13–28), is described in the battle narrative in a surprisingly "neutral" manner when it states that Ahab, who had disguised himself as a rank-and-file soldier, was fatally struck in a gap between his plates of armor by an arrow shot "at a venture/randomly/by happenstance" (1 Kings 22:34).

After Ahab's death, Ahaziah ruled only two years, apparently the victim of an injurious fall. Either under Ahaziah, or his successor Jehoram, Mesha of Moab rebelled against Israel and refused to pay the huge annual tribute of lambs and wool (2 Kings 3:4–5). Jehoram secured Jehoshaphat's help, supplemented by Edomite forces, in a punitive expedition against Moab (2 Kings 3:6–25). Initially successful, the invading army withdrew when it was panicked by the Moabite king's ritual sacrifice of his son in a desperate bid to turn the tide of battle (2 Kings 3:26–27). Jehoram, in league with the Judahite king Ahaziah, attacked Ramoth-Gilead, which was still occupied by Aram=Damascus, now ruled by Hazael. Jehoram was gravely wounded and forced to return to Jezreel to recover, while the army remained in the field. The unnamed "king of Israel" at war with Aram-Damascus who appears in several of the Elisha narratives is apparently understood by the narrator to be Jehoram (2 Kings 5:5–8; 6:8–8:6), but, given the weak position of Israel vis-à-vis Damascus described therein, it is likely that he was Jehu or Jehoahaz.

JUDAH—869–841 / 870–842
    JEHOSHAPHAT: 1 Kings 15:24; 22:1–36, 41–50; 2 Chronicles 17—20
    JEHORAM: 2 Kings 8:16–24; 2 Chronicles 21
    JEHOAHAZ=AHAZIAH: 2 Kings 8:25–29; 9:21–24, 27–29; 2 Chronicles
        22:1–9

Jehoshaphat made peace with Israel, accepted Athaliah of the house of Omri as wife for his son Joram, and joined Israel in two unsuccessful military ventures, one with Ahab against Aram-Damascus (1 Kings 22:1–36) and a second with Jehoram against Moab (2 Kings 3:6–27). Building fortifications and storehouses, he was in a strong position vis-à-vis adjacent powers. Edom, whose fugitive prince Hadad had threatened Solomon's control of southern Transjordan, nonetheless remained under Judahite hegemony administered by a deputy (*niṣṣāv*), and Jehoshaphat received gifts, if not formal tribute, from Philistines and Arabs (2 Chron. 17:11). Rejecting help from Ahaziah of Israel, Jehoshaphat built Phoenician-style ships at Ezion-geber on the Gulf of Akabah in hopes of establishing maritime trade to the south and east, as Solomon had done, but his fleet was wrecked. An attack of Moabites and Ammonites by way of En-gedi on the Dead Sea was repulsed (2 Chron. 20:1–30). Domestically, Jehoshaphat is said to have appointed judges in the fortified cities of Judah, while priests and esteemed family heads in Jerusalem were assigned to decide disputed cases (2 Chron. 19:8–11). He also eliminated *haqqades*, "the sacral objects/male cult personnel" (=the *qĕdēšîm* of 1 Kings 15:12) that Asa had failed to exclude from the cult of Yahweh at Jerusalem.

On ascending the throne, Joram of Judah killed all his brothers and some officials for reasons unstated (2 Chron. 21:4). Edom again revolted and appointed its own king, and Libnah in the Judahite foothills became independent. Philistines and Arabs attacked Judah and killed all the king's sons except his youngest, Ahaziah, who ascended the throne after Jehoram died of a disease of the bowels (2 Chron. 21:16–22:1). Ahaziah's brief reign was cut short when, while campaigning with Jehoram of Israel against Ramoth-Gilead, he was assassinated during Jehu's bloody coup against the Omrid dynasty (see below).

ISRAEL—841–753 / 842–747
  JEHU: 2 Kings 9–10
  JEHOAHAZ: 2 Kings 13:1–9
  JEHOASH: 2 Kings 13:10–25
  JEROBOAM II: 2 Kings 14:23–29; Amos 7:10–17

Like Omri, Jehu was designated king by an uprising of the army during a campaign in the field. He immediately seized the initiative to eliminate opposition by exterminating all members of the house of Omri-Ahab, as well as all members of the Judahite royal family who happened to be visiting in the north at the time of the coup. He is credited with being an ardent supporter of the cult of Yahweh who destroyed the temple of Baal in Samaria that Ahab had erected and murdered all professed adherents of Baal. By murdering the queen mother, Jezebel of Tyre, he effectively broke off diplomatic, and presumably also economic, relations with that Phoenician city, just as his murder of Judahite royalty severed the ties between Israel and Judah that had developed under the Omrid dynasty. This "isolationist" policy encouraged Hazael of Damascus to take control of all Israelite territory in Transjordan. Under Jehu's successor, Jehoahaz, Damascus pressed its attacks against Israel to the point that Jehoahaz's chariot force was decimated and he was left with modest infantry troops. This phase of his reign is described in a manner reminiscent of the book of Judges in that, taking pity, "Yahweh gave Israel a deliverer" (2 Kings 13:5), This unnamed "deliverer" has been taken to be the Assyrian king, Adad-nirari III, who campaigned against Damascus during this period, although it may be more likely that the "deliverer" is the prophet Elisha, who encouraged and inspired Israelite kings to fight against Damascus (2 Kings 6:8–23; 13:14–19). Indicative of the selective enforcement of ritual murder of captives, Elisha advised the king of Israel (Jehoram? Jehu? Jehoahaz?) not to slay captured Damascene troops but to "wine and dine" them before returning them home, presumably to serve as a warning to the king of

Damascus to cease from raiding Israel, a message that the Syrian monarch clearly heard and acted on (2 Kings 6:21–24).

Under the next king, Jehoash, Israel began to recover some of the cities taken by Aram-Damascus, and even managed to plunder the temple and palace in Jerusalem when the Judahite king, Amaziah, insisted on an ill-conceived contest of arms with Jehoash (see below). Jehoash's son, Jeroboam II, is credited with restoring the borders of Israel from Hamath in north central Syria to the Dead Sea and recovering territories in Transjordan that had been lost to Damascus. The king's far-ranging victories are said to have been prophesied by a certain Jonah ben Amittai (2 Kings 14:25; cf. Jonah 1:1), but according to the prophet Amos, the booming prosperity of Jeroboam II's reign brought mounting affluence to an Israelite elite at the expense of harsh and unjust conditions for many Israelite commoners (Amos 1:1; 7:10–17). This prosperous era in the reign of Jehu's dynasty came to an abrupt end when Jeroboam's son was assassinated after only six months in office.

JUDAH—841–740 / 842–733
ATHALIAH: 2 Kings 8:17, 26; 11:1–16; 2 Chronicles 22:10–23:15; 24:7
JOASH: 2 Kings 11—12; 2 Chronicles 24:1–27
AMAZIAH: 2 Kings 14:1–14, 17–20; 2 Chronicles 25
AZARIAH=UZZIAH: 2 Kings 14:21–22; 15:1–7; 2 Chronicles 26

Athaliah, daughter of Omri and mother of the murdered King Ahaziah, assumed the role of queen. She is said to have killed off all the royal family who had not already been killed by Jehu and is credited with sponsorship, but not the actual building, of a temple for Baal in Jerusalem, analogous to Ahab's temple for Baal in Samaria. Within a few years, a young Davidic prince who survived the killings was installed as king in a coup instigated by the priest Jehoiada and the palace guard. Athaliah was assassinated and the Baal cult suppressed.[40] When he attained his majority, Joash undertook extensive repairs of the Jerusalem temple that had been long delayed because priests misappropriated the funds given for that purpose. The king instituted a graft-free system for collecting and channeling contributions to the temple renovation. In the course of devastating Israel, Hazael of Damascus extended his conquests as far as Philistine Gath on the western border of Judah. Joash of Judah averted an impending attack on his kingdom by sending Hazael a large payment that he took out of the temple and palace treasuries, repeating the strategy employed by Asa when he "bought" the aid of Aram-Damascus against hostile Israel (1 Kings 15:16–20). The Chronicler explains Joash's subjection to Aram-Damascus as a result of the king's backsliding into idolatry after the death of Jehoiada, his mentor-priest, even going so far as to kill Zechariah, Jehoiada's son, which precipitated Joash's own violent death (2 Chron. 24:17–27).

After a thirty-eight-year reign, Joash was assassinated at the hands of two of his household officials. Once having established firm control of the kingdom, Joash's son Amaziah avenged his father's murder by killing his assassins. Following a successful military campaign against Edom, Amaziah brashly challenged Jehoash of Israel to do battle. The armies clashed at Bethshemesh on Judah's western border, and Amaziah was defeated. Jehoash proceeded to break down a long section of the wall around Jerusalem and plundered the temple and palace treasuries. This would appear to have been the opportune moment for the northern kingdom to incorporate Judah, but no such attempt was made by Jehoash. Subsequently, a conspiracy against Amaziah forced him to flee to Lachish, where he was captured and killed. Chronicles reports that after his victory over the Edomites, Amaziah worshiped their gods, and because of this apostasy was defeated by Jehoash of Israel (2 Chron. 25:14–24).

Azariah=Uzziah, son of Amaziah, enjoyed a long and prosperous reign over Judah that coincided with the expansive regime of Jeroboam II in Israel. Apart from his recovery of the port of Elath from Edom, Azariah's accomplishments are recorded only in Chronicles. He waged war against Philistine cities and planted Judahite settlements in a section of Philistine territory (2 Chron. 26:6), fought against Arabs and Meunites (2 Chron. 26:7; from Maon in Transjordan or the Minaeans of southern Arabia?), and received tribute from Ammon (2 Chron. 26:8). To enhance his military power, Azariah strengthened the fortifications of Jerusalem, reorganized his army, and improved its weaponry (2 Chron. 26:9, 11–15). The royal holdings in herds and crops were productively managed by capitalizing on regional economic specialization: herds were grazed in the Negeb, cereals were grown in the foothills and the coastal plain, and vineyards and orchards were cultivated in the hill country (2 Chron. 26:10). However, Azariah became leprous, and his son Jotham, in the capacity of chief steward, governed the people as coregent until his death.

ISRAEL—753–723 / 747–724
    ZECHARIAH: 2 Kings 15:8–12
    SHALLUM: 2 Kings 15:10, 13–15
    MENAHEM: 2 Kings 15:11, 17–22
    PEKAHIAH: 2 Kings 15:23–26

PEKAH: 2 Kings 15:25, 27–31; 16:5–9; Isaiah 7:1–6
HOSHEA: 2 Kings 17:1–4

After the forty-year reign of Jeroboam II, Israel was ruled by six kings in the span of twenty-three years, four of them assassinated by their successors and a fifth removed from office by the Assyrians prior to their siege and capture of Samaria. The Jehu dynasty ended when Shallum assassinated Zechariah, son of Jeroboam II, after a six-month reign. Shallum was in turn struck down after only one month by Menahem, who delivered a punishing blow to Tappuah because it was a city that did not recognize his rule. Under Menahem the political turmoil in Israel was exacerbated by the sudden imperious intrusion of Assyria into Syro-Palestine, initiated by the expansionist policies of Tiglath-pileser III. In order to avert an attack by the Assyrian king and to consolidate his grip on the throne, Menahem paid tribute of a thousand talents of silver that he exacted from "all the men of means" within his kingdom. The per capita exaction of fifty shekels computes to a levy on 60,000 persons. Menahem's son, Pekahiah, ruled briefly before he was murdered by Pekah, one of his military officers.

To fend off the Assyrians, Pekah entered a military alliance with Rezin of Damascus, and the two together put pressure on Ahaz of Judah to join them (Isa. 7:5–6). Ahaz refused and turned instead to Assyria for protection from the military threat that Israel and Damascus posed to Judah. In response to Judahite submission to Assyria, Tiglath-pileser conquered Galilee and Gilead and deported the populace, reducing Israel to less than half its former size, now consisting solely of the highland territory of Ephraim and Manasseh. Not long afterward, Pekah lost his ally Rezin when Assyria terminated the kingdom of Aram-Damascus. Hoshea assassinated Pekah and accepted Assyrian hegemony by pledging payment of annual tribute to the recently enthroned king Shalmaneser V. In a sharp turnabout, Hoshea subsequently rebelled against Assyria by withholding the tribute and courting support from Egypt. Shalmaneser removed Hoshea from office, captured Samaria after a lengthy siege, deported its populace to scattered locations in Upper Mesopotamia, and resettled captives from Mesopotamia in Israel to replace the rebellious deportees.

This marked the end of the kingdom of Israel, which thereupon became a province of the Assyrian empire. The eclectic objects and forms of worship among the surviving Israelites and the immigrants transplanted by Assyria are recounted, including the repatriation of a deported Yahweh priest who "resided in Bethel and taught them how they should 'fear' [i.e., worship] Yahweh" (2 Kings 17:28), with the mixed result that "they feared [worshiped] Yahweh but also served their own gods," which the narrator expands to say, "So these nations feared Yahweh, and also served their graven images; their children likewise, and their children's children—as their fathers did, so they do to this day" (2 Kings 17:33, 41). The narrator here makes an assessment rooted in his own setting, which is probably no earlier than the late Judahite monarchy and may be as late as the Judahite restoration in the late sixth or fifth centuries.

JUDAH—750–686 / 759–698
    JOTHAM: 2 Kings 15:32–38; 2 Chronicles 27
    AHAZ: 2 Kings 16; 2 Chronicles 28; Isaiah 7
    HEZEKIAH: 2 Kings 18–20; 2 Chronicles 29–32; Isaiah 36—39; Proverbs 25.1

Jotham, who had served for some time as coregent with his father Azariah, engaged in building activities in Jerusalem and elsewhere in Judah. He warred with the Ammonites and imposed tribute on them (2 Chron. 27:5). Ahaz began to feel the menacing presence of Assyria in the region when Pekah of Israel and Rezin of Damascus tried to force him into an alliance against the Assyrians. Jerusalem was under siege, and Edom on the southeast and the Philistines on the southwest seized this moment of Judahite vulnerability to attack (2 Chron. 28:16–18). Ahaz appealed directly to Assyria for deliverance, offering a large payment, and as a newly pledged vassal, he introduced an Assyrian or Damascene style altar to the temple in Jerusalem. It is unclear whether the adoption of this altar signaled desertion of the cult of Yahweh or was a mode of adapting Yahweh worship to Assyrian or Damascene cultic conventions.[41] In response to Ahaz's submission to Assyria, Tiglath-pileser took military action against Pekah and Rezin, who were forced to abandon their siege of Jerusalem. Shorn of much of its territory, Israel was reduced to a mountain enclave in Ephraim and Manasseh and within a decade lost its independence as a sovereign state (2 Kings 17:5–41; 18:9–12). It is thus evident that Judah had a hand in precipitating the demise of the northern kingdom, although there is every reason to believe that the weakened state of Israel would eventually have fallen to Assyria.

Hezekiah, Ahaz's successor, is credited with religious reforms, including demolishing a cult object in the form of a bronze serpent said to have been fashioned by Moses (cf. Num. 21:6–9, which attributes curative powers to the image). Hezekiah is also said to have magnanimously invited survivors of the fall of Israel to participate in the Judahite observance of Passover, but only a handful of northerners accepted his invitation (2 Chron. 30:1–11, but cf. 30:18, which presumes a much larger but ill-informed and "impure" northern participation).

On the military front, Hezekiah campaigned against the Philistines. Inheriting vassal obligations to Assyria, Hezekiah at first remained loyal even when other Syro-Palestinian states were rebelling. Eventually, however, he became a ringleader in revolt against Assyria, for which he made careful preparations by fortifying Jerusalem and securing its water supply against siege. Sennacherib invaded Judah and gained control of the entire country outside Jerusalem. One strand in the tradition implies that the siege was lifted when Hezekiah submitted and paid tribute to Sennacherib (2 Kings 18:14–16), but two other explanations of the sparing of Jerusalem are offered: that Sennacherib abandoned the siege when he heard of political disturbances at home (2 Kings 19:7, 37), and that a plague devastated the Assyrian army (2 Kings 19:35–36). In this period, Hezekiah received a delegation from Merodach-baladan, a Babylonian ruler, with whom he shared detailed information about the contents of the state treasury and armory, presumably with the thought of joining in yet another rebellion against Assyria (2 Kings 20:12–19). In spite of his rebellion, Hezekiah was retained by the Assyrians as the vassal king of Judah.

JUDAH—697–586 / 698–586

   MANASSEH: 2 Kings 21:1–18; 2 Chronicles 33:1–20
   AMON: 2 Kings 21:19–26; 2 Chronicles 33:21–25
   JOSIAH: 2 Kings 21:24; 22:1–23:30; 2 Chronicles 34—35
   SHALLUM=JEHOAHAZ: 2 Kings 23:31–34; 2 Chronicles 36:1–4; Jeremiah
      22:11 (cf. 1 Chron. 3:15)
   ELIAKIM=JEHOIAKIM: 2 Kings 23:34–24:6; 2 Chronicles 36:4–8; Jeremiah
      26; 36:1–2, 20–32
   [JE]CONIAH=JEHOIACHIN: 2 Kings 24:8–16; 25:27–30; 2 Chronicles
      36:9–10; Jeremiah 27:1–3; 29:1–2; 52:31–34
   MATTANIAH=ZEDEKIAH: 2 Kings 24:17–25:21; 2 Chronicles 36:11–21;
      Jeremiah 27:1–3; 29:5; 32:1–5; 34; 37:1–39:10; 51:59–60; 52:1–11.

Little is said about politics under Manasseh, whose sixty-year reign was the longest enjoyed by any king of Judah or of Israel. He is reported to have "shed very much innocent blood," but the disturbances referred to cryptically are unexplained. Chronicles claims that he was taken captive to Babylon by the Assyrians on suspicion of disloyalty and then restored to his throne, following which he became an exemplary king by reversing his previous religious apostasy, with the one exception that he allowed worship to continue at the high places, "but only to Yahweh their God" (2 Chron. 33:10–17). This alleged "conversion" of Manasseh ill accords with the assessment of the narrator of Kings who attributes the fall of Judah to the enormity of Manasseh's sin, which outweighed the good accomplished by Josiah (2 Kings 21:10–15; 23:26–27). Manasseh's son Amon was assassinated by palace officials, who were immediately put to death by "the people of the land," following which they chose Josiah, Amon's son, to be king.

The new king, Josiah, undertook major temple repairs, during which a neglected book of laws was uncovered. In solemn ceremony, the king, his officials, and the people subscribed to this document as "the law of the land." It is widely assumed that the scroll of laws was some version of the biblical book of Deuteronomy. Implementation of the book's cultic laws involved expunging from the temple many cultic practices devoted to "foreign gods," closing down all places of worship other than the Jerusalem temple, and destroying the former Israelite state shrine at Bethel, along with all the open-air shrines in the northern countryside. Kings dates Josiah's reforms to his eighteenth year in office, but Chronicles reports that the reforms began already in his twelfth year, perhaps even as early as his eighth year (2 Chron. 33:3–7). After an auspicious start in reviving the state of Judah, Josiah was killed in a confrontation or battle with pharaoh Neco that took place at Megiddo as Egyptian forces were marching through Palestine to engage a distant enemy in upper Syria, one version saying that Josiah "went to meet" Neco (2 Kings 23:29) and the other stating that Josiah "went out against" Neco to do battle with him (2 Chron. 35:20–22).

Shallum=Jehoahaz, son of Josiah, ruled for a mere three months before pharaoh Neco deposed him and installed his brother Jehoiakim as his vassal in Judah, imposing tribute which Jehoiakim raised by taxing his subjects, as Menahem had done in Israel. Jehoiakim is remembered for killing the prophet Uriah, who had spoken against his regime (Jer. 27:20–23), and for contemptuously destroying a scroll containing the dictated words of Jeremiah (Jer. 36:1–2, 20–26). Neo-Babylonia soon replaced Egypt as the hegemonic power in Palestine, and Jehoiakim paid Nebuchadnezzar tribute for three years before refusing further payment. Babylonia, assisted by its Syro-Palestinian auxiliary troops, besieged Jerusalem, during which time Jehoiakim died and was replaced by his son Jehoiachin. When Jerusalem was taken, Jehoiachin and a large number of royal family members, civil and military officers, and artisans were taken into captivity—8,000–10,000 according to one tradition (2 Kings 24:14, 16), and 3,023 according to another (Jer. 52:28).

Mattaniah=Zedekiah, Jehoiachin's uncle, was appointed king by the

Babylonians, probably as stand-in for the deported Jehoiachin. Zedekiah was torn between pro- and anti-Babylonian factions in Judah, eventually choosing to rebel in hopes of support from neighboring states, including Egypt (Jer. 27:1–3). Direct communication between Zedekiah and his Babylonian overlord is twice mentioned, once by means of two officials sent to Babylon by Zedekiah (Jer. 29:3), and a second time by a personal visit of Zedekiah to Babylon (Jer. 51:59). Zedekiah's vacillating relationship with Jeremiah is reported in some detail (Jer. 32:1–5; 34; 37:1–39:10). During an extended siege by the Babylonians, Zedekiah brokered the release of Jerusalem's slave population, but this emergency-prompted manumission was rescinded when the siege was lifted (Jer. 34:8–22).

With the capture of the city, Jerusalem's political, military, and religious facilities were destroyed by burning down temple, palace, and all other public buildings and demolishing the walls that enclosed and protected the city as an administrative and commercial center. Seventy-some religious, civilian, and military leaders of Judah were executed, and many others were deported (832 persons, Jer. 52:29). A few years later a third deportation occurred (745 persons, Jer. 40:7; 52:30). Those who were not taken away in the deportations under Jehoiachin and Zedekiah are described as "the poor people of the land" to whom were assigned cultivation of vineyards and fields, but the number of these impoverished Judahite agrarians is not stated (2 Kings 24:15; 25:12; Jer. 52:15–16). So ended the sovereign state of Judah. There is a brief glimpse of Jehoiachin in exile when it is reported that Evil-merodach, the Babylonian king who succeeded Nebuchadnezzar, showed favor to Jehoiachin by allowing him to eat at the king's table (2 Kings 25:27–30).

Characteristics of Israel's Centralized Politics in Biblical Texts

What understanding of centralized politics in ancient Israel is communicated by the narrative descriptions of the Hebrew Bible? Certain salient points stand out.

Political History Depicted in Confusing Montage. Several features of the biblical accounts make them difficult to fathom as witnesses to Israel's monarchic politics. One is the matter of sources. The narrating voice in Samuel–Kings cites three written sources where fuller information about the kings can be found, with the implication that these sources were excerpted to compose the biblical history and that they were still accessible at the time of writing. The sources cited in Kings are the Acts of Solomon (1 Kings 11:41), the Chronicles of the Kings of Israel (throughout 1–2 Kings beginning at 1 Kings 14:19), and the Chronicles of the Kings of Judah (throughout

1–2 Kings beginning at 1 Kings 14:29).[42] Chronicles cites many more such sources, frequently attributed to seers and prophets.[43] It is obvious that other sources besides those cited were employed in composing Samuel–Kings. Uncredited sources in 1 and 2 Samuel cluster around Samuel, Saul, and David, and those drawn upon in 1 and 2 Kings concern prophets, political coups, and cultic reforms.

This is not the place to evaluate the reliability or speculate about the contents of the cited sources, or to conjecture about the uncited sources that were drawn on. Our purpose at this juncture is rather to observe how the selective incorporation of diverse sources has affected the range, shape, and coherence of the political reportage. The result of this multisource origin for Samuel–Kings and Chronicles is that they present a montage of materials whose varying genre structures, topical foci, and ideological shapes are juxtaposed rather than smoothly integrated. Many gaps and incoherencies stand between the traditions incorporated in Samuel–Kings and the narrator's effort to shape them into a master narrative. Basically the same may be said of Chronicles, except that the author has purchased a larger measure of ideological coherence, both by omitting many troublesome narratives that appear in Samuel–Kings and by bearing down insistently on a close cause-effect relationship between cultic performance and the good or ill fortunes of kings and their subjects.

The synchronic chronology, while offering a surface framework to the narratives, does not resolve the problem of the disconnectedness in genres, topics, and ideologies. Within the reigns of kings, the order of narrated events and the time lapse between events is often unclear. Some of the Elisha narratives cannot be securely connected to a particular royal reign. Also, since some kings with short reigns are given more "press" than those with lengthier reigns, it is no small task for the reader to envison the time spans involved and to estimate the political "weightiness" of particular kings. Moreover, by structuring the account in successive self-contained panels devoted to each ruler, the effect is a paratactic recital of one reign after another that eschews long-term trends and patterns from reign to reign while focusing on the heads of state as the central actors and movers of events. The monarchs appear foregrounded against an assortment of officials and a largely undifferentiated body of subjects. The effects of this paratactic literary method on the time sense of the reader and on the possibilities for perceiving the coherence of events in Kings bear close attention. As one commentator has astutely observed,

> In this system, chronology is linear only in a very general sense.
> Actually, the author starts and finishes one reign before beginning

another, regardless of how far ahead of some absolute chronology this procedure takes the reader. Consequently, the reigns overlap where a king who is as yet unknown in the onward progression of time suddenly appears as a figure in the reign of his counterpart in north or south. . . . Time flows ahead, then back, then far ahead again, until finally the reader faces the exilic situation, presumably the period in which the author-editor wrote. Monarchical history in fact consists of discrete time periods—or under the aspect of literary content, enclosed blocks of tradition, none clearly subordinate to another, all linked with the barest of connective tissue. . . . Sometimes the author-editor simply juxtaposes two regnal periods, without an explicit bridge. . . . The work is an extended parataxis, regnal periods arranged like links in a chain, the "story" told without a strictly linear flow of time.[44]

Particularly perplexing is the disproportion and imbalance in the treatment of the course of events from a political perspective. Certain kings receive major attention, but what is said of them relates primarily to their involvement in cult and temple. The critical moments in the development of the northern monarchy that issued in the reign of Omri and the accomplishments of his entire dynasty are only superficially treated. The reign of Jehu following his coup is a blank. The "intrusive" Elijah and Elisha narratives are centered on the prophets and only fragmentarily related to political developments, which are not "fleshed out" by the narrator. What appear to have been prosperous and expansionist periods in the regimes of Jeroboam II of Israel and Azariah of Judah are passed over in a few verses. The "dark age" of Manasseh's long rule is disposed of with theological generalizations.

The recurrent disproportions between what is said and unsaid about the political history cannot be satisfactorily explained by imagining that the narrator used all the sources available to him and that he would certainly have told us more if he knew more, granted of course that the finite limits of his sources played a conditioning role in the composition. Nor can these disproportions be attributed to the carelessness of the narrator, for there are too many signs of deliberation in the construction of the work. We are left, as one observer has noted, with an account that is highly purposive in its design and execution, characterized by

imbalance in the complete narrative with its apparent overattention to the activities of Elisha and certain kings to the detriment of a comprehensive picture of the last century and a half of the history of Israel and Judah. The consistent nature of this "imbalance" identifies it as deliberate. In other words, there is a clear *selection* of certain materials from historical sources to the exclusion of others, and the emphasis that the writer places upon the activities of Elisha, Hezekiah, Jehu, Isaiah and Josiah betrays a preference for certain themes and examples of those themes in the actions of historical persons.[45]

Insofar as there is interpretive reflection on the course of political events, it is provided almost exclusively by a religious metadiscourse that pivots on the fidelity to Yahweh of rulers and their subjects conceived as a corporate whole. The "preference for certain themes" is decidedly oriented to the rhythm of cultic decline and cultic renewal. The criteria by which kings and their subjects are judged have no certain relevance or appropriateness to their actual calculations and behaviors amid the political and religious choices they faced. In short, although we are given considerable information about political events, we are given no controlling political perspective, but rather a network of analogies posed in cultic terms, since "these framework appraisals weave a metahistorical pattern of analogies and repetitions, a system of echoes and anticipations which unify the work at a conceptual level apart from the constraints of time and space."[46]

As a consequence of this preoccupation with the proper cult of Yahweh, communicated by means of a segmented and paratactic literary structure, the tumult of events recounted in Kings and Chronicles suffers from a decided lack of attention to the specifically political factors that "pushed" the course of events in one direction or another. In particular, the cast of characters in the political drama is not adequately delineated, since little information is given about the political agendas of kings, bureaucrats, and the various sectors of the general populace. In proposing political perspectives appropriate to the history recounted, the critical imagination of the interpreter must put together scenarios that go "behind" and "beyond" the narrator's fundamentally religious montage.

One People in Two Polities. The synchronic chronology aims at drawing a close connection between the political fortunes of Israel and Judah based on the premise that they share a fundamental unity in spite of their fractured history.[47] This synchronic literary device makes sense only if the traditionists were working with some notion, however hazily conceived, of an inclusive Israel encompassing the political entities Israel and Judah as members of one religiocultural community. In spite of its unrelenting condemnation of northern rulers, this synchronizing scheme shows that the author of Kings wishes to present the two states in a "love-hate" relationship, their fierce feuds articulated ambivalently as "a family quarrel" for which no resolution is reached. The split between north and south is already adumbrated in the struggle between the House of Saul and the House of David which, unresolved by the initial consent of all Israel to

David's rule, is passed on to Solomon as "a time bomb" that eventually ruptures the unity of the state. Chronicles, while ignoring northern politics except as they enter directly into Judah's history, exhibits a similar ambivalence but proposes a distinctive resolution of the conflict by allowing for repentant survivors of the fallen northern state to join the cult community of Yahweh in Jerusalem, but the offer from Hezekiah receives scant response. However, no "family reunion" between northerners and southerners was ever achieved, either during the monarchy or later under colonial conditions.

Given the strong selective biases of Samuel–Kings and Chronicles and the uncertain circumstances of their composition, it is pertinent to ask: Is the concept of inclusive Israel that haunts the narrators solely a nostalgic construct in hindsight, or was it a concept shared by rulers and subjects during the monarchic history recounted by Samuel–Kings and Chronicles? For reasons to be discussed in chapter 5, it is the sense of this study that the traditionists do correctly identify a commonality in the populations of Israel and Judah that entailed shared sociocultural and religious traditions and practices that ran deeper than the political "union" accomplished under David and Solomon. It is precisely this shared identity that is expressed in the prestate traditions of tribal Israel. This is not to say that the traditionists of Samuel–Kings and Chronicles have put a convincing "spin" on the content or thrust of the shared repertory of inclusive Israel in monarchic times, since it is patent that their primary interpretive categories derive from a later religious Yahwistic "orthodoxy" and "orthopraxis." Nonetheless, it seems to me that Samuel–Kings and Chronicles have grasped the fundamental point of a shared identity that, although unable to sustain political union, nevertheless endured amid the political divisions and, at the same time, endlessly complicated those divisions.

Gaining and Keeping Political Power. Succession to the throne is a matter of prime importance in the monarchic narratives. Success or failure in establishing and sustaining continuity of leadership is carefully noted at the beginning and end of royal reigns. Circumstances attending the termination of each royal incumbency are dutifully noted, the largest number by natural death (twenty-one kings), many by assassination (thirteen kings), and some through removal from office by a conquering foreign power (four kings) or death in battle (two kings). The high incidence of assassinations is striking. The political identity and motives of the assassins, and those parties who supported them, are either unreported, obscurely noted, or tendentiously described. The latter is especially the case in Chronicles, with its predilection for cut-and-dried religious motivations for the regicides.

Nonetheless, there are discernible differences in the patterns of assassination in the two kingdoms.

Eight of the reported cases of regicide occurred in the state of Israel. Three attempts at sustaining dynasties were cut short by assassination. The "dynasties" of Jeroboam I and Baasha at the fountainhead of the northern kingdom, and of Menahem not long before the fall of the northern kingdom, did not survive the deaths of their would-be "founders" by more than two years. Two other dynasties were more enduring. The House of Omri extended through four rulers from 882 to 843 B.C.E., and the House of Jehu embraced five rulers from 842 to 747 B.C.E. All five of these dynastic endeavors were terminated by assassinations. A further regicide occurred in the interim between Baasha's and Omri's reigns. Two more assassinations followed the eclipse of the Jehu dynasty. In all eight instances, it was the assassin who took the vacated throne. A number of these northern assassinations were military coups, and it is possible to explain them by personal ambition. It is apparent, however, as with Jehu and the last kings of Israel, that shifts in religious and political policies were often entailed and that no easy separation can be made between personal ambition and social, political, and religious sentiment as factors in these violent changes of regime. Instead of usurpations by "lone assassins," these violent shifts in political leadership represented wider convulsions in state and society that are only partially discernible in the terse and cryptic sources.[48]

It comes as somewhat of a surprise that the enduring dynasty of David in Judah was punctuated by five assassinations, although none dislodged the Davidic lineage, if indeed that was the intention of any of the assassins, Athaliah included. Joram murdered all his brothers and some officials after ascending the throne (2 Chron. 26:4). Ahaziah, who at the time of Jehu's coup was on a joint military operation with Joram of Israel, was killed by Jehu along with other visiting members of the Judahite royal household as part of the usurper's extirpation of the Omrid line (2 Kings 9:27–28; 10:12–14). A century later, Ahaz was apparently targeted for the same fate as Ahaziah when Pekah of Israel and Rezin of Damascus plotted to replace him as king with "the son of Tabeel" (Isa. 7:5–6).[49] Athaliah, daughter of Omri and mother of Ahaziah through an intermarriage that linked the two royal houses, reportedly seized the throne and killed off the remaining members of the Davidic household, except for the boy Joash, who was sequestered and eventually put on the throne in a palace revolt that led to the queen's execution (2 Kings 11). Two named officials of Joash assassinated him (2 Kings 12:20–21), but were executed by his son Amaziah (2 Kings 14:5), who was in turn assassinated by unnamed Jerusalem court conspirators (2 Kings 14:19–20). A century and a half later, unnamed officials of Amon assassinated him, but were put to death by "the people of the land" who then elevated Josiah to the throne (2 Kings 21:23–24).

All of the assassinations in Judah were intradynastic murders that did not displace the Davidic line, even during the eight years that Athaliah was queen. This accounts for a major difference between assassinations in the two kingdoms. Assassins in Israel customarily killed off all members of the king's household because they were intent on establishing new dynasties, whereas in Judah the incumbent kings Joash, Amaziah, and Amon alone were targeted by assassins, who did not aspire to usurp the Davidic line but only to seat a different Davidic ruler. Joram's murder of his six brothers and some state officials may have been motivated by a fear that the valuable gifts and holdings his father had given to the brothers would threaten his hold on the kingship (2 Chron. 21:1–4). Considering that Solomon similarly killed off potential rivals (1 Kings 2), Joram's purge of his blood relations may well have been duplicated by other rulers north and south. Jehu's murder of Ahaziah of Judah, together with a party of forty-two royalty visiting their counterparts in Israel, is a special case of assassination carried out across state jurisdictions, probably with the intent of rooting out all Phoenician influence in neighboring Judah. Jehu's purge of Judahite royalty is implicated in similar killings attributed to Ahaziah's mother Athaliah.

Athaliah's murder of "all the royal family" is more difficult to explain. She is clearly cast in the mold of her sister-in-law Jezebel as a notorious Baal-worshiper. According to Chronicles, her baleful influence not only corrupted her son Ahaziah (2 Chron. 22:3), but it is further claimed that after her execution, "the sons of Athaliah, that wicked woman, broke into the house of God and used all the dedicated things of the house of Yahweh for the Baals" (2 Chron. 24:7). The narrator, without openly saying so, appears to attribute to Athaliah a dark plot to establish an exclusively Baal-affiliated dynasty. The difficulty with this innuendo is twofold. In the first place, the introduction of Baal temples in Samaria and Jerusalem was not intended to replace the Yahweh cult but to supplement it in recognition of diplomatic ties with Phoenicia. There is no indication that Athaliah attempted to suppress Yahweh worship, and it is noteworthy that her name carries the theophoric component "Yah," as does her son Ahaziah's name. Second, if Athaliah killed off all the Davidides that Jehu had missed, presumably including her own sons along with any other of Ahaziah's sons by other wives, who could have carried on the new dynastic line? And why would she want to complete the decimation of the Judahite royal family that Jehu, the murderer of her sister-in-law Jezebel, had launched, especially when it would leave her without progeny or kin to start another dynasty? And, in the mind of the Chronicler, who could these surviving "sons of Athaliah" (2 Chron. 24:7) have been other than sons by Joram and thus of the Davidic line which, apart from Joash, she had supposedly extirpated at the time of her usurpation? Or does the Chronicler have in mind that Athaliah remarried a non-Davidide and raised up sons to establish a dynasty of her own, and, if so, how did they escape execution along with their mother?

In spite of the surprising ease with which readers have accepted her depiction at face value, it appears that Athaliah is badly misrepresented in the biblical account and is more plausibly understood as trying to provide a caretaker government in the wake of Jehu's murder of her son and many other members of Judahite royalty, leaving perhaps only Joash. It seems to me less far-fetched than the biblical scenario to imagine that Athaliah was serving as guardian of her grandson Joash and that she was assassinated in a palace plot aimed at removing her Phoenician-tainted influence on the young ruler.[50]

Polemical Versions of State Religion. In the biblical accounts, kings are depicted as exercising ultimate oversight of the state religion. They build and renovate temples, supervise temple worship, introduce and suppress cults, launch reform initiatives, officiate on important religious occasions, and appoint priests to carry out routine cultic duties. These religious functions of royalty in Israel and Judah are congruent with similar royal duties in other ancient Near Eastern states.[51] Far and away the major interest of Samuel–Kings and Chronicles in royal religion in united Israel and in Judah is the work of kings as builders and renovators of temples[52] and as reformers who purge the Jerusalem temple cult of foreign accretions.[53] Little is said about northern kings as temple builders and sustainers. Jeroboam's sanctuaries at Dan and Bethel are noted as illegitimate alternatives to Jerusalem, and Ahab builds a Baal sanctuary that Jehu "reforms" by obliterating it. The erection of a Yahweh temple in Samaria is omitted, leaving the impression that the sole sanctuary in the capital was Ahab's Baal temple.

On the whole, the involvement of the Israelite states in religious affairs is recounted in a disappointingly schematic and sporadic manner. To be sure, the summary evaluations of rulers seldom fail to pontificate on their performance as custodians of the cult, with only occasional remarks on other aspects of their statecraft, but in most instances the condemnations rendered are vague and stereotypical in the extreme. Certain of the narratives make up for this deficiency in descriptive detail only in limited measure, since large stretches of narrative tradition in Samuel–Kings have little or nothing to say about royal religion. The far fuller religious reportage in Chronicles adds little to our knowledge since, even more than Samuel–Kings, it patently idealizes the acts of "good" kings and castigates the acts of "bad" rulers with embellishments of dubious reliability. Moreover, the Chronicler's inflated descriptions of the musical and sacrificial programs of the Jerusalem temple, and of the priestly orders in charge of the cult, belong to the practice of the rebuilt temple rather than to the temple of the monarchic era.[54]

In the reports on religious affairs during the united monarchy, Saul is pictured as a flawed Yahwist who disobeys priestly instructions and violates his own decree not to consult mediums (1 Sam. 13:8–14; 15; 28:3–10). David is credited with bringing the ark to Jerusalem (2 Sam. 6:12–19) and passionately desiring to build a temple in Jerusalem (2 Sam. 7:1–17). Although he is advised by a prophet not to erect a temple, David purchases high ground for an open-air altar to mark the site of the future sanctuary (2 Sam. 24:18–25). Solomon devoutly worships Yahweh at Gibeon (1 Kings 3:3–4) prior to erecting a lavishly ornate temple in Jerusalem staffed by an official priesthood and splendidly provisioned with abundant sacrifices (1 Kings 6—8). David, however, runs afoul of Yahweh when he takes a census of his subjects, for which the kingdom is afflicted with a plague (2 Sam. 24:1–17), and Solomon marries foreign women and worships their gods, for which he suffers the even more drastic penalty of losing the greater part of his kingdom when the northern tribes rebel (1 Kings 11:1–13). As a consequence of Solomon's religious lapse, the solemn promise of an everlasting Davidic dynasty and an inviolate temple cult is put into profound jeopardy with the threat of an imminent drastic reduction of his kingdom and the foreshadowing of an eventual end to the kingdom altogether (1 Kings 8:46–53).

Although somewhat more nuanced and restrained in certain details than Chronicles, the account in Kings also evaluates the religious policies and practices of the rulers of Israel and Judah according to an inflexible set of criteria couched in stereotypical rhetoric and reiterated stock phrases. They are voted "up" or "down" as good or bad kings, depending on how diligently or how poorly they have preserved the cult of Yahweh as the narrator imagined that cult to have been at the time. In the state of Israel, Jeroboam I sets a baleful chain of judgments in motion by initiating idolatrous worship of golden calves at Dan and Bethel (1 Kings 14:7–16), and the northern kings who follow him are invariably excoriated for "doing evil in the sight of Yahweh" and "provoking Yahweh to anger" in that they "did not depart from the sin of Jeroboam." Ahab compounds the sin of

Jeroboam by building a Baal temple in Samaria and erecting an image to the goddess Asherah (1 Kings 16:31–33). Much is made of the life and death struggles against Baal worship in Israel conducted by Elijah (1 Kings 18—19), Elisha (2 Kings 1:1–16), Jehu (2 Kings 10:18–31), and in Jerusalem by Jehoiada (2 Kings 11:17–18). The sole king of Israel whose religious stance is partially lauded is Jehu who "wiped out Baal from Israel," but this positive appraisal is immediately qualified by the observation that he did not suppress the worship of the golden calves (2 Kings 10:28–29).

In Judah, Rehoboam tarnishes the House of David by permitting *bāmôt* ("high places," local outdoor altars of sacrifice), *maṣṣēbôt* (stone pillars representing male fertility), '*ašērîm* (wooden poles representing female fertility), and *qādēš* ("holy objects or persons," often taken to be male temple prostitutes, 1 Kings 14:22–24). Running as a leitmotif throughout the accounts of Judahite kings, even those who otherwise are said to have done "what was right in the sight of Yahweh," is their abject failure to remove the high places, until Hezekiah demolishes them (2 Kings 18:4), Manasseh rebuilds them (2 Kings 21:3), and Josiah once again destroys them in Judah and in Samaria (2 Kings 23:5, 8–9, 13, 19). A Baal temple in Jerusalem during the reign of Athaliah is destroyed at her death (2 Kings 11:18), but altars to Baal are built by Manasseh (2 Kings 21:3), and vessels made for the Baal cult are taken from the Jerusalem temple and destroyed by Josiah (2 Kings 23:4). In addition to Baal and Asherah worship and the prohibited high places that appear from Rehoboam onward, in later Judahite reigns we hear of kings who sacrifice their sons by immolation (2 Kings 16:3; 23:10; 2 Chron. 33:6; cf. a similar practice by a Moabite king, 2 Kings 3:27) and of astrological cults and sun worship involving images of horses and chariots in the temple precincts (2 Kings 21:5; 23:4–5, 11).[55]

In short, all the Judahite kings are branded with cultic laxity or perversion with the exception of Hezekiah and Josiah, who are praised for purging Jerusalem and Judah of proscribed cultic practices and objects without exception (2 Kings 18:1–6; 23:1–25). These purges are directed at such curious objects of veneration as a bronze serpent with magical powers attributed to Moses (2 Kings 18:4; cf. Num. 21:6–9) and woven hangings or coverings for an image of Asherah (2 Kings 23:7). Moreover, in the final years before the capture of Jerusalem, Ezekiel reports that a cult employing animal imagery, mourning rites for Tammuz, and sun worship was carried on within the temple precincts, only a few decades after the wholesale cultic "cleanup" carried out by Josiah (Ezek. 8:15–18). All of these citations of cultic irregularities beg certain crucial questions. By whose standards are the kings judged, and at what point in time were these standards formulated? How widely were these standards actually adhered to in the state cult, and how extensive was their acceptance among Judahites at large?[56] Permeating and shaping this torrent of condemnations directed at the kings of Israel and Judah, we can identify two criteria at work, one of "place" and the other of "substance."

The criterion of place is formulated as a *Jerusalem/non-Jerusalem* binary opposition, mandating the *sole* legitimacy of worship practiced in the Jerusalem temple and the corresponding illegitimacy of *all* worship conducted apart from Jerusalem. This means not only that all religious praxis in the northern kingdom is invalid, but that religious sacrifice and celebration anywhere in Judah outside Jerusalem is invalid and is to be extirpated. Standing in contradiction to this criterion, as we have noted, are stories about northern prophets and their sympathizers who worship Yahweh far from Jerusalem without any qualms and with no criticism by the narrator. Moreover, this criterion of sole worship at Jerusalem is further undermined by the narrator's claim that it was precisely Yahweh who mandated the secession of the northern tribes in the first place, but as a penalty on Solomon and not as a ban on Yahweh worship to punish the departing tribes. Finally, the narrator's admission that, for the first two hundred years of its existence, worship in the reduced state of Judah was conducted at "high places" throughout the kingdom without interference from rulers convincingly argues that the royal sanctuary of Solomon in Jerusalem was never intended to be the sole site of Yahweh worship.

The criterion of substance is formulated as a *Yahwistic/non-Yahwistic* binary opposition, specifying that worship in the Jerusalem temple vs. worship elsewhere is not merely an issue of proper location but rather a matter of religious authenticity. Only the Jerusalem cult recognizes and honors Israel's deity. Worship elsewhere is by definition worship of "other gods," since the exclusionary criteria for valid worship do not for a moment allow that a true Yahwist has any other recourse than to bring prayers and sacrifices to the Jerusalem temple. Thus the cultic criteria of place and substance are inextricably fused together.

Besides the northern prophets who behave in ignorance of these strict criteria for worship, there is one equivocation in the Chronicler's assessment of kings. Unlike Kings, Chronicles pictures Manasseh as repenting of his gross religious crimes and actually reversing his cultic atrocities, with the proviso that "the people, nevertheless, still sacrificed at the high places, but only to Yahweh their God" (2 Chron. 33:17). Here alone is a breach in the tight linkage of the criteria of place and substance of worship acknowledged openly. Otherwise, the Jerusalem monopoly on the Yahweh cult is

rigorously applied in the narrators' metacommentary on the religious policies of the two kingdoms. Jeroboam I is derisively judged to be worshiping golden calves as brute material objects that have no connection with
the worship of Yahweh (cf. Exodus 32), in spite of the near certainty that
the calf images functioned symbolically in a manner similar to the twelve
oxen on which the great basin in Solomon's temple rested (1 Kings 7:23–26).
That Jehu did not destroy these calf shrines corroborates their Yahwistic
identity (2 Kings 10:29). The worship of Judahites at their high places is
constantly slurred and anathematized by association with the stone pillars
and wooden poles representing the cults of Baal and Asherah.

Finally, the intertwined criteria of Jerusalem vs. non-Jerusalem worship
and Yahwistic vs. non-Yahwistic worship are brought full circle by the
inclusion in the narratives about Jeroboam I of the story of a prophet who
announces that the Bethel sanctuary, recently founded by the king, will one
day be destroyed. Placed three hundred years in advance of fulfillment of
the prophecy, the confrontation dramatically anticipates the desecration of
the Bethel cult site by Josiah as one aspect of his strict enforcement of the
Jerusalem cult monopoly (cf. 1 Kings 13 with 2 Kings 23:15–20, and note
that Josiah is explicitly named in 1 Kings 13:2).

The patently doctrinaire nature of these criteria clouds most of what is
said about royal religion in Kings and Chronicles. The anachronistic character of the standards of judgment is demonstrated by a nearly complete
obliviousness to the varied pragmatic motives of kings in adopting religious
policies of one sort or another, precisely motives that are sometimes
expressed and more often implied in the stories that the criteria are crudely
imposed upon. For example, in deciding to build temples at Dan and
Bethel, Jeroboam I reasons that "if this people [the populace of the state of
Israel] go up to offer sacrifices in the house of Yahweh at Jerusalem, then
the heart of this people will turn again to their lord, to Rehoboam king of
Judah, and they will kill me and return to Rehoboam king of Judah" (1
Kings 12:26–27). It could not be clearer that Jeroboam's cultic innovations
were not intended to reject allegiance to Yahweh but rather to elude political entrapment in a half-way separation from Judah by remaining implicated in its Jerusalem cult.

In similar vein, Ahab's building of a Baal temple in Samaria is the implementation of an interstate treaty protocol that accords his Tyrian wife the
diplomatic privilege of a place to practice her cult away from her homeland. This gesture does not signal a jettisoning of the Yahweh cult as the
official religion of the Israelite state in favor of the Baal cult.[57] Nor, as I have
argued above, is there any indication that Athaliah, as a Phoenician "trojan

horse" within Judah, was attempting to replace the Yahweh cult in Jerusalem with the Baal cult. Even the savage slaughter of Baal adherents by Jehu does not so much bespeak religious zeal as a ruthless political will to eliminate all opposition, since he takes no measures to reform the extant ways of worshiping Yahweh in the northern kingdom.

Furthermore, even the cultic measures deemed laudable in Kings and Chronicles give every indication of having been guided by political aims. Hezekiah's reported closure of Judahite high places may not have been solely, or even primarily, religiously motivated, for as a part of his strategy in preparation for rebellion against Assyria he may have sought not only to concentrate his military and economic assets in Jerusalem but also to supplement and reinforce them by drawing his cultic and ideological resources into the capital city.[58] The radical centralization of worship in Jerusalem attributed to Josiah entailed a centralizing fiscal policy that would reduce the percentage of state revenues siphoned off by local and regional "tax collectors," stimulate business with increased pilgrim traffic, and generally prosper the economy of Jerusalem.[59] Moreover, there are indications that by enforcing the laws of Deuteronomy Josiah had in mind extending the control of the state over family and lineage autonomy.[60] All such extra-religious factors in shaping religious institutions and practices, north and south, are studiously downplayed or passed over in the praise and blame dealt to the kings of Israel and Judah.

A comparison of differences in the ways that Kings and Chronicles apply the cultic criteria to regimes and events in monarchic times is highly instructive for assessing the political valences of these sources. It is striking that Kings often lets stand the contradiction between the cultic criteria and the narratives reported, whereas Chronicles repeatedly goes out of its way to make the narrative record "square" with the anachronistic religious criteria. The more heavy-handed moralistic interpretation of Chronicles is blatantly recurrent throughout its accounts of Judahite rulers. To begin with, not a word is said about Solomon initiating an idolatrous turn away from Yahweh, which first occurs in Judah when his son Rehoboam has been in office for three years (2 Chron. 11:17; 12:1), thereby precipitating the invasion of Judah by pharaoh Shishak as a direct punishment for Rehoboam's lapse from Yahweh worship (2 Chron. 12:2–12). After carrying out some religious reforms, Asa stumbles in his allegiance to Yahweh. He pays the king of Aram-Damascus to attack Israel instead of "relying on Yahweh," angrily imprisons the prophet who criticizes him, and "inflicts cruelties on some of the people." Shortly thereafter, Asa contracts a severe foot disease, improperly seeks help from physicians instead of from Yahweh, and dies within two years (2 Chron. 16:7–12). Jehoshaphat, who is credited with cultic and legal reforms, is nonetheless condemned by prophets for his alliances with Ahab and Azariah of Israel (2 Chron. 19:1–3; 20:35–37), and we are given the contradictory information that "he removed the high places" and that "the high places were *not* removed," with the blame for this failure apparently being shifted to the people of Judah (2 Chron. 17:6; 20:33).

Chronicles goes well beyond Kings in reciting a litany of Judahite rulers assassinated or devastated by diseases, and of diplomatic and military defeats inflicted on them and their people, invariably because of cultic crimes. As in Kings, three successive Judahite kings (Joash, Amaziah, and Azariah) are said to have done "what is right in the eyes of Yahweh" but failed "to remove the high places." Chronicles, however, luridly ties the royal misfortunes and untimely deaths more closely to cultic wrongdoing. Joash, following the death of his mentor Jehoiada the priest, deserts Yahweh and murders Jehoiada's son Zechariah, as a result of which Aram-Damascus severely defeats him and he dies by assassination (2 Chron. 24:17–27). Amaziah, following a smashing victory over the Edomites, turns to worshiping their gods, boastfully taunts Israel into doing battle with him, is defeated by Jehoash, and finally is assassinated in a Judahite conspiracy (2 Chron. 25:14–28). Azariah=Uzziah, after a pious and prosperous reign, "grows proud," tries to offer a sacrifice in the temple reserved for priests, and is struck with leprosy that forces him to live apart and relinquish the conduct of state affairs to his son as coregent (2 Chron. 26:16–21). Ahaz, who is presented as an utterly faithless king, is punished when Judah is ravished by Aram-Damascus and Israel, and Ahaz's desperate payment of tribute to Assyria is said "not to have helped him," contrary to the account in Kings (2 Chronicles 28; cf. 2 Kings 16:7–9). Moreover, the copy of an altar Ahaz saw in Damascus and erected in the Jerusalem temple, described ambiguously in Kings as possibly, or even probably, an altar of Assyrian design for Yahweh worship (2 Kings 16:10–18), becomes in Chronicles many altars "in every corner of Jerusalem" devoted explicitly to worship of "the gods of Damascus" that became "the ruin of him, and of all Israel" (2 Chron. 28:22–24).

Even the best of Judahite kings, although praised for their cultic reforms as in Kings, do not escape the critical eye of the Chronicler. Hezekiah, who in Kings is compelled to pay tribute when Sennacherib invades Judah, pays no such tribute; on the contrary, surrounding states bring gifts to Hezekiah once the Assyrian siege is lifted (2 Chron. 32:22–23). Nonetheless, after being spared death from a grave sickness, "Hezekiah did not make return according to the benefit done him, for his heart was proud" (2 Chron. 32:25), and his reception of envoys from Babylonia, openly criticized by a prophet in Kings, invites the Chronicler's muted comment that "God left him to himself, in order to try him and to know all that was in his heart" (2 Chron. 32:31; cf. 2 Kings 20:12–19). Josiah, who is tragically killed by pharaoh Neco, is faulted for bringing on his own death because he "did not listen to the words of Neco from the mouth of God" when the pharaoh expressly warned him, "Cease opposing God, who is with me, lest he destroy you" (2 Chron. 35:20–24). This way of accounting for Josiah's death is apparently meant to explain why Huldah's prophecy that he would die "in peace" was countermanded (2 Chron. 34:26–28), a discrepancy that Kings lets stand without explanation. It can be safely said that Chronicles carries the "Deuteronomistic" moral-theological axiom of cultic obedience vs. disobedience issuing in political well-being vs. woe to a far greater extreme than does Samuel–Kings.[61]

My point in this recital of the way breaches of the criteria for legitimate worship are woven into the narratives is to suggest that there are two impulses at work in Kings and Chronicles that come to expression both in similar and different ways, and that these impulses stand in pronounced tension with one another. The one impulse is to assemble known traditions about the monarchic past of Israel, united and divided. The other impulse is to pass judgment on rulers and state policies according to how scrupulously they upheld the cult of Yahweh or how perversely they departed from it. The problem in interpreting the sources as records of religious belief and practice in the monarchic past is that the assembled traditions repeatedly belie the Jerusalem-centered, monotheizing cult of Yahweh that the retrospective conception of the narrators and collectors of the traditions insist on imposing on them. According to our best understanding, the presumed consensus about cultic criteria invoked by the narrators comes from very late in the monarchy, or as a "total package" from a time after the fall of Judah. The criteria are articulated in the didactic instructions (*tôrôt*) of the book of Deuteronomy, and it is the cultic worldview of Deuteronomy that the narrators of Kings and Chronicles are drawing on as they collect, arrange, and comment on traditions that in large measure derive from circles lacking such a rigorous unified understanding of the cult of Yahweh. Furthermore, the cultic agenda advanced in Deuteronomy, Samuel–Kings, and Chronicles gives every appearance of deriving from reformist circles that are fighting to have their version of the cult become the established one in postmonarchic milieus where the scope and content of Yahwistic belief and practice are as yet ill-defined and fluid.[62]

So how can we separate between the "tight" cultic criteria of the reformist narrators and the "loose" cultic world of many of the narratives the reformists preserve and censoriously comment on? There are two clues. The initial clue lies in the sharp tension and frequent contradiction between the untidy and equivocal details and dynamics of many of the narratives and the smoothly confident pronouncements of the metanarrators. It can be seen that again and again they miss altogether or seriously distort the motives and meanings of rulers and state institutions by overdetermining the secular flux of events with retrojected cultic-sacral meanings. The second clue appears in the measurable differences in the way the reformist metanarrators of Kings and the reformist metanarrators of Chronicles treat the traditions at their disposal. We are able to compare their accounts ruler by ruler, noting what is omitted from one but found in the other, how they accent and elaborate shared narratives, how they apply their reformist criteria to explain the course of events, and indeed what sorts of events they feel an urgent need "to explain."[63]

When we thus compare Kings and Chronicles, it is clear that Samuel–Kings has preserved a much larger "pool" of traditions that are less homogenized in themselves and less overmastered by the reformist agenda. Many more twists and turns of events and unaccountable actions escape the reformist filter in Samuel–Kings. Although heavy enough in their metacommentary, they are content to allow a fair number of "loose ends" in the stories, with less resort to dogmatic and harmonizing explanations at every turn. Chronicles, on the other hand, censors and shapes what it shares with Samuel–Kings into a closer correspondence between narrative and metanarrative. It tries to explain many more political outcomes as the direct result of cultic fidelity or infidelity. This is not the place to speculate in detail as to why the Chronicler's reformist narration is so rigorous. It almost certainly has to do with the milieu in which Chronicles was written, a milieu probably later than that of Samuel–Kings, in which the main points of the Deuteronomic cultic agenda were established but in which the constitution and personnel of a restored temple, as well as the relationship of Judahite Yahwists to Yahwists in Samaria, were still unsettled issues. Suffice it to say that, if we had only the Chronicler's version of monarchic history, it would be easy to discount, or even dismiss it, as an impenetrable fantasy with the merest veneer of history.

With the two versions of monarchic politics in hand, however, we can perhaps legitimately conjecture that the distance standing between Samuel–Kings' "looser" version and Chronicles' "tighter" version is a rough measure of the distance between Samuel–Kings and the "still looser" clusters of traditions it has drawn upon. If Samuel–Kings seems more "secular" in its concerns than Chronicles, it is fair to conclude that many of its traditions in their precollected and preedited form were even "more secular" in their orientation and concerns than they now appear as glossed and "explained" by a Deuteronomic reform perspective. By "secular" we do not necessarily mean devoid of religious concerns, but rather less interested in the particulars of cultic practice as the quintessence of being Israelite or Judahite, and more interested in the day-to-day range of economic, social, and political affairs, including religion as part of the warp and woof of community life.

Above all, if Samuel–Kings inadvertently shows a much more "diverse" and "unsystematized" assortment of religious beliefs and cultic practices than does Chronicles, it seems reasonable to conclude that many of its traditions in their precollected and preedited forms were even "more diverse and unsystematized" than they now appear in Deuteronomistic dress. Accordingly, by hypothesizing a distance between Samuel–Kings and its assembled traditions that approximates the distance between Chronicles and Samuel–Kings, we are in a position to use our critical imagination to offer tenable scenarios of ancient Israelite politics, once the biblical data are brought into conversation with archeological data and extrabiblical texts and played off against data and models from comparative social sciences.

Shifting and Declining Diplomatic and Military Fortunes. Alongside religious affairs, and often intertwined with them, diplomatic and military facets of state politics are prominently featured in the biblical accounts. Saul's warfare with the Philistines and with Ammon, Moab, and Edom is reported, followed by David's victories over those same enemies, plus Aram-Damascus and Aram-Zobah, issuing in Israelite hegemony over those neighboring polities to the east and north of Israel and Judah. That hegemony is already eroding in the reign of Solomon when Aram-Damascus breaks away from Israelite control and an Edomite who flees to Egypt becomes Solomon's "adversary" but is blocked by pharaoh from organizing immediate military resistance against Solomon. Edom remains under the control of Judah until it revolts in the reign of Joram and installs its own king. Subsequently, Amaziah deals a severe blow to Edom, but, while Ahaz is preoccupied with the threat from Pekah and Rezin, Edom succeeds in recapturing Elath. Domination of Moab is inherited by separated Israel, but after the death of Ahab, Mesha of Moab revolts, and Moab henceforth remains independent of Israel and Judah.

Aram-Damascus becomes the most tenacious and persistent of Israel's foes during the ninth century, as the two states wage a seesaw struggle, and

Aram-Damascus also threatens Judah on two occasions. The Omrid kings from Ahab on are in a nearly constant state of war with Damascus, and Ahab meets his nemesis on the battlefield at the hands of Damscene forces after he rejects prophetic advice not to engage them (1 Kings 22). The later ninth-century rulers of Jehu's dynasty fare even worse from repeated incursions by Damascus. Assyria looms as the dominant power in Syro-Palestine in the mid-eighth century, bringing the northern kingdom to an end and subjecting Judah to vassalage for nearly a century. After a brief hiatus, Neo-Babylonia assumes the role of dominant power and terminates the southern kingdom. Egypt figures early and late as an enemy, when Shishak invades Israel during Rehoboam's reign (1 Kings 14:25–28) and when Neco kills Josiah and imposes vassalage on Judah in the interim between Assyrian and Neo-Babylonian ascendancy in Syro-Palestine (2 Kings 23:29–35).

Diplomacy, hand in glove with warfare, is also reflected at many points in the narrative. David and Solomon establish close ties with Phoenician Tyre (2 Sam. 5:11; 1 Kings 5:1–12), a bond that is resumed by the Omri-Ahab dynasty (1 Kings 16:31) and cut off by Jehu (2 Kings 9:30–37). Solomon marries an Egyptian princess and receives Gezer as dowry (1 Kings 3:1) and is visited by the queen of the south Arabian kingdom of Sheba (1 Kings 10:1–10). Aram-Damascus is alternately on friendly and hostile terms with the separated kingdoms. Asa of Judah persuades Aram-Damascus to break its ties with Israel and come to his aid against Baasha (1 Kings 15:16–22). Ahab imposes a moderate settlement on Aram-Damascus after defeating its army (1 Kings 20:30b-34). Under Jehu and Jehoahaz, Aram-Damascus gains the upper hand and dominates Israel relentlessly for several decades (2 Kings 13:3–4, 7), but Jehoash begins to reverse Israel's losses to Damascus (2 Kings 13:5, 14–25). Joash of Judah avoids a similar fate by making a large payment to Hazael of Aram-Damascus (2 Kings 12:17–18).

The Elisha narratives report unusually intimate contacts with Damascus. Naaman, commander of the Damascene army, comes to Israel in order to be healed of his leprosy by the king, but it is Elisha who heals him (2 Kings 5), and Elisha himself journeys to Damascus to instigate the assassination of Ben-hadad by one of his officers, Hazael, fulfilling a commission earlier given to Elijah (1 Kings 19:15; 2 Kings 8:7–15). There is no close parallel to this overt intervention of an Israelite prophet in the internal affairs of a foreign state, although there are looser affinities with Isaiah of the Exile's advocacy of Cyrus the Persian while living under Babylonian rule, as also with the didactic legends of Jonah, Daniel 1—6, and Esther. Pekah, in an anti-Assyrian maneuver, enters a league with Rezin of Aram-Damascus, and together they attempt to force Judah into an anti-Assyrian alliance (2 Kings

16:5; Isa. 7:1). Both during the Assyrian siege of Jerusalem in the reign of Hezekiah and the Neo-Babylonian siege of Jerusalem in the reign of Zedekiah, Judah seeks military assistance from Egypt, which proves ineffectual (2 Kings 18:21; 19:9; Jer. 37:5–10; 44:30).

The relations between the separated kingdoms of Israel and Judah are strained or openly belligerent throughout much of their parallel histories. Early in the era of the divided kingdoms, Abijam of Judah defeats and takes territory from Jeroboam I, and Baasha threatens Judah. However, under the Omri dynasty the two kingdoms achieve a rapprochement, as a result of which Jehoshaphat joins forces with Ahab against Aram-Damascus and again with Joram against both Aram-Damascus and Moab. The close relation between the two kingdoms is sealed by the wedding of Ahab's sister Athaliah to Jehoshaphat's son Jehoram. With the murder of Ahaziah of Judah by Jehu during the latter's coup and the murder of Athaliah in Judah, we hear of no more collaborative contacts between the two kingdoms. Some decades later, Amaziah of Judah provokes war with Jehoash of Israel and is roundly defeated. Toward the end of the northern kingdom, Pekah of Israel, joined by Aram-Damascus, attacks Judah but is forced to withdraw when Ahaz enlists the help of Assyria. A century later, as Assyrian control of Palestine declines, Josiah of Judah raids the territory of the former northern kingdom in order to impose religious reforms.

By and large, the accounts of these military and diplomatic operations are sparse on details.[64] The regions contested, such as Gilead or the border between Israel and Judah, and the cities under siege, such as Samaria, Jerusalem, Gibbethon, Ramoth-gilead and Kirhareseth, are sometimes named. Military strategy and tactics are erratically mentioned; however, the size and weaponry of the armies are generally treated formulaically, with mention of chariotry and infantry, while the numbers of troops mustered or slain, when stated, are typically given in large figures rounded off to thousands. When battles and sieges are most fully described, prophets are given a key role, and the motif of divine intervention stylizes the military action, to such an extent in the book of Chronicles that some of the battles are described as virtual religious processions and rituals.

Apart from the debacles attending the fall of both kingdoms, the territories that exchange hands after these battles or the terms imposed by the victors are infrequently or problematically described. For example, the territorial control that David actually achieves from his victories in Transjordan and Syria is obscure (2 Sam. 8:1–14; 10).[65] With respect to diplomatic relations, we are only now and then informed of the terms of the many treaties reported or implied when states establish peaceful relations or act in concert. The intensity and harshness of diplomatic exchanges are disclosed in the severe treaty terms that Nahash of Ammon tries to impose on Jabesh-gilead (1 Sam. 11:1–2) and Ben-hadad of Damascus on Samaria (1 Kings 20:1–11), as also in the demeaning treatment of David's diplomatic envoys by Hanun of Ammon when they arrive to attend the funeral of his father (2 Sam. 10:1–6) On the other hand, Ahab offers moderate terms to Ben-hadad in defeat, requiring only a return of conquered territory and some trading concessions (1 Kings 20:20b–34). The intimidating propaganda that is an ingredient of Assyrian diplomacy and warfare is given elaborate rhetorical exposition in the meeting of Judahite and Assyrian officials outside the walls of Jerusalem besieged by Sennacherib (2 Kings 18:19–37 // Isa. 36:4–20; 37:8–13).[66]

When we adhere as closely as possible to what the biblical traditions recount concerning Israelite interactions with other states, the perspective on wider ancient Near Eastern politics offered is understandably one-sided. We are allowed to see interstate diplomatic and military affairs only from an Israelite viewpoint. Moreover, the selectivity of political data, characteristic of the biblical traditions in general, is particularly prominent with respect to foreign affairs. Because we are fortunate to possess independent records from some of these states, we are able to identify certain omissions in the biblical narratives, as we shall note when we review the body of extrabiblical information relevant to our subject. If we had only the biblical accounts to go by, we would have no idea of the major role played by Assyria in Syro-Palestinian politics during the dynasties of Omri and Jehu, nor would we correctly understand the international alliance politics at work in the transition from Assyrian to Egyptian to Neo-Babylonian imperial control of Judah. Furthermore, a number of engagements with foreign states are reported both in Israelite and Judahite records and in the records of the opposing powers. Thus, we have "winner" and "loser" accounts of Moab's revolt against the Omrid dynasty and of the fall of the kingdoms of Israel and Judah. Interestingly, the one partial mitigation of the chauvinist perspective of the biblical traditions is our information on separated Israel. While it is true that the politics of the northern kingdom are related to us from a Judahite perspective, the Judahite traditionists claim to make use of records surviving from the fallen kingdom of Israel, and certainly the substance of those traditions was derived from northern sources of one sort or another. Consequently we are accorded occasional glimpses of how the state of Israel and the state of Judah viewed one another, both in their hostile and collaborative contacts.

Building Projects as Monuments to State Power. Building projects of kings are noted with some frequency.[67] David builds a royal residence in Jerusalem and strengthens the city's fortifications (2 Sam. 5:9, 11). Solomon is celebrated for constructing the temple (1 Kings 6), but it is clear that the temple is only one edifice in a larger architectural design that includes an assembly hall serving also as treasury and armory, a pillared portico, a judgment hall, a palace for himself, and another for his Egyptian wife (1 Kings 7:1–8). Much as the temple is exalted in the tradition, its status as a "royal chapel" for Solomon is underscored by the report that he spends nearly twice as long building his palace as in building the temple (1 Kings 6:38; 7:1). Among his other public works, Solomon strengthens the wall of Jerusalem, constructs the Millo, which is probably a "landfill" to make level terrain for additional building in the hilly capital (1 Kings 9:15), and builds or expands Hazor, Megiddo, Gezer, lower Beth-horon, Baalath, and Tamir (1 Kings 9:15–17). He is further credited with establishing unnamed store-cities and sites to house his chariots and horses (1 Kings 9:15), as well as building a fleet of ships at Ezion-geber to trade with Ophir [south Arabia, east Africa, India?] (1 Kings 9:26–28). Jeroboam I builds royal residences in Shechem, Penuel, and Tirzah, and erects shrines at Dan and Bethel (1 Kings 12:25–30; 14:17). Omri founds and fortifies Samaria as his capital (1 Kings 16:24), and Ahab builds a house of Baal in Samaria and an ivory-paneled residence for himself (1 Kings 16:32; 22:39).

All subsequent building projects are ascribed to kings of Judah. Asa builds fortified cities (2 Chron. 14:6), and Jehoshaphat constructs fortresses and store-cities (2 Chron. 17:1–2). Azariah=Uzziah establishes settlements in the territory of Ashdod, (re)builds Elath on the Gulf of Aqabah, constructs towers in Jerusalem, and places towers and cisterns in the wilderness for his many herds (2 Chron. 26:2, 6, 9–10). Jotham builds an upper gate in the temple, strengthens the Ophel wall in Jerusalem, constructs cities in Judah, and places forts and towers on the wooded hills (2 Chron. 27:3). Hezekiah is remembered for making a conduit and pool that brings water inside Jerusalem from the spring Gihon in preparation for siege, repairing the broken wall of Jerusalem and constructing a second outer wall, and strengthening the terraced slopes of the city (2 Kings 20:20; 2 Chron. 32:30; cf. Isa. 7:3; 22:8b–11). Manasseh is also credited with an outer wall around Jerusalem (2 Chron. 33:14). One of the sons of Josiah, presumably Jehoiakim, is said to have built a great house for himself with spacious upper rooms and ornate interior decoration (Jer. 22:13–16). The building activities reported are largely devoted either to embellishing and strengthening the royal temple-palace complexes in Samaria and Jerusalem or to providing defensible fortifications and military depots throughout the land, while two of the projects are for the economic purposes of launching a merchant fleet and provisioning royal herds.

This focus on the monumental construction of administrative and ceremonial centers, dubbed "the acropolis phenomenon,"[68] accentuates the centralizing thrust of both states, such that all space within the center, whether it be Jerusalem or Samaria, is "administrative space" and all space outside the center is "administered space." Moreover, a principal aim of "display" architecture is overtly ideological, to symbolize the power and glory of the state and to induce cooperation from subjects.[69]

Funding the State Apparatus. The economic programs of a few kings are reported. Of these, Solomon's fiscal policies and sources of income are most extensively described. Far briefer reports are provided for other monarchs, but enough is said to suggest a range of royal economic practices, concerning which the prophetic books provide occasional illuminating details.

Saul, the first king of Israel, comes from a family of sufficient means that his modest entourage can be accommodated on his own estate in Gibeah and supported from his own resources and from the resources of those who volunteer service to him. In two Saulide traditions there are references to royal obligations on subjects and royal grants to subjects that look suspiciously like retrojections from later monarchic practices: a person who distinguishes himself in extraordinary service to the king may be declared "free," that is, exempt from customary obligations (1 Sam. 17:25), and appointment to command posts in the army may be accompanied by grants of fields and vineyards (1 Sam. 22:7–8a).[70]

At his death, the lands of Saul pass into David's possession, a portion of which David assigns to the support of Saul's grandson Meribaal under the management of the servant Ziba with his fifteen sons and twenty servants (2 Sam. 9:7, 9–13). David's resources to support his administrative center at Jerusalem appear to be largely derived from personal holdings, such as the town of Ziklag awarded him by Achish of Gath (1 Sam. 27:6) and booty and tribute taken from the states he defeated in Transjordan and southern Syria, and from the voluntary gifts of wealthy supporters. Persons of means in Transjordan provide David and his army with provisions when they retreat in the face of Absalom's revolt (2 Sam. 17:27–29), and, one of these, Barzillai, is invited to come with David to Jerusalem and be provided for at the royal court (2 Sam. 19:31–40). This provisioning of favored persons at the Jerusalem court is possibly among the emoluments alluded to when the Judahites deny that they have been more favored in this regard than the northern tribes (2 Sam. 19:42). All in all, it appears that David is able to defer taxing his subjects by putting together an economic base consisting of personal holdings, contributions of wealthy families who support his regime, and booty and tribute from his foreign conquests.[71] That David provides stipendiary land grants to his officials is perhaps hinted at by references to the adjacent fields of Joab and Absalom (2 Sam. 14:30) and to the estate of Abiathar (1 Kings 2:26).

Solomon introduces a more rational and thoroughgoing policy of fiscal support drawn from taxation of his subjects' produce and labor power and from adroit exploitation of foreign trade.[72] His division of the kingdom into administrative districts provides the Jerusalem court with an abundant supply of food and ample feed for the horses in his chariot forces (1 Kings 4:7–19, 22–29). The agricultural surplus over and above domestic needs, in the form of grain and fine oil, is traded abroad for building materials and skilled artisans (1 Kings 5:1–12). The manual labor for his building projects is conscripted from his subjects (1 Kings 5:13–18; 9:5–23). Solomonic wealth is augmented by tribute from conquered regions, long-distance trade in luxury items, and franchise fees and taxes imposed on Israelite merchants and tolls exacted from transit trade (1 Kings 10:14–15). In the process of acquiring horses and chariots from Anatolia and/or Egypt for his own army, Solomon makes a profit by supplying some of these weapons of war to north Syrian states (1 Kings 10:28–29). The tradition speaks grandiloquently of Solomon's lavish supply of gold, but his fiscal vulnerability shows up starkly when he cedes twenty cities in Galilee to Hiram of Tyre in order to make up for his trade deficit with Phoenicia (1 Kings 9:10–14).

Information on the economic enterprises of later kings is sketchy. In separated Israel, although no details are given, the close ties of the Omri-Ahab dynasty with Tyre suggest trade relations, including imported building materials and skilled artisans, of the sort that Solomon had earlier established with Phoenicia. The rivalry between the northern kingdom and Aram-Damascus involves establishing trading concessions in one another's capital cities of Samaria and Damascus, depending on which state holds the upper hand at any given moment (1 Kings 20:34). The royal responsibility to provide for large numbers of horses and mules is reflected in Ahab's desperate search for water and feed during a time of acute famine (1 Kings 18:5–6). A sizable tribute of mutton and wool comes to the northern kingdom from its vassal Moab during the reigns of Omri and Ahab, but this income is lost when Moab revolts after Ahab's death (2 Kings 3:4–5).

In Judah, sporadic tribute seems to come from Edom, Ammon, and Philistia. Otherwise, the tradition does not remark much on the sources of royal income. Under Joash, we hear of an assessment on the populace for temple repairs, as well as voluntary gifts, which the king regularizes by instituting a system of collecting, counting, and distributing the temple funds intended to prevent priestly diversion or embezzlement of revenues (2 Kings 12:4–5). One unresolved issue in state finances is whether temple revenues are included as a percentage of taxes collected by the crown or are drawn independently from temple lands and fees provided by worshipers. All in all, the sacral office of the king, charged with religious responsibilities, suggests that state taxes provide for the upkeep of the cult.[73] Severe blows to the state economy are reported when the wealth stored in the Jerusalem temple and palace treasuries is plundered by foreign conquerors (1 Kings 15:25–27; 2 Kings 14:13–14; 24:13) or drawn upon by Judahite monarchs to curry favor with other states (1 Kings 15:18–19; 2 Kings 12:17–18) or to pay tribute or indemnity imposed upon Judah (2 Kings 18:15–16). That the contents of the state treasuries can be a "bargaining chip" in interstate alliances is indicated by the visit of Merodach-baladan's envoys to survey the treasury and armory of Hezekiah (2 Kings 20:12–15).

The Solomonic traditions reflect optimal conditions in which the state treasuries are augmented by foreign tribute and trade, but even that storied monarch falls into "deficit spending." As the kingdom breaks apart and Aram-Damascus, Assyria, and Neo-Babylonia bring pressure to bear on Israel and Judah, the contents of the state treasuries are "drawn down" to the point that demands for payments to foreign powers can be met only by passing on the costs to the general populace. Menahem of Israel "pays off" Assyria in order to secure his hold on the crown by assessing all the kingdom's "men of means" fifty shekels of silver each (2 Kings 15:19–20), and, in order to raise the gold and silver tribute demanded by Egypt, Jehoiakim of Judah taxes his subjects (2 Kings 23:33–35). Indeed, it is highly probable that it was common for payments of bribes, tribute, and indemnity to foreign states to be passed on to the populace in the form of special taxes.

Administering the State Apparatus. Although many offices and their incumbents are named, the overall administration of the state is nowhere comprehensively described, probably because nothing comparable to "a flow chart" of government existed in the sources. Only for David and Solomon are lists of officials provided, and even then only in the case of two of Solomon's officials are we given some specification of their duties and how they were carried out. Evidently the officials in these lists are functionaries in the larger bureaucratic system of the kingdom, each responsible for a particular branch or activity of government, but with no more to go on than brief titles for most of these officers, their actual duties and jurisdictions are open to various interpretations. This is less a difficulty for the military and religious officers than for those in charge of civil affairs.[74]

Comparing the two lists, we learn that five offices instituted by David are continued by Solomon, and three or four new offices are added. Lacking such lists for later kings, it is not certain that the bureaucratic profile of the kingdoms of Israel and Judah continues along the same lines. To be sure, most of the official titles in David's and Solomon's rosters appear here and there in later reigns (e.g., 2 Kings 18:18; 22:3–4), but not consistently so, and often the principal officials mentioned in narratives of the divided kingdoms and prophetic books bear titles different from those in service to David and Solomon. Many of the descriptors of leaders are common nouns that designate members of a class of persons rather than official titles. Moreover, at times the combinations of leaders who appear in particular narratives are so diverse as to appear randomly conjoined.

Precisely where we might expect some orderly survey of the branches of officialdom, none is forthcoming. For example, when the Judahite officials executed or exiled by the Neo-Babylonians in 598 and 586 are alluded to in Kings, and in some instances named, they are either lumped into broad categories, such as "officials" and "princes," or, when the account is more precise, do not correspond to the Davidic and Solomon officials (2 Kings 24:10–17; 25:18–21). The *sārîs,* mentioned in royal regimes both north and south, has as its primary denotation "eunuch," a castrated male especially prized as chamberlain of royal harems (2 Kings 9:32).[75] However, other references to *sārîsîm,* as is the case with the equivalent term in Mesopotamia, designate officials in a variety of civil and military positions. By and large, references to leaders and officials in the prophetic books are of limited help, since they are mostly ambiguous generic terms for groups of leaders, such as *śārîm, 'ăvādîm, ḥôrîm,* and *yôšěvîm,*[76] or named dignitaries lacking titles. Numerous sayings in the book of Proverbs devoted to kingship and court behavior do not single out royal officials or describe administrative practices.

The roles that the sons of the king may have played in state administration are touched upon only obliquely. It is said that David's sons are priests (all of them?; 2 Sam 8:18), and it is possible to interpret Absalom's solicitation of support for his rebellion by hearing pleas for justice at the city gate as the exploitation of his assigned post as a preliminary "hearing officer" to screen cases to be brought to the king's attention (2 Sam. 15:1–6). The sons of the king certainly posed a potential source of royal instability as they jockeyed for succession to the throne or even rose up against their father, and it is likely that coregency arrangements were intended in part to keep the appointed successor in line and to marginalize his disappointed or disgruntled brothers. "Middle-level" administrative assignments for the king's sons were apparently made by Rehoboam when, in addition to designating his son Abijam as "chief prince" and heir to the throne, "he distributed some of his sons through all the districts of Judah and Benjamin" (2 Chron. 11:22–24). Apparently fearing the power of his brothers, who received sizable donations from their father Jehoshaphat, including military positions, Joram of Judah murders not only his brothers but a number of high officials as well (2 Chron. 11:22–24).

ISRAEL'S COLONIAL POLITICS

The most striking feature of the biblical sources regarding Israelite colonial politics is that, while they contain more circumstantial information than the sources for prestate Israel, they are not as abundant as the sources for the politics of monarchic Israel. More seriously, on key issues of chronology and political substance they are garbled or opaque. Moreover, unlike the information on Israelite state politics, the biblical data on colonial times are discontinuous in their concentration on widely separated historical moments: on the immediate aftermath of the fall of Judah (586–582 B.C.E.), on the release of the Judahite deportees by Cyrus (538 B.C.E.), on the rebuilding of the Jerusalem temple (520–516 B.C.E.), on the careers of Ezra and Nehemiah (458–398 B.C.E.), and on the Maccabean revolt (175–164 B.C.E.). The late Hasmonean dynasty is documented outside the Hebrew Bible in 1 and 2 Maccabees, included in the Roman Catholic canon of the Old Testament (142–68 B.C.E). The longer intervening periods are undocumented in the Hebrew Bible except as certain highly legendary writings, such as Daniel 1—6 and Esther, or the ruminations of Ecclesiastes are construed to provide general impressions of colonial conditions in Judah and the Diaspora.

The paucity and confusion of sources for Israelite colonial politics is more than a little disconcerting, since it is widely believed that the bulk of the Hebrew Bible was compiled and/or written precisely in this colonial period. If the hypothesis is correct that much of the Hebrew Bible was composed or compiled after both kingdoms had fallen, it means that those who produced the traditions as they stand had much more to say about prestate and statist politics than they did about the colonial politics of the very times in which they lived.

This puzzling political "information gap" for the colonial era is conceivably explainable in a number of ways, either singly or in combination. One possibility is that the final authors of the Hebrew Bible regarded preexilic times as "the golden age" of Israel's life, and were "depoliticized" by the destruction of the Israelite and Judahite states. A second possibility is that they deemed it advisable to avoid writing about recent events so as not to displease their Persian overlords. A third possibility is that information about certain periods of colonial politics was unavailable to the final authors of the Hebrew Bible. A final possibility is that advocates of conflicting programs for restoring Judah were so preoccupied with legitimating their agendas by documenting and appealing to the more distant Israelite past that they had little time or interest to record the events unfolding in their lifetime. The "readings of the past" represented by Deuteronomy–Kings, Ezra–Nehemiah, Chronicles, the Priestly source of the Pentateuch, Haggai–Zechariah, Isaiah 40—66, and the Psalms are sufficiently different that they attest to divergent and clashing concerns and strategies for reconstituting communal life in Judah.

Whatever the reasons for the precipitous decline of history-like traditions, we are forced into a large measure of conjecture about the political conditions in which the Hebrew Bible was formulated and in which the earliest "Judah-ism(s)" began to take shape.[77] Even with the aid of Judahite and Diaspora writings not included in the Hebrew Bible, such as those in the Apocrypha and Pseudepigrapha, we have but a sketchy outline of the political fortunes of Judah during its subjection to the successive hegemony of Neo-Babylonia, Persia, and the Hellenistic kingdoms. Archaeological data and texts additional to the Hebrew Bible, Apocrypha, and Pseudepigrapha are of further help in grasping the colonial politics of Judah/Samaria and the Diaspora, but they are not decisive on many issues of interpretation.

Neo-Babylonian Political Hegemony

In spite of the prominence of the theme of exile in biblical texts, neither the general conditions of colonial Jewish life in Judah, Babylon, and Egypt under Neo-Babylonian rule nor the internal and external political factors that shaped and circumscribed their communities are described in any great detail in biblical traditions. The Judahite survivors of the fall of Jerusalem who fled to Egypt are wholly lost to view (2 Kings 25:26; Jer. 41:16–43:13). The deportation of Judahite leaders to Babylonia is accorded only the briefest mention (2 Kings 24:11–16; 25:11; 2 Chron. 36:20; Jer. 39:9); otherwise, these deportees crop up in the books of Jeremiah (24; 29) and Ezekiel (1:1–3; 3:15; 8:1; 14:1–3; 18:1–2, 19, 25; 20:1–3; 33:10, 30–33; 37:11), and they constitute the assumed audience of Isaiah 40—55.

The fate of those left in Judah is glimpsed briefly in Jeremiah and alluded to in the book of Lamentations. For the period immediately following the destruction of the state of Judah, we learn that Nebuchadnezzar commissioned Gedaliah, a holdover official from the fallen regime, to serve as "governor" (literally, "he appointed Gedaliah over them," 2 Kings 25:22, or "in the cities of Judah," Jer. 40:5). Installed at Mizpah, just to the north of devastated Jerusalem, Gedaliah gathered to his company the armed forces who had escaped into the countryside and Judahites who had fled to Moab, Ammon, and Edom (2 Kings 25:22–24; Jer. 40:7–12). Gedaliah's administration was cut short when he and his staff and a unit of Neo-Babylonian soldiers, as well as a large band of pilgrims from the north, were killed by Ishmael, "of the royal family," at the instigation of Baalis, king of Ammon (2 Kings 25:25; Jer. 40:13–41:18). Of reputed Davidic lineage, Ishmael may have had a revival of the Judahite kingdom as his ultimate aspiration, but his striking down of Gedaliah with a small band of assassins, followed by swift flight back to his base in Ammon, seems less a serious bid to reestablish an independent state of Judah in one stroke than a "spoiling" gesture intended to cripple the administration of Judah undertaken by natives who were collaborating with the Neo-Babylonians. A large company of Judahites who had rallied to Gedaliah, fearing reprisals from the Neo-Babylonians, fled to Egypt, taking with them the prophet Jeremiah, who had strongly advised against leaving the land. (2 Kings 25:26; Jer. 41:11–43:13). A third deportation of 745 Judahites in 582 B.C.E. may have been a Neo-Babylonian reprisal for the assassination of Gedaliah and consequent difficulties in establishing secure imperial rule over Judah (Jer. 52:30).

With the murder of Gedaliah and the flight of a large body of his loyalists to Egypt, nothing more is narrated about political conditions in Judah for the remaining decades of Neo-Babylonian domination. This abrupt "gap" in the Judahite history reinforces "the myth of the empty land," which eventually becomes an idée fixe in the ideology of the restored Judahite community.[78] Some references to life in Judah are filtered through poetic allusions in the book of Lamentations. Most of the complaints in these publically performed laments bewail the decimated Judahite political and religious infrastructure, but the fifth lament decries the humiliation and hardship of life in the conquered land. The conquerors are referred to only as "strangers" and "aliens" (5:2), and may refer not only to the Neo-Babylonians but also to the Edomites as opportunists, sympathizers, allies, or agents of the empire (cf. 4:21–22). The deplorable conditions are voiced in stereotypical lament language that may contain allusions to an impost on the necessities of life, such as water and wood (5:4) and forced labor at agrarian tasks, such as grinding grain and hauling wood (5:13). In an apparent departure from the Assyrian practice of exchanging populaces between conquered lands, there is no biblical record of the Neo-Babylonians introducing captives from elsewhere to replace the deported Judahites.

However, there is evidence that Edomites from Transjordan encroached on southern Judahite territory with tacit Neo-Babylonian approval, if not outright encouragement.[79]

The former personnel of the Judahite bureaucracy who had not been executed (2 Kings 25:18–21) were summarily removed from their posts and forcibly resettled in Babylonia at sites such as Tel-Aviv, Tel-meleh, Tel-harsha, Cherub, Addan, Immer and Casiphia (Ezek. 3:15; Ezra 2:59; 8:17). The settlements prefaced with "tel," that is, a mound or heap of ruins, suggest that some of these locations were deserted sites where the Judahite captives were segregated from the Babylonian populace and perhaps assigned the task of rebuilding them. Their work regimens and the terms of their detention are not spelled out.

Prophetic writings report that certain of the Judahites in Babylonia, refusing to accept that their detention would be prolonged, agitated for an early release, while others became demoralized and morose. Ezekiel, himself one of the deportees to Babylon, refers to elders who consulted him although they put little credence in the prophet's expectation of a lengthy banishment from Judah (Ezek. 14:1–3; 20:1–3; 33:30–33). Whether these elders were an informal group of traditional leaders or a body designated by the Neo-Babylonians to keep order and provide limited home rule among the deportees is not evident, although the latter may be implied by a letter that Jeremiah writes "to the elders of the exiles" with the approval of King Zedekiah and presumably of the Neo-Babylonian authorities as well (Jer. 29:1–3). Prior to the destruction of the state of Judah, Jeremiah indicates that prophets among the first wave of Babylonian deportees were agitating for a speedy return to Judah, and Jeremiah warns two of them that they are in danger of execution by the Neo-Babylonians for their subversive activities (Jer. 29:20–23). One leader among the exiles, Shemaiah ben Nehelam, possibly a priest or prophet, assumes the authority to write to a Jerusalem priest instructing him to curb the pro-Babylonian activity of Jeremiah, who regarded Nebuchadnezzar as "the servant of Yahweh," divinely appointed to punish Judah for its cultic and social wrongdoings (Jer. 29:24–32; cf. 27:1–7). This information from Jeremiah and Ezekiel comes from the years between the first and second deportations, 598–586 B.C.E., when the survival of an independent state of Judah still hung in the balance. With the fall of Judah and the devastation of Jerusalem, there are no further indicators of the circumstances of life in the deported community.

Only one narrative report breaks the decades-long silence about the Judahites taken to Babylonia, and that is an account of the favor shown to Jehoiachin, the Judahite king who had been detained in Babylon since the first deportation in 598. At the accession to the throne in 561 of Evil-merodach, Nebuchadnezzar's son, it is recounted that Jehoiachin was released from prison (house arrest?), given a seat of honor, provided special rations, and allowed to eat regularly at the Neo-Babylonian monarch's table (2 Kings 25:27–29 // Jer. 52:31–34). Nothing is said about the motive or intention of Evil-merodach in elevating Jehoiachin's status in captivity, nor is there any indication of the repercussions of this change of fortune on the deported community as a whole.

The only remaining biblical light on the Judahites in Babylonia comes from the poet-prophet of Isaiah 40—55, who addresses them toward the end of the exile, in approximately 550–538 B.C.E. The highly elusive poetic idiom yields no explicit details of their life conditions but does suggest some inferences. It is apparent that the captives, or at least a good number of them, have retained their communal identity as Judahites and Yahwists, but they are deeply demoralized by their political and ideological power-lessness. The poet-prophet intervenes in a political debate about the future of the deported community, whether to acquiesce in Neo-Babylonian hegemony or to favor, and even to work subversively, for the seizure of Babylon by Cyrus of Persia, who is looming large as a serious threat to Neo-Babylonia and as a potential liberator of the captive Judahites. The extreme derision of the prophet toward Babylonian culture and religion implies that assimilation to the conquerors' ways of life and worship exerted a strong attraction on his audience. This frontal attack on all things Babylonian may further imply that, over the decades, some Judahites had been drawn into mainstream Babylonian life, possibly in commerce or government service, and were therefore satisfied with their life conditions, a situation that the legends of Daniel 1—5 may distantly reflect.

Persian Political Hegemony

The most astonishing aspect of the political orientation of Isaiah 40—55 is that the poet-prophet openly champions Cyrus, the Persian, as the imminent deliverer of the Judahite deportees and the restorer of Jerusalem. Cyrus, invested with divine authority, is even hailed as the "shepherd" and "anointed" of Yahweh, God of Israel (Isa. 44:28; 45:1). The lavish rhetoric of Isaiah 40—55 can be reasonably decoded to mean not only that the poet-prophet expects Cyrus to conquer Babylon and restore his compatriots to Jerusalem but that he anticipates Cyrus' conversion to Israel's God and the elevation of Jerusalem to the status of religious capital of the Persian empire.[80] As for the attitude of Isaiah 40—55 toward the Judahites still living in their homeland, his assumption is that they will welcome the return of the exiles and readily accept their leadership in the form of an oligarchy replacing the defunct Davidic dynasty.[81]

The poet-prophet was correct about two of his hopes for Cyrus: the Persian did conquer Babylon, and he did release the Judahite captives to emigrate and reestablish Judah as a province of the Persian Empire, should they so desire. He was wrong in his other hopes, for Cyrus did not convert to Israel's religion, and he did not establish Israelite religion as the official faith of the empire. What he did was to recognize Judahite religion as one of many authentic local and regional cults within the empire. Not only was this not an elevation of the Yahweh cult to the supreme religion of the empire, it was not even preferential treatment for the Judahite religion, but one instance of a policy of toleration toward all cults as long as their adherents remained loyal to Persia. Moreover, the struggles over leadership in restored Judah following the return of the exiles indicate that those who remained in Judah during the exile did not compliantly accept the ideas and the programs of those who returned after decades in Babylonia. Nor is it by any means certain, as is sometimes assumed, that there was unanimity of viewpoint among those returning or among those who had remained in the land.[82]

The biblical profile of Cyrus as a benign ruler and benefactor of Judahites, in contrast to the nearly total dislike, even abhorrence, of Assyrian and Neo-Babylonian kings, sets the tone for a largely positive assessment of Persian hegemony throughout the biblical traditions. Although there are some indications of Judahite antipathy toward Persia, even open resistance against its rule, in the prophetic books of Haggai and Zechariah, the evidence for an actual revolt in 520–515 B.C.E. is based on obscurities in the biblical texts that have been taken to indicate deliberate censorship of an overt rebellion.[83] In any case, lack of Persian confidence in Zerubbabel, the governor of Judah who was also of the Davidic line, may be indicated by his disappearance from the record and by the fact that later governors of Judah were non-Davidic. Among the abundant prophetic oracles against foreign nations, there is none directed against Persia. In later legends, composed in post-Persian times, when Persian kings are about to allow the murder of Jews by royal decree, they are pictured as either acting against their personal desire or out of ignorance of the facts (Daniel 6; Esther).

The accounts in Ezra–Nehemiah of the reestablishment and governance of Judah in the Persian era, supplemented by the prophetic books of Haggai and Zechariah, are evidently composed of confusedly interlaced sources that make it difficult to determine the chronology of the stages of restoration and the exact rebuilding and reforming measures to be assigned to each stage.[84] According to the narrative line of Ezra–Nehemiah, the action unfolds in four stages with different leaders attached to each phase: the initial return of exiles to Jerusalem and the laying of plans to rebuild the temple under Sheshbazzar; the erection of the temple under the leadership of Joshua, high priest, and Zerubabbel, lay leader; the implementation of religious reforms by Ezra, priest and scribe; and the military, cultic, and political consolidation of the province by Nehemiah as governor.

There are obscurities and disputed points of interpretation at each of these stages. Sheshbazzar is a shadowy figure whose alleged accomplishments seem negated by the necessity of Joshua and Zerubbabel "to start from scratch" in building a temple. In some passages Joshua and Zerubbabel are coequal religious and civil leaders in Judah, but in others Zerubbabel's role is obscured and even effaced.[85] Ezra's commission of unspecified duration began in 458 B.C.E, if the biblical chronological synchronism refers to Artaxerxes I (Ezra 7:1, 7), while Nehemiah served as governor of Judah from 445 to 433 B.C.E, whereupon he returned to Persia for an unexplained reason, only to come back to Judah for a further undated term of office (Neh. 2:1; 13:6–7). Ezra's work is thus said to have preceded Nehemiah's, but there are several indications that Nehemiah's political reforms may best be regarded as having laid the groundwork for Ezra's subsequent religious reforms. On occasion the two leaders are referred to as collaborating authorities, as though Ezra was still active when Nehemiah arrived in Judah, but these look suspiciously like artificial editorial linkages (Neh. 8:9; 12:26). Ezra may actually have begun his work in 398 B.C.E., if the aforementioned Persian ruler was Artaxerxes II rather than Artaxerxes I. In any event, no chronology of Ezra and Nehemiah succeeds in resolving all the historical problems posed by the traditions.

For the entire Persian period, only the narrated activities of Ezra and Nehemiah throw any considerable light on political developments in restored Judah. Ezra is commissioned by the emperor to go to Judah and promulgate "the law of your God and the law of the king," appointing judges and magistrates to enforce the laws on pain of banishment, confiscation of goods, imprisonment, or death (Ezra 7:25–26). This charge is carried out by a public reading of "the book of the law of Moses," followed by a covenant of the entire community to observe its stipulations (Neh. 8:1–10:39). While some of the laws may be inferred from the text (Neh. 10:30–39), not enough is said to identify this lawbook conclusively with any of the law corpora contained in the Hebrew Bible. Ezra further compels all male members of the community, on threat of forfeiture of goods and banishment, to assemble in order to expose and dissolve mixed marriages, a measure which seems unanimously adopted (Ezra 9—10).

The reported reform measures of Nehemiah are more numerous than Ezra's. Greatest attention is devoted to his rebuilding of the walls of Jerusalem, which entailed a refortification of the city (Neh. 2:11–4:23). The populace of Jerusalem, chiefly occupied previously by community leaders, was enlarged by resettling one-tenth of the rural inhabitants within its walls and reordering settlements throughout the province (Nehemiah 11). Commercial activities on the Sabbath were forbidden (Neh. 13:15–22). The funding of priests and Levites was firmly secured (Neh. 10:32–39; 13:10–13; 14:30–31). Mixed marriages were prohibited but, contrary to Ezra's requirement, those already contracted were not dissolved; however, a son of the high priest who had married a daughter of Sanballat of Samaria was expelled from office and possibly from the province (Neh. 13:23–28).

The status of the restored Judahite community within the Persian imperial administration is clouded by the paucity, elusiveness, and fluctuation in the terms assigned to officials and in the specification of their jurisdictions and duties. Judah was clearly a subdivision within the large satrapy known as "Beyond the River," consisting of the entirety of Syro-Palestine to the west and south of the Euphrates River. Some historians have concluded, however, that Judah was not officially constituted as a province prior to Nehemiah's arrival as governor, being included for the first century of Persian rule within a larger province whose headquarters was in Samaria. This hypothesis would account administratively for the interference that the Judahites experienced from Samarians, in consort with other regions bordering on Judah, who sought to frustrate the rebuilding of the temple in Jerusalem at the end of the sixth century and the fortifying of Jerusalem in the mid-fifth century. If such were the case, leaders in Judah prior to Nehemiah would have been deputized by Persia as emissaries with designated powers to restore aspects of the communal infrastructure but without full autonomy outside the jurisdiction of Samaria. Recent finds of seal impressions and stamps have tended, however, to support the view that Judah was an independent province from the beginning.[86] Even so, Judah seems to have been little more than "a skeleton province" under Sheshbazzar, subsequently strengthened under Zerubbabel, and in decline again until the advent of Ezra and Nehemiah.

In the period 520–516 B.C.E., two prophetic books indicate that Zerubbabel, the governor, and Joshua, high priest in Judah, worked together in supervising the rebuilding of the Jerusalem temple (Hag. 1:1;

2:1, 4; Zechariah 3—4), which accords with what is said of them in Ezra–Nehemiah, even though the titles "governor" and "high priest" are not assigned them (Ezra 2:1; 3:2, 8; 4:3; 5:2; Neh. 12:1). This practice of a bipartite sharing of civil and religious oversight of Judah by lay and priestly leaders seems to have continued on into later Persian and Hellenistic times, although the biblical data on the lines of succession in the two offices are scant indeed.[87] The infrastructure of the provincial government and society is, however, far from clear. An inventory of the terms for lesser civic officials, communal leaders, and subgroups of the populace in Ezra–Nehemiah yields little confidence in the consistency or precision of their usage.[88] It appears that the sources drawn on to compose Ezra–Nehemiah employed a range of leadership terms elastically, and that the author did not attempt to standardize usages, either because it seemed unimportant to do so or because precise knowledge of the administrative structure and social organization of Judah was beyond the author's knowledge. It is pertinent that a similar imprecision in titles for administrative officials on various levels has been noted in the extrabiblical sources on the Persian empire.[89]

Probably the single most baffling obstacle to an understanding of internal political developments in Persian Judah is Ezra–Nehemiah's conception of who populated colonial Judah and who took the lead in shaping its social and religious institutions. The template for understanding Persian Judah in Ezra–Nehemiah is dominated by the premise that the totally depopulated land of Judah was repopulated and its institutions restored and purified by the survivors and descendants of the Judahites deported to Babylonia in 598, 586, and 582 B.C.E. The authentic "people of Israel" is the *gôlāh,* the community of exiles who have preserved the true faith in Yahweh and who return to a desolate "empty land" in order to "start afresh" by renouncing the unfaithfulness to God that had destroyed the states of Israel and Judah. An extensive geneaological list of returnees under Zerubbabel and Joshua (Ezra 2 // Neh. 7:6–73) separates those returnees entitled to membership in the community from those without entitlement, and Nehemiah consults this "book of genealogy" presumably to verify and perhaps to update its pedigrees (Neh. 7:5). Accordingly, the elusive references to "the people(s) of the land(s)" that characterize the opponents of the returnees are explicitly or implicly applied to external enemies, particularly Samarians, but also Ammonites, Arabs, and Ashdodites. Despite this recurrent motif of enmity between Judah and its neighbors, it is noteworthy that Judahite noblemen were in a cordial oath-bound relationship with Tobiah (Neh. 6:15–19), who was either the governor of Ammon or an influential ally of Sanballat, governor of Samaria, both leaders stigmatized as ardent enemies of the religiopolitical establishment in Judah (Neh. 2:10, 19; 4:1–3, 7; 6:1, 12, 14). During Nehemiah's absence from Jerusalem, priests even allowed Tobiah to take up quarters in the temple (Neh. 13:4–9).

In contrast to their preoccupation with external enemies, the accounts of the restoration of Judah de novo by the *gôlāh* take no account of the majority of Judahites who had not been deported at the fall of the state and whose descendants still lived in Judah, with the possible exception of the indebted Judahites who protest their loss of property and debt enslavement at the hands of fellow Judahites (Neh. 5:1–13).[90] Moreover, while the general thrust of Ezra–Nehemiah is to show the restored Judahites as harmoniously of one heart and mind, there are repeated references to divisions in the community and even resistance to Ezra and Nehemiah. In the absence of any acknowledgment of a continuing Judahite population that had never been deported, the numerous mixed marriages that are prohibited in the future by Nehemiah and radically dissolved by Ezra can only be explained as illicit alliances between men of the *gôlāh* and non-*gôlāh* women understood as foreigners from surrounding regions. Such mixed alliances thus stand in sharp contradiction to the premises of the genealogical lists which imply, if they do not directly demand, that proper Judahite marriages must be between members of the authenticated body of returnees from "exile." To extirpate these mixed marriages, Ezra threatens confiscation of property and banishment against those who refuse to address this issue (Ezra 10:7–8) and Nehemiah resorts to beating and hair-pulling to enforce oaths to abstain from future intermarriages (Neh. 13:25–27).

All in all, the commanding conception in Ezra–Nehemiah of a cohesive and triumphal body of returnees entering an empty land, untroubled by the presence of already established inhabitants and in unalterable conflict with the peoples surrounding Judah, utterly fails to make sense of the biblical texts, since they picture a community with severe internal strains and many ties with the populace of adjacent provinces. If we factor in the ignored long-standing Judahite populace and the ambivalent relations with Judah's neighbors, a whole new perspective on the complexity of the processes of "restoration" becomes both necessary and conceivable.[91]

If the relation of returning Judahites both to the older resident populace and to surrounding peoples is ignored and distorted in the religiopolitical and cultural ideology of Ezra–Nehemiah, the role of Persia in the reconstitution of colonial Judah stands out with unmistakable clarity. In spite of all the difficulties in discerning the exact course of events and the contours of the factional struggles involved in the securing of a stable Judahite community, the biblical traditions are abundantly clear in claiming that it was

Persian imperial policy to establish Judah as a viable part of its colonial system of administration. In doing so, Persian rulers issued directives for the repopulation and for the religious and political consolidation of provincial Judah. Moreover, the Persians dispatched exiled Judahites with specific commissions and powers to carry out the several tasks necessary to strengthening the religious, cultural, military, and civil infrastructure of Judah, providing them with fiscal resources and military protection at critical junctures. This project to build up Judah under Persian aegis did not happen in one stroke but was spread out over a century or more, suffering setbacks as well as renewed advances, apparently because of limited resources and contested leadership in Judah and because of distractions and interruptions in the Persian court during times of transition from one Persian monarch to the next when rebellions flared up in the farflung empire. The linchpin for establishing a secure Judah was a rebuilt temple, around which the religious loyalties of the populace could be rallied and whose priestly instructions and rituals could cement a sense of communal solidarity. But although the temple was in place by 516 B.C.E., it took many decades, and perhaps as long as a century or more, to regularize its leadership and standardize its practice. Interestingly, in Ezra–Nehemiah, once its rebuilding is recounted (Ezra 1:2–4; 3:8–13; 6:3–5), the temple receives only incidental attention (Neh. 2:8; 6:10–11). Moreover, since religious practice could not exist in a vacuum, during the same period it was necessary to build up the economic resources, military defenses, and civil structures that could enable the religion to take hold in practice and in ideology. Indeed, the temple not only served the cult but was closely implicated in economic, social, and political affairs. The hypothesis that rebuilt Judah was ruled by "a citizen-temple community" with religiopolitical rights and privileges belonging to its members that were not automatically extended to all inhabitants of the land, and that provided them social and economic advantages as well, goes some distance toward clarifying the form of colonization that Persia encouraged as well as the friction between those "inside" and those "outside" the establishment.[92]

Hellenistic Political Hegemony

Restricting our purview to the Hebrew Bible, there is little to say about the politics of Judah in the Hellenistic age, since the Hebrew Bible has no narrative reports concerning Hellenistic rule in Palestine. In prophetic writings, Greece is mentioned as one of Tyre's many trading partners and as the destination of Jews sold into slavery by Phoenician cities (Ezek. 27:13; Joel 3:6

[Heb. 4:16]). In these instances, as also in two vaguer contexts (Isa. 66:19; Zech. 9:13), the reference is to pre-Macedonian Greece prior to Alexander's invasion of Asia. Some have claimed unconvincingly to find veiled references to Hellenistic times in the obscure imagery of Zechariah 9—14, and although it is probable that Ecclesiastes was written in Ptolemaic times and that its dour assessment of kings is formed with Ptolemaic government immediately in mind, the wisdom genre in which the remarks are cast does not provide historical precision.

In the apocalyptic visions of Daniel, the Macedonian kingdom is "the fourth beast" and "the he-goat" that sprouts "horns=successor kings," culminating in a rampaging ruler who desecrates the temple in Jerusalem (7:7–8, 19–27; 8:5–12, 20–25). Although unnamed, Alexander and Antiochus Epiphanes IV are clearly the first and last of this series of Hellenistic rulers. That the author of Daniel was fairly well informed about the breakup of Alexander's kingdom and the successive rule of Ptolemies and Seleucids over Palestine is evident in a coded visionary review of the struggle between unnamed "kings of the south" and "kings of the north," once again culminating in the desecrating savagery of a northern king (11:2–39). While the historical details in this visionary account are elusive, they are coherent in recounting waves of destructive warfare between the Ptolemies and Seleucids, extending over a century in time. The "vision" further attests to the severe impact of this warfare on Judah, situated geopolitically between the warring parties, with Judah's leaders drawn into the conflicts by aligning themselves with one combatant or the other. All the allusions to Hellenistic rulers in these visions end abruptly in the hiatus between the desecration of the Jerusalem temple in 167 B.C.E. and its restoration in 164 B.C.E.

In contrast to its narrative discourse about the earlier Assyrian, Neo-Babylonian, and Persian hegemonies over Palestine, the Hebrew Bible thus refers to Hellenistic dominion only in the elusive overheated rhetoric of Daniel's apocalyptic imagery. Moreover, what this source tells us is presented under the fiction that Daniel, living in the Babylonian exile, is foretelling events that would occur hundreds of years in the future. The reticence of Daniel to speak plainly about politics is part of the convention of the apocalyptic genre and in no way due to political ignorance or disinterest on the author's part. Nonetheless, the stormy domestic and regional politics that suffuse the book remain deliberately veiled. This means that the last stage in the history recounted in the narratives of the Hebrew Bible is the reforming activity of Nehemiah in the latter part of the fifth century, or that of Ezra in the early fourth century, if he is placed in the reign of Artaxerxes II.

We are obliged to turn to Hellenistic historiography and to Judahite writings that were excluded from the later rabbinic canon in order to fill out our understanding of politics in this critical period. Of foremost importance are the books of Maccabees. First Maccabees, written in Hebrew, relates the Maccabean uprising against the Seleucids and the course of the independent Hasmonean dynasty from 175 to 134 B.C.E. Second Maccabees, an epitome of a longer work in Greek, tells only of the Maccabean revolt, beginning shortly before 175 and concluding in 161 B.C.E.[93] First Maccabees, composed in a style imitative of earlier biblical narratives, offers a more sustained and coherent political history than any comparable portion of the Hebrew Bible. Second Maccabees, on the other hand, is cast in the flamboyant style of a historical romance. Together these books give us richly detailed accounts of Palestinian politics in the second century B.C.E. While in broad agreement about many of the major events in the years 175–161 B.C.E., they have quite different religious and political assessments of those events.

Interestingly, 1 and 2 Maccabees occupy the anomalous position of being either "biblical" or "nonbiblical," depending on the perspectives of later Jewish and Christian communities. They are "nonbiblical" for the rabbinic Jewish canon and for the Protestant Christian canon, whereas they are "biblical" for the Roman Catholic canon and for the canons of some Eastern Christian churches. Within the confines of this chapter's overview of the politics of the Hebrew Bible, strictly speaking, 1 and 2 Maccabees fall outside our purview. If we are content to end our account of Israelite politics with the last reported history in the Jewish-Protestant canon, then we need take no further account of these Hellenistic histories. Since, however, a number of books within the Hebrew Bible were either written or edited in final form later than the time of Ezra–Nehemiah, including Daniel as a near contemporary of 1 and 2 Maccabees, a proper estimate of Israelite politics as a matrix of the literature of the Hebrew Bible needs to extend beyond Nehemiah to include late Persian and Hellenistic times. Accordingly, in this study we shall return to 1 and 2 Maccabees when we take up a critical assessment of the politics of ancient Israel in chapter 5.

Characteristics of Israel's Colonial Politics in Biblical Texts

For colonial politics we have a much reduced pool of information presented in literary montages that are even more confused and elusive than the accounts of the kingdoms of Judah and Israel in Kings and Chronicles. The skeletal chronology extends only as far as Ezra and Nehemiah, and the spotty political narrative ends with them. The conditions in Judah and among the *gôlāh* from the fall of Jerusalem to the rebuilding of the temple are at best only briefly referred to or implied in Lamentations and in Jeremiah, Ezekiel, and Isaiah 40—66. The period from the rebuilding of the temple to the coming of Ezra is a virtual blank, except as the undated prophetic book of Malachi may refer to its dispirited social and religious conditions. The "high points" of the rebuilding of the temple and the reforms of Ezra and Nehemiah are fraught with problems. Thereafter we have no account of happenings in Judah for more than two centuries until the Maccabean revolt. "Exile" and "Return" as major biblical motifs are simply not fleshed out with substantial detail. Judah during the Neo-Babylonian period is a virtual tabula rasa, and its undeported populace does not appear actively in the process of restoration.

Consequently, to discern the shape of the restored Judahite polity on the basis of the biblical traditions is no simple matter. It is clear that Judah is not an independent state with a king or ruling oligarchy that has a monopoly of force in its domain. It is an enclave or province under the sovereignty of Neo-Babylonia and Persia with appointed governors, only a few of them being named. Gedaliah, made governor of Judah after the fall of Jerusalem, directs an agrarian pacification program with the assistance of Judahite army units and a contingent of Neo-Babylonian soldiers (Jer. 40:7–12; 41:3). Under the Persians, Sheshbazzar lays the foundation of the temple. At the end of the fifth century, a high priest, Joshua, shares power with the governor, Zerubbabel, and together they lead in reconstructing the temple. Aspirations to make Zerubbabel king over an independent Judah are openly expressed in Haggai and Zechariah, but we have no report of whether they were acted on or what became of Zerubbabel. Ezra, although of priestly lineage, is not high priest, and Nehemiah, the governor, freely intervenes in religious matters. A clear delineation of duties between high priest and governor is lacking.

The delegated authorities in Persian Judah are dependent on the decisions of the imperial court in major policy matters, such as rebuilding the temple and repairing the walls and fortifications of Jerusalem, since these are measures that distinguish the status of the province and empower it politically, militarily, and commercially to serve Persian interests in the region. Similarly, the commission to Ezra to restore religious law in Judah is an act of imperial Persian policy, which is described as embracing "the law of your God and the law of the king" (7:28). If this is not a tautology, imperial laws over and above the religious law were endorsed as "a package deal." Violations of these laws were severely punishable to the point of death. Presumably, the various reforms undertaken by Ezra and

Nehemiah are understood as actions within the twofold law of God and king. A vexed issue is whether the religiocultural community circumscribed by Ezra was identical with the Persian province of Judah. On the surface it would seem to be so, but a community defined in such strict terms would have had doubtful place for large numbers of Judahites who did not satisfy Ezra's criteria but were still part of the populace subject to Persia. It is arguable that at first there was a separation between the reforming religious community and the larger polis, the former constituting the core of leadership approved by Persia, which only over time brought the whole province into its way of viewing politics and practicing religion. Again, because of a dearth of solid information, this must remain speculative.

In political terms, administration of the province proceeds by a combination of one-time reform measures and continuing administrative procedures. The latter are not spelled out in much detail, but it is noted that governors customarily receive a food allotment raised by payments of food, wine, and silver from the provincial populace (Neh. 5:14–15). Although Nehemiah waives this source of income, as governor he is presumably responsible for seeing that "the king's tax" on cultivated land is collected (Neh. 5:4). He also exercises the power to raise and allocate funds for the temple personnel. Although Ezra piously refuses military security when embarking on his mission, Nehemiah is accompanied by Persian "officers and mounted troops" (Neh. 2:9). The Judahites who rebuild the walls of Jerusalem are armed at Nehemiah's instruction in the face of physical threat from Samarian and other authorities (Neh. 4:7–23), who decades earlier interrupted the rebuilding of the temple (Ezra 4:23).

Particularly uncertain is the extent to which the reported reforms of Ezra and Nehemiah are successful at the time and how long-lasting they prove to be. Taken at face value, they seem to "carry the day" in instituting regularized civil and religious life in Judah. Yet they face strong opposition from surrounding provinces and resistance among Judahites, particularly to prohibition/abolition of mixed marriages and severance of ties with Samarians and Ammonites. During the period between Nehemiah's two visits to Judah, reform measures supposedly in effect are breached, and he has to take action to reinstitute them. Serious socioeconomic deprivation among Judahites forces Nehemiah to enforce a cancellation of debts that could jeopardize his role as guarantor of the provincial taxes due to imperial Persia. The books of Ezra–Nehemiah certainly end on a triumphal note, but the ensuing historical silence for two centuries leaves us no basis for judging the longevity of their accomplishments.

Of interest are the attitudes toward the hegemonic empires expressed in biblical literature. Jeremiah and Ezekiel are pro-Babylonian, but the authors of Lamentations in Judah and Isaiah 40—55 in Babylonia are hostile toward their overlords, and a series of anti-Babylonian oracles have been appended to the book of Jeremiah (Jeremiah 50—51). In the legends of Daniel, Judahite youth become servants in the Neo-Babylonian royal court and are severely tested in adherence to their faith. Nebuchadnezzar, initially a harsh tyrant, undergoes a dramatic conversion (Daniel 2—4), but his unrepentant son Belshazzar is overthrown by Darius the Persian (Daniel 5).

The Persian empire receives by far the most favorable treatment of any power that exercised sovereignty over Israel. Cyrus is profusely praised in Isaiah 40—55 and is lauded for his decree to release the Judahite detainees and rebuild the Jerusalem temple (2 Chron. 36:22–23; Ezra 1:1–4). In Ezra–Nehemiah Persia is the benevolent sponsor and protector of Judahite restoration. Significantly, there are no oracles against Persia in the Hebrew Bible. The one threat against Persian hegemony occurs in the prophecies of Haggai and Zechariah, who champion Zerubbabel as future king of Judah, yet without express animus against Persia per se but in the "messianic" expectation that all the kingdoms of the earth will be overthrown as the Davidic state arises to replace them (Hag. 2:21–23) In the legends of Daniel, Darius the Persian is a less malevolent king than either Nebuchadnezzar or Belshazzar, the Neo-Baylonians (Daniel 6), and in the visions of Daniel, Persia is not nearly the world-ravager that the Hellenistic kingdoms are (Daniel 7—11). In Esther, Persia is the cipher for a clumsy regime that can be manipulated by a scheming opportunist but, once his nefarious plot is uncovered, is willing to see that justice is done. Of course Daniel and Esther are wildly extravagant in their legendary portraiture and appeared to be decisively colored by the Maccabean-Hasmonean conflicts with the Seleucid empire.

Amidst the exaggerated drama of these legends, a double political dynamic is discernable: on the one hand, Judahites are learning that it is possible to participate in the wider culture, including service to foreign governments, without forfeiting their identity; and, on the other hand, imperial powers are learning that it is possible to accommodate the particularities of Judahite culture and religion without jeopardizing their rule. This accommodation between foreign overlords and their Judahite subjects is eventually gravely threatened by the Maccabean crisis, in which the Seleucid empire breaks the tacit accommodation that had been developing throughout the Persian era and apparently had not been fundamentally disturbed under the Ptolemaic regime. It could be said that there runs through restoration and Diaspora Judahite traditions the *explicit minimal goal* of preserving and developing a self-determined culture and religion within a larger foreign sovereignty. Simultaneously, however, this "half a loaf" goal is also shadowed by an *implicit maximal hope* of achieving full Judahite sovereignty unimpeded by foreign rule. This "maximal hope" announced in different forms by the author of Ezekiel 40—48 and by Haggai and Zechariah had to await realization until an unusual combination of domestic and international circumstances made an independent Judahite state possible in the last half of the second century B.C.E.

CHAPTER 4

The Ancient Near Eastern Matrix of Israelite Politics

The politics that is immediately germane to ancient Israel is the politics of the ancient Near East. This is the slice of "world-historical time" that provides the necessary perspective for viewing ancient Israelite politics. Ancient Near Eastern politics span a vast panorama extending over nearly three thousand years, from the so-called "dawn of civilization" through the Hellenistic era. Two of the handful of locations in the world where state politics arose independently were located in the ancient Near East, the one in Egypt and the other amid the Sumerian states of Mesopotamia. From these original centers in the Nile and Tigris-Euphrates valleys, the state form of organization spread widely over the entire area, in part by conquest and in part by imitation. Irrigation agriculture formed the economic base of these early pristine states, with an accompanying development of trade in finished goods and raw materials. The "secondary" states that spread out over the region depended on rainfall agriculture and became rivals or allies in trade, diplomacy, and warfare, or eventually fell under the imperial control of stronger states. Energetic peoples from the periphery of centralized polities, stimulated and emboldened by their contacts with strong states and adapting to new conditions, intruded into the existing state domains and took over the reigns of power in a process that has been called "interstitial emergence."[1]

THE EMERGENCE OF THE STATE IN THE ANCIENT NEAR EAST

For several millennia prior to state emergence, autonomous agrarian and pastoral settlements in the region had ordered their small-scale societies in nonhierarchic patterns. Leaders were answerable to social norms that barred them from appropriating the surplus of individual producers for personal gain or from creating a communal surplus fund that they could unilaterally impose and administer. Differences in wealth that show up in the archaeological record are best explained as larger shares of the produce assigned to leaders for the performance of their ceremonial and redistributive services to the corporate body. As improvements in irrigated agriculture and stockbreeding fostered increased crop and animal yields, denser habitation in the river valleys brought more complex economic and social functions and interests into play, which in turn required the negotiating of communal priorities in allocating resources and determining the rights and duties of actors in the public sphere. In this novel situation, some leaders in these communities began to convert the power they exercised at the will of the community into a power they exercised in their own right over the community without necessary consent of all affected parties or the backing of a popular majority. In practical terms, this meant that they could divert economic surplus to ends chosen by them without veto by the community at large. These ends included the building and maintenance of large administrative complexes from which their power radiated outward over a wider hinterland.

Taking responsibility for the oversight of the societal functions that had previously been decentralized, these central complexes of palaces and temples became the administrative and ceremonial nerve centers of the larger society. In keeping with their self-conception as the commanding authority for the entire community, the state functionaries adopted lavish lifestyles. In order to convert their asserted authority into effective power over the social whole, they developed bureaucracies to administer state policies. Writing and record keeping, apparently first developed to facilitate commerce, became an instrument in state administration and a medium for celebrating and enshrining state achievements. Large portions of the agrarian and pastoral surplus were required to support this hierarchic establishment. From its inception, the state claimed to secure social justice and domestic order, with the head of state as the ultimate human executer and guarantor of these communal benefits. Religious beliefs and practices served to legitimize the existing state structure as the channel through which divine blessings were bestowed on the governed community. Objections to state rule and noncompliance with the decisions of its officials were met not only with the solemn warrants and sanctions of religion but also, when necessary, with armed coercion. Military force was mustered to protect the commanding center against domestic threats and to enforce compliance with state enactments. Likewise, as more and more states asserted their sovereign authority, irreconcilable territorial claims prompted armed clashes among them.[2]

The precise circumstances in which decentralized societies in Egypt and Mesopotamia crossed the threshold into state societies remain an enigma.

It is impossible to give a definitive answer to vexed questions about the sequences of events that led to the emergence of the state or to isolate a single factor that "triggered" this chain of events. There are contending explanatory theories, but none of them can be conclusive because there is no documentation of the moment—or more likely the extended time span—of transition from the nonstate mode of human social life to the first states. The way existing states have functioned, together with scattered documentation about the rise of additional states once the initial "threshold to statehood" was crossed, offers some clues. These clues, however, do not lead to a single-factor explanation of the rise of state politics, but rather to a cluster of factors that may have worked in varying combinations from situation to situation. We leave aside the notion that the state is a self-evident response to an intrinsic human drive to seek submission to and dependence on external authority. This grounding of the state in "human nature" is neither an explanation nor a theory, being untestable and, as we shall see, belied by considerable historical evidence.[3]

It is worth noting the main theories about the causal factors in the rise of statehood, if only because they articulate significant aspects of the workings of centralized polities. The *social contract* explanation of the state is that a number of socially equal individuals, in order to protect their interests, compacted voluntarily to create a sovereign authority over them. The *functionalist* explanation is that the first architects of the state were persons skilled at finding solutions to the new challenges of economic and social complexity, as it were "an aristocracy of merit," to whom others deferred as deserving to exercise authority over the community. The *managerial* explanation is that certain economic challenges, such as building and maintaining large-scale irrigation systems, became so complex as to require the coordination that only a central power could exercise. The *military* explanation is that armed conquest and defense provided the occasion for one people to dominate another and for the victorious community to grant political power to those of their members who had achieved military success. The *social class* explanation is that a group within the community who had personally appropriated communal property, or who were aspiring to do so, instituted the state to legitimate and defend their project of self-aggrandizement.

Some element of truth seems to reside in each explanation, at least for the institution of particular states over the course of history, but none seems to be wholly adequate as an explanation of the first moves to statehood, or of the rise of all subsequent states, or of the astonishing tenacity of the state as the preeminent form of political organization once it gained momentum.

The social contract theory relies heavily on the notion of community as a loose association of autonomous individuals, but it does not easily square with the corporate traditionalism of nonstate societies. The modicum of truth in its claim is that some states may have arisen roughly in this manner, such as the democratic city-states in Greece and possibly the Phoenician mercantile city-states, but as a generalized model it is dubious. The functionalist theory seems excessively naive in believing that the most gifted persons in a society were those to whom nonstate populaces happily ceded fundamental powers, even in the formation of pristine states. Many state leaders have been exceptionally gifted persons, but over the entire history of statehood, in whatever forms it has taken, there are abundant examples of mediocre, effete, and even pathological political leaders. The managerial theory overlooks the reality that nonstate societies have managed to cope with considerable technological innovation without resorting to statehood. The element of truth in this argument is that the added difficulties of managing complex technology may provide a tempting occasion to let some members of the community take charge in exchange for greatly increased powers in other areas of communal life. The military theory appears to presuppose the prior existence of centralized state power, leaving unexplained how centralized military power originated in the first conquest state. The grain of truth in the theory is, that once militaristic states exist, nonstate peoples are exposed to conquest and, to avoid it, they are tempted to adopt a centralized polity to counter the states that threaten them. The social class theory does not really explain how a group within a nonstate society could muster sufficient power to break away from preceding social norms and initiate state hierarchy. The merit of its claim is that the state as an organizational structure, involving an executive head and an administrative bureaucracy, depends upon the support of a privileged stratum of the populace whose favored position is protected and reinforced by centralized authority and power in a kind of synergistic cycle that aims at self-perpetuation.

The outcome of spirited debate about the principal factors in provoking the emergence of the state form of social organization is not conclusive. In the judgment of the author, the social contract and functionalist arguments are particularly weak, and the managerial argument is overly economist. The military and social class arguments seem to have greater cogency. Taken together, they suggest a fusion of force and persuasion that enabled some members of a society, in which all shared in approximate benefits of production, to separate themselves sufficiently from prevailing communal norms and practices to take command of a surplus of authority and power that successfully transcended and subordinated the dispersed "lesser" authorities of society at large. Whatever the decisive impulses to statehood, it is a matter of record that once states gained a foothold in Mesopotamia and Egypt, they continued as the dominant overarching structure of social organization with only temporary interruptions and reversals. Breaks between large-scale political regimes, as in the so-called Intermediate Periods in Egypt and at the decline of Mesopotamian regimes, did not initiate any permanent renewal of nonstate social organization, but rather introduced eras of temporary political exhaustion and rivalry among contenders for the reestablishment of state rule. In short, after the collapse of particular state regimes, new versions of state politics arose to continue the old order. So the puzzle remains: how did the state get this power in the first place, and how did it manage to keep that power in an enduring institution, even as particular regimes rose and fell?

A major limiting factor in our knowledge about the emergence and triumph of the state form of political order is that the ancient Near Eastern state held a monopoly on writing about itself that largely restricts our knowledge to the perspective of the rulers, so that little is disclosed about the criticisms and organized opposition of the ruled. In truth, we know almost nothing about those who opposed state structures and still less about what, if any, alternative ways of organizing society they may have espoused and, on occasion, attempted to implement. Metaphorical traces of opposition to the state have been claimed for myths, such as the Babylonian Creation Epic, in which victorious Marduk represents the triumphal state and slain Tiamat, out of whose carcass the "civilized cosmos" is created, represents the sinister forces resisting the state. Similarly, the mythic assignment of humans to the role of servants of the gods, whose life will thereby be made easier, may be read as a sanction against those who would flout the authority and privilege of temple and palace. However, social and political realities are so refracted and obliquely reflected in myths that such claims have little historical diagnostic value beyond their clear assertion that humans at large are to serve both the gods and the states endorsed by the gods.

The case of ancient Israel is of interest in this regard. The Israelite tribal period involved a form of decentralized self-rule that met the needs of its highland agrarians and pastoralists but proved vulnerable to internal power grabs and external military threats. Although Israel's venture into statehood appeared two thousand years after state politics had come to dominate the ancient Near East, it preserved traditions about the misgivings and outright opposition of some members of society to the drift toward state politics. It is worth considering that the sorts of resistance to the imposition of the state expressed in Israelite traditions were similar to those that greeted the initial and subsequent steps to statehood elsewhere in the ancient Near East. In this indirect fashion, Israelite political life may provide a window on general processes in early state formation. Although the evidence is heavily stacked in favor of the "benevolent" state, there is good reason to believe that states did not arise, nor did they perpetuate themselves, solely or even primarily, from the free and informed consent of the populace they ruled.

Nor is it plausible to adopt the notion that, whether welcomed or not by their subjects, the state was an "inevitable" form of social organization corresponding either to the innate needs of humans or to the complexity of social organization. Nineteenth-century studies of the state were predominantly evolutionary in perspective. It was widely presumed that the movement from prestate to state organization and the subsequent advance of the state in complexity, territorial sweep, and political power were, so to speak, predetermined by an internal social logic. Research in the latter part of the twentieth century suggests that the entrenchment and advance of centralized sociopolitical organization in antiquity was less even and continuous than the dominant evolutionary paradigm of preceding studies proposed. Even though the overall course of history is toward the spread and enhancement of state power, particular societies have not followed the full evolutionary course, and there have been "devolutions" in other societies that have reached the brink of statehood and then failed to consolidate the state structure. This combination of overall augmentation of political power with marked regional and local variations has yielded a more modest "neoevolutionary" perspective. Nonetheless, both evolutionists and neoevolutionists assume a certain dynamic toward state formation and the enhancement of state power that makes it appear "natural," while the more decentralized forms of social organization appear either as "stepping stones" to greater centralization or as erratic "interruptions" to the primary plot of expansive state politics.

This triumphalist reading of the rise and growth of the state, whether full-blown or muted, not only downplays the many interruptions and detours in the development of the state throughout history. It also overlooks the relatively late appearance of the state in the whole sweep of human social life that extended over thousands of years in neolithic times. During this period there appear to have been recurrent social conditions in which communities might have handed over nonrecallable power to their leaders. That on numerous occasions they did not do so suggests that the state per se is hardly a "natural" phenomenon.[4] Moreover, when the state did emerge, it appeared independently only in a very few places (principally in Mesopotamia, Egypt, India, China, Mexico, and Peru).[5] Once ensconced, the state mode of social organization possessed tremendous power to invade and replace more decentralized modes. If we alter our perspective by recognizing that the appearance of the state was neither "natural" nor "inevitable," we are free to view the rise of the state as "fortuitous," even "serendipitous," a particular social experiment that proved of great utility for accomplishing certain social goals and, once embarked on, not easily reversed or modified. To say that the state arose fortuitously is not to say that it arose arbitrarily, as though, for instance, it could have arisen in sparsely populated mountain, plateau, or desert regions where resources and population were widely dispersed. Although it is problematic, as we have noted, to isolate any single overriding factor in the rise of those initial pristine states, it is evident that the social contexts where the state appeared displayed density of population, concentrations of agrarian and natural resources, and complex social organizational patterns that hierarchic control could attempt to coordinate and dominate with a growing measure of success. These state-generating contexts formed "social cages" from which dissenting social constituencies could not easily flee.[6]

The evolutionary and neoevolutionary paradigms of state politics carry another danger that can be very destructive of attempts to understand how state power may have been experienced by those who were moving to statehood for the first time. This would be true, for example, of the early Mesopotamians and Egyptians, but it would also apply to people elsewhere in the Near East as they adopted state organization in those cases where it was not imposed on them by conquest. The leaders who implemented the state structure and the general populace that supported, opposed, or were indifferent to its adoption would not necessarily have had a preestablished model of the state in mind. Under those circumstances, where a new form of social organization was emerging, it is safe to say that neither the rulers-to-be nor the subjects-to-be knew where political hierarchy was taking them, and that they could be easily "blindsided" by unanticipated turns in the course events with system-shaping consequences for good or for ill according to the varied standpoints of the participants. Rather than the singular notions of a "power coup" by leaders or a "contractual leap forward" by a consenting community as explanations for the emergence of the state, we might do better to think of "incremental" or "creeping" statism, since the full score of gains and losses for leaders and subjects could not have been adequately foreseen. Certainly the Israelite political traditions reflect this sort of ambivalence toward the state and a limited understanding of the direction in which centralized rule was carrying the society.

With a loosening of the paradigm of state inevitability, we can study politics as an account of how it has worked, both in its prestate and state forms, without the assumption that its course of development has been pre-determined. Most importantly, we can look at each instance of politics in terms of its own distinctive history. Comparisons of the histories of partic-ular polities will be relevant, but we will be careful not to have formed a single master paradigm of state politics that may obscure the particularities of the state under examination. Accordingly, our focus from this point on will be the Near Eastern matrix of state politics in which Israel arose. This approach to the politics of ancient Israel is especially advisable because Israel was not one of those first pristine states, but a late-emerging sec-ondary state, and thus an heir, however diffusely, of long-standing statist political organization to which it was exposed during its formative tribal decades. Israel came on the scene only after nearly two thousand years of state experience in its wider environment. Because Israel was in frequent interaction with other states, and at times dominated by them, it is incum-bent on us to understand the structures and strategies of those states as they formed a political matrix for the specifically Israelite political trajectory. Consequently, to do justice to the political experience of Israel it is neces-sary to view it within the wider context of antecedent and contemporary state cultures at each stage of its political journey.

To take such a broad but cautious historical comparative approach is not to decide in advance how much, or in what ways, politics in Israel may have borrowed directly from these Near Eastern states. In fact, our primary interest will not be in the vexed issue of Israelite "borrowing" from other cultures and polities, which has sometimes led biblical studies into a chase after "parallels" either torn out of context or nonexistent on closer exami-nation. It is always possible, at times probable, that what look at first glance like deliberately borrowed features were independent responses to similar circumstances or were elements mediated and diffused throughout a shared political environment. Likewise, we are not disposed to jump to conclusions about features of Israelite politics that appear distinctive, particularly to attribute them to Israel's religious uniqueness, which is in itself a problem-atic issue. Our aim is rather to set a stage for understanding Israel's politi-cal life as one instance of a much broader sector of "world-historical time."[7]

ANCIENT NEAR EASTERN POLITICAL TRAJECTORIES: STRUCTURES AND STRATEGIES

The two primary foci of Ancient Near Eastern politics were Mesopotamia and Egypt, where archaeology attests to a gradual increase of agrarian pro-ductivity and social complexity over many centuries preceding the formation of states in the Tigris-Euphrates and Nile valleys in 3000–2800 B.C.E. As political developments unfolded, the politics of the adjacent regions of Anatolia and Iran were eventually drawn into the story, along with Grecian Macedonia. The politics of Syro-Palestine, within which ancient Israel was situated, were closely connected to politics in the major power centers, but, apart from the maritime Phoenician city-states that founded colonies and stimulated Mediterranean trade, the Syro-Palestinian states were never "prime movers" in the exercise of political power beyond their own region.[8]

We shall briefly trace the political fortunes of states in the ancient Near East within three extensive time spans, from 3000 to 1500 B.C.E., from 1500 to 538 B.C.E., and from 538 to 63 B.C.E., attempting to identify patterns and trends in the conceptualization and exercise of political power that are relevant for an understanding of ancient Israelite politics.[9] The decision to make these chronological breaks may appear arbitrary, but it is defensible in the light of the significant differences in politics that characterize the three periods amid the undoubted continuity that linked them. In the initial era, from 3000 to 1500 B.C.E., the principal states are Mesopotamian and Egyptian. In the second era, from 1500 to 538 B.C.E., Anatolian and Syro-Palestinian states appear alongside the older powers. In the third phase, from 538 to 63 B.C.E., Iranian and Greek Macedonian states enter the arena of ancient Near Eastern politics.

Admittedly, the proposed task is daunting, both because of the sheer volume of the relevant data and because of fundamental disagreements among scholars of the ancient Near East concerning theories about the role of political power in relation to economy, society, religion, and culture and about the interactions among those public spheres in particular political regimes over the immense span of time involved. In one sense this should be reassuring to biblical scholars, who are sometimes tempted to think that other stretches of ancient history are much more clearly understood than the history of ancient Israel. However, as the volume of information about ancient Near Eastern politics increases and methods for analyzing the data proliferate, former certainties are unsettled, and reconstellations of data generate contending interpretations that fail to reach consensus on many central issues. Of course this diversity of interpretation among historians of antiquity may be "cold comfort" to biblical scholars, who are themselves frustrated by the reopening of historical issues about ancient Israel once regarded as more or less satisfactorily resolved.[10]

Mesopotamia from 3000 to 1550 B.C.E.

In lower Mesopotamia, between 3000 and 2800 B.C.E., a dozen or so Sumerian city-states arose with sizable urban centers that held sway over rural hinterlands of irrigated agriculture and sheepherding.[11] These city-states shared a common language, culture, and worship, by turns cooperating and competing economically, often resorting to war with one another, so that political prominence rotated among several states over several centuries. The political regimes cooperated with temple establishments in dividing the agricultural and pastoral surplus garnered from the general populace, many of whom worked on royal or temple estates. The production and allocation of the economic surpluses called for a considerable managerial bureaucracy and systematic record keeping. Literacy was confined to a small circle of scribes. Land grants were assigned to government personnel. In some city-states, councils or assemblies of leading citizens may have held consultative powers,[12] and, although state and temple were the dominant institutions, private transactions in land and goods seem to have been allowed. Religious thought envisioned a pantheon of deities, corresponding to the multiple political power centers and their domestic hierarchies. Political leaders were viewed as representatives of the gods with entitlements to rule and responsibilities to sustain order and justice in their realms. Trade for luxury goods and for the raw materials Sumer did not possess, in return for its grain, wool, and manufactured goods, reached far up the river valley and into the deserts and mountains that bordered the valley. In this way, Sumerian culture spread far afield, and there is evidence of trading contacts with India and Egypt from early dynastic times.

In the period 2400–2200 B.C.E., political power shifted northward to the middle Tigris-Euphrates valley, as Sargon and Naram-Sin of Akkad established a rudimentary empire that dominated the formerly autonomous Sumerian city-states and less effectively extended its power northward as far as Syria and eastward into Iran.[13] The language of this upstart state was Akkadian, adapted to the cuneiform script of Sumer, and the state made a point of appropriating the old Sumerian literary and religious culture in bilingual versions. Tribute was garnered and trade was facilitated by military expeditions, which were limited, however, by the difficult logistics of moving and supplying armies at great distances from their home bases.[14] Administration of the subject Sumerian states was carried out by the heads of the subject city-states; elsewhere administration was episodic and fragile. The decline of Akkad opened the middle and lower valley to the Guti, a mountain people from the east, not likely the first among many intruders who were to taste the benefits of Mesopotamian economic productivity and to seek to control it for themselves.

From 2100 to 1950 B.C.E., after the relatively brief reign of the highland Guti, political power once again returned to Sumerian city-states. This time, however, there was more conflict among the city-states, who entertained imperial ambitions, no doubt stimulated by the Akkadian example. In the so-called Ur III period, the rulers of that city mounted an empire that rivaled the ambitions of the Akkadian empire, although not its equal in territory controlled. Monumental palaces and temples were built, irrigation systems were improved and extended, trade was promoted, and a strong administrative apparatus was in place throughout lower Mesopotamia. The fertility of the lower valley probably reached its peak in this period; thereafter, the leaching of salt into the soil and poor maintenance of the irrigation works seem to have led to a gradual decline in productivity over the next millennium.[15] In the end, the rulers of Ur were no more successful in coherently administering conquered regions outside of Sumer than the Akkadians had been. Following the decline of Ur, in the period 1950–1800, Isin and Larsa in turn became the dominant lower Mesopotamian powers, but without the imperial reach of Ur III. The Elamites, an eastern mountain people who had long been interactive with Sumerian culture, briefly controlled Sumer before being repulsed.[16]

Once again, from 1800 to 1550, the pendulum of Mesopotamian political power swung in favor of the middle Tigris-Euphrates valley. Amorites from Syria, who had migrated into the valley from Syria over decades of time, formed kingdoms in several regions of Mesopotamia during the Old Babylonian period, the most powerful being located in Babylon.[17] Adopting the Sumero-Akkadian cultural tradition, including the "sacred" Sumerian language and the Akkadian "secular" language, the dynasty of Hammurabi ruled for some decades over an empire that dominated the length and breadth of the valley more effectively than any predecessor state had been able to do. Governors appointed by the crown replaced city-state rulers in Sumer and possibly also in formerly independent states north and northwest of Babylonia. The royal regime succeeded in weakening the economic clout of the temples and opened up entrepreneurial opportunities for ambitious laity. The space for landowners and merchants to engage in business on their own, while limited, seems to have been a feature of Mesopotamian states from the beginning. Under the Old Babylonians, however, more scope to "private" transactions in land and goods was permitted. Although this has been described as a process of "secularization," the economic retrenchment of the temples was not accompanied by rejection of religious faith and practice, since the ideology of the state continued to rest on religious premises. The cultural and ideological aspirations of the state were articulated in a collection of customary laws endorsed by Hammurabi that recognized differentials in social status among his subjects.[18] The foundation myth of the Babylonian state, possibly composed some centuries later in the Middle Babylonian period, is contained in the Enuma Elish, a creation story that recounts how the "young" god Marduk defeated the "senior" gods and clinched his victory by establishing Babylon as his privileged cult center.[19]

As Old Babylonian power ebbed by 1600 B.C.E., political control of Mesopotamia fragmented. Kassites from the eastern highlands ruled over middle and lower Mesopotamia, while the kingdom of Assyria emerged to its north on the upper Tigris River, the kingdom of Mitanni arose to the northwest of Assyria, and still farther to the northwest the Hittite kingdom was forming in central Anatolia. The long-standing geopolitical dynamic of a succession of single ascendant lower and middle Mesopotamian states that sustained economic ties with regions on their periphery, sometimes dominating them politically, was gradually shifting toward more complex multistate competition among contenders of roughly equal power over an expanded region involving upper Mesopotamia, Anatolia, and Syria. The harbinger of this diversification of political power was already evident in the last half of the third millennium when states such as Ebla in north Syria and Mari on the middle Euphrates attained considerable power with which Mesopotamian regimes had to reckon. Recent excavations at Tell Beydar and Tell Mozan disclose similarly strong political centers in the Upper Khabur valley to the north of Mari.[20]

Key developments in this first phase of the Mesopotamian political trajectory may be summarized as follows:

1. The state emerged securely as a political power network that proved effective in coordinating and dominating the kinship, economic, and ideological power networks within a circumscribed territory that could be controlled from an urban center.

2. The state developed administrative bureaucracies to carry out its programs of economic and military control as it drew upon expanding surpluses to maintain irrigation canals, to stimulate long-distance trade, and to erect royal palaces, fortifications, and ceremonial temples. Systematic record keeping smoothed the flow of goods and coordinated the work of government personnel. Land grants to high officials for as long as they served the state were customary.[21]

3. The state shaped a command economy by allocating the sizable resources it mustered through taxation, trade, and, when possible, through booty and tribute. In addition to large government and temple estates, there were landholders and merchants of means who had a measure of freedom to buy and sell, as long as they fulfilled their obligations to the state. Thus, alongside the preeminent command economy there was a limited market

economy, whose scope tended to expand over the centuries without ever becoming the primary sector of ancient Near Eastern economies.[22]

4. Temple establishments were vital as the generators of the state ideology that buttressed loyalty to the crown and accordingly received a generous share of the economic surplus. These temples maintained a considerable freedom from direct state control, although their autonomy diminished over time. The state was conceived as executing the will of the gods. Military victories and times of prosperity were evidence of divine favor, whereas the setback and collapse of dynasties or regimes were often rationalized as punishment by the gods for royal neglect of the cult or outright cultic infractions.[23] In the ideology of corporate laments, defeated city-states bemoaned the loss of their patron deities who were humiliated or displaced by the gods of the conquerors. Concurrent with the cults of the state gods, there was a multiplicity of private and family gods and religious practices, including divination and magic.

5. Changes in political regimes in Mesopotamia, and elsewhere in the ancient Near East, have frequently been attributed to "waves" of immigrants who overwhelmed the resident populace and set up new states. The major waves identified have been "Akkadian," "Amorite," and "Aramean." It is now widely agreed that it is more accurate to speak of intermittent "streams" of newcomers who over time became a sizable part of the populace and, when older regimes faltered, were able to provide new infusions of political energy.[24] In fact, some scholars deny that we can detect certain signs of sizable immigration into Mesopotamia and say that, at most, we may speak of "trickles" rather than "streams" of newcomers. In addition to the gradual "streams/trickles" of immigration, there were periodic "incursions" of militant pastoralists such as the Guti and Kassites who, with a relatively small number of warriors, overthrew weakened regimes and took over as heads of state.

Many historians continue to regard some of the clusters of people named in the ancient records as "ethnic groups." This ill-defined label, however, gives the impression of our knowing more than we actually know about them. A "minimalist" definition of an ethnos as a people who believe themselves to be of common ancestry and identity and who are so recognized by others, while tenable for well-documented peoples, is difficult to apply to groups in antiquity in the absence of evidence.[25] A "maximalist" definition, including features such as a collective name, a common myth of descent, a shared history, a distinctive shared culture, an association with a specific territory, and/or a sense of solidarity, is more diagnostically satisfying.[26] However, other than the collective name, we have little information pertinent to the other criteria for most of the alleged "ethnic groups" in the ancient Near East. Thus, it is not evident that we gain insight by using the ethnicity category, and may even impair our understanding by reifying groups into hard-and-fast identities that they may not have possessed. The general impression we gain of the Mesopotamian cultural and political world over the centuries is that it was heterogeneous, and, although by no means a "melting pot" of diverse identities, at least a world in which multiple sociocultural groups coexisted and interacted under "the umbrella" of the values, traditions, and institutions spawned in the early Sumerian city-states. Some of these sociocultural groups may have possessed self-identity strong enough to be thought of as "ethnic," but others may have been looser aggregations of people according to one or another criterion of language, territory, cultural style, class position, legal status, or occupational activity.

6. The oscillation of dominant political power between the lower and middle Tigris-Euphrates valley is a noteworthy feature of this period: from Sumerian city-states (lower valley), to Akkadian kingdom (middle valley), back to Sumerian city-states and the Ur III kingdom (lower valley), and thence to the Old Babylonian kingdoms (middle and upper valley). This swing of the political power pendulum reflects the strong, economically productive infrastructure of both regions with their capacity to supply the resources necessary to support a state apparatus. It also reveals the decided "wear and tear" on states as they struggled to perpetuate their ascendancy militarily and administratively. In other words, power tended "to slip away" from political centers toward peripheral regions in which new centers arose to eclipse the former centers now in decline.

7. Attempts of the lower and middle valley kingdoms to extend their control over greater distances were of limited success. Akkadian, Ur III, and Old Babylonian states managed to dominate regions in the upper Tigris-Euphrates valley and into the plateaus, mountains, and deserts bordering the valley. But this control, beyond raids and expeditions that recovered booty, was sporadic and fragile in areas outside the lower and middle valley. Although these regimes are customarily called "empires," they were far less coherent and efficient than later ancient Near Eastern empires beginning with the Neo-Assyrians. Cumbersome modes of communication and transportation, sluggish military logistics, and weak administration of the imperial periphery prevented the kinds of sustained control that were possible in the areas proximate to the capital cities of Akkad, Ur, and Babylon and other urban centers in the imperial heartland.[27]

8. Despite the infirmity of these early Mesopotamia states in securely controlling and integrating all the regions over which they held actual or

nominal power, their economic and cultural influence radiated far beyond the areas they directly dominated. People on the valley fringes, in the mountains to the north and east and in the desert to the south and west, as well as inhabitants of the north Syrian plain, were drawn into trading networks with the Mesopotamian states and increasingly exposed to the lure of the valley's economic productivity, literate culture, and institutions of political centralization.[28] As the valley political centers weakened, these "marginal" people, who were often more pastoral than agrarian in their way of life, periodically penetrated the valley and from time to time established new regimes. Without radically displacing the existing populace, they added a layer of sociopolitical power and new infusions of culture. This means that the "newcomer" regimes were not simply "outsiders," since by the time they came to power they were already resident in the valley or had long been in contact with and affected by Mesopotamian culture. A distinction can perhaps be drawn between those people who had long been resident in the valley in considerable numbers, such as the Akkadians, Amorites, and Arameans, and those fewer in number who came more abruptly by military incursion and often remained there as governing elites, such as the Guti, the Elamites, and the Kassites. The latter have been described as "marcher lords," and the role of these incursions of power from beyond Mesopotamia gained in importance in subsequent periods.[29]

9. Finally, while we note the rise and fall of many political regimes, they all appear to have been variations on a form of tributary bureaucratic state that adopted similar forms of political organization to address similar problems of social control. Furthermore, whatever the background of the successive elites, they aligned themselves with traditional Sumerian values and ways of life and added their respective contributions to an accumulating Mesopotamian intellectual, artistic, and political culture that became Sumero-Akkadian and, in centuries to follow, a more inclusive Mesopotamian "way of life," successfully maintaining its continuity and coherence until the end of the Neo-Babylonian empire, and even thereafter was recognized as one venerable segment in the Persian and Hellenistic eras.[30] However, owing to skewed evidence, the extent to which this "high culture" of the bureaucratic states penetrated the general populace is uncertain.

Egypt from 3000 to 1500 B.C.E.

When the state is first documented in Egypt, it already forms a unified government that controls the entire Nile valley from Aswan to the Mediterranean Sea. Tradition has it that this unification was imposed by a ruler from the southern reaches of the Nile valley (Upper Egypt) who conquered

the northern Nile delta (Lower Egypt). That the unification proceeded from
south to north is borne out by archaeological evidence, but it also suggests
that unification took place incrementally rather than in a single stroke.[31]
The Egyptian state crystallized somewhat later than the Mesopotamian city-
states, and while there is disputed evidence of Mesopotamian influence in
architecture and in the development of hieroglyphics, the Egyptian political development was essentially indigenous. While the course of the state
throughout Egyptian history was to remain more stable than Mesopotamian
states, it was not without its times of turmoil and decline. The greater
coherence and stability of Egyptian politics is understandable in terms of
the Nile valley's relative geographical isolation and the concentration of its
population into territory in the narrow Nile valley, which could be more
easily pacified and administered by central government than was the case
with the more geographically open and far-flung regions of Mesopotamia.
In this regard, the Syro-Palestinian states, including those of ancient Israel,
generally lacked natural boundaries, and thus had much more in common
with the geopolitically vulnerable Mesopotamian states than with the more
protected Egyptian state.

Egyptian rulers, bearing the title of pharaoh ("great house"), held preeminent power in all areas of public life and were regarded as divine when
representing the gods in ceremonial functions. Their modes of rule are not
well documented, since we possess no Egyptian law codes or state decrees.
We know of no conciliar bodies such as those claimed for some Mesopotamian city-states. In principle, pharaoh owned all land, but there was a
distinction between royal estates and the fields cultivated by peasants subject to taxation. Slavery was limited to foreign captives, but Egyptian commoners were subject to conscription on labor projects. Government
personnel were at first drawn chiefly from kinsmen of the pharaohs, but
over time, as the administrative apparatus proliferated, bureaucratic offices
were opened to others.[32] The state was constituted by the union of about
forty provinces, called nomes,[33] beginning with the Nile valley and later
incorporating the delta. Each nome was initially headed by a relative of the
pharaoh in order to ensure loyalty to the crown, but a drift toward decentralization and regional autonomy again and again presaged the decline of
dynasties. Regional nobility exercised considerable power that could but-
tress or undermine pharaonic rule. Urbanization in Egypt was much less
obvious than in Mesopotamia. State capitals were primarily royal and temple establishments with attendant crafts and small industries. Memphis, one
of Egypt's first seats of government, was established at a point near the division between the long narrow Nile valley of Upper Egypt and the broad

Nile delta of Lower Egypt. Priesthoods of the many Egyptian deities were often a political power factor, since pharaohs sought their favor and ideological endorsement. The priests of Amon in Thebes and Ra in Memphis-Heliopolis were particularly active in throwing their weight behind one or another pharaoh. Indeed, some pharaohs rose from priestly ranks.

The Early Dynastic Period (First–Third Dynasties) is reckoned from 3000 to 2700 B.C.E., followed by the Old Kingdom during the period 2700 to 2200 B.C.E. (Fourth–Eighth Dynasties). The state's command of society and economy is epitomized in the Old Kingdom royal pyramid tombs, designed and decorated by skilled engineers and craftsmen and built by conscripted peasant labor. Its decline was marked by growing decentralization, with regional authorities usurping powers once reserved to the royal court. Trade in precious metals and timber was conducted with the adjacent regions of Sinai, Nubia, and Syro-Palestinian coastal cities. Beyond the level of raids and skirmishes to keep open trading contacts to the south and west, there was minimal warfare, since there were no threatening neighboring states and, with sufficient resources on hand or available by trade, Egypt had no imperial ambitions farther afield. The First Intermediate Period, from 2200 to 2000 (Ninth–Eleventh Dynasties), saw the dissolution of centralized rule, with various regional dynasties vying for power. This era is later evoked as a time of social chaos and economic want, although it must be remembered that this dire judgment is rendered by later dynasts, who prided themselves on having restored unified rule to the land.[34]

Egypt was again unified from 2000 to 1750 in the Middle Kingdom, which was initiated by a dynasty from Thebes in Upper Egypt (Twelfth–Thirteenth Dynasties). Although its rulers resided in a new capital located a short distance south of Memphis, they erected temples and tombs in Thebes, a process that reached its lavish culmination during the New Kingdom. Amon, the chief Theban god, was fused with Ra, the Heliopolitan deity, to form Amon-Ra as the preeminent national deity. Under the Middle Kingdom, strenuous efforts were made to strip the monarchs of their independent powers. Trade was expanded, and Egypt's first imperial ventures were undertaken into Nubia. With the strengthening of central government, an expanded sector of "professional" administrators, scribes, soldiers, artisans, and merchants arose in counterbalance to the provincial governors.[35]

From 1750 to 1550, Egypt again lapsed into the divided rule of the Second Intermediate Period (Fourteenth–Seventeenth Dynasties). "Asiatics," known as Hyksos, ruling from Avaris in the delta, extended their control midway up the Nile valley, but they were unable to defeat Theban dynasties in Upper Egypt. That the Hyksos came in a mass invasion from bases in Palestine, as later tradition claimed, is now sharply questioned. It is more likely that growing communities of Syro-Palestinian traders and adventurers residing in the delta produced their own Egyptianized Semitic dynasties. The result was an amalgam of Asiatic and Egyptian cultures. When Theban dynasties restored "proper" Egyptian rule, they stigmatized the delta dynasties they defeated as barbarian "foreigners." When the next wave of "native" Egyptian rulers began to extend their rule into Syro-Palestine, they cultivated the xenophobic myth of "barbarian" Hyksos to validate their imperial ventures.[36]

Key developments in the first Egyptian political trajectory may be summarized as follows:

1. With the emergence of written records, the Egyptian state had already achieved unification of the entire length of the Nile valley up to Aswan under a single political regime. Competing political centers in Egypt, of the sort we encounter in the first phase of documented Sumerian politics, had been transcended by the advent of recorded history. This was accomplished not by an urban-centered regime that coordinated and lived off diverse agrarian, pastoral, small industrial, and commercial economies, but by a patrimonial political order presiding over a fundamentally homogeneous ecology whose desert perimeters prevented escape of its inhabitants from "the social cage" of a dense populace in a confined area.

2. The major qualification to this claim of a homogeneous Egyptian ecology is the undoubted difference between the narrow four-hundred-mile Nile valley of Upper Egypt and the delta of Lower Egypt, where several widely fanning branches of the Nile meandered toward the sea through a patchwork of fields, pastures, and marshes. The delta, seldom a center of far-reaching political power, was nonetheless difficult to pacify effectively and can be seen as a factor in the constant threat of destabilization to the unified dynasties that reigned from Upper Egypt. When unified rule lapsed, warring regional regimes were usually divided along the geographical fault line between the delta and the river valley. There is a rough equivalence between the dual power centers of middle and lower Mesopotamia and of Lower and Upper Egypt, but the major difference may have been that the shifts in centralized power in Mesopotamia, fueled by migrations and incursions of "marcher lords" did not occur in Egypt until late Assyrian times, with the possible exception of the Hyksos. Moreover, the delta region, while harboring enough power to contribute to the demise of weakened dynasties ruling from Lower Egypt, failed to establish centralized rule on its own until the decline of the New Kingdom. The Hyksos delta dynasties,

although the dominant power in Egypt for two centuries and probably more indigenous than once thought, were unable to extend their rule over the entire Nile valley.

3. The Egyptian state developed around an exceedingly "high" conception of the pharaoh as avatar of the gods and lord of the entire Egyptian domain, and the early dynasties strove to keep major court appointments within the ruler's kinship network. A large administrative bureaucracy, comparable to that in Mesopotamia, and perhaps even larger, gradually led to the accrual of power by provincial governors and professional court personnel. This dispersal of power attendant on the growth of bureaucracy led to the undermining of central rule in the First and Second Intermediate Periods, when contending dynasties struggled for ascendancy. Unfortunately, we know less about the details of administrative organization in Egypt than in Mesopotamia. The office of the vizier, second in command to the pharaoh, through whom all lines of communication between pharaoh and the other high officials were channeled, was not duplicated by any ancient Near Eastern state, and appears to have been a measure to keep the independent power of bureaucrats in check.[37]

4. The command economy of the Egyptian state was more all-embracing than its Mesopotamian counterpart, there being no indication of an economic sector independent of the state. This need not mean, however, that the economy was always effectively under the control of the royal court. The tendency of provincial governors to develop unchecked powers, prompting them eventually to form independent dynasties, indicates that it was a major challenge for the central state apparatus to keep stringent control over the widely dispersed economic productivity of the land. Put otherwise, since there was not a recognizable private economy, the way to prosperity for aspiring Egyptians was to secure a place in the central administration or to create rival centers of political power that sought local and regional control of human and natural resources.[38]

5. Temples figured prominently in Egyptian politics by providing the ideology of divine kingship and by buttressing loyalty to the state. As in Mesopotamia, many gods, at first connected with particular shrines, were known to the populace and were variously appealed to, and sometimes combined, to supply legitimacy to political regimes. The temples seem not to have had the measure of freedom from royal control that characterized Mesopotamian temples. In fact, the trajectories of temple-state relations seem to have been reversed in the two areas: in Mesopotamia, the initially independent temples were increasingly brought under state restrictions, whereas in Egypt, temples, at first under state control, gained considerable

freedom over time, and their priesthoods became important players in the struggle among claimants to the pharaonic office.[39]

6. The relation of the Egyptian state to the encompassing society and culture is, on the one hand, seemingly harmonious. The relative homogeneity of language and culture over the whole Nile region, especially when compared with the heterogeneity of Mesopotamian society, certainly contributed toward a monochromatic political culture with sweeping claims to sovereignty.[40] On the other hand, the frequent disruptions of unified rule and the rivalries for succession within dynasties reveal a state apparatus that was vulnerable to repeated collapses and replacements by new attempts at effective rule. The political volatility and turbulence of Egyptian statehood, seemingly as endemic as the political rivalry in Mesopotamia, may reflect considerable cultural differences, especially between Upper and Lower Egypt, that are masked by the more uniform political rhetoric. The relations of society and culture to politics are made all the more difficult to discern because of the paucity of information about Egyptian daily life of the sort we possess for Mesopotamia. Until the Hyksos, the internecine dynastic struggles were represented as "family fights." The shock of the Hyksos regime, simplistically attributed by later dynasties to a massive invasion by foreigners, was rather that Asiatic peoples and cultures were beginning to penetrate Lower Egypt and that Egyptian fortunes would henceforth necessarily be tied more closely to developments in Syro-Palestine and the regions of Asia beyond.

Mesopotamia, Anatolia, and Syro-Palestine from 1500 to 538 B.C.E.

A decidedly new phase of ancient Near Eastern political life develops from 1500 B.C.E. onward. Mesopotamia was no longer dominated by a single polity, as had been the case for varying stretches of time under Akkad, Ur III, and the Old Babylonian "empires." The region was fragmented into the rival states of Kassite Babylonia, Assyria, and Mitanni, further complicated by the emergence of the kingdom of Hatti in Anatolia and by Egyptian penetration of Syro-Palestine under the New Kingdom (see below).[41] The spread of light horse-drawn chariots, brought by the pastoral invaders to the east and north of Mesopotamia, unsettled the military edge enjoyed by armies of the old regime, consisting of infantry and unwieldy chariots with solid wheels drawn by wild asses. The shift in weaponry and tactics contributed to the turbulence of interstate conflicts. The first wave in state domination of large territories that had characterized the first millennium and a half of ancient Near Eastern history had played itself out. Limited by cumbersome administration and thrown off balance by new infusions of elites that the trade and military ventures of the early empires had helped to politicize, previous concentrations of political power were now decentered and diversified among several counter-balancing polities. These states engaged in elaborate rituals of diplomacy that included "gift"-giving and intermarriage to establish alliances and build coalitions, at the same time each was dominating lesser polities in their sphere by means of suzerain-vassal treaties. Warfare among them was frequent as the balance of power shifted from moment to moment.

By 1200, the competing major power centers were diminished or swept away by Aramean pastoralists from the desert fringe and by Aegean Sea Peoples who settled along the Syro-Palestinian coast.[42] The Hittite kingdom was obliterated, along with smaller coastal states such as Ugarit, and Egypt retreated from its Asiatic empire, leaving maritime Phoenician city-states[43] and small Aramean kingdoms in interior Syria, such as Carchemish and Damascus, to their own devices. In this context of highly dispersed local and regional powers, the states of Israel, Ammon, Moab, and Edom arose in the mountains and plateaus of interior Palestine without interference from stronger states. Among the older regimes, only Assyria survived, limited to control of Babylonia, until its resurgence in the ninth century.

Technological advances in this period had far-reaching political impact. Iron gradually replaced bronze as the preferred metal for military and agricultural purposes. The widespread availability of iron meant that, unlike bronze, its production was no longer an assured state monopoly. The spread of iron tools boosted agriculture in the rain-watered regions outside the irrigated valleys and thus strengthened peasant families, as well as contributing to an increase in local and medium-distance trade.[44] At the same time, the development of alphabetic writing made literacy more accessible beyond a narrow circle of professional scribes, thus further reducing the assured cultural monopoly of state regimes, although there is no indication of widespread literacy.[45] It is even possible to speak of a "cosmopolitan" culture spreading among advantaged groups throughout the entire ancient Near East, affecting Egypt as well, and stimulating exchanges among peoples more widely and intensively than ever before and less hindered by protectionist states.[46]

With the collapse of former empires of dominion and the weakening of those states that survived, the various power networks gained greater freedom of maneuver, particularly as more assertive artisan and commercial interests escaped restrictive state control, favoring the development of politically "looser" societies and polities with "multipower actors."[47] Oligarchies in Phoenicia and newly founded Aramean kingdoms in interior Syria tempered royal rule with more confederate polities. Even in Assyria, the one surviving sizable kingdom, nobility and merchants gained a voice in government. Over large areas of Syro-Palestine and northern Mesopotamia, local agrarian and pastoral communities acquired greater autonomy, while industry and commerce were in the hands of "free-floating" artisans, mariners, merchants, and nomadic traders. This "multiactor" development was not democracy of the sort that later emerged in Greece, but in addition to stimulating freedom of movement and enterprise among town dwellers and nomads, it no doubt brought some relief for the majority of people who labored on the land. To the extent that agricultural production was improved, local trade was stimulated, and states were less involved in massive public works requiring heavy taxation, peasants gained some benefits from the widespread "decentering" of political power in this period. Our assessment on this point is of course qualified by how little is known about how common people were affected by state activities or what they thought about the states to which they were subject. The one partial exception is in the indirect witness of Israel's prestate traditions, which describe the emergence of the tribal confederation of Israel during this very period.

The retreat of the imperialist state, however, did not prevent the smaller states from warring with one another, and there existed no decisive impediment against some state eventually attempting to dominate ever larger regions if it could find the opportunity and means to do so. Assyria thrust briefly into northern Syria in the twelfth century, but weaker rulers followed and it was not until the ninth century that Assyria was able to mount sustainable efforts at imperial expansion in southern Mesopotamia, in the mountains of eastern Anatolia, and deep into Syro-Palestine as far as the kingdoms of Israel and Damascus.[48] Following yet another retraction of its sphere of power, the Neo-Assyrian empire was launched in full fury by Tiglath-pileser III in 740 B.C.E., and a succession of vigorous kings, reigning for more than a century, went on to fashion the largest and administratively most successful ancient Near Eastern empire to date, which at its high-water mark invaded and dominated Egypt for two decades.[49] Fully integrating the technologies of infantry with iron weaponry and horse-drawn chariots, supplemented by new methods of siege warfare, the Assyrian army was formidable. It incorporated auxiliary units from defeated regions, as well as mercenary forces, and it was only as the percentage of non-Assyrian troops sharply increased toward the end of the empire that its tight discipline and morale declined precipitously.

The Assyrian government functioned through a well-organized bureaucracy, the logistics of which were capable of mustering the human and nat-ural resources necessary for its support. The populace included a sizable body of free landholders, who provided the backbone of state power. As the most northeasterly of the Mesopotamian states, Assyria had long expe-rience in trading and warring with the mountain peoples on its borders. The Assyrian heartland, while not as rich in agrarian surpluses as middle and southern Mesopotamia, was well situated geographically, and the pro-nounced convergence of its political, military, social, and ideological net-works provided a secure foundation for expansion abroad. In order to pacify conquered regions and integrate them economically to the net ben-efit of the homeland, Assyria had to overcome the weaknesses that had frustrated every previous attempt to build viable empires. Toward this end, Assyria succeeded in fashioning political instruments and policies that worked hand in glove with its military undertakings and its goal of trans-ferring economic surpluses from the periphery to the center of empire.[50]

As the Assyrians advanced into foreign territories and forced their polit-ical regimes to capitulate, the conquered king or an appropriate native replacement was accorded vassal status involving mutual pledges of loyalty and the payment of annual tribute to the imperial coffers. As long as the tribute was paid and no rebellions attempted, domestic affairs were left in the hands of the vassal ruler. Increasingly, when tribute was withheld or declined or open rebellions broke out, Assyria resorted to incorporating the offending region as a province of the empire and appointing an Assyrian governor, who could ensure greater social and political stability and expe-dite regular payment of taxes to the crown. At the height of empire, virtu-ally the entire Assyrian domain had been given provincial status, with only a few peripheral regions exempted, Judah being one. The compliance of vassal rulers and provincial populations required force or the credible threat of force. No ancient Near Eastern empire, Assyria included, ever wielded military manpower sufficient to mount the permanent occupation of conquered territories. The Assyrians established garrisons at critical points to serve as "trip wires" against recalcitrant or openly rebellious natives, but they depended principally on a large standing and conscripted army that could crush resistance. The slow pace at which these armies could move was never fully overcome, but the logistics of military supply was smoothed by the tight administration of loyal vassal states and provinces that could provision armies in transit to more distant battles and provide auxiliary troops as needed. Furthermore, the Assyrians "lived off the land" of resistant or rebellious regions by requisitioning crops and ani-mals at will.

A second measure, designed to break the will and capacity of conquered regions to rebel, was the wholesale forced deportation of ruling classes and their skilled servants, who were resettled in distant parts of the empire. Probably hundreds of thousands of people were transferred in large-scale population exchanges between regions, so that Mesopotamians, for example, found themselves relocated in Syro-Palestine and inhabitants of Syro-Palestine were settled in Mesopotamia. This was the fate that befell the upper classes of Israel in 722 B.C.E. In practice, this policy meant that large parts of the empire, especially those most resistant to Assyrian rule, were peopled with subjects bereft of former social ties, speaking different languages, and steeped in different cultures, thereby sharply reducing the possibility that they could cooperate subversively. Moreover, this policy of population exchanges on a grand scale was wonderfully suited to the economic needs of the empire. Those uprooted and transplanted included a high percentage of persons with administrative, military, and artisan experience, who formed a captive pool of skilled labor that the Assyrians could deploy as needed. In this way, the Assyrians supplemented their own human resources by recruiting the best talent of their captives.[51]

Finally, the Assyrian ideological network was fueled by a distinctive version of Mesopotamian religion, broadly dependent on the old Sumero-Akkadian traditions, but with a distinctive militaristic twist typified by "the terror-inspiring" deity Ashur at the head of the pantheon. It was in this deity's name that the kings of Assyria laid claim to dominion wherever its arms, conceived as the direct expression of Ashur's ferocious lordship, could reach. Vassal treaties were sealed with an oath to this imperial god, and rebels against his will could expect speedy retribution. However, Ashur never shook off his virtual identification with the kingdom named after him. He never became a transcultural god worshiped widely in the manner of earlier Mesopotamian deities such as Ishtar and Ea. Beyond formal deference to Ashur required at the political level, his worship seems never to have been imposed upon, or even commended to, non-Assyrians. Although Assyrian kings delighted in claiming continuity with preceding culture and religion, and even collected ancient texts in Ashurbanipal's library, they lacked the cultural and religious cosmopolitanism of earlier Mesopotamia until late in their history, to the extent that one is tempted to call the Assyrians the first ideological "nationalists." Assyria's xenophobia, however, was lodged in the ruling elite and did not permeate the general Assyrian populace sufficiently to create a cohesive national culture.[52]

With all its advances in developing a highly integrated military-administrative apparatus, the Assyrian empire came to a surprisingly sudden end. Royal succession had never been secure in Assyria, with coups and assassinations often punctuating the transition between kings. But when struggle for the throne broke out between Ashurbanipal and his rebellious brother, the empire proved vulnerable to a combination of forces. The army, now heavily staffed with foreign auxiliaries and mercenaries, was overextended and had been forced out of Egypt under Ashurbanipal's predecessor. The formerly disciplined administration was under strain to deliver diminishing surpluses to the heartland. Without new conquests, Assyria had to depend on already overexploited territories to sustain "the burden of empire." The catalytic factor in this precarious situation was the emergence of two threatening powers: an Aramean dynasty from Chaldea in far southern Mesopotamia that championed a Neo-Babylonian renascence and a federation of militarized pastoralists from Iran that went under the name of Medes. When these two "marcher lord" forces formed an alliance and attacked the Assyrian capital, it fell in 612 B.C.E. A remnant of Assyrian troops and administrators who fled westward and set up base in Haran were defeated three years later.

The Chaldean dynasty established its residential and administrative capital in Babylon, so that the center of gravity in Mesopotamian politics shifted to the middle Mesopotamian region, where the Akkadians, Old Babylonians, Guti, and Kassites had once ruled.[53] The city of Babylon was lavishly rebuilt by Nebuchadnezzar, who returned to the core of Sumero-Akkadian culture with some debt to Assyrian monumental architecture and mural design. The Assyrians had boldly asserted that their patron deity Ashur was simultaneously the architect and lord of their rapidly expanding empire. The Neo-Babylonians "went them one better" by appropriating the Middle Babylonian creation story to reaffirm that the authority and power of the old Sumerian gods had been seized by Marduk, who in fashioning Babylon accomplished a virtual "new creation" in a sea of sociopolitical chaos. A seamless connection was thereby asserted between cosmic order and the political order achieved by the Neo-Babylonians. Oddly, however, the last ruler of the dynasty, Nabonidus, turned his back on the Marduk cult by elevating the cult of the moon god Sin, located at Haran in northern Mesopotamia, to the highest rank within the empire.[54]

In spite of its grandiose claims, Neo-Babylonian rule prevailed for less than a century, from 612 to 538 B.C.E. During its relatively brief hegemony, revived Babylon appropriated the military and administrative advances of the Assyrians by keeping a close watch on conquered regions and deporting the leadership of states that resisted its rule. Apparently, however, the Neo-Babylonians did not exchange populations in the deliberate manner of the Assyrians, or, at most, on a much smaller scale. Accordingly, Judahite leaders were deported to Babylonia but no foreign captives replaced them as had been the case in Israel under Assyrian hegemony. The brevity of Neo-Babylonian rule is attributable to at least two factors. For one thing, the alliance of "convenience" that had joined Neo-Babylonians and Medes in the overthrow of Assyria did not last. Each party went its own way in subsequent decades and eventually clashed head-on. While the Neo-Babylonians controlled the arc of the Tigris-Euphrates valleys and Syro-Palestine, the Medes were establishing dominance over the ring of mountains and plateaus in Iran and Anatolia, along the eastern and northern perimeter of the Fertile Crescent, thereby denying or complicating Neo-Babylonian access to the resources of those regions from which the Assyrians had greatly benefited. Before long, a "marcher lord" within the Medean confederation, Cyrus of Anshan, galvanized the loosely organized members of the confederation into a powerful striking force, which soon turned against Babylon. A second contributor to Neo-Babylonian vulnerability was strife within its ruling class. In polemical documents of the time, it is claimed that Cyrus's success in seizing the city and toppling the Chaldean regime was aided by Babylonian priests whom Nabonidus had alienated in his neglect of the Marduk cult. It is also probable, due to an extended absence of Nabonidus from Babylon, that state administration and military preparedness had been neglected, leaving the city vulnerable to attack and prompting a Babylonian governor and army commander to defect to Cyrus at a critical moment in the defense of the capital.

Egypt from 1500 to 538 B.C.E.

Once Hyksos rule was overthrown, the New Kingdom (Eighteenth–Twentieth Dynasties), having unified all of Egypt, launched conquests in Palestine and southern Syria, ending two centuries later in a stalemate with the Hittites, who dominated northern Syria. With the eclipse of the New Kingdom, yet another period of disunity followed, as rival kingdoms in Tanis and Thebes by turns cooperated and contended for power (Twenty-First–Twenty-Fourth Dynasties). When later dynasties from time to time united the land (Twenty-Fifth–Twenty-Sixth Dynasties), they were unable to reestablish an Asiatic empire, in spite of occasional efforts to foment and support Syro-Palestinian rebellions against the Assyrians and Neo-Babylonians. So defensive was Egypt's position that it was invaded and briefly administered by Assyria in the seventh century. The rise of ancient Israel coincided with the decline of the New Kingdom. Weaker Egyptian dynasties that followed, because they were geographically proximate to Israel, could from time to time attempt to play a role in Palestinian affairs, but in the end none of their interventions proved of decisive geopolitical importance.

In undertaking its imperial ventures into adjacent Asia, the New Kingdom strategy was both military and economic, its twin aims being interdependent for their success.[55] By establishing a buffer zone in the Syro-Palestinian corridor, Egypt sought to prevent a recurrence of infiltration or invasion by Asiatics such as it had experienced under the Hyksos. In the process, it aimed to secure a regular flow of tribute from its vassals and, in particular, to dominate the lucrative international trade that passed through the corridor by land and by sea. The Egyptian imperial administration was looser than that of the contemporary Hittites or of the later Assyrians. After major military campaigns, defeated city-state rulers served as "regents" of the Egyptian crown and were responsible for annual tribute. Egyptian civil officers exercised sporadic oversight of the regents. Egyptian troops, garrisoned at a few points throughout the conquered regions, were relatively ineffectual in keeping the regents from warring among themselves. To secure compliance from vassals, as well as to garner booty and captives for state labor projects, from time to time Egypt relied on major military campaigns, but with ephemeral results.

The New Kingdom was internally disturbed by the reformist rule of pharaoh Akh-en-Aton, who elevated the worship of Aton, the sun disc, to the status of sole national deity, and a political struggle ensued with the Theban priesthood who served Amon.[56] With the failure of this reform effort, subsequent Ramesside rulers moved their capital to the delta in order better to oversee the Asiatic empire, while remaining faithful to the pre-reform cult of Amon-Ra that affirmed allegiance to the traditional religious loyalties of Upper and Lower Egypt disrupted by Akh-en-Aton. The Ramesside pharaohs renewed Egypt's Asiatic empire for a time, but were checked and forced into abandonment of the conquered territories by internal weaknesses and by the Aegean migrations that had overwhelmed the Hittite empire and penetrated Syria and Palestine.

The following Egyptian dynasties were often headed either by Libyans who had moved into the delta from the west or by Nubians who had extended their rule up the Nile from interior Africa.[57] These new political actors were not barbarian outsiders, for Egyptian culture and religion had greatly influenced them prior to their rise to power, intermixing with their indigenous ways of life. In this regard, they probably did not differ greatly from the Hyksos, but the "Hyksos panic" was not repeated, because Egypt had by now become a more multicultural society, owing to the New Kingdom's "opening into Asia," and no "pure" nativist Egyptian political force had the power to restore "the good old days." While there were momentary spurts of power that briefly united the entire land, or that permitted occasional raids into Syro-Palestine and tenuous promises of support to Syro-Palestinian rebels against Assyria and Neo-Babylonia, these regimes were simply unable to mount a permanent threat to Asiatic powers. To the contrary, Assyria invaded and ruled Egypt for two decades, and later the Persians extended their control over the Nile valley for more than a century. Egypt's one moment of imperial renewal was in 609–605, during the brief political vacuum between Assyrian and Neo-Babylonian control of Palestine, when pharaoh Neco of the Saite Dynasty was able to depose Jehoahaz and appoint Jehoiakim to the throne in Judah and collect tribute before being driven out of Palestine by the Neo-Babylonians following the Battle of Carchemish. Nonetheless, in the events that led to the fall of the kingdoms of Israel and Judah, leadership factions in both states turned to Egypt in the vain hope that they could escape the onslaughts of Assyria and Neo-Babylonia. It is also of note that Israelites and Judahites, both as mercenaries and as refugees, made their way to Egypt in the seventh and sixth centuries, forming the nuclei of dispersed Yahweh-worshiping communities that were to grow enormously in Hellenistic times.[58]

Mesopotamia, Egypt, Anatolia, Iran, and Macedonia from 538 to 63 B.C.E.

At this point our separate treatment of Mesopotamian and Egyptian politics ceases, and it becomes necessary to consider both regions as subsets of one larger political matrix that includes not only Mesopotamia, Anatolia, and Syro-Palestine, but also Iran and the centers of Greek culture and politics in the eastern Mediterranean as they begin to impact events and institutions in the ancient Near East and, at the end of our study, the looming entrance of Rome into the Near East.

Cyrus, as founder of the Persian empire, fell heir to the former domains of the Neo-Babylonian and Median empires, which instantly gave him control over territory that exceeded even the outermost limits of Assyrian dominion.[59] Under his successors, the empire was extended eastward to the Indus valley, north and west over the whole of Anatolia, and southwest over the Nile valley. The political organization and administration necessary to hold together the far-flung empire was a severe test for the Persian rulers, but they proved equal to the task over the two centuries that they ruled a larger territory with a more polyglot population than had any previous Near Eastern imperial regime. The Persians built on many of the strategies developed by the Assyrians, but with cultural and ideological inducements that tempered the military terrorism that had been Assyria's major weapon, and they added a considerable repertory of administrative strategies. They improved roads to facilitate military and commercial movement, and they enlisted the help of Phoenician and Greek city-states to exploit the advantages of maritime warfare and trade. Coinage, originating from Anatolia/Asia Minor, came into widespread usage as a medium of exchange that prospered commerce.

After the initial conquests of Cyrus, subsequent rulers concentrated on administration of the sprawling empire, which was divided into twenty large districts, known as satraps, each with its own governor and bureaucratic apparatus.[60] Satraps were further subdivided into smaller provinces. Sizable numbers of the Persian elite became residents throughout the empire, not only those who ran the organs of government but also the noble class and their entourages, who were assigned large land grants. To ensure political loyalty and fiscal honesty among the administrators of this vast empire, the royal court instituted a security force independent of the satraps and their staffs, whose responsibility it was to investigate and audit the performance of the imperial civil service. As an aspect of their aim to rule as much as possible by persuasion, the Persians tried to strengthen local and regional social, cultural, and religious bonds. Many of the people deported by the Assyrians were encouraged and assisted in returning to their homelands, among them the descendants of the former elite of the kingdom of Judah, and an effort was made to restore temples and their paraphernalia that had been looted or had fallen into neglect under the Neo-Babylonians. Local communities, such as restored Judah and Egypt, were encouraged to codify their traditional laws as the basis of semiautonomous judicial systems.[61] In all this, of course the highest authority remained the Persian imperial court, which required that taxes be raised for its support and which did not hesitate to intervene in critical "trouble spots," proving themselves to be as ruthless in putting down rebellions as the Assyrians had been.

By the beginning of the fifth century, Persians came into increasing conflict with Greek city-states, some of which they controlled in Asia Minor and others that remained independent on the Greek mainland, in particular, Athens. A thriving trade between Greece and Persia was occasion both for cooperation and for rivalry that broke into open warfare. Athens gave assistance to anti-Persian uprisings in Egypt. Persia, with an eye on control of the lucrative Greek maritime trade, embarked on two major invasions of mainland Greece and was twice defeated and driven back when the normally divided Greek city-states united to defend themselves (490–479 B.C.E.).

A state of stalemated tension and sporadic warfare continued, complicated by the fact that Persia ruled over the Greek colonies in Asia Minor, some of whom sided with Persia because of their fear of Athens and Sparta. In ensuing decades, while Athens and Sparta depleted one another in the Peloponnesian War, Egypt broke free of Persian rule for several decades but was reconquered shortly before the demise of the Persian empire.[62]

Not surprisingly, in the estimation of Greeks the Persian empire was an unbridled "despotism," in contrast to the "democracy" enjoyed by many of the Greek city-states. Just as the extent and nature of Greek democracy requires qualification, so monolithic despotism does not accurately describe the mixture of political structures and processes that held the Persian empire together. The grip of the central imperial regime in Persia was firm and demanding, but it no more controlled all levels of social and political life than had preceding empires, and it could succeed only by working flexibly with local and regional power networks whenever possible. This combination of a single overarching political regime and multiple lesser centers with their own forms of social and cultural identity and self-expression contributed to a cosmopolitan culture, at least among the Persian and non-Persian elites in all the provinces. The foundation for this multicultural development was laid at the start when the Persians, an Indo-European people from Iran, overran the Semitic, Egyptian, and Anatolian Greek worlds. Adopting Aramaic as their official tongue, the Persians realized that to maintain control over such a diverse population it would be necessary to operate under a broad cultural and ideological canopy that did not trumpet their "national" superiority as the Assyrians had done. Nor could they rely on simply appropriating the proud Mesopotamian heritage, since they not only brought their own long-standing Median-Persian legacy into the empire, but they also had to cope with the equally proud Egyptian and Anatolian Greek heritages. The Persians had a resource for projecting a cosmopolitan basis for their empire in their allegiance to Zoroastrianism, which recognized Ahura Mazda as the single beneficent deity. At the same time, they could equate this divine being with other gods worshiped throughout the empire, whose cults they made no effort to exterminate, other than to destroy those temples involved in political insurrection.[63]

The weakened Greek city-states were incorporated into Philip's Macedonian empire, and his son Alexander launched an invasion of mainland Asia that overwhelmed the Persian empire within a few short years (334–330 B.C.E.) The Macedonian army that tipped the balance of power against Persia was superior in weaponry, tactics, discipline, and morale.[64] The Persian "federal" system of rule that gathered so many peoples into its fold, strained by the struggle to recapture Egypt and disturbed by rebellions of its governors in Asia Minor and elsewhere, was unable to field troops with sufficient unity of purpose and effective enough generalship to prevail against the hard-driving Macedonians.

With Alexander the Great's conquest of Persia, a new and more assertive cultural cosmopolitanism spread over the ancient Near East. The Persian political structures were inherited and adapted by Alexander and his successors but with ample provision for the foundation of Greek-style city-states and military colonies that planted the seeds of Greek thought and culture, which were to have far-reaching effects transcending the rise and fall of particular political regimes.[65] At Alexander's early death without a successor, his vast empire fell apart into territories ruled by his warring generals, the two major winners being Ptolemy, who controlled Egypt and Palestine, and Seleucus, who reigned over Syria, Asia Minor, and Mesopotamia. Although the Macedonians were Greek in language and culture, they were not primary carriers of Greek political democracy. Philip of Macedon had defeated the separate Greek city-states and incorporated them in his kingdom before his son Alexander moved against Persia. The Macedonians recognized and tolerated semiautonomous city-state polities, even founding them when it served their imperial purposes, but always they were treated as subjects and instruments of royal rule, just as the Phoenician and Anatolian Greek city-states had been subject to Persian royalty. On balance, there is little qualitative difference between the political "despotism" of the Persians and the political "despotism" of the Hellenistic kingdoms that followed.

In Egypt, the Ptolemies established an elaborate bureaucracy, owing something to older Egyptian practices, enabling them to tax and conscript their subjects with considerable efficiency, including those living in Palestine under their control throughout the third century.[66] They actively sponsored Greek culture, including establishment of a renowned library in Alexandria. They melded the accoutrements of Greek culture with Egyptian traditions, including attribution of deity to themselves as successors of the pharaohs. The Seleucids, ruling from Antioch in Syria, had a much larger realm to control, seem not to have been the equal of the Ptolemies as administrators, and were often in fiscal crisis. Ptolemaic and Seleucid armies clashed repeatedly over control of Palestine, with the Ptolemies prevailing until the Seleucids took control at the beginning of the second century.

Beneath the highest echelon of imperial rule, Palestine consisted of Judah and a number of older Phoenician and declining Philistine city-states, together with several newer Greek city-states. As Ptolemies and Seleucids clashed over control of Palestine, they offered various emoluments and concessions to these Palestinian entities in order to gain their support. The first Seleucid ruler of Palestine was generous to Judah, but a subsequent king intervened in strife between Judahite factions who favored and opposed Hellenistic culture and backed rival candidates for the Jerusalem high priesthood. Antiochus Epiphanes threw his full support behind the pro-Hellenistic forces in Judah and joined them in trying to syncretize the worship of Yahweh and to prohibit the customary religious practices of circumcision, Sabbath observance, temple worship, and reading of the Torah. The ensuing conflict erupted in civil war among Judahites and spawned a colonial guerilla resistance against Seleucid interference. Owing to stubborn resistance in Judah and dissension within the Seleucid regime, within a few years Judah regained religious freedom, followed before long by the establishment of an autonomous Judahite Hasmonean kingdom that lasted until the Romans brought it to an end a century later. The Hasmonean rulers, although stemming from a movement that had been anti-Hellenistic, operated as petty Hellenistic rulers who subjected much of non-Judahite Palestine to their dominion.[67]

During the Ptolemaic and Seleucid eras, large numbers of Judahites migrated to Egypt, some seeking political refuge and many more looking for economic advantage. Greek became their daily language, and although retaining their religious practices, they were profoundly influenced by Hellenistic culture.[68] Both the Seleucid and Ptolemaic kingdoms survived into the first century, when they fell to Roman conquest, the former in 64 B.C.E. and the latter in 30 B.C.E. The Hasmonean kingdom was absorbed by Rome in 63 B.C.E. This development marks a suitable point to conclude our review of ancient Near Eastern political trajectories amid which Israelite and Judahite politics were conducted.

SUMMARY ASSESSMENT OF ANCIENT NEAR EASTERN POLITICS

Over three millennia, a series of centralized political regimes arose in Mesopotamia and Egypt, in the Syro-Palestinian corridor connecting those two regions, and in Anatolia. In due time, regimes springing from Iran and Greek Macedonia spread their dominion over the ancient Near East. Amid the welter of historical details, we may identify certain defining features in the structures and strategies of these state polities.

Primacy of State Power. These political networks were constituted as the most comprehensive and authoritative institution within societies, with rights and powers to command and coordinate the functions and resources of the other spheres of society. States arose and were perpetuated when economic surpluses were sufficient to support them and when social diversity and inequality invited the establishment of a public instrument for coordinating and allocating economic resources and social statuses.

Maintenance of State Power. The effectiveness of these states in implementing their formal entitlement to command and coordinate societal networks depended on many variables that could weaken or strengthen their performance. The authority of states was not a simple "given," since, once established, the sovereign claim had to be reproduced from moment to moment and from generation to generation. Typically the centralized "executive power" of the state had to contend with challenges from other domestic power centers, such as merchants, landholders, and priesthoods, as well as its own bureaucrats. In order to secure and hold political power, state rulers wielded a combination of persuasion and force. Political success depended on the complex interaction of many covariables, such as the delegation of state duties to an administrative bureaucracy that could be held accountable; the availability of human and natural resources; the cooperation or resistance of domestic social, economic, and ideological power networks; and fluctuations in diplomacy and warfare with other states. The "making" and "breaking" of ancient Near Eastern states was a recurrent feature of the political history we have reviewed.

State Economy. The major states of the ancient Near East were largely monarchic bureaucracies operating from an administrative and ceremonial center, while lesser states followed more or less similar patterns in the organization of their resources. The main sources of state revenue were agricultural and pastoral surpluses gathered from rural subjects, income from royal estates, profits from trade, and tribute from conquered lands. A major power difference among states was whether they could marshal optimal resources domestically and reach out to dominate other states or regions sufficiently to draw tribute from them and to control the flow of trade. In order to sustain the flow of revenues and to "live up" to their claims to serve and protect their subjects, states took responsibility for enhancing agrarian and craft production, adjudicating disputes among subjects, quelling civil unrest and insurrections, and protecting the state territory from outside attack. The perceived balance between the "costs" in taxation, conscription of labor, and other state measures that regulated the populace, on the one hand, and the "benefits" in productivity and security, on the other hand, worked to strengthen or weaken political regimes.

State Administration. Political power radiated outward from the governing center to the periphery of states.[69] This "periphery" is to be understood both spatially and socioeconomically. As a general rule, state power was expressed spatially by the ability to exert control over the whole of its claimed territory, determined by such factors as geographical accessibility and effectiveness in the chain of command by which government policies were carried out. Also, as a general rule, state power was expressed socioeconomically by the ability to exert control over the social and economic networks, both the activities of bureaucrats who did its bidding and of nobility, merchants, and priests, who in many instances held power bases outside of government service. Political regimes declined and were overthrown when they could not control their spatial and socioeconmic peripheries.

While a good deal is known from various texts concerning titles and functions of officers in state administration, this information is sufficiently scattered and sporadic, and sometimes so contradictory, that it has been impossible to reconstruct a complete profile of state administration in any of the ancient Near Eastern polities. Interestingly, we seem to come nearest to well-rounded reconstructions in the case of the early Sumerian states and the late Ptolemaic Empire, but even in those cases there are considerable gaps and uncertainties. If the ancient Near Eastern royal courts prepared handbooks for administrators detailing their duties or developed flowcharts of administrative processes, they have been lost. More likely, the administrative staffs of antiquity did not exhibit the elaborated "rationality" of bureaucracy in the modern West, and the model of a civil service that endures independent of changes in government may be applicable only to certain limited offices, such as scribes and priests. Some interpreters of these ancient state administrations have preferred to call them "patrimonial" rather than "bureaucratic," in order to stress that administrators did not serve an abstract "state" but were personal servants of the monarch. Be that as it may, we note that, by whatever means, certain vital functions of government could be carried out only by persons delegated to do so, and if they failed in a major way, the commanding "center" of the state could not sustain its authority and power over the "periphery."[70]

State Ideology. Political power was buttressed by the ideological power of religion. Amid all the diversities of gods, myths, and rituals, it was a constant that states drew upon indigenous religions to legitimate their entitlement to rule and to rally support from the populace. In a minority of cases, as in Egypt, political rulers were divinized in their cultic roles; elsewhere, they were generally conceived as the privileged deputies of the gods.[71] The temple priesthoods were indispensable to political order, but the relationship between rulers and priests was often rocky, since states were inclined to garner the benefits of religious ideology while curtailing the economic and social power of religious institutions. The legitimacy of aspiring new political regimes was typically buttressed by appropriation of venerable "culture deities," particularly in Mesopotamia and Egypt, while each of the states in Anatolia and Syro-Palestine had analogous patron deities. Religious blessings on the royal office did not always protect occupants of the throne, for usurpations and assassinations were a recurrent feature in these states. Deposed kings were stigmatized by their successors as slothful or apostate in failing to carry out their religious mandate. When states expanded into empires, it was typical not only to assert the special status of the conquerors' god(s), but also to accommodate the gods of the conquered within a redesign of the pantheon of deities.

State Fragility. The popularized notion that ancient Near Eastern states were unadulterated "oriental despotisms" is clearly mistaken.[72] Contrary to the impression that these ancient regimes were static monoliths under the absolute control of their rulers, it is manifest that they seldom, if ever, dominated their societies as totally as they trumpeted in their public display of edicts, inscriptions, art, and architecture. Indeed, state regimes were "momentary" concentrations of power overlaying diverse social and economic groups with competing interests. The balance among these groups, if unsettled, could erode or topple political regimes. These "moments" of sustained political order might last in any state for decades, even for as long as a century or more, and enfeebled regimes might retain power if the domestic and foreign forces opposing them were weak and divided, but the overall record is not one of unbroken continuity and longevity of regimes.[73] New regimes could be founded on military achievements but could last only if they were able to orchestrate and administer a balance among the major economic and social players in their realm. In short, the ancient Near Eastern states were not totalitarian "despotisms," although particular states were more or less authoritarian. Nor should we regard those regimes in which councils or assemblies of leading citizens may have exercised consultative powers as "democracies" or "republics." It is probably better to recognize tendencies toward a loosening of centralized control as "multiactor" societies arose in which politics had to take greater account of dispersed sources of power, but the renewed empires of domination, such as Assyria and Persia, were able to broaden and reconfigure their administrative structures and ideological formulations to limit political power-sharing with these multiple social actors.

States as Aspiring Empires. In Mesopotamia beginning with Akkad and in Egypt beginning with the Middle Kingdom, strong states attempted to dominate weaker states in order to counter real or perceived threats from abroad, to enhance their wealth, and to consolidate their legitimacy by quelling domestic opposition.[74] These imperial ventures were fitful and only partially successful until the Assyrians managed to combine military and administrative strategies to greater effect. Subsequent Persian and Hellenistic empires elaborated and improved the Assyrian strategies. Empires had all the domestic difficulties of nonexpansive states, plus additional problems. The extended spatial periphery of the empire strained communication and military campaigning. The socioeconomic periphery was expanded with the aim of laying tribute to all the networks of economic production and social reproduction within conquered regions, including the enlistment of cooperating comprador groups to "normalize" imperial domination. However, this reach for power over conquered peoples could "backfire" by awakening noncooperation and passive resistance and lead to open rebellion, especially when the imperial center weakened, as frequently occurred when the imperial army was hard pressed to fight on several fronts, or just after the death of a ruler before his successor was able to secure his power base. Moreover, the farther imperial power extended its reach, the greater the risks of insubordination or rebellion by subject populaces and imperial administrators. The imperial gains in state security, additional revenues from conquered regions, and overall prestige could easily be offset by the costs in personnel and materials to pacify and administer the empire.

Ephemeral States amid Ongoing Cultures. The embedment of these ancient Near Eastern political networks, as well as the social, economic, and ideological networks, within wider "cultures" or "civilizations" is apparent. In Mesopotamia, the early Sumero-Akkadian tradition was sustained down to the Neo-Babylonian era,[75] and the Egyptian cultural tradition was perpetuated to the very end of the Ptolemaic regime.[76] These cultural complexes consisted of religious beliefs and practices, literary texts, artistic conventions, and folkways that persisted from political regime to political regime. As far as we can judge, the primary carriers and perpetuators of these cultural complexes were bureaucrats and professionals who worked in the state and temple bureaucracies. What is not known, because we have only scanty, indirect access to the popular oral culture, is how far this common "high culture" penetrated into the mass of the populace and could be counted on as a kind of tacit consensual bond between rulers and ruled. Rulers were constrained to accommodate themselves to the received cultural traditions, even as they worked to expand and reshape them, but the extent to which this cultural pressure came "from below" remains indeterminate.[77] As the Mesopotamian and Egyptian cultural traditions converged under the Persians, a more expansive cosmopolitan outlook emerged from the interface and interaction among Persian, Mesopotamian, Egyptian, and Greek cultures. Hellenization of the ancient Near East inserted yet another cultural horizon that was even further disengaged from particular political regimes, in that it posited a potentially universal culture for all "rational/civilized" peoples. In practice this cosmopolitan Hellenistic culture was both resisted and combined in various ways with the indigenous ancient Near Eastern cultures.

Multilingual Diplomacy and Multilingual States. The complex interface of culture and politics is particularly evident in the languages used for discourse within the social and political networks of ancient Near Eastern polities.[78] We should in principle distinguish the following sociolinguistic spheres: the official language used for the conduct of internal state business, the language of international diplomacy, the language spoken by political and social elites, the language(s) spoken by the subject populace. Although the evidence is far from complete, it is clear that often different languages were operative within one polity. Presumably, the greatest linguistic homogeneity was in the earliest Sumerian city-states and in Egypt prior to the Middle Kingdom. Akkadian speakers became dominant in middle Mesopotamia, and their language of empire became the diplomatic lingua franca of the ancient Near East for more than a thousand years. Amorites brought yet another linguistic vehicle into Mesopotamian culture, although it never became a bureaucratic or diplomatic language. Aramean immigrants formed the demographic base of later Mesopotamia regimes, and their Aramaic tongue replaced Akkadian as the medium of interstate politics until Greek prevailed under the Hellenistic kingdoms. Beneath the level of interstate communication, however, particular regimes often employed other languages for official purposes, and these would not necessarily be identical with the spoken languages of the political elites, whose scribes kept the records. Still farther down the social ladder, the populace might share one or more languages that differed from the "political tongues" of those who ruled them. This polyglot factor is a strong indicator of the diversity of peoples and cultures that were "thrown together" under a single political power network and an index of the failure of "nation-states" to emerge with distinctive national identities shared by the rulers and the ruled. It appears that it was the Assyrian elite who strove hardest to carve out a distinctive "national" identity within the general domain of Sumero-Akkadian culture, but Assyria's military and administrative accomplishments were not matched by a melding of the populace into a sense of being a singular, unified people that could outlast the demise of the state.[79]

JUDAH AND ISRAEL AS ANCIENT NEAR EASTERN STATES

From the preceding description of the ancient Near Eastern political trajectory, it is possible to characterize the politics of ancient Israel as a subset within the larger family of regional states. Without ignoring historical details or precluding innovation in Israelite politics, we are in a position to recognize structures and strategies in Israelite statehood that were typical of other ancient Near Eastern polities. This orientation provides a perspective that is lacking when we treat Israelite politics solely in terms of its textual evidence or in terms of generalized political theory that does not take the ancient Near Eastern specifics into account.

The Temporal Scale. On a temporal scale, Israelite politics fall within the last one-third of the historical trajectory we have traced, emerging in prestate form around 1200 B.C.E. and in statist form after 1000 B.C.E., whereas the Mesopotamian and Egyptian states could trace back their beginnings over two thousand years, to 3000–2800 B.C.E. This immense difference in time scale is easily forgotten in the light of the "foreshortening" effects of the cursory and impressionistic references to earlier ancient Near Eastern polities and cultures in the Bible itself and in many studies devoted to ancient Israel. On the other hand, the biblical traditionists "compensated" in a measure for the relative "youthfulness" of Israel by tracing their ancestor Abraham to Ur and Haran in upper Syria and dating him more than one thousand years before the founding of the Israelite monarchy.

The Spatial Scale. On a spatial scale, Israelite polities were among the small to mid-sized states of the ancient Near East, comparable in territorial extent to many other Syrian and Palestinian states. At best, occasional Israelite domination of adjacent small-scale states never lasted for long, and Israel never attempted, much less succeeded, in conquering Egypt or Mesopotamia. Although the diversity of regional ecologies and climate could sustain a moderate level of subsistence, Israelite territories possessed limited natural and human resources for mounting major political initiatives against other regions. This limitation on the power potential of the Israelite state is easily overlooked when focus is put on the grandiose account of Solomon's empire, or when the bellicose expansionist rhetoric of Israelite royal psalmody is taken too literally.

The Independence-Dependence Scale. On an independence-dependence scale, Israelite polities enjoyed autonomous statehood for approximately five of the nearly twelve centuries we are examining: for four centuries under royal dynasties, at first united and then divided into northern and southern kingdoms, and for nearly a century under Judahite Hasmonean rulers. The period of autonomy was shorter by more than a century for the northern kingdom, which was overthrown in 722 B.C.E., and attenuated for the southern kingdom during the nearly century and a half when it was a vassal state of Assyria and Neo-Babylonia. But autonomous statehood was not the sole or primary indicator of Israelite identity. At its inception, Israel was an association of tribes with considerable freedom from outside control, but not as yet forming a state. In the long interval between the fall of the kingdom of Judah in 586 B.C.E. and the founding of the Hasmonean state in 145 B.C.E., the Judahite community was subject to Neo-Babylonian, Persian, and Hellenistic empires. Thus, for the entirety of the Israelite political trajectory from the late eighth century onward, Israelite politics were played out within the shadow, and often under the thumb, of much stronger powers whose spheres of dominion controlled or threatened them. The brief revival of Israelite political independence under Josiah in seventh-century Judah, as well as the longer Hasmonean regime in the second and first centuries, was made possible because of weaknesses in the imperial powers. Within the context of regional politics, Israel was often a significant player on a par with other Syro-Palestinian states, but in the international context it was never a major political force.

The Geopolitical Scale. In geopolitical terms, however, the geographical location of Israel was strategically significant out of proportion to its tenuous political strength. Israel's strategic value was both commercial and military. The major land routes that connected the Nile and Tigris-Euphrates valleys, together with highways connecting South Arabia and the Mediterranean coast, passed through southern Palestine along a constricted corridor between the sea and the desert. Local regimes or imperial powers that could control these routes profited from tolls on transported goods and, if they chose, could apply a "choke hold" on transit trade. Although only in their brief expansionist moments were Israel and Judah able to control these routes, their very proximity to them drew the attention of stronger states with high stakes in international trade. It was also along these highways that armies of conquest marched in two directions, from Egypt into Asia and from Mesopotamia/Syria toward Egypt. As the last settled region in western Asia before reaching the Sinai desert, Palestine served both as a buffer zone for Egypt against foreign invasion and as the staging area for Asiatic empires to launch invasions of Egypt. Therefore, influence on or actual dominion over Israel and Judah was a prime goal of imperial powers seeking to control the nexus of roads that converged in the Syro-Palestinian corridor.

Political Division and Diminished State Power. The potential political power of ancient Israel was aborted by its division into two kingdoms from 930 B.C.E. onward. Israel, the northern kingdom, was the more populous and economically prosperous, although less geographically defended from without and less socially cohesive. Although the two kingdoms shared cultural and linguistic traditions, as well as manifestations of the cult of Yahweh, they were able to collaborate only on rare occasions and were never able to agree on a common royal house, once the split had occurred. Since the ancient Near Eastern political collectivities we have noted were prone to break up into smaller political entities, the rupture in the kingdom of David at Solomon's death is no great surprise.

In their failing to reunite, the two kingdoms were also typical of the difficulty of separated political entities reuniting, except as subunits of larger empires. In fact, were it not for the biblical tradition that treats the northern and southern kingdoms as part of a larger cultural and religious Israel, there is little basis for treating the two polities together, other than as instances of the larger phenomenon of small Syro-Palestinian states that cooperated in alliance and competed in diplomacy and war. In strictly political terms, the arbitrariness of treating the states of Israel and Judah in combination, distinguished from surrounding states, has been overlooked by many biblical historians, who operate on the overriding premise that since Israel and Judah shared a common religion they were "natural twins" in politics. While conceding the shared culture and religion of the two states, as well as recognizing their geographical contiguity, the thrust of this inquiry into their politics seeks to counter the "artificiality" of isolating the Israelite and Judahite kingdoms from the larger field of Syro-Palestinian states.

State Transmission and Cultivation of Prestate Traditions. One respect in which Israel and Judah are distinctive is the extent to which they preserved traditions about their prestate society and the steps that led to the formation of a state. This sort of information is notoriously lacking in other ancient Near Eastern states, since the formative circumstances occurred largely in a preliterate or subliterate period. Where we have references to the founding of states in the ancient Near East, they are either vaguely mythological or are cast so as to give heroic prominence to the state founder. Just what credence to give to the prestate Israelite traditions, anomalous as they are for the ancient Near East, remains a matter of dispute. For historical analogies it is necessary to go outside the ancient Near

East to other societies where we have information about such prestate social formations, and it is unclear in what respects these formations, distant in time and space, are comparable to ancient Israel.[80] Entailed in such comparisons is the issue of why Israel and Judah should have preserved extensive prestate traditions when other states in their political environment did not.

Small-Scale Tributary Monarchies. Structurally, the kingdoms of Israel and Judah were small-scale monarchies, constituted as tributary states that drew on the agrarian and pastoral surplus of subjects to sustain a privileged way of life for the crown and the bureaucracy that ran domestic and foreign affairs of state. In this, they were "duplicates" of such states throughout the Syro-Palestinian corridors, functioning on the pattern of the larger kingdoms and empires that so often intruded on them, with necessary adjustments and reductions of scale and intensity in the administrative machinery of state. In this connection, we need to note that we have rather fuller information on the Judahite bureaucracy than on the Israelite bureaucracy. The data for Israel, however, has to be recognized as "redrafted" by the Judahite redactors who preserved northern traditions after the fall of Samaria. The effective power of the Israelite and Judahite states rested on securing cooperation, or at least compliance, from influential landholders and merchants, but the notion that leading citizens formed a consultative body with formal powers to affect the crown, of which we have traces elsewhere in the ancient Near East, rests on disputed evidence. The king did not own land beyond certain royal estates, which could be acquired and augmented in various ways: by inheriting the patrimony of previous kings, by taking land vacated by owners, by confiscation of criminals' property, by gift or purchase from Israelites, and by foreign conquest and annexation.[81] The impact of tributary rule, however, was felt far beyond the royal estates through the state's power to shape the subsistence economy in its own interests by taxation and commercial subsidies that skewed production and exchange to the advantage of people of means.[82] This intermesh between state power and the civil networks of Israel and Judah, with strong regimes holding the upper hand, seems more accordant with Mesopotamian arrangements of the political economy than with Egyptian protocol in which the state, at least when it was strong, had more commanding power.

The Dubious Claim of Participatory Government. The tendency of Western historians and political theorists, biblical scholars included, to regard Israel as the harbinger of democratic freedom and civil rights is highly misleading. This judgment depends heavily on selective reading of provisions of biblical law codes and an anachronistic understanding of biblical covenant language in the "social contract" tradition of later Western political theory.[83] In the actual political practices related in biblical traditions, it is difficult to distinguish Israel and Judah as being "freer" or more protective of "citizen rights" than other states at the time. The frequent claim that, at least in monarchic Judah, there was a council or body of free citizens ("the people of the land") that significantly reined in state power is dubious.[84]

While much of the unfavorable light thrown on the monarchy in biblical traditions can be attributed to the anachronistic monotheistic viewpoint of late traditionists, a fair share of the criticisms concern socioeconomic injustices inflicted or permitted by the crown. These criticisms, prominent in prophetic narratives and oracles but also more temperately expressed in wisdom literature, do not appear to have produced measurable institutional or policy changes in the conduct of the tributary states. Jehu's "revolution," reputedly at the instigation of a prophet, brought little if any positive benefit to the northern kingdom. The biblical lawcodes may reflect efforts at judicial reforms under the monarchy that were not long lasting, as in the case of Josiah. The sociopolitical source and import of these reforms are less than clear: were they initiated by social sectors seeking "to rein in" monarchic power, or were they instances of the state "coopting" and blunting efforts to restrain its powers?[85]

In any event, the considerable scope of criticism of state rule expressed in the finished biblical literature is no doubt due in part to the jaundiced eye of late Judahites who had outlived the fallen state and constituted themselves as a religiocultural enclave within the Persian empire. There seems to be no comparable global indictment of an ancient Near Eastern state's weaknesses and failures to serve its subjects delivered from the perspective of survivors of the defunct polity who have formed, as it were, a countercommunity. The condemnations of ancient Near Eastern dynasties and state regimes, which are plentiful, are mainly delivered by subsequent dynasties and regimes who are claiming to do "a better job" than their predecessors. Perhaps the nearest ancient Near Eastern analogy to Israelite critiques of its own monarchy are the "prophetlike" ex post facto indictments of Egyptian dynasties delivered to reigning pharaohs who are expected to correct the ancient wrongs that still prevail, but the social context generating these radical criticisms is unknown (cf. "The Admonitions of Ipu-wer," *ANET,* 441–44).

The Struggle for Dynastic Continuity. The difficulties in sustaining dynastic continuity are clear enough in the biblical record, especially in the northern kingdom. Yet even Judah, which managed to sustain the Davidic dynasty for well over three hundred years, was not without precarious moments in the succession of its rulers. The "liminal dangers" in the transfer of political power are abundantly illustrated in the political histories of other ancient Near Eastern states. Even the most powerful kingdoms and empires experienced "continuity crises" when strong rulers produced weak heirs, when members of the royal family fought over succession to the throne, or when usurpers seized power to found new dynasties. Assassinations and military coups were an ever-present threat to political regimes. In some states, there was a rule or tradition for the eldest son to succeed to the throne, but this was not invariably followed, and other states seem to have had no such protocol, so that rulers had to designate their successors and hope that their wishes would prevail. Within the dynasties of Israel and Judah, there is no clear evidence for any established rule regarding royal succession, so that even if there was a presumption that the eldest son should inherit power, this did not prevent other claimants, whether from within or without the royal family, from seizing office.[86]

The State and Judicial Institutions. The judicial role that is ascribed to the king in the Israelite states accords with the ancient Near Eastern custom of regarding the king as "chief judge," with responsibility to uphold justice in the realm.[87] As a rule, however, judgments were carried out through existing civil administration, reaching down to the level of village judiciaries, with the king serving symbolically, if not always in practice, as court of highest appeal. The Mesopotamian collections of laws are issued in the name of kings, but they appear to formalize and endorse customary procedures and rulings rather than to offer entirely new prescriptive codes. By contrast, none of the biblical law compilations is attributed to a king, which is probably best explained by the late redaction of these collections, after the Israelite states had disappeared, a perspective undergirded by the ideology of Yahweh as Israel's sole "king." The attribution of these biblical law collections to the stewardship of Moses, the traditional founder of the Israelite polity, accords with the retention of prestate traditions claiming the origins of Israel to have preceded the emergence of the state. There is no reason to believe that the actual day-to-day dispensing of justice in Israel differed markedly in form or content from jurisprudence in other states, although this remains a highly disputed issue. In my judgment, this conclusion is supported by the content of biblical laws, which, while somewhat more protective of human life and less severe in enforcing property rights than was the case with non-Israelite laws, nonetheless display considerable commonality with known laws from throughout the ancient Near East.[88]

States Transformed into Religiocultural Enclaves. The status of Judah under Persian and Hellenistic rule as a religiocultural enclave within an empire is familiar as one of the strategies of late empires. Rather than rule by uprooting local ruling elites and inspiring terror, as the Assyrians had tended to do, Persian and Hellenistic empires attempted, wherever possible, to incorporate existing cohesive social groupings as instruments of imperial order. By granting a measure of "home rule" over internal affairs in Judah, including religious practice and customary law, the empire aimed to secure maximum cooperation and loyalty from native authorities. A dual local leadership of civil and priestly high officials was approved by Persia and honored by the Ptolemies and Seleucids. In this way local communal interests and values could be linked to imperial rule, envisioned as the protector of diversity within its unified embrace. This colonial political order provided an incubator for Judahite culture and religion to take root and grow under the aegis of a reformist group or groups who redrew the concept of Israel in essentially "apolitical" or "transpolitical" terms. At the same time local politics was vigorously pursued to the extent allowed in the process of giving internal definition to the restored community.

The State and Religious Ideology. The religious ideology of the Israelite states accords closely in its structure and effects with other state ideologies. The complication in grasping the Israelite state ideology lies in the monotheistic claim that the completed Hebrew Bible projects. There is little doubt that the Judahite enclave in Persian and Hellenistic times was fundamentally monotheistic in its devotion to Yahweh, even as there were major disputes over how that monotheistic faith should be institutionally expressed. Nevertheless, the earlier monarchic religious ideologies in Israel and Judah are problematic. With respect to Judah, it is widely agreed that certain of the Psalms embody a "royal theology" that derives from monarchic times and expresses a "high" view of the Davidic king as representative of God on earth, thus having much in common with similar sanctification of royalty throughout the ancient Near East (e.g., Psalms 2; 18; 72; 89; 110).[89] But it is far from clear how widely this ideology was shared by Judahites, and, furthermore, it was characteristic of ancient Near Eastern states that the cult recognized and supported by political regimes was not enforced on all its subjects beyond the immediate realm of state protocol and ritual. The observance of other cults among the populace was normally accepted as a natural correlate of the concept of multiple gods and goddesses.

All in all, acknowledgment of considerable latitude in belief and practice, both between and within different cults, is probably the most accurate way to understand the "religious demographics" of Israel and Judah that were welcomed, or at least countenanced, by their political regimes prior to Josiah's reforms. Judging by the pronounced antistatist sentiments in various biblical traditions, certainly in the northern kingdom and very likely in Judah, the royal theology of Yahweh as unreserved champion of the state would have been held in suspicion, or expressly rejected, by many subjects of the crown. Moreover, religious sentiments and practices that derived from the prestate period were in all likelihood cherished independent of the royal appropriation and revamping of the cult of Yahweh. By and large, the states of Israel and Judah were officially committed to the Yahweh cult, with occasional preference for the Baal cult, but there are many indications that other cults were observed among the populace at large, and that worship of Yahweh could accommodate features of other cults in a manner that was later to be judged illicit by the monotheistic advocates who brought the biblical traditions to their final literary form.

In short, it is reasonable to regard the meeting and mixing of religion and politics in pre-Persian Israel as basically similar to the nexus between state and religion in other ancient Near Eastern states. To be sure, this "multicultic" perspective on pre-Persian Israel flies in the face of biblical editorial claims that from its inception Israel was fundamentally monotheistic and that the many reported departures from "the true faith" were to be "explained away" as reprehensible apostasies. It is all the more difficult to reorient our thinking on this point because Judaism and Christianity have traditionally accepted the biblical claim of Israelite monotheism from Abraham onward.

CHAPTER 5

Critically Imagining the Politics of Ancient Israel

Working with the biblical accounts of politics in the context of the politics of the ancient Near East, supplemented by relevant archaeological data and comparative sociology and anthropology, I shall now attempt some readings of Israelite politics as a project of the critical imagination. The *critical* aspect of this project proceeds according to generally accepted canons of historical reasoning. The *imaginative* aspect of the project acknowledges that a critical reconstruction is necessarily shaped by the imaginative vision of the historian. Historical imagination differs from historical fantasy and from historical fiction by closely following available sources and taking no liberties with known data without explaining the reasons for doing so. Historical imagination shares with fantasy and fiction in the conjuring of a rounded, intuitive, and meaning-laden reading of the subject, but it does so by constantly factoring in multiple types of evidence and proposing how they are connected in a fresh construal. Historical imagination employs various analytical methods and provisional hypotheses within the format of a "thought experiment" or "postulational model" that traces and joins chains of events and webs of relationships that ramify in many directions.[1]

ISRAEL'S DECENTRALIZED POLITICS

As we have seen, the biblical traditions about the so-called patriarchs, about Moses and the exodus Israelites, and about the tribes led by Joshua and assorted judges, purport to tell of Israel's fortunes before it became a state. These traditions in Genesis through Judges constitute a very sizable portion of the Hebrew Bible. We have also observed that the inclusion of such a body of traditions is unique in the ancient Near East. This is not to say that other polities lacked such traditions, but rather to say that the written records of those polities do not include such traditions beyond the sketchiest allusions to prestate times. Either these prestate traditions were forgotten by the time historical recollections were being written down, or they were deemed irrelevant to the events that the state rulers and their literati wanted to preserve in writing. Considering that Mesopotamian, Egyptian, and other ancient Near Eastern states regularly represent the work of their rulers as establishing "civilized" order in their societies by overcoming natural and human chaos with the help of the gods, it appears that they did not regard events that occurred before the state emerged as worthy of present recollection. To their minds, the disorder of prestate times did not possess any sort of intelligible history to relate.

If we follow this interpretation of the lack of ancient Near Eastern prestate traditions, we are then prompted to ask: why was it that ancient Israel "broke ranks" with other states in preserving a considerable volume of prestate traditions? To hazard an answer to this question it is necessary to make some judgments about the date of the biblical prestate traditions in order to determine what settings or functions these traditions had within the institutional life of ancient Israel. Since the issue of date and setting for these traditions is exceedingly vexed, we have no scholarly consensus among biblical historians to draw upon but must offer a fresh hypothesis and the reasons for advancing it. In offering this hypothesis, we are not concerned at this stage with the credibility of the prestate traditions as such. To that important question we shall return. For the moment we are attempting to understand who had an interest in creating and preserving such traditions and with what purpose in mind.

Whence the Prestate Traditions?

Several answers, singly or in combination, have been given to that question by biblical scholars:

Actual Prestate Origins. A first proposal is that at least some of the traditions were created by Israelites who lived in the prestate society, traditions that survive as fragments and torsos within later literary collections;

Early State Origins. A second contention is that many of the traditions were created under state auspices near the beginning of the monarchy as part of the foundation myths of the states of Israel and Judah (in historical-critical analyses, normally viewed as J and E versions of pentateuchal, and possibly hexateuchal, traditions);

Late State Origins. A third hypothesis is that many of the traditions were created under state auspices near the close of the monarchy as part of an effort to reform and expand the state of Judah in the last decades before its demise, and/or shortly afterward, in order to explain the fall of the state (normally viewed as one or two editions of the Deuteronomistic History in Joshua through Kings);

Colonial Origins. A fourth alternative is that many or all of the traditions were created under scribal/priestly auspices during the reconstruction of Judah as an enclave within the Persian or Hellenistic empire as part of the foundation myth of this religiocultural community (normally viewed as the P version of the Pentateuchal traditions and the Chronicler's history that parallels and supplements Kings and, on some views, including all the pentateuchal traditions and the Deuteronomistic History).

Supporting evidence has been advanced with considerable plausibility for each of these positions.[2] In the above formulation, the qualifying terms "at least some," "many," and "all" with reference to the biblical traditions are intended to accommodate the range of scholarly opinions that combine two or more of the four stated options in varying combinations and with differing nuances.[3] The complexity of judgments about source dating and reliability follows of course from the recognition that biblical traditions give every indication of being *cumulative* and *temporally depth-dimensional.* This means that sources attributable to a particular time customarily include accounts of a more distant past, which raises the critical question of how accurately the later traditions have transmitted information and historical contexts from earlier times. Amid the variety of views on this issue, there is widespread concurrence that prestate traditions were still being created in Persian/Hellenistic times when the concluding touches were put on the biblical narrative traditions. But how early did the formation of traditions about premonarchic Israel begin? Were all of the prestate traditions created at this late stage when Israel was no longer politically independent (option 4 above)? Or, were some of the prestate traditions created earlier while the state still existed (options 2 and/or 3), and even earlier during the actual prestate period (option 1)?

Why Were Prestate Traditions Preserved?

The hypothesis of this study, as already suggested in chapter 3, is that many of the prestate traditions did arise in the period before the establishment of the state, and that a major reason for their perpetuation in the final version of the Hebrew Bible is that by the time the Hebrew Bible was finalized, the Israelite states had disappeared and there was a strong cultural and religious desire to reconnect with the period before those states arose. The motivation to present the earliest possible traditions was driven by a "legitimation crisis," as the intellectual elite of restored Judah sought to authorize their leadership within a securely validated Israelite community whose origins could be traced to the distant past. But if these "old" traditions were not simply fabricated in toto to satisfy contemporary needs, how was it possible that traditions created in prestate times could have been preserved during Israelite statehood? What reasons were there for literate leaders in the Israelite state(s), or for intellectuals outside government circles, to value and transmit prestate traditions when other ancient Near Eastern literati did not?

In my view, prestate traditions survived during the monarchy principally due to two political dynamics, the first concerning efforts *to establish the state* and the second regarding efforts *to reform the state*. Regarding state establishment, the "intelligentsia" of the united monarchy invoked a premonarchic "foundation myth" to certify that the disparate highlanders of southern Judah and northern Israel, presently subject to single-state rule, actually had been one people all along and thus properly owed their loyalty to a central political regime. When this unified regime broke apart at the secession of the northern tribes, the new state of Israel in the north drew on prestate traditions to offer its own version of "prehistoric" times that upstaged Judah in favor of the northern tribes.[4] Concerning attempted state reformation after the fall of the northern kingdom, a reform in Judah aimed at restoring the larger territory once ruled by David and Solomon with Jerusalem as its center, and as an aspect of that project, yet another appeal to prestate traditions was made, which aimed at tracing the unity of the people to ancient tribal times. Subsequently, survivors of Judah's downfall who had supported the reform effort perpetuated its notion of the premonarchic unity of tribal Israel.

Taken together, these state-inspired appeals to prestate conditions, some friendly and some critical of the state, indicate the precarious nature of the Israelite state that was not able to establish itself solely on the grounds of a royal charter "from on high,"[5] but had to contend with the tribalized sentiments and habits of its subjects by showing how the state grew legitimately out of the tribal order and served, or at least claimed to serve, the best interests of all its subjects. The division into two states, each making polemical claims about the prestate period, served to keep prestate traditions alive but at the same time contributed to divergent and conflicting versions of the common origin that both states affirmed.

So the full hypothesis favored in this study concerning the reason for the prominence of prestate traditions in ancient Israel is as follows: actual prestate traditions (option 1) were preserved under the monarchy because they were weapons in the struggle to justify an initial unified state, then a breakaway state (option 2), and finally a hoped-for reunified state (option 3), and this mélange of prestate traditions was preserved, supplemented, and edited in the restored Judahite community as a way of claiming its origins in a distant tribal past (option 4), thereby relegating the monarchy to the status of a failed and outmoded enterprise no longer necessary for a religiocultural community capable of thriving in the absence of Israelite political autonomy. The colonial traditionists included the accounts of the Israelite monarchies as the necessary bridge to their own times, permeated by their conviction that the monarchic "subversions" and "inversions" of proper Israelite norms and practices reinforced their own "restitution" of those norms and practices, which they believed to derive from prestate times.

How Credible Are the Preserved Prestate Traditions?

When the presence of prestate traditions in ancient Israel is hypothesized in this way, it becomes clear that, once the state emerged, *all* the contexts in which prestate traditions were either created or preserved were polemically charged situations. Perhaps there were those outside of the state regimes who recounted the prestate traditions, but if so, their interest in them was also polemical, for they were seeking to validate a kin-based culture and society endangered by the state, whereas the governmental interests during the monarchy and the priestly interests that shaped the final form of the traditions displayed a pronounced tendency to subordinate kinship relations to the state or to the later religiocultural community in restored Judah. So we are bound to ask, what assurance do we have that these alleged prestate traditions, shaped and transmitted by statist and colonial concerns, are credible witnesses to what took place before the state was founded? If we concede that these traditions underwent a long process of transmission and reformulation before receiving their final form, and that they served over the centuries as ideological ammunition in political infighting, how is it possible to distinguish between aspects of the traditions that give us believable access to prestate conditions and aspects of the traditions that are largely or wholly later constructs?

In short, the hypothesis that traditions from prestate times were transmitted during the monarchy and finally preserved in restoration Judah does not verify the reliability of those traditions but only establishes the *possibility of their reliability,* which must be determined not by fiat but by critical discrimination. Our first step then is to assess what is said about decentralized tribal politics and to offer reasons to believe that valid prestate traditions have survived amid all the polemical storms through which they passed from generation to generation.

We have seen in chapter 3 that the traditions about ancient Israel prior to the monarchy lack any reliable account of the sequential history of the community or any detailed description of the forms of social organization that prevailed. The narrative pictures a founding family migrating first to Canaan and then to Egypt, where it proliferates into twelve tribes. Fleeing from Egypt, these tribes settle in Canaan. The chronological succession of these stages is schematic, and the events recounted lack verification from any other source. The entire construction of these prestate traditions is that of a literary foundation myth of the origins of a people conceived as a self-conscious unity from its nuclear beginnings under Abraham. Is it possible to extract from these traditions any tenable understanding of prestate Israel if we do not have the history of its formation and have only a smattering of information about the constitution of its "tribes"? This task of probing the authenticity of the prestate traditions would be hopelessly uncontrolled if we were unable to locate any "fixed points" outside the traditions themselves.[6] As it stands, in spite of heroic efforts to prove otherwise, we have no such controls over the patriarchal and Mosaic traditions. Fortunately, however, we do have two Archimedean points to assist us in assessing the Joshua–Judges traditions.

The anchor points are provided by one Egyptian text and by a range of archaeological data. According to the stela of Egyptian pharaoh Merneptah, his army defeated a people called "Israel" during a campaign in Canaan in approximately 1207 B.C.E.[7] Although the size, location, and social arrangements of this people are unstated, the reference indicates the presence of an entity called "Israel" within Canaan two centuries before the founding of the monarchy.[8] During those same two centuries archaeology reveals a proliferation of small agrarian/pastoral villages in the Canaanite highlands in the areas extensively referred to in the biblical traditions as settled by Israelites. While nothing in the remains "proves" that these were Israelite settlements, it is a sound inference that it was this region and its populace that formed the demographic and material resource base of the first Israelite state.[9] The predominance of clusters of single-family dwellings, together with an absence of fortifications and public buildings, suggests local social organization intent on adaptation to a marginal environment for subsistence farming and herding. The biblical portrait of "tribes," with shifting leadership beyond the local level, is broadly accordant with the archaeological data, which, to be sure, cannot vouch for the historical accuracy of any single detail in the traditions.

In the absence of informative inscriptions, ascertaining the sociopolitical organization on the basis of the material remains has proven to be an intractable problem. Whether local organization was based on village or clan/lineage networks, or some combination, and whether the society as a whole formed a segmentary kinship system of the sort known from anthropological investigations, cannot be deduced with certainty. Nor can it be determined if "tribe" is more than a rough regional designation, nor is it clear precisely by what process the "tribes" cooperated through consultation and joint action. What does appear to be established by the Merneptah stela and the archaeology of the highlands is that a population of cultivators and herders, at least some of whom bore the name Israel, lived in the regions of Canaan where the state of Israel subsequently arose, and furthermore that the biblical characterization of this population as politically decentralized and socially linked in village and kin arrangements is authentic.

The status and role of women in the traditions about early Israel accord with a model of flexible leadership in which women such as Miriam (Ex. 15:20–21; Num. 12:1–2) and Deborah (Judg. 4:4–10; 5:1, 12) could exercise ritual, judicial, and military powers. These traditions reflect the circumstances of a decentralized peasant society in which men and women shared closely in the labor process and in the labor surplus. The household in village clusters, as yet unregulated by state power, was the center of most social activity, and the public sphere, being the extension of collective household concerns, offered more opportunities for women *and* men to take part in leadership capacities. Under the centralized monarchy, women were increasingly excluded from public roles in government and religion. Two clarifications about the place of women in the unfolding Israelite society are advisable. It is noteworthy that in many biblical narratives, in both the tribal and monarchic periods, women exercise initiatives within and beyond the family sphere that have a decisive effect on the course of events. This significant participation of women in shaping events can best be explained by distinguishing between *authority,* understood as "the culturally legitimated right to make decisions and command obedience," and *power,* understood as "the ability to effect control despite or independent of official authority." In the fundamentally patriarchal Israelite society, men held the formal authority, but women were able nonetheless to wield informal power in many contexts and situations.[10] The limited, often improvisational, exercise of informal power by women should not obscure the fact that they were subject to the male heads of families and eventually to state authority and power that largely reinforced the nuclear patriarchal family, which was in turn increasingly isolated from the supportive kin networks that had characterized the tribal period.[11]

The repertory of religious beliefs and practices of these highlanders is only sparsely represented in the archaeological record.[12] No religious inscriptions and no burials containing religious objects have been found, and little in the way of undisputed cultic structures or cultic paraphernalia has survived. It seems likely that an open-air installation in the hills of Manasseh north of Shechem, in which a small bronze bull figurine was found, was cultic in nature, but the assertion that structures on Mt. Ebal were a place of ritual sacrifice has not found general acceptance.[13] Small female figurines in abundance were presumably prized by women to aid in pregnancy and birth, and it is likely that they are representations of a goddess such as Asherah.[14] It is not only religious inscriptions that are lacking, but any inscriptions beyond alphabetic scratchings and personal names on ceramics and arrowheads, and it is not only special religious structures that are absent, but also public buildings of any sort.[15] Burials were presumably in shallow graves that have left no traces.

So the meager material indicators about religion are of a piece with the scant material indicators about judicial practices, military affairs, and social organization in general. This skimpy material evidence for religion does not of course mean that these people were without religion. A fortiori, we can posit that, like all ancient Near Easterners, early Israelites were religious. Patently, this Israelite prestate society relied on oral communication and pursued its social and religious life through institutions that did not require written records or administrative and ceremonial centers lodged in public structures. Apparently the religion was observed in homes and open-air spaces. The archaeological profile broadly accords with the biblical accounts of a simple cult in which sacrifice was offered both by laity and a dispersed rural priesthood, and in which festivals connected to the agricultural seasons and episodic warfare were observed.[16] No names of deities, nor objects that can be certainly associated with particular deities, turn up in the archaeological record. We possess only the biblical indicators that the primary deity was Yahweh, but that other cults were honored, particularly that of Baal.

Archaeological surveys indicate that there were rather different ecologies and settlement patterns in the central highlands of Ephraim and Manasseh, in contrast to the southern highlands of Judah.[17] Of the two regions, Judah was more isolated topographically and had a smaller population and a stronger pastoral economy. This differentiation tends to support a number of indications in the biblical traditions that Judah stood apart from the cooperative arrangements among the other tribes until late in the tribal period or possibly even as late as the reign of Saul. The initially independent prestate histories of the central and southern tribes help to explain the breakup of the united kingdom into separate states in the two regions. Extensive biblical references to Israelite settlements in Galilee[18] and in Gilead[19] are not as certainly supported by archaeological evidence, but since those regions are mountainous enclaves with conditions similar to the central highlands, it is likely that Israelite groups were settled there.

Moreover, the Merneptah stela is useful for assessing the biblical traditions of the exodus and conquest. To be sure, the frequent ploy of trying to harmonize the incident related in the stela with the biblical account of escape from Egypt and conquest of Canaan is fruitless. The Merneptah stela has no bearing on whether Israelites were in Egypt, since the battle occurs in Canaan, and it gives insufficient detail to connect it with anything in the biblical conquest narratives.[20] What the stela does attest to is the hostile encounter of Egyptians and Israelites at the beginning of the spread of village settlements over the highlands. It also is evident that, although Merneptah claims to have destroyed Israel and may have defeated it militarily, the affected populace survived. Moreover, Merneptah's campaign was part of the continuing endeavor of the Nineteenth Dynasty to maintain control over Palestine, even as its grip on the region was weakening and in less than a hundred years was ended.

Nonetheless, Merneptah's campaign, and other Egyptian thrusts into Palestine during the first half of the twelfth century, may be the historical matrix of the traditional motifs of Israel's bondage in and deliverance from Egypt. Continuing Egyptian imperial claims on Canaan impacted the inhabitants of Palestine differentially. The geographically exposed lowland city-states, astride major trade routes and offering agricultural abundance, were subjected to vassalage as long as the Egyptian empire could sustain itself in Asia. The more remote highlanders, off the main trade routes and without abundant resources, were both less attractive and less vulnerable to direct Egyptian intervention. Instead, the city-states' rulers, already prone to fighting among themselves, had a stake in dominating the highland populace that was being enlarged by people fleeing difficult conditions in the city-states. Because of their disunity, however, the city-states were limited in their efforts to pacify and impose tribute on the highland settlements. A military and political vacuum was thus created in which the highlanders might astutely cooperate to keep both the Egyptians and the city-states at bay.

From the Israelite perspective, the immediate threat from the city-states, themselves vassals of Egypt, overlapped with and was driven by the more distant threat from Egypt, inasmuch as both the city-states and Egypt pursued tribute-demanding policies that struck at the heart of the independent livelihood of free agrarians and pastoralists in the highlands. Eventually this Egyptian-Canaanite dominion was taken over by the Philistines, who came to ascendancy on the southwest Palestinian coast in the early twelfth century and extended their control over the old Canaanite city-states during the following century and a half. In a sense, then, the Israelites faced a hegemonic threat that was conceived as embracing Egyptian, Canaanite, and Philistine components, shifting variously according to the balance of power among these centralized states and city-states. In terms of the formation of early Israelite tradition, what appears to have happened is that all these hostile relations with Egypt and Egyptian surrogates *in Canaan* were "gathered up" into the paradigm of a single mass captivity *in Egypt,* and, similarly, all the successes of Israelites in eluding Egyptian-Canaanite-Philistine control *in Canaan* were condensed and projected into the paradigm of a single mass deliverance *from Egypt.*[21] Admittedly, this hypothesis about the generative matrix for the bondage-exodus themes does not exclude the possibility that some group or groups within Israel had been in Egypt. It is rather to say that the formulation of the themes need not have been dependent on any actual Israelite presence in Egypt, which in any case continues to be undemonstrable.

Nevertheless, it is far from clear at what period the Egyptian bondage-exodus themes arose in Israel. Many earlier scholars argued that these themes did indeed arise in premonarchic times, but this claim depends on how one dates the earliest narrative strata in Exodus and whether the Song of the Sea in Exodus 15 reflects premonarchic cultic celebration.[22] Most current theories of Pentateuchal composition would place the origin of the bondage-exodus themes in later monarchic times. Even if the themes are relatively late as they stand, obviously distorted by their grandiose depiction of events, they do correctly identify Egypt as the major threatening power in the environment of prestate Israel, an aura of oppression that could extend to Canaanite and Philistine city-states, and eventually to Assyria, Neo-Babylonia, Hellenistic empires, and Rome. Speaking for the early emergence of the bondage-exodus theme is that once the Egyptian empire in Syro-Palestine collapsed before the end of the twelfth century, Egypt was never again more than a transitory threat to Israel until the Hellenized Ptolemaic empire in the third century. Indeed, more often than not, Egypt was looked to by Israel and Judah as a political ally against Assyria and Neo-Babylonia. The Egyptian domination of Judah, which fell within a five-year period (609–604 B.C.E.) during the hiatus between Assyrian and Neo-Babylonian hegemony, appears to have been too transitory to have served as the generative matrix for the Exodus traditions.[23]

A number of prestate traditions relate armed clashes with other peoples in the vicinity of prestate Israel, such as the Moabites and Ammonites from Transjordan and the Midianites, who appear to have been forming a nomadic commercial empire based in the desert fringe to the east and south of Canaan. Biblical traditions claim "kinship" ties with Moab and Ammon, probably on the basis of social and cultural similarities, although to date the slowly increasing archaeological data on Moab and Ammon is still too minimal to draw firm conclusions. Later, under monarchic government, the three states were often in conflict, and it is not improbable that disputed claims to territory in Transjordan erupted in armed clashes in the prestate period. With the slackening of trade and weakening of rule over the countryside attending the decline of Late Bronze cities, it is plausible that Midianites sought to extend their control and influence into Canaan but were repulsed by Israelite tribesmen.[24]

All in all, the content and organization of the traditions in Joshua and Judges are heavily militaristic, which at first glance does not sit well with the archaeological evidence of unfortified Israelite settlements. Since the prestate traditions are presented as though a united Israel is conquering the whole of Canaan, the frequency and scale of warfare has no doubt been grossly exaggerated. Even so, it is to be noted that Israel's victories all occurred in open country and did not involve siege warfare, with the exception of a terse note about Jericho, which does not accord with the other traditions that recount the capture of the city.[25] The numbers of Israelite combatants reported often run into the thousands, but one way of computing the actual size of Israel's militia proposes that the total volunteer army that all the tribes could field in concert was no more than five thousand men.[26] Moreover, there is no record of all the tribes fighting together until the Philistine wars under Saul. Probably many of the conflicts were raids or skirmishes. The highland Israelite cultivators could not have greatly increased their production and doubled their population within two hundred years if they had been drained by constant large-scale warfare.

There is one last piece of evidence in support of the retention of prestate traditions in the finished form of the Hebrew Bible. This bit of evidence concerns the literary depiction of the Israelite highlanders both in song and in prose. A fair number of poems in Genesis through Judges make a strong claim to being largely premonarchic compositions, in some cases retouched by later hands.[27] They exhibit a combination of fierce belligerency toward enemies, strong depictions of in-group loyalties, a high premium on large families, exuberant delight in the produce of field and herd, and naive confidence that their deity supports them in work and war. When supplemented by narratives that exhibit similar qualities in their plots and characterizations, together with annals and lists that display archaic features, there is a decidedly authentic aura about the social world portrayed.[28]

There are arcane notations and idiosyncratic behaviors that seem more like cultural "survivals" than studied "inventions." Many of these features work against the grain of the editorial framework of the traditions in that the Israelites are more often disunited than united, sometimes fight among themselves, make allegedly forbidden treaties with locals, and observe religious practices deemed illicit in later biblical tradition. It is impossible to prove conclusively that these features are solely premonarchic, both because early and later literary materials are erratically intermixed and because the rural life of monarchic Israel may well have retained many of these same characteristics at least until the Deuteronomic reform in the seventh century. Still, in their cumulative effect, it is reasonable to believe that many of the conditions and circumstances of prestate Israel are reflected in these poems and narratives.[29] Yet, with all that said, the sum total of the information they yield does not produce a connected history, nor does it articulate a rounded picture of social organization and interaction among "the tribes of Israel." Instead of a historical portrait, the traditions sketch a sociocultural collage or broken mosaic.

In sum, I have contended for the following characterization of prestate Israel.

1. Agrarian and pastoral highlanders bearing the communal name "Israel" were present in Canaan by the end of the thirteenth century, and their village settlements spread over the central highlands during the following two centuries.

2. The forms of social organization in prestate Israel were focused at the local level, involving village and lineage groupings, and included intermittent cooperation at the level of regional tribes. The details of social organization are no more than hinted at from archaeology, and the biblical data are sketchy and uncoordinated by any comprehensive description of the society.

3. The paucity of material evidence concerning the deity or deities worshiped and the sites, rituals, and paraphernalia employed in the religion of prestate Israel is broadly congruent with the biblical traditions that speak of songs, sacrifices, and festivals at open-air sites involving laity and at most a modestly developed and empowered priesthood.

4. It is probable that Judah in the southern highlands remained outside extensive connections with the central tribes until the verge of the monarchy. Israelite settlements in Gilead and Galilee probably maintained contact with the central highland tribes.

5. The highland Israelites struggled to retain autonomy over against imperial claims by Egypt, with whom they clashed militarily on at least one

occasion, and also from domination by Canaanite and Philistine city-states. The clash of Israelites with Egyptians in Canaan probably provided the historical context for developing the mythic paradigm of all Israel as once captive in Egypt and subsequently delivered from Egypt, a paradigm that may already have begun to take shape in prestate times.

6. In addition to threats from Egypt, Canaanite city-states, and Philistines, Israel experienced border conflicts with Moab and Ammon and an incursion by nomadic Midianites. Many of these conflicts were probably on a small scale and not sufficient to prevent Israel from improving its agrarian and pastoral economy and enlarging its population.

7. Many songs and narratives set in prestate times contain archaic and idiosyncratic features that are best understood as survivals of that first phase of Israelite society and culture. Nonetheless, they fall short of providing a history of the times or a descriptive inventory of social structure and process.

In short, the biblical traditions about prestate Israel provide "glimpses" and "echoes" of a people among whom social power was broadly distributed in local settings. This decentralized power aimed to preserve and prosper loosely affiliated agrarian/pastoral communities in the face of harsh environmental conditions and hostile political forces. Cooperation within and among these communities was impelled by the need to band together to maximize productive labor, to secure domestic justice, and to provide self-defense. A number of models drawn from anthropology and social history have been proposed as analogical templates of prestate Israel; however, given the decided limitations of our data, these models are neither conclusive nor necessarily exclusive of one another.

Among available theoretical models for understanding prestate Israel, it has been proposed that highland Israel was *a frontier society,* where settlers of independent spirit from the more economically developed coastal city-states struggled to adapt to new ecological challenges without obligations to state authority. These settlers were "pushed" by economic and political decline in the city-states and "pulled" by opportunities to build a new life in the highlands.[30] The need to establish social order without state power suggests other interpretive models. The concept of *a retribalizing society* underscores that the settlers did not have a single preexistent social organization but developed their own by building on the kinship ties of various immigrant groups and improvising additional social networks as needed.[31] The notion that this was a *a segmentary society* stresses the similarity of the Israelite acephalic social structure to many prestate societies observed in anthropological studies.[32] The proposal that early Israel was a *chiefdom,* or a cluster of chiefdoms, rests on indications of ranking among its leaders.[33] More recently, in place of the stark choice between an egalitarian or a hierarchical social order, on the basis of archaeological evidence it has been proposed that early Israel was a *heterarchy,* consisting of some regions with developed chiefdoms and others with far less centralized social arrangements.[34] These concepts of frontier society, retribalizing society, segmentary society, chiefdom, and heterarchy are in themselves elastic enough to encompass different modes of social organization. In particular, the concept of heterarchy suggests that we may have been mistaken in our assumption that all sectors of Israelite society were at the same level of social organization. Thus, for lack of sufficient social information about early Israel, these models function as broad descriptors that do not specify detailed social scenarios so much as provide ways for the critical imagination to grasp the turbulent conditions and precarious processes in which earliest Israel emerged.

The role of religion in the emergence of prestate Israel, although scarcely as all-determinative as the biblical scenario alleges, must nonetheless have been considerable. The highland settlers brought religious beliefs and practices with them, of which we may gain some impression from scattered references in the biblical traditions and from what we know of Canaanite religions apart from the Bible. Amid these cults, devotion to the cult of Yahweh arose. It did not deny the existence of other gods. It may not even have required the exclusive adherence of its followers, and insofar as some Yahwists may have asserted that claim, the Yahweh cult certainly did not win the allegiance of all Israelites. In the absence of a state, one cannot speak of Yahwism as "the official religion." Other cults flourished alongside the worship of Yahweh. The bronze bull from Manasseh and the ubiquitous female figurines give measurable support to the prevalence of the Baal and Asherah cults, either separately practiced or in some fashion appropriated by, or even merged with, the Yahweh cult. It is a reasonable conjecture that the appeal of the cult of Yahweh lay in its success in equating the three vital interests of Israelite society with divine intentionality and potency: Yahweh as fertilizer of fields and wombs, Yahweh as enforcer of communal justice, and Yahweh as leader of the armies. Other cults could make convincing claims in one or two of these spheres, but the "inclusive coverage" of the Yahweh cult may have proven especially attractive, even to the point of eliciting a primary, or even exclusive, commitment from many Israelites who were looking for protection in all the domains of daily life.[35]

In terms of the world-historical time of ancient Near East politics, the local emergence of Israel fits within a paradigm of "center and periphery" as contending loci of power. In our overview of ancient Near Eastern politics, we noted a repeated pattern of expanding and contracting centers of power that oscillate between dominating and losing control over their peripheral territories and peoples. As the political center weakens, peripheral areas may be left to their own devices for considerable periods of time before a new power center exerts dominance. Prestate Israel represented just such an "interstitial emergence," one of many such "devolutions" in the sweep of ancient Near Eastern history. The juncture at which Israel arose coincided with the widespread attrition and retrenchment of Late Bronze state power that extended over the whole of Syro-Palestine, Anatolia, and northern Mesopotamia.[36] It would be three centuries before hegemonic states once again dominated the ancient Near East. What is singular about prestate Israel is that its distinctive "voice" has been retained in a literary corpus dominated by voices speaking from later state contexts. Moreover, these prestate memories were cultivated not simply as antiquarian curiosities but as a vital part of the ongoing cultural and religious traditions of later Israel. In particular, they served as a kind of socioreligious "check" or "damper" on Israelite thought about the authority and power of states, and no doubt constrained and shaped the structures and strategies of the Israelite states.

ISRAEL'S POLITICS CENTRALIZED IN A SINGLE STATE

Why the Move to Statehood?

Until recent decades, biblical historians, reliant on a single-factor explanation, found little difficulty in identifying the conditions that led to the rise of the state in ancient Israel. The biblical traditions foreground the urgent need for a united military command to counter the external threat of the Philistines as the occasion for the election of Saul as commander in chief and king. This seemed to be the necessary and sufficient explanation for the rise of the Israelite state. In the light of state formation theory, however, the military factor cannot be taken in isolation from other forces at work. Comparative studies of the emergence of numerous "secondary" states disclose that such polities seldom, if ever, have arisen solely because of an external threat unless they are overrun by another power and state organization is imposed on them. There are significant internal forces at work to dispose toward statehood, such as growing economic and social inequality, breakdown of the judicial system, civil strife, and population pressure. In particular societies, either an external threat or any of the cited internal disturbances may be the "trigger" in precipitating state formation that has been prepared for by additional factors that may not appear on the surface of reported events.

Moreover, the impression that it would be "natural" for tribally organized societies and chiefdoms to evolve into states is not borne out by political anthropology. To the contrary, a well-balanced tribal system, even with a strong redistributive chiefdom, resists the concentration of dispersed social power in state organs. Tribes and chiefdoms are less "steps to statehood" than they are "evolutionary culs-de-sac." Indigenous states arise only when there is some fundamental dislocation in the power networks of a decentralized society, such that the old system has become dysfunctional, and a new allocation of power takes place. It is not that tribes agree to increase their effectiveness by rearranging or augmenting existing social power, so that the state is basically "more of the same" old power. Rather, the state is "a new breed of power," power structured and asserted in an entirely new way, such that it becomes power "apart from the tribe" and power "over the tribe." As we have previously noted, this is not to say that the social actors who institutionalize centralized political power are always aware of the "big step" they are taking, since the far-reaching consequences of political centralization may not become apparent until the state has been in operation for some time.

It is true of course that prestate societies may choose leaders for special tasks in the face of challenges and crises that cannot be met by existing leadership arrangements. The appointment of the military "judges" in Israelite traditions typifies such "special assignments." These appointments are conceived as temporary measures that lapse once the immediate task is completed. Thus, insofar as the tribes designated Saul as commander in chief of their armed forces, there would have been no grant of further powers, and thus no office of "king" to occupy once the miliary crisis passed. There have been many instances of decentralized peoples uniting under a single military command without resorting to state organization, as, for example, among the Germanic and Celtic people who resisted Rome and the Amerindians who defended against immigrant Europeans. The external threat, dire as it was, did not "trigger" a set of other factors disposing toward centralized politics. It was, therefore, not "inevitable" that, once Saul was chosen military leader, an Israelite state would follow. Indeed, even with the choice of David, it is not at first evident that he was more than a very effective military commander, functioning as a redistributive chief rather than as a king. In the process of state formation, there is often "a liminal zone" between the old prestate order and the operative state order, in which old arrangements persist as the new modes of power are fitfully but steadily coming into force. This sort of halting movement from tribe to state seems to best describe the developments in the "reigns" of Saul, David, and Solomon as described in the biblical traditions. Instead of a "leap" to statehood, one should rather say that the traditions imply "eroding" tribalism in tandem with "creeping" or "incremental" statism.[37]

What developments in Israel's prestate society would have predisposed a movement toward statehood? For one thing, it is probable that there was a growing imbalance in the size and productivity of land holdings. Relative social equality during the initial settlement seems to have secured to all families the right of access to land, but the land policies of the tribes were probably not so programmatic as to have provided parcels of equal size or fertility to all households, and if there was actual land redistribution from time to time, as some believe, it may have been confined to small tracts in village commons.[38] Furthermore, the diversity of terrain, soil types, and climatic conditions resulted in some cultivators and pastoralists prospering while others fell behind. Famine, disease, and untimely deaths probably placed a heavier burden on some families than others. Certain men of wealth and prestige may have had chiefly stature, as is perhaps presupposed by the terse list of so-called minor judges.

Although the ethic of many tribal societies stresses mutual aid to members in need, as is implied in the earliest "legal" provisions of the Bible, the village system of justice administered by elders may not have been equal to checking aggressive violators of this ethic. Even though the communal ethic espoused by the cult of Yahweh was premised on a just order to protect the integrity of all family units, the upholding of this ethic may have depended on moral suasion and religious sanctions that lacked means of assured enforcement and that were not necessarily honored by elements of the populace who were not adherents of the cult of Yahweh. Big landholders and aspiring tribal leaders were tempted to use the ideal of mutual aid as an occasion to build up a following of clients who might, when "push came to shove," serve as "private gangs" in disputes with other landholders or to secure political leverage in tribal decision-making.[39] Moreover, there are indications that some judicial and priestly functionaries victimized rather than protected their clients. As regional trade, interrupted with the decline of Egyptian hegemony, began to revive, the more prosperous Israelites were in a position to profit from it. Finally, there were regional loyalties and enmities that frustrated cooperation in maintaining a trustworthy system of justice and that interfered with efforts to mobilize tribal military units in timely and effective self-defense.

These hypothesized "cracks" in the socioeconomic solidarity of the tribes may not have been dire enough in themselves to precipitate state formation by the dawn of the tenth century. The tribal order might very well have continued for some time had it not been for threatening developments in the areas surrounding the Israelite highlands. Centralized state power in Canaan had been exceedingly weak during the first century and more of Israelite settlement in the highlands. Egypt was withdrawing from Asiatic empire. The old Canaanite city-states were weakened by economic decline and the intrusion of the Sea Peoples into coastal regions. The Philistines were only slowly consolidating their foothold in the Canaanite lowlands. Ammonites and Moabites could threaten Israelite settlements in Transjordan but were no serious danger to the Cisjordan highlanders. Midianite raiders could harass Israel but not subject it. It was an optimal "power vacuum" for the implantation and cultivation of decentralized tribal life, but the "window of opportunity" for tribal life began to close rapidly toward the end of the eleventh century. A league of Philistine city-states, headed by a military aristocracy that had assimilated to Canaanite culture, extended its control over the whole length of the coastal plain and across the lateral Esdraelon valley to the Jordan River. With tighter military discipline, improved body armor, and a mix of weaponry and tactics better suited to mountainous warfare than their city-state predecessors, the Philistines posed an ominous threat to Israel. Their strategic goal seems to have been to lay claim to the grain-growing breadbasket of the highlands by subjecting Israel to vassal status.[40] In the meantime, the Ammonites and Moabites were growing more aggressive toward Israel in Transjordan.

The theory of "environmental and social circumscription" has been proposed as one way to understand the rise of states. It posits that under population pressure and land scarcity, there is an increased competition for resources among sectors of the community that cries out for a definitive resolution adjudicated, legitimated, and enforced by a single sovereign power. Resource scarcity and demographic growth thus combine to create a socioeconomic "pressure cooker" that can be "vented" only by centralized political intervention. Although population in Israel had grown remarkably over some two centuries, it had started from a very low baseline, so it is questionable that the carrying capacity of the land had reached the kind of absolute "overload" possible in the more fertile riverine valleys. However, the earliest settlements were on the most easily cultivated and grazed lands, so that over time expansion could occur only by clearing virgin lands, requiring heavy labor and often new agrarian and horticultural skills. The frontier was thus "closing" territorially and socially, in that there were fewer places to flee to for those who were most in need of a new beginning. The concept of "social caging" may be more applicable to early Israel than the notion of "circumscription," since it does not require competition for scarce resources due to population growth but stresses the need to coordinate and regularize increasingly complex socioeconomic relations. In a sense then, two trajectories of "circumscription" or "caging" were working to put pressure on the old tribal system: internally Israelites were constrained by diminished arable land and more complex social relations, and externally they were constrained by aggressive states that sought to lay tribute to their produce.[41]

There are several questions posed to the critical imagination in assessing the first phase of centralized politics in ancient Israel. The above proposed matrix of factors contributing to state formation in Israel answers one of the questions: since Israel prospered as a tribal society for two hundred years, why did it resort to state politics when it did? But there are other equally challenging questions: What were the steps taken to establish and strengthen the state? At what point in the process did Israel become a state, and what sort of state was it? In what spheres of society did the state exert its sovereignty, and with what effects or transformations in society at large? How did the social power networks subtended by the state affect the operations of centralized power? What forms did state administration take? What role did the cult of Yahweh play in political institutions and ideology? Who were the supporters and who the opponents of state rule? What were the gains and losses of statehood for Israel as a social community? How did the Israelite state impact non-Israelite peoples? The biblical traditions supply answers to some of these questions, more or less completely and more or less convincingly, but others can be answered only by inference or analogy.

How Did the State Secure Its Hold?

The steps to statehood as described in Samuel–Kings show a steady increase in the extension and consolidation of state powers. Saul was made commander of the tribal levies in order to expel the encroaching Philistines who had established outposts or garrisons in the hill country. His headquarters were on his family estate at Gibeah. A large structure unearthed at the possible site of Gibeah is not certainly assignable to his reign, and, in any case, it is a fortification rather than a palace. He had no detectable non-military powers beyond the capacity to reward followers with honors and possibly with modest land grants.[42] There is no indication of taxation or conscription beyond the outlay of men and supplies for the tribal levies, which, given the seriousness of the Philistine threat, were probably readily volunteered for the most part. There is no account of Saul's keeping records, nor is there evidence of his role as head of the judicial system or as pontiff of the religious cult. In keeping with his limited exercise of power, there was no discernible state bureaucracy. In his functions, Saul seems no more than a military chief.

On the other hand, the biblical traditions picture Saul and his supporters as assuming that his powers would devolve to his successors, which implies dynastic pretensions and thus aspirations to permanence of rule reaching beyond the Philistine crisis.[43] To the extent that this is not a naive case of ex post facto reporting, these aspirations beyond the power actually assigned to Saul may reflect the intentions of leading citizens, drawn from his tribe of Benjamin and the adjacent tribes of Ephraim and Manasseh, to consolidate and perpetuate the office. It appears that Saul's "falling out" with David in itself did not indicate competition for dynastic kingship but rather rivalry over who was the most skilled and loyalty-evoking military leader.

The death of Saul in battle resulted in the baton of Israel's military leadership passing to David, whose career as a military adventurer suited him well for the role. He established himself as head over Judah and bode his time until he was able to win the consent of northern leaders to rule over all the tribes. However, up until his capture of Jerusalem as his capital-to-be, there are no clear signs that David's "rule" was any more committed to efforts to regulate the populace or draw income from them than Saul's had been. We are still at the stage of a military chief, although one whose ambition and calculated moves suggests a leader who was amenable to expanding his powers beyond the military realm. He opened up the pathway to fuller power by decisively defeating the Philistines, clearing the way for him to seize Jerusalem as the territorial base for his regime's sovereignty over the tribes. The list of David's officers indicates that he maintained a standing army supplemented by Philistine mercenaries, that he conducted diplomacy, kept state records, and appointed priests over the state cult. Moreover, the king is pictured as "chief justice" to whom appeal could be made in disputed matters of law (2 Sam. 15:2; cf. 4:4–11; 21:3–6).

Although David's rule following his establishment in Jerusalem contained several of the marks of unambiguous state power, certain customary features of statist politics were lacking. He did not build lavishly. Nor does he appear to have taxed his subjects to raise state revenues. Traditional reports that he wanted to build a temple but was advised against it, and that he undertook a census, probably with taxation in mind, for which he was condemned, imply that David's ambition was held in check by the independent social and religious sensibilities of his tribal subjects. At most, his demands on the populace may have consisted of limited military conscription and forced labor to supply the army and to work on modest building projects.

In spite of his manifest successes, and the "kid gloves" with which he treated the tribes, David's rule was shaken by two revolts, one within his own household and the other an uprising of northern tribes. The personal ambition of his son Absalom was able to play on grievances about David's slack administration of justice, and Sheba's revolt seems to have been rooted in northern resentment of domination by a Judahite who "played favorites" with his own tribe. As for entitlement to succession to the throne, ancient Near Eastern states followed differing practices. Apparently the most frequent custom was for the eldest son to succeed to the throne, but many exceptions are known to have occurred.[44] David apparently did not unequivocally designate an heir, and only on his deathbed was there extracted from him a designation that may or may not have been his desired choice. As we earlier noted, this sort of instability in royal families and dynasties appears again and again throughout the history of the Israelite states, and in this respect is comparable to the difficulties in securing stable transitions of rule in states throughout the Near East, including the most powerful Mesopotamian, Anatolian, and Egyptian regimes.

One aspect of David's rule is not addressed in the biblical traditions, and that is the mixed character of the populace who comprised his subjects. This oversight follows from the view of late editors who understood the original tribal allotments to have comprised all the territory that fell within the state. It is evident, however, that David's rule staked a claim on the lowlands and valleys that had never been occupied by Israelites and thus embraced the territories and populations of former Canaanite city-states. Whether these formerly non-Israelite regions were administered in any manner different from David's tribal constituencies is unknown. It has been suggested that these regions, unlike the tribes, were subject to taxation, but we have no evidence to this effect. It is scarcely to be doubted, however, that the inclusion of a sizable population that lacked specifically Israelite traditions, laws, and culture, as well as the cult of Yahweh, will have created a heterogeneous body of subjects, some of whom were now "Israelite" only in the political sense that they were subjects of the Davidic state of Israel.[45] It is not certain that the differences between these two state constituencies were ever fully overcome. In any case, worship of Yahweh as the state deity did not mean the instantaneous or universal worship of Yahweh among all subjects of the newly founded state of Israel. Not only were there those in the old tribal society who observed other cults, but worship of various Canaanite deities would have prevailed among the inhabitants of the city-states that David drew into his kingdom. There is no indication that David attempted to impose the cult of Yahweh as obligatory on all his subjects. Thus, the heterogeneity of the tribalists was amplified by the heterogeneity of the larger state population that incorporated tribalists and urban and rural residents of city-states who had previously lived apart from the Israelites.

After eliminating the Philistine threat, David's foreign military campaigns carried him into Transjordan and northward toward southern Syria. His conquests of Ammon, Moab, and Edom, themselves in the process of transition to statehood, yielded considerable booty and were followed by the imposition of tribute. Defeats inflicted on Syrian forces that are said to have come to the aid of the Transjordan states are recounted in a highly confused manner, and the sort of control or influence that David was able to exercise over Syrian states is vaguely reported.[46] It is possible that the booty and tribute David extracted from Transjordan was able to supply his revenue needs without taxing his own subjects, especially since he was not engaged in extensive building. If the scenario of his reign that we have proposed is correct, it is understandable that David was remembered with fondness as a king who "saved" Israel militarily and socioeconomically at a relatively low cost to his subjects.

Under David the lineaments of state sovereignty, and the structures to enforce it, began to take shape. It was a "lean" state, lacking architectural splendor and an ostentatious aristocracy, and treading lightly in its demands on the new subjects.[47] Foreign wars were able to carry the major costs of this rule. It was, however, a state that depended heavily on the astuteness of its head, for it bore within its subjects deep divisions between the northern and southern tribes and between the old tribal populace and the newly annexed city-state inhabitants. And while it professed the cult of Yahweh, this was not the exclusive religion of the populace, and the Yahwistic ideology promoted by the state was not identical to, or even compatible with, the beliefs and practices of many of its subjects.

Solomon abandoned the caution of his father David by taking aggressive steps to increase and consolidate state power, but in the process seems to have strained the productive capacity of his subjects and exacerbated the social and cultural divisions that David had managed to contain with some success. The major undertakings of Solomon lay in royal building projects, enlargement of the military, taxation, trade, diplomacy, and state ideology. He doubled the size of his Jerusalem capital by erecting a palace and temple and is credited with building fortifications at key points as defensive measures to preserve the conquests of David. Whereas David had relied principally on infantry, Solomon is said to have developed chariot forces to increase the mobility and striking power of his armed forces. Whereas David felt compelled to terminate plans to tax his subjects, Solomon divided his kingdom into districts for the express purpose of supplying revenues to the crown. Although David may have introduced limited labor conscription, the scale of Solomon's public works vastly increased the need for forced labor to transport materials and work on construction. Solomon capitalized on his strategic position as a transit point between Egypt, Syro-Mesopotamia, and South Arabia to exact commercial tolls and to speculate in the sale of horses and chariots. In diplomacy, Solomon worked out an intermarriage arrangement with Egypt and a commercial treaty with Tyre involving exchange of Israelite grain for Tyrian timber, shipbuilders, and artisans to design and erect his public buildings, as well as tapping into luxury trade with South Arabia. In the service of state ideology, Solomon's temple for Yahweh focused and symbolized the divine blessing on state power. To accomplish all these enhancements of state power, Solomon increased the state bureaucracy.

The unraveling of Solomon's kingdom came rapidly at his death. The weaknesses in his program of expanded and consolidated power can be pieced together from various details in the biblical traditions. The increase in revenues to support his building projects, armaments, and expanded bureaucracy depended upon taxed agrarian surpluses from his subjects and a favorable balance of trade with other states. That Solomon had to cede territory to Tyre in payment for imports indicates a serious fiscal deficit. This forfeit of Israelite territory means that he was running low on gold and silver bullion and on surpluses of grain and oil to exchange for needed imports. The shortfall in agricultural surpluses was probably due in large part to his forced labor program, in which Israelite peasants were expected to do state labor in transport and construction while simultaneously maintaining the productivity of fields and herds. The revolt of Damascus and disturbances in Edom may also have affected his profits from transit trade. Solomon had thus undertaken a more ambitious program of state-sponsored "development" than he had human and natural resources to implement. While Damascus and Edom could take advantage of this weakness, there were no neighboring states strong enough to challenge Solomon's regime in head-on warfare. It remained for disaffection among his subjects to terminate his grandiose projects.

The biblical traditions that report the political achievements of Solomon are supplemented by traditions that laud his wealth and wisdom and that locate his eventual failure in sexual passion that drove him to acquire large numbers of foreign wives and concubines whose religious cults contaminated his otherwise enviable rule. This focus on sex and idolatry diverts attention from the sociopolitical reasons for Solomon's downfall. It ignores the social and economic consequences of his forced development program.[48] Nonetheless, it is probable that there are historical kernels of truth in the embellished claims to Solomonic wealth and wisdom. As for "wealth," Solomon presumably amassed more riches and displayed them more conspicuously than ever before seen in Israel. Bureaucrats, merchants, and big landholders prospered, but the great majority of peasants and herders suffered a decline in their standard of living as they struggled to meet state demands for their labor and produce.

As for his "wisdom," Solomon's expansion of state power on several fronts required court records and enlargement of the scribal corps that David had first appointed. The scribal branch of government in Mesopotamia and Egypt was the setting for the cultivation of wisdom traditions, and it is probable that Solomonic scribes began to do the same. However, the report that Solomon himself authored proverbs, fables, and songs means no more than that he was the royal sponsor of scribal activities, and the claim that he was personally a very wise man is belied by his thirst for excess beyond his actual means. As for his "sexual passion and idolatry," the tradition grossly exaggerates the number of Solomon's foreign wives and concubines and entirely misses the point that these were diplomatic marriages signifying that Solomon had international stature. High-level diplomatic marriages, entailing the recognition and practice of foreign cults alongside the official state cult, were a staple of ancient Near Eastern politics. The actual objections to Solomon's rule among his subjects had nothing to do with polygamy and idolatry, but rather with the forced labor he imposed on them and the way he monopolized the worship of Yahweh in Jerusalem as the ideology endorsing his reign.

Was Tenth-Century Israel an Actual State?

The foregoing characterization of the reigns of Saul, David, and Solomon is premised on a critically imaginative reading of the biblical sources in the context of ancient Near Eastern politics and political anthropology. Amid all the overlays and distortions in the biblical traditions, they retain a credible sketch of the movement to statehood in Israel. This confidence, however, is not shared by more skeptical interpreters, both on textual and on archaeological grounds.[49] The objectors claim that the large amount of literary embellishment and fantasy in the traditions engulfs the minimal "factual" data, to the extent that some go so far as to see David and Solomon as wholly imaginary figures "fronting" for an alleged "united monarchy" that never existed. Furthermore, in the case of Solomon, they note that the archaeological record is surprisingly meager for a regime supposedly noted for its monumental architecture, and little of his alleged wealth has left a trace. In the view of most archaeologists, Jerusalem is an archaeological blank in the tenth century. Indeed, there is now general concurrence that certain structures formerly attributed to the Solomonic era, and thought to be an iron smelter (proven erroneous) and stables (only possibly so), belong to a later century. A number of building projects at regional centers may not be datable more precisely than within a time span from the mid-tenth to the mid-ninth centuries. Finally, it is argued that the small population and low level of socioeconomic development in Israel could not have sustained the "empire" attributed to David and Solomon.[50] So the question persists: what credence can be given to the reported political achievements of David and Solomon?

In dialogue with these objections, it must be admitted that they give pause to facile trust in the biblical traditions. In particular, they caution us to "scale down" traditional notions about the territorial scope, sociopolitical complexity, and royal opulence of the united monarchy, promoted by the late biblical elevation of David and Solomon to the stature of archetypal progenitors of just and prosperous rule. But does a "scaled down" version of their reigns accord with the archaeological record and with estimates of the demographic and socioeconomic infrastructure of prestate Israel? The paucity of archaeological data does not count decisively one way or another.[51] Given subsequent destruction and rebuilding in Jerusalem, it is not surprising that there are no archives or royal buildings surviving from the tenth century B.C.E. Apart from Jerusalem, Solomon's building projects were at strategically placed military and administrative centers. Excavations at some of these locations, such as Hazor, Megiddo, and Gezer, have uncovered casemate walls, monumental gates, and public buildings consistent with centralized state planning, but there is disagreement among archaeologists as to whether these public works are from the tenth or the ninth century. Although its interpretation is much disputed, in the opinion of most interpreters the fragment of an Aramaic stela from ninth-century Dan refers to the "House of David" and thus would seem conclusively to rule out the view that David was a purely fictitious figure.[52] But even if this is so, the terse reference tells us nothing about the nature and scope of the rule of this "House of David," and in no way vouches for the splendor attributed to Solomon's reign.

Perhaps more crucial to the viability of a tenth-century Israelite state is

the rather small population scattered in modestly productive rural settlements. Could a centralizing state emerge with such sparse resources? And
could that state have had a Judahite power base, when Judah was much
less populous and economically developed than the northern tribes? At this
point, ancient Near Eastern history and political anthropology come to our
aid. Small states could and did arise on rather slender infrastructures, especially when power shifts occurred in larger states in their vicinity. For
example, Ammon, Moab, and Edom in Transjordan developed into tribal
kingdoms on a "weaker" demographic and economic foundation than
Israel enjoyed, and even though their emergence as "kingdoms" was probably a century or more later than Israel's, they do illustrate the tenability of
modest state formations that are fragile and liable either to subsequent
growth or to decline and extinction.[53] Depending on combinations of internal and external forces, these ventures toward statehood might fail, or they
might stabilize at a modest level, or in exceptional circumstances, their ruling class might dominate other states briefly or go on to form large-scale
empires with lasting effects. There are many gradations in the movement
from the incipient state to the full-scale state and many opportunities for
arrested growth, retrogression, and collapse. It is entirely consistent with
the archaeological and anthropological evidence that David and Solomon
may have aimed for a strongly centralized state but were unable to realize
it because their aspirations collided with the stubborn resistance of a large
part of the populace, whose loyalties were tenaciously local and thus only
tenuously committed to support of a centralized polity, especially when the
state intruded sharply on their subsistence economy and began to exploit
and depress it.

Given the uncertainties surrounding the extrabiblical evidence and the
decided tendency of biblical traditions to exalt David as model king and
master musician and Solomon as exemplar of wealth and wisdom, there is
a further way to understand at least some of the political accomplishments
attributed to them. It has been proposed that measures taken by later kings,
north and south, have been assigned to David as dynastic founder and to
Solomon as temple builder in order to add concrete detail to their legendary luster.[54] Viewed as anachronisms, David's conquests in Transjordan
and Syria may be echoes of later monarchic campaigns against those
regions. Solomon's division of his realm into twelve districts, but omitting
Judah, may be seen as the act of a northern ruler, such that Solomon's
actual undertaking to subject the north to administrative control was of
more limited success. In that event, Solomon would have had more difficulty collecting taxes and conscripting labor battalions than the traditions

now imply. One might go so far as to say that the named functionaries in David's and Solomon's administration may be represented as filling offices or having powers that did not develop until later in the monarchy. The ties of David and Solomon with Tyre, and of Solomon with Egypt and South Arabia, as well as Solomon's trading ventures, might be explained as retrojections from later royal regimes. However, such a hypothetical reduction in Davidic-Solomonic accomplishments cannot be carried too far, if only because the cataclysmic breakaway of the north at his death indicates that Solomon had conscripted sufficient labor for state projects that he awakened deep resentment among northerners. Moreover, friendly ties with Tyre did not extend beyond the Omri dynasty in the north, and the diplomatic links to Egypt and South Arabia did not subsequently loom large in the later divided kingdoms.

All in all, in the instance of what has been called "the united monarchy" of Israel, it is plausible to posit incipient and early state formation that was launched as a "power grab" by a popular Judahite military chief who for a time was able adroitly to balance the disparate groups in his realm while operating from a newly founded capital uncompromised by tribal rivalries. David's time of service under Achish of Gath may have provided him with a Philistine urban model for his rule at Hebron, but in moving to Jerusalem he had to come to terms with the preexistent tribes whom he subordinated to his rule, but whose social base and latent political power he could not eliminate.[55] With the backing of a loyal army, and by taking booty and tribute from weaker adjacent regions in place of excessive demands on the tribes, David was able to "keep the lid" on internal opposition. His successor Solomon attempted to rationalize and consolidate the regime by taxation and forced labor but ran up against ecological and human obstacles that frustrated his best efforts. He simply did not have the natural resources and popular consent to wield the intensive political and economic power he aspired to. Moreover, the attempt to appropriate the cult of Yahweh as the ideology of the state was not convincing to enough subjects, especially in the north, to keep the state intact.

Viewed in this way, once the immediate Philistine threat was repulsed, the state venture was only "united" loosely under David as a tribal kingdom. When Solomon sought to consolidate his realm as a territorial kingdom, in which the state would sharply subordinate the tribes, his regime lost legitimacy and aborted, leaving in its wake two weakened polities that, despite periodic renewals of power in both states, were never again to be joined. Thus it can be seen that the vaunted political "unity" of north and south under David and Solomon was institutionally precarious, even though their claims to sovereignty set political precedents that were potent enough to secure the dominance of centralized state rule in Israel and Judah for future generations. In sum, for less than a century, Israel was ruled by a "single" regime, but under that singular rule the body politic was only precariously "united."

ISRAEL'S POLITICS CENTRALIZED IN TWO RIVAL STATES

In an earlier chapter we surveyed the episodic biblical data on the politics of the kingdoms of Israel and Judah. How does this information fare when viewed in connection with extrabiblical references, archaeological remains, the wider ancient Near Eastern political trajectory, and analogies from social history and political anthropology? In short, the biblical data appear to be tenable in many respects, even demonstrably accurate in a few instances, but not uniformly reliable. The primary impediment in the biblical accounts is the marked tendency to read later religious judgments and interpretations into earlier situations. This tendency has not only introduced "misreporting" of events and motives, but it has also strongly influenced the selection of the material to be reported, with kings and issues that are deemed to have been of "religious" significance receiving the lion's share of attention. Nonetheless, since religion was closely intertwined with politics, even accounts that highlight religion may intentionally or inadvertently provide insights into the "secular" import of events.

We are not narrowly interested, however, in whether extrabiblical texts, archaeology, ancient Near Eastern politics, and comparative social sciences "confirm" or "disconfirm" the biblical accounts, since such a project easily degenerates into a disjointed and reactionary treatment of the subject matter. We are chiefly interested in what additional information "outside sources" may provide about politics in ancient Israel and, in particular, what new "angles of vision" they may offer for synthesizing and interpreting old and new information. The greatest value of comparative textual, archaeological, and political studies is that they enable us to get a little closer to political realities as they were known to their participants and thus to secure independent and alternative ways of reading biblical traditions that in themselves tend to "slide over" material conditions and, in many cases, appear to be out of touch, and even at cross purposes, with the thought and action world of the politics recounted.[56]

Our first "take" on Israelite politics viewed apart from the Bible is to present a brief assessment of material remains recovered by archaeology within Palestine from the tenth to the early sixth century, with a view to estimating the likely parameters of state development both synchronically and diachronically. Our second "take" will be to see how the particulars of the politics of Israel and Judah are confirmed, enlarged, nuanced, or corrected by comparative information drawn from the records of other ancient Near Eastern states that provide a number of synchronisms with Israelite history.

Israelite and Judahite Archaeological Data

For our foray into extrabiblical evidence to assist us in discerning the lineaments of Israelite statehood, we turn first to Palestinian material remains, including texts and inscriptions. The volume of archaeological data is vast, and the more limited epigraphic finds are increasing steadily, so that it is necessary to limit our focus to materials that appear to be most pertinent to Israelite politics. Those who naively assume that "the hard facts" of archaeology are more easily and definitively demonstrated than the obscurities of biblical texts will necessarily be disappointed by the "subjective" element in archaeological interpretation. The effort to read political institutional history in material remains is impeded by the fact that until recent years archaeologists have done little to offer a sociopolitical synthesis and analysis of their findings, and when they have drawn political inferences from the material finds, they have frequently been compromised by questionable "harmonizations" with biblical texts. Currently a sizable number of archaeologists are engaged in fruitful studies of the material foundation of state formation in Israel.[57] To date, however, broader issues of political structure and the scope and power of Israelite states in domestic and foreign affairs have for the most part been only cursorily explored with reference to the archaeological record. Nevertheless, a trajectory of Israelite statehood drawing on extrabiblical information can now be traced in broad outline.

Material Remains. From around the middle of the tenth century, and extending throughout the history of the Israelite states, there is ample evidence of developing cities with walls and fortifications, public buildings, water tunnels, workshops, and residential quarters. Much of the building, especially in the administrative-military complexes, is on a sufficient scale to have required organized labor that only a central authority could have mustered. Efforts at town planning—evident in the layout of walls and gates, the grouping of structures of various types, and the street patterns—likewise argue for centralized design aimed at coordinating site functions.[58] The governmental structures, usually on raised platforms and separated from the rest of the city, together with larger dwellings distinguished from the majority of modest housing, indicate the presence of an elite set off symbolically and socioeconomically from the populace at large. These material traces of political centralization are usually not securely datable to the reigns of particular kings as recorded in the biblical record, so that, as we have noted, whether particular structures in northern cities such as Megiddo, Hazor, and Gezer were the work of Solomon or of Omri-Ahab remains a matter of some dispute. Moreover, in the absence of telltale contents, the function of some structures remain open to conjecture; for instance, are the rectangular pillared buildings found at several sites stables, storage rooms, barracks, or bazaars? But there can be little doubt that, whenever precisely built, the architectural, engineering, and artisanal sophistication involved in their construction strongly argues for state planning and oversight. This is the case even if, as suspected, much of the work at least initially was executed by Phoenician architects and artisans. To assemble and fund the foreign artisans engaged in the projects would have necessitated diplomatic and logistical skills orchestrated by a centralized political authority.

The pattern of settlements is amenable to analysis by archaeological "central place theory,"[59] an analytic model that ranks settlements by size, commonly arranged in "a three-tier hierarchy," with large sites as commanding centers, mid-size sites as nodes mediating between larger and smaller sites, and small towns and villages as the terminal points of actions initiated by the centers and mediated by the nodes. The network of small towns and villages constitutes the essential agrarian and pastoral infrastructure on which the entire state apparatus depends for the sustenance of its personnel and for revenues to underwrite its civil, commercial, military, and religious operations. The size of sites, their pattern of distribution, and their identifiable functions provide a framework for grouping, analyzing, and interpreting the archaeological information in ecological and sociopolitical terms.

Although their archaeological recovery leaves much to be desired, Jerusalem in Judah and Samaria in Israel commend themselves as the commanding centers of their respective states. Built-over Jerusalem has produced scattered remains, none of which come with certainty from the royal acropolis. The surviving elements of the Samarian royal acropolis have been excavated but the remainder of the city has not been explored. The apparent size of the two sites suggests that Samaria, from its founding in the early ninth century, and Jerusalem, at least from the latter part of the eighth century, were the largest cities and the governmental nerve centers in their respective kingdoms. The political economy of Samaria is documented by receipts written on broken pottery from the late ninth or early eighth century, recording consignments of oil and wine, either as taxes to the royal coffers or as delivery of produce to officials from the estates granted them as perquisites of office. Finely wrought decorative ivories from the Samarian acropolis reveal a taste for luxury items and the means to procure them, while numerous lavish rock-cut tombs in the vicinity of Jerusalem in the late eighth and seventh centuries attest to the prosperity enjoyed by its elite.

A number of second-rank centers were distributed through both kingdoms at strategic locations for administrative and military purposes and probably also to protect and facilitate trade. Chief among these in the north were Dan, Hazor, Megiddo, and Gezer, and in the south Lachish and Beersheba. In a number of cases, the residential quarters in these centers were relatively small, suggesting that those who lived within the walls were government personnel, while the "civilian" population lived in towns and villages in the vicinity. These centers, strongly fortified and replete with public buildings, served as "conduits" to translate state decisions into effective actions in the outlying regions of the kingdom and as "trip wires" against impending military attacks. Religious structures and installations are not certainly identified in most of these locations, with the exception of Dan, where an impressive ninth-century cultic precinct accords with the biblical report that Jeroboam I established Dan as one of the two "official" centers of worship in the northern kingdom to replace Jerusalem.

At the lower settlement level were walled towns and unwalled villages. The towns were primarily residential. Structures that may have served public functions were on a smaller scale and less ornate than buildings in the primary centers. Small industrial workshops for processing oil and wine, making pottery, and producing textiles appeared with some frequency. Storage jars with the names of four towns stamped on their handles may have been assigned to, or manufactured at, those locations as part of civil or military administration in late eighth-century Judah. Luxury goods in the form of jewelry, fine vessels, and decorative ivories were scarce or nonexistent, being concentrated predominantly in the commanding centers and second-rank sites.

Hundreds of small villages were interspersed among the larger sites. These villages were occupied by farmers, horticulturalists, and herders. The domestic architecture of the villages consisted of minor variations on the three- or four-room pillared house, probably with a second story, that had been typical of prestate highland settlements. The houses were fronted by courtyards or animal folds and often accompanied by storage pits and sometimes by cisterns. These simple dwellings were functionally adaptive to basic needs for human and animal shelter, cooking facilities, storage of tools and modest crop surpluses, and retention of rain water. Unadorned pottery and some tools appear, but luxury goods and cultic objects are rare. It is relevant for assessing the living standards of most of the populace to note that the same basic house plan is found in urban domestic quarters set apart from the large public buildings and the homes of the governing elite.

The demarcation line between "town" and "village" is not a simple function of spatial dimension or number of inhabitants, but had to do with social homogeneity/heterogeneity and sociopolitical complexity/simplicity. Certain prosperous villages might actually be more populous than small towns. Towns show a propensity toward a mixture of social statuses without necessarily close kinship ties, and they appear to be the terminal points in the administrative-military chain of command that required protection by defensive walls. Given the incidence of small industrial production, towns were probably also regional market centers. Villages, on the other hand, tended to be monofunctional as the living quarters for people who worked the surrounding fields, orchards, and pastures and were cooperatively linked by kinship ties and shared labor agreements. These unwalled villages were too numerous and dispersed to be defended against attack; consequently, at the approach of enemy armies, villagers would seek refuge in the walled settlements. This concatenation of urban-administrative and agrarian-pastoral settlements more nearly suggests a "four-tier" hierarchy of sites, consisting of capital cities, regional military-administrative sites, provincial towns, and local villages, rather than the more usual "three-tier" arrangement posited in central place theory.[60]

A subject that has often been ignored in discussing the Israelite states is the issue of their scale relative to other states nearby and more distant. The large numbers in biblical census figures and in biblical battle reports have tended to induce inflated notions of population, to take only one indicator of political scale. As we have seen, in recent discussions among archaeologists and historians, the question has arisen as to whether population and production of surplus had reached a sufficient threshold in Israel to support a strong state, or even any state at all, as early as the tenth century. Population estimates are based on criteria such as the number of persons estimated to occupy an acre of space within settlements displaying particular building patterns, the population density supportable by the estimated available food supply, and comparison with more recent census figures in areas settled in a presumably similar manner.[61] These estimates have a very wide margin of error, but in general nowadays they are greatly reduced from the high figures proposed prior to refinements in demographic studies. It is estimated that major centers in Israel and Judah held 1,500–3,000 inhabitants on average, with Jerusalem and Samaria at the upper end of the scale, perhaps with 5,000–8,000 inhabitants until a marked increase occurred in the eighth century that may have tripled or quadrupled the number of their inhabitants. Provincial towns might have had populations of 500–1,000, while villages fell in the range of 50 to a few hundred inhabitants. It is evident that the largest cities in Israel and Judah were a fraction of the size and population density of Mesopotamian and north Syrian political centers.

The reduced scale of Israelite urbanism was directly related to the irregular mountain terrain and marginal-rainfall agriculture, which contrasted with the more fertile breadbasket resources of Mesopotamia and north Syria. The overall population of Israel and Judah at the time of their separation into two states may be roughly calculated at no more than 100,000, with probably 75 percent living in the northern kingdom. This figure waxed and waned, according to historical circumstances, but never approached the much greater density that developed in late Hellenistic and Roman times. The total population of Israel and Judah at mid-eighth century could be generously estimated at 400,000, with Israel continuing as the more populous kingdom. In the seventh century, Judah's population may have been on the order of 100,000 to 150,000. Of the total populace, probably a large majority always lived in villages, although greatly affected by the political economy of cities. Moreover, the urban-rural ratio could be skewed by ecological and historical conditions. In the reduced territory of seventh-century Judah, for example, up to one-half of the populace may have lived in Jerusalem and its environs.

Texts and Inscriptions. Although Palestinian texts and inscriptions are not nearly so plentiful as the written finds from Mesopotamia, Egypt, and north Syria, they selectively but vividly illuminate political conditions. We have already mentioned a ninth-century Aramaic stela from Dan, apparently recording warfare between Israel and Aram-Damascus, which in the view of most interpreters refers to the dynasty of David,[62] and we have noted that the Samarian Ostraca document the role of the state in the domestic political economy.[63] A late eighth-century dedicatory inscription carved into a rock-cut tunnel to bring water within Jerusalem's walls is identifiable as part of Hezekiah's preparations against an Assyrian siege.[64] Also from the late eighth century, an elaborate rock-cut tomb outside Jerusalem belongs to a steward whose name is only partially preserved and who may well have been the royal steward Shebna condemned by Isaiah for making just such extravagant preparations for his burial (Isa.

22:15–19).[65] The last days of independent Judah are attested in military letters from Lachish that tell of frenzied efforts to defend against the Neo-Babylonian invasion in 588–586 B.C.E., complicated by divisions within Judah's leadership as to the proper foreign policy to pursue in the face of great-power domination.[66] Also, as Judah was under attack by Neo-Babylonians and their Edomite allies, military letters from the fortress of Arad in the Negeb recount rations assigned to troops and efforts to shore up positions against the Edomites.[67] The rare voice of a lowly harvest worker speaks in a late seventh-century letter, found near Yavneh-Yam, in which he pleads with an official to return the garment that his been wrongfully taken from him, presumably as security for a debt.[68]

The most plentiful written materials are the carved seals and seal impressions, used to stamp papyrus documents that have long since disintegrated.[69] Accompanied frequently by graphic designs, these artifacts name the owner of the seal and often his official title. The fund of names and offices recorded on these seals corresponds in considerable measure with names and offices referred to in Kings, Isaiah, and Jeremiah, and it is likely that some of these seals belonged to the persons named in those biblical books. The names "Jeroboam" and "Uzziah" on two of the seals are probably kings Jeroboam II of Israel and Azariah=Uzziah of Judah, although officials in their service, rather than the rulers themselves, are the owners of the seals. Recently, the seals of two Judahite kings, Ahaz and Hezekiah, have been discovered.[70]

Inscriptions and drawings from Kuntilleth Ajrud,[71] a way station in northern Sinai on the route to the Red Sea, are best known for their reference to "Yahweh of Samaria and his Asherah," which, together with similar inscriptions found in a tomb near Hebron,[72] attest to goddess worship among some Yahweh worshipers in the last half of the ninth century or first half of the eighth century. Additionally, however, the explicit association of Yahweh with Samaria, the mixture of Israelite and Judahite pottery forms, and the imitation of Phoenician-style artistic motifs at a location in the far south suggest close and collaborative relations between the northern and southern kingdoms. Fragments of a text in an atypical Aramean dialect from late eighth-century Deir Allah in the mid-Jordan valley recite sayings of the seer Balaam that bear many similarities to the biblical tradition concerning the same prophet in Numbers 22—24.[73] While the provenance of the text is not Israelite, the parallels and overlaps in person, plot, and theme between the two Balaam traditions indicate a sharing of religious traditions between Israel and Transjordanian peoples. The blending of religion and politics is apparent in the discovery of a shrine at the military outpost of

Arad, bearing some resemblances in its plan and orientation to the Jerusalem temple and seemingly in active use until late in the eighth century. Furthermore, although the evidence is ambiguous, a late seventh- or early sixth-century cult site near Arad contains a mixture of Judahite and Edomite pottery and a reference to the Edomite deity, Qaus, which may indicate that Judahite troops or settlers in the area were exposed to or actually participated in Edomite cultic practices.[74]

Non-Israelite Texts and Inscriptions

A second foray into extrabiblical information about monarchic politics elicits numerous explicit, and some implicit, references to the kingdoms of Israel and Judah in the state records of other powers. In a number of instances, Assyrian and Neo-Babylonian sources report on events that are also related in the biblical traditions, providing chronological "synchronisms" that enable us to give absolute dates to the biblical enumerations of royal reigns.[75] Of particular importance for present purposes, these conjunctions of biblical and extrabiblical reports on the same events provide a two-sided view of "what really happened," disclosing both agreements and disagreements in the sources. Some of the allusions to Israel and Judah in other state records actually extend our knowledge of Israelite political history because they relate events that are not touched on in the Bible.

Early in the reign of Rehoboam, about 924 B.C.E., the Egyptian ruler Sheshonk I carried out an extensive campaign throughout southern Palestine and left a list of the cities he raided and at least partially destroyed. This pharaoh, called Shishak in the Bible, is said to have destroyed fortified towns in Judah and taken gold and silver from Rehoboam of Judah (1 Kings 14:25–28; 2 Chron. 12:1–12). Sheshonk's list does not include Jerusalem, but it attests to extensive destruction of fortresses in the Negeb and brings Sheshonk's army to Gibeon, a short distance northwest of Jerusalem. The apparent aim of the pharaoh's sweep through Philistia, Judah, and Israel was to reestablish control of trade routes that Egypt had dominated under the New Empire. The timing of the campaign, shortly after the breakup of Solomon's kingdom, took advantage of weakened political power in Palestine. The accuracy of Sheshonk's list has been questioned on the grounds that he may be making excessive claims; however, corroboration of his campaign, though not the conquest of every site listed, appears in the fragment of a Sheshonk stela found at Megiddo.[76]

In 853 B.C.E., Shalmaneser III of Assyria began a series of campaigns into Syro-Palestine, and he boastfully reports on the battle of Qarqar during the first campaign.[77] He faced a coalition of twelve states and tribal groups that included the kingdom of Israel under Ahab. The largest contingents were contributed by Aram-Damascus (20,000 infantry), Hamath, and Israel (10,000 infantry each). Ahab is said to have provided the largest number of chariots, although the stated 2,000 has been adjusted downwards by some scholars to 200 or even 20 chariots.[78] The Assyrian annals have a tendency to inflate numbers of casualties in order to exalt their victories, and in this case Shalmaneser even claims a total defeat of the enemy coalition. This is belied by the fact that he retreated following the battle, and in his subsequent three campaigns into northern Syria he did not penetrate beyond Qarqar. Putting aside squabbles among themselves—including friction and warfare between Israel and Aram-Damascus—the Syro-Palestinian states by combining forces succeeded in blocking Assyrian advances for more than a decade. Ahab's participation in the alliance is not mentioned in the Bible. Either the biblical sources were uninformed about this battle or chose to ignore it, possibly because of animus against Ahab or because the conflict was felt to have taken place too far away to have significant consequences for Israel and Judah. Although Shalmaneser reports that Ammonites opposed him, there is no mention of Moab, Edom, and Judah. Since these three states were either vassals or allies of Israel at the time, it is entirely possible that their military contingents were counted among Ahab's forces.[79]

In 841 B.C.E., on his fifth western campaign, Shalmaneser III succeeded in conquering Aram-Damascus and exacting tribute from Israel and other states in Syro-Palestine no longer able to confront him in an effective coalition. Barring the debated reference of uncertain date to David in the Tel Dan stela, Jehu has the distinction of being the first Israelite to be named in a non-Israelite text and the only Israelite king known to have been represented graphically, although Judahite soldiers and captives are pictured on Sennacherib's relief of the capture of Lachish in 701. Carved in an obelisk panel, Jehu is shown bowing before Shalmaneser as his courtiers present tribute consisting of gold, silver, gold vessels and goblets, tin, royal ceremonial scepters, and precious wooden objects, perhaps javelins.[80] This is yet another event in Israel's foreign relations that is unnoted in the Bible. One can speculate that this submission to a foreign power was embarrassing to traditionists who viewed Jehu as a Yahweh loyalist striving to rid Israel of foreign ties. However, in breaking off diplomatic relations with Phoenicia, Jehu had surely helped to foster disunity among the Syro-Palestinian states, thereby creating an opening for Shalmaneser to exploit. It is probable, however, that the dissolution of the anti-Assyrian coalition began earlier when Hazael usurped the throne in Damascus and initiated an attack on Israel.[81]

The stela of King Mesha of Moab, dated about 840–820, gives a more detailed account of hostilities with Israel during the Omri dynasty than is found in 2 Kings 3:4–27.[82] Both accounts concur that Omri, or his son Ahab, had conquered Moab but that after some time Mesha rebelled. It appears that Mesha seized an opening for rebellion when the Hamath-Damascus-Israel alliance against Assyria collapsed and Israel was engaged in resumed hostilities with Damascus. However, the two accounts do not flesh out this sketchy scenario in the same manner or even with reports of the same events. The biblical account refers to the Israelite conquest only by inference when it notes Mesha's withholding of the annual tribute of sheep and wool, and it details the unsuccessful effort of Joram to defeat Mesha by a surprise attack on Moab from the southwest. In contrast, Mesha reports on his seizure of three Israelite settlements, two in the northwest of his kingdom and one nearer to his centrally located capital at Dibon.

How the "mismatched" events of the two accounts are to be related, both in content and chronology, is open to various reconstructions. The Mesha stela is probably a building dedication set up to honor the state deity, Chemosh, for whom the king has built a sanctuary, along with many other structures, including a royal palace, fortifications, reservoirs, and roads, as well as rebuilding ruined towns or fortresses. Stressing the support of Chemosh, Mesha states that he slaughtered all the Israelite inhabitants of two of the towns as a "dedication" to the deity and brought booty that included Israelite cultic objects to the Chemosh sanctuary. He recites the commands of Chemosh to make war against Israel and details a nighttime attack against one of the cities. Yahweh is named as the defeated Israelite deity, in counterpoint to Chemosh the triumphant Edomite deity. In fact, the conduct of the military operations and the ritual slaughter of captives is so remarkably similar to the style and ideology of biblical accounts of "holy war" that many interpreters were at first inclined to regard the Mesha stela as a forgery, but on paleographic grounds its authenticity is now undisputed.[83] This "holy war" schema, so pervasive in Joshua and recurrent in parts of Samuel and Kings, is championed in the seventh-century law code of Deuteronomy 20, but its actual historical practice has been open to question. On the strength of the Mesha stela, however, it is clear that the concept and practice of ritual slaughter of captives was operative in greater Palestine at least two centuries earlier than the probable date of Deuteronomy 20. It appears that Deuteronomy seized upon known sporadic outbreaks of ritual warfare and generalized them into an obligatory program for Israel, notwithstanding how frequently its harsh stipulations are ignored or contravened in biblical war narratives.[84]

Resuming Assyrian aggression in Syro-Palestine after a lapse of three decades, Adad-nirari III, probably in 796 B.C.E., dealt another blow to Aram-Damascus and collected an immense tribute in gold, silver, iron, precious cloth, and ivory-decorated furniture. In the same campaign he received tribute from Joash of Israel, along with Tyre and Sidon, but the nature of the Israelite tribute is unstated, and, once again, it is not reported in the Bible.[85] Since both Jehu's and Joash's submissions to Assyria were apparently voluntary, unlike the armed resistance mounted by Damascus, the direct effects felt in Israel would have been chiefly economic. Indirectly, however, Assyria's maneuvers in Syro-Palestine greatly affected relations between Israel and Damascus. Once Shalmaneser withdrew from the west after 841 B.C.E., Damascus was free to attack and conquer parts of Israel, but with reassertion of Assyrian power by Adad-nirari III, Damascus was weakened, and Joash was able to recover territories that had been lost to Damascus for decades. These ups and downs in the relations of two states formally under Assyrian dominion indicates that at this stage in the Assyrian empire, prior to the tighter integration achieved from Tiglath-pileser III onward, considerable latitude existed for its tributary states to war with one another. From the Assyrian point of view, this interstate conflict among its political dependencies was certainly preferable to their banding together in rebellion against Assyria.

Following Assyria's sustained penetration of Syro-Palestine beginning with Tiglath-pileser in 744 B.C.E., Israel vacillated between submission to Assyria and open rebellion. Menahem of Israel paid a sizable tribute to Tiglath-pileser[86] before a new ruler, Pekah, openly rebelled against Assyria. Exasperated with Israel's fickle allegiance, Assyria terminated Israel's status as a vassal kingdom when it captured Samaria in 722, in one of the last campaigns of Shalmaneser V. His successor, Sargon II, taking credit for the city's conquest, rebuilt the city in 720 and installed a provincial administration with an Assyrian governor.[87] More than 27,000 officials and leading citizens were deported and replaced by captives from other conquered regions, including "distant Arabs." The uncertainty of Assyrian numbers is reflected in variant reports that a contingent of either fifty or two hundred Israelite chariots was incorporated into the Assyrian army. This report is indicative of the stronger measures taken by Assyrian imperialism beginning with the reign of Tiglath-pileser in 744. It corresponds roughly with the biblical report, although the latter gives no number of those deported and it names more regions from which new settlers were drawn than does the Assyrian report.

A decade prior to the fall of Samaria, Ahaz of Judah voluntarily submitted to Assyria to escape pressure put on him by Israel and Damascus, who had once again joined in an anti-Assyrian alliance. His successor, Hezekiah, remained loyal to Assyria until the death of Sargon II in 705, whereupon he became a ringleader in an alliance of Palestinian rebels and withheld tribute. After securing his hold on the empire, Sennacherib invaded Judah and besieged Jerusalem. This campaign is more fully treated in biblical and Assyrian texts than any other of the confrontations between Israel or Judah and a foreign power.[88] The two accounts concur on a few major points, but there are many contradictions and omissions between them, and as might be expected, each gives a more favorable "slant" to its own side in the conflict. Both agree that Hezekiah capitulated and paid heavy tribute, that the siege was lifted, and that Hezekiah was retained as vassal king. The biblical report attributes the lifting of the siege and the retention of Hezekiah on the throne to two unreconciled reasons: the Assyrian army was devastated by "the angel of Yahweh" [a plague?] (2 Kings 19:35) and/or Sennacherib withdrew when he faced political dissension at home that led to his assassination (2 Kings 19:36–37), which in fact did not occur for another twenty years. In his annals, however, Sennacherib is in no haste and under no pressure to leave Palestine before he has complected the reorganization of Judah, which he reduces in size by granting much of its territory to Philistine city-states while increasing the annual tribute.

The damage inflicted on Judah must have been extensive. The Kings account only hints at the devastation of the countryside claimed by Sennacherib, including the destruction of forty-six walled sites, one of them being Lachish, whose siege and capture are dramatically pictured on a mural in his palace. The Bible also says nothing about the deportation of the populace, while Sennacherib claims to have "driven out" more than 200,150 Judahites without replacing them with new settlers. This figure is certainly preposterous, for it is unlikely that there were that many people in Judah outside of Jerusalem to begin with, and a denuding of the rural populace would have left Hezekiah without any agrarian infrastructure to support his continuing rule and to deliver the imposed tribute to Assyria. A massive deportation of captives would have made sense only if Sennacherib was converting Judah from a vassal state to a province replete with Assyrian administrators and an infusion of captive peoples from elsewhere in the empire, as had been Sargon's policy in Samaria. The Assyrian and biblical records agree that no such radical shift in Judah's colonial status occurred.[89]

Assyria's "leniency" in retaining Hezekiah as his vassal calls attention to an anomalous feature of Assyrian imperial policy in Palestine that invites explanation. When Syrian and north-central Palestinian states, including Israel, were finally subdued by Assyria, they were turned into imperial provinces with Assyrian governors. It is noteworthy, however, that the Phoenician and Philistine coastal states, and the interior states of Judah, Ammon, Moab, and Edom were allowed to remain vassal states with native rulers. Since the coastal states were thriving trade emporiums, it is likely that the Assyrians did not want to meddle in the successful conduct of trade as long as they were able to skim off the desired profits. Possibly for the same reason, the interior Palestinian states were spared provincialization because it was through their territories that profitable trade passed between Arabia, Egypt, and the Phoenician and Philistine ports. In any event, the fact that Judah remained a vassal state, and did not experience the resettlement on its soil of peoples from other parts of the empire, allowed it to preserve a far greater demographic, social, cultural, and religious coherence than was possible in the northern kingdom. This same advantage accrued to Judahites after the collapse of their state, since the Neo-Babylonians did not resettle outsiders in Judah when they reorganized it as an imperial province.

For the events during the last years of Judahite political independence, the Neo-Babylonian Chronicles provide one valuable clarification of the biblical record and one important synchronism.[90] In the terse reports of Kings and Chronicles, the motives and circumstances surrounding the death of Josiah at the hands of pharaoh Neco are obscure. Until the discovery of the Neo-Babylonian Chronicles it had been assumed that, as Assyria neared collapse, the Egyptian army was dispatched to Syria in order to join in the defeat of its long-time enemy. With that understanding, it was difficult to explain why pharaoh Neco killed Josiah at Megiddo, since Neco and Josiah would have had a common interest in hastening the downfall of Assyria. Surprisingly, however, the Neo-Babylonian Chronicles inform us that Egypt had in fact switched sides in the international power struggle and was seeking to shore up the weakened Assyrians with a view to precluding Neo-Babylonian hegemony over Syro-Palestine. In order to prevent the Egyptians from coming to the aid of the remnant of Assyrians who had withdrawn to Haran after the fall of Nineveh, it appears that Josiah intercepted Neco's army at Megiddo "to fight with him" (as 2 Chron. 35:20–22 reports) and not simply "to meet him" (as in 2 Kings 23:29); alternatively, what began as a diplomatic meeting escalated into armed conflict or a skirmish in which Josiah was seized and executed by the Egyptians.

The Neo-Babylonian synchronism with Judahite history "zeroes in" on the siege and capture of Jerusalem in 598–597 B.C.E. The brief account of

Nebuchednezzar's campaign reads, "[The king of Akkad] encamped against the city of Judah and on the second day of the month of Adar he seized the city and captured the king. He appointed there a king of his own choice, received its heavy tribute which he sent back to Babylon."[91] This contemporary report from the Neo-Babylonian perspective concurs with the biblical account on certain central points: the capital city of Judah, that is, Jerusalem, was besieged and captured; Judah's king was removed; a new king was installed; and sizable booty was carried to Babylon. It does not name either the dethroned king or his replacement, nor does it give an inventory of the booty or mention the deportation of the rebellious king and his officials, as in the fuller biblical account (2 Kings 24:1–16). Regrettably, the extant portions of the Neo-Babylonian Chronicles break off at 595/594 B.C.E., and thus provide no account of the capture of Jerusalem in 586 B.C.E. The terse report for 598–97 is typical of the restrained and lapidary style of the Neo-Babylonian Chronicles, in comparison with the histrionic bombast and greater detail of the Assyrian annals. Moreover, the Chronicles are astonishingly frank about military difficulties and reversals, as when they report on a battle with Egyptians in 601–600 B.C.E., "The King of Egypt heard and mustered his army. In open battle they smote the breast of each other and inflicted great havoc on each other. The king of Akkad and his troops turned back and returned to Babylon."[92] After this military setback, Nebuchadnezzar admits to taking a year off to reorganize and reequip his army before returning to Syro-Palestine.

Neo-Babylonian ration lists from the later reign of Nebuchadnezzar record oil allotments to Jehoiachin, king of Judah,[93] who according to Kings had been deported to Babylon in 598–97 B.C.E. (2 Kings 24:12, 25) and was eventually "promoted" from imprisonment to a privileged place at the Babylonian king's table (2 Kings 25:27–30). The ration list does not single out Jehoiachin for special honor but simply lumps him among a large number of captives from Ashkelon, Tyre, Byblos, Arvad, Egypt, Medea, Persia, Lydia, and Greece.

Synthesis of Biblical and Extrabiblical Data on the Monarchy

Our review of the extrabiblical data suggests the following conclusions and implications concerning state development in Israel and Judah:

Modest Political Centralization. The material evidence unequivocally supports the existence of a centralized state in Israel from the early ninth century and in Judah from the late eighth century. Comparable corroboration of a Davidic-Solomonic "united" Israel hovers in uncertainty due to disagreements over dating the pertinent archaeological finds, although the majority view of archaeologists appears to regard the disputed monumental building in the north as tenth century in date and thus Solomonic. Also, the Tel Dan stela seems to posit a Davidic dynasty in Jerusalem by some indeterminate date in the ninth century. The paucity of material remains in Jerusalem prior to the late eighth century is a "nil" factor because of subsequent destruction and rebuilding on the probable locations of the city of David and the temple and palace of Solomon. An impressive stepped stone rampart may have been the podium on which David's acropolis was built, but the dating of this structure is problematic, and no buildings of the Davidic period survive.[94] The "gaps" in architectural and artifactual evidence for the northern kingdom prior to Omri and for Judah between Rehoboam and Hezekiah may be accounted for in part by the weakened condition of the northern and southern components of the former regime of David and Solomon once their effort at political unification failed. Concluding, as I have, that David and Solomon attempted a political unification that was undermined by internal social and economic contradictions, it is to be expected that the deficiencies in their efforts will have been inherited by the northern and southern leadership in heightened measure, considering the division of resources between the two kingdoms and the increasing intervention of foreign powers in Palestinian affairs. Characteristic of the Davidic-Solomonic regime was a structural lopsidedness in a demographic and economic infrastructure that was far stronger in the north than in the south, but whose political center administered from the weaker southern base. The abrupt sundering of this structurally imbalanced kingdom led to severe consequences for both kingdoms, and especially so for Judah.

A Larger, More Multicultural and Cosmopolitan Northern State. When the kingdom broke apart, the north carried away the bulk of the populace and the most developed economy, while cutting itself free of the administrative apparatus that had been wielded by the south. No doubt averse to heavy-handed political rule of the sort they had rebelled against, northerners had reason to move slowly for several decades before Omri arose to establish a commanding center with monumental architecture and a bureaucratic apparatus that approximated and perhaps exceeded Solomon's. It is also probable that the consolidation of political power in the north was slowed by pharaoh Sheshonk's destructive campaign shortly after the schism and by conflict with Aram-Damascus. Interpreting the northern political development as a cautious process of institutional trial and error is further indicated by the biblical report that the northern capital was located at no less than three different sites before Omri built Samaria. This shifting of the political center, together with a series of military coups that grabbed political power, probably reflected a struggle among sectional interests in the ecologically and culturally diverse north. Omri was able to establish a secure political center only after putting down a rival whom biblical tradition says was followed by half the populace, which may very well have reflected a division between those who favored a stronger centralized state, which Omri eventually provided them, and those who favored a weaker political regime. The north was able to revive more quickly than the south because of its decided advantages in agricultural output and trade, the latter helped along by Israel taking up treaty relations with Tyre of the sort that Judah could not easily maintain because the bulk of agricultural exports desired by Tyre was now under the control of Israel.

A Smaller, More Monocultural and Insular Southern State. When the north withdrew from southern dominion, Judah was left with a capital and an administrative apparatus but with a severely reduced populace and economic infrastructure. Sheshonk's raids in the Negeb and across northwest Judah were further debilitating to Judah's economic position. In Transjordan, Ammon and Moab now fell within Israel's sphere of influence, with only Edom remaining in Judah's tenuous control. Subsequent Davidic rulers are reported to have built fortifications in various parts of Judah, but before the time of Hezekiah we do not have material evidence for these projects, and whatever further building may have been done in Jerusalem has been effaced from the archaeological record. In the military clashes between Israel and Judah that occurred from time to time, Judah stood to suffer the greater loss, since its capital lay only a few miles south of the border with Israel. According to the biblical record, Jerusalem was once captured by a northern king and on a second occasion brought under siege by the north, whereas there is no report of a Judahite penetration deep into Israel, much less of any Judahite threat to the capital at Samaria. When Israel and Judah were collaborative under the Omri dynasty, Judah was clearly the subservient ally of Israel. It would appear that only in the eighth century, possibly beginning with Uzziah, was Judah able to achieve sufficient political and economic strength to close some of the "developmental" gap between south and north, but there is precious little archaeological evidence to support this hypothesis, which is based on biblical and extrabiblical textual grounds.

Two States Struggling under Imperial Pressure. With Israel's demise, it appears that Judah was an immediate beneficiary. By virtue of Judah's voluntary submission to Assyria, Ahaz and Hezekiah enjoyed favored trade relations stabilized by the Assyrian hegemony over the entire region.

Moreover, judging from the archaeological evidence that Jerusalem was greatly expanded at this time, increasing its population severalfold,[95] it is highly probable that many refugees from the fallen state of Israel fled south, bringing with them a pool of administrative, military, and artisan skills to enhance the southern kingdom, as well as literary and religious traditions that fructified Judahite society. To be sure, a grave setback was suffered when Hezekiah rebelled against Assyria and rural Judah was devastated in retaliation, with a large part of western Judah ceded to Philistine states.[96] But once Hezekiah, properly chastened by the Assyrians, resumed his role as a faithful vassal king, political and economic conditions seem to have stabilized through the following seventy-some years of Assyrian dominion, although the biblical and archaeological data are scant for this period. Free of the Assyrian yoke under Josiah, Judah expanded territorially, and the institution of draconian policies of fiscal and cultic centralization brought renewed prosperity to Jerusalem, but with a probable depression of social and economic life in the Judahite hinterlands for those inhabitants who were not a part of the political and military establishment. Judahite settlements and fortresses extended into the Negeb to protect trade with the Red Sea and Egypt. For a time under Josiah, Judah was free of tribute payments to the faltering Assyrian empire, but at Josiah's death tribute was reimposed on Judah, first by Egypt and later by Neo-Babylonia. In the final two decades of Judahite independence, the state was riven by factional infighting in highest government circles between those who favored continuing submission to Neo-Babylonia and those who argued for revolt.[97]

State Involvement in Foreign Trade. The extent and character of state involvement in trade is rather well attested from extrabiblical data. Philistine, Phoenician, Cypriot, and Greek pottery appear with sufficient frequency to indicate that commercial ties between Israel and Judah and surrounding states were considerable. Settlements in the Negeb and the pottery and inscriptions from Kuntilleth Ajrud attest to overland trade between Judah and a port on the Red Sea, while Tel Qasile served as an outlet to the Mediterranean.[98] Transit trade to and from Transjordan, Arabia, Egypt, Philistia, and the Mediterranean-Aegean regions traversed Judah, while Israel played a similar role in the movement of goods to and from coastal Phoenicia and inland regions in Transjordan and southern Syria. Despite repeated hostilities between north and south, international trade continued to pass along the coastal highway that was fitfully controlled by Israel and Judah, depending on their political fortunes from period to period. Direct trade between Israel and Judah no doubt occurred even though limited by the fact that for the most part they had only similar goods to exchange. The biblical record credits the launching of interstate commercial ventures to Solomon, and the Omrides are pictured as establishing diplomatic and commercial ties with Tyre and Damascus. Archaeological evidence throws little light on the Solomonic role in sponsoring trade, but the Omri-Ahab royal buildings and luxury items uncovered in Samaria indicate Syro-Phoenician influence of the sort to be expected as part of extensive commercial and cultural exchanges between Israel, Tyre, Damascus, and other regional states. Moreover, the tribute in gold and silver that Jehu delivered to Shalmaneser III and the profusion of luxury items Sennacherib collected from Hezekiah imply royal treasuries that were augmented by international trade. It is probable that interstate trade was either conducted under royal auspices or heavily regulated by the state.

State Involvement in the Domestic Economy. The domestic economy rested on a broad base of small farmers and herders, many of whom were independent producers whose struggle for subsistence was often imperiled by drought, by money-lending indebtedness to big landholders and merchants, and by state agents collecting taxes and imposing corvée. As lands were lost to unpaid debts, many of the small producers became tenants, hired laborers, or workers on royal estates. Local markets provided for exchange of goods and services offered either by the direct producers or by merchant intermediaries. Little is known about interest rates or prices, but judging by information from other ancient Near Eastern economies, they were probably subject to sharp fluctuation, which generally worked to the disadvantage of those in the weakest economic position. Royal estates directly provisioned government personnel and produced surpluses that may have been made available domestically to those who had the purchasing power. In the main, however, the fine oil and wine from royal estates and from the orchards and vineyards of prosperous civilians were consigned to the export market in order to acquire building materials, precious metals, and luxury items.

In short, domestic production and foreign trade conditioned one another, with varied gains and losses accruing to different sectors of the populace. Both the archaeological data and references to socioeconomic conditions in prophetic texts point to a process of agricultural intensification to boost export trade and to enrich the crown, with severe repercussions on small cultivators who were excluded from the benefits of this developmental spiral. These periods of state-sponsored intiatives to enhance the economy to the advantage of the state apparatus and the upper social strata seem to have been at their height under Jeroboam II in Israel and under Hezekiah and Josiah in Judah. The appearance in eighth- and seventh-century Judah of pottery vessels of standard sizes and weights with marked values suggests that the state took a hand in regulating weights and measures. Whether there were state-instituted price controls is not known.

The State and Literacy. The extent of literacy in Israel and Judah has been much debated, especially as the fund of inscriptions has increased in recent decades. Opinions vary from the judgment that writing was confined within a narrow stratum of officials to a belief that functional literacy was widespread in the general populace. In many discussions on this issue, the criteria for determining "literacy" are not carefully specified. Do we mean reading and/or writing? What level of mastery over what range of communication acts is presupposed? What technical, cultural, and social factors encouraged or impeded the spread of literacy, however defined?[99]

In answering these defining questions, the epigraphic evidence is far from conclusive. Many of the inscriptions can be identified as belonging to governmental contexts, and it is certainly to be expected that scribes and glyptic artisans would be able to read and write. So-called "scribal schools" may have consisted of no more than master scribes giving "on the job" training to apprentices who would eventually take their places. However, how far literacy extended into the bureaucracy and civilian elite, and beyond into society at large, cannot be ascertained from present evidence. The numerous seals bearing the names of officials and other socially prominent persons do not in themselves prove that their owners, in contrast to the artisans who fashioned them, were literate. The Lachish and Arad letters suggest that some military officers were literate. Beyond official circles, the evidence for literacy is more problematic. Some of the fairly crude inscriptions in tombs may indicate the hand of commoners or at least of persons outside the scribal establishment. The Yavneh Yam petition of a poor harvester was probably dictated and not written in his own hand, but it does suggest that in some instances literate communication was available to nonliterate folks. The actual social and political need for literacy appears to have been modest, since most transactions were carried out orally. Ordinary business dockets could be kept with minimal literacy, but there may have been nongovernmental "private secretaries" who could draw up contracts and financial ledgers. Ritual texts, composed either in premonarchic times or at Jerusalem and other monarchic shrines, may well have been given written form, but they would have been largely accessible to worshipers only in their oral rendition. Neither premonarchic nor monarchic ritual needs would seem to have required more than small circles of literate laity and/or priests.

The distinctions between facility in speaking, reading, and writing a language become apparent in interstate diplomatic and commercial contacts. Given the proximity of Israel and Judah to several states with which they had diplomatic, commercial, and military interaction, it is likely that many government officials, and not only scribes, were at least minimally conversant in other Semitic tongues and dialects and probably also in Egyptian and eventually in Greek. In the case of merchants engaged in interstate trade, it can be presupposed that they were fluent enough in the foreign tongues necessary to carry on business transactions. Under the later Assyrian empire the need for multilingualism may have diminished as Aramaic became the lingua franca throughout the empire. The services of state scribes could be enlisted when important "high level" oral agreements required written documentation. Functional literacy, sufficient to the tasks of state administration, was certainly present in Israel and Judah, but the level and range of competency in reading and writing, and the scope of its reach beyond court circles, remains unclear.

COMPARABILITY OF ISRAEL AND JUDAH
TO OTHER ANCIENT NEAR EASTERN STATES

The issue of the comparability of the Israelite and Judahite states to other ancient Near Eastern polities, often posed as a question of Israelite "distinctiveness" or "uniqueness," is extremely complex.[100] Too often the comparison has been made solely or primarily in terms of their respective religions, sometimes motivated by an apparent compulsion to find some way in which Israel was "really different" from, or even "superior" to, contemporary states and societies. In this attempt at "comparison," I shall briefly consider material culture and technology, arts and crafts, literature, religion, and political institutions in that order.

In *material culture and technology,* Israel and Judah were broadly similar to other inland states such as Ammon, Moab, Edom, and Damascus, with Judah showing more affinities with the pastorally dominant Transjordan kingdoms and Israel more nearly on a par with Damascus in its agrarian foundations. The contention that aspects of the material culture, such as pottery forms and domestic architecture, are uniquely Israelite has not fared well since these supposedly "unique" elements are found beyond the sphere of Israelite occupation. More importantly, to the degree that Israelite material culture represented a particularized adaptation to highland conditions, it is best viewed as a subset of wider Palestinian culture, with few signs of having introduced innovative technology to the region.[101] The material achievement of Israelite highlanders consisted, it seems, of the resourceful combination of already existing agrarian technologies, as in constructing cisterns, grain pits, and terraces, in order to create a productive adaptation to marginal growing conditions.[102] Israel and Judah also shared some material affinities with Philistia and Phoenicia, but the prominence of the maritime economy in the coastal states constituted a marked difference in culture and even in polity in the case of the Phoenician cities, which remained in the control of commercial oligarchies.

In terms of monumental architecture, it has been observed that ashlar masonry and ornamental details such as proto-aeolic capitals and stone balustrades are better represented in Israel and Judah than in Phoenicia, from which they are often alleged to have originated; if this is more than a matter of accidental archaeological finds, it may indicate that Israel first, and Judah later, perfected these architectural features.[103] With respect to the technology of written scripts, it has been proposed that the development of the alphabet by experimentation over centuries, beginning as early as 1800 B.C.E., reached its acme and was even perfected in Israel.[104] Specific contributions of early Israelites to the development of the alphabet, however, are simply undemonstrated, although it is evident that alphabetic script was available in tribal Israel and was employed in what are widely regarded as early biblical texts such as the Song at the Sea and the Song of Deborah.

Israelite *arts and crafts* are seldom discussed as a body of work,[105] and the allegedly slim Israelite repertory has often been explained by a preference for "the word" over "the image," and specifically by the prohibition against images of the divine, which is claimed to have put a damper on all representational art. Furthermore, it is difficult to determine at times if particular objets d'art, such as the Samarian ivories or the proto-aeolic capitals, were imported, made by hired non-Israelites, or crafted by Israelites accomplished in techniques and styles from abroad. There are reasoned responses to all these difficulties. To begin with, it is highly problematic whether the verbal/visual dichotomy holds up as a sweeping characterization of Israelite sensibility. Also, the date, scope, and actual affect of the prohibition of images of the deity are uncertain. In actuality, arts and crafts are clearly present in Israel and Judah, and representational artifacts are considerable, witnessed, for example, by the bronze bull from Samaria, ceramic figurines in female form worn as necklaces, animal and human designs on seals, and crude pictures on tomb walls and in the caravansary at Kuntilleth Ajrud, the latter possibly picturing Yahweh and his consort Asherah. There is no good reason to deny that these were all made by Israelites and that some of them had an iconic function in religious belief and practice.

Without a doubt, Israelite arts and crafts in no way matched the profusion of Mesopotamian and Egyptian representational art. More to the point, however, is a comparison with other Syro-Palestinian states, rather than with states on the scale of Egypt and the Mesopotamian polities. Although little comprehensive comparison appears to have been undertaken based on a close study of artifactual evidence, it appears to me that Israel and Judah were not especially deficient in arts and crafts, nor for that matter especially advanced, when compared with neighboring states on more or less the same scale of social complexity and with roughly the same form of political economy. In truth, the lines between Canaanite-Israelite-Philistine-Phoenician-Syrian art cannot be drawn categorically, since reciprocal influences among all the Syro-Palestinian states and cultures are apparent, not to mention the embracing impact of Egyptian, Mesopotamian, and Hittite art on the entire Levant.

In terms of *literary production,* we have two bodies of evidence. One is the literature preserved in the Hebrew Bible, substantial portions of which I have argued stem from monarchic times. Most, if not all, the genres represented in the monarchic contributions to the Hebrew Bible are also found elsewhere in the ancient Near East.[106] Until recently, it seemed sufficient to acknowledge a generalized Israelite debt to this literature, accompanied by a singling out of this or that close similarity between Israelite and Mesopotamian/Egyptian/Hittite writings, as with the Babylonian Creation Epic, the Egyptian Hymn to Aton, and the Hittite suzerain-vassal treaties. It becomes ever clearer, as biblical scholars attend to the work of ancient Near Eastern specialists, that much of this earlier comparative study was atomistic, ignoring the context of the literature in both cultures by confining itself to philological and form critical matters and to the narrow, largely undecidable issue of whether the biblical texts borrowed directly from extrabiblical texts. The distribution of similar literary genres, motifs, and conventions over large parts of the ancient Near East suggests that those in Israel and Judah who could read and write and had familiarity with foreign literary traditions and practices, and possibly certain foreign writings themselves, would have been variously exposed to and affected by literary production from abroad.

What distinguishes the Israelite writings above all is that those texts eventually woven into the Hebrew Bible underwent a lengthy process of supplementation, redaction, preservation, and transmission that extended their life enduringly beyond the temporal horizon of the ancient Near East. The other ancient Near Eastern texts did not survive in a living tradition but were only recovered over the last two centuries. Nonetheless, it is growingly evident that there were bodies of Mesopotamian literature that underwent complex processes of collection, redaction, arrangement, and transmission over centuries of time before the eclipse of the ancient Near East, and that it is appropriate to speak of these collections as having the honorary and regulative status of "canons."[107] These venerable Mesopotamian texts are primarily to be distinguished from the Hebrew Bible in that they never came to form the basis of an organized religion that perpetuated them as scripture. The point here is not to diminish the literary excellence of the Hebrew Bible, but rather to stress that its varied contents, written over close to a thousand years, bear a close stylistic, thematic, and ideological relationship with texts from surrounding cultures and that these compositions, before they were aggregated in the Hebrew Bible, existed as separate pieces with various aims and functions that had counterparts elsewhere in the wider ancient Near Eastern literary environment.

The other body of Israelite written evidence consists of texts and inscriptions not included in the Bible, some of which we have described earlier in this chapter. These texts, minimal and fragmentary as they are, presumably stem from some of the same literate environments in which writings eventually gathered into the Hebrew Bible were produced. Why we have so few such extrabiblical Israelite writings when compared to the canonical corpus is probably best accounted for by the nature of the primary writing material in use at the time. Mesopotamian and north Syrian texts survived because they were written on clay tablets or stone stelas. Egyptian texts survived because they were either inscribed on walls or penned on papyrus preserved by the dry climate. In Palestine, there is minuscule evidence of wall inscriptions and clay tablets. Papyrus, the common Palestinian writing material, disintegrated from the wet winter climate, except in those few instances where the texts were hidden away in arid regions, or were copied and recopied because someone wished to preserve them, as apparently was the case with works that became "biblical." The Israelite and Judahite inscriptions we have are on pottery sherds, rock-cut inscriptions, plastered walls, and seals or seal impressions. Thus, we are cautioned against assuming that Israel, Judah, and the other south Syrian and Palestinian states produced only the modicum of writing that has so far come to light, of which the longest specimen is probably the Mesha stela. Their writings on papyrus, if not preserved by recopying, would have perished long ago, leaving us in the dark as to how voluminous they may have been.

In accounting for Israel's prominence as the most prolific producer of surviving literature among the Syro-Palestinian states, with only Ugarit's mythological and administrative texts approaching Israel's output, we should be asking: who in Israel had the interest to preserve a considerable number of these older texts by copying and recopying them? Once we remove the biblical canonical factor operative in postmonarchic times, a reasonable assessment of Israelite and Judahite monarchic literature in relation to contemporary ancient Near Eastern literature suggests that they shared broadly similar venues. If there is a greater versatility and creativity in Israelite and Judahite writing in monarchic times than elsewhere in Syro-Palestine, it does not appear to be due to their composition under state auspices but to other sectors of society that operated in critical dialogue with the state, such as prophetic, priestly, and wisdom circles that were able to maintain a distance from total cooptation by the state.

With respect to *religion,* the extrabiblical evidence does not speak for an exclusive Yahwistic cult in Israel or Judah, much less a monotheistic one, during monarchic times. Unfortunately, the relevant evidence is meager and inconclusive, but there does not appear to be any aspect of the religion of Israel and Judah in monarchic times that distinguished it as markedly different from the religions of other contemporary states. There are indications that the official state religion of Israel and Judah was the cult of Yahweh at least in most periods, to which the high incidence of Yahwistic theophoric names among the kings and officials of Judah, increasing greatly in the eighth and seventh centuries, bears witness. This is evidenced for ninth-century Israel by the Mesha stela and for late seventh- and early sixth-century Judah by the Lachish and Arad letters.

But what sort of Yahweh cult? The Kuntilleth Ajrud and Khirbet el-Qom inscriptions from ninth- or eighth-century Judah, the former with an admixture of Israelite pottery and Phoenician motifs, link Yahweh with a female consort Asherah, regarded as anathema in postexilic biblical tradition. The book of Jeremiah reports that women survivors of the destruction of Jerusalem in 586 expressed their ardent devotion to "the Queen of Heaven," perhaps equatable with Astarte, a goddess not always distinguishable from Asherah. One or more Semitic goddesses are referred to in the worship of fifth-century Jews who had fled to Egypt, where they served as mercenaries in the Egyptian army. The book of Ezekiel reports that an array of non-Yahwistic cults and practices were prevalent even within the Jerusalem temple precincts prior to the fall of the city.

The cumulative archaeological and biblical evidence leads us to wonder about the actual repertory of beliefs and practices in the cult of Yahweh during the monarchic era.[108] It is apparent that we cannot trust the judgment of polemical biblical sources, whether they are monarchic or later, to give us a realistic or well-proportioned account of religious belief and practice prior to the decisive move toward exclusive monotheism in postexilic times. Rather, we should say that these sources, by their very polemical stance, indicate that the structure and content of the Yahweh cult was in flux, with partisans for one or another position clashing vehemently and at times violently. The political implications of these religious conflicts are far from clear, but in general it seems that the forces pushing exclusive Yahwism tended to be insular and isolationist, while those that favored a more hybrid Yahwism, willing to accommodate and embrace aspects of other religious outlooks and practices, were more cosmopolitan and internationalist.

A major factor in enhancing one or another of these understandings of the Yahweh cult was the recurrence of political crises precipitated by foreign aggression, which finally destroyed both kingdoms. As the Assyrian and Neo-Babylonian juggernauts bore down on Judah, the political center invoked Yahweh as protector of the political establishment. The populace was pushed to opt for reliance on Yahweh as celebrated in the royal cult, or to identify with a "revisionist" Yahweh as articulated by prophets or Deuteronomists, or to rely on other deities either in contention with or partially assimilated into the cult of Yahweh. Thus, although the biblical text assumes a standard, communally agreed-upon cult of Yahweh, which many people abandoned when they should have known better, a close reading of the text combined with extrabiblical data indicates that the very predominance of the Yahweh cult, as well as its precise beliefs and practices, was still under heated dispute. Throughout the monarchy, Yahweh was in the process of formation as a concept and as an object of worship, as were also the proper places and rites of worship, not to mention the legitimacy of competing priesthoods.

In terms of *political institutions,* Israel and Judah were similar to other tributary monarchies in Syro-Palestine. With modest differences, the political administration of agrarian/pastoral states throughout the region was similarly articulated, the major variant being the Phoenician city-states with a maritime commercial orientation. One point on which Israelite and Judahite politics has been repeatedly distinguished in the history of biblical interpretation is their alleged foundations in a covenantal arrangement between rulers and ruled. This contention has taken a number of forms. It was long argued that the rapid change of dynasties in Israel attested to a form of "charismatic" leadership, in which acclamation was required by a spokesperson for the Yahweh cult and concurrence by popular assembly.[109] This may explain in part the rise of Jeroboam as the first ruler of the northern kingdom, but thereafter the disrupted dynasties are more often than not led by military coups, even if they invoked a religious veneer to validate their seizures of power. Some have detected traces of "primitive democracy" in Mesopotamian and Syrian states that Judah in particular is thought to have developed to a higher degree by requiring that rulers consult with an assembly or council of citizens. It is noted that David had to forge a compact with the elders of the northern tribes in order to secure their assent to his rule, that "covenants" possibly of the same sort recurred in the reigns of Joash and Josiah, and that an obscure group called "the people of the land" was active in the choice of certain successors to the Davidic throne. However, it is not surprising that David, as the first successful political centralizer, had to come to terms with tribal elites. The later monarchic "covenants" are theologically colored, and the identity of "the people of the land" remains clouded, perhaps the best guess being that they were groups of powerful landholders and merchants but not necessarily a formally constituted body with defined powers.[110]

As far as the extrabiblical evidence is concerned, there is no support for this contention of a special covenantal foundation to Israelite politics that would be particularly different from the theopolitical justification of regimes throughout the ancient Near East, which seem never at a loss in claiming divine mandates as their ultimate foundation. This is not to deny that covenantal thinking existed in monarchic Israel and Judah but simply to say that its claims on the actual formation and conduct of regimes are problematic.[111] According to the biblical record, northern and southern kings alike repeatedly behave in an independent manner that does not suggest that they are under priestly, conciliar, or popular control. It is quite possible to recognize that covenantal/conciliar thinking, both religious and secular, probably stemming from tribal times, was current in Israelite and Judahite circles without being able to make much of an impact on the state. Kings might seek to appropriate such sentiments to their advantage, as seems likely with Hezekiah and Josiah, but that they subjected themselves unequivocally to covenantal restraints dictated by religious traditions and mechanisms is highly dubious. It is, in fact, questionable whether any of the Syro-Palestinian tributary states, dependent as they were on exploiting the surpluses of their overwhelmingly agrarian and pastoral producers, could have prospered, or survived, had they adhered to policies of social and economic justice of the sort advocated by Israelite and Judahite prophets and priests.[112]

THE POLITICAL AGENDA OF ISRAEL AND JUDAH

Taking into account the several lines of evidence concerning the states of Israel and Judah, how shall we characterize them in terms of their local and regional specificity and as exemplars of ancient Near Eastern polities? One way of organizing and conceptualizing the data is to view these states as networks of institutional power controlled by authorities whose goal it was to secure, defend, replenish, expand, legitimate, and bequeath their inherited power base indefinitely through time. The daily routines and episodic crises that occupied the attention of political leaders entailed the marshaling of sufficient means to preserve, extend, and exploit the natural and human sources of power that constituted their assets as the highest authorities in their domains.

There were several imperative tasks that any state ruler or regime had to carry out in order to thrive, or even to survive. One was to secure an orderly *transfer of power* from ruler to ruler and from regime to regime. For the current paramount ruler, this meant securing his hold on office as quickly and decisively as possible and assuring that his position would be passed on intact to his successor. A second critical task was the *defense of the functional integrity of the state* against foreign and domestic threats to its stability and continuity. A third task was the periodic *replenishment of the natural and human resources* eroded by time and circumstance and the efficient garnering of those resources to fund the operations of the state. A fourth task was to strive for the *expansion of the resource base* of the state, either through territorial acquisition, diplomatic maneuvers, or intensification of production and efficiency of tax collection within existing borders. A fifth imperative was the *legitimation of the regime's right to rule,* which could be achieved by providing leadership perceived as advantageous to a majority of the populace, or at least to those subjects who exercised power in nonstate social networks, and also by articulating an ideology that gave cosmic grounding to the regime's right to rule and to pursue its policies of the moment.

In these fundamental regards, Israel and Judah were no different from their neighbor states and no different from the great powers such as Assyria and Egypt. All of them had to face this congeries of distinguishably separate but closely interconnected tasks as the fundamental requisite of "successful" politics. To fail in any one of these tasks could have debilitating ripple effects on other tasks, weakening and eventually toppling single rulers or entire states. And since the impulse to preserve and extend state power was endemic to every state, the interaction between states was necessarily a zero-sum game in which there were necessarily losers as well as winners, each state's achievements tending to be gained at the expense of one or more other states. The most that could be achieved by any ruler was that the state he ruled would be a winner under his regime. The zero-sum competition between states was mirrored in a similar field of contending social actors within states, who were variously satisfied or dissatisfied with their lot as domestic subjects of regimes they either supported wholeheartedly, complied with reluctantly, resisted as they were able, or openly rebelled against.

In one sense, this model of state tasks is so general that it is unremarkable, even truistic, to the extent that it is applicable to all states throughout human history. Nevertheless, this profile of the fundamental imperatives of ancient Near Eastern polities has diagnostic value for looking at how any particular state implemented the critical tasks intrinsic to its viability as a power network. It forces the observer to consider facets of state power that may not be documented or alluded to in the sources concerning particular states. It does not, of course, tell us in advance about the numerous ways in which those tasks could be carried out, nor does it predict the precise combinations of successes and failures that marked the erratic course of actual states. Nonetheless, using this repertory of state tasks, we can reflect on the particularities of the politics of Israel and Judah in the context of the network of states in which they regularly participated. To reduce the multiplicity of data to a manageable form, we shall look at the implementation of the state tasks in Israel and Judah by means of two sets of concentric relationships that can be analytically distinguished even as they are recognized as reciprocally interconnected. The first is the concentric *external* relations between Israel and Judah, their neighboring states, and more distant megastates. The second is the concentric *internal* relations between the political centers of Israel and Judah, the primary political and economic beneficiaries of both political regimes, and the majority of subjects less tangibly benefited, or seriously disadvantaged, by state power.

Foreign Affairs and the Political Agenda of Israel and Judah

Relations between Israel and Judah. Once Israel and Judah separated into two sovereign entities occupying adjacent territories, the attempts of each to secure and enhance their viability sometimes collided in a straight-out winner-loser contest and less frequently cooperated to the benefit of both states. The two kingdoms were embroiled in a series of border clashes during the first half century after they parted ways, in which each state was jockeying to establish a frontier that would be strategically advantageous. This was a more urgent matter for Judah, since it needed to secure the largest possible buffer zone on its northern border to serve as a protective shield for the nearby capital at Jerusalem. These periodic struggles seem to have been little more than skirmishes that only modestly altered the border between them. At one point, however, when the struggle was going poorly for Judah, Asa made a substantial payment to Damascus to relieve Judah by attacking Israel from the northeast. More serious warfare broke out a century later when Amaziah, flushed by a victory over Edom, felt bold enough to engage Israelite forces that were recovering from long subjection to Damascus. The biblical account pictures Amaziah as the reckless challenger and Joash of Israel as at first dismissively declining hostilities before reluctantly agreeing. This quaint ceremonious exchange is put in question by the report that the battle occurred at Beth-shemesh in Judah, which implies that Israel rather than Judah was spoiling for the fight and seized the initiative. The result was a resounding defeat of Judah, demolition of a section of Jerusalem's walls, and plunder of the royal treasury. In the closing decade of Israel's independence, Israel joined with Damascus to compel Judah to enlist in an anti-Assyrian alliance, but their siege of Jerusalem was broken when Ahaz of Judah appealed to Assyria for help. Although these hostilities between Israel and Judah accomplished little that was to the long-term gain of either state, it is evident that they were intense, with both belligerents willing to call on the aid of another state to assist them when "push came to shove."

Instances when hostilities between Israel and Judah played a direct part in overturning the reign of particular kings in either state, while relatively few, are indicative of the ferocity of their rivalry. The most blatant case was Jehu's assassination of Ahaziah of Judah, the unfortunate ally of his chief target, Jehoram of Israel. It seems likely that Amaziah of Judah was assassinated by some of his officials as a result of the humiliating defeat Israel inflicted on his forces, a defeat due at least in part to the king's overconfidence. The intent of Pekah of Israel and Rezin of Damascus in besieging Jerusalem was not only to force Judah to join them in an anti-Assyrian alliance, but also to replace Ahaz with the son of Tabeel, probably the scion of a Transjordanian family loyal to the northern kingdom. Had they been successful, the Davidic dynasty would have ended. Instead, Ahaz turned the tables on the besiegers by calling for Assyrian assistance, which led directly to the assassination of Pekah by a pro-Assyrian Israelite who took the throne.

Positive relations between Israel and Judah developed during the Omrid dynasty, at the instigation of Israel as part of a grand design of alliance-building that would benefit all the states involved. A compact of peace was secured between the two states when Jehoshaphat's son, Jehoram, married Athaliah, Omri's daughter. This opened the way to Judahite military success against Edom, improved commercial ties with Philistia and Arabia, and even fostered a venture in trying to reopen maritime trade via the Red Sea. It also freed Israel to focus on military coalition building to face the Assyrian threat from the north, and to develop its commercial ties with Tyre and Damascus. Later in the Omrid dynasty, as the anti-Assyrian coalition collapsed, Israel twice called on Judahite forces to join in renewed hostilities against Damascus, first under Jehoshaphat and later under his grandson Ahaziah; and when Moab rebelled against Israelite domination, Israel pressed Judah to join in a counterattack against Moab launched from Judahite territory. The impression we gain from these accounts is that Israel was by far the stronger member of the alliance and that Judah was under considerable compulsion to involve itself in Israel's military ventures in Transjordan.

Cordial and cooperative relations between Israel and Judah were shattered by Jehu's murder of Ahaziah and a large part of the Judahite royal family when he annihilated all descendants and partisans of Omri. By killing Jezebel, whose marriage to Ahab had sealed alliance with Tyre, Jehu also shattered his connections with Tyre. As the wider south Syro-Palestinian network of alliances collapsed, including ties between Israel and Judah, the north now stood alone against the advancing Assyrians who, after taking tribute from Israel and Damascus, pulled back for several decades leaving Damascus free to devastate Israel and Judah. This is a singularly clear instance of the conjunction of the political interests of Israel, Judah, and other neighboring states that for a brief time strengthened all parties against Assyria, but could not be sustained, as the small states turned to fighting among themselves, thus allowing Assyrian dominion to gain its first firm foothold in southern Syria and northern Palestine.

Although there is no explicit biblical or extrabiblical reference, it seems probable that in the first half of the eighth century Israel and Judah came to peaceful terms, if not an actual alliance. There is no report of their joining forces in military campaigns or otherwise directly cooperating. However, as the power of Damascus declined and Assyria was occupied elsewhere, both states appear to have expanded their territory and prospered commercially and agriculturally under the long reigns of Jeroboam II of Israel and Azariah=Uzziah of Judah. This decades-long recession of foreign intrusion into Israel and Judah was comparable to the international power vacuum that had permitted the emergence of the Davidic-Solomonic state two centuries earlier. As in the preceding century, the leading edge of this military expansion and economic prosperity was provided by Israel, whose demographic and economic foundations and strategic position continued to mark it as the stronger of the two states.

Just as abruptly as in the ninth century, however, this period of Israelite-Judahite harmony was cut short by the renewed imperial thrusts of Assyria, which led soon to the demise of Israel as an independent state and to the reduction of Judah to vassal status. Judah refused to cooperate with Israel and Damascus in an anti-Assyrian alliance and, to save itself, capitulated to Assyria without a fight.

As for the impact of the royal ideologies of Israel and Judah on their interstate relations, we have minimal information. The editorial hand shaping the biblical accounts is clearly Judahite, in that it condemns all northern rulers as apostates from the true theopolitical order of Judah. When, however, we examine the narratives about the two kingdoms apart from their editorial framework, it is not at all clear that either treated the other as religiously apostate or that religion per se precluded their cooperation when political circumstances were favorable in the eyes of both parties.

Because the biblical traditions are Judahite in their present form, we have only scattered details about northern royal ideology. It was clearly Yahwistic, but under Omri it did allow Baal worship in the capital of Samaria, as part of the diplomatic privileges extended to Jezebel, the Tyrian wife of Ahab. Fierce fighting between advocates of Yahweh and advocates of Baal over which should be the state deity are reported in the prophetic traditions about Elijah. The biblical tradition claims that Jezebel initiated the struggle, but that claim falters under close examination, since it was not customary for cults granted political status as a diplomatic privilege to attempt to extirpate the cults of the host country. In any case, the Baal cult was eliminated as a state religion by Jehu, although Baalistic practices continued among the general populace. State sanctuaries were also situated at Dan and Bethel on the southern and northern borders, and Shechem and Shiloh appear to have been revered as old north Israelite cultic centers. The specific components of royal rites and the religious conceptions of kingship in the northern kingdom are obscure.

Southern royal ideology is better attested in traditions about the sanctity of Zion-Jerusalem and the Davidic dynasty. Elements of royal rites and concepts of the king as the adopted son of Yahweh are found in narratives and psalms, but nothing like a complete ritual program survives.[113] The motif of a promissory covenant with David ensuring the endurance of his dynasty is attested (2 Samuel 7; Psalms 2; 110),[114] but it is not clear how early that motif entered Judahite political tradition, and it is even less clear that a covenant between each Davidic ruler and the people of Judah was a regular feature of a ruler's coronation, nor are the political terms and implications of the alleged covenant reconstructable. It is also evident that later claims to a "purer" Yahwistic faith in Judah are dubious in the light of many reported details of non-Yahwistic cults and practices, or of illicit Yahwistic practices, that extend to the final years of the kingdom. In developing his interstate ties, Solomon is said to have contracted marriages that brought his wive's cults into Jerusalem; specifically mentioned are the cults of Phoenician Sidon, Ammon, and Moab.

Although one or another of the religious practices deemed apostate by the editors of Kings is said to have been eliminated by certain Judahite rulers, the reform measures are incomplete and have no lasting success. It is abundantly clear that alternatives to a strict Yahweh cult were never entirely eliminated from official circles. Royal diplomatic marriages to foreign wives would still entail the introduction of their cults in Jerusalem, even if they remained peripheral or subordinate to the dominant state cult of Yahweh. Interestingly, although the house of Baal in Jerusalem is associated with Athaliah by implication, and it is further implied that she sponsored Baal worship in place of Yahweh worship, it is not claimed that she built the house, or even that she patronized it, or that she attempted to elevate the Baal cult to the status of sole official religion. In fact, Athaliah bears a Yahwistic name, but that Jezebel was her sister-in-law appears to have been enough to cast on her the innuendo of a like zeal for Baal. It is quite possible that the house of Baal in Jerusalem was an older establishment, even from Solomon's time, or that, if it was built for Athaliah as a concession to the Baal worship of her family of origin, it was simply a subordinate diplomatically privileged cult that did not aspire to preempt the primacy of the Yahweh cult.[115]

All circumstances considered, it seems that each state preferred its own version of royal Yahwistic ideology, but with allowances for other cults that had varying success in maintaining themselves and that in various ways seem to have influenced the cult of Yahweh. The key point seems to be that each ideology was politically bound to the state, so that disputes on religious matters were not claims about the general superiority of one religion over another. It is politically significant that when the two states had reasons to cooperate, their respective ideologies did not prevent them from doing so.

Relations with Neighboring States. The pattern of oscillation between interstate hostility, neutrality, and cooperation that we have seen in the relations between Judah and Israel is duplicated in their relations with other states in southern Syria and Palestine. Sometimes the stances of Israel and Judah toward these other states were aligned, but more often they were at variance, since all the states in the larger region resolutely pursued policies that seemed momentarily advantageous to each. It was extremely difficult for these states to align their diplomatic and military strategies in order to cooperate over any considerable period of time.

The movement toward cooperation among them, spearheaded by the Omrid rulers of Israel, was driven both by commercial considerations, since none of these small states was self-sufficient in basic resources, and by military considerations, since none of them was powerful enough to resist Assyria, Egypt, or Babylonia single-handedly. These urgent needs were countered by an undertow of divisiveness stemming from disputes among themselves over their expansive, sometimes "miniimperial," strategies toward one another, by the instability of regimes, and by the difficulty of sustaining unity when the immediate threat of larger powers receded. Of course cooperation among them was not made any easier by the astuteness with which Assyria, Egypt, and Neo-Babylonia employed "divide and conquer" tactics to drive wedges between the smaller states at every opportunity. The viability of Israel and Judah as self-sustaining states was thus at times enhanced, but far more often jeopardized, by their embroilment in the maelstrom of regional small-state politics. Overall, it is not evident that Israel or Judah showed favoritism toward one another based on shared demographics, history, culture, or religion, except for the regional geopolitical strategy of the Omrid dynasty. The notion of an inclusive Israel, stressed by the narrator(s) of Kings,[116] was not powerful enough in the long run to overrule centrifugal self-interests in both kingdoms amid the rough and tumble of Syro-Palestinian politics.

Damascus and Tyre, as states adjacent to Israel on the northeast and the northwest, were significant factors in the ebb and flow of northern state power. As long as there were cordial ties with both states, Israel stood to gain commercially from maritime trade with Tyre and overland trade with Damascus, and as long as the anti-Assyrian alliance that involved Israel and Damascus held firm, peaceful regional conditions prospered domestic productivity and smoothed the flow of trade. Once the anti-Assyrian alliance collapsed, Israel and Damascus reverted to warfare over territory in northern Transjordan, and the lucrative trade with Tyre was imperiled by Jehu's murder of Jezebel. The loss of Moab and the alienation of Judah following Jehu's murder of Ahaziah left Israel alone and exposed to two or three decades of devastation and virtual vassalage by an aggressive Damascus.

Prior to the Omrid dynasty, Asa of Judah had paid Damascus to enlist its military help when border warfare with Israel was threatening the Jerusalem regime. Later, when Jehu ruthlessly severed Israel's alliance with

Judah, the southern regime was probably pleased to see Israel getting its "just deserts" at the hands of Damascus. However, Damascus so thoroughly trounced Israel that its military sweeps extended into Philistia, and an attack on Judah was averted only when Joash made a substantial payment to Hazael of Damascus. It is likely that Joash's weakness in the face of Damascus was a factor in his assassination. Damascus loomed once again as a threat to Judah when, in coalition with Israel, it tried to force Ahaz to join them against Assyria.[117]

Tyre was among the seafaring Phoenician city-states strung along the Mediterranean coast north of Acco that had successfully weathered the incursion of the Sea Peoples, among them being the Philistines who eventually settled on the coast south of Carmel. Sidon was first to found a series of colonies throughout the Mediterranean, and Tyre followed suit, establishing, among others, the Punic colony of Carthage in North Africa. Tyre, Sidon, and Byblos became the commercial conduits between the Greek world and the ancient Near East, purveyors of the alphabetic script and developed and accomplished artisans in the fashioning of luxury goods. Phoenicia was acting "true to form" when it supplied building materials, as well as expertise in architecture, crafts, and seafaring, for Solomon and later for the Omrid dynasty, gaining in return agricultural products and access to trade with Arabia. The entente between Phoenicia and Israel was broken by the isolationist policy of Jehu. While the close ties were never restored, it is possible that, as both Israel and Judah regained their strength under Jeroboam II and Uzziah, trade between the Phoenician coast and the Israelite-Judahite hinterland was encouraged and regularized by both parties. Like the other Syro-Palestinian states, the Phoenician city-states were compelled to pay tribute to Assyria, beginning in the mid-ninth century, and repeatedly so from Tiglath-pileser III onward as the Assyrian empire encroached ever more deeply into Syro-Palestine. Tyre survived siege by Shalmaneser V, but its control and influence over other Phoenician city-states was diminished, and Esarhaddon, as he mounted his invasions of Egypt, reduced Tyre's power even further. Nevertheless, Tyre remained a functioning vassal city-state in whose administration the Assyrians intervened with great care, since they were dependent on the maritime prosperity that Phoenicia provided them in tribute and trade. The city of Tyre, divided between a mainland settlement and an island port capable of being provisioned by sea, was highly resistant to military conquest.

Following in the strategic footstops of the Assyrians, the Neo-Babylonians struggled to bring the Phoenician city-states under firm control as they prepared for invasion of Egypt. Nebuchadnezzar laid siege to Tyre for more than a decade before both parties came to a negotiated settlement. Phoenician connections with post-Solomonic Judah are attested in the alleged presence of Tyrian and Sidonian envoys at a meeting in Jerusalem to consider revolt against Neo-Babylonia, presumably spearheaded by Zedekiah without success (Jer. 27:3). Phoenician colonies were largely Mediterranean coastal trading emporiums, but Phoenicians did found some inland settlements in northern Syria. None is known to have been established in Palestine, and there are no records of warfare between any of the Phoenician city-states and Israel or Judah. The effective "weapons" of Phoenicia were not military but commercial, and they wielded them skillfully even when they had to accommodate to Assyrian and Neo-Babylonian hegemony.[118]

The Transjordanian states of Ammon, Moab, and Edom were important for Israel and Judah to the extent that they lay athwart north-south and east-west highways that carried trade between the Mediterranean coast, north Syria, Egypt, and South Arabia. David and Solomon had dominated these regions, but subsequent rulers of Israel and Judah had mixed success in hanging on to them. Moab fell within Israel's power sphere, but northern kings were too weak to enforce control of Moab until it was reconquered by the Omrid dynasty, enabling Israel to profit from sizable tribute of animals and wool. When Moab rebelled in the waning years of the Omrid dynasty, Mesha's ferocious ritual slaughter of Israelite captives may have been sparked by memory of a brutal massacre of male Moabites by Joab, David's general (2 Sam. 8:2), and during the dark years of Israel's subjection to Damascus, Moabite raiders attacked Israel (2 Kings 13:20–21). Moab paid tribute to successive Assyrian kings from Tiglath-pileser to Ashurbanipal and was generally reluctant to join other regional states in rebellion; although it did initially join a revolt against Sargon, it recanted in time to avoid punishment. Part of Moab's obligation to Assyria included sending laborers to Lebanon to cut and transport timber for building projects and providing troops for campaigns against Egypt and Arabian tribes. Neo-Babylonia inherited Assyria's dominion over Moab, and Moabites were among the vassals who attacked Jerusalem when Jehoiachim withheld tribute from Nebuchadnezzar (2 Kings 24:2). Some years later, Moab was said to have been among the Phoenician and Palestinian states that Zedekiah ineffectually attempted to enlist in rebellion against Neo-Babylonia (Jer. 27:2). In 582, Nebuchadnezzar defeated and subjected Moab (Josephus, *Antiquities*, 10.181–82).[119]

Ammon became independent at the breakup of Solomon's kingdom. According to the Chronicler, Ammonites, Moabites, and Edomites attacked

Jehoshaphat in the wilderness of Judah between Jerusalem and the Dead Sea, but the tradition is problematic (2 Chron. 20:1, 10, 20, 22–23). Ammon was among the coalition of regional states that opposed Shalmaneser III at the battle of Qarqar, indicating cordial relations with Israel at the time. Uzziah and Jotham of Judah are reported to have received tribute from Ammon, the latter for at least a three-year period (2 Chron. 26:8; 27:5). Ammon was one of the Neo-Babylonian vassals that participated in raids against Jerusalem during Jehoiakim's reign. Rumor had it that Baalis, king of Ammon, instigated the assassination of Gedaliah, Neo-Babylonian governor of Judah after 586, at the hands of a surviving member of the Judahite royal family (Jer. 40:14). If so, Ammon may have been openly rebelling against Neo-Babylonia and perhaps hoping to incite Judah to renewed rebellion under the leadership of the assassin Ishmael, who was of Davidic lineage. If Moab was drawn into the same insurrection, we may have the reason for Nebuchadnezzar attacking Ammon and Moab in 582, and perhaps at that time abolishing the kingship in both lands.[120]

Unlike Moab and Ammon, who gained their independence when Solomon's kingdom broke apart, Edom, which had been garrisoned by David, seems to have remained in Judahite hands under the supervision of a deputy governor (2 Sam. 8:14; 2 Kings 22:47). The continued control of Edom apparently allowed Jehoshaphat to attempt to restore Red Sea maritime trade, but during his son's reign Edom revolted and set up its own king (2 Kings 8:20). Decades later, Amaziah raided Edom but did not conquer it (2 Kings 14:7). The Red Sea port of Elath, which may have been retaken during Judahite expansion under Uzziah, was recovered by Edom while Ahaz was occupied with the Israelite-Damscene siege of Jerusalem (2 Kings 16:6). Edom, in company with the other Transjordanian states, paid regular tribute to the Assyrians from Tiglath-pileser III to Ashurbanipal, and like Moab provided conscript labor and troops for their overlords. When the Neo-Babylonians mustered their vassal forces against Jerusalem, Edom is not named among the attackers. The hostility of biblical traditions toward Edomite behavior at this time seems to have been directed at the settlement of Edomites in southern Judah following the fall of Jerusalem. Ascertaining the details of Edomite-Judahite relations is complicated by the apparent extended use of "Edom" to include a large part of the eastern Negeb into which Edomites had been moving for decades prior to the fall of the kingdom of Judah.[121]

In their interchanges with Israel and Judah, Edom and Moab in particular may not have been operating in all periods as unified or stable polities. Tribal or kin-related social organization was strong in all three lands, and the line between strong chiefdoms and tribal kingdoms may have oscillated from period to period. Ammon appears to have had the most stable and developed monarchic rule, with Moab often split between its northern tableland and southern mountains, and Edom probably least focalized around any single governing center.

The Philistine city-states of Gaza, Gath, Ashkelon, Ashdod, and Ekron, located on the coast to the southwest of Judah, are sometimes named individually in the records and sometimes referred to collectively as "Philistines." For the most part, each Philistine state pursued its own strategies, and thus they were seldom, if ever, united. Although David blocked their attempt to dominate the highlands of Israel and Judah, they remained independent throughout subsequent centuries, engaging in intermittent warfare with Israel and Judah. They battled with Israel after the split of the kingdoms (1 Kings 15:27; 16:15) and, more than a century later, joined Edom and the Arab tribes in a seesaw struggle with Judah. As the last "jumping off" point for Egypt, they were repeatedly embroiled in the imperial endeavors of Assyria, Egypt, and Neo-Babylonia, sometimes as compliant satellite states and sometimes as rebels. Tiglath-pileser III installed local rulers in the Philistine city-states as vassals and put down rebellions, as did his successors Sargon II and Sennacherib. In the revolt against Sennacherib, presumably led by Hezekiah of Jerusalem, only Ashkelon and Ekron participated, the latter as the result of a popular revolt that delivered the king Padi, who remained loyal to Assyria, into the hand of Hezekiah for detention. When the revolt had been suppressed, Sennacherib awarded the loyal Philistine city-states with large parts of the territory of western Judah. In order to conquer Egypt, Esarhaddon tightened his grip on the Philistine city-states. Even though they themselves were not maritime powers on the scale of the Phoenician ports, the Philistine city-states did provide access to the sea, in addition to their favorable location astride the coastal highway, so that it was in the interest of Judah either to dominate them or to be on good relations with them. One can perhaps legitimately speculate that, no matter what the status of diplomatic relations between Philistine city-states and Judah, those engaged in trade probably found ways to sustain the exchange of goods that was profitable for the ruling elites.[122]

As for the royal ideologies of Judah and Israel vis-à-vis neighboring states, the fullest information comes from the report of a military clash between Israel and Moab in the mid-ninth century. Mesha's stela, which reports the Moabite king's successful revolt against domination by the Omrid dynasty, indicates that he regarded his triumph as the achievement of the god Chemosh, in direct opposition to the Israelite god Yahweh. The presumed contest between the Tyrian Baal and the Israelite Yahweh during the Omrid dynasty is of a different order, since it involved two states in close diplomatic connection who were adhering to the international protocol of the time, which provided for a foreign deity to be given diplomatic status in a host state. It remains an unsettled issue as to whether Ahab and Jezebel actually intended to pose an exclusive choice between Baal and Yahweh, and it may be further questioned whether the Elijah of tradition is correctly represented as fanatically insistent on the exclusive worship of Yahweh at the state level. The prevailing conception in interstate affairs seems to have been that when states were in league, they honored one another's religious cults, but when they were at war, their deities were believed to be at war with one another and thus totally engaged in battle on behalf of their devotees.

Certain traditions referring to earlier times also have a bearing on this issue of the interface of state deities. A confused tradition in Judges 11 concerning territorial claims between Ammon and Israel, which incongruously identifies the Moabite god Chemosh as the chief Ammonite deity, articulates the concept of "ordeal by battle," with the victorious party justified in concluding that its deity has won "the test" (Judges 11:27). The reported capture of the ark by the Philistines during the days of Samuel's leadership, and its subsequent return to Israel, is another intriguing tradition. According to some interpretations, it reflects the motif of capture of an enemy's gods, which might be displayed in the victor's capital but might also on occasion be returned to the conquered devotees as a "magnanimous" symbolic gesture.[123] The biblical records of the divided monarchy and the parallel extrabiblical documents have little to say about this sort of overt confrontation of deities. The address of the Assyrian official to Hezekiah and the besieged inhabitants of Judah (2 Kings 18:19–35) bespeaks the cunning of Assyrian propaganda, but the argument as elaborated appears to have been shaped from a later Judahite reformist perspective. No doubt, royal state ideologies played a part in international relations, including the sealing of treaties, but their deployment in the sector of interstate relations we are surveying is not known in any great detail. Spotty references, however, do appear in prophetic literature. Hosea announces that Assyria will carry off the golden calf, analogous to the Philistine seizure of the ark (Hos. 10:5–6), and Ezekiel refers to a Neo-Babylonian/Judahite treaty sworn to by the deities of both parties (Ezek. 17:1–21).

Relations with the Great Powers. The history of Israelite and Judahite relations with the great powers of the ancient Near East has been recited earlier, and our review of state relations in Syro-Palestine has noted the many instances in which the affairs of the small states, including Israel and Judah, were entangled. During the periods when the great powers were quiescent and uninvolved in Syro-Palestine, regional states were able to pursue their goals unfettered by the intrusion of imperial powers. It was in just such a "great-power vacuum" that tribal Israel arose and became a state under David and Solomon. Similar recessions of foreign power permitted Israelite political ascendency under Omri and Jeroboam II and Judahite florescence under Azariah=Uzziah and again under Josiah.

With the exception of pharaoh Sheshonk's invasion of Judah and Israel, which was not followed up by further Egyptian actions, Israel and Judah continued without threat from great powers until the Assyrian invasion of Syria in the mid-ninth century. Momentarily blocked by the coalition of states in which Israel participated, Assyria returned after a decade to impose its formal dominion over Israel and its neighboring states to the north. Occupied elsewhere for some decades, Assyria returned to reassert its dominion at the opening of the eighth century. Another period of relief from foreign intervention ensued, only to be followed by renewed and sustained Assyrian dominion at mid-century, issuing shortly in the demise of the northern kingdom.

Judah, lying just outside the area of Assyrian dominion until Tiglath-pileser III's campaigns in the last part of the eighth century, enjoyed two centuries without threats from the major powers. However, when the advancing Assyrian conquests reached Judah, it succumbed voluntarily, later unsuccessfully rebelled, and thereafter remained under Assyrian tutelage as a vassal state until the waning of the Assyrian empire. The brief revival of Judahite independence under Josiah probably occurred within the orbit of Egyptian power in the wake of Assyrian withdrawal from Palestine and Syria. Egypt tightened its control on Judah as it prepared to face off with the Neo-Babylonians. With Egyptian defeat, the Neo-Babylonians assumed dominion over Judah until, after successive rebellions, its state structure was demolished.

The impact of the great powers on the ability of Israel and Judah to carry out the vital functions of statehood was both direct and indirect. The most direct impact was the annual tribute required of subject states by the imperial conquerors. The lists of tribute goods in the Assyrian annals give an idea of the substantial payments exacted in precious metals and luxury goods. These payments laid waste to the royal treasuries which had been amassed from a variety of revenue sources, such as government-sponsored commerce, tolls on transit trade, taxation of the general populace, and, on occasion, tribute taken from other small states. When Israel or Judah rebelled, heavy indemnity payments were customarily added to the annual tribute. In voluntarily submitting to Assyria, Menahem of Israel paid tribute "in advance" in order to curry favor and secure from his overlord lenient terms that would assure him a secure vassal status, and it is likely that Ahaz of Judah did the same when he turned to Assyria to lift the siege of Jerusalem by Israel and Damascus. It is further reported that Menahem raised the thousand talents of silver by a levy on propertied citizens ("men of means"), at a rate of fifty shekels each, which yields a total of 60,000 persons taxed if the payment was required in one lump sum, but possibly a smaller number if the payment was spread over more than one year. In Judah, pharaoh Neco imposed a tribute of a talent of gold and one hundred talents of silver, which Jehoiakim secured by assessing a tax on "the people of the land," roughly equivalent to "the men of means" taxed by Menahem.

Further, imperial control over Israel and Judah resulted in disruption of agriculture and stockbreeding due to devastation of fields, orchards, and pasturage during military campaigns. Amid the turbulence of invasion and siege it was difficult to tend fields, orchards, and flocks, as villagers fled to walled cities or were impressed into military service. The flow of trade was likely to be similarly diminished. Of course, the imperial powers prided themselves on establishing peace and prosperity in the regions brought under their control, but this claim is open to serious question in the light of Assyrian and Neo-Babylonian policies. Despite the "civilizing" rhetoric of imperial powers, the overall aim of their policies was to maintain loyal subjects whose productivity would swell the empire's coffers. To do so, imperial powers had to establish a measure of social and economic stability, but the imperial ledger sheet of success was calculated not by the benefits accorded to subjected colonial peoples but by the accumulation of wealth and power in the imperial heartland. This self-serving imperial program was especially evident in the regions reorganized and incorporated as Assyrian provinces, as was the fate of the northern kingdom, but it was also at work in vassal states such as Judah. The survival and expansion of empires absolutely depended on their drawing from conquered regions surpluses that would at least offset the costs of their military and administrative investments and optimally would "turn a profit."

The indirect effects of imperial politics on Israel and Judah were far-reaching. The overshadowing presence of empires impacted the stability of smaller state regimes, as factions within the state establishment opted for divergent strategies to oppose or to collaborate with the hegemonic states that threatened them. The series of short reigns and assassinations in the closing decades of Israelite independence, as well as the shifting loyalties and tenuous power of the Judahite kings who followed Josiah, amply illustrate the difficulty of sustaining continuity and coherence of leadership in small states under heavy external pressure. Moreover, as we have noted, the intrusion of the great powers added yet another layer of complexity to the already tangled relations among the small states. Under pressure from Assyria, Damascus and Israel could by turns be enemies or allies, and Judah under Hezekiah and later under Zedekiah made strenuous efforts to develop antiimperial coalitions with Philistine and Transjordan states that had been historic enemies. Some of these solicited states responded favorably, others remained aloof, and some either joined the imperial powers' counterattack or benefited from the spoils of Judah's defeats. It was difficult for any of these small Syro-Palestinian states to know who might be relied upon as friend or foe, as the patterns and balances of power shifted frequently and unpredictably over time. Israel and Judah were just as vulnerable as other Syro-Palestinian states in this regard.

The challenge of legitimizing Israelite and Judahite regimes in the face of imperialist military power and ideological contestation was demanding. The "proof" of the legitimacy of political order was in the power to assert and maintain control over all contrary centers and claims of power. Religion was the primary purveyor of ideological power. When ancient Near Eastern documents treating the relations of states mention religion, in most instances they carry the explicit or implicit claim that the gods favor whatever state of affairs is recorded or endorsed in the documents. Annals of military campaigns and victories celebrate the triumphs of the winner's god(s), the obverse of which is the defeat and humiliation of the loser's god(s). Treaties between states regularly call upon the gods of all parties to sanction compliance with the treaty terms, with dire threats of divine punishment for those who would dare to violate them.

In Judah, royal psalms sung in the Jerusalem temple participate in this political theology as they assert the manifestation of Yahweh's supremacy through the capacity of the king and his armies to dominate other nations and their deities. The Davidic and Zion motifs of the sanctity and universal sway of Yahweh and his anointed are, to be sure, highly mythological in the grandiosity of their claims, but they are nonetheless rooted in the tenacity with which the rulers of all states—however small and weak—strove to ground their existence in divine will and to surround their office with religious trappings. The speech attributed to the Assyrian emissary who attempted to dissuade Jerusalemites from following Hezekiah in rebellion, while obviously colored by its pro-Judahite telling, is premised on a thoroughly ancient Near Eastern concept that the Assyrians honed to perfection: that the deity of the conquerors is more powerful than all other gods and thus it is useless for states to depend upon their own lesser gods to deliver them. Of course, there was no simple one-to-one correspondence between states and religious cults. The worship of particular deities often predated and subsequently outlived states in which they were honored. Various manifestations of the same god might be paramount in several states, including those at war with one another, as, for example, in the Baal-worshiping states of Syria and Phoenicia and in the Yahweh-worshiping states of Israel and Judah.

The ongoing rise and fall of states and their deities posed serious problems of meaning for political and religious collectivities whenever they were on the losing side in diplomatic and military contests. One way of dealing with the threatened collapse of meaning in the wake of such political loss was to explain the loss as divine "punishment" for some "sin" against the gods. When the Assyrians experienced reversals, they were sometimes explained by a ruler's failure to support the royal cult in a proper manner or by his impiety in destroying a temple whose sanctity should have been respected. The present form of the biblical accounts of the states of Israel and Judah is rife with such explanations, and it is easy to see that to a large extent they are sweeping ex post facto explanations from the point of view of Judah-oriented Yahweh worshipers looking back after the states had fallen. Nonetheless, it would have been true to state theology at the time to look for cultic infractions as the reasons for political setbacks. The "purges" and "reforms" attributed to Jehu in the north and to Hezekiah and Josiah in the south, however overlaid by later constructions, may very well have been driven, at least in part, by the desire to "purify" religious practices in order to secure for the state the endangered blessing of Yahweh.

In some cases it is apparent that religious reforms served very practical administrative purposes. To the extent that Hezekiah may have closed high places throughout Judah, the measure may have been a part of his plan to concentrate all material and religious resources in Jerusalem, in preparation for his rebellion against Assyria. Josiah's alleged reforms along similar lines may have been intended to strengthen the political and fiscal power of Jerusalem over against middle and lower echelons of the bureaucracy that were draining away resources at the expense of the political center. Faced with the relentless and overbearing military power and religious ideology of Assyria, the felt need of the state to be on the best possible footing with

Yahweh would have been acute, and for the Judahite regime that meant a strengthening and purifying of the cult of Yahweh in Jerusalem. Insofar as this was a step on the way to eventual monotheism, the concentrating of official worship at Jerusalem may best be viewed as a kind of "political monolatry" intended to maximize and legitimate the power of the state. Whether there were comparable reforms of the Yahweh cult in the capital of Samaria, or in the state shrines at Dan and Bethel, is not evident in the sources, although it appears that the prophet Hosea sounded the need for just such cleansing of forms of worship that did not sufficiently distinguish between Baal and Yahweh.[124]

Domestic Affairs and the Political Agenda of Israel and Judah

Relations within the Political Center. The political center may be regarded as that body of people within the state who made the principal decisions to deploy political power in order to secure, defend, replenish, expand, and legitimate the governing institutions. In the absence of written state constitutions and the dearth of archival records, the scope and configuration of the political centers in Israel and Judah can only be approximately determined.[125] The political center would, in any event, have included the monarch, members of the royal family, the chief officers of the main branches of government responsible for the chains of command that carried out state decisions, and advisors to the court who might have official assignment or might be consulted on an ad hoc basis. Influential members of the royal family would have included sons of the monarch, one of whom may have been coregent in certain reigns, other close male relatives, and the queen mother, who is often named in the notations about Judahite kings. The chief officers would have included a commander-in-chief of the army, a secretary of state or protocol officer, a chief scribe responsible for state records and diplomatic correspondence, a steward in charge of the royal household and its estates, an administrator of the tax system, an overseer of conscripted labor, and one or more chief priests. The exact duties accompanying the official titles that appear in biblical lists and narratives, which are fuller for Judah than for Israel, are subject to a range of interpretations, and it may be that there were offices of high rank not mentioned in the sources.

Presumably these chief officials were directly accountable to the king, and it is both reasonable and supported by the sources that they would have consulted with one another, both at the summons of the monarch and at their own prompting as occasion required. There is no certainty that they formed a cabinet that met with regularity and adhered to stated rules and fixed agendas. There is also no evidence, as has been sometimes claimed, that there existed a council or assembly of chief citizens with consultative or legislative powers. The collectivity called "the people of the land," who had great political clout at certain junctures in Judahite politics, is not depicted as a formal state body but as an influential bloc of citizens, varying in composition from time to time, who acted in concert to shape the state in line with their convergent interests. It is apparent that some forceful chief officials exercised decisive influence on the crown, as is reported of Joab, David's army commander, and of the family of Shaphan under Josiah and subsequent Judahite rulers. The leading bureaucrats enjoyed emoluments of office that included not only their day-to-day support but also the assignment of estates whose proceeds were theirs to dispose of for personal profit. Whether these estates were theirs to enjoy only so long as they held office (prebendal estates) or were held in perpetuity and thus inheritable by their descendants (patrimonial estates) is not evident. There is a definite tendency in monarchic state administration for prebendal estates to evolve into patrimonial estates under weak rulers, but the terms of bureaucratic estate-holding in Israel and Judah are not spelled out. There are, however, indications in the biblical records and in seal impressions that offices were sometimes held within one family over two or more generations, which in itself would both signify and promote a drift from prebendal to patrimonial holdings.[126]

Unity of viewpoint and action within the political centers of Israel and Judah is both what the ruling elites hoped for in the pursuit of their goals and "the public face" or "propaganda spin" that they put on their policies and actions. Such asserted unity fluctuated dramatically, if only because the clusters of interests that found expression in the state apparatus were not easily prioritized and may in fact at times have been contradictory. Each new challenge to state authority and power might precipitate realignment of the cliques or factions within the bureaucracy. Fissures within the political center could be exploited by domestic parties and foreign powers that sought to bring about changes in the state regime or to force it to submit to imperial control. The most expansive political narratives in the Hebrew Bible reveal frequent tensions and conflicts within the ruling center over such issues as the royal succession in the reign of David, the proper state religious policy under Ahab, and the correct stance to adopt toward threats from foreign powers during the last decades of Israel's and Judah's independence. Many of the assassinations and power coups related in the biblical records are depicted as originating within the political center by army commanders, "servants" of the king, and even by members of the royal family. The cohesion of the political center could be eroded by weak and indecisive rulers, by contention among rivals for succession to the throne, by ambitious bureaucrats striving to carve out private power domains, by adverse harvests and food shortages, by failure to meet the grievances of socially powerful sectors of the populace, by serious military reversals, and by disputes over how to respond to threats from abroad. In sum, it is evident that the governing effectiveness of the political center could not be safely taken for granted by any ruler but had to be constantly reassessed, reorganized, and shored up in the face of changing circumstances within and beyond state boundaries.

Relations between the Political Center and Its Primary Beneficiaries. The precise line between bureaucrats directly in the service of the crown and other major players in Israelite society and politics who stood to benefit from state policies and actions cannot be clearly drawn. The bureaucratic arms of the central regime reached in widening circles to encompass provincial and local jurisdictions. While the levels and functions of the bureaucratic hierarchy are not spelled out, military and forced labor conscription and collection of taxes required a network of personnel serving the state. It is likely that levies of labor and revenues were laid on social entities such as villages or, in some instances, on categories of freeholders. Full-time agents of the crown doubtless organized the implementation of these imposts, but their success depended on the cooperation of village elders, who were probably responsible for fulfilling quotas of conscripted labor and taxed goods.

The gray area where governmental appointees worked with civil leaders at regional and local levels of administration was a ground for contestation between the demands of the state and the concerns of local communities to harbor and control their resources. This contestation deepened in times of scarcity of resources due to crop failures, debt foreclosures, warfare, or excessive state demands. Local leadership warily assessed the performance of the central authorities in delivering the promised benefits of economic prosperity, domestic law and order, and protection from foreign powers, carefully weighing the goods and values received against the costs of surrendering local resources to the state. This calculus by local leadership was complicated by an ebb and flow in the capacity of the state to justify itself ideologically and/or to enforce its will on the subject populace. Likewise, the capacity and readiness of the state to provide special incentives for cooperation by local leaders, such as tax concessions or assistance in agricultural development and public safety, had a marked effect on the willingness of grass-roots leaders to "deliver the goods" to Samaria or Jerusalem.

Insofar as the state prospered in realizing its goals of securing, defending, replenishing, expanding, and legitimating political power, certain sectors of the populace wielding social power stood to benefit appreciably from governmental policies and projects. Chief among these beneficiaries would have been big landholders and merchants. But, again, no absolute divide can be drawn between civil and governmental beneficiaries of the state. In addition to their possession of landed estates granted by virtue of their office, it is likely that state officials also carried on land acquisition and commercial ventures "on the side." Social, economic, and political networks were enmeshed. This entanglement could prompt divided loyalties, as state officials pursued interests outside the bounds of their assigned duties, and citizens of wealth and social standing prospered at times from a burgeoning state and suffered loss or decline when the state languished or took crippling actions against them. In good times there might well be sufficient resources to enrich both the state and the wider circle of wealthy landholders and merchants, but in times of retrenchment due to drought, declining trade, or diplomatic and military reversals, the division of diminished resources could become an arena of acute struggle between the political center and its dependent beneficiaries.

In Israel, under the Omrids and Jeroboam II, and in Judah, under Uzziah, the early reign of Hezekiah, and the reforms of Josiah, state prosperity no doubt spilled over to the advantage of wealthy and socially prominent citizens. But in hard times, illustrated by the levies of Menahem on Israelite men of means and of Jehoiakim on prosperous Judahites in order to pay tribute to Assyria and Egypt, those who had come to expect the state to prosper and enhance their positions could be cruelly disappointed. To be sure, nongovernmental elites often had little immediate alternative but to comply with the state, but their shaken confidence in and loyalty to heavy-handed regimes offered fertile ground for plots to replace the discredited rulers with those more protective of the conspirators' socioeconomic interests.

It is apparent, therefore, that the relations within the political center and the center's relations with its traditional beneficiaries were complexly intertwined and delicately balanced. The political center required the consent and cooperation of its leading citizens, and the leading citizens required a state structure to protect and enhance their wealth and status. But whenever the interests of center and beneficiaries clashed, there was fertile soil for political instability and for the emergence of peripheral domestic power centers that could enfeeble the central regime to the point of ineffectuality or strike it down with the concurrence of disaffected leaders in civil society and in governmental service. Because the social and economic interests of subordinate state officials and of leading citizens of means frequently overlapped, and in some cases were identical, weakened state rule could invite insubordination and conspiracy among officials who, in coalition with their civilian counterparts, sought to replace the reigning monarch. This state of affairs seems to be precisely what is referred to rather obscurely in the biblical records as conspiratorial initiatives of "the people of the land," that is, leading citizens, and/or "servants of the king," that is, state officials, to assassinate kings they opposed and to install kings who would be compliant with their priorities and policy preferences.

When a broad alignment of interests among leading figures in state service and civil society developed, it was possible to enlist the army in backing a seizure of state power. The rifts that were opened up by these struggles for control of the state might extend deep into civil society, to the point that the struggle between Tibni and Omri for the throne of Israel approximated a civil war, said to have lasted for four years, in which the populace was evenly split between the two contestants. Even if this is a rhetorical exaggeration, it attests to the social chaos that political rivalries both reflected and exacerbated. The same disintegration of the social fabric appears to have attended the succession of royal usurpers in the last years of the kingdom of Israel and the enervating battles between pro- and anti-Babylonian political sympathizers preceding Judah's eclipse, extending even to the murder of Gedaliah after the fall of Jerusalem.

Relations between the Political Center and the General Populace. Given the frequent claim that biblical traditions place great value on all members of the community, it is somewhat surprising that there is precious little information in the Hebrew Bible to single out the impact of the central government on subjects of the state who had little wealth or social power or to indicate the attitudes of these rank-and-file citizens toward the state. References to the wider public are normally undiscriminating in their generality, and the narratives that highlight individuals vis-à-vis the political center are minimal, apart from the encounter of prophets with political authorities, which requires special consideration.[127]

There are, to be sure, numerous references to "all the people" or "all Israel" that signify the general populace gathered on important occasions, such as the dedication of the temple, the assembly of northerners to deliberate on Rehoboam's kingship, the gathering on Mt. Carmel for the contest between Yahweh and Baal, those summoned to hear Jehu's address at Samaria, the crowd at Joash's coronation, and the assembly called by Josiah for a reading of the law. In the last two instances, the people join kings Joash and Josiah in covenants of loyalty to Yahweh. It is obvious that the descriptor "all the people" is hyperbole, since the entire populace could not possibly have been in attendance on any of these occasions. The import of the term is rather to indicate the general will of the people expressed in the unanimity of mind and action on the part of all those present. In fact, we scarcely hear the actual voices of the people assembled. For example, the grievances of northerners expressed to Rehoboam and their subsequent announcement of separation from the House of David, as well as the acclamation of Yahweh as God by the people on Mt. Carmel, are delivered in unison as if by a massed chorus. It is evident that the sole function of "all the people" is to corroborate the actions of their political and religious leaders. The refusal of the northerners to acquiesce in Rehoboam's rule is sign enough for the Judahite editor of the story that they are politically treasonous and religiously apostate.

Interestingly, there are a few instances of subjects who approach kings as petitioners with complaints of injustice for which they seek redress. The woman of Tekoa asks David to reprieve her only son from capital punishment (2 Sam. 14:4–11); two harlots who claim the same child bring their dispute to Solomon (1 Kings 3:16–28); a starving woman who shared her cannibalized son with another woman complains to a king of Israel when the second woman reneges on her promise to do likewise (2 Kings 6:24–31); and a woman of Shunem appeals to a king of Israel to restore the house and land that someone has expropriated while she was living abroad (2 Kings 8:1–6). Each of these incidents has a somewhat different narrative function and might be dismissed as folkloric "window dressing," except for the account of Absalom's currying of favor among petitioners who come to David for judgment but receive no hearing because "no one is delegated by the king to hear you" (2 Sam. 15:1–6). This report suggests that there was a possibility for complaints to be brought to the king in his role as chief justice of the land, which he might settle with the help of deputized assistants. Who was eligible for such a royal hearing, and whether it was often granted, is unclear, especially in light of the neglect of royal justice that Absalom played upon to stir up his revolt.

These stories about suppliants of royal justice trade on the motif of "the just king," widespread in the ancient Near East and abundantly attested in biblical psalms and prophecies, often with exalted rhetoric, but the actual participation of the king in the administration of justice is seldom mentioned. For the most part, it is believed that administration of justice was in the hands of local elders, and that only selected cases came to the king's attention. The Deuteronomic lawbook prescribes a court in Jerusalem where a priest or priests and a judge are to decide cases "too difficult" for local settlement (Deut. 17:8–13), but the king is not said to be responsible for appointing them, and if this provision was ever enacted, it was probably only in the reign of Josiah. There is a report that early on in Judah Jehoshaphat appointed judges throughout Judah and a corps of priests and heads of families in Jerusalem "to decide disputed cases" (2 Chron. 19:4–8), but the claim is strongly colored by the Chronicler's theology and reads like a retrojection of Deuteronomy's appellate court scheme into a much earlier time. Administration of justice in local jurisdictions is attested in the north when the trumped-up charges against Naboth are brought in the presence of the elders and nobles of Jezreel, who impose the death sentence on him (1 Kings 21:5–14), although Naboth, in possession of a vineyard and living in proximity to the palace, was probably a man of some means. Presumably, however, the same local judicial system would have applied to all members of the community, whatever their social station.

We possess one bit of extrabiblical information about how a poor petitioner might seek redress of a wrong. It appears in a letter dictated by a reaper who claims that, even though he has finished harvesting and storing the grain, his overseer has taken his cloak without reason. The aggrieved suppliant asks an unnamed official to intervene and see to it that his cloak is returned. The text, found in a small fortress in the coastal plain, dates to the last part of the seventh century B.C.E., when Judah under Josiah was expanding into former Philistine territory. The suppliant may have been a corvée worker whose cloak was taken as security to make certain he finished his work, or perhaps as a penalty imposed by the overseer for allegedly not completing his work. The official approached may have been a district governor or the army commander in charge of the fortress. Interestingly, a relevant biblical law forbids keeping overnight a debtor's cloak given in pledge, since the outer garment also served as a blanket for the indigent (Ex. 22:26–27), and a prophet alludes to "garments taken in pledge" as floor coverings beside altars for the drunken revelry of social oppressors (Amos 2:8). That the wronged field worker thought it neither fruitless nor too dangerous to appeal to an official "over the head" of his boss indicates that he entertained some confidence in invoking governmental authority "to do the right thing," although we have no way of knowing how typical this hapless reaper's petition was or how frequently such appeals brought corrective results. In any event, his plea is reminiscent of the Egyptian text entitled "The Eloquent Peasant," which relates a similar wrong that the plaintiff pursued through several judicial levels until his case was heard in pharaoh's court.[128]

A special case is represented by the reports of prophets who confronted kings or royal officials, sometimes to console and encourage them, but more often to challenge and condemn them. Such direct encounters are reported to have been initiated by Nathan, Ahijah of Shiloh, Jehu ben Hanani, Elijah, Elisha, Amos, Isaiah, and Jeremiah. In a few instances the meetings were instigated by the political center itself, as with Micaiah ben Imlah, Elisha, Isaiah, and Jeremiah. Other prophetic words directed at kings and/or the ruling establishment may have been delivered only at a distance from the royal court, such as the critiques of Hosea, Micah of Moresheth, and Zephaniah. This is not the place to inquire into these encounters in all their variety of circumstance and message. The primary question here is whether or not we are able to regard these prophets as "ordinary" subjects of the crown. There is the disputed issue of whether some of the prophets held office in the royal court or the state cult. Moreover, there is an unre-solvable question about the socioeconomic status of particular prophets. How we view the religiopolitical and socioeconomic location of prophets has a direct bearing on the extent of their contact with ordinary Israelites and the extent to which they represented the feelings and concerns of sub-jects of the crown who were not among its chief beneficiaries.

Although there is no satisfactory generalization concerning the social location of prophets, it should be noted that prophets articulated a wide range of opinion and judgment about high politics that repeatedly under-scored the destructive effects of the political center on ordinary subjects of the state. This was particularly true in matters of debt servitude and land-grabbing, which impoverished small holders, in tandem with corruption of justice, which denied protection and redress to the victims. Indeed, some of the prophets take on the virtual role of "ombudsmen" on behalf of the victims of injustice, but this does not appear to be a position officially assigned to them by the state. Prophets are also critical of religious abuses and foreign policies that embroil the populace in wars and deportations.

In assessing their criticisms, it is admittedly not possible to know if all these prophetic words about state politics, or even their gist, were spoken in monarchic times, since their messages have been collected, edited, and expanded in poststate conditions. Nor can we draw a firm line in their crit-icisms between the abuses of political leaders and the abuses of privileged landholders and merchants not in government service. This may simply reflect the way in which the political center and its privileged beneficiaries worked in close coordination. It is at any rate clear that prophetic advocacy of the right of disprivileged Israelites to sustainable livelihood and fair treatment by those holding political power or favored by state power is expressed repeatedly. Not only the words attributed to prophets, but some of the narratives about them, particularly in the case of Elisha, paint a picture of very harsh conditions for ordinary Israelites, due to famine, debt, and siege warfare. Indeed the bands of prophets around Elisha appear to be drawn from lower levels of society, and their conventicles are at least directed in part at providing socioeconomic security for these prophetic disciples and their families.[129]

All in all, the large majority of subjects in Israel and Judah are little evident in the biblical traditions. They do not display any direct voice in government, although they are the targets of governmental actions that require of them taxation to support the crown, assessments to fund the state religion, corvée labor on public projects, and impressment into military service. The burden that these obligations placed upon the people is summarized eloquently in words attributed to Samuel when Israel seeks a king (1 Sam. 8:10–18). It has been common to see this text as an ex post facto judgment on the reign of Solomon, but whenever it was composed, it aptly describes the reservations and resistances of independent-minded subsistence farmers that doubtless formed an undertow throughout the history of the kingdoms. Although we have few details as to how these exactions were organized and administered, or at what levels of demand they operated from king to king, it is certain that the states could not have functioned without considerable demands on the populace and without at least a moderate level of compliance. While the deathblow was delivered to both states by an imperial power, the domestic health of Israel and Judah depended in large measure on the morale of their subjects in feeling reasonably well served by political authorities and on the readiness of the general populace to respond to state demands without excessive coercion. The scattered, and largely indirect, evidence we possess on the degree of consent and compliance granted to the political center by the general populace points in two directions: on the one hand, general compliance, whether due to actual consent or to fear and inertia; on the other hand, considerable disquiet, resistance, and, on occasion, open rebellion.[130]

ISRAEL'S COLONIAL POLITICS

We have seen that the reports of the trajectory of Israel's colonial politics related in the Hebrew Bible are sketchy, discontinuous, and opaque to the point of requiring a large measure of speculation in attempting to comprehend the political conditions in which the predominantly cultural and religious traditions of the colonial era took shape. The highly selective biblical scenarios of colonial times give the impression that the cultural and religious vitality and creativity of Judah was sustained solely by the Babylonian exiles, at whose initiative the homeland was restored within a viable political framework sponsored by a benign Persian Empire. Once the temple was rebuilt and civil and religious order secured, Judah became the stable center of a people unified in all essential cultural and religious matters. On this telling of colonial politics, the Judahites and Samarians who remained in the land and the dispersed Judahites who did not return to the homeland have no place in the story. These absent elements of colonial politics need to be supplied by information from other sources and by a large measure of inferential reasoning.

Extrabiblical Data: Material and Textual Evidence

In Neo-Babylonian Judah there is evidence of the destruction of Jerusalem and of a number of sites in the shephelah and Negeb, but in Benjamin and around Bethlehem occupation continued. Burial finds include jewelry and other prestige items,[131] suggesting that "the poor of the land" were not the sole occupants of Judah. Little new building is evidenced apart from Tell en-Nasbeh, probably to be identified as Mizpah, the headquarters of the Neo-Babylonian province. While Jerusalem was extensively destroyed, there are some signs of continuing modest habitation in and around the city. No new cultural or political elements are evident in the material remains; instead, "close scrutiny shows that the real turning point in terms of material culture came only at the end of the sixth century when Persian authority was established, new pottery types appear and Attic ware was imported from Greece."[132] The limited archaeological evidence suggests that the Babylonian provincial administration may not have been as intensive or exacting as prior Assyrian and subsequent Persian governance.

In Persian Judah, there is evidence of rebuilt and newly founded settlements in Judah proper and garrisons at sites in Judah, the Negeb, and northern Sinai. A considerable corpus of seals and bullae attests to the presence of native officials, merchants, and scribes, as do many stamped handles from jars probably assigned to collect taxes in kind. Silver coinage and Greek pottery become increasingly common in the late Persian period, attesting to a thriving trade in international goods. The boundaries of the Persian province of Yehud=Judah are disputed, some scholars including the lowlands and coastal plain and others restricting the province to the hill country and its desert fringe, an issue that archaeological data do not appear to resolve in the absence of documentation. Estimates of the population of Persian Judah have been significantly downsized in recent years, throwing doubt on the nearly 50,000 returnees claimed in Ezra 2=Nehemiah 7:1–70. One recent estimate, based on an exhaustive review of the archaeological data, claims a population of about 13,000 prior to the mid-fifth century, increasing to about 20,000 thereafter. Estimates of the population of Jerusalem range from 1,500 to 4,500 at most. The vast majority of settlements were small villages.[133]

Although there are no texts from Judah itself, a well-preserved collection of late fifth- to early fourth-century Aramaic papyri from a military colony in upper Egypt illuminates the cultural, legal, and religious conditions of life in one dispersed community of Judahites who maintained connections with Jerusalem and Samaria but did not slavishly follow the practices of either home community.[134] In addition, fragmentary legal or administrative papyri have been found attached to bullae from Samaria belonging to a group of upper-class citizens who fled the capital when Alexander crushed a rebellion in Samaria. Among them the family of Sanballat, governor of Samaria, is mentioned.[135] As for information about Judahites who remained in Babylonia, we encounter several Judahite names in the documents of a business house in Nippur operated by the Murashu family.[136] Josephus, in writing of Persian and Hellenistic Judah, often differs from and supplements the biblical accounts, but his reliability on many matters is subject to dispute.[137]

In the late Persian and Ptolemaic periods, Greek traders and settlers are increasingly evident in coastal Palestine, with the previous Phoenician-style architecture giving way to Hellenistic design.[138] Cities with a majority Greek population and polity are founded, largely in the coastal region, but also in Samaria and the Judahite shephelah. The Zenon papyri from mid-third century Egypt reveal that the Ptolemies tightened the economic exploitation of Palestine by developing and supervising estates that exported oil and wine.[139] Josephus reports on the political machinations involved in the Ptolemaic appointment of governors, high priests, and tax farmers in Judah, a competitive struggle that continued under Seleucid rulers as reported in 1 and 2 Maccabees.

Ben Sira, writing in Jerusalem about 175 B.C.E., is the only securely datable Judahite document in the long interval between Ezra–Nehemiah and the books of Daniel and Maccabees. This wisdom book celebrates temple and high priesthood and also exalts "torah." The author offers a rambling resume of Israelite history that covers many persons and themes of the Pentateuch and Prophets, but it is by no means clear that he is familiar with the finished form of those collections. Moreover, he does not recognize a closed canon of holy books, claiming in fact that his writing is on a par with the existing inspired books. Ben Sira makes no mention of Ezra but moves directly from Nehemiah's building projects to praise of his contemporary, the high priest Simon ben Onias. In encompassing several streams of Judahite tradition in his encyclopedic mind, Ben Sira betrays little direct interest in politics, writing it seems in "the calm before the storm" of Maccabean-Hasmonean turmoil.[140]

The considerable building projects of Maccabean and Hasmonean Judah are evident not only in Judah itself but in other parts of Palestine to which Hasmonean rule was extended by conquest. These include palaces and fortifications and some private dwellings. Some of this building may have been undertaken by Seleucid rulers during their efforts to pacify Palestine. Tombs of wealthy Hasmonean families are numerous in Jerusalem and its environs. While Hasmonean coins show a revival of the old Hebrew script, in place of the Aramaic script prevalent in Judah since the Persian period, there is an increase in Greek names among Judahites, including Hasmonean rulers, and the architecture and political culture of the Hasmoneans are thoroughly Hellenistic.[141]

While the archaeological remains and inscriptions from the colonial period are helpful in setting certain parameters for political developments and allow us to fill in a few details, they are insufficient to make up for the lack of a connected political history in the Hebrew Bible. It is only when we reach the Maccabean-Hasmonean period that a fairly full account of Judahite politics can be rendered.

From Centered Autonomous Politics to Dispersed Dependent Politics

With the collapse of the state of Judah in 586 B.C.E., Israelite politics ceased to be autonomous, with the exception of the brief revival of the Hasmonean state in 140–63 B.C.E. Fundamental political rights and powers now rested with the great empires within which Judah functioned as an administrative subunit. Considerable self-determination was allowed in matters deemed by the empires to be "internal affairs," but the sovereign powers essential to conduct diplomacy and warfare with other states and to raise and allocate revenues were reserved to the Neo-Babylonian, Persian, and Hellenistic overlords. The Judahite elite who served as administrators in the imperial systems were constrained by their obligations to the empires and by the need to remain in as favorable a position as possible with their fellow Judahites. The subordinate governing elite were deemed successful by the empires when they kept Judah politically pacified and economically profitable, and they were deemed successful by Judahites when they were able to gain from the empires concessions that enlarged the sociocultural and religious spheres for self-determination and improved the economic lot of the populace. Obviously, these two desiderata were not easily reconciled in formulating and enforcing administrative policies.

Moreover, the dispersion of Judahites throughout the ancient Near East, a majority of whom never returned to Judah, further decentered and diversified the political arrangements under which the heirs of Judahite culture and religion lived in such varied regions as Egypt, Babylonia, Arabia, and Syro-Palestine. The combination of dependent Judahite politics and dispersed Judahite communities had significant consequences.

For one thing, it is probable that the political arrangement in Judah was not duplicated in any other of the communities where dispersed Judahites lived. Judah, as a province of empire, was governed internally by a native administrative elite that was in direct touch with the imperial center. We have no evidence that Judahites elsewhere within the empires were constituted as provinces or districts within the imperial structure. Such information as we have about Judahites in Egypt during Persian and Hellenistic times indicates that their cultural and religious distinctiveness was on the whole recognized and tolerated but nevertheless subject at times to hostility and outright violence. The reasons for this relative "political disenfranchisement" of dispersed Judahites are not hard to come by. They probably never formed a majority of the populace in any of the regions they inhabited. More importantly, in these regions there had been no prior Judahite political entities, such as the former state of Judah represented in Palestine, which could have been convenient for the empires to reconstitute as viable administrative units.[142]

There is a second, often overlooked, consequence of this dependent political arrangement. Although Judah proper held some decisive advantages over the dispersed Judahites, it lacked the political power to enforce its religiocultural viewpoints outside its own borders except by persuasion. The persuasive power of restored Judah's religiocultural leadership rested on ideological and pragmatic grounds. Ideologically, restored Judah claimed continuity with the Judahite and larger Israelite past rooted in territory and tradition. Judah was the "homeland" of all dispersed Judahites, initially in a geographical sense and subsequently in a metaphorical sense. Pragmatically, restored Judah could offer particular institutional, ritual, and literary achievements as models for how dispersed Judahites might organize their cultural and religious life. Nonetheless, the geographical distance and difference in local conditions meant that the communities of dispersed Judahites charted their own courses without slavish imitation of the homeland. The Elephantine community of Judahites in Egypt at the end of the fifth century was probably typical of other such dispersed communities in its relations with the homeland. It consulted both with Jerusalem and Samaria on religious matters, but it had a temple, in defiance of Deuteronomic law, and it incorporated minor deities alongside Yahweh in its worship.

These loose, even optional, connections between the Judahite center and the Judahite periphery are probably due in part to there being less of a unified front on cultural and religious matters in Judah than often imagined. The considerable variety of streams of tradition represented by Deuteronomic, Priestly, Chronistic, prophetic, and wisdom literary corpuses may not have been as smoothly harmonized as implied by the usual view that the Pentateuch was canonized around 400 B.C.E. and the Prophets around 200 B.C.E. It remains unclear what body of laws Ezra is reported to have brought to Judah in the mid-fifth century, and if we mean by canonization that a uniform mode of interpreting and deriving standardized practice based on holy books has been established, then it can be correct to claim canonization only toward the end of the first century C.E.[143]

A fair summary of the interface between Judahite politics and Judahite culture and religion in the colonial period might be as follows. Although Judah was stripped of political sovereignty, sufficient politically protected social space was created for Judahite culture and religion to develop along multiple tracks, one in the restored homeland and the others in dispersed communities throughout the Near East. There were broad family resemblances among these Judahite communities but no unanimity that could be enforced, because of the absence of direct political leverage and because, even in Judah proper, no single harmonized version of culture and religion was established amid controversies and accommodations that fell short of producing a singular "Judaism."[144]

The Political and Transpolitical Matrix of the Hebrew Bible

We can correctly speak of the political factor in the development of the Hebrew Bible in a twofold sense. In the first place, there could have been no integral ongoing development of Judahite culture and religion without the political integument provided by the empires that permitted a restored Judah and largely tolerated Judahite cultural and religious practices throughout the ancient Near East. In this context, Judah as a province of empires was the "anchor point" of this far-flung development, because even when its specific practices were rejected or sharply modified, it served as a territorial and socioreligious reference point that provided a reservoir of memory and tradition, as well as a contemporary way of life to be taken into account by Judahites everywhere. Second, the lineaments of the development of the literary traditions that came to form the Hebrew Bible betray the significance of political factors in their production and preservation. Each of the several streams of tradition is stamped by issues of political power, both in their stance toward foreign nations and in their understanding of how power should be distributed and exercised in the Judahite community. These streams of tradition sometimes anachronistically overlay the political conditions of tribal and monarchic Israel with the obscuring veil of colonial political conditions. At other times they maintain a knowledgeable separation between colonial and precolonial ways of life, successfully preserving the outlines and considerable details of the precolonial past. That the specifics of the internal Judahite power struggles after 586 B.C.E. are so often "veiled" in the traditions, making the Haggai–Zechariah and Ezra–Nehemiah reports more the exception than the rule, suggests the operative reality of a pronounced political component in determining what was written and preserved, as well as what was omitted or suppressed.

On the other hand, the eclipse of Judahite political sovereignty did have what we may call "transpolitical" consequences and effects on the course of the culture and religion. The sovereign empires had no particular stake in the shape that Judahite culture and religion might take, beyond assuring that it would not disrupt their rule. The interventions of Persia in the missions of Ezra and Nehemiah were intended to stabilize and strengthen the province against Egyptian and Greek threats to the region. From the Persian perspective, the reforms of Ezra and Nehemiah were political measures, but there are reasons, as we have seen, for questioning the overwhelming success attributed to these reforms in supposedly securing cultural and religious homogeneity in Judah. At best, it is probable that the "mixed bag" of reforms solidified Jerusalem as a cultural and religious center where the ongoing multiple strains of Judahite belief and practice could be fought over and worked out. Furthermore, since the religious leaders of Judah and of the dispersed Judahite communities knew that there was no available sovereign political power to impose their views on one another or to compel them into a common accord, they had to resort to cultural and religious resources of ideological and pragmatic persuasion.

In this colonial climate of a recession of political power as the primary means of organizing culture and religion, state power fell under increasing suspicion and discredit. The way the monarchies of Israel and Judah are presented reflects a divided mind about political power. As Judahite communities outlived the Neo-Babylonian and Persian empires, community values and practices that "transcended" particular polities were enhanced as the basis of social solidarity. While politics was an ever-present reality, its ultimate value for shaping the community was discounted by many Judahites. This depreciation of politics as the primary force in human affairs is further reflected in the prophetic and wisdom traditions. A deepening monotheistic conviction that looked to a deity who was the final arbiter of history proceeded in tandem with the experience of a rich and vigorous communal life that, although vulnerable to the vicissitudes of imperial politics, was not felt to be finally determined by political arrangements. This "coming to terms" with politics both as an unavoidable present reality and as a long-term irrelevance was of course shattered by the intervention of the Seleucid empire into an internal Judahite cultural and religious dispute. The outburst of apocalyptic literature accompanying this harsh reintroduction of sovereign politics into the life of the community luridly displays the contempt with which political power was viewed when it attempted unilaterally to impose cultural and religious order.

Hasmonean "Exceptionalism"

Against the backdrop of four hundred years of Judah's subservience to great empires, the Maccabean revolt and Hasmonean regime come as a great surprise. However, with the delicate interface between politics and the spheres of culture and religion in mind, it is not so difficult to understand the Maccabean-Hasmonean "anomaly." Indeed, from the vantage point of the second-century B.C.E. upheaval in Judah, we can test some of our conclusions about politics in preceding periods of Israelite/Judahite history.

The Maccabean uprising is best understood as the escalation of civil conflict in Judah into a political rebellion sparked by heavy-handed Seleucid intervention in support of one party to the domestic dispute. Hellenistic ideas and practices were being adopted by an upper stratum in Jerusalem who countenanced a "liberalization" of religion and favored reconstituting Jerusalem as a Greek polis within the Seleucid empire. More traditional Judahite leaders opposed these moves, and the contest between the two policies focused on appointment of the high priest. For some time, under Ptolemies and Seleucids it seems that appointments of the native Judahite elite to offices in the provincial administration had often been sold to the highest bidders. In this instance, hostilities broke out between the two parties, and the Seleucid court intervened in support of the Hellenizing Judahites and went so far as to proscribe widely accepted Judahite religious beliefs and practices based on temple worship and adherence to the Torah, probably by this point more or less identical with the present Pentateuch.

A strong, militarized resistance movement, coinciding with Seleucid difficulties at home and abroad, restored the traditional religious practices but left unresolved the extent of Hellenistic thought and custom that would be compatible with traditional Judahite religion.

The resistance coalition that won back the space for cultural and religious freedom in Judah broke apart when some members decided to push for full political independence, probably with mixed motives of personal aggrandizement and a desire to safeguard Judah against future interventions by unstable Seleucid rulers. Again international circumstances were favorable to this undertaking, and the Hasmonean dynasty of independent Judahite rulers prevailed for eighty years before being swept away by advancing Roman power. The Hasmoneans were opposed on traditional grounds because of their cooptation of the kingship and high priesthood, since they lacked the Davidic and Aaronid credentials specified by tradition. They were also opposed on political and socioeconomic grounds because of their indulgence in luxury and the cruelty of their treatment of opponents. The roots of the later, more clearly articulated Sadducean, Pharisaic, and Essene "parties/movements" are located in the Hasmonean maelstrom. The Pharisaic and Essene tendencies were anti-Hasmonean, while the Sadducean inclinations were pro-Hasmonean. The Essenes withdrew from the political sphere, while representatives of the other movements became embroiled in struggles to shore up, overthrow, or moderate Hasmonean rule. The last years of Hasmonean rule, marked by inner-dynastic fights, were unpopular with a cross-section of leading Judahites who eventually appealed to Rome to put an end to their dismal reign, although they did not anticipate the extreme measures that Pompey would take in granting their petition.

Was There a Distinctive Ancient Israelite Polity?

What perspective does this Hasmonean venture throw on the Israelite politics we have been examining in this study? In my judgment, the Hasmonean state and the earlier Israelite/Judahite monarchies shared certain similarities in the way they related both to Israelite/Judahite culture and religion and to the surrounding political culture. In both instances, we observe a formal adherence to the Yahwistic cult, attended by the adoption of political forms and practices resonant with the wider environment that were often at odds with indigenous culture and religion and that spawned a deepening split between rulers and ruled. The kingdoms of Israel and Judah during the tenth to sixth centuries B.C.E. adopted a form of tributary state that corresponded closely with similar small to medium-sized states in

Syro-Palestine. The dynastic claims of the rulers of these kingdoms were in tension, and at times open conflict, with many of their subjects, owing to their perceived violation of the traditional protections of kin and village networks, which found expression in ways of understanding the cult of Yahweh in sharp disagreement with state religious ideology. The eventual destruction of both kingdoms was anticipated, and probably contributed to, by recalcitrant subjects whose views were articulated by a number of prophets.

The Hasmonean kingdom of the late second and early first century B.C.E. adopted a form of the tributary state that corresponded closely to Hellenistic kingdoms in their environment. The Hasmoneans aggressively conquered large parts of Palestine, at their apex of power actually approximating the effective size of the Davidic-Solomonic kingdom. Their armies even supplied mercenary troops to a faction of Syrians fighting over control of the Seleucid throne. They imposed Yahwistic religion on some of the conquered areas. They encouraged "new wealth" through expanded conquest and commerce and showed minimal regard for the socioeconomic and religious scruples of their more traditional subjects, both those possessed of "old wealth" and the depressed peasantry. They were ruthless in executing their domestic opponents. In their final decades, the Hasmoneans were scarcely distinguishable from the Seleucids whose abusive intervention in Judah their forebears had opposed.

It seems to me that the conclusion to be drawn from this contextual and typological comparison between the precolonial monarchies of Israel and Judah and the late colonial Hasmonean kingdom is patently clear. The Israelite people never managed to develop a political structure that matched the creativity and novelty of the culture and religion they exhibited. Moreover, beyond a general aspiration that their form of rule should be accordant with religious ideals and respectful of ordinary Judahites, they never developed a conception or model of political order as a viable alternative to the tributary state. The visions they entertained harked back vaguely to tribal comradeship, or longed for a truly righteous king, or projected harmonious rule by the righteous after foreign and domestic sinners would be annihilated. All these nostalgic and utopian visions, powerful as protests against abusive politics, offered religious loyalties as the basis for resolving the dilemmas inherent in the exercise of corporate power. But the hoped-for religious solidarity was itself an issue of political dispute, and the premised derivation of the ends and means of political order from religious solidarity remained unspecified.[145]

This "failure" to produce a distinctively Israelite political order is not in any way surprising. Nowhere in antiquity do we find such political innovation outside of Greek "democracy," which was itself sharply compromised by contradictions of class and gender and eventually swamped by empires. In spite of the development of republican and democratic institutions of government in recent centuries, it cannot be said that there is as yet any resolution of the tension and conflict between religious beliefs and practices and the exercise of sovereign power. Nonetheless, communities and nations reliant on Jewish and Christian traditions and values have sought to draw political inspiration and even practical political directives from the Hebrew Bible.[146] These brave undertakings, in various ways striving to provide an integral merger of religion and politics, have never produced satisfying results in the long run, on either political or religious grounds. In all their various permutations, biblically derived "theopolitics" continually replicate the frustrating failures and contradictions of ancient Israel's political experience. It is perhaps this very "disconnect" between religion and politics that constitutes one aspect of the enduring attraction of the Hebrew Bible, since in its pages we are invited to rehearse critically and imaginatively the political dilemmas that still bedevil us in a modern/postmodern world simultaneously interconnected by advancing economic and cultural "globalization" and divided by entrenched local, regional, and national loyalties under the rubrics of "multiculturalism," "ethnocentrism," and "nationalism."

The Politics of Ancient Israel

In the course of this inquiry, I have surveyed what the Hebrew Bible has to say about ancient Israelite politics and how the Israelite states were situated in their ancient Near Eastern matrix. Joining extrabiblical material and inscriptional testimony with comparative social science perspectives, leavened by historiographic and political theory, I have gone on to propose a critically imaginative reading of the changeful course of political power in tribal, monarchic, and colonial Israel.

SUMMING UP ANCIENT ISRAELITE POLITICS

Certain of my conclusions bear repeating:

1. With the aid of archaeological and extrabiblical texts and the guidance of newer historiographic theory, I have placed considerable confidence in the capacity of the biblical sources to give us trustworthy scenarios of the political life of ancient Israel beginning with tribal times, despite their sketchy, sometimes distorted, detail and their preoccupation with religion.

2. Factoring in ideological criticism, I have stressed that the biblical political scenarios are complexly expressive both of the dominant colonial ideology that shaped and framed the finished Hebrew Bible and of ideological perspectives prevalent in tribal and monarchic Israel that have been retained, perhaps unwittingly, within the completed whole.

3. Drawing on the rich reservoir of ancient Near Eastern studies, I have shown that Israel's political structures and strategies were typical of its time and place, exhibiting a mixture of political strength and fragility in which aspiring states faced limits to their efforts to dominate culture and society and to assert their power over against other states.

4. Taking account of advances in our understanding of Israelite religion, I have argued that the cult of Yahweh, while a creative force in the tribal era and the official state religion under the monarchy, was neither dominant

enough nor sufficiently unified in its diverse manifestations to shape the politics of the Israelite states in a decisive manner, even though various versions of Yahwism were enlisted in political causes and conflicts.

5. Combining all my sources and methods of inquiry, I have concluded that no special "covenant" politics, in contrast to covenant traditions in society and religion, are discernible in the conduct of the Israelite states and that there was no distinctive Israelite polity involving the regular participation of its members, who remained "subjects" rather than "citizens" of their respective states.

6. Finally, I have concluded that what proved to be distinctive of ancient Israel was not its politics but rather its literature and religion, in which the states of Israel and Judah played an important but ancillary role, and that this specialness of Israel, which is not detectable during the monarchy, emerged only over the centuries following the fall of the states.

The import and implications of these conclusions deserve to be spelled out. If the Israelite states were like other ancient Near Eastern states and were not decisively shaped by religious beliefs and practices that were themselves polymorphous and often in conflict, how do we account for the emergence of religiocultural communities among the survivors of the fallen states of Israel and Judah? This is close to Max Weber's famous question, "Hence we ask, how did Jewry develop into a pariah people with highly specific peculiarities?", recognizing of course that Weber ignored the popular pejorative meaning of "pariah" when he used it as technical jargon to refer to a "guest" people who are "hosted" in a larger society, a meaning that is better represented by the term "marginal people."[1]

We can approach this question by assessing the respective roles of culture and religion and of politics as they interacted in the shaping of Israelite communal life. I believe we can properly posit a developing core of culture and religion in preexilic Judah that carried over into the dispersed Judahite communities, who retained their identity and traditions. A similar core in northern Israel no doubt enabled the Samarian/Samaritan community to outlive the fall of the state, as well as groups of deported northern Israelites of whom we have only a smattering of information. These "core" cultural and religious identities, stemming from tribal and monarchic times, were sufficiently autonomous that they did not require any centralized political or religious authority to sustain them by decreeing and enforcing uniformity of belief and practice upon them.

The origin point of this core religiocultural identity was located in the old familial and communitarian culture of premonarchic Israel. This prestate culture was carried on in the predominantly village- and family-centered

society that the centralized states were never able to alter in any fundamental way, even though the state's political economy repeatedly threatened it—and, under Solomon and Josiah, attempted radically to subject it to
the state. This heterogeneous decentralized culture entailed various forms of
Yahwism, as well as other cults. It was precisely this familial/communitarian
substratum, sustained throughout the monarchy, that wove a "safety net"
enabling dispersed Judahites to retain continuity with their past while cre-
atively adapting to new conditions of life.

Having said this, however, credit must be given to the Israelite states for
providing a protective integument in which, with no conscious contribution
on their part, the heterogenous familial/communitarian culture and religion
could prosper. If we imagine a scenario in which the independent Israelite
states had not arisen, it is doubtful that the loosely coordinated tribal culture and religion of Israel could have developed a strong, enduring tradition and way of life, had they been dominated in the tenth and ninth
centuries by Philistia, Egypt, Damascus, or Assyria, rather than by indigenous states. This unwitting protective role of the native state is illustrated
by the relative weakness of north Israelite culture and religion after the fall
of Israel in the eighth century, compared to the more virile culture and religion of Judah. Israel experienced only two hundred years of statehood
before it was harshly suppressed by Assyria, whereas Judah went on to
profit not only from another 150 years of political independence but also
from an infusion of northern culture and religion brought by refugees who
fled to Judah after the fall of Samaria.

There is yet another credit that must be accorded the Israelite states for
an unwitting contribution to the thriving communities of colonial Judahites.
It was the state establishment that led the way in cultivating writing and literacy, even though within a circumscribed circle, and it was this circle that
apparently recorded what we know of tribal and monarchic politics. The
availability of writing to persons with other agendas allowed the written
retention of prophetic, wisdom, and covenant-legal traditions that stood in
tension, or outright conflict, with the state. It is safe to say that the under-
girding infrastructure of familial/communitarian traditions that gave body to
colonial Judahites might well have been lost without the literate Judahite
"intellectuals" who preserved traditions in writing and went on to create
other texts, eventuating in the collections that in time formed the Hebrew
Bible. It was no doubt these same intellectuals who took the lead in shaping religious beliefs and practices in the colonial era.

The imperial politics of the great powers also had an inadvertent role to play
in the fashioning of colonial Judah. The sharp encounters of the kingdoms

of Israel and Judah with Assyria and Neo-Babylonia, in the face of which Judahite culture and religion—infused with refugee Israelites and their traditions—not only held their ground but prospered, prepared their colonial descendants to resist homogenization in the cultures of their overlords. By good fortune, the Neo-Babylonian, Persian, and Hellenistic empires retreated considerably from the harshest measures of the Assyrian empire and by design attempted to incorporate existing cultures, religions, and forms of home rule within their overarching sovereignty. This policy not only enabled a restoration of Judah proper but also allowed Judahites dispersed throughout the empires to develop their own manner of life.

Nevertheless, if the primary core of Judahite survival and subsequent growth lay in its culture and religion, enabled by indigenous and foreign polities that tested its endurance while also securing conditions for its survival, it must be stressed that this very culture and religion was not a single coherent and unifying resource. The diverse manifestations of what it meant to be "Israel" in colonial times are well illustrated by the variegated traditions finally brought together in the Hebrew Bible, as also by the evidences of multiple forms of "Judah-ism" in Judah itself and throughout the Dispersion. Seen from without, the marginalized life of these colonial Judahites could appear culturally and religiously cohesive, but as experienced from within the community, many differences were acknowledged and contested.

In short, neither statist politics nor a central religious authority was able to resolve the long-standing issues over who was included and who was excluded from the community of Israel, and on what terms. Only with the rabbinic establishment in the late first and second centuries C.E. were the boundaries of Israel drawn with more emphatic clarity and its sacred literature circumscribed by consensual authority. But before that rabbinic settlement was reached, Judah was racked by three revolts, one against the Seleucids and two against Rome, accompanied by civil discord that divided the community over issues of culture and religion as much as over political issues. Neither the Hasmonean dynasty nor the temple establishment could achieve consensual agreement among Judahites as to who they were, how they should treat one another, how they should worship, and how they should be governed.

THE LEGACY OF ANCIENT ISRAELITE POLITICS

The legacy of ancient Israel provides us with no distinctive politics and with no template for translating culture and religion into a viable polity. Ancient

Israel's politics have been mined for the support of the divine right of kings, revolution against unjust authority, covenanted commonwealths, liberal democracy, nationalism, capitalism, and socialism. This is not only because the scriptural authority invested in the Hebrew Bible has repeatedly tempted proponents of sociopolitical systems to claim its legitimation, but also because the unsystematized and unreconciled political structures, practices, and viewpoints expressed in the Hebrew Bible contain elements that appear to have certain affinities with a wide spectrum of modern political systems. The nearest "whole view" of ancient Israelite politics I have been able to conjure in my critical imagination is that of a tributary agrarian monarchy, preceded by some form of loose association of "tribes" exercising diffused power and authority, and followed by semiautonomous religiocultural enclaves incorporated into monarchic empires. None of these political forms is transferable into contemporary politics. They cannot be transferred as a whole, or in selected parts, if only because the course of world history has unfolded far beyond the adequacy of ancient models to do more than inform us of the sources of some of our notions and sentiments about politics and to highlight political dilemmas that have been with us since the dawn of civilization. The modern state of Israel, committed to its biblical roots, has not been able to recuperate a coherent biblical politics that can resolve the conflicting claims of religious nationalism and liberal democracy.[2] Various attempts to conceive the United States of America theopolitically as a "New Israel" have foundered on the shoals of religious diversity and liberal democracy.[3]

The gulf between culture/religion on the one hand and politics on the other was never successfully bridged in ancient Israel, nor has it ever been, in the long and uneasy relations between these two divergent networks of social power. The rise of liberal democracies, with their separation of church and state, attests to the systemic weaknesses and gross abuses of polities grounded in religion, while leaving unsettled the ontological and moral foundations of these religiously neutral polities.[4] This is not to say that there is no basis for judging between political systems and particular political establishments. It is rather to say that our judgments must involve a web of pragmatic, moral, religious, and philosophical considerations, and that insofar as we draw upon the Hebrew Bible for political guidance, it will be at the level of selective guidelines or principles that we choose to extract from the mélange of biblical perspectives.

In conclusion, I would point to the religious dimension of ancient Israel as both a persistent source of "utopian" or "eschatological" hope in the achievement of peace and justice in human affairs and as an equally enduring source of impediments to the realization of peace and justice. What I have to say on this point, I believe, applies in principle to the three scriptured monotheistic religions of Judaism, Christianity, and Islam. In my estimation, it is the conjunction of scripture and monotheism that has generated both high hopes for peace and justice and constant frustrations of those hopes.

First, monotheism has encouraged a worldwide vision of peace and justice, while simultaneously nurturing the belief that "we" monotheists—of a particular type—are the sole or superior carriers of that peace and justice, all too easily dividing the world into "us" and "them."

Second, scripturization of religion has connected monotheists with rich traditional resources, while simultaneously promoting a rules-oriented literalism that ignores the cultural relativism of the texts and spawns divisions and open warfare among those who disagree in their interpretation and application of the rules.

Third, scriptured monotheism inculcates the view that God is in control of history and has mandated that humans are to collaborate in the achievement of the divine purposes, while simultaneously leaving its adherents "high and dry" as to how to translate the divine revelation into full-orbed social and political institutions and practices.

I put these contradictory propositions without any clarity about their resolution, and, in any case, the epilogue to a study of ancient Israelite politics is not the place to pursue them.[5] I will only point out how deeply rooted all these internally contradictory propositions already are in late colonial and rabbinic Israel, and I have no doubt the same is true of earliest Christianity and Islam. I will comment in particular only on the third point above, namely, the gap between the assertion of divine control over human history and the insistence on human participation in the divine intentions.

In the course of my inquiry into the biblical texts that disclose ancient Israelite politics, I became increasingly aware of the different "modes" or "voices" in which the texts spoke. Many texts recount vivid and engrossing narratives about political agents who make critical choices, narratives that rely entirely on immanental descriptions of human motives, ambitions, and plans leading to actions and consequences that, from the narrative's perspectives, could have gone in a number of directions. Other texts, however, purport to contain the very mind and word of God, not only judging what is right and wrong in the conduct of the political actors, but declaring that it was God who acted to bring about consequences that from the narrative's point of view were effected by the political players themselves. This disjunction in the biblical record between divine and human "causation" in human affairs has been aptly called "the dual causality principle" and may be decoded into philosophical language as the paradox of freedom and determinism.[6]

Without trying to explore or unravel this disjunction, I want only to emphasize how sharply this limits the instructiveness of the Hebrew Bible, both for a clear view of how politics operated in ancient Israel and for appropriating biblical texts for political reflection in our world. In order to undertake my critically imaginative construal of ancient Israelite politics, I chose to sidestep the problem methodologically by excluding from my primary sources those parts of the Hebrew Bible that in my view offered metadiscourse on God's assessment of and intervention in Israelite politics. There are of course many other ways of coping with this enigma of the alternating divine and human voices. However, even those who make the most strenuous efforts to harmonize the two voices are left with inconsistencies and gaps in their interpretation that allow for very different kinds of political outlooks, both in theory and practice.

So as not to conclude on an entirely negative note, I underscore my thesis that the basically undistinguished politics of ancient Israel preserved the record of its prestate communitarian life and "gave cover" to a cultural and religious matrix from which the remarkable literature and thriving religion of multiple colonial Judah-isms eventually issued in a more unitary Judaism. Ironically, we are able to look back upon those politics solely because of the tenacious survival of the texts and the religious beliefs and practices accompanying them. Without this literature and religion, ancient Israelite politics would hardly be worth a second look.

Notes

Chapter 2

1. Raymond Boudon and Francois Bourricaud, *A Critical Dictionary of Sociology* (Chicago: Univ. of Chicago Press, 1989), 267.

2. I am indebted to Michael Mann (*The Sources of Social Power. Vol. 1, A History of Power from the Beginning to A.D. 1760* [Cambridge: Cambridge Univ. Press, 1986], 1–33) for a "networks" model of the ingredients of public power, in preference to the more customary partition of society into "dimensions" or "levels." The network metaphor signals the mutually conditioning and ever fluctuating interplay between overlapping "circuits of power." I differ from Mann, who employs "social power" as a covering term for all the power networks, in that I include social power as a network alongside his economic, military, political, and ideological power networks, in order to accommodate the kinship and village-based social organization of Israel that preceded and later coexisted with native and foreign hierarchic political power. Norman Yoffee ("Too Many Chiefs? [or, Safe Texts for the '90s]," in *Archaeological Theory: Who Sets the Agenda?* ed. N. Yoffee and A. Sherratt [Cambridge: Cambridge Univ. Press, 1993], 72) refers to "institutional groupings of partly overlapping and partly opposing fields of action that lend the possibility of instability, as well as stability, to overarching social institutions."

3. These "stateless societies" or "ordered anarchies" are illustrated by John Middleton and David Tate (*Tribes without Rulers: Studies in African Segmentary Systems* [London: Routledge & Kegan Paul, 1958, with new preface, 1970]) and treated more theoretically by Pierre Clastres (*Society against the State* [New York: Zone Books, 1989]).

4. On defining the state, see Morton H. Fried and Frederick M. Watkins, "State," *IESS* 15:143–57 and Ronald Cohen and Elman R. Service, eds., *Origins of the State: The Anthropology of Political Evolution* (Philadelphia: Institute for the Study of Human Issues, 1978), 2–5. Mann follows Weber closely in defining the state as "a differentiated set of institutions and personnel embodying centrality, in the sense that political relations radiate outward to cover a territorially demarcated area, over which it claims a monopoly of binding and permanent rule-making, backed up by physical violence" (*Sources,* 37).

5. Sheldon S. Wolin, *Politics and Vision: Continuity and Innovation in Western Political Thought* (Boston/Toronto: Little, Brown & Co., 1960), 7.

6. Aiden Southall, "Orientations in Political Anthropology," *Canadian Journal of African Studies* 3 (1969): 42–52.

7. Herbert Kaufman, "The Collapse of Ancient States and Civilizations as an Organizational Problem," in *The Collapse of Ancient States and Civilizations,* ed. N. Yoffee and G. L. Cowgill (Tucson: Univ. of Arizona Press, 1988), 219–35.

8. On dispersed power in stateless societies, see Middleton and Tate, *Tribes without Rulers,* 1–31, and Ted C. Lewellen, *Political Anthropology: An Introduction,* 2d ed. (Westport, Conn.: Bergin & Garvey, 1992), 26–35.

9. Among the state typologies most frequently thought to be applicable to ancient Israel are those that express a sliding scale of political power and complexity, such as inchoate early state, typical early state, transitional early state, and mature state (Henri J. M. Claessen and Peter Skalnik, eds., *The Early State* [The Hague: Mouton Publishers, 1978], 22–23, 589–93) and those that characterize forms of economic production or forms of domination, e.g., the patrimonial state (Max Weber, *Economy and Society: An Outline of Interpretive Sociology* [Berkeley, Calif.: Univ. of California Press, 1978], 1009–69), the agrarian state (Gerhard E. Lenski, *Power and Privilege: A Theory of Social Stratification* [Chapel Hill, N.C.: Univ. of North Carolina Press, paperback ed., 1984], 189–296), the Asiatic state (Karl Marx, described and discussed in Lawrence Krader, *The Asiatic Mode of Production: Sources, Development, and Critique in the Writings of Karl Marx* [Assen: Van Gorcum, 1985]), the tributary state (Samir Amin, *Class and Nation Historically and in the Current Crisis* [New York: Monthly Review Press, 1980], 46–70), to which may be added the more recently emphasized patron-client state (Niels Peter Lemche, "Kings and Clients: On Loyalty between the Ruler and the Ruled in Ancient 'Israel,'" *Semeia* 66 [1995]: 119–32; "Justice in Western Asia in Antiquity; Or: Why No Laws Were Needed!" *Kent Law Review* 70 [1995]: 1695–1716). Ronald A. Simkins ("Patronage and the Political Economy of Monarchic Israel," in *Semeia* [*The Social World of the Hebrew Bible: Twenty-Five Years of the Social Sciences in the Academy*], forthcoming) argues that a patron-client mode of production dominated the "lesser" household, statist, and trade modes of production throughout the monarchy.

10. With respect to the problems involved in the use of typologies and evolutionary schemes in sociological theorizing, see Christopher Lloyd, *The Structures of History* (Oxford/Cambridge, Mass.: Blackwell, 1993), 66–88, and as employed in biblical studies, Niels Peter Lemche, "On the Use of 'System Theory,' 'Macro Theories,' and 'Evolutionistic Thinking' in Modern Old Testament Research and Biblical Archaeology," *SJOT* 4:2 (1990): 73–88; reprinted in Charles E. Carter and Carol L. Meyers, eds., *Community, Identity, and Ideology: Social Sciences Approaches to the Hebrew Bible* (Winona Lake, Ind.: Eisenbrauns, 1996), 273–86.

11. Mann (*Sources,* 30–31, 173–74, 530–32) picks up on Wolfram Eberhard's term "world time" (*Conquerors and Rulers: Social Forces in Modern China,* 2d rev. ed. [Leiden: E. J. Brill, 1965], 13–16) to expand on the process of power development throughout "world-historical time," a process neither evolutionary nor teleological, but which emerges in particular states with profound effects on the world around them. This process demands that all comparisons of states must respect the historical configurations in which they appear. The concept of world-historical time is taken up with qualification by John Gledhill ("Introduction: the Comparative Analysis of Social and Political Transitions," in *State and Society: The Emergence and Development of Social Hierarchy and Political Centralization,* ed. J. Gledhill, B. Bender, and M. T. Larsen [London: Unwin Hyman, 1988], 2–4, 9–10). Without using

the term, and depending on a more Marxist analytic apparatus, Eric R. Wolf (*Europe and the People without History* [Berkeley, Calif.: Univ. of California Press, 1982]) illustrates this sort of world-historical contextualization by analyzing the impact of European power systems both on the European lower classes and on "primitive" peoples since 1400 A.D. World-historical time is not to be automatically equated with Wallerstein's world system theory, which is more economist in its approach, nor does it begin with an axiomatic positing of universal history but rather seeks amid historical particularities to work toward a characterization of how these particularities have shaped various "subworlds" that reciprocally affect one another and may imply the potential for one world history. However, my employment of the concept of "local-historical time" nested within "world-historical time" follows a reverse pathway from that of Mann, who focuses on the initiative of leading centers of organized power in both stimulating and constraining lesser power centers, while the interest of the present study is in the ways that the "lesser" power center Israel was stimulated and constrained by the "greater" power centers in its space-time world. Put differently, I seek to understand what it means to recognize that while Israel is the focus of my study, Israel was decidedly not the power center of its sector of world-historical time.

12. Mann, *Sources,* 531–32, 538–41.

13. The past treatment of ancient Israelite politics is characterized on the one hand by poorly theorized descriptive histories and on the other hand by technical studies on particular institutions and practices, similarly weak in theory and often uncontextualized in the wider field of Israelite politics. A bibliography of major histories of Israel and Judah published in the nineteenth and twentieth centuries, compiled by John H. Hayes and J. Maxwell Miller (*Israelite and Judaean History* [Philadelphia: Westminster Press, 1977], xxv–xxix), contains no title that includes the term "politics" or "political," indicative of the assumption that to recount Israel's history in broadest terms is tantamount to recounting its politics. I am not aware that recent histories of Israel have shown any advance in this regard. Despite its title, Henri Cazelles, *Histoire politique d'Israël des origines à Alexandre le Grand* (Paris: Desclée, 1982) draws exclusively on historiographic literature without any attention to specific issues in political administration or theory. The scholar who came nearest to focusing on Israelite politics as a theoretical issue was Albrecht Alt, in his influential essays on "The Formation of the Israelite State in Palestine" and "The Monarchy in the Kingdoms of Israel and Judah" (*Essays on Old Testament History and Religion* [orig. pub. 1930, 1951; Oxford: Basil Blackwell, 1966], 171–259), but even Alt failed to incorporate any resources from political science. Until the last couple of decades, most of the overt discussion of Israelite politics has been devoted to the issues that Alt formulated and the positions he advocated, many of which now appear outmoded or peripheral. The more theoretically sophisticated work on Israelite politics that has emerged in recent times has yet to find expression in a large-scale analytic or synthetic work. David Biale (*Power and Powerlessness in Jewish History* [New York: Schocken Books, 1986], 3–57), building on the work of Amos Funkenstein and Ismar Schorsch, took a first step in the needed direction by claiming politics as an integral dimension of Israelite/Jewish life both in biblical and Talmudic times, in contrast to polarized emphases on Jewish "passivity" or occasional revolutionary "activism," but his treatment of the biblical era is

terse, reliant on older research, and the political theory he cites is largely postbiblical Jewish. Nevertheless, the pointedness and clarity of Biale's inquiry derives from his concern to understand the politics of modern Israel as a Jewish state.

14. The spirited debate over what sort of genre is represented by biblical history-like traditions is haunted by a sense that they evidently do not correspond to either of the Western prose genres of fiction and nonfiction and are thus neither "historiography" nor "historical novel(s)." Interestingly, in exploring this puzzlement from different angles, both Frank M. Cross (*From Epic to Canon: History and Literature in Ancient Israel* [Baltimore/London: Johns Hopkins, 1998], 22–29) and Daniel Boyarin ("Placing Reading: Ancient Israel and Medieval Europe," in *The Ethnography of Reading,* ed. J. Boyarin [Berkeley, Calif.: Univ. of California Press, 1993], 10–37) locate the genre conundrum in the orality that underlies and shapes the literary text. Cross proposes that the most appropriate genre for Israel's history-like narratives is "traditional epic," with its closest affinity in Homeric epic, while Boyarin hesitantly states that the genre must be read by us as "didactic fiction," a genre approximated by the rabbinic category of "mashal/parable." Others have found a genre affinity between biblical narrative and the Gilgamesh Epic (David Damrosch, *The Narrative Covenant: Transformations of Genre in the Growth of Biblical Literature* [San Francisco: Harper & Row, 1987], 51–143) or between biblical narrative and the Histories of Herodotus (Jan-Wim Wesselius, *The Origin of the History of Israel. Herodotus' Histories as Blueprint for the First Books of the Bible,* JSOTSup [Sheffield: Sheffield Academic Press, forthcoming]).

15. Norman K. Gottwald, "Biblical Views on 'Church-State' Relations and Their Influence on Existing Political Ideologies," in *The Hebrew Bible in Its Social World and in Ours,* SemeiaSt (Atlanta: Scholars, 1993), 365–83.

16. Philip R. Davies (*In Search of 'Ancient Israel',* JSOTSup 148 [Sheffield: Sheffield Academic Press, 1992]) and Niels Peter Lemche (*The Israelites in History and Tradition* [Louisville, Ky.: Westminster John Knox, 1998]) have strenuously rebutted the notion of a unified continuous historical subject "Israel" prior to the postexilic period with some justification, given the facile way Israelite identity is posited in many studies. A leading contention in James R. Linville (*Israel in the Book of Kings: The Past as a Project of Social Identity,* JSOTSup 272 [Sheffield: Sheffield Academic Press, 1998]) is that the book of Kings is nervously preoccupied with the boundaries of Israelite identity and that its ambivalent and shifting nomenclature for the "Israelite" actors in the book of Kings reflects disputes over exclusiveness/inclusiveness issues in the colonial Judahite community when it was most likely composed. Somewhat similarly, E. Theodore Mullen Jr. (*Narrative History and Ethnic Boundaries: The Deuteronomistic Historian and the Creation of Israelite National Identity,* SemeiaSt [Atlanta: Scholars, 1993]) focuses on the formation of Israelite identity as a central preoccupation of the entire Deuteronomistic corpus but is more conventional in his dating of the work.

17. Hans-Joachim Zobel, "*yĕhûdâ,*" *TDOT,* 4:482–99; "*yiśrā'ēl,*" *TDOT,* 6:397–420; G. von Rad and K. G. Kuhn, "*yiśrā'ēl,*" *TDNT,* 3:356–69; Graham Harvey, *The True Israel: Uses of the Names Jew, Hebrew, and Israel in Ancient Jewish and Early Christian Literature,* AGJU 35 [Leiden/New York/Cologne: E. J. Brill, 1996). On the uses of Israel and Judah in the books of Kings and Chronicles, see Linville, *Israel in the Book of Kings,* 16–37, 91–104, and H. G. M. Williamson, *Israel in the Books of Chronicles* (Cambridge: Cambridge Univ. Press, 1977), 1–10, 126–30.

18. "Hymn of Victory of Mer-ne-Ptah (The 'Israel Stela')," trans. John A. Wilson (*ANET,* 376–78); and see my chap. 5, 163–67, nn. 8, 20.

19. Zobel, *"yiśrā'ēl,"* 399–401, summarizes the case for the meaning "El reigns/is supreme" in preference to "El strives/contends."

20. Norman K. Gottwald, *The Tribes of Yahweh: A Sociology of the Religion of Liberated Israel, 1250–1050 B.C.E.* (2d corrected printing, Maryknoll, N.Y.: Orbis, 1981; reprint with new introduction, Sheffield: Sheffield Academic Press, 1999), 493–97; Zobel, *"yiśrā'ēl,"* 411–12. Frank M. Cross has plausibly proposed that the proper name Yahweh arose as an epithet for El in the form *'ēl zū* (or *dū) yahwī ṣaba'ōth,* "El who creates the (armed) hosts," referring by double entendre to the armed hosts of heaven and the armed hosts of Israel (*Canaanite Myth and Hebrew Epic: Essays in the History of the Religion of Israel* [Cambridge: Harvard Univ. Press, 1970], 65–71), and see the discussion in Gottwald, *Tribes,* 682–85.

21. Zobel, *"yĕhûdâ,"* 491–94; Roland de Vaux, *The Early History of Israel* (Philadelphia: Westminster Press, 1978), 540–52.

22. Linville, *Israel in the Book of Kings,* pursuing a reading strategy of literary attribution, observes that "the myth of the schism is strangely perverse; it produces two liminal 'Israels,' neither one complete, and neither one expendable" (175); see his discussion of "Alternative Israels" and "Rights to a Name," 176–91.

23. H. G. M. Williamson (*Israel in the Books of Chronicles* [Cambridge/New York/Melbourne: Cambridge Univ. Press, 1977], 102–10, 126–30, 139–40) concludes that the Chronicler "wished to emphasize that Judah was still an integral part of Israel in its full sense, despite its name Judah" (106) and further to demonstrate "that a faithful nucleus [in Judah] does not exclude others [from northern Israel], but is a representative centre to which all the children of Israel may be welcomed if they will return" (140).

24. This larger, inclusive Israel may be thought of as "imagined" in the sense of Benedict Anderson's anthropological description of the concept of nation as "an imagined community . . . conceived as a deep, horizontal comradeship" expressed in shared history and tradition (*Imagined Communities: Reflections on the Origin and Spread of Nationalism,* rev. ed. [London/New York: Verso, 1991], 6–7). Like Anderson, Anthony D. Smith (*The Ethnic Origins of Nations* [Oxford: Blackwell, 1986], 6–125) stresses the cultural roots of nationalism but goes beyond Anderson in delineating what he takes to have been ethnic solidarities in antiquity, including many of the sociopolitical entities of the ancient Near East, which in his view were forerunners and adumbrations of modern nations. Smith acknowledges the difficulties in knowing to what extent the group consciousness expressed in elite texts from antiquity was shared by the general populace and in determining whether the ancient proper names, presumed to speak of population groups, were more or less territorial, political, or "ethnic." What may be occurring in the protean and elastic biblical concepts of "Israel" is a groping toward the formation of a group identity that does not yet have firm boundaries or singular institutional expression, such that "the sum of all the literary 'Israels' cannot be taken as expressing a total, trouble-free self-image" (Linville, *Israel in the Book of Kings,* 37). Accordingly, in the present study I pointedly avoid use of the word set "ethnos/ethnic/ethnicity" because of the extreme multivalency of meaning attached to it, which is either so vague as to be of doubtful diagnostic value or so precise as to be unverifiable from our sources. See my chap. 4, 125–26, nn. 25–26.

25. The term Samaritan(s) is the Greek rendering (*samareîtai*) of Hebrew Samarians (*šōmerōnîm*) which occurs in the Hebrew Bible only in 2 Kings 17:29, referring to the inhabitants of northern Israel, in keeping with its usage in eighth-century Assyrian texts. Ezra–Nehemiah never uses the term "Samaria(n)" to refer to Judah's northern opponents. Although 2 Kings 17 certainly looks with disdain on these practitioners of religious syncretism, it shows no familiarity with the postexilic cult community of Yahweh-worshiping "Samaritans," who referred to themselves as Keepers or Guardians of the Law (*šāmērîm*). Later rabbinic tradition called them Cuthites (2 Kings 17:24, 30). In this study I deliberately use only the term "Samarian(s)", so as to avoid an anachronistic reification of the later fixed enmity between the two religious communities connoted by the customary word pair "Samaritans" vs. "Jews." It appears that a total breach between Judahite and Samarian Yahwists did not occur until the second century B.C.E. Further on the Samaritans, see Robert T. Anderson, "Samaritans," *ABD*, 5: 940–47; James D. Purvis, "The Samaritans and Judaism," in *Early Judaism and its Modern Interpreters* (Philadelphia: Fortress/Atlanta: Scholars, 1986), 81–98; R. J. Coggins, *Samaritans and Jews: the Origins of Samaritanism Reconsidered* (Atlanta: John Knox, 1975); and Ingrid Hjelm, *The Samaritans and Early Judaism: A Literary Analysis,* JSOTSup 303 (Sheffield: Sheffield Academic Press, 2000), who provides a critical overview of major hypotheses about Samaritan origins and explicates what is said of them in Samaritan, Jewish, Christian, and Hellenistic literature.

26. Frank M. Cross, "Samaria and Jerusalem in the Era of Restoration," in *From Epic to Canon,* 173–202; John H. Hayes and Sara R. Mandell, *The Jewish People in Classical Antiquity: From Alexander to Bar Kochba* (Louisville, Ky.: Westminster John Knox, 1998), 25–27.

27. The extent of the dispersion of Judahites in the sixth century B.C.E. and the subsequent histories of these Yahweh-worshiping communities are very imperfectly known. The Egyptian dispersion is best documented by the late-fifth-century Elephantine texts (*ANET,* 491–92) and by traditions about relations between Judah and the large Judahite community in Alexandria in the third and second centuries, where biblical writings were translated into the Greek Septuagint. It is noteworthy that even though the Judahite military colonists in Elephantine sought counsel on religious matters from both Jerusalem and Samaria, they built their own temple in disregard of the exclusive claims of the rival sanctuaries at Jerusalem and Gerizim. Moreover, they recognized lesser deities alongside Yahweh. It is also reported that during the Maccabean uprising a fugitive Jerusalem high priest established a temple to Yahweh at Leontopolis in Egypt (Lester L. Grabbe, *Judaism from Cyrus to Hadrian.* Vol. 1, *The Persian and Greek Periods* [Minneapolis: Fortress, 1992], 266–67). The third-century Letter of Aristeas and the second-century Sibylline Oracles, Book 3, from Alexandria, show a decided cordiality and openness toward Greek culture (George W. E. Nickelsburg, *Jewish Literature between the Bible and the Mishnah: A Historical and Literary Introduction* [Philadelphia: Fortress, 1981], 161–69).

The Babylonian dispersion, the posited origin of the initiative to restore Judah in Ezra–Nehemiah, is virtually undocumented in Persian and Hellenistic times. Jacob Neusner (*A History of the Jews in Babylonia.* Vol. 1, *The Parthian Period,* South Florida Studies in the History of Judaism 217, reprint of rev. ed. [Atlanta: Scholars,

1999, 1969], 10–15) introduces our scant information about the early settlements of Judahites in Babylonia with the remark, "Very little is known, however, about Babylonian Jewry before the first century B.C.E., and still less about Jews in Mesopotamia and Iran proper. Few references to the Jews in the trans-Euphrates territories of the Seleucids survive" (11). The book of Tobit and the Letter of Jeremiah in the Protestant Apocrypha probably derive from Mesopotamia in the late third or early second centuries (Nickelsburg, *Jewish Literature,* 30–38). Tobit is pictured as a deeply pious northern Israelite Yahwist who was carried to Nineveh after the fall of Samaria in 722 B.C.E., which hints at the high probability that exiled Judahites on occasion linked up with exiled Israelites who had retained their Yahwistic allegiance. Although Tobit gives a pronounced "nod" to the sanctity of the Jerusalem temple, its folk piety fraught with magical elements does not appear closely aligned with the religious practices known in postexilic Judah. Tobit's familiarity with the polytheistic story of Ahikar, even turning its hero into a Yahweh devotee, is echoed in the appearance of a manuscript of the book of Ahikar in the Egyptian Elephantine community. Gordon Darnell Newby (*A History of the Jews in Arabia from Ancient Times to Their Eclipse under Islam* [Columbia, S.C.: Univ. of South Carolina Press, 1988]), 14–23) reports scant information on the early Judahite settlements in Arabia, although there is conjecture that Judahite soldiers may have served in Nabonidus's army during the several years the Neo-Babylonian king spent at Tema in north Arabia. Moreover, even within Judah itself, there was no monochromatic Judahite cultural and religious identity, as vividly attested by the Qumran community that broke away from the Jerusalem establishment in the second century. The Qumran library is generally understood to have collected writings from many sources that express a variety of unsystematized views about the proper institutional and ideological shape that Judahite religion should take (John J. Collins, "Dead Sea Scrolls," *ABD,* 2:85–101).

28. As late as the first century C.E., both the text and the canon of the Hebrew Bible were in flux. Diverse local texts and editions of what were to become "biblical" books were cited in support of the religious and political stances of rival groups. These eventual biblical works coexisted with a much wider range of works also considered religiously authoritative by one group or another in Judah or the Diaspora. Cross argues persuasively that it was the Pharisee Hillel and his disciples, beginning in the early first century C.E., who took up the project of standardizing the text of a series of works they regarded as authoritative, and it was this assemblage of books in three parts (Law, Prophets, and Writings) that came to form the Hebrew canon as we know it. The labors of the Hillel school did not eliminate all rival books until the period between the two Jewish revolts (70–135 C.E.), when the Pharisaic movement triumphed in its bid to become the official shapers of rabbinic Judaism (*From Epic to Canon,* 205–29).

29. Gerhard von Rad, "*yiśrā'ēl,*" *TDNT,* 3:358.

30. "Judaism" as an abstract Greek noun paired with "Hellenism" first appears in the second century B.C.E. (2 Maccabees 2:21; 8:1; 14:38). The process by which the culture and religion of Judah were abstracted and distilled into an encompassing descriptor for the beliefs and practices of the Yahweh cult, whether within or beyond Judah proper, must have been long and complex. In an effort to conceptualize this development, Philip R. Davies ("Scenes from the Early History of

Judaism," in *The Triumph of Elohim: From Yahwisms to Judaisms,* ed. D. V. Edelman [Grand Rapids, Mich.: Eerdmans, 1995], 145–82) distinguishes three stages: (1) a Judahite culture, composed of habits and customs, that was not yet conceptualized; (2) a Judahite culture that was conceptualized as a particular way of life that included religion, which he calls "Juda-ism"; and (3) a Judahite culture regarded as a "covering" term for the beliefs and practices of Yahweh worshipers everywhere, and thus "Judaism." But just as, in the second stage, there were a number of competing versions of "Juda-ism," so, in the third stage, there were alternative and rival "Judaisms" until the Rabbinic period in the second century c.e. Linville (*Israel in the Book of Kings,* 27) helpfully proposes that the distinction between Davies' second and third stages is made clearer by referring to the second stage as "Juda*h*-ism" rather than "Juda-ism." Davies sums up the principled basis of his distinctions, "Recognizing that Judaism *has* a beginning, not in the mists of antiquity or in some other inaccessible source, but in historical and cultural events and processes, is an important first step in a *historical* approach to this religion. . . . 'Judaism' is not a 'given' at the outset (nor at the end, for that matter) but something that participates fully in the ever-changing flux of human thought and behavior" (153–54). Robert P. Carroll ("Israel, History of [Post-Monarchic Period]," *ABD,* 3:567–76) likewise cautions against a monolithic reification of "Judaism" in the postexilic era, even when qualified as "early Judaism." Just as I refrain from the use of the term Samaritans to refer to Samarians, so I refrain from anachronistic reference to Jews and Judaism during the historical span of this study, since those terms all too easily obscure and mystify the diversity of developments that only slowly produced a consensus understanding that can be called Judaism. This of course in no way denies that rabbinic Judaism had deep roots in its Judahite predecessors.

31. James Pasto ("When the End Is the Beginning? Or When the Biblical Past Is the Political Present: Some Thoughts on Ancient Israel, 'Post-Exilic Judaism,' and the Politics of Biblical Scholarship," *SJOT* 12:2 [1998]: 191–92) in stressing a large measure of continuity between the preexilic and postexilic Judahite populace and culture, observes as follows, *"the fact is that the term 'Judaism' is only minimally attested in the sources for the Second Temple period. . . .* It is 'Israel,' rather than 'Judaism' that was and remained the premier term of self-reference for 'Jews' from at least the fourth century b.c.e. and until their 'westernization' in the eighteenth and nineteenth centuries c.e." (author's italics). Pasto further cautions that the term "Judaism" in Maccabees may not mean the "religion" or "way of life" of Judahites but rather "siding/collaborating with the Judahite party" against the Hellenizers. The thrust of his remarks is that the "ism" in Judaism is informed by ancient Hellenistic and modern Western secular sociopolitical categories, and especially by anti-Semitic religious thought that permeated nineteenth-century biblical scholarship.

Regrettably, in much scholarly discourse, Judaism is misleadingly reified as a religion "jump-started" after the exile in a radical departure from earlier Israelite culture and religion. In an effort to resist this splitting of preexilic and postexilic Israelite culture and religion into two entirely different phenomena, Marc Zvi Brettler ("Judaism in the Hebrew Bible? The Transition from Ancient Israelite Religion to Judaism," *CBQ* 61 [1999]: 429–47) proposes to broaden the nomenclature of Judaism to cover the preexilic period: "I believe that the most satisfactory solution is to expand the use of the term 'Judaism(s)' into the preexilic period, thereby reflecting the continuity of tradition and practice. Given the scholarly tendency to divide Judaism into periods, we might even speak of the biblical period in terms of 'emergent' or 'earliest' Judaism" (445). Although I applaud Brettler's motivation, I think an expanded use of "Judaism" would obscure the long, slow development from a nonmonotheistic, scriptureless, and diversified preexilic Israelite culture and religion into the monotheistic, scriptured, and relatively homogeneous culture and religion that was reached under rabbinic Judaism.

32. Davies (*"'Ancient Israel,'"* 32–35, 66–70) and Thomas L. Thompson (*The Mythic Past: Biblical Archaeology and the Myth of Israel* [New York: Basic Books, 1999], 15, 164–68, 213–14) are insistent on these synchronisms as the only secure historical anchor points in the biblical monarchic narratives.

33. Against those who claim that the biblical narratives are historically reliable because they are so often "plausible" and "lifelike," Thomas L. Thompson (*Early History of the Israelite People: From the Written and Archaeological Sources* [Leiden/New York/Cologne: E. J. Brill, 1992], 388) makes the pertinent rejoinder that fiction excels in precisely such qualities of "believability." My point here is that much of the allegedly historical biblical reportage is neither very good fiction nor very believable in a fictive sense, precisely because of its hodgepodge of genres and styles, its oscillations between minute details and sweeping generalizations, and its gaps and incongruities in reciting events. The biblical narratives' manner of reporting events does not make a convincing historical novel out of Genesis–Kings, in contrast to short novellas that appear here and there within the text, such as the Joseph story or the Davidic court history, nor does it have the coherence of an ethnographic "travelogue" such as Herodotus produced.

34. On the vexed issue of how we are to assess the reliability of particular textual claims about what happened in Israel's history, interpreters obviously employ an array of expressed or unexpressed criteria to which they give differential weight in judging textual assertions to be "erroneous," "possible," "probable," or "certain." In this respect, biblical historians are no different from historians as a whole, since historical research is not itself a single method but an arsenal of methods that can be, and regularly is, variously employed, and the subject matter of history is amorphous until some delineations are made by the historian as to what is to be included and excluded. Norman K. Gottwald ("Triumphalist versus Anti-triumphalist Versions of Early Israel: A Response to Articles by Lemche and Dever in Vol. 4 [1996]," *CurBS* 5 [1997]: 20–26) posits a "historicity continuum" whose opposed poles feature historical information about specific persons, places, and events (H1 data) at one end of the spectrum and historical information about social, cultural, and political structures and processes lacking or meager in space-time specifics (H2 data) at the other end of the spectrum. Particular "historical" references fall variously along this continuum. Marc Z. Brettler (*The Creation of History in Ancient Israel* [London/New York: Routledge, 1995], 142–43) suggests that it is helpful to test the validity of biblical historical claims in the way that truth claims are treated under different forms of legal adjudication: either proven "beyond a reasonable doubt," as in criminal cases, or established by "a preponderance of evidence," as in civil law. Both Gottwald's and Brettler's formulations encourage the extension of historical probability to include textual claims that stricter "factually proven" approaches would exclude, but neither proposal as stated has been convincingly operationalized to

deal with the complexity of evidential factors relevant to most, if not all, historical truth claims in biblical texts.

35. I have adopted this biblical sociopolitical periodization into tribal, monarchic, and colonial eras as the organizing principle for my textbook, *The Hebrew Bible—A Socio-Literary Introduction* (Philadelphia: Fortress, 1985; see chart 12, 602–6), while simultaneously recognizing that the biblical writings, although adhering to this periodization, were in most instances *not* composed or compiled in the periods they either describe or claim to originate from, according to attributed authorship. In practice, this means that the sociopolitical chronology and the literary chronology of ancient Israel are not in any sort of direct one-to-one alignment. The result is that both the sociopolitical horizons and the literary horizons have to be reconstructed hypothetically, both separately and in relation to one another in a process that cannot avoid a measure of circular reasoning. Thus, it is not at all surprising that there are numerous, sharply differing versions of how the social and literary histories diverge and/or converge.

36. Jack Goody (*The Logic of Writing and the Organization of Society* [Cambridge: Cambridge Univ. Press, 1986]) spells out the major differences in communication involved in literate and nonliterate societies and polities in early Mesopotamia and West Africa, with some references to Israel. Susan Niditch (*Oral World and Written Word* [Louisville, Ky.: Westminster John Knox, 1996], 39–59) notes that the epigraphic finds from monarchic Israel are either for circumscribed military or commercial purposes or symbolic iconic purposes, attesting to a strong oral bias in the culture.

37. Those scholars, such as Philip R. Davies and Thomas L. Thompson, who place no confidence in the sociocultural existence of Israel before the monarchy, are swayed in part by the inconsistent and anachronistic nomenclature used to characterize the corporate entities described in the prestate traditions, whereas those of us who give cautious credence to prestate Israel, while acknowledging the linguistic and historical anachronisms, follow social historical and political anthropological models for how states are formed within already functioning decentralized societies (Gottwald, *Tribes;* Frank S. Frick, *The Formation of the State in Ancient Israel: A Survey of Models and Theories,* SWBA, 4 [Decatur, Ga: Almond Press, 1985]; Frith Lambert, "The Tribe/State Paradox in the Old Testament," *SJOT* 8/1 [1994]: 20–44; Paula M. McNutt, *Reconstructing the Society of Ancient Israel* [Louisville, Ky.: Westminster John Knox, 1999]). If I read him rightly, Niels Peter Lemche appears to be somewhat ambivalent on this issue. In recent publications, he characteristically maintains his skepticism about the textual accounts of the tribal period, as well as of earlier and later periods, but he also draws on social historical and political anthropological data in such a fashion that he creates an ecological and sociopolitical Palestinian environment in which a tribal Israel would be perfectly conceivable, even though he stops short of pursuing this line of inquiry, which he had tentatively begun to do in his earlier books, *Early Israel: Anthropological and Historical Studies on the Israelite Society Before the Monarchy,* VTSup 37 (Leiden: E. J. Brill, 1985), 407–35, and *Ancient Israel: A New History of Israelite Society* (Sheffield: JSOT Press, 1988), 75–117. This "setup" of conditions for a social reconstruction of early Israel, which Lemche does not follow up on, is especially pronounced in his *Prelude to Israel's Past: Background and Beginnings of Israelite History and Identity*

(Peabody, Mass.: Hendrickson Publishers, 1998) but also implicit in *The Israelites in History and Tradition,* both of which contain provocative "leads" for critical imaginative reenactments of tribal life.

38. Perceptive readings of how political power increased and "migrated" in the ancient Near East appear in Mann, *Sources,* 73–249, and William H. McNeill, *The Rise of the West: A History of the Human Community with a Retrospective Essay* (1963; reprint, Chicago: University of Chicago Press, 1991), 29–166.

39. Most general political and cultural histories of the ancient Near East give minimal attention to a macro comparison of Israel with its neighbors, and what is said is primarily devoted to its religion. From the side of sociology, Talcott Parsons (*Societies. Evolutionary and Comparative Perspectives* [Englewood Cliffs, N.J.: Prentice-Hall, 1966], 95–108) and S. N. Eisenstadt (*The Origins and Diversity of Axial Age Civilizations* [Albany, N.Y.: SUNY Press, 1986], 1–25) have offered brief comparative reflections on Israel in its larger context but likewise focused on Israel's religion and are meager on historical contexts. While the general histories of McNeill and Mann provide excellent macro frameworks on the ancient Near East, they have surprisingly little to say about Israel.

40. Although many historians of ancient Israel are irritated by the reiterated claim of scholars such as Davies, Lemche, and Thompson that most historical reconstructions of ancient Israel have been too reliant on uncritical paraphrasing of the biblical narratives, I am convinced that their cautionary message has performed a valuable service in raising epistemological and methodological consciousness, in sharpening argumentation, and in profitably reopening issues long thought to have been conclusively settled. Whatever the outcome of the debates on particular issues, I am confident that biblical studies are being strengthened by the minimalist challenge. See the unsympathetic critique by Ian W. Provan ("Ideologies, Literary and Critical: Reflections on Recent Writing on the History of Israel," *JBL* 114 [1995]: 585–606) and the rejoinder by Philip R. Davies ("Method and Madness: Some Remarks on Doing History with the Bible," *JBL* 114 [1995]: 699–705).

41. Terry Eagleton (*Criticism and Ideology: A Study in Marxist Literary Theory* [London: Verso, 1976], 68–69) draws an intriguing analogy between the way a dramatic production enacts and reconstitutes the ideology of a dramatic text, on the one hand, and the way a literary text enacts and reconstitutes the ideology of an age or social sector and thereby reveals something of its relations to history, on the other. As in the case of Fuentes, whom I quoted at the close of chap. 1, Eagleton is working with literary texts of novelistic fiction that do not have the same genre conventions as historiography. Yet it seems to me, genre differences notwithstanding, that the way fiction relates to "real life" throws light on the series of "slippages" that every historian encounters between reported data, the genres in which they are reported, the ideologies informing the reportage, and the ideological vision of the historian, a series of "slippages" that must be bridged by the creative imagination of the historian in order to gain access, however refracted, to the ideologies of the history under study. In this sense, historiography may be seen as a "dramatic" or "fictive" production even as it consciously strives to stay as close as possible to "what really happened." Mario Liverani (*Prestige and Interest: International Relations in the Near East ca. 1600–1100 B.C.*, History of the Ancient Near East / Studies 1 [Padova: sargon srl, 1990], 285–95) articulates the subtle "triangular pattern"

between event, ideology, and account, noting that ideology not only shapes the account but constitutes the medium or "grid" in which political events are enacted and understood by their participants, and only with some sense of operative ideologies in antiquity can political historians link single events in patterns that lend them meaning.

42. Lynn Hunt, "History as Gesture; or, the Scandal of History," in *Consequences of Theory: Selected Papers from the English Institute*, 1987–88, ed. J. Arac and B. Johnson (Baltimore; Johns Hopkins, 1991), 103.

43. Norman K. Gottwald, "Rhetorical, Historical, and Ontological Counterpoints in Doing Old Testament Theology," in *God in the Fray: A Tribute to Walter Brueggemann*, ed. T. Linafelt and T. K. Beal (Minneapolis: Fortress, 1998), 11–23.

44. Biblical scholarship has long recognized such ideological factors as the "tendency" of texts and the "preunderstanding" of interpreters, but only over the last decade or so has it consolidated these concerns under the rubric of ideological criticism. See David Jobling and Tina Pippin, ed., *Ideological Criticism of Biblical Texts*, *Semeia* 59 (1992); The Bible and Culture Collective, *The Postmodern Bible* (New Haven: Yale Univ. Press, 1995), 272–308; and David J. A. Clines, *Interested Parties: The Ideology of Writers and Readers of the Hebrew Bible*, JSOTSup 205 (Sheffield: Sheffield Academic Press, 1995), 9–25; and Norman K. Gottwald, "Ideology and Ideologies in Israelite Prophecy," in *Prophets and Paradigms: Essays in Honor of Gene M. Tucker*, ed. Stephen B. Reid, JSOTSup 229 (Sheffield: Sheffield Academic Press, 1996), 136–49. Jacques Berlinerblau ("Ideology, Pierre Bourdieu's *Doxa*, and the Hebrew Bible," in *Semeia [The Social World of the Hebrew Bible: Twenty-Five Years of the Social Sciences in the Academy]*, forthcoming) questions the widely held assumption among biblical scholars that ideologies are "voluntaristic," i.e., consciously held and deliberately employed by a single class, in contrast to the view that ideologies are "hidden," i.e., unconsciously held, often obliquely expressed, and widely shared by sectors of a social formation who are most likely to be victimized by them.

45. I have discussed this issue in connection with the "ideological confrontation" between Dever and Lemche over the historicity of biblical texts (Gottwald, "Triumphalist versus Anti-Triumphalist Versions of Early Israel," 26–36). Noteworthy instances of willingness to scrutinize one's ideology as a biblical interpreter are Daniel Patte, *Ethics of Biblical Interpretation: A Reevaluation* (Louisville, Ky.: Westminster John Knox, 1995) and David Jobling, *1 Samuel*, Berit Olam (Collegeville, Minn.: Liturgical Press, 1998), 3–37, wherein the authors sustain a pronounced autobiographical voice as they trace their changeful ideological journeys and evaluate what an admitted ideology implies for the ethical integrity and social practice of the interpreter. Roland Boer (*Novel Histories: The Fiction of Biblical Criticism* [Sheffield: Sheffield Academic Press, 1997]) includes himself in a bar conversation with Martin Noth, George Lukacs, and Walter Scott in a work that calls on the genres of historical novel, science fiction, and utopian literature to deconstruct the alleged objectivism of biblical criticism.

46. This author's ideological perspectives are more fully grounded autobiographically in the prolegomenon to Norman K. Gottwald, *The Hebrew Bible in Its Social World and in Ours*, xv–xxix, and elaborated in several of the articles in part 3 ("A Social Critical Theology") and part 4 ("Social and Political Ethics") in the same volume. Quite a number of studies have analyzed the ideological underpinnings of

my biblical interpretations, among which I mention: Walter Brueggemann, review of *Tribes of Yahweh, JAAR* 48 (1980): 44–51, reprinted in *The Bible and Liberation: Political and Social Hermeneutics,* ed. N. K. Gottwald and R. A. Horsley, rev. ed. (Maryknoll, N.Y.: Orbis, 1993), 227–35; Robert Morgan and John Barton, *Biblical Interpretation* (Oxford: Oxford Univ. Press, 1988), 152–54; David Jobling, "Sociological and Literary Approaches to the Bible: How Shall the Twain Meet?" *JSOT* 38 (1987): 85–93; P. T. Chikafu, "The Audience Presupposed in the Conquest, Infiltration, and Revolt Models: A Sociological Analysis," *JTSA* 84 (Sept. 1993): 11–24; Leo G. Perdue, *The Collapse of History,* OBT (Minneapolis: Fortress, 1994), 69–109; and Roland Boer, "Deutero-Isaiah: Historical Materialism and Biblical Theology," *BibInt* 6/2 (April 1998): 181–204.

Chapter 3

1. Norman K. Gottwald (*The Tribes of Yahweh: A Sociology of the Religion of Liberated Israel, 1250–1050 B.C.E.* [2d corrected printing, Maryknoll, N.Y.: Orbis, 1981; reprint with new preface, Sheffield: Sheffield Academic Press, 1999], 237–341) presents an extended analysis of the societal nomenclature for premonarchic Israel from literary, historical, and anthropological perspectives.

2. The fluid and protean character of biblical terms for communal leaders is widely acknowledged. For example, Robert North ("Palestine, Administration of [Judean Officials]," *ABD,* 5:86–90), on concluding his review of manifold attempts to attach stable significations to the terms for preexilic political authorities, remarks, "Really *all* the above biblical terms for civil authority are shifting and interchangeable" (88), and he finds that this is even more evident in the postexilic nomenclature. T. R. Hobbs (*2 Kings,* WBC 13 [Waco, Tex.: Word], 256) observes, "Many official bureaucratic titles tend to retain their original designation while at the same time the specific function of the official so designated has changed." To be sure, context at times supplies considerable certitude about the meaning of any single occurrence of a term, but that same meaning cannot be safely presupposed for other occurrences, which must in each instance be examined afresh.

3. Ronald E. Clements (*Abraham and David: Genesis XV and its Meaning for Israelite Tradition* [London: SCM Press, 1967]) finds the figure of Abraham to be shaped as a prototype of David, and Joel Rosenberg goes even farther (*King and Kin: Political Allegory in the Hebrew Bible* [Bloomington/Indianapolis: Indiana Univ. Press, 1986]) when he claims that "Genesis is . . . nothing short of a companion work to II Samuel, a 'midrash,' if you will, upon the Davidic history" (xiii). Gary A. Rendsburg ("Biblical Literature as Politics: The Case of Genesis," in *Religion and Politics in the Ancient Near East,* ed. Adele Berlin, Studies and Texts in Jewish History and Culture [Bethesda, Md.: Univ. Press of Maryland, 1996], 47–70) offers an alternative political allegorization of Genesis, and S. David Sperling (*The Original Torah: The Political Intent of the Bible's Writers* (New York/London: New York Univ. Press, 1998]), broadens the biblical political allegory to cover the entire Pentateuch. More theoretically, Roland Boer ("National Allegory in the Bible," *JSOT* 74 [1997]: 95–116) expands the work of Rosenberg, Schwartz, and Bal on political allegory in the Hebrew Bible with reference to a parallel conversation among Jameson, Ahmad, and Sprinker on national allegory in contemporary literature.

4. The social organizational structure of premonarchic Israel hypothesized in Gottwald, *Tribes* (see n. 1 above) is highly schematic and best viewed as an analytic/synthetic exercise that tries to make sense of the society imagined by the literary portrait of early Israel when historical-critical and anthropological assessments are factored into the reconstruction. Niels Peter Lemche (*Early Israel: Anthropological and Historical Studies on the Israelite Society Before the Monarchy*, VTSup 37 [Leiden: E. J. Brill, 1985], 80–290) makes a wide-ranging critique of my reconstruction, working with different historical critical hypotheses and anthropological analogues. So many variables are entailed in modeling early Israelite society that I would not care to defend my schema in all respects, but I continue to advocate this sort of endeavor, especially when joined in dialogue with counterschemas, in order to clarify the scope and limits of biblical data and to bring to light the unresolved issues. Paula M. McNutt (*Reconstructing the Society of Ancient Israel* [London: SPCK/Louisville: Westminster John Knox, 1999], 75–103), noting the uncertainties that persist, provides a lucid summary and appraisal of recent hypotheses about the social organization and structure of the tribal period.

5. The political scientist Aaron Wildavsky (*The Nursing Father: Moses as a Political Leader* [University, Ala.: Univ. of Alabama Press, 1984]) "plays" figuratively with Moses as the shaper of four different types of political designs or "regimes": slavery, anarchy, equity, and hierarchy. The point of interest in his work is that the Moses narratives are so "political" in their public scope and yet so devoid of the particulars of any single sociopolitical system that Wildavsky is able to abstract from them a range of ideal-typical regimes that do not rest on any historical reconstruction but rather on a deployment of literary imagination structured by political leadership paradigms. He argues, as have others, that the habits of mind and method in structural and political anthropology are conceptually similar to the mind-set and rules of rabbinic exegesis (13–16).

6. Gottwald, *Tribes,* 555–83.

7. For reviews of the biblical and extrabiblical evidence on the semantic force of *šōphēṭ,* see Martin S. Rozenberg, "The Šōfĕṭîm in the Bible," *ErIsr* 12 (1975): 77*–86*; Tomoo Ishida, "The Leaders of the Tribal League 'Israel' in the Premonarchic Period," *RB* 80 (1975): 514–30; and Keith W. Whitelam, *The Just King: Monarchical Judicial Authority in Ancient Israel,* JSOTSup 12 (Sheffield: Sheffield Academic Press, 1979), 50–61.

8. Gottwald, *Tribes,* 507.

9. Lemche, *Early Israel,* 245–72, stresses a preference for lineage structure over clan structure for an understanding of early Israelite society. However, Adam Kuper ("Lineage Theory: A Critical Retrospect," *Annual Review of Anthropology* 11 [1982]: 71–95) finds the lineage or descent group model "threadbare" and doubts that there are any societies "in which vital political and economic activities are organized by a repetitive series of descent groups" (92). It appears that both lineage and clan configurations, as currently discerned in anthropology, are of fairly limited utility for making sense of the biblical social unit called *mišpāḥāh* and its connections with the *bēth-'āv* and the *šēvet/maṭṭeh,* primarily because the biblical data are so equivocal on the points that distinguish clan and lineage. See McNutt (*Reconstructing the Society,* 83–85, 99–100), who notes, "Both lineages and clans are unilineal groups that perceive themselves as being descendants of a particular individual. But they

are different in that the genealogy of a lineage is more permanent, reflecting both real and postulated kinship between its members, while a clan genealogy varies according to particular clan segments, and its members, who assume common ancestry, cannot demonstrate their genealogical connections" (83–84).

10. James W. Flanagan ("Chiefs in Israel," *JSOT* 20 [1981]: 47–73) and Frank S. Frick (*The Formation of the State in Ancient Israel*, SWBA 4 [Decatur, Ga.: Almond Press, 1985], 71–97) argue for the presence of chiefdoms in tribal Israel. On the other hand, the imprecision in the concept of "chief," which covers a range of differing leadership arrangements spread across egalitarian, rank, and centralized societies, makes it of elusive value as a model for interpreting archaeological data in the judgment of Norman Yoffee ("Too Many Chiefs? (or, Safe Texts for the '90s)," in *Archaeological Theory: Who Sets the Agenda?* ed. N. Yoffee and A. Sherratt [Cambridge: Cambridge Univ. Press, 1993], 60–78), and presumably he would have similar strictures against applying chiefly models to ancient textual data. McNutt (*Reconstructing the Society*, 114–42), building on Flanagan and Frick, presents a nuanced argument for chieftainship in Israel as predecessor to the state.

11. Gottwald (*Tribes*, 358–75) traces the twelve-tribe concept in both its versions to the differing administrative practices of David and Solomon, the tribal format omitting Levi originating under Davidic administration (in which tribes were integral to the state infrastructure) and the tribal format including Levi stemming from Solomonic administration (in which tribes were of diminishing importance to the conduct of state affairs). To date I have not encountered serious objections to this proposal.

12. Gale A. Yee ("Ideological Criticism: Judges 17—21 and the Dismembered Body," in *Judges and Method: New Approaches in Biblical Studies*, ed. G. A. Yee [Minneapolis: Fortress, 1995], 146–70), in arguing that these narratives conduct "a propaganda war" against the Levitical clergy as part of the attempt of Josiah and the Deuteronomist "to break up the tribal body in service to the monarchy" (167), obviates the impulse to explain the tribal centralization featured in them as a faithful reflection of premonarchic sociopolitical organization. Yee's anti-Levitical reading of the text leaves room for the more frequently proposed anti-Saulide polemic in that the concubine's rapist-murderers are Benjaminites.

13. The mainline position of historical critical scholarship for more than a century has regarded Chronicles as dependent on Samuel–Kings for those passages they hold in common, whereas opinions have been various concerning the other sources of Chronicles (Robert H. Pfeiffer, "Chronicles, I and II," *IDB*, 1:578–80). Recently, however, A. Graeme Auld (*Kings without Privilege: David and Moses in the Story of the Bible's Kings* [Edinburgh: T. & T. Clark, 1994]) has contended that where they overlap, Kings and Chronicles draw on an earlier story of the Davidic dynasty. See also Baruch Halpern, "Sacred History and Ideology: Chronicles' Thematic Structure—Indications of an Earlier Source," in *The Creation of Sacred Literature: Composition and Redaction of the Biblical Text*, ed. R. E. Friedman (Berkeley, Calif.: Univ. of California Press, 1981), 35–54. Two recent volumes conveniently arrange the parallels between Chronicles, Samuel–Kings, and other biblical texts, accompanied by introductions and critical notes: John C. Endres, William R. Millar, and John Barclay Burns, eds., *Chronicles and its Synoptic Parallels in Samuel, Kings, and Related Biblical Texts* (Collegeville, Minn.: Liturgical Press,

1998), and W. R. Brookman, *A Hebrew-English Synopsis of the Old Testament: Samuel, Kings, and Chronicles* (Peabody, Mass.: Hendrickson Publishers, 2000). For more on the sources of Kings and Chronicles, see nn. 42–43 below.

14. For a review of scholarly opinions on the two *mišpāṭîm* attributed to Samuel, see Tomoo Ishida, *The Royal Dynasties in Ancient Israel: A Study on the Formation and Development of Royal-Dynastic Ideology* (Berlin/New York: Walter de Gruyter, 1977), 40–41.

15. Mephibosheth, "from the mouth of shame" or "from the mouth of Bosheth=the god Shame" (in 2 Sam. 4:4; 8:6; 16:1; 19:24; 21:6), appears to be a demeaning alteration of the original name Meri(b)baal (retained in 1 Chron. 8:34; 9:40). The substitution of bōšeth/Bosheth for Baal, in addition to stigmatizing the use of the Baal component in an Israelite name, may intend to eliminate the necessity of saying, or even seeing, the despised name of "Baal" in the royal family (Diana V. Edelman, *ABD*, 4:696–97, 701–2).

16. It is usual for interpreters to understand the elders who compact with David in 5:3 as the same northern elders in 3:17–18, but the stress on "*all* the tribes" (v. 1) and "*all* the elders" (v. 3) leaves open the possibility that the "Israel" of this text is larger Israel and that the northern and southern tribes are jointly involved in the elevation of David as king over a new political entity rather than "appending" the northern tribes to the already existing kingdom of Judah (so Linville, *Israel in the Book of Kings,* 118).

17. On David's wars and the extent of his kingdom, see J. Maxwell Miller and John H. Hayes, *A History of Ancient Israel and Judah* (Philadelphia: Westminster Press, 1986), 179–85. Baruch Halpern ("The Construction of the Davidic State: An Exercise in Historiography," in *The Origins of the Ancient Israelite States,* JSOTSup 228, ed. V. Fritz and P. R. Davies [Sheffield: Sheffield Academic Press, 1996], 44–75), citing the literary devices of Assyrian display inscriptions and annals that put "a maximal spin on the real events" (52), finds similarities in the reports of David's Transjordanian and Syrian campaigns that inflate limited military and diplomatic ventures by means of the typical "method of royal inscriptions to aggrandize by implication, to lead the reader without prevaricating" (67).

18. See Tomoo Ishida, "Solomon," *ABD,* 6:107–8 for a graphic layout displaying the officers of David and Solomon comparatively in side-by-side columns.

19. Tryggve N. D. Mettinger (*Solomonic State Officials: A Study of the Civil Government Officials of the Israelite Monarchy,* ConBOT 5 [Lund: Gleerup, 1971], 63–69) discusses the uncertainties surrounding the status of "the friend of the king," who appears only during the reigns of David and Solomon, and concludes that he was the intimate counselor of David, given official title under Solomon, but superseded in the divided monarchy by *yō'ēṣ,* the generic term for "counselor."

20. E. A. Speiser, "Census and Ritual Expiation in Mari and Israel," *BASOR* 149 (1958): 17–25. But note the caution that nothing like the modern practice of counting an entire populace was known in the ancient Near East prior to the Roman imperial censuses (so Frederick Mario Fales, "Census, Ancient Near East," *ABD,* 1:882–83).

21. The regions from which Solomon imported horses and chariots are problematic: the meaningless MT reading *miqwê* is commonly corrected to *miqqūwē* or *miqqô',* "from Kue" = Cilicia, a region in Anatolia, and *miṣrayim,* Egypt, is fre-

quently construed as a misreading for Musri (also in 2 Kings 7:6), likewise located in Anatolia (John Gray, *I and II Kings. A Commentary*, OTL, 2d rev. ed. [Philadelphia: Westminster Press, 1970], 264 nn.g,h, 268–69). On the other hand, Yutaka Ikeda ("Solomon's Trade in Horses and Chariots in Its International Setting," in *Studies in the Period of David and Solomon and Other Essays*, ed. T. Ishida [Tokyo: Yamakawa-Shuppansha, 1982], 215–38) retains Egypt in the text and argues for the historical authenticity of the reported trade, claiming that it does not refer to large-scale trade in military equipment but to especially prized and costly horses and chariots used for ceremonial display purposes. Some recent commentators contend that the text derives from later monarchic times when overland trade in horses and chariots is attested in Assyrian sources; see, e.g., Nadav Na'aman, "Sources and Composition in the History of Solomon," in *The Age of Solomon: Scholarship at the Turn of the Millennium*, ed. L. K. Handy (Leiden/New York/Cologne: E. J. Brill, 1997), 70–72.

22. For a detailed discussion of possible solutions to the textual, geographical, and historical problems in reconstructing the Solomonic administrative districts, see Simon J. DeVries, *I Kings*, WBC 12 (Waco, Tex.: Word, 1985), 63–74.

23. J. Alberto Soggin, "Compulsory Labor under David and Solomon," in *Studies in the Period of David and Solomon*, 259–67. Muhammad A. Dandamayev ("Slavery, Ancient Near East/Old Testament," *ABD*, 6:58–65) situates the Israelite state corvée in relation to known forms of slavery in the ancient Near East.

24. On the high officials of David and Solomon, see John Bright, "The Organization and Administration of the Israelite Empire," in *Magnalia Dei: The Mighty Acts of God*, ed. F. M. Cross et al. (Garden City, N.Y.: Doubleday, 1975), 193–208; Benjamin Mazar, "King David's Scribe and the High Officialdom of the United Monarchy of Israel," in *The Early Biblical Period: Historical Studies*, ed. S. Ahituv and B. Levine (Jerusalem: Israel Exploration Society, 1986), 126–38; Abraham Malamat, "Organs of Statecraft in the Israelite Monarchy," in *BARead* 3 (1970): 163–98; Mettinger, *Solomonic State Officials*; Udo Rüterswörden, *Die Beamten der israelitischen Königszeit*, BWA(N)T 117 (Stuttgart: Kohlhammer, 1985).

25. Ishida, "Solomon," *ABD*, 6:108.

26. Instances of indeterminacy in the use of "Israel" (either northern kingdom or inclusive Israel) or of double entendre (both northern kingdom and inclusive Israel) occur in 2 Sam. 5:1–3 (see n. 16 above) and in 2 Kings 17, where the inclusive "people of Israel" delivered from Egypt in vv. 7–8 narrows down to the northern kingdom of Israel in vv. 9–18 (note "images of two calves," v. 16). After abruptly implicating Judah in the cultic crimes of Israel, it is said that "Yahweh rejected all the seed of [inclusive] Israel" (vv. 19–20).

27. A loose parallel to the synchronized history of Kings appears in the Assyrian Synchronistic History (Chronicle 21) published with introduction and commentary by A. K. Grayson (*Assyrian and Babylonian Chronicles* [Locust Valley, N.Y.: J. J. Augustin Publisher, 1975], 51–56, 157–70), which recounts battles fought between contemporary Assyrian and Babylonian kings from the early fifteenth to the early eighth centuries. In most cases, the Assyrian king is named first and the synchronization is no more exact than to say "at the time of [king x]." Just as Kings pronounces a generalized condemnation on Israel vis-à-vis Judah, the Synchronistic History lauds Assyria at the expense of Babylonia, which is claimed to have

repeatedly violated an age-old agreement between the two parties concerning the boundary line separating them ("May the praises of Assyria be lauded for[ever]. May the crime of Sumer and Akkad be bruited abroad through every quarter," 170). The Assyrian document, however, is narrow in its topical scope and lacks the complexity and ambivalence with which Kings treats the relations between Israel and Judah. A Synchronistic King List of Assyrian and Babylonian rulers from the time of Ashurbanipal is an even more distant parallel to Kings, since it contains no narrative (Grayson, 200).

28. The array of difficulties in working with the relative dates supplied for each king, and the different ways in which the variables are "adjusted" to develop a self-consistent chronology, are well illustrated by comparing and contrasting the following reconstructions: Mordechai Cogan, "Chronology, Hebrew Bible," *ABD,* 1:1005–11; Simon J. DeVries, "Chronology of the OT," *IDB,* 1:584–89; John H. Hayes and P. K. Hooker, *A New Chronology for the Kings of Israel and Judah* (Atlanta: Scholars, 1988); and Edwin R. Thiele, *The Mysterious Numbers of the Hebrew Kings* 3d ed. (Grand Rapids, Mich.: Eerdmans, 1983).

29. Thiele, *Mysterious Numbers,* has succeeded in reconciling *all* the biblical numbers in MT, but only by positing a complex combination of coregencies, undocumented events, shifts in calendars, and changes in the calculation of regnal years. His manipulation of the variables is as arbitrary as those of other proposed chronologies, and it can be fairly said that he purchases coherence at the expense of parsimony. Although I used Thiele's chronology with reservations in Gottwald, *The Hebrew Bible—A Socio-Literary Introduction* (Philadelphia: Fortress, 1985), xxix, I am no longer convinced that it has an "edge" on other chronologies such as those of DeVries and Cogan. John Gray has put the state of chronological studies of Kings precisely, "Difficulties and discrepancies are admitted by all . . . and, on the basis of the biblical evidence alone, taken at its face value, no final certainty may be achieved in the chronology of Kings" (*I and II Kings,* 56).

30. The steps entailed in converting the relative biblical dates into absolute dates derived from Assyrian and Neo-Babylonian records are lucidly described by DeVries ("Chronology of the OT," 585).

31. The absolute dates that can be assigned to particular biblical events are listed in tabular form by Cogan ("Chronology, Hebrew Bible," 1007).

32. On coregencies, see Gray, *I and II Kings,* 65–68, and Thiele, "Coregencies and Overlapping Reigns," *JBL* 93 (1974): 176–89.

33. See nn. 28–29 above.

34. Dennis T. Olson, "Pekah" and "Pekahiah," *ABD,* 5:214–16.

35. John Strange, "Joram, King of Israel and Judah," *VT* 25 (1975): 191–201; Maxwell Miller and John H. Hayes, *A History of Ancient Israel and Judah* (Philadelphia: Westminster Press, 1986), 280–82.

36. A. M. Honeyman, "The Evidence for Royal Names among the Hebrews," *JBL* 67 (1948): 13–26.

37. On the nature of Jeroboam's cult, Wesley I. Toews (*Monarchy and Religious Institutions under Jeroboam,* SBLMS 47 [Atlanta: Scholars, 1993]), after a thorough review of the evidence, concludes "that the religious policies and institutions advocated by Jeroboam drew upon ancient Israelite traditions, and that they were Yahwistic, and that they were perceived as legitimate practice in the Israelite state

during the period of Jeroboam and probably for a long time thereafter, perhaps until the time of Hosea" (147). Toews' judgment is in line with the views of most scholars who have written on the subject (see Carl D. Evans, "Jeroboam," *ABD,* 3:742–43). Frank M. Cross (*Canaanite Myth and Hebrew Epic: Essays in the History of the Religion of Israel* [Cambridge: Harvard Univ. Press, 1973], 73–75) elucidates the old Israelite cult traditions revived by Jeroboam, and remarks, "Apparently, Jeroboam's real sin was in establishing a rival to the central sanctuary at Jerusalem, not in the introduction of a foreign god or a pagan idol" (75).

38. Athaliah is identified both as the daughter of Omri (2 Kings 8:18) and the daughter of Ahab (2 Kings 8:26). H. J. Katzenstein ("Who Were the Parents of Athaliah?" *IEJ* 5 [1955]: 194–97) and Winfried Thiel ("Athaliah," *ABD,* 1:511) cogently argue that she was a daughter of Omri and sister of Ahab.

39. On the *ḥērem* as ritual destruction of captive persons and goods, see Norbert Lohfink, "*ḥāram,*" *TDOT* 5:180–99; Philip D. Stern, *The Biblical Ḥerem: A Window on Israel's Religious Experience,* BJS 211 (Atlanta: Scholars, 1991); and on the sociopolitical significance of the practice, Gottwald, *Tribes,* 543–50.

40. Athaliah was the only reported female head of state in Israel and Judah, but the narrator, regarding her as a usurper of the Davidic line, refrains from giving her the title *malkâh,* "queen." The mothers and wives of kings are often named, and sometimes they play a large role in the narratives, e.g., Jezebel and Athaliah. Three are identified as a *gĕvîrâh,* "great lady/queen mother": Maacah, mother of Asa (1 Kings 15:13), Athaliah, mother of Ahaziah (2 Kings 10:13), and Nehushta, mother of Jehoiachin (Jer. 13:18; 29:2). See Carol Smith, "'Queenship' in Israel? The Cases of Bathsheba, Jezebel and Athaliah," in *King and Messiah in Israel and the Ancient Near East,* JSOTSup 270, ed. J. Day (Sheffield: Sheffield Academic Press, 1998), 142–62. On the plausibility of the Kings' account of Athaliah's reign, see the discussion under "Gaining and Keeping Power" and n. 50 below.

41. The common older view that Ahaz's altar was in the service of a foreign cult imposed by Assyria (Gray, *I and II Kings,* 635) is now generally abandoned (see T. R. Hobbs, *2 Kings,* 215–18), largely as a consequence of two studies demonstrating that it was not Assyrian policy to impose their religious practices on conquered peoples beyond the formal acknowledgment of the overlord's deity when signing treaties (John W. McKay, *Religion in Judah under the Assyrians* [London: SCM Press, 1973] and Mordechai Cogan, *Imperialism and Religion: Assyria, Judah, and Israel in the 8th and 7th Centuries B.C.E.,* SBLMS 19 [Missoula, Mont.: Scholars, 1974]).

42. On the stated sources of Kings, see James A. Montgomery, *A Critical and Exegetical Commentary on the Book of Kings,* ICC, rev. ed. (New York: Charles Scribner's Sons, 1951), 24–45; Gray, *I and II Kings,* 9–36, and Steven W. Holloway, "Kings, Book of 1–2," *ABD,* 4:70–73.

43. On the stated sources of Chronicles, see Edward L. Curtis and Albert A. Madsen, *A Critical and Exegetical Commentary on the Books of Chronicles,* ICC (New York: Charles Scribner's Sons, 1910), 17–26; Jacob M. Myers, *I Chronicles,* AB 12 (Garden City, N.Y.: Doubleday, 1965), xlv–lxiii; and Ralph W. Klein, "Chronicles, Book of 1–2," *ABD,* 1:996–97. Benjamin Maisler (Mazar) ("Ancient Israelite Historiography," *IEJ* 2 [1952]: 82–88) argues that while both Kings and Chronicles drew on government and temple records, the bulk of their sources came from prophetic circles and in his view constitute "the pearls of Israelite historiography,"

an assessment more literary and religious than strictly historical. For more on the sources of Kings and Chronicles, see n. 13 above.

44. Burke O. Long, *I Kings with an Introduction to Historical Literature,* FOTL 9 (Grand Rapids, Mich.: Eerdmans, 1984), 22. Long further contends that Herodotus and the Deuteronomist share similar paratactic literary conventions. Richard D. Nelson ("The Anatomy of Kings," *JSOT* 40 [1988]: 44) remarks on the paratactic synchronisms, "This temporal 'folding over' pattern unites the stories of Judah and Israel into a single story which the reader is unable to untangle." Perhaps it is better to say that the several strands intending to tell "a single story" are not easily "untangled" by the reader.

45. Hobbs, *2 Kings,* xxvii.

46. Long, *I Kings,* 26.

47. A major point in Linville, *Israel in the Book of Kings,* is that Kings adheres resolutely to a notion of larger Israel as inclusive of both kingdoms. Mullen (*Narrative History,* 258–86) and Gary N. Knoppers (*Two Nations under God: The Deuteronomistic History of Solomon and the Dual Monarchies,* HSM 52 [Atlanta: Scholars, 1993], 1:2–7, 54–56) are in fundamental agreement, although they differ as to the historical horizon(s) from which the narrator(s) of Kings articulate this ecumenical Israel. Mullen and Knoppers are comfortable with a two-edition placement of the Deuteronomistic History in the late seventh and mid-sixth centuries, while Linville, exceedingly doubtful of ascertaining the compositional history and the sociohistorical locus, favors a later indeterminate context in postexilic times.

48. Tomoo Ishida (*The Royal Dynasties in Ancient Israel: A Study of the Formation and Development of Royal-Dynastic Ideology,* BZAW 142 [Berlin/New York: Walter de Gruyter, 1977], 151–82) discusses the assassinations at length in his treatment of dynastic succession in the two kingdoms, and attributes those in the northern kingdom to factors such as military failures of certain kings, tribal rivalries, and antagonism between rulers and people, with tribal rivalries being decisive in his view. Ishida's analysis pays scrupulous attention to the biblical data but does not probe the social, economic, and political dimensions in great depth, in large part because the major interest of his study is to prove, contra Albrecht Alt, that the dynastic principle was adhered to not only in Judah but throughout the history of the northern kingdom (see chap. 5, n. 109).

49. "The son of Tabeel" has been variously identified as a son of Azariah or Jotham by a Syrian princess from the Tabeelite tribe, and thus a Davidic prince (W. F. Albright); a descendant of an important north Israelite family, later known as the Tobiads, who probably received Transjordanian estates as a reward for loyalty to Pekah of Israel (B. Mazar); and the ruler of Phoenician Tyre, who was offered the Judahite throne to induce him to join the anti-Assyrian alliance of Israel and Damascus (A. Vanel). See John H. Hull Jr., "Tabeel," *ABD,* 6:292.

50. Although differing in many details, the commentaries and scholarly literature are nearly unanimous in accepting the account of Athaliah's "usurpation" of the Judahite throne at face value. I have found but one source that shares the main outlines of my view that her rule, although irregular, was legitimate. Mullen (*Narrative History and Ethnic Boundaries,* 21–32) likewise favors the view that Athaliah, in the role of queen mother, acted as interim head of state and guardian of the young Joash until such time as he would be old enough to assume the throne. Her hus-

band Joram's murder of all his brothers, followed by Jehu's massacre of further members of the Judahite royal household, left Joash as the sole male survivor of Davidic lineage. In order to assure dynastic continuity, and particularly to block any move by Jehu to take over the rule of Judah, Athaliah acted peremptorily, but she could have done so only with a strong support group. Patricia Dutcher-Walls (*Narrative Art, Political Rhetoric: The Case of Athaliah and Joash*, JSOTSup 209 [Sheffield: Sheffield Academic Press, 1996], 154) makes the similar point that Athaliah could hardly have acted without a strong faction backing her, but although she employs a model of factional politics in agrarian monarchies, Dutcher-Walls does not question the biblical account of Athaliah's intent to exterminate the Davidic dynasty. Mullen, on the other hand, adds the intriguing point that the absence of a regnal formula for Athaliah may not be due in the first instance to the Deuteronomist's aversion to her, although it served his purpose well, but may reflect rather the absence of any regnal formula in his sources, precisely because as queen mother preparing Joash to rule she was not, and did not claim to be, a rightful occupant of the throne other than in an interim capacity. Mullen (29, n. 25) reports that the legitimacy of Athaliah's interim rule has also been suggested by H. Reviv ("On the Days of Athaliah and Joash," *Beth Mikra* 47 (1970/71): 541–49 [Heb.]) and by C. Levin (*Der Sturz der Königen Atalja. Ein Kapitel zur Geschichte Judas im 9. Jahrhundert v. Chr.* [Stuttgart: Katholisches Bibelwerk, 1982], 83–90). The attempt of Hannelis Schulte ("The End of the Omride Dynasty: Social-Ethical Observations on the Subject of Power and Violence," *Semeia* 66 [1995]: 135–37, 144–45) to supply a plausible political rationale for Athaliah's "monstrous" murders by explaining them as a measure to protect Judah's "open borders" policy toward neighboring states is a strained defense of the biblical account.

51. A. Leo Oppenheim, *Ancient Mesopotamia: Portrait of a Dead Civilization,* rev. ed. (Chicago: Univ. of Chicago Press, 1977), 95–109; Erik Hornung, "The Pharaoh," in *The Egyptians,* ed. Sergio Dandoni (Chicago: Univ. of Chicago Press, 1997), 283–313.

52. Arvid S. Kapelrud, "Temple-Building: A Task for Gods and Kings," *Or* 32 (1963): 52–62; Victor (Avigdor) Hurowitz, *I Have Built You an Exalted House: Temple Building in the Bible in the Light of Mesopotamian and Northwest Semitic Writings,* JSOTSup 115 (Sheffield: JSOT Press, 1992).

53. On the cultic reforms of kings, see Gösta W. Ahlström, *Royal Administration and National Religion in Ancient Palestine* (Leiden: E. J. Brill, 1982), and Richard H. Lowery, *The Reforming Kings: Cults and Society in First Temple Judah,* JSOTSup 120 (Sheffield: JSOT Press, 1991).

54. William Riley, *King and Cultus in Chronicles: Worship and the Reinterpretation of History,* JSOTSup 160 (Sheffield: JSOT Press, 1993). Marti J. Steussy (*David: Biblical Portraits of Power* [Columbia, S.C.: Univ. of South Carolina Press, 1999], 125–26) aptly denotes the Chronicler's concept of the monarchy, "The Chronicler's David is paradigmatic rather than unique. . . . His Israel is more congregation than nation, defined by its temple preparations rather than transitions in political status. . . . This emphasis on worship creates a bridge across the discontinuity of Jerusalem's fall, connecting monarchic Judah to Persian Yehud."

55. J. Glen Taylor, *Yahweh and the Sun: Biblical and Archaeological Evidence for Sun Worship in Ancient Israel,* JSOTSup 111 (Sheffield: Sheffield Academic Press, 1993).

56. Susan Ackerman (*Under Every Green Tree: Popular Religion in Sixth-Century Judah,* HSM 46 [Atlanta: Scholars, 1992]) studies the sixth-century cultic "abominations" condemned in Jeremiah 7 and 44, Ezekiel 8, Isaiah 57 and 58 at a point in Judah's history when, according to Kings and Chronicles, the monarchic cult reforms had been carried out, and concludes that, not only were these "abominable" practices widespread, but they were regarded by their devotees as thoroughly Yahwistic. In her summary remarks, Ackerman says, "Most of the manifestations of popular religion which I have described are native to the west Semitic sphere and even to Israel, and they are indigenous in the practice of Yahwistic religion . . . sixth-century Yahwism was characterized by a diversity which extends far beyond the parameters seemingly established by the biblical text. Indeed, it is only too obvious that there can be no one definition of what Yahwism was in the exilic period. . . . The priestly/deuteronomistic/prophetic version of what exilic Yahwism was is only that: a version" (215–16). Mark S. Smith (*The Early History of God: Yahweh and the Other Deities in Ancient Israel* [San Francisco: Harper & Row, 1990], xix–xxxiv, 154–57) speaks of a complex twofold process of Israelite convergence with and divergence from Canaanite and other ancient Near Eastern religions, a process that extended into and beyond the exile.

57. Martin A. Cohen, "In All Fairness to Ahab: A Socio-Political Consideration of the Ahab-Elijah Controversy," *ErIsr* 12 (1975): 87*–94*.

58. Baruch Halpern ("Jerusalem and the Lineages in the Seventh Century B.C.E.: Kinship and the Rise of Individual Moral Liability," in *Law and Ideology in Monarchic Israel,* ed. Baruch Halpern and Deborah W. Hobson, JSOTSup 124 [Sheffield: Sheffield Academic Press, 1991], 27, 47–48, 73–74, 77–79) seeks to show how Hezekiah's policy of political centralization disrupted the rural lineage systems and ancestor cults. James Pasto ("When the End is the Beginning . . . ," 185–86) likewise views Hezekiah's domestic policies as aimed at mobilizing a common front against Assyria.

59. William E. Claburn, "The Fiscal Basis of Josiah's Reform," *JBL* 92 (1973): 11–22, derived from his "Deuteronomy and Collective Behavior" (Ph.D. diss., Princeton Univ., 1968), and Shigeyuki Nakanose, *Josiah's Passover. Sociology, and the Liberating Bible* (Maryknoll, N.Y.: Orbis, 1993), 32–112.

60. Naomi Steinberg, "The Deuteronomic Law Code and the Politics of State Centralization," in *The Bible and the Politics of Exegesis: Essays in Honor of Norman K. Gottwald on His Sixty-Fifth Birthday,* ed. D. Jobling et al. (Cleveland: Pilgrim Press, 1991), 161–70.

61. In current biblical scholarship there is a decided reaction against treating Deuteronomy and the hypothetical "Deuteronomic School" as the necessary source of theological motifs in other biblical books that bear greater or lesser resemblance to style and motifs in Deuteronomy and the Deuteronomistic History; see, e.g., the articles in Linda S. Schearing and Steven L. McKenzie, eds., *Those Elusive Deuteronomists: The Phenomenon of Pan-Deuteronomism,* JSOTSup 268 (Sheffield: Sheffield Academic Press, 1999), especially those by Richard Coggins (22–35), Norbert F. Lohfink (36–66), and Robert R. Wilson (67–82), and the postscript by McKenzie (262–71). While mindful of this caution and fully aware that many biblical streams of tradition speak of obedience and disobedience as issuing in rewards and punishments, my reason for speaking of "the 'Deuteronomistic' moral-theological

axiom" in this instance is that Chronicles deliberately reproduces the Deuteronomistic judgments of the book of Kings and goes on to heighten and intensify them.

62. The protracted history of Yahwism in its movement from one among many cults to the achievement of an exclusive status among Judahites, as well as the process of its "refinement" in which many earlier features of the Yahweh cult were shed and anathematized, is traced in Mark S. Smith, *The Early History of God,* and various aspects of the monotheizing process are treated in Diana V. Edelman, ed., *The Triumph of Elohim: From Yahwisms to Judaisms* (Grand Rapids: Eerdmans, 1995). Robert K. Gnuse (*No Other Gods: Emergent Monotheism in Israel,* JSOTSup 241 [Sheffield: Sheffield Academic Press, 1997]), drawing on the accumulated evidence, evaluates a number of proposals that have been offered for reconstructing the contributing factors and emergent stages in the development of monotheism.

63. Steven L. McKenzie (*The Chronicler's Use of the Deuteronomistic History,* HSM 33 [Atlanta: Scholars, 1984]) usefully classifies the textual data on the extent and manner of the Chronicler's departures from Kings, quite apart from his particular conclusions about Chronicles' attestation to multiple editions of Kings.

64. Yigael Yadin (*The Art of Warfare in Biblical Lands,* 2 vols. [New York: McGraw-Hill, 1963]), profusely illustrated, draws on a wide range of textual and archaeological data to document military weaponry and strategy in the ancient Near East, significantly filling in the lacunae in biblical information on the subject.

65. Halpern, "Construction of the Davidic State" (cf. n. 17).

66. Mordechai Cogan and Hayim Tadmor (*II Kings: A New Translation with Introduction and Commentary,* AB 11 [Garden City, N.Y.: Doubleday & Co., 1988], 242–43) note parallels to Rab-shakeh's speech from Assyrian records of high officials who address besieged cities and of affinities with the rhetoric of diplomatic persuasion used in 2 Kings, which are further developed by C. Cohen ("Neo-Assyrian Elements in the First Speech of the Biblical Rab-šaqê," *IOS* 9 [1979]: 32–48).

67. Victor Hurowitz (*I Have Built You an Exalted House,* 126) concludes, "Comparisons of the structures of more than twenty extra-biblical building accounts and four biblical building accounts has shown that there is practically no difference between the biblical accounts and the accounts which have reached us from different areas and different periods. . . . They are all typical, routine ancient Near Eastern building stories" (126).

68. Ahlström, *Royal Administration,* 18–26.

69. The political and ideological power of monumental architecture and murals in Mesopotamian regimes are discussed by Julian Reade, "Ideology and Propaganda in Assyrian Art," in *Power and Propaganda: A Symposium on Ancient Empires,* Mesopotamia 7, ed. M. T. Larsen (Copenhagen: Akademisk Forlag, 1979), 329–43, and by Carl Nylander, "Achaemenid Art," in *Power and Propaganda,* 345–59. Carol Meyers (*ABD,* 6:359–61) discusses the importance of the religious symbolism of the Jerusalem temple in focusing and cementing political loyalty to the Davidic dynasty.

70. Mettinger (*Solomonic State Officials,* 80–89) details the sources of royal holdings and the types of land grants by the crown to officials and supporters; see chap. 5, n. 42.

71. Norman K. Gottwald, "The Participation of Free Agrarians in the Introduction of Monarchy to Ancient Israel: An Application of H. A. Landsberger's Framework for the Analysis of Peasant Movements," *Semeia* 37 (1986): 81–82.

72. Chris Hauer Jr. ("The Economic and National Security in Solomonic Israel," *JSOT* 18 [1980]: 63–73) offers some "dollars and cents" calculations of Solomon's exorbitant expenditures. To the contrary, David C. Hopkins ("The Weight of the Bronze Could Not Be Calculated," in *The Age of Solomon*, 300–311), reflecting the current doubt about the grandeur of Solomon's reign, warns that there is no way to convert the biblical figures on Solomon's wealth into meaningful economic values "because we lack the data necessary to relate such numbers to the Solomonic gross national product or gross national consumption or any other broad economic indicator" (301). Joseph R. Rosenbloom ("Social Science Concepts of Modernization and Biblical History: The Development of the Israelite Monarchy," *JAAR* 40 [1972]: 437–44), while alert to the way David, and especially Solomon, "pushed" centralization "to the breaking point," does not gain any appreciable insight by invoking current modernization theory to illuminate their endeavors, based as that theory is on very different foundations in contemporary capitalism.

73. Frank Crüsemann ("State Tax and Temple Tithe in Israel's Monarchical Period" [unpublished paper from the SBL Sociology of the Monarchy Group, annual meeting, 1983]), noting that the assessment and collection of separate state and cult revenues are first described in postexilic texts, favors the view that the preexilic states collected cultic revenues as an aspect of a sacrally legitimated kingship. Phyllis Bird, in response to Crüsemann, observes that any such system of state collection of temple revenues would not have applied to local and regional sanctuaries supported by families or clans, or to the landed endowments of priesthoods. Carol Meyers (*ABD*, 6:361) observes that references to kings emptying the temple treasuries in order to meet extraordinary expenses signifies that at least some state revenues were kept in the temple precinct, probably because it was a safe place at the heart of the royal acropolis. A sharp separation between state funds and temple funds may not be sustainable, given that religion was an arm of government and that kings seemed to enjoy discretionary control over temple funds.

74. The offices of *mazkîr* and *sōphēr*, which I have rendered respectively as "herald/protocol officer" and "secretary/chief scribe," in particular have found no scholarly consensus as to their duties; see Joachim Begrich, "Sōfēr und Mazkīr," *ZAW* 58 (1940–41): 1–29, and Mettinger, *Solomonic State Officials*, 25–62. Rüterswörden, in *Die Beamten*, argues that the topmost cohort of officials was called *śārîm*, for which *rō'š*, *rav*, *pāqîd*, and *'al-* [with attached sphere of responsibility], were synonyms. In his view, other officials were of lesser rank. Saul was attended only by *'ăvādîm*, "servants," and although David had *śārîm*, they first appear in the list of Solomon's officials. This positing of a two-tier rank in the official titles, in itself questionable, does not help appreciably in understanding their duties. More to the point is Rüterswörden's contention that the *śārîm* were not only patrimonial appointees in personal service to the king but also representatives of the upper echelons of society, with the result that their socioeconomic status and their political status, derived from different sources, sometimes served to solidify loyalties to the crown and at other times created divisions and dissension in the royal establishment.

75. The office of *sārîs* has been particularly perplexing. Its core meaning is "eunuch," a castrated male who often served as chamberlain in royal harems, and seemingly this is its sense in 2 Kings 9:32. Elsewhere in biblical texts and through-

out the ancient Near East, *śārîsîm* occupy a variety of civil and military offices, and it is disputed whether the holders of this title were in every instance actual eunuchs (see Cogan and Tadmor, *II Kings*, 112).

76. On *yōšěvîm* in the sense of "rulers, persons in authority" [i.e., those "sitting" in the seat of authority], see Gottwald (*Tribes*, 512–34), who extends this meaning, already identified by Alt and Cross-Freedman, to many additional biblical passages, with greater or lesser certainty in particular contexts. To my knowledge, this sense of the term for "rulers" has not been further investigated in recent years.

77. Concerning the notion of "Judah-ism," even diverse "Judah-isms," in the colonial period, intended to avoid the notion that Yahwistic religion achieved a precise boundable form prior to rabbinic times, see my discussion in chap. 2, "'Israel' and 'Judah' as Ambiguous Historical Agents," and especially nn. 30–31.

78. Robert P. Carroll, "The Myth of the Empty Land," *Semeia* 59 (1992): 79–93; Hans M. Barstad, *The Myth of the Empty Land: A Study in the History and Archaeology of Judah During the 'Exilic' Period* (Oslo: Scandinavian Univ. Press, 1996).

79. On Edomite incursions and settlements in Judah, see J. R. Bartlett, "Edom," *ABD*, 2:291–93.

80. Norman K. Gottwald, *All the Kingdoms of the Earth: Israelite Prophecy and International Relations in the Ancient Near East* (New York: Harper & Row, 1964), 330–46.

81. Norman K. Gottwald, "Social Class and Ideology in Isaiah 40—55: An Eagletonian Reading," *Semeia* 59 (1992): 43–57, with responses by John Milbank (59–71) and Carol A. Newsom (73–78).

82. For divergent analyses of the factional leadership conflicts in restoration Judah, see Paul D. Hanson, *The Dawn of Apocalyptic* (Philadelphia: Fortress, 1979); Brooks Schramm, *The Opponents of Third Isaiah. Reconstructing the Cultic History of the Restoration*, JSOTSup 193 (Sheffield: Sheffield Academic Press, 1995); and Stephen L. Cook, *Prophecy and Apocalyptic: The Postexilic Social Setting* (Minneapolis: Fortress, 1995). Precisely because the biblical texts are typically elusive in their identification of the factions or parties at odds with one another, a profile of social groups in restoration Judah, as well as their relation to particular ideologies and programs of action, remain tantalizingly problematic. This indeterminacy of group identities is a major obstacle to writing a history of the Judahite restoration.

83. The references in Zechariah 3:1, 6; 6:11 to Joshua, the high priest, and in Zechariah 4:6–10 to Zerubbabel, the governor, relate the two figures in a confused manner, but when they are read together in context, it is evident that the "branch" of 3:8 and 6:12 is none other than Zerubbabel, who is touted as the future king of Judah. The plural "crowns" in 6:11, 14 makes it virtually certain that the name of Zerubbabel once stood in this passage alongside Joshua.

84. With regard to Ezra–Nehemiah as sources for reconstructing the stages of return and restoration, the source critical and historical issues at stake are reviewed in Gottwald, *The Hebrew Bible*, 428–38, 514–22, and in Lester L. Grabbe, *Judaism from Cyrus to Hadrian*, Vol. 1, *The Persian and Greek Periods* (Minneapolis: Fortress, 1992), 1–145. More recent studies employing literary critical and sociohistorical methods are reported by Tamara C. Eskenazi, "Current Perspectives on

Ezra–Nehemiah and the Persian Period," *CurBS* 1 (1993): 59–86, and Charles E. Carter, *The Emergence of Yehud in the Persian Period: A Social and Demographic Study,* JSOTSup 294 (Sheffield: Sheffield Academic Press, 1999), 249–324. The fullest recent attempt at a historical reconstruction of colonial Judah in the imperial Persian context is Jon L. Berquist, *Judaism in Persia's Shadow: A Social and Historical Approach* (Minneapolis: Fortress, 1995), which is strong in its explication of developments in the Persian Empire that impacted Judah but requires supplementation and modification from the archaeological, demographic, and economic data for Judah proper that Carter brings to the subject.

85. See n. 83 above.

86. Cross, *From Epic to Canon,* 180–82; Carol L. Meyers and Eric M. Meyers, *Haggai, Zechariah 1—8,* AB 25B (Garden City, N.Y.: Doubleday, 1987), 13–16.

87. Cross (*From Epic to Canon,* 152–58, 161–64), summoning a wide range of extrabiblical evidence including the genealogy of Samarian governors, reconstructs the line of high priests from Joshua (b. ca. 570) to Onias I (b. ca. 345). He identifies the practice of naming sons after their grandfathers, so-called papponymy, whereby the names of high priests are repeated in successive generations, and notes that the same practice appears among the Samarians and Ammonites. Meyers and Meyers (*Haggai, Zechariah 1—8,* 9–17), who carry their analysis only as far as the end of the fifth century, subscribe to Cross's list of high priests and add their own reconstruction of the succession of governors from Sheshbazzar to Nehemiah.

88. Norman K. Gottwald, "The Expropriators and the Expropriated in Nehemiah 5," in *Concepts of Class in Ancient Israel,* ed. Mark R. Sneed, South Florida Studies in the History of Judaism 201 (Atlanta: Scholars, 1999), 4 n. 2.

89. Christopher Tuplin, "The Administration of the Achaemenid Empire," in *Coinage and Administration in the Athenian and Persian Empires,* ed. Ian Carradice (Oxford: British Archaeological Reports, 1987), 116–18, 127–28; commented on by Meyers and Meyers (*Haggai, Zechariah 1—8,* 15–16).

90. Gottwald, "The Expropriators and the Expropriated," 1–6.

91. Pasto ("When the End is the Beginning?" 189–90) remarks, "Ezra–Nehemiah, of course, speak of Zerubbabel and Joshua as returning Exiles. However, we must at least accept the possibility that this is part of the wider ideology of Exile and Return in these texts, one that transforms natives into returnees. . . . While it is not to be doubted that returning Exiles came to play a prominent role in the post-586 society, . . . one critical question arises: if we did not have Ezra–Nehemiah and the tradition of the returning Exiles would we have any indication that 'restoration' was carried out *by anyone but members of the Judean population that remained in the land?* . . . All of this together suggests a general continuity of the native population of Judah through and beyond Babylonian deportations" (author's italics).

92. The concept of restored Judah as a temple community that supplied the governing framework for politics and economics has been developed by Joel Weinberg, a sample of whose work appears in *The Citizen-Temple Community,* JSOTSup 151 (Sheffield: JSOT Press, 1992). His main thesis has been sympathetically received, albeit with qualifications, by Daniel L. Smith (*The Religion of the Landless: The Social Context of the Babylonian Exile* [Bloomington, Ind.: Meyer-Stone Books, 1989], 106–8) and Joseph Blenkinsopp ("Temple and Society in Achaemenid Judah," in *Second Temple Studies 1: Persian Period,* JSOTSup 117

[Sheffield: Sheffield Academic Press, 1991], 22–53); whereas Carter (*The Emergence of Yehud,* 294–307) concurs with H. Kreissig (*Klio* 66 [1984]: 35–39) that the Judahite citizen-temple community proposed by Weinberg is so atypical of other such known communities that his hypothesis is precarious and unproven.

93. Thomas Fischer, "First and Second Maccabees," *ABD,* 4:439–50; Jonathan A. Goldstein, *I Maccabees,* AB 41 (Garden City, N.Y.: Doubleday, 1976) and *II Maccabees,* AB 41A; Garden City, N.Y.: Doubleday, 1983).

Chapter 4

1. On "interstitial emergence," see Michael Mann, *The Sources of Social Power.* Vol. 1, *A History of Power from the Beginning to A.D.* 1760 (Cambridge: Cambridge Univ. Press, 1986), 15–19.

2. The gradual accumulation of power, exempt from societal veto, leading to state formation in the ancient Near East has been described at length by historians and anthropologists, e.g., Charles R. Redman (*The Rise of Civilization: From Early Farmers to Urban Society in the Ancient Near East* [San Francisco: W. H. Freeman & Co., 1978], 177–322); Mann (*Sources,* 73–129); but there is no consensus on what precipitated the "leap" or "drift" to statehood or which of several possible contributing factors carried the greatest weight. Norman Yoffee ("Mesopotamian Interaction Spheres," in *Early Stages in the Evolution of Mesopotamian Civilization,* ed. N. Yoffee and J. J. Clark [Tucson, Ariz./London: Univ. of Arizona Press, 1993], 257–69) shows how archeological evidence in Mesopotamia attests to the steady growth of commercial and cultural "interaction spheres" during the prestate Ubaid and Uruk periods, creating the preconditions and potentialities for state formation, but he does not attempt to identify what aspect of social relations "catalyzed" the emergence of the first states.

3. Dissatisfactions with "single factor" explanations of the rise of states and a preference for "multicausal" theories are detailed in Mann, *Sources,* 49–63; Henry T. Wright, "Recent Research on the Origin of the State," *Annual Review of Anthropology* 6 (1977): 379–97; Christine W. Bailey, "The State of the State in Anthropology," *Dialectical Anthropology* 9 (1985): 65–91. Henri J. M. Claessen and Peter Skalnik (*The Early State* [The Hague: Mouton Publishers, 1978]), after reviewing prevailing theories about state origins (5–17), propose their own refinements based on twenty-one cases of early states widely distributed geographically (622–29). Gerda Lerner (*The Creation of Patriarchy* [New York/Oxford: Oxford Univ. Press, 1986]), acknowledging a matrix of enabling factors in the rise of the state, argues that the overlooked precondition for political hierarchy lay in the prior conversion of women into commodity-like resources that could be exchanged or bought and enslaved as war captives, which eventually led to the capture or purchase of men as slaves. Once women and some men could be subordinated in this manner, the foundation was laid for the emergence of social classes and the rise of the state. In Lerner's terms, "Thus, the enslavement of women, combining both racism and sexism, preceded the formation of classes and class oppression. Class differences were, at their very beginnings, expressed and constituted in terms of patriarchal relations. Class is not a separate construct from gender; rather class is expressed in genderic terms (213). . . . The archaic state in the Ancient Near East

emerged in the second millennium B.C. from the twin roots of men's sexual dominance over women and the exploitation by some men of others. From its inception, the archaic state was organized in such a way that the dependence of male family heads on the king or the state bureaucracy was compensated for by their dominance over their families. Male family heads allocated the resources of society to their families the way the state allocated the resources of society to them. The control of male family heads over their female kin and minor sons was as important to the existence of the state as was the control of the king over his soldiers" (216). In focusing incisively on the gender component, Lerner has introduced an element almost entirely lacking in previous and ongoing studies of the precipitating factors in the emergence of ancient Near Eastern states.

4. The archaeologically validated aversion of stateless societies to political centralization for millennia prior to the first appearance of states is evident throughout Europe, Africa, and Oceania. Mann (*Sources,* 63–70) reviews this often overlooked "end of general social revolution," and remarks, "Most of the prehistory of society saw no sustained movement toward stratification or the state. Movement toward rank and political authority seems endemic but reversible" (67), and concludes emphatically that "*no general social evolution occurred beyond the rank societies of early, settled neolithic societies*" (69–70; author's italics).

5. Among the so-called "pristine" states, Mann (*Sources,* 74–75) includes Sumer, Egypt, Indus valley, North China, Mesoamerica, and Peru for "a probable total of six independent cases," noting that some add Minoan Crete, Elam, and East Africa. Robert McC. Adams (*The Evolution of Urban Society: Early Mesopotamia and Prehispanic Mexico* [Chicago/New York: Aldine Publishing Co., 1966], 21–22) accepts the same six independent cases, noting that the important distinction is "between voluntary states and externally imposed or inspired ones." On the other hand, William H. McNeill (*The Rise of the West: A History of the Human Community with a Retrospective Essay* [Chicago/London: Univ. of Chicago Press, 1991], 64–69, 94, 167–69, 239–43) is skeptical of pristine states beyond Sumer and Egypt, stressing strong external influence or stimulus in all other early states.

6. The process that Mann (*Sources,* 39–49 passim, 67–69) calls "social caging," when external flight from authority or internal choice of an alternative authority are precluded, closely resembles the environmental and social "circumscription" theory of Robert L. Carneiro ("A Theory of the Origin of the State," *Science* 169 [1970]: 733–38).

7. In developing the concept of "world-historical time" as a way of formulating comparisons that are historically informed, Mann (*Sources,* 173–74) objects to the direction that neo-Weberian comparative sociology has taken toward global but overly static analyses that gather examples from diverse stages of social-power development and are thus insufficiently historical to grasp the power dialectic within states and between states that are contemporary and states that succeed one another. While granting much of value in their studies, Mann finds that the works of John H. Kautsky (*The Politics of Aristocratic Empires* [Chapel Hill, N.C.: Univ. of North Carolina Press, 1982]), Reinhard Bendix (*Kings or People: Power and the Mandate to Rule* [Berkeley, Calif.: Univ. of California Press, 1978]), and S. N. Eisenstadt (*The Political Systems of Empires* [New York: Free Press, 1963/1969]) share a largely cyclical rather than developmental view of social power in ancient

and premodern polities. For the purposes of my study of ancient Israelite politics in its wider Near Eastern setting, Mann has been a more fertile source for framing my project than any of the named "neo-Weberians," even as I have gained insights from their characterizations of particular features of ancient "bureaucratic" or "aristocratic" empires. Similarly, Gerhard E. Lenski's analysis of agrarian societies in *Power and Privilege: A Theory of Social Stratification* (Chapel Hill, N.C.: Univ. of North Carolina, 1966/1984), currently more widely influential in biblical studies than the work of any other comparative sociologist since Weber, does not provide the historical leverage and nuance needed to locate ancient Israel among its political neighbors. On "world-historical time," see also chap. 2, n. 11.

8. The mercantile colonies established around the Mediterranean by Phoenician city-states represent an exceptional case, but apart from their importance in trade and in transmitting an alphabetic script to Greece, they did not have great political influence on the politics of Syro-Palestine. See Brian Peckham, "Phoenicia, History of," *ABD*, 5:349–57; William A. Ward, ed., *The Role of the Phoenicians in the Interaction of Mediterranean Civilizations* (Beirut: American Univ. of Beirut, 1968).

9. In addition to the relevant sections of the comprehensive histories of Mann (*Sources*, 73–249) and McNeill (*Rise of the West*, 29–166, 277–94), I have drawn on Jack M. Sasson (*Civilizations of the Ancient Near East*, 4 vols. [New York: Charles Scribner's Sons, 1995]; including a splendid "Timeline of Ancient Near Eastern Civilizations," vol. 1, viii–xi) and the following sources specific to subregions of the ancient Near East. I am particularly indebted to Jack Sasson for his careful perusal of this chapter and for a number of suggestions and corrections that have improved my presentation.

On Mesopotamia and Egypt: William W. Hallo and William K. Simpson, *The Ancient Near East. A History* (New York: Harcourt Brace Jovanovich, 1971); Amélie Kuhrt, *The Ancient Near East, c. 3000–330 B.C.*, 2 vols. (London/New York: Routledge, 1995); Daniel C. Snell, *Life in the Ancient Near East, 3100–332 B.C.* (New Haven, Conn./London: Yale Univ. Press, 1997), a lucid account for nonspecialists with a particular focus on social and economic history.

On Mesopotamia: Dominique Charpin, "The History of Ancient Mesopotamia: An Overview, *CANE*, 2:807–29; I. M. Diakanoff, ed., *Ancient Mesopotamia: Socio-Economic History* (Moscow: Nauka Publishing House, 1969); Hans J. Nissen, *The Early History of the Ancient Near East 9000–2000 B.C.* (Chicago/London: Univ. of Chicago Press, 1988); A. Leo Oppenheim, *Ancient Mesopotamia: Portrait of a Dead Civilization*, rev. ed. with Erica Reiner (Chicago/London: Univ. of Chicago Press, 1977); J. Nicholas Postgate, *Early Mesopotamia: Society and Economy at the Dawn of History* (London: Routledge, 1992); D. T. Potts, *Mesopotamian Civilization: The Material Foundations* (Ithaca, N.Y.: Cornell Univ. Press, 1997); Michael Roaf, *Cultural Atlas of Meospotamia and the Ancient Near East* (New York/Oxford: Facts on File, 1990); Wolfram von Soden, *The Ancient Orient: An Introduction to the Study of the Ancient Near East* (Grand Rapids, Mich.: Eerdmans, 1994); Norman Yoffee, "The Economy of Ancient Western Asia," *CANE*, 3:1387–99.

On Egypt: John Baines and Jaromír Málek, *Atlas of Ancient Egypt* (New York: Facts on File, 1980); Edward Bleiberg, "The Economy of Ancient Egypt," *CANE*, 3:1373–85; Barry J. Kemp, *Ancient Egypt* (London: Routledge, 1991); H. Kees, *Ancient Egypt: A Cultural Topography* (Chicago: Univ. of Chicago Press, 1961);

William J. Murname, "The History of Ancient Egypt: An Overview," *CANE*, 2:691–717; Georg Steindorff and Keith C. Seele, *When Egypt Ruled the East*, rev. ed. (Chicago: Univ. of Chicago Press, 1957); B. G. Trigger, Barry J. Kemp, David O'Connor, and Alan B. Lloyd, *Ancient Egypt: A Social History* (Cambridge: Cambridge Univ. Press, 1983), with superb bibliographical essays; P. J. Vatikiotis, *The History of Egypt*, 3d ed. (Baltimore: Johns Hopkins, 1986); John A. Wilson, *The Burden of Egypt* (Chicago: Univ. of Chicago Press, 1951).

On Hittites: O. R. Gurney, *The Hittites*, rev. ed. (London/Baltimore: Penguin Books, 1981); "The Hittite Empire," in *Power and Propaganda: A Symposium on Ancient Empires*, ed. M. T. Larsen (Copenhagen: Akademisk Forlag, 1979), 167–89.

On Assyria: A. Kirk Grayson, "Mesopotamia, History of (Assyria)," *ABD* 4:732–55; Kuhrt, *The Ancient Near East*, 2:473–501; A. T. Olmstead, *History of Assyria* (Chicago: Univ. of Chicago Press, 1923); H. W. F. Saggs, *The Might That Was Assyria* (London: Sidgwick & Jackson, 1984).

On Neo-Babylonia: Kuhrt, *The Ancient Near East*, 2:589–621; H. W. F. Saggs, *The Greatness That Was Babylon* (New York: Hawthorn Books, 1962).

On Persia: Pierre Briant, *Histoire de l'empire perse de Cyrus à Alexandre* (Paris: Fayard, 1996); J. M. Cook, *The Persian Empire* (New York: Shocken Books, 1983); Richard N. Frye, *The Heritage of Persia* (Cleveland: World Books, 1962); *The History of Ancient Iran* (Munich: C. H. Beck, 1984); Kuhrt, *The Ancient Near East*, 2:647–701; A. T. Olmstead, *The History of the Persian Empire* (Chicago: Univ. of Chicago Press, 1948).

On the Macedonian Empire: Pierre Briant, *Alexander the Great: Man of Action, Man of Spirit* (New York: Harry N. Adams, 1996); N. G. L. Hammond, *A History of Macedonia* (Oxford: Clarendon Press, 1972); C. B. Welles, *Alexander and the Hellenistic World* (Toronto: A. M. Hakkert, 1970).

On the Ptolemaic Kingdom: Roger S. Bagnall, *The Administration of the Ptolemaic Possessions outside Egypt*, Columbia Studies in the Classical Tradition 4 (Leiden: E. J. Brill, 1976); Edwyn R. Bevan, *A History of Egypt under the Ptolemaic Dynasty* (London: Methuen & Co., 1927).

On the Seleucid Kingdom: Edwyn R. Bevan, *The House of Seleucus*, 2 vol. (1902; reprint, New York: Barnes & Noble, 1966); H. Seyrig, "Seleucus I and the Foundation of Hellenistic Syria," in Ward, ed., *The Role of the Phoenicians*, 53–63.

10. William W. Hallo, "Biblical History in its Near Eastern Setting: The Contextual Approach," in *Scripture in Context: Essays on the Comparative Method*, ed. C. D. Evans, W. H. Hallo, and J. B. White (Pittsburgh: Pickwick Press, 1980), 1–26.

11. Kuhrt, *The Ancient Near East*, 1:27–44. Details of this Sumerian cultural and sociopolitical florescence are vividly illustrated and mapped in Roaf, *Cultural Atlas*, 58–93.

12. Thorkild Jacobsen, "Primitive Democracy in Ancient Mesopotamia," *JNES* 2 (1943): 159–72. McNeill remarks that the better term for the phenomenon might be "primitive oligarchy" (*Rise of the West*, 40, n. 15). Jacobson's hypothesis has not been sustained in subsequent research.

13. Kuhrt, *The Ancient Near East*, 1:44–55; Aage Westenholz, "The Old Akkadian Empire in Contemporary Opinion," in Larsen, *Power and Propaganda*, 107–23; Roaf, *Cultural Atlas*, 96–100.

14. A. D. Crown ("Tidings and Instructions: How News Travelled in the Ancient Near East," *JESHO* 17 [1974]: 265) reports various estimates on the distance ancient

Near Eastern army units could travel in one day, ranging from thirteen to twenty miles, with one scholar claiming thirty miles for Assyrian infantry. Based on much fuller data on the later Macedonian army (Donald W. Engel, *Alexander the Great and the Logistics of the Macedonian Army* [Berkeley, Calif.: Univ. of California Press, 1978]), Mann concludes that on average ancient Near Eastern armies of conquest could move no more than about twenty miles in a day and, more importantly, that after three days they would be dependent on such supplies as they could seize in enemy territory (*Sources,* 137–42).

15. For details on the long-term detrimental effects of salinization on the alluvial soils of Mesopotamia and the arduous work of building and maintaining irrigation canals, see Potts, *Mesopotamian Civilization,* 12–29.

16. On Sumerian Ur III, Isin, Larsa, and the Elamites: Kuhrt, *The Ancient Near East,* 1:56–80; Roaf, *Cultural Atlas,* 100–112.

17. On the Old Babylonians: Kuhrt, *The Ancient Near East,* 1:108–17; Samuel A. Meier, "Hammurapi," *ABD,* 3:39–42; Roaf, *Cultural Atlas,* 120–21; Jack M. Sasson, "King Hammurabi of Babylon," *CANE,* 2:901–15.

18. "The Code of Hammurabi," trans. Theophile J. Meek (*ANET,* 163–80); "Laws of Hammurabi," in Martha T. Roth, *Law Collections from Mesopotamia and Asia Minor,* SBLWAW 6, 2d ed. (Atlanta: Scholars Press, 1997), 71–142.

19. "The Creation Epic," trans. E. A. Speiser (*ANET,* 60–72); "The Creation Epic: Additions to Tablets V–VII," trans. A. K. Grayson (*ANET,* 501–3).

20. I am indebted to Jack Sasson for calling my attention to the recent discoveries at Tell Beydar and Tell Mozan in the Upper Khabur valley, which are in process of publication in *Subartu* and other journals of Mesopotamian studies.

21. Clyde Curry Smith, "The Birth of Bureaucracy," *BA* 40 (1977): 24–28; McGuire Gibson and Robert D. Biggs, eds., *The Organization of Power: Aspects of Bureaucracy in the Ancient Near East,* SAOC 46, 2d ed. (Chicago: The Oriental Institute, 1991). For more on bureaucracy in antiquity, see n. 70 below.

22. Karl Polanyi (*Trade and Market in the Early Empires: Economies in History and Theory,* ed. K. Polanyi, C. M. Arensberg, and H. W. Pearson [New York: The Free Press, 1957], 12–26, 243–69) argued for "marketless trading" in ancient Mesopotamia, favoring reciprocity and redistribution over exchange categories, and substantive over formal economic theories, for a proper understanding of ancient economies. This issue has been much debated, with most scholars finding market economizing present in some degree, but not on the scale rather naively assumed before Polanyi's work. Timothy Earle ("Prehistoric Economics and the Evolution of Social Complexity: A Commentary," in *Prehistoric Production and Exchange: The Aegean and Eastern Mediterranean,* ed. A. B. Knapp and T. Stech [Los Angeles: Institute of Archaeology, 1985], 106–11) proposes that the substantive and formalist approaches to economics are compatible, since the former looks at the social constraints on economic activity while the latter considers how people come to decisions within those constraints. Robert C. Hunt ("The Role of Bureaucracy in the Provisioning of Cities: A Framework for Analysis of the Ancient Near East," in Gibson and Biggs, *The Organization of Power,* 158–63) details how market and redistributive exchange mechanisms might both have been operative in distributing food to urbanites, for example, in the Ur III period. A brief summary of the debate appears in Daniel C. Snell, *Life in the Ancient Near East,* 149–52.

23. Johannes Renger, "Interaction of Temple, Palace, and 'Private Enterprise' in

the Old Babylonian Economy," in *State and Temple Economy in the Ancient Near East,* ed. E. Lipiński, OLA 5 (Louvain: Departement Orientalistiek, 1979), 1:249–56.

24. Kathryn A. Kamp and Norman Yoffee ("Ethnicity in Ancient Western Asia during the Early Second Millennium B.C.: Archaeological Assessments and Ethnoarchaeological Prospectives," *BASOR* 237 [1980]: 85–104) summarize the "waves" and "streams" immigrant hypotheses, favoring the latter as qualified by "enclosed nomadism," which recognizes the side-by-side coexistence of pastoralists, cultivators, and town dwellers over large parts of Mesopotamia.

25. Kamp and Yoffee ("Ethnicity in Ancient Western Asia") operating with the "loose" definition of an ethnic group (88), display confidence that ethnic "self-consciousness" can be traced archaeologically in material marks of symbols, behaviors, values, and economic/political strategies (96–97). The evidence they offer concerning Amorite ethnic identity seems dubious (97–99). Anatoly M. Khazanov ("Ethnicity and Ethnic Groups in Early States," in *Pivot Politics: Changing Cultural Identities in Early State Formation Processes,* ed. M. van Bakel, R. Hagesteijn, and P. van de Velde [Amsterdam: Het Spinhuis, 1994], 67–85) adopts a similarly loose understanding of ethnicity and goes on to find monoethnic, monolingual, and polyethnic early states, a number of them in the ancient Near East. Far more cautious is Ronald Cohen ("State and Ethnicity: the Dialectics of Culture and Polity," in M. van Bakel et al., eds., *Pivot Politics,* 47–66), who objects to ethnicity as a monolithic category: "Ethnicity is an extremely mercurial concept. It gains in entity as varying forms of identity lump on top of one another, and loses concreteness as these identifications begin to create more separable identities each overlapping" (50 n. 2). Yoffee elsewhere refers to how social group identities are "cobbled together" (Yoffee and Clark, eds., *Early Stages,* 269). My misgiving about ethnic labels is this: how can we know exactly, or even approximately, what "varying forms of identity" were "lumped on top of one another" or "cobbled together" among ancient Near Eastern peoples?

26. Anthony D. Smith (*The Ethnic Origins of Nations* [Oxford: Blackwell, 1986]), employing a "tight" delineation of ethnicity (22–31) that works well for groups about which we have adequate information, such as Jews, Armenians, and Greek Orthodox, makes a laudable but problematic attempt to find ethnic groups throughout the ancient Near East, using the Elamites as a test case illustrative of other peoples (70–71). Smith's historical and sociocultural analyses are thorough and impressive, especially his characterization of the Assyrian society, and they certainly show that groups of people forming majorities or minorities in the ancient Near East states had varying kinds and degrees of sociocultural homogeneity. But he falls short of showing that any of these groups satisfy his own criteria for ethnicity. Smith's distinction between group identities that are carried by a core of rulers who overlay populations that do not share their views ("lateral-aristocratic") and group identities shared by concentrated or scattered populations ("vertical-demotic") is instructive in clarifying some of the different ways that group identity can be expressed culturally and politically (76–89). Anthony Leahy ("Ethnic Diversity in Ancient Egypt," *CANE,* 2:225–34), while failing to clarify what he means by "ethnic," argues from artistic and linguistic evidence for the presence in Egypt of people of varied physical and cultural features from earliest times for whom the Nilotic culture did form a veritable "melting pot" or "sacred canopy."

27. On the failure of Akkad, Ur III, and the Old Babylonian kingdom of

Hammurabi to become effective empires, Mann argues that these states were not truly territorial or unitary but "federal" in their unintegrated oversight of social power networks. "Concentrated coercion" by military means could not prevent social power from spreading beyond governmental control and undermining the centralized political institutions (*Sources*, 174–76). Analytic light is thrown on the fragility of empire building by Robert D. Sack (*Human Territoriality: Its Theory and History* [Cambridge: Cambridge Univ. Press, 1986]), who, categorically rejecting the dubious belief in an innate territorial instinct, defines territoriality as a control strategy consisting of "the attempt by an individual or group to affect, influence, or control people, phenomena, and relationships, by delimiting and asserting control over a geographic area" (19). He spells out trends and complexities in the growth of territoriality through history, noting that the potential for control has been realized to varying degrees and that effective territoriality always requires sustained and shrewd effort to achieve and maintain. Daniel Miller ("The Limits of Dominance," in *Domination and Resistance*, ed. D. Miller, M. Rowlands, and C. Tilley [London: Unwin Hyman, 1989], 63–79) draws on anthropology, social history, and social theory to focus on the multifactorial nature of political power that precludes the complete or permanent elimination of counterideologies and counterforces within its realm.

28. The far-reaching effects of Mesopotamian societies in "politicizing" the outlying desert and mountain peoples through the circulation of goods, ideas, and people, together with the reciprocal impact of the fringe areas on the valley centers, are detailed in McNeill, *Rise of the West*, 98–109, and Mann, *Sources*, 78–82, 130–33, 163–66, 179–80. Gil J. Stein (*Rethinking World-Systems: Diasporas, Colonies, and Interaction in Uruk Mesopotamia* [Tucson, Ariz.: Univ. of Arizona Press, 1999]) contends that insufficient weight has been given to the initiative of outlying local cultures in the shaping of colonialism, exchange, and secondary state formation in ancient societies, and proposes "distance-parity" and "trade-diaspora" models for assessing interregional relations. The once-fashionable habit of labeling peoples "barbarian" or "civilized" is now usually either eschewed or carefully qualified (McNeill, for example, refers to "high barbarism"), because as an oppositional semantic pair the terms stereotype the "inferior outsiders" as uncultured and brutal, ignore their many contributions to the culture of the "superior insiders," and beg the question of the actual human value and overall benefits of the increased social complexity that distinguishes "higher civilization." Bennett Bronson ("The Role of Barbarians in the Fall of States," in *The Collapse of Ancient States and Civilizations*, ed. N. Yoffee and G. L. Cowgill [Tucson, Ariz.: Univ. of Arizona Press, 1988], 196–228) supplies a demystifying definition: "A *barbarian* is simply a member of a political unit that is in direct contact with a state but that is not itself a state . . . it is perfectly possible for a barbarian to be civilized insofar as he may be literate . . . , or technologically sophisticated . . . , or appreciative of the great tradition of nearby states. . . . He is a barbarian not because he is uncultured but because he is on the outside looking in" (200).

29. On "marcher lords" from the deserts and mountains as "pioneers of hegemonic empires," see Mann, *Sources*, 130–33, 174–76, 181–82.

30. Norman Yoffee, "The Late Great Tradition in Ancient Mesopotamia," in *The Tablet and the Scroll: Near Eastern Studies in Honor of William W. Hallo*, ed. M. E. Cohen, D. C. Snell, and D. B. Weisberg (Bethesda, Md: CDL Press, 1993), 300–308.

31. Barry J. Kemp, "Unification and Urbanization of Ancient Egypt," *CANE*,

2:679–90. Jac. J. Janssen ("The Early State in Ancient Egypt," in Claessen and Skalnik, *The Early State*, 215–18) concludes that: "the early Egyptian state is like a foundling without known parents" (218). It seems, however, that the same might also appropriately be said of the early Mesopotamian state.

32. On pharaoh, bureaucracy, and the general populace: see Janssen, "The Early State in Ancient Egypt," 218–28; Oleg Berlev, "Bureaucrats," in *The Egyptians*, ed. Sergio Donadoni (Chicago/London: Univ. of Chicago Press, 1997), 87–119.

33. For maps of the nomes of Upper and Lower Egypt, see Baines and Málek, *Atlas of Ancient Egypt*, 154–55.

34. On the Old Kingdom and First Intermediate Period: Kuhrt, *The Ancient Near East*, 1:135–60; Baines and Málek, *Atlas of Ancient Egypt*, 30–35.

35. On the Middle Kingdom: Kuhrt, *The Ancient Near East*, 1:161–73; Baines and Málek, *Atlas of Ancient Egypt*, 40–42.

36. On the Second Intermediate Period and the Hyksos: Kuhrt, *The Ancient Near East*, 1:173–82; Donald B. Redford and James M. Weinstein, "Hyksos," *ABD*, 3:341–48; Thomas L. Thompson, *The Mythic Past: Biblical Archaeology and the Myth of Israel* (New York: Basic Books, 1999), 138–49.

37. On the concentration and dispersal of Egyptian governmental powers: Barry J. Kemp in Trigger et al., *Ancient Egypt*, 174–82.

38. A revisitation of the public/private economy debate appears in Michael Hudson and Baruch Levine, eds., *Privatization in the Ancient East and Classical World: A Colloquium Held at New York University, November 17–18, 1994*, Peabody Museum Bulletin 5 (Cambridge, Mass.: Peabody Museum of Archaeology and Ethnology, 1996).

39. H. Goedicke, "Cult-Temple and 'State' during the Old Kingdom in Egypt," in Lipiński, *State and Temple Economy*, 1:113–32.

40. On the cultural homogeneity of Egypt, Mann remarks, "The pharaoh controlled one consolidated 'organization chart,' centered on the Nile, uniting economic, political, ideological, and a modicum of military power. . . . A consequence of this extraordinary degree of social and territorial caging was that Egyptian culture seems virtually unitary. . . . The degree of common cultural participation in a single (and, naturally, highly unequal) society was unique. This was as close an approximation to a unitary social system—the model of society I am rejecting in this work—as we find throughout recorded history" (*Sources*, 113–14), and Anthony Smith asserts that "the union of the two kingdoms, and the powerful religious influence of Memphis' priesthood, soon subordinated any regional cultures to the all-Egyptian culture of the rulers. There is perhaps no other example of so uniform and homogenous a cultural profile in antiquity, where the culture of the upper strata so profoundly penetrated the social and economic life of the dependent strata" (*The Ethnic Origins of Nations*, 89). I am not so much rejecting this view, especially when Egypt is compared to Western Asia, as I am cautioning against overstating the case in near absolute terms.

41. The complicated interactions among the Kassite, Assyrian, Mitannian, Hittite, and Egyptian states from ca. 1500 to 1200 B.C.E. are discussed in the text and displayed on the maps in Roaf, *Cultural Atlas*, 132–48.

42. It was common in early studies of the "collapse" of the Late Bronze Age states to stress natural disasters and cultural disintegration, but the disasters have

not been determinable, and while the old regional system certainly disintegrated and state power was obliterated or sharply reduced, recent studies stress that it was not a setback to ongoing communal life but a creative transition to new power arrangements. See William H. Hallo, "From Bronze Age to Iron Age in Western Asia: Defining the Problem," in *The Crisis Years: The Twelfth Century B.C. from beyond the Danube to the Tigris*, ed. W. A. Ward and M. S. Joukowsky (Dubuque, Iowa: Kendall/Hunt Publishing Co., 1989), 1–9; J. D. Muhly, "The Crisis Years in the Mediterranean World: Transition or Cultural Disintegration?," in Ward and Joukowsky, eds., *The Crisis Years*, 10–26; Mario Liverani, "The Collapse of the Near Eastern Regional System at the End of the Bronze Age: The Case of Syria," in *Centre and Periphery in the Ancient World*, ed. M. Rowlands, M. T. Larsen and K. Kristiansen (Cambridge: Cambridge Univ. Press, 1987), 66–73.

43. Addressing the issue of how the Phoenician city-states managed to survive the onslaught of the Sea Peoples, Patricia M. Bikai ("The Phoenicians," in Ward and Joukowsky, *The Crisis Years*, 132–41) proposes that they allied with the Sea Peoples in the interest of promoting trade.

44. On the effects of iron on agriculture and commerce: James D. Muhly, "Mining and Metalwork in Ancient Western Asia," *CANE*, 3:1501–21.

45. On literacy and the alphabet: Herman Vanstiphout, "Memory and Literacy in Ancient Western Asia," *CANE*, 2:181–96; Jeremy A. Black and W. J. Tait, "Archives and Libraries in the Ancient Near East," *CANE*, 2:197–209; William Whitt, "The Story of the Semitic Alphabet," *CANE*, 4:2379–97.

46. McNeill (*Rise of the West*, 110–12) refers to a "cosmopolitan civilization" by the fifteenth century B.C.E. in which states carried on "a lively diplomatic, commercial, and cultural intercourse." However, Liverani correctly observes that this thriving Bronze Age intercourse was monopolized by palace regimes. With the demise or retreat of large centralized states after 1200, room was opened up for "free-floating" artisans and commercial agents in the cities and for smaller communities to repopulate the hinterlands that had been neglected by former state regimes. Liverani (Rowlands, Larsen, and Kristiansen, eds., *Centre and Periphery*, 67–68, 72) outlines the contrasting socioeconomic and political patterns in Late Bronze and Early Iron Age Syria.

47. Mann (*Sources*, 532–38) organizes his analysis of ancient Near Eastern history around the ideal types of *the multipower-actor state*, wherein "decentralized power actors competed with one another within an overall framework of normative regulation" and *the empire of domination*, which "combined military concentrated coercion with an attempt at state territorial centralization and geopolitical hegemony" (533–34). He sees these as poles in a continuum of uneven collective power development. Among the multipower-actor states he includes Sumerian, Phoenician, Anatolian, and Greek city-states, while Akkad, Assyria, Persia, and later Rome are "classic" empires of domination. The important point for Mann is that these two forms of power organization developed dialectically but without any pre-ordained outcome or any single-factor explanation that we can identify in retrospect. That the kingdoms of Israel and Judah may have exhibited features of Mann's multipower-actor state may be indicated by the prophetic and legal traditions that seem to have stood outside, or at least in tension with, the political center and its royal theology.

48. Israel Eph'al, "On Warfare and Military Control in the Ancient Near Eastern Empires: A Research Outline," in *History, Historiography, and Interpretation: Studies in Biblical and Cuneiform Literature,* eds. H. Tadmor and M. Weinfeld (Jerusalem: Magnes Press/Leiden: E. J. Brill, 1983), 88–106; H. W. Saggs, "Assyrian Warfare in the Sargonid Period," *Iraq* 25 (1963): 145–54.

49. On Assyrian success in overcoming previous weaknesses in imperial policies, to become the first "revitalized empire of domination," see Mann, *Sources,* 231–37, and R. J. van der Spek ("Assyriology and History: A Comparative Study of War and Empire in Assyria, Athens, and Rome," in *The Tablet and the Scroll: Near Eastern Studies in Honor of William W. Hallo,* ed. M. E. Cohen, D. C. Snell, and D. B. Weisberg [Bethesda, Md.: CDL Press, 1993], 262–70), who spells out the dynamics of interstate and domestic power struggles that impelled these three states into militarism and imperial expansion. John Kautsky (*The Politics of Aristocratic Empires,* 7) notes that, in the absence of technology and state policies to increase agricultural and pastoral production, the shrinking tax base could press political regimes into wars of territorial expansion, often ill-advised, in an attempt to enlarge their resources.

50. On Assyrian imperial administration: A. Kirk Grayson, "Assyrian Rule of Conquered Territory in Ancient Western Asia," *CANE,* 2:959–68; Kuhrt, *The Ancient Near East,* 2:531–40; Peter Machinist, "Palestine, Administration of (Assyro-Babylonian)," *ABD,* 5:69–76; Simo Parpola and Kazuko Watanabe, eds., *Neo-Assyrian Treaties and Loyalty Oaths,* SAAS 2 (Helsinki: Helsinki Univ. Press, 1988). On the economic dimensions of Assyrian empire: N. B. Jankowska, "Some Problems of the Economy of the Assyrian Empire, in Diakanoff, *Ancient Mesopotamia: Socio-Economic History,* 253–76; J. N. Postgate, "The Economic Structure of the Assyrian Empire," in Larsen, ed., *Power and Propaganda,* 193–221.

51. On Assyrian deportation policies: Busteney Oded, *Mass Deportation and Deportees in the Neo-Assyrian Empire* (Wiesbaden: Reichert, 1979).

52. On Assyrian ideology: Kuhrt, *The Ancient Near East,* 2:505–19; Mario Liverani, "The Ideology of the Assyrian Empire," in Larsen, ed., *Power and Propaganda,* 297–317. Anthony D. Smith's "lateral-aristocratic" form of group ideology well describes the Assyrian elite, at least in the last two centuries of their empire (*The Ethnic Origins of Nations,* 100–105).

53. On Neo-Babylonians: Kuhrt, *The Ancient Near East,* 2:589–622; D. J. Wiseman, *Nebuchadrezzar and Babylon* (Oxford: Oxford Univ. Press, 1983); Roaf, *Cultural Atlas,* 192–93, 198–203.

54. P.-A. Beaulieu, *The Reign of Nabonidus, King of Babylon 556–539 B.C.,* Yale Near Eastern Researches 10 (New Haven, Conn.: Yale Univ. Press, 1987).

55. On the Egyptian New Kingdom: Baines and Málek, *Atlas of Ancient Egypt,* 42–48; Paul J. Frandsen, "Egyptian Imperialism," in Larsen, ed., *Power and Propaganda,* 167–89; Kuhrt, *The Ancient Near East,* 1:185–224, 317–30; David O'Connor, *Ancient Egypt,* 183–232; G. Steindorff and K. Seele, *When Egypt Ruled the East.*

56. Donald B. Redford, "Akhenaten," *ABD,* 1:135–37; Cyril Aldred, *Akhenaten, Pharaoh of Egypt: A New Study,* rev. ed. (London: Thames & Hudson, 1988).

57. On the Libyan, Nubian, and later native Egyptian Dynasties, and the domination of Egypt by Assyria and Persia: Kuhrt, *The Ancient Near East,* 2:623–46;

David O'Connor and Alan B. Lloyd in Trigger et al., *Ancient Egypt*, 249–348; Baines and Málek, *Atlas of Ancient Egypt*, 42–48.

58. Joseph M. Modrzejewski, *The Jews of Egypt: From Rameses II to Emperor Hadrian* (Princeton, N.J.: Princeton Univ. Press, 1995), 21–26.

59. On Persia: Kuhrt, *The Ancient Near East*, 2:647–791; Roaf, *Cultural Atlas*, 203–15.

60. On Persian imperial administration: J. M. Cook, *The Persian Empire*, 77–90, 102–12, 167–82; Christopher Tuplin, "The Administration of the Achaemenid Empire," in *Coinage and Administration in the Athenian and Persian Empires*, ed. Ian Carradice (Oxford: British Archaeological Reports), 109–66. For a map of the satrapies, see Roaf, *Cultural Atlas*, 208–9. Reflecting on the results of an ongoing workshop on Achaemenid History, Heleen Sancisi-Weerdenburg ("The Quest for an Elusive Empire," in *Achaemenid History*. Vol. 4, *Centre and Periphery*, ed. H. Sancisi-Weerdenburg and A. Kuhrt [Leiden: Netherlands Institute of the Near East, 1990], 263–74) points out how little is actually known of the administration and ideology of the Persian Empire as they operated on local and regional levels: "When one decides to look from the bottom, it is often hard to see the empire. In other words, it is very difficult to perceive the impact, let alone the administrative structure of, the Achaemenid empire" (263). In recommending the use of anthropological models to narrow the gap between historians of Persia who stress the unity of the empire and archaeologists who stress its cultural and political diversity, she describes a dynamic in Achaemenid studies very like the tensions and divisions of approach among historians of ancient Israel.

61. On Persian initiatives to codify the laws of Egypt and Judah: Gösta W. Ahlström, *The History of Ancient Palestine from the Palaeolithic Period to Alexander's Conquest*, JSOTSup 146 (Sheffield: Sheffield Academic Press, 1993), 876–79; Geo Widengren in John H. Hayes and J. Maxwell Miller, eds., *Israelite and Judaean History* (Philadelphia: Westminster Press, 1977), 515.

62. On Greek-Persian relations: Hermann Bengston, ed., *The Greeks and the Persians* (New York: Delacorte Press, 1968). Mann discusses the ambivalent Greek attitudes toward the Persians (*Sources*, 214–16) and reasons for the Greek triumph over the Persians (240–46).

63. On Persian ideology: Heleen Sancisi-Weerdenburg, "The Construction and the Distribution of an Ideology in the Achaemenid Empire," in M. van Bakel et al., eds., *Pivot Politics*, 101–19.

64. Frank E. Adcock, *The Greek and Macedonian Art of War* (Berkeley, Calif.: Univ. of California Press), 1957; Donald W. Engel, *Alexander the Great and the Logistics of the Macedonian Army*.

65. On the Macedonian Empire and Hellenistic Culture: Samuel K. Eddy, *The King Is Dead: Studies in the Near Eastern Resistance to Hellenism 334–31 B.C.* (Lincoln, Neb.: Univ. of Nebraska Press, 1961); F. E. Peters, *The Harvest of Hellenism: A History of the Near East from Alexander the Great to the Triumph of Christianity* (New York: Simon & Schuster, 1970); W. W. Tarn, *Hellenistic Civilisation*, 3d rev. ed. (New York: New American Library, 1952).

66. Roger S. Bagnall, *The Administration of the Ptolemaic Possessions outside Egypt* (Leiden: E. J. Brill, 1976), 11–24, 180–83, 213–51; Peter Schaefer, "Palestine under Ptolemaic Rule," in Miller and Hayes, eds., *Israelite and Judaean History*, 571–75.

67. Norman K. Gottwald, *The Hebrew Bible—A Socio-Literary Introduction* (Philadelphia: Fortress, 1985), 439–56; Peter Schaefer, "Palestine under Seleucid Domination" and "The Hasmonean Dynasty," in Miller and Hayes, eds., *Israelite and Judaean History,* 576–611; Solomon Zeitlin, *The Rise and Fall of the Judaean State: A Political, Social and Religious History of the Second Commonwealth.* Vol. 1, *332–37 b.c.e.* (Philadelphia: Jewish Publication Society of America, 1962).

68. Elias J. Bickerman, *The Jews in the Greek Age* (Cambridge/London: Harvard Univ. Press, 1988); Victor Tcherikover, *Hellenistic Civilization and the Jews* (Philadelphia: Jewish Publication Society of America/Jerusalem: Magnes Press, 1961).

69. In spite of frequently expressed reservations about the adequacy of center/periphery political theory, it remains analytically useful if not rigidly or mechanically applied; see Rowlands et al., eds., *Centre and Periphery,* 1–73.

70. Michael G. Morony ("'In a City without Watchdogs the Fox Is the Overseer': Issues and Problems in the Study of Bureaucracy," in Gibson and Biggs, eds., *The Organization of Power,* 5–14) cautions against facilely conceiving the administrative arm of states in antiquity as necessarily "bureaucratic" in the full-blown modern sense of a tightly organized, impersonally operated, and rule-governed system. Employing sociopolitical theorizing about bureaucracy, he raises questions concerning ancient Near Eastern patterns of governance through appointed officials. He is able to find a range of discontinuous evidence on some points, but on many aspects of bureaucracy the ancient sources are disconcertingly silent, at least in some cases suggesting loose, even haphazard, organization, more "patrimonial" than "bureaucratic" in Weber's usage.

71. Henri Cazelles, "Sacral Kingship," *ABD,* 5: 863–64; John Baines, "Ancient Egyptian Kingship: Official Forms, Rhetoric, Context," in *King and Messiah in the Ancient Near East: Proceedings of the Oxford Old Testament Seminar,* ed. J. Day, JSOTSup 270 (Sheffield: Sheffield University Press, 1998), 16–53; W. G. Lambert, "Kingship in Ancient Mesopotamia," in Day, ed., *King and Messiah,* 54–70.

72. Karl A. Wittfogel (*Oriental Despotism: A Comparative Study in Total Power* [New Haven, Conn./London: Yale Univ. Press, 1957]) argued that ancient states arose in "hydraulic societies" as managers of complex irrigation works, a monocausal theory that has been found empirically weak, and he further envisioned these states as exercising "total power" on analogy with the Soviet state under Stalin. The intellectual and political roots of the distorted views of Western scholars concerning Asia and the Middle East are traced and critiqued by Edward W. Said, *Orientalism* (New York: Random House, 1978).

73. In contending for significant ruptures and discontinuities between state regimes in early Mesopotamia, Piotr Michalowski ("Charisma and Control: On Continuity and Change in Early Mesopotamian Bureaucratic Systems," in Gibson and Biggs, eds., *The Organization of Power,* 45–57) remarks: "There has been a strong tendency to view Mesopotamian history as a continuous affair, one in which better and ever bigger 'empires' followed one another, teleologically focused on achieving national greatness. This continuum was broken by a number of 'Dark Ages' which were overcome and after a period of reconstruction, progress marched on. I think it is fair to say that currently few scholars would identify with such a position. As became evident, . . . the norm of political organization during the third

and early second millennia was the city-state and the so-called empires of the Dynasties of Akkad and Ur III, as well as the short period of glory under Hammurabi and Samsu-iluna, lasted in each case for no more than a few generations. In fact, the whole time of unity of Sumer and Akkad up to the end of the Old Babylonian period consisted of two hundred and thirty years, at the most. . . . The overt recognition of these ruptures and discontinuities is of crucial importance for the study of bureaucratic systems, for each of these states had to be created anew, at least to a certain extent, and the sad fact is that we know next to nothing about the important early years of their formation" (46–47).

74. R. J. van der Spek ("Assyriology and History," in M. E. Cohen et al., eds., *The Tablet and the Scroll,* 262–70) perceptively details the intense international and domestic pressures that often pushed heads of states into imprudent wars that proved ruinous, finding very similar dynamics in Assyria, Athens, and Republican Rome.

75. Norman Yoffee, "The Late Great Tradition in Ancient Mesopotamia."

76. Baines and Málek, *Atlas of Ancient Egypt,* 52–55.

77. Smith (*The Ethnic Origin of Nations,* 70–73), in a discussion of "the problem of 'social penetration,'" notes that we are poorly informed as to how extensively the high culture and ideology of political elites in antiquity were shared by the general populace, and Norman K. Gottwald ("Early Israel and the Canaanite Socio-Economic System," in *Palestine in Transition: The Emergence of Ancient Israel,* eds., D. N. Freedman and D. F. Graf, SWBA 2 [Sheffield: Almond Press, 1983], 25–37) observes, "A still unanswered question is the extent to which the ideologies of the ancient Near Eastern centralized states succeeded in creating popular cultures that cemented the populace in a common world view. Is it possible that we assume naively the same level and breadth of ideological cohesion for these ancient ideologies that we do for later historical religions such as Judaism, Christianity, Islam, Hinduism, and Buddhism?" (32).

78. For a brief historical contextualization of languages in the ancient Near East, see Kuhrt (*The Ancient Near East,* 4–6), who states that about fifteen languages are known to have been in use at various times, along with approximately seven systems of writing. For fuller treatment, see the multiauthored articles on Sumerian, Semitic, Egyptian, Indo-European, and other less-understood languages of the ancient Near East in *CANE,* 2:107–79; also "Languages," *ABD,* 4:155–229.

79. Smith (*The Ethnic Origins of Nations,* 100–5) attributes the dissolution of Assyrian ethnic identity, so total that it did not survive the fall of the state, to cultural syncretism and the intermixing of the Assyrian population with other peoples during its last two centuries of empire.

80. See, e.g., Norman K. Gottwald, "Icelandic and Israelite Beginnings: A Comparative Probe," in *The Labour of Reading: Desire, Alienation, and Biblical Interpretation: Essays in Honour of Robert C. Culley,* ed. F. C. Black et al., SemeiaSt (Atlanta: Scholars, 1999), 209–24. Very few crosscultural studies of sociopolitical institutions have included ancient Israel. An exception is Guy E. Swanson (*The Birth of the Gods: The Origin of Primitive Beliefs* [Ann Arbor, Mich.: Univ. of Michigan Press, 1960]), who tests Durkheim's theory about the social origin of religious beliefs by examining the correlation between sociopolitical complexity and varieties of belief, including monotheism, in fifty societies, among which are Middle

Kingdom Egypt, Augustan Rome, and Israel in the time of the judges. For a summary and critique of his methods and conclusions, see Gottwald, *Tribes*, 625–27, 639–41.

81. Mettinger (*Solomonic State Officials: A Study of the Civil Government Officials of the Israelite Monarchy*, ConBOT 5 [Lund: Gleerup, 1971], 80–87) details the various means by which kings could accumulate property without violating custom or law.

82. Marvin L. Chaney has meticulously uncovered the prophetic textual evidence for state intervention in the economy during the eighth and seventh centuries by means of a calculated strategy of agricultural intensification entailing a shift from subsistence cropping to the production of wine and oil for export, with dire effects on the viability of peasant life: "Bitter Bounty: The Dynamics of Political Economy Critiqued by the Eighth-Century Prophets," in *The Bible and Liberation: Political and Social Hermeneutics,* ed. N. K. Gottwald and R. A. Horsley (Maryknoll, N.Y.: Orbis, 1993), 250–63; "Whose Grapes? The Addressees of Isaiah 5:1–7 in the Light of Political Economy," in *Semeia* [*The Social World of the Hebrew Bible: Twenty-Five Years of Social Sciences in the Academy*], ed. R. A. Simkins and S. L. Cook, forthcoming). The bureaucratic managerial interventions necessary to provision ancient Near Eastern cities are carefully plotted through all the stages of production, extraction, transport, storage, processing, and distribution of food by Robert C. Hunt ("The Role of Bureaucracy in the Provisioning of Cities," in Gibson and Biggs, eds., *The Organization of Power,* 141–68). Hunt is able to draw on fairly full economic data from early Mesopotamia, and while it is obvious that Israelite states were involved in the same provisioning tasks, the textual and archaeological information for Israel and Judah is deficient in comparison.

The relevant archaeology is detailed by John S. Holladay Jr. ("The Kingdoms of Israel and Judah: Political and Economic Centralization in the Iron IIA–B [Ca. 1000–750 B.C.E.]," in *The Archaeology of Society in the Holy Land,* ed. T. E. Levy [New York: Facts on File, 1995], 368–98). Holladay "tests" the archaeological evidence by using an anthropological study of the legal systems of 184 societies in which class and wealth distinctions increased with an increase of the forces of production (Katherine S. Newman, *Law and Economic Organization: A Comparative Study of Preindustrial Societies* [Cambridge: Cambridge Univ. Press, 1983]). He concludes that there was a decided trend toward wealth accumulation but that the data from rural Israel and Judah necessary to measure the economic impact on the populace are so meager as to provide little information on land alienation and agricultural intensification (391–92). William G. Dever ("Social Structure in Palestine in the Iron II Period on the Eve of Destruction," in Levy, ed., *The Archaeology of Society,* 416–30), reviewing the archaeology of the seventh and early sixth centuries, while concurring that the evidence is "inconclusive," nonetheless believes that the archaeological data in sum, when taken together with biblical texts, speaks for pronounced state control of the economy (418–20). In sum, the textual and archaeological data yield scattered, and not always congruent, testimony about the extent and details of agricultural intensification. However, when Israelite agriculture is viewed comparatively through the lens of anthropological studies of highland cultivation by small landholders who are highly dependent on strategies of risk-spreading and optimization of labor (for details, see David C. Hopkins, *The Highlands of Canaan: Agricultural Life in the Early Iron Age,* SWBA 3 [Decatur, Ga.: Almond Press, 1985]), it is obvious that the survival of these small farmers could be easily threatened by state taxation and import-export policies of the sort we have reason to believe were implemented by the states of Israel and Judah.

83. Daniel J. Elazar (*The Covenant Tradition in Politics.* Vol. 1, *Covenant and Polity in Biblical Israel: Biblical Foundations and Jewish Expressions* (New Brunswick, N.J./London: Transaction Publishers, 1995) gives a particularly eloquent expression of the view that modern notions of covenantal politics rest on ancient Israelite covenant beliefs and practices; he argues that "the only record we have of a fully covenantal civilization is that of ancient Israel as portrayed in Scripture" (10). Ira Sharkansky (*Ancient and Modern Israel: An Exploration of Political Parallels* [Albany, N.Y.: State Univ. of New York Press, 1991] and *Israel and Its Bible: A Political Analysis* [New York/London: Garland Publishing, 1996]), attending to historical criticism of the Bible, is far more restrained in finding fairly minimal, and always problematic, continuities between ancient Israelite politics and the exigencies of politics in the modern world, as exemplified by the contemporary state of Israel. In biblical studies, arguments for covenantal and legal restraints on Israelite kingship have been made by Gerhard von Rad ("The Royal Ritual in Judah," in *The Problem of the Hexateuch and Other Essays* [New York: McGraw-Hill, 1966], 222–31) and by Baruch Halpern (*The Constitution of the Monarchy in Israel,* HSM 25 [Atlanta: Scholars, 1981], 175–256). However, as Keith A. Whitelam observes, "many of these passages [cited by von Rad and Halpern] are extremely ambiguous and notoriously difficult to date," and furthermore, they exhibit "the striking differentiation between the ideal presentation of the duties of kingship and the stark reality of a society subject to the widespread powers of a highly centralized agrarian monarchy" ("King and Kingship," *ABD,* 4:46). See also n. 89 below.

84. Hayim Tadmor ("'The People' and the Kingship in Ancient Israel: The Role of Political Institutions in the Biblical Period, *"Journal of World History* 11 [1968]: 3–23), while asserting the ultimate sovereignty of the people as the basis of royal authority, finds no evidence for representative bodies who had a major voice in choosing kings or affecting their policies; such interventions as appear are ad hoc and apart from any perceivable constitutional system.

85. There is a difference in emphasis among interpreters of the "royal reforms." Frank M. Cross ("Kinship and Covenant in Ancient Israel," in *From Epic to Canon: History and Literature in Ancient Israel* [Baltimore/London: Johns Hopkins, 1998], 3–21) stresses the reform programs of D and P as reconstructions and resurrections of early tribal league covenantal institutions that sought to counter "high Judaean" royal ideology, whereas others underscore how the reform measures were "coopted" by monarchy to strengthen its position. On debt easements, see Marvin L. Chaney, "Debt Easement in Israelite History and Tradition," in *The Bible and the Politics of Exegesis: Essays in Honor of Norman K. Gottwald on His Sixty-fifth Birthday,* ed. D. Jobling et al. [Cleveland: Pilgrim Press, 1991], 127–39; on Deuteronomic laws concerning women and the family, see Naomi Steinberg, "The Deuteronomic Law Code and the Politics of State Centralization," in D. Jobling et al., eds., *The Bible and the Politics of Exegesis,* 161–70; and on Deuteronomic restriction of Passover to Jerusalem, see Shigeyuki Nakanose, *Josiah's Passover: Sociology and the Liberating Bible* (Maryknoll, N.Y.: Orbis, 1993), 32–112. These two impulses

to reform are not, however, mutually exclusive; they belong together dialectically. As pressures for reform arose from outside the monarchic establishment, astute leaders within state circles would promulgate reform measures to serve state interests.

86. On royal succession rules and practices in Israel and the ancient Near East, see Tomoo Ishida, *The Royal Dynasties in Ancient Israel*, BZAW 142 (Berlin/New York: W. de Gruyter, 1977), 151–70 passim.

87. Keith A. Whitelam, *The Just King: Monarchical Judicial Authority in Ancient Israel*, JSOTSup 12 (Sheffield: JSOT Press, 1979).

88. On the relation of ancient Near Eastern and Israelite laws, see Samuel Greengus, "Biblical and ANE Law," *ABD*, 4:242–52; Frank Crüsemann, *The Torah: Theology and Social History of Old Testament Law* (Minneapolis: Fortress, 1996), 9–13; Raymond Westbrook, "Biblical and Cuneiform Lawcodes," *RB* 92 (1985): 247–65.

89. David Jobling, "Deconstruction and the Political Analysis of Biblical Texts: A Jamesonian Reading of Psalm 72," *Semeia* 59 (1992): 95–127, and Walter Houston, "The King's Preferential Option for the Poor: Rhetoric, Ideology, and Ethics in Psalm 72," *BibInt* 7 (1999): 341–67. Jobling, operating with a Marxist literary and political economic hermeneutic, and Houston, exhibiting a hermeneutic informed by liberation theology and political theology, differ on a number of points—such as the economic system presupposed by the psalm—but concur on the equivocation with which the king's advocacy of justice for the poor is set forth in Psalm 72. Houston concludes that "this ideology, which presents the king as caring for the poor of his own people but claiming tribute from foreign nations, contains a moral contradiction, as well as concealing the truth that the king was supported by domestic exploitation," but the attempt in the psalm to align the royal interests with the interests of the poor is achieved "at the expense of the doctrine of unconditional divine election, deriving the king's legitimacy from his fulfilment of the divine will in his 'option for the poor'" (363–64). Exploring Israel's economy as a weak variant of the Asiatic or tributary mode of production, Jobling suggests that the social contradictions of Psalm 72 may be related either to the "coexistence of a dominant tributary mode with a repressed communitarian mode of production" or to the reality "that the tributary mode cannot be installed in so *small* a society as Israel" (95).

Chapter 5

1. T. R. Carney (*The Shape of the Past: Models of Antiquity* [Lawrence, Kans.: Coronado Press, 1975], xvi–xvii, 21–23) describes the thought experiment or postulational model as follows: "It is employed when one wishes to search for some kind of pattern amongst a mass of data, especially if pattern and/or data are complicated and confusing. . . . The problem in such cases is that the investigation does not involve simply tracing one single causally connected chain or series of consequences. Instead, several complexes of interconnected variables and relationships are involved. These are in a ramifying set of causal relationships—they go in and out in every direction, like the roots of a banyan tree. . . . The analysis must be done as a whole or it cannot be done at all. Some form of pattern matching is called for" (21). Roger S. Bagnall (*Reading Papyri, Writing Ancient History* [London/New York: Routledge, 1995]) writes perceptively on the way philological and exegetical

studies of ancient texts are "interactively" and "recursively" linked to the forming and testing of hypotheses about the historical, cultural, and social matrix of the documents (1–8).

2. Niels Peter Lemche (*Prelude to Israel's Past: Background and Beginnings of Israelite History and Identity* [Peabody, Mass.: Hendrickson Publishers, 1998], 219–25) gives a balanced summation of pro and con arguments for attributing the pentateuchal traditions to the tenth, seventh, sixth, or fifth to third centuries B.C.E, and concludes, "All of the preceding suggestions regarding the dating of the Pentateuch provide compelling arguments. . . . I feel more persuaded by the fourth option [fifth to third centuries], but each theory carries its own internal logic that commands our attention" (225).

3. Richard Elliott Friedman ("Torah [Pentateuch]," *ABD*, 6:605–22) presents the state of the debate over the composition of the Pentateuch, arriving at largely traditional critical conclusions, while Albert de Pury ("Yahwist ['J'] Source," *ABD*, 6:1012–20), reviewing much of the same ground as Friedman, is highly skeptical of the documentary hypothesis. Some of the newer tendencies in pentateuchal studies were launched by John Van Seters (*Abraham in History and Tradition* [New Haven, Conn.: Yale Univ. Press, 1975]), who placed the earliest stratum of the Pentateuch in the exile, and by Rolf Rendtorff (*The Problem of the Process of Transmission in the Pentateuch*, JSOTSup 89 [Sheffield: JSOT Press, 1990]), who contended for autonomous "blocks" of pentateuchal traditions transmitted independently until their late redaction. Rendtorff ("The Paradigm Is Changing: Hopes—and Fears," *BibInt* 1 [1993]: 34–53) comments on how newer views of the composition of the Pentateuch complicate its use as a historical source. The breakup of classical critical views of the Deuteronomistic history is traced by Steven L. McKenzie ("Deuteronomistic History," *ABD*, 2:160–68) and by A. Graeme Auld "The Deuteronomists and the Former Prophets, or What Makes the Former Prophets Deuteronomistic?" in *Those Elusive Deuteronomists: The Phenomenon of Pan-Deuteronomism.* ed. L. S. Schearing and S. L. McKenzie, JSOTSup 268 [Sheffield: Sheffield Academic Press, 1999], 116–26).

4. In spite of the current scholarly tendency to deny the existence, or at least the recoverability, of an Elohist version of Israelite beginnings, a strong case for an integral E source is made by Alan W. Jenks (*The Elohist and North Israelite Traditions,* SBLMS 22 [Missoula, Mont.: Scholars, 1977]) and by Robert B. Coote (*In Defense of Revolution: The Elohist History* [Minneapolis: Fortress, 1991]). The revolution Coote refers to is the north's uprising, led by Jeroboam I, against the House of David.

5. Contrasting with the rather "secular" accounts of the rise of kingship in Israel is the Sumerian King List, composed at the beginning of the Sumerian revival after defeat of the Gutians. Intent on asserting the divine origin and unbroken continuity of Sumerian rule from antideluvian times (although transferred from city to city), the list opens with the formula, "When kingship was lowered from heaven . . .", which is repeated after the interruption of the flood, "After the Flood swept over (the earth) (and) when kingship was lowered (again) from heaven . . ." ("The Sumerian King List," *ANET,* 265–66).

6. Lemche (*Prelude to Israel's Past,* 1–65) explains at length the difficulties in finding external controls to evaluate the biblical portrait of premonarchic Israel.

7. "Hymn of Victory of Mer-ne-Ptah (The 'Israel Stela')," *ANET,* 376–8.

8. That the "Israel" of the stela bears the linguistic marker for "people/social group" rather than the linguistic marker for "land/country" is noteworthy. John A. Wilson (see preceding n. 7), remarks, "This is a valid argument [i.e., that Israel in the stela is a people and not a place]. Determinatives should have meaning. . . . The argument is good, but not conclusive, because of the notorious carelessness of Late-Egyptian scribes and several blunders of writing in this stela" (*ANET,* 378 n. 18). Frank J. Yurco ("Merneptah's Canaanite Campaign," *Journal of the American Research Center in Egypt* 23 [1986]: 189–215) claims that a mural, previously attributed to Rameses II, pictures Merneptah's campaign described in the stela and that one of the mural panels shows Israelites and Egyptians engaged in battle. There are two disputed points about this mural. Does it actually depict Merneptah's campaign, and are Israelites pictured? Donald B. Redford ("The Ashkelon Relief at Karnak and the Israel Stela," *IEJ* 36 [1986]: 188–200) not only rejects Yurco's reconstruction, but has serious doubts about the historical reliability of the Canaanite list in the stela. Itamar Singer ("Egyptians, Canaanites, and Philistines," in *From Nomadism to Monarchy: Archaeological and Historical Aspects of Early Israel,* ed. I. Finkelstein and N. Na'aman [Jerusalem: Israel Exploration Society/Washington, D.C.: Biblical Archaeology Society, 1994], 286–89) offers cautious support to Yurco and to the historical plausibility of Merneptah's thrust into Palestine, possibly into the hill country itself.

9. Israel Finkelstein, *The Archaeology of the Israelite Settlement* (Jerusalem: Israel Exploration Society, 1988); "The Great Transformation: The 'Conquest' of the Highlands Frontiers and the Rise of Territorial States," in *The Archaeology of Society in the Holy Land,* ed. T. E. Levy (New York: Facts on File, 1995), 349–63; William G. Dever, "The Israelite Settlement in Canaan: New Archaeological Models," in *Recent Archaeological Discoveries and Biblical Research* (Seattle/London: Univ. of Washington Press, 1990), 37–84; "Israel, History of (Archaeology and the 'Conquest')," *ABD,* 3:545–58. While differing on many points, Finkelstein and Dever concur that the archaeological data are broadly consistent with the kind of premonarchic society described in biblical texts. Even among scholars who have been dismissive of overly close correlations between archaeology and biblical history, there is a recognition that the refined archaeology of the last three decades contributes valuable knowledge of distribution of settlements, demographic shifts, and the economy and ecology of the Palestinian highlands, which must necessarily play a central role in efforts to reconstruct premonarchic social life (see Niels Peter Lemche, *The Israelites in History and Tradition* [Louisville, Ky.: Westminster John Knox/London: SPCK, 1998], 65–85).

10. This authority/power distinction, derived from Weber and now well documented in the ethnographic record (see Michelle Rosaldo and Louise Lamphere, eds., *Women, Culture, and Society* [Stanford, Calif.: Stanford Univ. Press, 1974]), is applied to ancient Israel by Carol Meyers (*Discovering Eve: Ancient Israelite Women in Context* [New York/Oxford: Oxford Univ. Press, 1988], 41–42). Drawing on archaeological and anthropological evidence, Meyers also develops the economic reasons for women having a greater share of social power in the tribal period than in later times.

11. Gerda Lerner (*The Creation of Patriarchy* [New York/Oxford: Oxford Univ. Press, 1986], 161–98) argues the all-embracing subordination of women to men in

biblical society and ideology, in continuity with the earlier subordination of women in Mesopotamian society and in parallel with the Aristotelian depreciation of women as "mutilated males." Insofar as women held status and power, it was almost entirely due to their attachment to men of status and power. See also Harold C. Washington, "Violence and the Construction of Gender in the Hebrew Bible: A New Historicist Approach," *BibInt* 5 (1997): 324–63.

12. Michael David Coogan, "Canaanite Origins and Lineage: Reflections on the Religion of Ancient Israel," in *Ancient Israelite Religion: Essays in Honor of Frank Moore Cross,* ed. P. D. Miller Jr. et al. (Philadelphia: Fortress, 1987), 115–24; William G. Dever, "The Contribution of Archaeology to the Study of Canaanite and Early Israelite Religion," in Miller et al., *Ancient Israelite Religion,* 209–47; Mark S. Smith, *The Early History of God: Yahweh and the Other Deities in Ancient Israel* (San Francisco: Harper & Row, 1990); Herbert Niehr, "The Rise of YHWH in Judahite and Israelite Religion: Methodological and Religio-Historical Aspects," in *The Triumph of Elohim: From Yahwisms to Judaisms,* ed. D. V. Edelman (Grand Rapids, Mich.: Eerdmans, 1995), 45–72.

13. Amihai Mazar, *Archaeology of the Land of the Bible 10,000–586 B.C.E.* (New York/London: Doubleday, 1990), 348–52.

14. Saul Olyan, *Asherah and the Cult of Yahweh in Israel,* SBLMS 34 (Atlanta: Scholars, 1988); Smith, *The Early History of God,* 80–97.

15. One or more large structures at Tel Masos in the northern Negeb may indicate commercial or administrative uses, but whether the site was in Israelite control is problematic (see Israel Finkelstein, "Arabian Trade and Socio-Political Conditions in the Negev in the Twelfth–Eleventh Centuries B.C.E.," *JNES* 47 [1988]: 241–52).

16. On the contrast of tribal and state cults in ancient Israel, see Gary A. Anderson, *Sacrifices and Offerings in Ancient Israel: Studies in Their Social and Political Importance,* HSM 41 (Atlanta: Scholars, 1988). On possible regulative effects of festivals on the agrarian economy, see Frank S. Frick, "Religion and Sociopolitical Structure in Early Israel: An Ethno-Archaeological Approach," in *Community, Identity, and Ideology: Social Science Approaches to the Hebrew Bible,* ed. C. E. Carter and C. L. Meyers (Winona Lake, Ind.: Eisenbrauns, 1996), 465–66.

17. Finkelstein (*Archaeology of the Israelite Settlement*) surveys the results of Iron I excavations and surveys in all regions (27–117) while focusing particularly on the territory of Ephraim (119–234); see also Israel Finkelstein and Zvi Lederman, eds., *Highlands of Many Cultures: The Southern Samaria Survey—the Sites,* 2 vols., Monograph Series 14 (Tel Aviv: Institute of Archaeology, Tel Aviv Univ., 1997), which is to be followed by a third volume integrating the historical, economic, and demographic data; Adam Zertal, "'To the Land of the Perizzites and the Giants': On the Israelite Settlement in the Hill Country of Manasseh," in Finkelstein and Na'aman, eds., *From Nomadism to Monarchy,* 47–69; Amihai Mazar, "Jerusalem and Its Vicinity in Iron Age I," in *From Nomadism to Monarchy,* 70–91; Avi Ofer, "'All the Hill Country of Judah': From a Settlement Fringe to a Prosperous Monarchy," in *From Nomadism to Monarchy,* 92–121.

18. Rafael Frankel, "Upper Galilee in the Late Bronze Age-Iron I Transition," in Finkelstein and Na'aman, eds., *From Nomadism to Monarchy,* 18–34; Zvi Gal, "Iron I in Lower Galilee and the Margins of the Jezreel Valley," *From Nomadism to Monarchy,* 35–46.

19. Magnus Ottosson, *Gilead: Tradition and History,* ConBOT 3 (Lund: Gleerup, 1969); "Gilead (Place)," *ABD,* 2:1020–22.

20. Gösta W. Ahlström (*Who Were the Israelites?* [Winona Lake, Ind.: Eisenbrauns, 1986], 37–42) and Lemche (*Israelites in History and Tradition,* 35–38) are in complete agreement that the Merneptah stela in no way supports the Sojourn and Exodus traditions, and both locate Israel of the stela in the highlands for different reasons, Ahlström favoring Israel as a territory and Lemche favoring Israel as a population group.

21. The hexateuchal Exodus-Conquest theme as a "root metaphor" for Israel's early experience in Canaan is advanced by Gottwald (*Tribes,* 214–15, 417, 508–9; "The Exodus as Event and Process: A Test Case in the Biblical Grounding of Liberation Theology," in *The Future of Liberation Theology: Essays in Honor of Gustavo Gutiérrez,* ed. M. H. Ellis and O. Maduro [Maryknoll, N.Y.: Orbis, 1989], 250–60 = Gottwald, *The Hebrew Bible in Its Social World and In Ours,* SemeiaSt [Atlanta: Scholars, 1993], 267–79). Keith W. Whitelam ("Israel's Traditions of Origin: Reclaiming the Land," *JSOT* 44 [1989]: 23–27, 31) cites African and Incan origin traditions of migration, palpably mistaken in their claims of a geographical trek by their ancestors. Such claims arose by converting political, commercial, or other contacts between two peoples into a spatial metaphor of "migration."

22. A detailed linguistic argument for the premonarchic origin of Exodus 15 is advanced by Frank M. Cross Jr. and David N. Freedman (*Studies in Ancient Yahwistic Poetry,* 2d ed. [Grand Rapids, Mich./Cambridge, UK: Eerdmans/Livonia, Mich.: Dove Booksellers, 1997], 31–45) and expanded ("The Song of Miriam," *JNES* 14 [1955]: 237–50). Freedman sketches the historical implications of a working hypothesis that Exodus 15 and Judges 5 are early poetic compositions that have been "prosaized" in the accompanying narrative passages ("Early Israelite History in the Light of Early Israelite Poetry," in *Unity and Diversity: Essays in the History, Literature, and Religion of the Ancient Near East,* eds. H. Goedicke and J. J. M. Roberts [Baltimore: Johns Hopkins, 1975], 3–35). It seems to me that the Cross-Freedman early dating of these poems on linguistic grounds is credible, but that Freedman's historical conclusions, while suggestive, remain conjectural. Steven Weitzman (*Song and Story in Biblical Narrative: The History of a Literary Convention in Ancient Israel,* Indiana Studies in Biblical Literature [Bloomington/Indianapolis: Indiana Univ. Press, 1997]), while not confident that the songs can be dated with certainty, believes that they arose as cultic compositions secondarily inserted into prose passages in keeping with a scribal convention typified by the eighth-century Piye Stela from Egypt.

23. If we assume that the Egyptian resurgence under the Saite Dynasty, beginning with Psamtik I (664–609 B.C.E.), brought Judah under the hegemony of Egypt as Assyrian control crumbled from ca. 630 onward, it might be posited that the Exodus-Bondage theme arose during Josiah's reign as a national liberation motif directed against Egyptian domination. This is unlikely, however, since references to deliverance from Egypt occur with some frequency in a number of prophetic books and Psalms that predate Josianic times. It seems to me that this conclusion is not invalidated by Niels Peter Lemche (*Early Israel: Anthropological and Historical Studies on the Israelite Society before the Monarchy,* VTSup 37 [Leiden: E. J. Brill, 1985], 306–85), who argues that none of these prophetic and psalm texts reflects

familiarity with the pentateuchal accounts of the Exodus. Since, however, they do attest to deliverance from Egypt as a well-known motif by the eighth century B.C.E., independent of the pentateuchal narratives, the motif could not have been first created under Josiah. This leaves open the possibility that the harsh encounter of Judah with Egypt in the last third of the seventh century enlivened the motif and contributed to its elaboration in the Deuteronomic traditions.

24. On the Midianites as a wide-ranging "protectorate" or "league" of nomads involved in commerce, see Otto Eissfeldt, "Protektorat der Midianiter über ihre Nachbarn im letzten Viertel des 2. Jahrtausends v. Chr.," *JBL* 87 (1967): 383–93; William J. Dumbrell, "Midian—A Land or a League?" *VT* 25 (1975): 323–37; Ernst A. Knauf, "Midianites and Ishmaelites," in *Midian, Moab, and Edom: The History and Archaeology of Late Bronze and Iron Age Jordan and North-West Arabia*, ed. J. F. A. Sawyer and D. J. A. Clines, JSOTSup 24 (Sheffield: JSOT Press, 1983), 135–46. A counterargument that Midianites were a settled people until well into the second millennium B.C.E. is mounted by Elizabeth J. Payne ("The Midianite Arc in Joshua and Judges," in Sawyer and Clines, eds., *Midian, Moab, and Edom,* 163–72). J. David Schloen ("Caravans, Kenites, and *Casus Belli*: Enmity and Alliance in the Song of Deborah," *CBQ* 55 [1993]: 18–38), translating Judg. 5:10b as "you who rule over Midian" and identifying the caravans of Judg. 5:6 as Midianite, posits a premonarchic alliance between Midian and Israel.

25. The introduction to the Israelite capture of Jericho implies a siege (Josh. 6:1), but the actual account describes a miraculous collapse of the city walls (6:2–21), and the prior story of the Israelite spies who negotiate with Rahab hints strongly at collaborators in Jericho who helped deliver the city to the Israelites (2:1–24). In the final redaction, the collaboration account is subordinated to the miraculous collapse account (6:17b, 22–23, 25).

26. George E. Mendenhall, "The Census Lists of Numbers 1 and 26," *JBL* 77 (1968): 52–66, followed by Gottwald, *Tribes,* 270–76. Mendenhall's argument that the same formula for radically reducing the "thousands" in the large numbers is used in the Chronicler's reports of premonarchic and early monarchic events is rebutted by Ralph W. Klein ("How Many in a Thousand?" in *The Chronicler as Historian,* eds. M. P. Graham, K. G. Hoglund and S. L. McKenzie, JSOTSup 238 [Sheffield: Sheffield Academic Press, 1997], 270–82). Klein allows, however, that Mendenhall may be correct about the "thousands" in some preexilic documents.

27. On premonarchic poetry: Cross and Freedman, *Ancient Yahwistic Poetry;* Gottwald, *Tribes,* 47–48, 278–82, 503–15; Lawrence E. Stager, "Archaeology, Ecology, and Social History: Background Themes to the Song of Deborah," *Congress Volume: Jerusalem, 1986,* ed. J. Emerton, VTSup 40 (Leiden: E. J. Brill, 1988), 221–34.

28. On narratives, annalistic notes, and inventories reflecting premonarchic social, political, and religious conditions, see Gottwald, *Tribes,* "Compendium of Historical Sources," 48–56, and extensive exegeses of texts throughout (see "Index of Biblical References").

29. It is noteworthy that Hermann Gunkel (*The Stories of Genesis: A Translation of the Third Edition to Hermann Gunkel's Commentary on the Book of Genesis,* trans. J. J. Scullion, ed. W. R. Scott [German orig. 1910; Vallejo, Calif.: BIBAL Press, 1994], 1–19), while strenuously arguing that the patriarchal traditions are imaginative

stories and not historical writing, nonetheless contends that many of the stories, such as Genesis 34 and 38, possess "a historical kernel" in the form of "a fragment of a tradition of an event that really happened." His point entails a frustrating paradox: we cannot date these happenings, nor can we reconstruct them in any detail, but we must not ignore the echoes and reminiscences of actual experiences and conditions of life, so that "the historical and the imaginative have been woven into the single, unified web which we now see." Gunkel is even willing to speak of *historical stories*, which weave an imaginative web around actual events, in contrast to *ethnological stories*, which narrate fictitious events in order to explain the relationships between peoples (18–19). Frith Lambert ("The Tribe/State Paradox in the Old Testament," *SJOT* 8/1 [1994]: 20–44) rests a part of his case for the survival of premonarchic traditions about tribal and city-state social organization on the way in which many biblical texts, whether describing premonarchic or monarchic times, tend to mix together bureaucratic and tribal terminology, which he accounts for as follows: "What we ultimately have is this: Within a bureaucratic framework of expression, we find a tribal core of subject matter; but that tribal core in its turn provides a framework for a sacred history, which is however *administered* (or presented) by a *state apparatus*. Here the paradox has come full circle" (author's italics) (23).

30. On Israel as a frontier society, see the exchange between the sociologist Gerhard Lenski in his review of *The Tribes of Yahweh* in *RelSRev* 6 (1980): 275–78, and Gottwald, "Two Models for the Origins of Ancient Israel: Social Revolution or Frontier Development," in *The Quest for the Kingdom of God: Studies in Honor of George E. Mendenhall*, ed. H. Huffmon et al. (Winona Lake, Ind.: Eisenbrauns, 1983), 5–24.

31. "Retribalization" is a concept introduced by Gottwald (*Tribes*, 323–28) in dialogue with Morton H. Fried (*The Evolution of Political Society: An Essay in Political Anthropology* [New York: Random House, 1967], 170–74), in response to his notion of tribes as "secondary formations" that take shape in confrontation with intrusive state polities. The concept suggested itself as a way of modeling the improvised, even "jerry-built," social structure of "tribal" Israel (see *Tribes*, 237–86). It is related in some respects to "revitalization" movements (including so-called nativist, messianic, or millennial cults) such as the Handsome Lake movement among the New York State Iroquois, described by Anthony F. C. Wallace (*Religion: An Anthropological View* [New York: Random House, 1966], 30–39, 157–66, 209–15). In my view, some of the processes and effects of retribalization in Israel may be illuminated by the improvisational social organization of the Plains Indians, who formed "composite tribes" out of peoples of diverse backgrounds, though sometimes of the same linguistic stock, who migrated from the eastern woodlands and the western Great Basin in order to develop an equestrian bison-hunting political economy that reached its peak from 1750 to 1850. Although weak in clan and lineage structure in some instances, these tribes were bound by ceremonial, social, and military sodalities and led by shifting chieftainships. In the last quarter of the nineteenth century, as this equestrian mode of life was coming to an end, the Ghost Dance revivalist movement that had originated in Nevada swept through the Plains tribes. See Marshall D. Sahlins, *Tribesmen,* Foundations of Modern Anthropology Series (Englewood Cliffs, N.J.: Prentice-Hall, 1968), 41–42; Peter Farb, *Man's Rise to*

Civilization as Shown by the Indians of North America from Primeval Times to the Coming of the Industrial State (New York: E. P. Dutton, 1968), 112–32; Thomas W. Overholt, "The Ghost Dance of 1890 and the Nature of the Prophetic Process," *Ethnohistory* 21 (1974): 37–63.

32. On Israel as a segmentary society: Frank Crüsemann, *Der Widerstand gegen das Königtum: Die antiköniglichen Texte des Alten Testaments und der Kampf um den frühen israelitischen Staat* (Neukirchen-Vluyn: Neukirchener Verlag, 1978), who builds on the work of the anthropologist Christian Sigrist, *Regulierte Anarchie. Untersuchungen zum Fehlen und zur Entstehung politischer Herrschaft in segmentaren Gesellschaften Afrikas* (Olten u. Freiburg im Breisgau: Walter, 1967); Gottwald, *Tribes,* 321–37; Frank S. Frick, *The Formation of the State in Ancient Israel: A Survey of Methods and Theories,* SWBA 4 (Sheffield: Almond Press, 1985). A counterview that early Israel was more "an association of chiefdoms" than a segmentary society is advanced by John W. Rogerson ("Was Early Israel a Segmentary Society?" *JSOT* 36 [1986]: 17–26), but his sharply posed opposition between segmentation and chiefdom, especially in settings where the chief has limited powers, is dubious. Of course, it must be granted that to claim segmentation for early Israel does not provide a detailed articulation of its social organization.

33. On early Israel as a chiefdom: James W. Flanagan, "Chiefs in Israel," *JSOT* 20 (1981): 47–73; Frick, *The Formation of the State,* 71–97.

34. Carol Meyers ("*Tribes* and Tribulations: Retheorizing Earliest 'Israel,'" in *The Tribes of Yahweh Twenty Years On,* ed. R. Boer [Sheffield: Sheffield Academic Press, forthcoming]), working with recent archaeological evidence that early Israel displayed a series of occupation zones with markedly different levels of sociopolitical complexity (recounted in R. D. Miller III, "A Social History of Highland Israel in the 12th and 11th Centuries B.C.E." [Ph.D. diss., Univ. of Michigan, 1998]), proposes that the concept of *heterarchy,* rather than hierarchy, best describes the differentiated distributions of authority and power that operated from region to region in tribal Israel in "lateral" networks that left space for various social roles that were not dominated by "top down" hierarchies controlling all domains of life. Meyers concludes, "While heterarchies may not be what is meant by 'egalitarian,' they may indeed be 'less hierarchical.' . . . And, 'less hierarchical' according to the heterarchic model imbues our understanding of early 'Israelite' life with new possibilities."

35. Gottwald (*Tribes,* 903–13) sets forth the argument that the special attraction of Yahwism consisted of its validation and empowerment, both organizationally and symbolically, of the agrarian way of life among highland tribalists: "'Covenantal' thinking in early Israel was not faith against culture but, more accurately, *faith sustaining Israelite retribalizing culture against Canaanite hierarchic culture.* . . . From the start, Israelite Yahwism *affirmed and sustained an alternative way of appropriating natural and social goods through an alternative culture*" (910). The major qualification I would now make in this claim is that the cult of Yahweh was as heterogeneous in its composition as were the people who formed Israel, and that it both coexisted and competed with other cults in premonarchic as well as in monarchic times (see Gottwald, "Recent Studies of the Social World of Premonarchic Israel," *CurBS* 1 [1993]: 182–85; *Tribes,* Preface to the Reprint, 1999, xl–xlvi).

36. On center-periphery relations in Palestine-Syria: Mario Liverani, "The

Collapse of the Near Eastern Regional System at the End of the Bronze Age: The Case of Syria," in *Centre and Periphery in the Ancient World*, ed. M. Rowlands, M. T. Larsen, and K. Kristiansen (Cambridge: Cambridge Univ. Press, 1987), 66–73; M. B. Rowton, "The Topological Factor in the *Hapiru* Problem," in *Studies in Honor of Benno Landsberger on His 75th Birthday*, Assyriological Studies 16 (Chicago: Oriental Institute, 1965), 375–87; "Dimorphic Structure and the Parasocial Element," *JNES* 36 (1977): 181–98.

37. Gottwald, "The Participation of Free Agrarians in the Introduction of Monarchy to Ancient Israel: An Application of H. A. Landsberger's Framework for the Analysis of Peasant Movements," *Semeia* 37 (1986): 77–106.

38. Given the great stress in biblical texts on allotments of land to ancestral families, the issue of whether there was village common land periodically redistributed to families is a moot point. Most earlier champions of redistributed holdings assumed that early Israel had been nomadic and that nomads practice redistribution, but both these assumptions are nowadays discredited. Marvin L. Chaney ("Ancient Palestinian Peasant Movements and the Formation of Premonarchic Israel," in *Palestine in Transition: The Emergence of Ancient Israel*, ed. D. N. Freedman and D. F. Graf, SWBA 2 [Sheffield: Almond Press, 1983], 64–65), basing his argument on settled peasant communes in Europe and the Middle East, as well as traces of such communal holdings in ancient Syria, concludes that biblical claims to restoration of land rest on "repartitional domain" (i.e., "a system of land tenure wherein the fields were held by the village as a whole and were periodically redistributed among its members to take account of demographic changes." Such redivision of land may be implied in Psalm 16:5–6 and Micah 2:5. Christopher J. H. Wright (*God's People in God's Land: Family, Land, and Property in the Old Testament* [Grand Rapids, Mich.: Eerdmans/Exeter: Paternoster Press, 1990], 66–70) is unpersuaded that all Israelite lands were subject to periodic redistribution, but allows that there may have been "a mixed economy" in which some fields and pastures were so allotted.

39. My caricature of "private gangs" may be given more precision by reference to the social outsiders who gathered around Abimelech (Judg. 9:4), Jephthah (Judg. 11:3), and David (1 Sam. 22:1–2). Alternatively, these groups may be viewed either in terms of patron-client arrangements, as in Niels Peter Lemche ("From Patronage Society to Patronage Society," in Fritz and Davies, eds. *The Origins of the Ancient Israelite States*, JSOTSup 228 [Sheffield: Sheffield Academic Press, 1996], 106–20), or in terms of social banditry, as in Chaney ("Ancient Palestinian Peasant Movements" 72–83). The point is that such ad hoc groupings arise in the interstices between established kin relations and customary social authorities.

40. Gottwald, *Tribes*, 414–17; Chaney, "Systemic Study of the Israelite Monarchy," *Semeia* 37 (1986): 66–67, who develops a proposal of Albrecht Alt, "Micha 2, 1–5, ΓΗΣ ΑΝΑΔΑΣΜΟΣ in Juda," in *Kleine Schriften zur Geschichte des Volkes Israels* (Munich: Beck, 1959), 3:373–81.

41. Robert Carneiro, "A Theory of the Origins of the State," *Science* 169 (1970): 733–38; "The Chiefdom: Precursor of the State," in *The Transition to Statehood in the New World*, ed. G. D. Jones and R. R. Krautz (Cambridge: Cambridge Univ. Press, 1981), 37–79. Michael Mann (*The Sources of Social Power*. Vol. 1, *A History of Power from the Beginning to A.D. 1760* [Cambridge: Cambridge Univ. Press, 1986],

75, 100) finds Carneiro's view, while overstating population pressure and militarism, partially congenial with his own model of "social caging." Robert B. Coote and Keith A. Whitelam (*The Emergence of Early Israel in Historical Perspective*, SWBA 5 [Sheffield: Almond, 1987], 144–47, 160, 165, 187) regard Carneiro's hypothesis about state origins as the most appropriate one for understanding the rise of the Israelite state.

42. Saul's innuendo that David may be promising land grants to win over Saul's retainers to his side is ambiguous as to whether Saul has already provided land grants to his courtiers (1 Sam. 22:7–8a). However, in terms of the resources controlled by the crown identified by Mettinger (*Solomonic State Officials*, 81–89), Saul would have had only his family's estate, and possibly land taken from the sanctuary at Nob (1 Sam. 22:18–19) and from Gibeonites (2 Sam. 21:1–6), to award his followers. Moreover, it would hardly have been apparent at this early stage in David's rise to power that he would eventually acquire sufficient means to make land grants to royal officials.

43. On Saul and the dynastic principle: Tomoo Ishida, *The Royal Dynasties in Ancient Israel: A Study on the Formation and Development of Royal-Dynastic Ideology*, BZAW 142 (Berlin/New York: Walter de Gruyter, 1977), 26–54.

44. On primogeniture: Ishida, *The Royal Dynasties*, 8, 155.

45. Wolfram Eberhard (*Conquerors and Rulers: Social Forces in Medieval China*, 2d rev. ed. [Leiden: E. J. Brill, 1965], 2–13), in a discussion of "Social System and Multiple Society," notes that Asian polities typically ruled over diverse "social layers" that often had little cultural connection with their rulers and little communication among themselves. The biblical tendency to label "Canaanites" as outsiders who corrupt "pure" Israelite society and religion masks the reality that Canaanites, understood as inhabitants of the Israelite state(s) who were not part of the heartland of premonarchic Israel, were fully incorporated under the rule of the Israelite polities. Gottwald (*Tribes*, 498–554) contends that hostility toward Canaanites in premonarchic Israel was directed at rulers and their military-political functionaries rather than at the Canaanite populace as a whole, and Karen Engelken ("Kanaan als nicht-territorialer Terminus," *BN* 52 [1990]: 47–63) understands "Canaanite" to refer to the urban way of life opposed by the early Israelites. Niels Peter Lemche (*The Canaanites and Their Land: The Tradition of the Canaanites*, JSOTSup 110 [Sheffield: JSOT Press, 1991]) claims that although extrabiblical sources do speak of an ill-defined area along the Syro-Palestinian coast as Canaan, the term in biblical sources refers either to "traders=Phoenicians" (in prophetic literature) or the pre- and non-Israelite inhabitants of the land who threaten Israelite integrity with corruption (in the Pentateuch and Deuteronomistic history). Although many aspects of Lemche's argument are disputed, he is doubtless correct that there never was a self-identified Canaanite ethnic, cultural, or political entity and that the biblical epithet "Canaanite" is, in the majority of its uses, an ideologically constructed foil to Israel.

46. On David's Transjordanian and Syrian wars: Baruch Halpern, "The Construction of the Davidic State: An Exercise in Historiography," in Fritz and Davies, eds., *The Origins of the Ancient Israelite States*, 44–75; Nadav Na'aman, "Sources and Composition in the History of David," in Fritz and Davies, eds., *The Origins of the Ancient Israelite States*, 170–86.

47. Christa Schäfer-Lichtenberger ("Sociological and Biblical Views of the Early

State," in Fritz and Davies, eds., *Origins of the Ancient Israelite States,* 78–105), employing the typological criteria of Henri J. M. Claessen and Peter Skalnik (*The Early State* [The Hague: Mouton Publishers, 1978]), concludes that David's regime constituted a state at uneven levels of development, with its "leanest" aspects falling in the areas of administration, stratification, and productivity of domestic and foreign surpluses. William M. Schniedewind (*Society and the Promise to David: The Reception History of 2 Samuel 7:1–17* [Oxford/New York: Oxford Univ. Press, 1999], 18–26) also perceives David's rule as a modest first step toward full statehood that was viewed in manifold, often highly idealized, ways in the subsequent history of interpretation, which he explicates by means of literary reader reception theory. His summation is apt: "Only within a unique configuration of historical circumstance and individual personality did a united and independent state emerge under David and Solomon. It lasted scarcely more than a generation, even according to the biblical account. Yet, through the nostalgic literary development of a golden age of David and Solomon, it lived on and grew" (17).

48. David Jobling, " 'Forced Labor': Solomon's Golden Age and the Question of Literary Representation," *Semeia* 54 (1991): 57–76, subsequently expanded with further historical-ideological and hermeneutical reflections and retitled as "The Value of Solomon's Age for the Biblical Reader," in *The Age of Solomon: Scholarship at the Turn of the Millennium,* ed. Lowell K. Handy (Leiden/New York/Cologne: E. J. Brill, 1997), 470–92.

49. For pro and con arguments concerning the integrity of the biblical portrait of a great Davidic-Solomonic empire, see the essays in Handy, ed., *The Age of Solomon,* with foreword by D. V. Edelman and postlude and prospects by the editor, and in Fritz and Davies, eds. *The Origins of the Ancient Israelite States,* with introduction by Davies. For more on current disputes over the dating of archaeological finds in the tenth–ninth centuries B.C.E., cf. Israel Finkelstein, "The Archaeology of the United Monarchy: An Alternative View," *Levant* 23 (1996): 177–87; Finkelstein, "Hazor and the North in the Iron Age: A Low Chronology Perspective," *BASOR* 314 (1999): 55–70; and William G. Dever, "Archaeology and the 'Age of Solomon': A Case Study in Archaeology and Historiography," in Handy, ed., *The Age of Solomon,* 217–51.

50. See David W. Jamieson-Drake, *Scribes and Schools in Monarchic Judah: A Socio-Archaeological Approach,* SWBA 9/JSOTSup 109 (Sheffield: Almond Press, 1991), and Hermann M. Niemann, *Herrschaft, Königtum, und Staat. Skizzen zur soziokulturellen Entwicklung im monarchischen Israel,* FAT 9 (Tübingen: J. C. B. Mohr, 1993), with rebuttals by Baruch Halpern, "The Construction of the Davidic State: An Exercise in Historiography," 44–75, and Christa Schäfer-Lichtenberger, "Sociological and Biblical Views of the Early State," 78–105, in Fritz and Davies, eds., *The Origins of the Ancient Israelite States.*

51. On alternative ways of interpreting the absence or scarcity of public buildings, monumental inscriptions, and epigraphic finds, see Schäfer-Lichtenberger, "Sociological and Biblical Views," 79–82.

52. Avraham Biran and Joseph Naveh, "An Aramaic Fragment from Dan," *IEJ* 43 (1993): 81–98; "The Tel Dan Inscription: A New Fragment," *IEJ* 45 (1995): 1–18; Baruch Halpern, "The Stela from Dan: Epigraphic and Historical Considerations," *BASOR* 296 (1994): 63–80; Frederick H. Cryer, "On the Recently-Discovered 'House of David' Inscription," *SJOT* 8/1 (1994): 3–19.

53. The loose nature of the Transjordanian polities is described by Øystein S. LaBianca and Randall W. Younker, "The Kingdoms of Ammon, Moab, and Edom: The Archaeology of Society in Late Bronze/Iron Age Transjordan (ca. 1400–500 B.C.E.)," in *The Archaeology of Society in the Holy Land,* ed. T. E. Levy (New York: Facts on File, 1995), 399–415. LaBianca ("Excursis: Salient Features of Iron Age Tribal Kingdoms," in *Ancient Ammon,* ed. B. MacDonald and R. W. Younker, Studies in the History and Culture of the Ancient Near East 17 [Leiden/Boston/Cologne, 1999], 19–23) treats Israel, Ammon, Moab, and Edom as broadly similar in their political organization. Ernst A. Knauf ("The Cultural Impact of Secondary State Formation: The Cases of the Edomites and Moabites," in *Early Edom and Moab: The Beginning of the Iron Age in Southern Jordan,* ed. P. Bienkowski, Sheffield Archaeological Monographs 7 [Sheffield: J. R. Collis, 1992], 47–54) contends that the relatively late archaeological evidence for Moabite and Edomite state formations (ninth and eighth centuries respectively) indicates that they were imitative of adjacent states in Cisjordan and southern Syria on whose economies they were dependent. This may suggest a progressive "wave" of state formations, starting from the Philistine city-states, extending to Israel, and eventually affecting Transjordan. The relevant point for our discussion is that Israel and the Transjordan communities did not simply copy city-state political organization but adapted it to encompass previously tribal peoples. Thus, tribal kingdoms, in contrast to city-states, were likely to be both broader in terms of the populaces they included and more dependent on securing the consent and cooperation of the ongoing tribal networks in their realm. James W. Flanagan (*David's Social Drama: A Hologram of Israel's Early Iron Age,* SWBA 7 [Sheffield: Almond Press, 1988], 304–8, 325–41) has drawn parallels between the meteoric careers of David and Ibn-Saud, the founder-king of Saudi Arabia, making the point that a strong and adroit leader can catalyze a larger political formation by engaging the loyalty of previously separated and hostile tribal communities.

54. The retrojection of later monarchic developments into the reign of Solomon, and their idealization, has been variously proposed by David C. Hopkins, "The Weight of the Bronze Could Not Be Calculated: Solomon and Economic Reconstruction," in Handy, ed., *The Age of Solomon,* 300–311; Herman M. Niemann, "The Socio-Political Shadow Cast by the Biblical Solomon," in *The Age of Solomon,* 252–99; and Ernst A. Knauf, "Le roi est mort, vive le roi! A Biblical Argument for the Historicity of Solomon," in *The Age of Solomon,* 81–95.

55. Juval Portugali ("Theoretical Speculations on the Transition from Nomadism to Monarchy," in Finkelstein and Na'aman, eds., *From Nomadism to Monarchy,* 17) conjectures that "several new sociospatial configurations were formed inside the Israelite social system, and coexisted in relationships of interaction and competition. These were the Israelite traditional *societas,* Saul's chiefdom, and David's urban *civitas.* David won this struggle . . . by 'enslaving' the Israelite *societas.* " David's initial *civitas* at Hebron "was a copy of the Philistine model." What is most interesting about Portugali's admitted "speculations" is that he draws on sociopolitical theorists such as Morgan, Engels, and Durkheim to emphasize "the systemic break in the transition from *societas* to *civitas,* " which, on his view, was effected by David. While I concur in the systemic break, it seems to me that under David's leadership it proceeded in a series of "cracks" or "fissures" in such a manner that the final break became apparent only when it proved impossible for popular sentiment "to reform"

the regime of Solomon and Rehoboam, leaving to the aggrieved populace the sole recourse of forming its own *civitas* in the hope that the new state might be more respectful of the Israelite *societas*.

56. John S. Holladay Jr. (Levy, ed., *The Archaeology of Society in the Holy Land,* 368) aptly states the terms on which archaeology is best suited to serve biblical studies: "Baldly put, the whole utility of archaeology as an independent materialistic perspective upon human culture is vitiated by carelessly enfolding it in a nonmaterialist matrix, even one derived from the highest ethical and moral principles. From this perspective, archaeology has much more to contribute to biblical study if it is conducted as a purely materialist pursuit in its own right than if it is somehow regarded as the 'handmaiden' to the study of the Bible."

57. See the essays in Levy, ed., *The Archaeology of Society in the Holy Land,* and in Israel Finkelstein and Nadav Na'aman, eds. *From Nomadism to Monarchy: Archaeological and Historical Aspects of Early Israel* (Jerusalem: Israel Exploration Society/Washington, D.C.: Biblical Archaeology Society, 1994).

58. Ze'ev Herzog, *Archaeology of the City: Urban Planning in Ancient Israel and Its Social Implications,* Monograph Series 13 (Tel Aviv: Institute of Archaeology, Tel Aviv Univ., 1997). For sites and topics in Palestinian archaeology, see Michael Avi-Yonah and Ephraim Stern, eds., *Encyclopedia of Archaeological Excavations in the Holy Land,* 4 vols. (Jerusalem: Israel Exploration Society and Masada Press, 1975–78), updated and expanded by Ephraim Stern, ed., *The New Encyclopedia of Archaeological Excavations in the Holy Land,* 4 vols. (Jerusalem: Israel Exploration Society & Carta/New York: Simon & Schuster, 1993). See also, Eric M. Meyers, ed., *The Oxford Encyclopedia of Archaeology in the Ancient Near East,* 5 vols. (New York/Oxford: Oxford Univ. Press, 1997). Recent surveys and analyses of the archaeology of the monarchy include William G. Dever, *Recent Archaeological Discoveries and Biblical Research* (Seattle/London: Univ. of Washington Press, 1990), 85–166; Amihai Mazar, *Archaeology of the Land of the Bible, 10,000–586 B.C.E.* (New York/London: Doubleday, 1990), 368–530; Gabriel Barkay in *The Archaeology of Ancient Israel,* ed. Amnon Ben-Tor (New Haven, Conn./London: Yale Univ. Press, 1992), 302–73; and Volkmar Fritz, *The City in Ancient Israel* (Sheffield: Sheffield Academic Press, 1995), 76–189.

59. On archaeological Central Place Theory as applied to monarchic Israel, see William G. Dever, "Archaeology and the 'Age of Solomon,'" 218–23. Gregory A. Johnson ("Aspects of Regional Analysis in Archaeology," *Annual Review of Anthropology* 6 [1977]: 479–508) assesses the technical and conceptual criticisms of Central Place Theory and concludes that it remains a useful analytic tool, provided its limits as an "ideal typical" construct are respected: "Most models of locational behavior are essentially unverifiable in that for the sake of generality they involve assumptions which are untestable or which cannot be expected to be met under real world conditions. Utility and testability, however, are not necessarily coterminous. Most authors [treated in the present review essay] agree that these models provide context within which the operation of real world processes may be understood" (501).

60. Dever ("Archaeology and the 'Age of Solomon,'" 222 n. 9) observes that Palestinian archaeologists differ in the number of "loosely defined" settlement tiers they identify, whether three (Dever and Mazar), four (Herzog), or five (Holladay).

61. On Iron Age demographics: Yigal Shiloh, "The Population of Iron Age Palestine in the Light of a Sample Analysis of Urban Plans, Areas and Population Density," *BASOR* 239 (1980): 25–35; Mogen Broshi and Israel Finkelstein, "The Population of Palestine in Iron Age II," *BASOR* 287 (1992): 47–60; Israel Finkelstein, "Environmental Archaeology and Social History: Demographic and Economic Aspects of the Monarchic Period," *Biblical Archaeology Today: Proceedings of the Second International Congress on Biblical Archaeology, Jerusalem, June 1990*, eds. J. Aviram and A. Biran (Jerusalem: Israel Exploration Society, 1993), 56–66; and Dever, "Archaeology and the 'Age of Solomon,'" 221–22. Dever remarks, "Despite many differing interpretations of specific data, there is a consensus that an estimate of ca. 100 persons per acre of inhabited domestic area gives the best results" (n. 8).

62. On the Tel Dan inscription, see n. 52 above.

63. "The Ostraca of Samaria," *ANET,* 321.

64. "The Siloam Inscription," *ANET,* 321; *ABD,* 6:23–24; K. A. D. Smelik, *Writings from Ancient Israel: A Handbook of Historical and Religious Documents* (Louisville: Westminster John Knox, 1991), 64–71.

65. N. Avigad, "The Epitaph of a Royal Steward from Siloam Village," *IEJ* 3 (1953): 137–52. Even though the broken name in the inscription does not allow us to know if this is precisely Shebna's tomb, the well-preserved title of "royal steward" and the sumptuous tomb indicate the privileged status and wealth of Judahite state officials in the eighth century B.C.E.

66. "The Lachish Ostraca," *ANET,* 321–22; *ABD,* 4:126–28; Smelik, *Writings from Ancient Israel,* 116–31; Dennis Pardee, *Handbook of Ancient Hebrew Letters,* SBLSBS 15 (Atlanta: Scholars, 1982), 67–114.

67. "Three Ostraca from Arad," *ANET,* 568–69; *ABD,* 1:336–37; Smelik, *Writings from Ancient Israel,* 101–15; Pardee, *Handbook,* 24–67.

68. "A Letter from the Time of Josiah," *ANET,* 568; Smelik, *Writings from Ancient Israel,* 93–100; Pardee, *Handbook,* 15–24.

69. The number of seals and seal impressions, especially from Judah, has grown by leaps and bounds over the last three decades. Ruth Hestrin and Michal Dayagi-Mendels (*Inscribed Seals: First Temple Period. Hebrew, Ammonite, Moabite, Phoenician, and Aramaic* [Jerusalem: Israel Museum, 1979]) reported on 136 seals known before the findings reported by Nahman Avigad (*Bullae and Seals from a Post-Exilic Judean Archive,* Qedem 4 [Jerusalem: Institute of Archaeology, the Hebrew Univ., 1976] and *Hebrew Bullae from the Time of Jeremiah* [Jerusalem: Israel Exploration Society, 1986]). With the publication of Robert Deutsch (*Messages from the Past: Hebrew Bullae from the Time of Isaiah through the Destruction of the First Temple* [Tel Aviv: Archaeological Center Publications, 1999], there are now over 500 published bullae. Avigad and Deutsch offer minimal historical and political interpretation of the bullae in their publications of the finds. Avigad expands somewhat on their historical implications in "The Contribution of Hebrew Seals to an Understanding of Israelite Religion and Society," in *Ancient Israelite Religion: Essays in Honor of Frank Moore Cross,* ed. P. D. Miller Jr. et al. Philadelphia: Fortress, 1987), 195–208, but has little to say about their implications for the structure of state administration. See n. 126 below.

70. On the Ahaz and Hezekiah seals, see Robert Deutsch, "First Impressions— What We Learn from King Ahaz's Seal," *BAR* 24/3 (May–June 1998): 54–56, 62;

Frank M. Cross, "King Hezekiah's Seal Bears Phoenician Imagery," *BAR* 25/2 (Mar.–Apr. 1999): 42–45, 60.

71. Kuntilleth 'Ajrud Inscriptions and Drawings: *ABD,* 4:103–9; Smelik, *Writings from Ancient Israel,* 155–62.

72. Khirbet el-Qom Inscriptions: Willam G. Dever, "Iron Age Epigraphic Material from the Area of Khirbet el-Kom," *HUCA* 40/41 (1969–70): 139–204; Smelik, *Writings from Ancient Israel,* 152–55.

73. Deir 'Alla inscriptions: *ABD,* 2:129–30; J. Hoftijzer and G. van der Kooij, *Aramaic Texts from Deir 'Alla* (Leiden: E. J. Brill, 1976); Smelik, *Writings from Ancient Israel,* 79–88.

74. Mazar, *Archaeology of the Land of the Bible,* 496–99.

75. The absolute dates established for events during the monarchy on the basis of Assyrian and Neo-Babylonian documents are listed by Mordechai Cogan, "Chronology, Hebrew Bible," *ABD,* 1:1007. Nadav Na'aman ("The Contribution of Royal Inscriptions for a Re-Evaluation of the Book of Kings as a Historical Source," *JSOT* 82 [1999]: 3–17) concludes that a comparison of biblical and extrabiblical "synchronisms" from the late tenth–ninth centuries shows the author of Kings to have had a small number of sources with limited information, from which he drew logical inferences not always compatible with historical reality.

76. "Lists of Asiatic Countries under the Egyptian Empire," *ANET,* 242–43; "The Campaign of Sheshonk I," *ANET,* 263–64; Benjamin Mazar, "The Campaign of Pharaoh Shishak to Palestine," *Congress Volume, Strasbourg 1956,* VTSup 4 (Leiden: E. J. Brill, 1957), 57–66.

77. Monolith Inscription of Shalmaneser III: *ANET,* 278–79; Jeffrey Kah-Jin Kuan, *Neo-Assyrian Historical Inscriptions and Syria-Palestine: Israelite/Judean-Tyrian-Damascene Political and Commercial Relations in the Ninth–Eighth Centuries B.C.E.* (Hong Kong: Alliance Bible Seminary, 1995), 27–40. For interpretations of the Neo-Assyrian historical texts pertinent to Syro-Palestine, see also A. K. Grayson, "Assyria: Ashur-dan II to Ashur-nirari V (934–745 B.C.)," in *CAH,* 2d ed. (Cambridge: Cambridge Univ. Press, 1982), 3/1:238–81; "Assyria: Tiglath-pileser III to Sargon II (744–705 B.C.)," in *CAH,* 2d ed. 3/2:71–102; Hayim Tadmor, "Assyria and the West: The Ninth Century and Its Aftermath," in *Unity and Diversity: Essays in the History, Literature, and Religion of the Ancient Near East,* ed. H. Goedicke and J. J. M. Roberts (Baltimore: Johns Hopkins, 1975), 36–48.

78. Nadav Na'aman ("Two Notes on the Monolith Inscription of Shalmaneser III from Kurkh," *Tel Aviv* 3 [1974]: 97–102) proposes that 2000 is a scribal error for 200, but Kuan (*Neo-Assyrian Historical Inscriptions,* 35 n. 104) counters that, granted numerous scribal errors in Assyrian inscriptions, there is no good reason to believe this figure to be any more exaggerated than the other numbers in the inscription. It might also be observed that the precise numbers of chariots may be less significant than the fact that Ahab contributed a larger chariot force than any other coalition partner. Interestingly, the size of Ahab's chariot force may lend indirect support to the tradition that Solomon invested heavily in chariotry. Since most of Solomon's chariot units were stationed in the north, they probably fell into the hands of the kingdom of Israel.

79. J. Maxwell Miller and John H. Hayes, *A History of Ancient Israel and Judah* (Philadelphia: Westminster Press, 1986), 270; favored also by Kuan, *Neo-Assyrian Historical Inscriptions,* 39–40.

80. The Black Obelisk of Shalmaneser III: *ANET,* 281; Kuan, *Neo-Assyrian Historical Inscriptions,* 62–66.

81. Kuan, *Neo-Assyrian Historical Inscriptions,* 53–57.

82. "The Moabite Stone," *ANET,* 320–21; *ABD,* 4:108–9; Smelik, *Writings from Ancient Israel,* 29–50; J. Andrew Dearman, ed., *Studies in the Mesha Inscription and Moab* (Atlanta: Scholars, 1989).

83. Thomas L. Thompson (*The Mythic Past: Biblical Archaeology and the Myth of Israel* [New York: Basic Books, 1999], 11–14) correctly points out the stereotypical literary motifs in the Mesha Stela, but in doubting that the stela gives trustworthy historical information because of its conventional literary "packaging," he fails to recognize that virtually all accounts of the deeds of ancient Near Eastern monarchs are fraught with stock phrases, motifs, and images that require discriminate assessment rather than blanket dismissal in deciding on the extent of their historical trustworthiness.

84. On the annihilation of captives (*ḥērem*): Walter Dietrich, "The 'Ban' in the Age of the Early Kings," in Fritz and Davies, eds., *Origins of the Ancient Israelite States,* 196–210; Gottwald, *Tribes,* 543–50.

85. The Calah Slab and el-Rimah Stela of Adad-nirari III: *ANET,* 281–82 [Calah Slab only]; Kuan, *Neo-Assyrian Historical Inscriptions,* 78–84. The slab makes terse reference to tribute imposed on "the house/land of Omri," while the stela reports that Adad-nirari "received the tribute of Joash of the land of the Samarians." These "summary inscriptions" do not indicate either the nature or amount of tribute, nor can the date of payment be securely fixed. Presumably the two reports refer to a payment of tribute associated with Adad-nirari's defeat of Damascus, which scholars date variously between 803 and 796 (see Kuan, 93–106).

86. Annals of Tiglath-pileser III: *ANET,* 283–84; Kuan, *Neo-Assyrian Historical Inscriptions,* 138–51. There are three, and possibly four, accounts of this Assyrian ruler's imposition of tribute on Menahem of Israel. The itemized payment of precious metals and luxury goods is reminiscent of the tribute that Shalmaneser III received from Jehu a century earlier.

87. Display Inscriptions of Sargon II: *ANET,* 284–86. Shalmaneser V is credited with the destruction of Samaria in 2 Kings, and in the Babylonian Chronicle 1 he is said to have "ravaged Samaria" (Kuan, *Neo-Assyrian Historical Inscriptions,* 195–97). But it is his successor, Sargon II, whose inscriptions claim the capture and rebuilding of Samaria. Hayim Tadmor ("The Campaigns of Sargon II of Assur," *JCS* 12 [1958]: 22–40, 77–100) has argued persuasively that Shalmaneser V died during or shortly after the siege of Samaria and that Sargon II completed the siege and/or rebuilt the city in the process of reorganizing the former kingdom of Israel as an Assyrian province. See also K. Lawson Younger Jr., "The Fall of Samaria in Light of Recent Research," *CBQ* 61 (1999): 461–82.

88. The Oriental Institute Prism of Sennacherib: *ANET,* 287–88. Summing up the devastation of Judah, the Nebi Yunus Slab (*ANET,* 288, col. 2), states, "I laid waste the large district of Judah and put the straps of my (yoke) upon Hezekiah, its king." The Assyrian reliefs of the siege and capture of Lachish during this campaign, showing the savagery of the siege and its grisly aftermath, are accompanied by the statement, "Sennacherib, king of the world, king of Assyria, sat upon a *nimedu-*throne and passed in review the booty (taken) from Lachish." The biblical account of the siege is in 2 Kings 18:13–19:37 with parallels in Isaiah 36—38 and 2 Chronicles 32.

89. A possible recourse is to regard the Assyrian claim to have deported 200,150 Judahites as a scribal error for 2,150, or even 150 (Gray, *I and II Kings,* 2d rev. ed., 673–74). Hayes and Miller (*A History of Ancient Israel and Judah,* 362) observe that "none of the kingdoms [involved in the revolt against Sennacherib] were transformed into Assyrian provinces as one would have expected. This was consistent with earlier Assyrian policy in which the seaport kingdoms and Judah along with Moab, Ammon, and Edom had been left as semi-independent kingdoms with kings from the ruling families or local populations."

90. Donald J. Wiseman (*Chronicles of Chaldean Kings [626–556 B.C.]: In the British Museum* [London: Trustees of the British Museum, 1961]) included revisions of the text of that portion of the Chronicles, from 616 to 609, previously published in C. J. Gadd, ed., *The Fall of Nineveh* (London: Humphrey Milford, Oxford Univ. Press, 1923). In *Nebuchadrezzar and Babylon* (Oxford: Oxford Univ. Press, 1985) Wiseman provides a historical discussion of the Chronicles and related texts.

91. Wiseman, *Chronicles,* 32–35, 73; *Nebuchadrezzar and Babylon,* 32–36.

92. Wiseman, *Chronicles,* 29–31, 71; J. A. Brinkman ("The Babylonian Chronicle Revisited," in Tzvi Abusch et al., eds., *Lingering over Words: Studies in Ancient Near Eastern Literature in Honor of William L. Moran* [Atlanta: Scholars, 1990], 74–75) accounts for the greater candor of the Babylonian record compared to Assyrian annals by pointing to limited evidence that the versions we possess were probably copied by "private" scribes without ties to palace or temple.

93. Ration list for Jehoiachin: *ANET,* 308.

94. Philip J. King, "Jerusalem," *ABD,* 3:748–51 summarizes the archaeology of Jerusalem up to the mid-1980s, noting the slim evidence from the tenth–ninth centuries. Various solutions to this "absence" of the city of David and Solomon are set forth by Amihai Mazar ("Jerusalem and Vicinity," in Finkelstein and Na'aman, eds., *From Nomadism to Monarchy,* 72–73). The most recent comprehensive report on Iron Age Jerusalem is Yigal Shiloh, "Jerusalem: The Early Periods and the First Temple Period: Excavation Results," in Stern, *The New Encyclopedia of Archaeological Excavations,* 2:701–11.

95. Magen Broshi, "The Expansion of Jerusalem in the Reigns of Hezekiah and Manasseh," *IEJ* 24 (1974): 21–26.

96. The Prism inscription of Sennacherib states, "His [Hezekiah's] towns which I had plundered, I took away from his country and gave them (over) to Mitinti, king of Ashdod, Padi, king of Ekron, and Sillibel, king of Gaza. Thus I reduced his country, but I still increased the tribute" (*ANET,* 288). A reminiscence of this ceding of Judahite territory to Philistine cities may appear in Isaiah 1:7.

97. The struggle between pro- and anti-Babylonian factions in the Judahite leadership during Zedekiah's reign is alluded to in the Lachish Letters and reported at some length in the book of Jeremiah. See Burke O. Long, "Social Dimensions of Prophetic Conflict," *Semeia* 21 (1981): 31–53, with a response by Norman K. Gottwald, 107–9; see also Gottwald, *All the Kingdoms of the Earth: Israelite Prophecy and International Relations in the Ancient Near East* (New York: Harper & Row, 1964), 270–93.

98. "Gold of Ophir," imported through the Red Sea port of Ezion-geber, is mentioned in the reigns of Solomon (1 Kings 9:28) and Jehoshaphat (1 Kings 22:49). An eighth-century text from the Mediterranean port of Tel Qasile speaks of "gold of

Ophir to Beth-horon, 30 shekels" (Benjamin Maisler [Mazar], "Two Hebrew Ostraca from Tell Qasile," *JNES* 10 [1951]: 265–67). The location of Ophir is unknown; some have proposed that Ophir refers not literally to the place of origin but to the metal's fine quality.

99. A. R. Millard ("Literacy [Israel]," *ABD,* 4:337–40) is confident of extensive literacy in ancient Israel, but others are far more cautious. Susan Niditch (*Oral World and Written World* (Louisville, Ky.: Westminster John Knox, 1996], 39–77), stressing the primacy of oral communication, observes that most of the extrabiblical texts and letters, coming in the main from the second half of the monarchy, are short and for pragmatic military or commercial purposes, while a few somewhat longer inscriptions are of a ritual, symbolic, or monumental character. Sean Warner ("The Alphabet: An Innovation and Its Diffusion," *VT* 30 [1980]: 81–90) challenges the assumption that availability of the alphabet would automatically increase literacy, since the functions of reading and writing were shaped and circumscribed by socioeconomic and political conditions to such an extent that general literacy has been achieved only during the last three hundred years.

100. Gottwald, *Tribes,* in dialogue with John Bright (592–99) and in general concurrence with Morton Smith and Bertil Albrektson (667–99) finds the distinctiveness of Israel to lie in the way the formative religious notions of Yahwism corresponded to the sociopolitical egalitarianism of premonarchic times. Peter Machinist ("The Question of Distinctiveness in Ancient Israel," in *Essential Papers on Israel and the Ancient Near East,* ed. F. E. Greenspahn [New York/London: New York Univ. Press, 1991], 420–42) locates the biblical claim to Israelite distinctiveness in its status as a relative newcomer in the ancient Near East seeking to develop a "counter identity" over against the great states and civilizations. Both positions depend upon dating many disputed biblical texts in the premonarchic and monarchic eras and presuppose an Israelite religiocultural self-awareness that is not closely attached to the centralized state and is, in some instances, antipathetic to the state.

101. Gloria London ("A Comparison of Two Contemporaneous Life-styles of the Late Second Millennium B.C.," *BASOR* 273 [1989]: 37–55) treats lowland "Canaanite" culture and highland "Israelite" culture as subsets of the same basic cultural repertory.

102. David C. Hopkins (*The Highlands of Canaan: Agricultural Life in the Early Iron Age,* SWBA 3 [Decatur, Ga.: Almond Press, 1985]) details the web of interlocking technical processes and cooperative labor investments necessary to secure a livelihood for Israel's agrarian/pastoral populace.

103. Since the earliest and finest examples of ashlar masonry and the proto aeolic capital carved in stone appear closely associated in Israelite royal architecture, Yigal Shiloh (*The Proto Aeolic Capital and Israelite Ashlar Masonry,* Qedem 11 [Jerusalem: Institute of Archaeology, Hebrew Univ. 1979], 82–91) reasoned that Israel was the innovator of these architectural features, but Mazar (*Archaeology of the Land of the Bible,* 471–75) cautions that the temporal priority of the Israelite examples may be due to the fact that Phoenician monumental building from the early Iron Age has not been uncovered. Most scholars have assumed that these elegant architectural features were introduced into Israel by the Phoenician craftsmen hired by Solomon, and probably by Omri as well, but Shiloh claims that the biblical texts represent Phoenicians as experts in woodwork and metal crafts, not in architectural design and masonry.

104. The principles and procedures involved in the early development of an alphabetic script are lucidly described and illustrated with a number of examples, accompanied by slides, in P. Kyle McCarter, *Ancient Inscriptions. Voices from the Biblical World* (Washington, D.C.: Biblical Archaeology Society, 1996), 67–80, and, for further details, see Frank M. Cross, "The Origin and Early Evolution of the Alphabet," *ErIsr* 8 (1967): 8*–24*. The socioeconomic location of those who first experimented with an alphabetic script has been the subject of considerable discussion. David Diringer (*The Alphabet: A Key to the History of Mankind,* 3d ed. [London: Hutchinson, 1968], 162) argued for the alphabet as a popular "democratic" script over against the elitist "theocratic" hieroglyphics from which it developed. It is worthy of note that the proto-Sinaitic inscriptions, from the sixteenth–fifteenth centuries, were made by Canaanite workers in Egyptian mines. Recently, protoalphabetic inscriptions from several centuries earlier have been discovered in Egypt, where they were carved by Semitic traders. It seems likely that the alphabet was developed not by professional scribes in state service but rather among social "outsiders" marginal to state establishments, such as manual laborers, artisans, and traders. However, the alphabet's superior facility in writing commended it soon enough to state purposes. S. Yeivin ("The Age of the Patriarchs," *RSO* 38 [1963]: 284–85) freely speculates that Israel's patriarchal families were the inventors of the proto-Sinaitic alphabet, or at least those responsible for developing and spreading the alphabet, but he offers no convincing evidence.

105. Mazar (*Archaeology,* 502–20 passim) briefly surveys the classes of objects constituting the arts and crafts of Israel and Judah. Many specimens are highly imitative of styles and motifs in surrounding cultures, and often of inferior craftmanship, but others show greater originality and superb execution.

106. The standard collection of ancient Near Eastern texts in English translation has long been James L. Pritchard, ed., *Ancient Near Eastern Texts Relating to the Old Testament,* 3d ed. with supplement (Princeton: Princeton Univ. Press, 1969). A newly projected three-volume compendium of ancient Near Eastern Texts (William W. Hallo and K. Lawson Younger Jr., eds., *The Context of Scripture: Canonical Compositions from the Biblical World* [Leiden/New York/Cologne, vol. 1, 1997; vol. 2, 2000]) will contain many more texts, including some found or published since the last edition of *ANET,* along with fuller introductions and notes. Moreover, the project is shaped by a studied rationale as to how best to view such texts comparatively in biblical studies. As Hallo remarks, "The new attitude . . . recognizes that the assessment of a biblical text, so far from ending with the identification of an extra-biblical parallel, begins there" (xxviii). See also *SBL Writings from the Ancient World Series,* ed. Burke O. Long and Simon B. Parker (Atlanta: Scholars, 9 vols. to date, 1990–), organized by discrete literary genres and/or regions.

107. Hallo ("The Concept of Canonicity in Cuneiform and Biblical Literature: A Comparative Appraisal," in *The Biblical Canon in Comparative Perspective: Scripture in Context IV,* ed. K. L. Younger Jr., W. W. Hallo, and B. F. Batto, Ancient Near Eastern Texts and Studies 11 [Lewiston, N.Y.: Edwin Mellen Press, 1991], 1–19) shows that the Mesopotamian cuneiform literature displays such canonizing features as systematic selection of literary works, tendency to produce a standardized text, a fixed arrangement of contents, and an established sequence in which books were to be read or studied. Jeffrey H. Tigay (*Empirical Models for Biblical Criticism,* ed.

J. H. Tigay [Philadelphia: Univ. of Pennsylvania Press, 1985], 21–52) argues that the evolution of the Gilgamesh Epic, traceable over a millennium and a half, throws light on the process of the development and final redaction of the pentateuchal traditions.

108. Mark S. Smith, *The Early History of God: Yahweh and the Other Deities in Ancient Israel* (San Francisco, Calif.: Harper & Row, 1990); Robert K. Gnuse, *No Other Gods: Emergent Monotheism in Israel*, JSOTSup 241 (Sheffield: Sheffield Academic Press, 1997); Susan Ackerman, *Under Every Green Tree: Popular Religion in Sixth-Century Judah*, HSM 46 (Atlanta: Scholars, 1992); Jacques Berlinerblau, "The 'Popular Religion' Paradigm in Old Testament Research: A Sociological Critique," *JSOT* 60 (1993): 3–26.

109. The case for a charismatic kingship in the northern kingdom was advanced by Albrecht Alt ("The Formation of the Israelite State in Palestine," in *Essays on Old Testament History and Religion* [Oxford: Basil Blackwell, 1966], 171–237; "The Monarchy in the Kingdoms of Israel and Judah," in *Essays*, 239–59), and it was convincingly rebutted by Giorgio Buccellati (*Cities and Nations of Ancient Syria: An Essay on Political Institutions with Special Reference to the Israelite Kingdoms*, Studi Semitici 26 [Rome: Istituto di Studi del Vicino Oriente, 1967]) and Tomoo Ishida (*The Royal Dynasties in Ancient Israel: A Study on the Formation and Development of Royal-Dynastic Ideology*, BZAW 142 [Berlin/New York: Walter de Gruyter, 1977]).

110. Joseph P. Healey, "Am ha'arez," *ABD*, 1:168–69; Ernst Würthwein, *Der 'amm ha'arez im Alten Testament*, BWA(N)T 17, Stuttgart: Kohlhammer, 1936); Ernest W. Nicholson, "The Meaning of the Expression 'am ha'arez in the Old Testament," *JSS* 10 (1965): 59–66.

111. Many discussions of the biblical notion and practice of covenant either ignore the role of covenant in state affairs or assume that the relations between heads and subjects of the Israelite states were regulated under the provisions of the religious covenant with Yahweh, even though the provisions supposedly governing the state are seldom mentioned. The instructions obligating the king to keep the Deuteronomic law (Deut. 17:14–20) are often taken as paradigmatic of customary covenantal measures restricting royal power in specified ways and/or authorizing power sharing with deliberative or consultative bodies of citizens. In actuality, the few references to covenants between kings and their subjects do not indicate any such details, and the so-called "law of the king" in Deuteronomy 17 reads more like a moral admonition than a binding limitation on the king.

112. Norman K. Gottwald (*All the Kingdoms of the Earth: Israelite Prophecy and International Relations in the Ancient Near East* [New York: Harper & Row, 1964], 350–77), strongly indebted to Martin Buber, tries to assess the mixture of pragmatic "realism" and theopolitical "idealism" in the political consciousness of prophets vis-à-vis the political consciousness of the rulers they criticized. Gottwald ("Ideology and Ideologies in Israelite Prophecy," in *Prophets and Paradigms: Essays in Honor of Gene M. Tucker*, JSOTSup 229 [Sheffield: Sheffield Academic Press, 1996], 143–49) evaluates the frequent charge that prophetic ideology was "false consciousness" or "impractical utopianism."

113. The strongest evidence of a role for the Judahite king in the Jerusalem temple cult is found in a series of "royal psalms" identified by Gunkel as Psalms 2, 18, 20, 21, 45, 72, 101, 110, 132, and 144:1–11 (Hermann Gunkel, *Einleitung in die*

Psalmen. Die Gattungen der religiösen Lyrik Israels [Göttingen; Vandenhoek & Ruprecht, 1933], 140–71). Apart from a few implied ritual acts, these texts do not allow us to reconstruct the liturgies in any detail, although the coronation of the king appears to have been the occasion of a number of these psalms. Additional psalms that celebrate the Kingship of Yahweh complicate the issue, but those who locate these psalms in a festival aimed at the renewal of cosmos and society, such as Mowinckel and Kraus, do not argue that the Israelite king enacted the role of deity, as was the case in some ancient Near Eastern cults.

114. William M. Schniedewind, *Society and the Promise to David,* treats the core promise to David in 2 Sam. 7:1–17 as "early political literature" from David's reign and traces its successive reinterpretations throughout the Hebrew Bible and into the late Second Temple period.

115. On Athaliah, see chap. 3, nn. 40, 50.

116. On notions of inclusive Israel, see chap. 2, nn. 22–24 and chap. 3, n. 47.

117. On Damascus: Horst Klengel, *Syria 3000 to 300 B.C.: A Handbook to Political History* (Berlin: Akademie Verlag, 1992), 190–226 passim; Wayne T. Pitard, *Ancient Damascus: A Historical Study of the Syrian City-State from Earliest Times until Its Fall to the Assyrians in 732 B.C.E.* (Winona Lake, Ind.: Eisenbrauns, 1987); Benjamin Mazar, "The Aramean Empire and Its Relations with Israel," *BA* 25 (1962): 98–120; Emil G. Kraeling, *Aram and Israel* (New York: Columbia Univ. Press, 1918).

118. On Tyre and Phoenicia: William A. Ward, ed., *The Role of the Phoenicians in the Interaction of Mediterranean Civilizations* (Beirut: American Univ. of Beirut, 1969); Gerhard Herm, *The Phoenicians: The Purple Empire of the Ancient World* (London: Gollancz, 1975); Martha S. Joukowsky, ed., *The Heritage of Tyre: Essays on the History, Archaeology, and Preservation of Tyre* (Dubuque, Iowa: Kendall/Hunt Publishers, 1992); F. Briquel-Chatonnet, *Les relations entre les cités de la côte phénicienne et les royaumes d'Israël et de Juda,* OLA 46 (Louvain: Departement Orientalistiek, 1992).

119. On Moab: J. Maxwell Miller, "Moab," *ABD,* 4:882–93; A. H. Van Zyl, *The Moabites,* Pretoria Oriental Series 3 (Leiden: E. J. Brill, 1960); Piotr Bienkowski, ed., *Early Edom and Moab: The Beginning of the Iron Age in Southern Jordan,* Sheffield Archaeological Monographs 7 (Sheffield: J. R. Collis, 1992); Klaas A. D. Smelik, *Converting the Past: Studies in Ancient Israelite and Moabite Historiography* (Leiden: E. J. Brill, 1992).

120. On Ammon: Jean-Michel de Tarragon, "Ammon, Ammonite," *ABD,* 1:184–96; Walter E. Aufrecht, *A Corpus of Ammonite Inscriptions,* Ancient Near Eastern Texts and Studies 4 (Lewiston, N.Y.: Edwin Mellen Press, 1989); Burton MacDonald and Randall W. Younker, eds., *Ancient Ammon.*

121. On Edom: Burton MacDonald, "Edom," *ABD,* 2:287–301; John R. Bartlett, *Edom and the Edomites,* JSOTSup 77 (Sheffield: JSOT Press, 1989); Piotr Bienkowski, ed., *Early Edom and Moab: The Beginning of the Iron Age in Southern Jordan.* Sheffield Archaeological Monongraphs 7 (Sheffield: J. R. Collis, 1992); Diana V. Edelman, ed., *You Shall Not Abhor an Edomite For He Is Your Brother: Edom and Seir in History and Tradition,* Archaeology and Biblical Studies 3 (Atlanta: Scholars, 1995).

122. On Philistia: H. J. Katzenstein and Trude Dothan, "Philistines," *ABD,* 5:326–33; R. D. Barnett, "The Sea Peoples," *CAH,* 3d ed, 2/2:371–78; Trude Dothan,

The Philistines and Their Material Culture (New Haven, Conn.: Yale Univ. Press, 1982); Carl S. Ehrlich, *The Philistines in Transition: A History from ca. 1000–730 B.C.E.*, Studies in the History and Culture of the Ancient Near East 10 (Leiden: E. J. Brill, 1996).

123. Patrick D. Miller Jr. and J. J. M. Roberts, *The Hand of the Lord: A Reassessment of the 'Ark Narrative' of I Samuel*, JHNES (Baltimore: Johns Hopkins, 1977).

124. Stephen L. Cook ("The Lineage Roots of Hosea's Yahwism," in *Semeia [The Social World of the Hebrew Bible: Twenty-five Years of the Social Sciences in the Academy]*, ed. Stephen L. Cook and Ronald A. Simkins, forthcoming) employs anthropological data on the often contentious relations between lineage and state priesthoods to argue that Hosea's cultic critique is predicated on the prophet's membership in a lineage-based northern priesthood that has been excluded from the state cult.

125. Identification of the constituent elements of the political center entails, at least implicitly, a class analysis of the wider Israelite/Judahite societies. Such a class analysis is seldom attempted by biblical exegetes, in part because of the notoriously sketchy social information and in part because of a general resistance to accepting class as an appropriate category for analyzing precapitalist societies (see Gottwald, "The Expropriated and the Expropriators in Nehemiah 5," 9–13). For the outlines of such a class analysis, see Norman K. Gottwald, "A Hypothesis about Social Class in Monarchic Israel in the Light of Contemporary Studies of Social Class and Social Stratification," in *The Hebrew Bible in Its Social World and in Ours*, SemeiaSt (Atlanta: Scholars, 1993), 139–64, with a summary chart on 164. This article is indebted to an unpublished essay by Anthony Mansueto, "From Historical Criticism to Historical Materialism" (seminar paper, the Graduate Theological Union, Berkeley, Calif., 1983). My analysis is rephrased and extended to several biblical texts in Norman K. Gottwald, "Social Class As an Analytic and Hermeneutical Category in Biblical Studies," *JBL* 112 (1993): 3–22. William G. Dever (Levy, ed., *The Archaeology of Society*, 427–29) groups scores of government and civil occupations into eleven social classes without specifying the relations of domination that obtained among them. Ronald A. Simkins ("Patronage and the Political Economy of Monarchic Israel," in *Semeia [The Social World of the Hebrew Bible: Twenty-Five Years of the Social Sciences in the Academy]*, ed. Stephen L. Cook and Ronald A. Simkins, forthcoming) finds the mechanism for class domination during the monarchy to have been a patron-client mode of production to which household and state economies were subordinated. Douglas A. Knight ("Political Rights and Powers in Monarchic Israel," *Semeia* 66 (1995): 93–117) prefers to speak of "national/local politics" instead of "central/peripheral politics," cautioning that "such a duality tends to diminish the experiences of those not located in the seats of national power. From the perspective of villagers, of course, their own contexts constitute the heart of life in the whole region, and the capital and urban culture are marginal and anomalous in comparison" (99). Further on the center/periphery model, see n. 36 above and chap. 4, nn. 69–70.

126. On the basis of the limited number of seals and seals impressions available at the time, Shmuel Yeivin ("Families and Parties in the Kingdom of Judah," in *Studies in the History of Israel and Its Land* [Tel Aviv: M. Nvuman, 1959], 250–93

[Hebrew]) proposed that high offices in eighth–seventh century Judah were characteristically occupied over generations by family "dynasties" (see his chart, 272–73). The vast new wealth of seals and bullae published by Avigad and Deutsch appear not yet to have been assessed comprehensively as a resource for understanding the bureaucracy of the Israelite states comparable to Yeivin's exemplary but outdated reconstruction. For bibliography on the seals and bullae, see n. 69 above.

127. Few historians of ancient Israel have explored the relation between the central government and the general populace in a systematic manner. A notable exception is Douglas A. Knight ("Political Rights and Powers"), with whose conclusions about rather distant and abrasive relations between them I am in basic agreement.

128. For the Judahite reaper's petition, see n. 68 above, and for the Egyptian text, see "The Protests of the Eloquent Peasant," *ANET,* 407–10.

129. Norman K. Gottwald, "The Plot Structure of Marvel or Problem Resolution Stories in the Elijah-Elisha Narratives and Some Musings on Sitz im Leben," in *The Hebrew Bible in Its Social World and in Ours,* 128–30.

130. Carney (*The Shape of the Past,* 118–23) articulates widely shared opinions on why there were no social revolutions in ancient states, attributing this fact to a lack of objective conditions and the absence of class consciousness among a fractured and generally apathetic populace. Certainly few ancient power upheavals can be identified as social revolutions involving wide sectors of the populace, although I have argued such for tribal Israel. It is relevant, however, that anthropological observations of contemporary peasant societies document extensive unrest and versatile forms of passive resistance and "foot dragging" that do not accord with popular apathy so much as recognize the powerful forces of domination arrayed against peasants (see James C. Scott, *Weapons of the Weak: Everyday Forms of Peasant Resistance* [New Haven, Conn.: Yale Univ. Press, 1985]; John Gledhill, *Power and Its Disguises: Anthropological Perspectives on Politics* [London/ Boulder, Colo.: Pluto Press, 1994], 80–93). Since these are not forms of resistance that regimes readily acknowledge, it is worth considering that the dominating voice of the official records from the ancient Near East, Israel and Judah included, will likely have muted or censored out widespread social discontent, preferring to describe their opponents either as foreign adversaries or domestic malcontents with limited following (see Gottwald, "The Expropriated and the Expropriators," 11–12). Robert P. Carroll ("Rebellion and Dissent in Ancient Israelite Society," *ZAW* 89 [1977]: 176–204) suggests that sociopolitical unrest and conflict in the world of the biblical writers are often indirectly expressed by displacing them into ancient times, as in the wilderness narratives of Exodus and Numbers, which recount severe conflicts between Moses and various persons and groups at odds with his leadership.

131. G. Barkay, "The Iron Age II–III," 372.

132. G. Barkay, "The Iron Age II–III," 373. Most surveys of sixth-century archaeological finds do not isolate them from the following Persian period, in part because until recently it was difficult to establish criteria for separating the two periods; see Charles E. Carter, *The Emergence of Yehud in the Persian Period: A Social and Demographic Study,* JSOTSup 294 (Sheffield: Sheffield Academic Press, 1999), 119–34.

133. Carter (*The Emergence of Yehud,* 134–213) reviews the archaeological evi-

dence as a basis for reconstructing site distribution and population, distinguishing between Persian I (538–450 B.C.E.) and Persian II (450–332 B.C.E.). The boundaries of Carter's reconstructed Persian Judah do not embrace the foothills and plains, which, if included, would yield a larger population.

134. The Elephantine papyri: *ANET,* 491–92; Bezalel Porton, "Elephantine Papyri," *ABD,* 2:445–55; Porton, *Archives from Elephantine: The Life of an Ancient Jewish Military Colony* (Los Angeles: Univ. of California Press/London: Cambridge Univ. Press, 1968).

135. The Samarian papyri: Douglas M. Gropp, "Samaria (Papyri)," *ABD,* 5:931–32; Frank M. Cross, "The Papyri and Their Historical Implications," in *Discoveries in the Wadi ed-Daliyeh,* ed. P. W. Lapp and Nancy Lapp, AASOR 41 (Cambridge: American Schools of Oriental Research, 1974), 17–29.

136. Matthew W. Stolper, "Murashu, Archive of," *ABD,* 4:927–28.

137. Louis H. Feldman, "Josephus," *ABD,* 3:985–89; L. H. Feldman and G. Hata, eds., *Josephus, The Bible, and History* (Detroit: Wayne State Univ. Press, 1989).

138. Ephraim Stern ("Between Persia and Greece: Trade, Administration, and Warfare in the Persian and Hellenistic Periods (539–63 B.C.E.)," in Levy, ed., *The Archaeology of Society,* 432–44) reviews the evidence for Greek trade, colonization, and architectural influence in Palestine, beginning already in the Persian period.

139. The Zenon Papyri: Victor A. Tcherikover and A. Fuks, eds., *Corpus Papyrorum Judaicarum* (Jerusalem: Magnes Press/Cambridge: Harvard Univ. Press, 1957), 1:1–47, 115–30; P. W. Pestman, ed., *A Guide to the Zenon Archive* (Leiden: E. J. Brill, 1981).

140. Alexander A. Di Lella, "Wisdom of Ben-Sira," *ABD,* 6:931–45; Philip R. Davies, "Scenes from the Early History of Judaism," in Edelman, ed., *The Triumph of Elohim,* 168–72.

141. Peter Schaefer, "The Hellenistic and Maccabean Periods," in Hayes and Miller, eds., *Israelite and Judaean History,* 549–59.

142. Victor A. Tcherikover (*Hellenistic Civilization and the Jews* [Philadelphia: Jewish Publication Society of America, 1961], 269–332) reviews what is known of the political status of Diaspora communities, including the interface between Jewish communities and Greek cities, noting such privileges and rights as were accorded the dispersed communities and the possibility for individual Jews to attain citizenship. More recent surveys with bibliographies are found in subentries under "Judaism," *ABD,* 3:1037–83 passim: in the Graeco-Roman period, 1048–50 (J. A. Overman and W. S. Green); in Egypt, 1061–72 (P. Borgen); in North Africa, 1072–73 (S. Applebaum); and in Babylonia, 1076–83 (M. Beer). See also Martin Goodman, ed., *Jews in a Graeco-Roman World* (Oxford: Clarendon Press, 1998).

143. The most satisfying proposal as to the process and timing of canonization of the Hebrew Bible is that of Frank M. Cross (*From Epic to Canon: History and Literature in Ancient Israel* [Baltimore/London: Johns Hopkins, 1998], 205–29). His hypothesis is summarized in chap. 2, n. 28.

144. On the literary evidence for diverse Dispersion "Judah-isms" that remained outside the control of Jerusalemite efforts to standardize them, see chap. 2, n. 27.

145. One of the few attempts by a biblical scholar to examine political power across the whole range of biblical history is by J. P. M. Walsh (*The Mighty from Their Thrones: Power in the Biblical Tradition,* OBT 21 [Philadelphia: Fortress,

1987]). His political analysis of the premonarchic period is broadly congruent with my *Tribes,* from which he has drawn "idealized" conclusions more in line with Mendenhall's views of Israelites' origins. As a result, his critique of monarchy lacks adequate political description, analysis, and placement of the states of Israel and Judah in their wider political context. As a result, centralized politics are made to look like a mode of power that could be easily renounced if only religious justice were put into practice, and the alternative implied seems to be a return to tribalism. In my judgment, the studies by David Biale, a historian of Judaism, and Ira Sharkansky, a political scientist, offer more satisfactory assessments of ancient Israelite politics; see chap. 2, n. 13, and chap. 4, n. 83.

146. One of the most exhaustive studies of the impact of Israelite political praxis and ideology on the subsequent history of politics is the four-volume work of Daniel J. Elazar, *The Covenant Tradition in Politics.* Vol. 1, *Covenant and Polity in Biblical Israel;* Vol. 2, *From Christian Separation through the Protestant Reformation;* Vol. 3, *The Great Frontier and the Matrix of Federal Democracy;* Vol. 4, *The Constitutional Matrix of Modern Democracy* (New Brunswick, N.J./London: Transaction Publishers, 1995–1998. Compared to the much briefer studies of Biale and Sharkansky, Elazar overstates the systematic unity of biblical politics and inflates the influence of biblical politics on subsequent eras, although the rich detail of his historical recital is immensely informative. More successful in showing the complex, ambivalent, and often disjunctive relations between the Bible and modern political thought are the essays in Kim Ian Parker, ed., *Liberal Democracy and the Bible* (Lewiston, N.Y./Queenston/Lampeter: Edwin Mellen Press, 1992); see the preceding n. 145.

Epilogue

1. Max Weber, *Ancient Judaism,* trans. and ed. Hans H. Gerth and Don Martindale (orig. pub. 1917–21; Glencoe, Ill.: Free Press, 1952), 5. Weber borrowed the term "pariah" from the caste system of India without any implication of anti-Semitism, but also it seems without due appreciation of the range of Jewish worldwide settlements and "high status" accomplishments that are not paralleled in the marginalized Indian castes. Robert E. Park, as cited by Gerth and Martindale in the preface (xxv), proposed the concept of marginality, which Gerth and Martindale accept as a suitable replacement for "pariah people," since it avoids the popular pejorative sense of the term and also takes into account that the marginal people may be of high or low status depending on social and cultural context.

2. Moshe Halbertal and Avishai Margalit (*Idolatry* [Cambridge/London: Harvard Univ. Press, 1992]) find that the biblical strictures on idolatrous paganism have carried over into subsequent Jewish denigrations of nonmonotheistic believers, including even the broad-minded Maimonides. Zeev Sternhall (*The Founding Myths of Israel: Nationalism, Socialism, and the Making of the Jewish State* [Princeton: Princeton Univ. Press, 1998]) documents how the Zionist founders of Israel widely assumed that a nationalist Jewish revival in an autonomous state would ensure domestic social justice, while ignoring the existence of the Arab "Other." Sternhall details, for example, how the influential Zionist theoretician Aaron David Gordon abhorred both capitalism and socialism and assumed—naively in retrospect—that the national

revival of Jews laboring on the land would lead to an abolition of capitalist inequities among a "brotherhood" of Jews without any need for socialist reconstruction of society and state. David Biale and Ira Sharkansky express similar equivocations and reservations about political power in the modern state of Israel; see chap. 2, n. 13; chap. 4, n. 83; chap. 5, n. 145.

3. Norman K. Gottwald, "Are Biblical and U.S. Societies Comparable? Theopolitical Analogies toward the Next American Revolution," in *The Hebrew Bible in Its World and in Ours* (Atlanta: Scholars, 1993), 307–23.

4. The essays in Kim Ian Parker's *Liberal Democracy and the Bible* (Lewiston, N.Y./Queenston/Lampeter: Edwin Mellen Press, 1992) focus primarily on the ambivalent rejection and appropriation of biblical political ideology and practice by modern political theorists. Scott Bader-Saye (*Church and Israel after Christendom: The Politics of Election* [Boulder, Colo.: Westview Press, 1999]) highlights some of the political consequences of the ongoing struggle between Judaism and Christianity over which faith is the legitimate heir of biblical election.

5. Norman K. Gottwald ("Biblical Views on 'Church-State' Relations and Their Influence on Existing Political Ideologies," in *The Hebrew Bible in Its Social World and in Ours,* SemeiaSt [Atlanta: Scholars, 1993], 365–83) proposes that democratic socialism comes closest to meeting certain criteria of biblical social justice but acknowledges that this assessment requires a selective judgment in the face of many biblical texts that are authoritarian, hierarchic, and supportive of existing wealth and power. M. Douglas Meeks (*God the Economist: The Doctrine of God and Political Economy* [Minneapolis: Fortress, 1989]), in a more theological mode, draws selectively on biblical texts to develop his theology of a God whose largesse in creation and redemption calls for a leveling of wealth and power throughout human societies, but he does not adopt a socialist solution, since he conceives of socialism solely as a hierarchically imposed political program.

6. Yairah Amit ("The Dual Causality Principle and Its Effects on Biblical Literature," *VT* 37 [1987]: 385–400) picks up the title phrase from Yehezkel Kaufmann, and in dialogue with Gerhard von Rad and I. L. Seeligmann, explains the dual causality principle in this way: "The readers of these stories may explain occurrences by two systems of interpretation—the divine system and the human system—without one system contradicting or invalidating the other" (391). Amit's chief interest lies in the literary effects of the dual causality principle. Her proposal to locate this dual causality principle of narration in late Assyrian times is inconclusive, as is von Rad's proposal to place its beginning in the Davidic-Solomonic kingdom. It seems more likely to me that this principle is exhibited already in old literature such as the Song of Deborah, although Amit may be correct that the frequent removal of God into the background of biblical narratives undergoes a later development, assuming "a prominent part in the struggle for a more abstract concept of God" (400). Roland Boer (*Jameson and Jeroboam,* SemeiaSt [Atlanta: Scholars, 1996]), 155–57) comments on the Kaufmann-Amit principle of dual causality with reference to 1 Kings 11–14 under the rubric of historical determinism: "The mixed success in realizing the dual causality principle indicates the fundamental ideological theme or ideologeme—which by default must be religious—operating in these texts. It is the problem of the way in which the divine may be understood to be involved in human affairs, the problem of the relationship between divine and

human which may be termed 'historical determinism' or 'providence.' To express it this way is to highlight the contradiction inherent within the ideologeme: human and divine dimensions, voluntarism and determinism, are not easy to reconcile. Thus, the dual causality principle is one way of dealing with the problem, more explicit divine control is another." (157) Both Amit and Boer leave many questions unaddressed, which suggests that the dual causality principle in Israelite literature and religious thought deserves further research and reflection. Richard Elliott Friedman (*The Disappearance of God: A Divine Mystery* [Boston: Little, Brown & Co., 1995]) approaches this shifting divine/human interface in a wide-ranging examination of both biblical Testaments, Nietzche and Death of God theology, and Jewish Kabbalah.

Bibliography

Ackerman, Susan. *Under Every Green Tree: Popular Religion in Sixth-Century Judah.* HSM 46. Atlanta: Scholars, 1992.

Adams, Robert McC. *The Evolution of Urban Society: Early Mesopotamia and Prehispanic Mexico.* Chicago: Aldine Publishing Co., 1966.

Adcock, Frank E. *The Greek and Macedonian Art of War.* Berkeley, Calif.: Univ. of California Press, 1957.

Aguilar, Mario I. "Rethinking the Judean Past: Questions of History and a Social Archaeology of Memory in the First Book of Maccabees." *BTB* 30 (2000): 58–67.

Ahlström, Gösta W. *The History of Ancient Palestine from the Palaeolithic Period to Alexander's Conquest.* JSOTSup 146. Sheffield: Sheffield Academic Press, 1993.

_____. *Royal Administration and National Religion in Ancient Palestine.* Leiden: E. J. Brill, 1982.

_____. *Who Were the Israelites?* Winona Lake, Ind.: Eisenbrauns, 1986.

Aldred, Cyril. *Akhenaten, Pharaoh of Egypt: A New Study.* Rev. ed. London: Thames & Hudson, 1988.

Alt, Albrecht. *Essays on Old Testament History and Religion.* Oxford: Basil Blackwell, 1966.

_____. "Micha 2, 1–5, ΓΗΣ ΑΝΑΔΑΣΜΟΣ in Juda." In *Kleine Schriften zur Geschichte des Volkes Israels.* Vol. 3. Munich: Beck, 1959. 373–81.

Amin, Samir. *Class and Nation Historically and in the Current Crisis.* New York: Monthly Review Press, 1980.

Amit, Yairah. "The Dual Causality Principle and Its Effects on Biblical Literature." *VT* 37 (1987): 385–400.

Anderson, Benedict. *Imagined Communities: Reflections on the Origin and Spread of Nationalism.* Rev. ed. London: Verso, 1991.

Anderson, Gary A. *Sacrifices and Offerings in Ancient Israel: Studies in Their Social and Political Importance.* HSM 41. Atlanta: Scholars, 1988.

Aufrecht, Walter E. *A Corpus of Ammonite Inscriptions.* Ancient Near Eastern Texts and Studies 4. Lewiston, N.Y.: Edwin Mellen Press, 1989.

Auld, A. Graeme. "The Deuteronomists and the Former Prophets, or What Makes the Former Prophets Deuteronomistic?" In *Those Elusive Deuteronomists: The Phenomenon of Pan-Deuteronomism.* Edited by L. S. Schearing and S. L. McKenzie. JSOTSup 268. Sheffield: Sheffield Academic Press, 1999. 116–26.

_____. *Kings without Privilege: David and Moses in the Story of the Bible's Kings.* Edinburgh: T. & T. Clark, 1994.

Avi-Yonah, Michael, and Ephraim Stern, eds. *Encyclopedia of Archaeological Excavations in the Holy Land.* 4 vols. Jerusalem: Israel Exploration Society and Masada Press, 1975–78. Updated and expanded by Ephraim Stern, ed., *The New Encyclopedia of Archaeological Excavations in the Holy Land.* 4 vols. Jerusalem: Israel Exploration Society and Carta, 1993.

Avigad, Nahman. *Bullae and Seals from a Post-Exilic Judean Archive.* Qedem 4. Jerusalem: Institute of Archaeology, Hebrew University, 1976.

_____. "The Contribution of Hebrew Seals to an Understanding of Israelite Religion and Society." In *Ancient Israelite Religion: Essays in Honor of Frank Moore Cross.* Edited by P. D. Miller Jr. et al. Philadelphia: Fortress, 1987. 195–208.

_____. "The Epitaph of a Royal Steward from Siloam Village." *IEJ* 3 (1953): 137–52.

_____. *Hebrew Bullae from the Time of Jeremiah.* Jerusalem: Israel Exploration Society, 1986.

Bader-Saye, Scott. *Church and Israel after Christendom: The Politics of Election.* Boulder, Colo.: Westview Press, 1999.

Bagnall, Roger S. *The Administration of the Ptolemaic Possessions outside Egypt.* Columbia Studies in the Classical Tradition 4. Leiden: E. J. Brill, 1976.

_____. *Reading Papyri, Writing Ancient History.* London: Routledge, 1995.

Bailey, Christine W. "The State of the State in Anthropology." *Dialectical Anthropology* 9 (1985): 65–91.

Baines, John. "Ancient Egyptian Kingship: Official Forms, Rhetoric, Context." In *King and Messiah in Israel and the Ancient Near East: Proceedings of the Oxford Old Testament Seminar.* Edited by J. Day. JSOTSup 270. Sheffield: Sheffield Academic Press, 1998. 16–53.

Baines, John, and Jaromir Malek. *Atlas of Ancient Egypt.* New York: Facts on File, 1980.

Barkay, Gabriel. "Iron II–III." In *The Archaeology of Ancient Israel.* Edited by Amnon Ben-Tor. New Haven, Conn./London: Yale Univ. Press, 1992. 302–73.

Barnett, R. D. "The Sea Peoples." *Cambridge Ancient History.* Edited by I. E. S. Edwards et al. 3d ed. 2/2. Cambridge: Cambridge Univ. Press, 1975. 371–78.

Barstad, Hans M. *The Myth of the Empty Land: A Study in the History and Archaeology of Judah during the 'Exilic' Period.* Oslo: Scandinavian University Press, 1996.

Bartlett, John R. "Edom." *ABD* 2: 287–95.

_____. *Edom and the Edomites.* JSOTSup 77. Sheffield: JSOT Press, 1989.

Beaulieu, P.-A. *The Reign of Nabonidus, King of Babylon 556–539 B.C.* Yale Near Eastern Researches 10. New Haven, Conn.: Yale University Press, 1987.

Becking, Bob. *The Fall of Samaria: An Historical and Archaeological Study.* SHANE 2. Leiden: E. J. Brill, 1992.

Begrich, Joachim. "Sōfēr und Mazkīr." *ZAW* 58 (1940–41): 1–29.

Bendix, Reinhard. *Kings or People: Power and the Mandate to Rule.* Berkeley, Calif.: Univ. of California Press, 1978.

Bengston, Hermann, ed. *The Greeks and the Persians.* New York: Delacorte Press, 1968.

Berlev, Oleg. "Bureaucrats." In *The Egyptians.* Edited by Sergio Donadoni. Chicago: Univ. of Chicago Press, 1997. 87–119.

Berlinerblau, Jacques. "Ideology, Pierre Bourdieu's *Doxa,* and the Hebrew Bible." *Semeia.* Atlanta: Scholars, forthcoming.

_____. "The 'Popular Religion' Paradigm in Old Testament Research: A Sociological Critique." *JSOT* 60 (1993): 3–26.

Berquist, Jon L. *Judaism in Persia's Shadow: A Social and Historical Approach.* Minneapolis: Fortress, 1995.

Bevan, Edwyn R. *A History of Egypt under the Ptolemaic Dynasty.* London: Methuen & Co., 1927.

_____. *The House of Seleucus.* 2 vols. 1902. Reprint. New York: Barnes & Noble, 1966.

Biale, David. *Power and Powerlessness in Jewish History.* New York: Schocken Books, 1986.

The Bible and Culture Collective. *The Postmodern Bible.* New Haven, Conn.: Yale Univ. Press, 1995.

Bickerman, Elias J. *The Jews in the Greek Age.* Cambridge: Harvard Univ. Press, 1988.

Bienkowski, Piotr, ed. *Early Edom and Moab: The Beginning of the Iron Age in Southern Jordan.* Sheffield Archaeological Monographs 7. Sheffield: J. R. Collis, 1992.

Bikai, Patricia M. "The Phoenicians." In *The Crisis Years: The Twelfth Century B.C. from beyond the Danube to the Tigris.* Edited by W. A. Ward and M. S. Joukowsky. Dubuque, Iowa: Kendall/Hunt Publishing Co., 1989. 132–41.

Biran, Avraham, and Joseph Naveh. "An Aramaic Fragment from Dan." *IEJ* 43 (1993): 81–98.

_____. "The Tel Dan Inscription: A New Fragment." *IEJ* 45 (1995): 1–18.

Black, Jeremy A., and W. J. Tait. "Archives and Libraries in the Ancient Near East." In *CANE.* Vol. 2. New York: Charles Scribner's Sons, 1995. 197–209.

Bleiberg, Edward. "The Economy of Ancient Egypt." In *CANE,* vol. 3. New York: Charles Scribner's Sons, 1995. 1373–85.

Blenkinsopp, Joseph. "Temple and Society in Achaemenid Judah." In *Second Temple Studies 1: Persian Period.* JSOTSup 117. Sheffield: Sheffield Academic Press, 1991. 22–53.

Boer, Roland. "Deutero-Isaiah: Historical Materialism and Biblical Theology." *BibInt* 6 (April 1998): 181–204.

_____. *Jameson and Jeroboam.* SemeiaSt. Atlanta: Scholars, 1996.

_____. "National Allegory in the Bible." *JSOT* 74 (1997): 95–116.

_____. *Novel Histories: The Fiction of Biblical Criticism.* Sheffield: Sheffield Academic Press, 1997.

Boudon, Raymond, and Francois Bourricaud. *A Critical Dictionary of Sociology.* Chicago: Univ. of Chicago Press, 1989.

Boyarin, Daniel. "Placing Reading: Ancient Israel and Medieval Europe." In *The Ethnography of Reading.* Edited by J. Boyarin. Berkeley, Calif.: Univ. of California Press, 1993. 10–37.

Brettler, Marc Zvi. *The Creation of History in Ancient Israel.* London: Routledge, 1995.

_____. "Judaism in the Hebrew Bible? The Transition from Ancient Israelite Religion to Judaism." *CBQ* 61 (1999): 429–47.

Briant, Pierre. *Alexander the Great: Man of Action, Man of Spirit.* New York: Harry N. Adams, 1996.

_____. *Histoire de l'empire perse de Cyrus à Alexandre.* Paris: Fayard, 1996.

Bright, John. "The Organization and Administration of the Israelite Empire." In

Magnalia Dei: The Mighty Acts of God. Edited by F. M. Cross et al. Garden City, N.Y.: Doubleday, 1975. 193–208.

Brinkman, J. A. "The Babylonian Chronicle Revisited." In *Lingering over Words: Studies in Ancient Near Eastern Literature in Honor of William L. Moran.* Edited by Tzvi Abusch et al. Atlanta: Scholars, 1990. 73–104.

Briquel-Chatonnet, F. *Les relations entre les cités de la côte phénicienne et les royaumes d'Israël et de Juda.* OLA 46. Louvain: Departement Oriëntalistiek, 1992.

Bronson, Bennet. "The Role of Barbarians in the Fall of States." In *The Collapse of Ancient States and Civilizations.* Edited by N. Yoffee and G. L. Cowgill. Tucson, Ariz.: Univ. of Arizona Press, 1988. 196–218.

Brookman, W. R. *A Hebrew-English Synopsis of the Old Testament: Samuel, Kings, and Chronicles.* Peabody, Mass.: Hendrickson Publishers, forthcoming.

Broshi, Magen. "The Expansion of Jerusalem in the Reigns of Hezekiah and Manasseh." *IEJ* 24 (1974): 21–26.

Broshi, Magen, and Israel Finkelstein. "The Population of Palestine in Iron Age II." *BASOR* 287 (1992): 47–60.

Brueggemann, Walter. Review of *The Tribes of Yahweh,* by Norman K. Gottwald. *JAAR* 48 (1980): 44–51.

Buccellati, Giorgio. *Cities and Nations of Ancient Syria: An Essay on Political Institutions with Special Reference to the Israelite Kingdoms.* Studi Semitici 26. Rome: Istituto di Studi del Vicino Oriente, 1967.

Burke, Peter. "History of Events and the Revival of Narrative." In *New Perspectives on Historical Writing.* University Park, Pa.: Pennsylvania State Univ. Press, 1992. 233–48.

Carneiro, Robert L. "The Chiefdom: Precursor of the State." In *The Transition to Statehood in the New World.* Edited by G. D. Jones and R. R. Krautz. Cambridge: Cambridge Univ. Press, 1981. 37–79.

_____. "A Theory of the Origins of the State." *Science* 169 (1970): 733–38.

Carney, T. R. *The Shape of the Past: Models of Antiquity.* Lawrence, Kans.: Coronado Press, 1975.

Carroll, Robert P. "Israel, History of [Post-monarchic Period]." *ABD* 3: 567–76.

_____. "The Myth of the Empty Land." *Semeia* 59 (1992): 79–93.

_____. "Rebellion and Dissent in Ancient Israelite Society." *ZAW* 89 (1977): 176–204.

Carter, Charles E. *The Emergence of Yehud in the Persian Period: A Social and Demographic Study.* JSOTSup 294. Sheffield: Sheffield Academic Press, 1999.

Carter, Charles E., and Carol L. Meyers, eds. *Community, Identity, and Ideology: Social Sciences Approaches to the Hebrew Bible.* Winona Lake, Ind.: Eisenbrauns, 1996.

Cazelles, Henri. *Histoire politique d'Israël des origines à Alexandre le Grand.* Paris: Desclée, 1982.

_____. "Sacral Kingship," *ABD* 5: 863–64.

Chaney, Marvin L. "Ancient Palestinian Peasant Movements and the Formation of Premonarchic Israel." In *Palestine in Transition: The Emergence of Ancient Israel.* Edited by D. N. Freedman and D. F. Graf. SWBA 2. Sheffield: Almond Press, 1983. 39–90.

_____. "Bitter Bounty: The Dynamics of Political Economy Critiqued by the Eighth-Century Prophets." In *The Bible and Liberation: Political and Social Hermeneutics.* Edited by N. K. Gottwald and R. A. Horsley. Maryknoll, N.Y.: Orbis, 1993. 250–63.

_____. "Debt Easement in Israelite History and Tradition." In *The Bible and the Politics of Exegesis: Essays in Honor of Norman K. Gottwald on His Sixty-Fifth Birthday.* Edited by D. Jobling et al. Cleveland: Pilgrim Press, 1991. 127–39.

_____. "Systemic Study of the Israelite Monarchy." *Semeia* 37 (1986): 53–76.

_____. "Whose Grapes? The Addressees of Isaiah 5:1–7 in the Light of Political Economy." *Semeia.* Atlanta: Scholars, forthcoming.

Charpin, Dominique. "The History of Ancient Mesopotamia: An Overview." In *CANE,* vol. 2. New York: Charles Scribner's Sons, 1995. 807–29.

Chikafu, P. T. "The Audience Presupposed in the Conquest, Infiltration, and Revolt Models: A Sociological Analysis." *JTSA* 84 (Sept. 1993): 11–24.

Claburn, William E. "The Fiscal Basis of Josiah's Reform." *JBL* 92 (1973): 11–22.

Claessen, Henri J. M., and Peter Skalnik, eds. *The Early State.* The Hague: Mouton Publishers, 1978.

Clastres, Pierre. *Society against the State.* New York: Zone Books, 1989.

Clements, Ronald E. *Abraham and David: Genesis XV and its Meaning for Israelite Tradition.* London: SCM Press, 1967.

Clines, David J. A. *Interested Parties: The Ideology of Writers and Readers of the Hebrew Bible.* JSOTSup 205. Sheffield: Sheffield Academic Press, 1995.

Cogan, Mordechai. "Chronology, Hebrew Bible." *ABD* 1: 1005–11.

_____. *Imperialism and Religion: Assyria, Judah, and Israel in the 8th and 7th Centuries B.C.E.* SBLMS 19. Missoula, Mont.: Scholars, 1974.

Cogan, Mordechai, and Hayim Tadmor. *II Kings: A New Translation with Introduction and Commentary.* AB 11. Garden City, N.Y.: Doubleday & Co., 1988.

Coggins, R. J. *Samaritans and Jews: The Origins of Samaritanism Reconsidered.* Atlanta: John Knox, 1975.

Cohen, C. "Neo-Assyrian Elements in the First Speech of the Biblical Rab-šaqê." *IOS* 9 (1979): 32–48.

Cohen, Martin A. "In All Fairness to Ahab: A Socio-Political Consideration of the Ahab-Elijah Controversy." *ErIsr* 12 (1975): 87*–94*.

Cohen, Ronald. "State and Ethnicity: The Dialectics of Culture and Polity." In *Pivot Politics: Changing Cultural Identities in Early State Formation Processes.* Edited by M. van Bakel, R. Hagesteijn, and P. van de Velde. Amsterdam: Het Spinhuis, 1994. 47–66.

Cohen, Ronald, and Elman R. Service, eds. *Origins of the State: The Anthropology of Political Evolution.* Philadelphia: Institute for the Study of Human Issues, 1978.

Collins, John J. "The Dead Sea Scrolls." *ABD* 2: 85–101.

Coogan, Michael David. "Canaanite Origins and Lineage: Reflections on the Religion of Ancient Israel." In *Ancient Israelite Religion: Essays in Honor of Frank Moore Cross.* Edited by P. D. Miller Jr. et al. Philadelphia: Fortress, 1987. 115–24.

Cook, J. M. *The Persian Empire.* New York: Schocken Books, 1983.

Cook, Stephen L. "The Lineage Roots of Hosea's Yahwism." *Semeia.* Atlanta: Scholars, forthcoming.

_____. *Prophecy and Apocalyptic: The Postexilic Social Setting.* Minneapolis: Fortress, 1995.

Coote, Robert B. *In Defense of Revolution: The Elohist History.* Minneapolis: Fortress, 1991.

Coote, Robert B., and Keith A. Whitelam. *The Emergence of Early Israel in Historical Perspective.* SWBA 5. Sheffield: Almond Press, 1987.

Cross, Frank M. *Canaanite Myth and Hebrew Epic: Essays in the History of the Religion of Israel.* Cambridge: Harvard Univ. Press, 1970.

_____. *From Epic to Canon: History and Literature in Ancient Israel.* Baltimore: Johns Hopkins, 1998.

_____. "King Hezekiah's Seal Bears Phoenician Imagery." *BAR* 25 (Mar.–Apr. 1999): 42–45, 60.

_____. "The Papyri and Their Historical Implications." In *Discoveries in the Wadi ed-Daliyeh.* Edited by P. W. Lapp and Nancy Lapp. AASOR 41. Cambridge: American Schools of Oriental Research, 1974. 17–29.

_____. "The Origin and Early Evolution of the Alphabet." *ErIsr* 8 (1967): 8*–24*.

Cross, Frank M., Jr., and David N. Freedman. "The Song of Miriam." *JNES* 14 (1955): 237–50.

_____. *Studies in Ancient Yahwistic Poetry.* 2d ed. Livonia, Mich.: Dove Booksellers, 1997.

Crown, A. D. "Tidings and Instructions: How News Travelled in the Ancient Near East." *JESHO* 17 (1974): 244–71.

Crüsemann, Frank. "State Tax and Temple Tithe in Israel's Monarchical Period." Paper presented at the annual meeting of the Sociology of the Monarchy Seminar, Society of Biblical Literature, 1984.

_____. *The Torah: Theology and Social History of Old Testament Law.* Minneapolis: Fortress, 1996.

_____. *Der Widerstand gegen das Königtum: Die antiköniglichen Texte des Alten Testaments und der Kampf um den frühen israelitischen Staat.* Neukirchen-Vluyn: Neukirchener Verlag, 1978.

Cryer, Frederick H. "On the Recently-Discovered 'House of David' Inscription." *SJOT* 8 (1994): 3–19.

Curtis, Edward L., and Albert A. Madsen. *A Critical and Exegetical Commentary on the Books of Chronicles.* ICC. New York: Charles Scribner's Sons, 1910.

Damrosch, David. *The Narrative Covenant: Transformations of Genre in the Growth of Biblical Literature.* San Francisco: Harper & Row, 1987.

Dandamayev, Muhammad. "State Gods and Private Religion in the Near East in the First Millennium B.C.E." In *Religion and Politics in the Ancient Near East.* Ed. Adele Berlin. Studies and Texts in Jewish History and Culture. Bethesda, MD: Univ. Press of Maryland, 1996. 35–45.

Davies, Philip R. *In Search of 'Ancient Israel.'* JSOTSup 148. Sheffield: Sheffield Academic Press, 1992.

_____. "Method and Madness: Some Remarks on Doing History with the Bible." *JBL* 114 (1995): 699–705.

_____. "Scenes from the Early History of Judaism." In *The Triumph of Elohim: From Yahwisms to Judaisms.* Edited by D. V. Edelman. Grand Rapids, Mich.: Eerdmans, 1995. 145–82.

Dearman, J. Andrew, ed. *Studies in the Mesha Inscription and Moab*. Atlanta: Scholars, 1989.

Deutsch, Robert. "First Impressions—What We Learn from King Ahaz's Seal." *BAR* 24 (May-June 1998): 54–56, 62.

———. *Messages from the Past: Hebrew Bullae from the Time of Isaiah through the Destruction of the First Temple*. Tel Aviv: Archaeological Center Publications, 1999.

Dever, William G. "Archaeology and the 'Age of Solomon': A Case Study in Archeology and Historiography." In *The Age of Solomon: Scholarship at the Turn of the Millennium*. Edited by Lowell K. Handy. Leiden: E. J. Brill, 1997. 217–51.

———. "The Contribution of Archaeology to the Study of Canaanite and Early Israelite Religion." In *Ancient Israelite Religion: Essays in Honor of Frank Moore Cross*. Edited by P. D. Miller Jr. et al. Philadelphia: Fortress, 1987. 209–47.

———. "Iron Age Epigraphic Material from the Area of Khirbet el-Kôm." *HUCA* 40/41 (1969–70):139–204.

———. "Israel, History of [Archaeology and the 'Conquest']." *ABD* 3: 545–58.

———. "The Israelite Settlements in Canaan: New Archaeological Models." In *Recent Archaeological Discoveries and Biblical Research*. Seattle: Univ. of Washington Press, 1990. 37–84.

———. *Recent Archaeological Discoveries and Biblical Research*. Seattle: Univ. of Washington Press, 1990.

———. "Social Structure in Palestine in the Iron II Period on the Eve of Destruction." In *The Archaeology of Society in the Holy Land*. Edited by T. E. Levy. New York: Facts on File, 1995. 416–30.

DeVries, Simon J. "Chronology of the OT." *IDB* 1: 584–89.

———. *I Kings*. WBC 12. Waco, Tex.: Word Books, 1985.

Diakanoff, I. M., ed. *Ancient Mesopotamia: Socio-Economic History*. Moscow: Nauka Publishing House, 1969.

Diamond, James S. *Homeland or Holy Land? The "Canaanite" Critique of Israel*. Bloomington, Ind.: Indiana University Press, 1986.

Dietrich, Walter. "The 'Ban' in the Age of the Early Kings." In *The Origins of the Ancient Israelite States*. Edited by V. Fritz and P. R. Davies. JSOTSup 228. Sheffield: Sheffield Academic Press, 1996. 196–210.

Di Lella, Alexander A. "Wisdom of Ben-Sira." *ABD* 6: 931–45.

Diringer, David. *The Alphabet: A Key to the History of Mankind*. 3d ed. London: Hutchinson, 1968.

Dothan, Trude. *The Philistines and Their Material Culture*. New Haven, Conn.: Yale Univ. Press, 1982.

Dumbrell, William J. "Midian—a Land or a League?" *VT* 25 (1975): 323–37.

Dus, Jan. *Theokratische Demokratie des alten Israel: Fünf Studien zur Geschichte Israels*. Frankfurt: Peter Lang, 1992.

Dutcher-Walls, Patricia. *Narrative Art, Political Rhetoric: The Case of Athaliah and Joash*. JSOTSup 209. Sheffield: Sheffield Academic Press, 1996.

Eagleton, Terry. *Criticism and Ideology: A Study in Marxist Literary Theory*. London: Verso, 1976.

Earle, Timothy. "Prehistoric Economics and the Evolution of Social Complexity: A Commentary." In *Prehistoric Production and Exchange: The Aegean and Eastern*

Mediterranean. Edited by A. B. Knapp and T. Stech. Los Angeles: UCLA Institute of Archaeology, 1985. 106–11.

Eberhard, Wolfram. *Conquerors and Rulers: Social Forces in Modern China.* Rev. ed. Leiden: E. J. Brill, 1965.

Eddy, Samuel K. *The King Is Dead: Studies in the Near Eastern Resistance to Hellenism 334–31 B.C.* Lincoln, Neb.: University of Nebraska Press, 1961.

Edelman, Diana V., ed. *You Shall Not Abhor an Edomite For He is Your Brother: Edom and Seir in History and Tradition.* Archaeology and Biblical Studies 3. Atlanta: Scholars, 1995.

Ehrlich, Carl S. *The Philistines in Transition: A History from ca. 1000–730 B.C.E.* Studies in the History and Culture of the Ancient Near East 10. Leiden: E. J. Brill, 1996.

Eisenstadt, S. N., ed.. *The Origins and Diversity of Axial Age Civilizations.* Albany, N.Y.: SUNY Press, 1986.

_____. *The Political Systems of Empires.* New York: Free Press, 1969.

Eissfeldt, Otto. "Protektorat der Midianiter über ihre Nachbarn im letzten Viertel des 2. Jahrtausends v. Chr." *JBL* 87 (1967): 383–93.

Elazar, Daniel J. *The Covenant Tradition in Politics.* 4 vols. New Brunswick, N.J.: Transaction Publishers, 1995.

Elliott, Mark A. *The Survivors of Israel: A Reconstruction of the Theology of Pre-Christian Judaism.* Grand Rapids: Eerdmans, 2000.

Endres, John C., William R. Millar, and John Barclay Burns, eds. *Chronicles and Its Synoptic Parallels in Samuel, Kings, and Related Biblical Texts.* Collegeville, Minn.: Liturgical Press, 1998.

Engel, Donald W. *Alexander the Great and the Logistics of the Macedonian Army.* Berkeley, Calif.: Univ. of California Press, 1978.

Engelken, Karen. "Kanaan als nicht-territorialer Terminus." *BN* 52 (1990): 47–63.

Eph'al, Israel. "On Warfare and Military Control in the Ancient Near Eastern Empires: A Research Outline." In *History, Historiography and Interpretation: Studies in Biblical and Cuneiform Literature.* Edited by H. Tadmor and M. Weinfeld. Jerusalem: Magnes Press, 1983. 88–106.

Eskenazi, Tamara C. "Current Perspectives on Ezra–Nehemiah and the Persian Period." *CurBS* 1 (1993): 59–86.

Evans, Carl D. "Jeroboam." *ABD* 3: 742–45.

Exum, J. Cheryl, ed. *Virtual History and the Bible.* *BibInt* 8 (2000).

Fales, Frederick Mario. "Census, Ancient Near East." *ABD* 1: 882–83.

Farb, Peter. *Man's Rise to Civilization as Shown by the Indians of North America from Primeval Times to the Coming of the Industrial State.* New York: E. P. Dutton, 1968.

Feldman, Louis H. "Josephus." *ABD* 3: 985–89.

Feldman, Louis H., and G. Hata, eds. *Josephus, the Bible, and History.* Detroit: Wayne State Univ. Press, 1989.

Finkelstein, Israel. "Arabian Trade and Socio-Political Conditions in the Negev in the Twelfth–Eleventh Centuries B.C.E.," *JNES* 47 (1988): 241–52.

_____. *The Archaeology of the Israelite Settlement.* Jerusalem: Israel Exploration Society, 1988.

_____. "The Archaeology of the United Monarchy: An Alternative View." *Levant* 23 (1996): 177–87.

_____. "Environmental Archaeology and Social History: Demographic and Economic Aspects of the Monarchic Period." In *Biblical Archaeology Today: Proceedings of the Second International Congress on Biblical Archaeology, Jerusalem, June 1990.* Edited by J. Aviram and A. Biran. Jerusalem: Israel Exploration Society, 1993. 56–66.

_____. "The Great Transformation: The 'Conquest' of the Highlands Frontiers and the Rise of Territorial States." In *The Archaeology of Society in the Holy Land.* Edited by T. E. Levy. New York: Facts on File, 1995. 349–63.

_____. "Hazor and the North in the Iron Age: A Low Chronology Perspective." *BASOR* 314 (1999): 55–70.

Finkelstein, Israel, and Zvi Lederman, eds. *Highlands of Many Cultures: The Southern Samaria Survey—The Sites.* 2 vols. Monograph Series 14. Tel Aviv: Institute of Archaeology, Tel Aviv Univ., 1997.

Fischer, Thomas. "First and Second Maccabees." *ABD* 4: 439–50.

Flanagan, James W. "Chiefs in Israel." *JSOT* 20 (1981): 47–73.

_____. *David's Social Drama: A Hologram of Israel's Early Iron Age.* SWBA 7. Sheffield: Almond Press, 1988.

Frandsen, Paul J. "Egyptian Imperialism." In *Power and Propaganda: A Symposium on Ancient Empires.* Edited by M. T. Larsen. Copenhagen: Akademisk Forlag, 1979. 167–89.

Frankel, Rafael. "Upper Galilee in the Late Bronze Age—Iron I Transition." In *From Nomadism to Monarchy: Archaeological and Historical Aspects of Early Israel.* Edited by I. Finkelstein and N. Na'aman. Jerusalem: Israel Exploration Society, 1994. 18–34.

Freedman, David Noel. "Early Israelite History in the Light of Early Israelite Poetry." In *Unity and Diversity: Essays in the History, Literature, and Religion of the Ancient Near East.* Edited by H. Goedicke and J. J. M. Roberts. Baltimore: Johns Hopkins, 1975. 3–35.

Frick, Frank S. "Cui Bono?—History in the Service of Political Nationalism: The Deuteronomistic History as Political Propaganda." *Semeia* 66 (1995): 79–92.

_____. *The Formation of the State in Ancient Israel: A Survey of Models and Theories.* SWBA 4. Decatur, Ga.: Almond Press, 1985.

_____. "Religion and Sociopolitical Structure in Early Israel: An Ethno-Archaeological Approach." In *Community, Identity, and Ideology: Social Science Approaches to the Hebrew Bible.* Edited by C. E. Carter and C. L. Meyers. Winona Lake, Ind.: Eisenbrauns, 1996. 448–70.

Fried, Morton H. *The Evolution of Political Society: An Essay in Political Anthropology.* New York: Random House, 1967.

Fried, Morton H., and Frederick M. Watkins. "State." *IESS* 15 (1968): 143–57.

Friedman, Richard Elliott. *The Disappearance of God: A Divine Mystery.* Boston: Little, Brown & Co., 1995.

_____. "Torah [Pentateuch]." *ABD* 6: 605–22.

Friedrich, Johannes. *Extinct Languages.* New York: Philosophical Library, 1957.

Fritz, Volkmar. *The City in Ancient Israel.* Sheffield: Sheffield Academic Press, 1995.

Frye, Richard N. *The Heritage of Persia.* Cleveland: World Books, 1962.

_____. *The History of Ancient Iran.* Munich: C. H. Beck, 1984.

Gadd, C. J., ed. *The Fall of Nineveh.* London: Humphrey Milford, Oxford Univ. Press, 1923.

Gal, Zvi. "Iron I in Lower Galilee and the Margins of the Jezreel Valley." In *From Nomadism to Monarchy: Archaeological and Historical Aspects of Early Israel.* Edited by I. Finkelstein and N. Na'aman. Jerusalem: Israel Exploration Society: 1994. 35–46.

Gibson, McGuire, and Robert D. Biggs, eds. *The Organization of Power: Aspects of Bureaucracy in the Ancient Near East.* 2d ed. SAOC 46. Chicago: Oriental Institute, 1991.

Gledhill, John. "Introduction: the Comparative Analysis of Social and Political Transitions." In *State and Society: The Emergence and Development of Social Hierarchy and Political Centralization.* Edited by J. Gledhill, B. Bender, and M. T. Larsen. London: Unwin Hyman, 1988. 1–29.

_____. *Power and Its Disguises: Anthropological Perspectives on Politics.* London: Pluto Press, 1994.

Gnuse, Robert K. *No Other Gods: Emergent Monotheism in Israel.* JSOTSup 241. Sheffield: Sheffield Academic Press, 1997.

Goedicke, H. "Cult-Temple and 'State' during the Old Kingdom in Egypt." In *State and Temple Economy in the Ancient Near East: Proceedings of the International Conference.* Edited by Edward Lipiński. Vol. 1. Louvain: Department Oriëntalistiek, 1979. 113–32.

Goldenberg, Robert. *The Nations That Know Thee Not: Ancient Jewish Attitudes Toward Other Religions.* New York: New York Univ. Press, 1998.

Goldstein, Jonathan. *1 Maccabees.* AB, 41. Garden City, NY: Doubleday, 1976.

_____. *2 Maccabees.* AB, 41A. Garden City, NY: Doubleday, 1983.

Goodman, Martin, ed. *Jews in the Graeco-Roman World.* Oxford: Clarendon Press, 1998.

Goody, Jack. *The Logic of Writing and the Organization of Society.* Cambridge: Cambridge Univ. Press, 1986.

Gottwald, Norman K. *All the Kingdoms of the Earth: Israelite Prophecy and International Relations in the Ancient Near East.* New York: Harper & Row, 1964.

_____. "Are Biblical and U.S. Societies Comparable? Theopolitical Analogies toward the Next American Revolution." In *The Hebrew Bible in Its World and in Ours.* SemeiaSt. Atlanta: Scholars, 1993. 307–23.

_____. "Biblical Views on 'Church-State' Relations and Their Influence on Existing Political Ideologies." In *The Hebrew Bible in Its Social World and in Ours.* SemeiaSt. Atlanta: Scholars, 1993. 365–83.

_____. "Early Israel and the Canaanite Socio-Economic System." In *Palestine in Transition: The Emergence of Ancient Israel.* Edited by D. N. Freedman and D. F. Graf. SWBA 2. Sheffield: Almond Press, 1983. 25–37.

_____. "The Exodus as Event and Process: A Test Case in the Biblical Grounding of Liberation Theology." In *The Future of Liberation Theology: Essays in Honor of Gustavo Gutiérrez.* Edited by M. H. Ellis and O. Maduro. Maryknoll, N.Y.: Orbis, 1989. 250–60.

_____. "The Expropriators and the Expropriated in Nehemiah 5." In *Concepts of Class in Ancient Israel.* Edited by Mark R. Sneed. South Florida Studies in the History of Judaism 201. Atlanta: Scholars, 1999. 1–19.

_____. *The Hebrew Bible—A Socio-Literary Introduction.* Philadelphia: Fortress, 1985.

_____. *The Hebrew Bible in Its Social World and in Ours.* SemeiaSt. Atlanta: Scholars, 1993.

_____. "A Hypothesis about Social Class in Monarchic Israel in the Light of Contemporary Studies of Social Class and Social Stratification." In *The Hebrew Bible in Its Social World and in Ours.* SemeiaSt. Atlanta: Scholars, 1993. 139–64.

_____. "Icelandic and Israelite Beginnings: A Comparative Probe." In *The Labour of Reading: Desire, Alienation, and Biblical Interpretation: Essays in Honour of Robert C. Culley.* Edited by F. C. Black et al. SemeiaSt. Atlanta: Scholars, 1999. 209–24.

_____. "Ideology and Ideologies in Israelite Prophecy." In *Prophets and Paradigms: Essays in Honor of Gene M. Tucker.* Edited by Stephen Breck Reid. JSOTSup 229. Sheffield: Sheffield Academic Press, 1996. 136–49.

_____. "The Participation of Free Agrarians in the Introduction of Monarchy to Ancient Israel: An Application of H. A. Landsberger's Framework for the Analysis of Peasant Movements." *Semeia* 37 (1986): 77–106.

_____. "The Plot Structure of Marvel or Problem Resolution Stories in the Elijah–Elisha Narratives and Some Musings on Sitz im Leben." In *The Hebrew Bible in Its Social World and in Ours.* SemeiaSt. Atlanta: Scholars, 1993.

_____. "Recent Studies of the Social World of Premonarchic Israel." *CurBS* 1 (1993): 163–89.

_____. "Rhetorical, Historical, and Ontological Counterpoints in Doing Old Testament Theology." In *God in the Fray: A Tribute to Walter Brueggemann.* Edited by T. Linafelt and T. K. Beal. Minneapolis: Fortress, 1998. 11–23.

_____. "Social Class and Ideology in Isaiah 40–55: An Eagletonian Reading." *Semeia* 59 (1992): 43–57, with responses by John Millbank (59–71) and Carol A. Newsom (73–78).

_____. "Social Class as an Analytic and Hermeneutical Category in Biblical Studies." *JBL* 112 (1993): 3–22.

_____. *The Tribes of Yahweh: A Sociology of the Religion of Liberated Israel 1250–1050 B.C.E.* 2d rev. ed. Maryknoll, N.Y.: Orbis, 1981. Reprint with new introduction, Sheffield: Sheffield Academic Press, 1999.

_____. "Triumphalist versus Anti-Triumphalist Versions of Early Israel: A Response to Articles by Lemche and Dever in Volume 4 (1996)." *CurBS* 5 (1997): 20–26.

_____. "Two Models for the Origins of Ancient Israel: Social Revolution or Frontier Development." In *The Quest for the Kingdom of God: Studies in Honor of George E. Mendenhall.* Edited by H. Huffmon et al. Winona Lake, Ind.: Eisenbrauns, 1983. 5–24.

Gottwald, Norman K., and R. A. Horsley, eds. *The Bible and Liberation: Political and Social Hermeneutics.* Rev. ed. Maryknoll, N.Y.: Orbis, 1993.

Grabbe, Lester L. *Judaism from Cyrus to Hadrian.* Vol. 1, *The Persian and Greek Periods.* Minneapolis: Fortress, 1992.

Gray, John. *I and II Kings: A Commentary.* 2d ed. OTL. Philadelphia: Westminster Press, 1970.

Grayson, A. Kirk. "Assyria: Ashur-dan II to Ashur-nirari V (934–745 B.C.)." CAH, 3/1. 2d ed. Cambridge: Cambridge Univ. Press, 1982. 238–81.

_____. *Assyrian and Babylonian Chronicles.* Locust Valley, N.Y.: J. J. Augustin Publisher, 1975.

_____. "Assyrian Rule of Conquered Territory in Ancient Western Asia." In *CANE*, vol. 2. New York: Charles Scribner's Sons, 1995. 959–68.

_____. "Assyria: Tiglath-pileser III to Sargon II (744–705 B.C.)." CAH, 3/2. 2d ed. Cambridge: Cambridge Univ. Press, 1982. 71–102.

_____, trans. "The Creation Epic: Additions to Tablets V–VII." In *ANET*. Edited by James B. Pritchard. 3d ed. Princeton: Princeton Univ. Press, 1969. 501–3.

_____. "Mesopotamia, History of (Assyria), *ABD* 4: 732–55.

Greengus, Samuel. "Biblical and ANE Law." *ABD* 4: 242–52.

Gropp, Douglas M. "Samaria [Papyri]." *ABD* 5: 931–32.

Gunkel, Hermann. *Einleitung in die Psalmen: Die Gattungen der religiösen Lyrik Israels*. Göttingen: Vandenhoek & Ruprecht, 1933. English translation: *Introduction to Psalms: The Genres of the Religious Lyric of Israel*. Translated by James D. Nogalski. Macon, Ga.: Mercer Univ. Press, 1998.

_____. *The Stories of Genesis: A Translation of the Third Edition of Hermann Gunkel's Commentary on the Book of Genesis*. Translated by J. J. Scullion. Edited by W. R. Scott. Vallejo, Calif.: BIBAL Press, 1994.

Gurney, O. R. "The Hittite Empire." In *Power and Propaganda: A Symposium on Ancient Empires*. Edited by M. T. Larsen. Copenhagen: Akademisk Forlag, 1979. 167–89.

_____. *The Hittites*. Rev. ed. London: Penguin Books, 1981.

Halbertal, Moshe, and Avishai Margalit. *Idolatry*. Cambridge/London: Harvard Univ. Press, 1992.

Hallo, William W. "Biblical History in Its Near Eastern Setting: The Contextual Approach." In *Scripture in Context: Essays on the Comparative Method*. Edited by C. D. Evans, W. W. Hallo, and J. B. White. Pittsburgh: Pickwick Press, 1980. 17–26.

_____. "The Concept of Canonicity in Cuneiform and Biblical Literature: A Comparative Appraisal." In *The Biblical Canon in Comparative Perspective: Scripture in Context IV*. Edited by K. L. Younger Jr., W. W. Hallo, and B. F. Batto. Ancient Near Eastern Texts and Studies 11. Lewiston, N.Y.: Edwin Mellen Press, 1991. 1–19.

_____. "From Bronze Age to Iron Age in Western Asia: Defining the Problem." In *The Crisis Years: The Twelfth Century B.C. from beyond the Danube to the Tigris*. Edited by W. A. Ward and M. S. Joukowsky. Dubuque, Iowa: Kendall/Hunt Publishing Co., 1989. 1–9.

Hallo, William W., and William K. Simpson. *The Ancient Near East: A History*. New York: Harcourt Brace Jovanovich, 1971.

Hallo, William W., and K. Lawson Younger Jr., eds. *The Context of Scripture: Canonical Compositions from the Biblical World*. 2 vols. New York: E. J. Brill, 1997–2000.

Halpern, Baruch. *The Constitution of the Monarchy in Israel*. HSM 25. Atlanta: Scholars, 1981.

_____. "The Construction of the Davidic State: An Exercise in Historiography." In *The Origins of the Ancient Israelite States*. Edited by V. Fritz and P. R. Davies. JSOTSup 228. Sheffield: Sheffield Academic Press, 1996. 44–75.

_____. "Jerusalem and the Lineages in the Seventh Century B.C.E.: Kinship and the Rise of Individual Moral Liability." In *Law and Ideology in Monarchic Israel*. Edited by Baruch Halpern and Deborah W. Hobson. JSOTSup 124. Sheffield: Sheffield Academic Press, 1991. 11–107.

_____. "Sacred History and Ideology: Chronicles' Thematic Structure—Indications of an Earlier Source." In *The Creation of Sacred Literature: Composition and Redaction of the Biblical Text.* Edited by R. E. Friedman. Berkeley, Calif.: Univ. of California Press, 1981. 35–54.

_____. "The Stela from Dan: Epigraphic and Historical Considerations." *BASOR* 296 (1994): 63–80.

Hammond, Mason. "The Indo-European Origin of the Concept of a Democratic Society." *Symbols* (Dec. 1985): 10–13.

Hammond, N. G. L. *A History of Macedonia.* Oxford: Clarendon Press, 1972.

Hanson, Paul D. *The Dawn of Apocalyptic.* Philadelphia: Fortress, 1979.

Harvey, Graham. *The True Israel: Uses of the Names Jew, Hebrew, and Israel in Ancient Jewish and Early Christian Literature.* AGJU 35. Leiden: E. J. Brill, 1996.

Hauer, Chris, Jr. "The Economic and National Security in Solomonic Israel." *JSOT* 18 (1980): 63–73.

Hayes, John H., and P. K. Hooker. *A New Chronology for the Kings of Israel and Judah.* Atlanta: Scholars, 1988.

Hayes, John H., and Sara R. Mandell. *The Jewish People in Classical Antiquity: From Alexander to Bar Kochba.* Louisville, Ky.: Westminster John Knox, 1998.

Hayes, John H., and J. Maxwell Miller. *Israelite and Judaean History.* Philadelphia: Westminster, 1977.

Healey, Joseph P. "Am ha'arez." *ABD* 1: 168–69.

Herm, Gerhard. *The Phoenicians: The Purple Empire of the Ancient World.* London: Gollancz, 1975.

Herzog, Ze'ev. *Archaeology of the City: Urban Planning in Ancient Israel and Its Social Implications.* Monograph Series 13. Tel Aviv: Institute of Archaeology, Tel Aviv Univ., 1997.

Hestrin, Ruth, and Michal Dayagi-Mendels. *Inscribed Seals: First Temple Period. Hebrew, Ammonite, Moabite, Phoenician, and Aramaic.* Jerusalem: Israel Museum, 1979.

Hjelm, Ingrid. *The Samaritans and Early Judaism: A Literary Analysis.* JSOTSup 303. Sheffield: Sheffield Academic Press, 2000.

Hobbs, T. R. *2 Kings.* WBC. Waco, Tex.: Word Books, 1985.

Hoftijzer, J., and G. van der Kooij. *Aramaic Texts from Deir 'Alla.* Leiden: E. J. Brill, 1976.

Holladay, John S., Jr. "The Kingdoms of Israel and Judah: Political and Economic Centralization in the Iron IIA-B (ca. 1000–750 B.C.E.)." In *The Archaeology of Society in the Holy Land.* Edited by T. E. Levy. New York: Facts on File, 1995. 368–98.

Honeyman, A. M. "The Evidence for Royal Names among the Hebrews." *JBL* 67 (1948): 13–26.

Hopkins, David C. "The Weight of the Bronze Could Not Be Calculated." In *The Age of Solomon: Scholarship at the Turn of the Millennium.* Edited by L. K. Handy. Leiden: E. J. Brill, 1997. 300–11.

_____. *The Highlands of Canaan: Agricultural Life in the Early Iron Age.* SWBA 3. Decatur, Ga.: Almond Press, 1985.

Hornung, Erik. "The Pharaoh." In *The Egyptians.* Edited by Sergio Dandoni. Chicago: Univ. of Chicago Press, 1997. 283–313.

Houston, Walter. "The King's Preferential Option for the Poor: Rhetoric, Ideology, and Ethics in Psalm 72." *BibInt* 7 (1999): 341–67.

Hudson, Michael, and Baruch Levine, eds. *Privatization in the Ancient Near East and Classical World: Colloquium Held at New York University, November 17–18, 1994.* Peabody Museum Bulletin 5. Cambridge: Peabody Museum of Archaeology and Ethnology, 1996.

Hull, John H., Jr. "Tabeel." *ABD* 6: 292.

Hunt, Lynn. "History as Gesture; or, the Scandal of History." In *Consequences of Theory: Selected Papers from the English Institute, 1987–88.* Edited by J. Arac and B. Johnson. Baltimore; Johns Hopkins, 1991. 91–107.

Hunt, Robert C. "The Role of Bureaucracy in the Provisioning of Cities: A Framework for Analysis of the Ancient Near East." In *The Organization of Power: Aspects of Bureaucracy in the Ancient Near East.* Edited by McGuire Gibson and Robert D. Biggs. 2d ed. SAOC 46. Chicago: Oriental Institute, 1991. 141–68.

Hurowitz, Victor (Avigdor). *I Have Built You an Exalted House: Temple Building in the Bible in the Light of Mesopotamian and Northwest Semitic Writings.* JSOTSup 115. Sheffield: JSOT Press, 1992.

Ikeda, Yutaka. "Solomon's Trade in Horses and Chariots in Its International Setting." In *Studies in the Period of David and Solomon and Other Essays.* Edited by T. Ishida. Tokyo: Yamakawa-Shuppansha, 1982. 215–38.

Ishida, Tomoo. "The Leaders of the Tribal League 'Israel' in the Premonarchic Period." *RB* 80 (1975): 514–30.

———. *The Royal Dynasties in Ancient Israel: A Study on the Formation and Development of Royal-Dynastic Ideology.* BZAW 142. Berlin: Walter de Gruyter, 1977.

———. "Solomon." *ABD* 6: 105–13.

Jacobsen, Thorkild. "Primitive Democracy in Ancient Mesopotamia." *JNES* 2 (1943): 159–72.

Jamieson-Drake, David W. *Scribes and Schools in Monarchic Judah: A Socio-Archaeological Approach.* SWBA 9. JSOTSup 109. Sheffield: Almond Press, 1991.

Jankowska, N. B. "Some Problems of the Economy of the Assyrian Empire." In *Ancient Mesopotamia: Socio-Economic History.* Edited by I. M. Diakanoff. Moscow: Nauka Publishing House, 1969. 253–76.

Janssen, Jac. J. "The Early State in Ancient Egypt." In *The Early State.* Edited by Henri J. M. Claessen and Peter Skalnik. The Hague: Mouton Publishers, 1978. 218–28.

Jenks, Alan W. *The Elohist and North Israelite Traditions.* SBLMS 22. Missoula, Mont.: Scholars, 1977.

Jobling, David. "Deconstruction and the Political Analysis of Biblical Texts: A Jamesonian Reading of Psalm 72." *Semeia* 59 (1992): 95–127.

———. *1 Samuel.* Berit Olam. Collegeville, Minn.: Liturgical Press, 1998.

———. "'Forced Labor': Solomon's Golden Age and the Question of Literary Representation." *Semeia* 54 (1991): 57–76.

———. "Sociological and Literary Approaches to the Bible: How Shall the Twain Meet?" *JSOT* 38 (1987): 85–93.

———. "The Value of Solomon's Age for the Biblical Reader." In *The Age of Solomon: Scholarship at the Turn of the Millennium.* Edited by Lowell K. Handy. Leiden: E. J. Brill, 1997. 470–92.

Jobling, David, and Tina Pippin, eds. *Ideological Criticism of Biblical Texts. Semeia* 59 (1992).

Johnson, Gregory A. "Aspects of Regional Analysis in Archaeology." *Annual Review of Anthropology* 6 (1977): 479–508.

Joukowsky, Martha S., ed. *The Heritage of Tyre: Essays on the History, Archaeology, and Preservation of Tyre.* Dubuque, Iowa: Kendall/Hunt Publishers, 1992.

Kamp, Kathryn A., and Norman Yoffee. "Ethnicity in Ancient Western Asia during the Early Second Millennium B.C.: Archaeological Assessments and Ethnoarchaeological Prospectives." *BASOR* 237 (1980): 85–104.

Kapelrud, Arvid S. "Temple-Building: A Task for Gods and Kings." *Or* 32 (1963): 52–62.

Katzenstein, H. J. "Who Were the Parents of Athaliah?" *IEJ* 5 (1955): 194–97.

Katzenstein, H. J., and Trude Dothan. "Philistines." *ABD* 5: 326–33.

Kaufman, Herbert. "The Collapse of Ancient States and Civilizations as an Organizational Problem." In *The Collapse of Ancient States and Civilizations.* Edited by N. Yoffee and G. L. Cowgill. Tucson, Ariz.: Univ. of Arizona Press, 1988. 219–35.

Kautsky, John H. *The Politics of Aristocratic Empires.* Chapel Hill, N.C.: Univ. of North Carolina Press, 1982.

Kees, H. *Ancient Egypt: A Cultural Topography.* Chicago: Univ. of Chicago Press, 1961.

Kemp, Barry J. *Ancient Egypt.* London: Routledge, 1991.

_____. "Unification and Urbanization of Ancient Egypt." In *CANE*, vol. 2. New York: Charles Scribner's Sons, 1995. 679–90.

Kessler, Rainer. *Staat und Gesellschaft im vorexilischen Juda: Vom 8. Jahrhundert bis zum Exil.* VTSup 47. Leiden: E. J. Brill, 1992.

Khazanov, Anatoly M. "Ethnicity and Ethnic Groups in Early States." In *Pivot Politics: Changing Cultural Identities in Early State Formation Processes.* Edited by M. van Bakel, R. Hagesteijn, and P. van de Velde. Amsterdam: Het Spinhuis, 1994. 67–85.

King, Philip J. "Jerusalem." *ABD* 3: 747–66.

Klein, Ralph W. "How Many in a Thousand?" In *The Chronicler as Historian.* Edited by M. P. Graham, K. G. Hoglund, and S. L. McKenzie. JSOTSup 238. Sheffield: Sheffield Academic Press, 1997. 270–82.

Klengel, Horst. *Syria 3000 to 300 B.C.: A Handbook to Political History.* Berlin: Akademie Verlag, 1992.

Knauf, Ernst A. "The Cultural Impact of Secondary State Formation: The Cases of the Edomites and Moabites." In *Early Edom and Moab: The Beginning of the Iron Age in Southern Jordan.* Edited by P. Bienkowski. Sheffield Archaeological Monographs 7. Sheffield: J. R. Collis, 1992. 47–54.

_____. "Midianites and Ishmaelites." In *Midian, Moab, and Edom: The History and Archaeology of Late Bronze and Iron Age Jordan and North-West Arabia.* Edited by J. F. A. Sawyer and D. J. A. Clines. JSOTSup 24. Sheffield: JSOT Press, 1983. 135–46.

_____. "Le roi est mort, vive le roi! A Biblical Argument for the Historicity of Solomon." In *The Age of Solomon: Scholarship at the Turn of the Millennium.* Edited by L. K. Handy. Leiden: E. J. Brill, 1997. 81–95.

Knight, Douglas A. "Political Rights and Powers in Monarchic Israel." *Semeia* 66 (1995): 93–117.

_____. "Whose Agony? Whose Ecstasy? The Politics of Deuteronomic Law." In

Shall Not the Judge of All the Earth Do What Is Right? Studies on the Nature of God in Tribute to James L. Crenshaw. Edited by David Penchansky and Paul L. Redditt. Winona Lake, Ind.: Eisenbrauns, 2000. 97–112.

Knoppers, Gary N. *Two Nations under God: The Deuteronomistic History of Solomon and the Dual Monarchies.* Vol. 1. HSM 52. Atlanta: Scholars, 1993.

Krader, Lawrence. *The Asiatic Mode of Production: Sources, Development, and Critique in the Writings of Karl Marx.* Assen: Van Gorcum, 1985.

Kraeling, Emil G. *Aram and Israel.* New York: Columbia Univ. Press, 1918.

Kreissig, H. "Eine beachtenswerte Theorie zur Organisation altvorderorientalischer Tempelgemeinden im Achämenidenreich." *Klio* 66 (1984): 35–39.

Kuan, Jeffrey Kah-Jin. *Neo-Assyrian Historical Inscriptions and Syria-Palestine: Israelite/Judean-Tyrian-Damascene Political and Commercial Relations in the Ninth–Eighth Centuries B.C.E.* Hong Kong: Alliance Bible Seminary, 1995.

Kuhrt, Amélie. *The Ancient Near East, ca. 3000–330 B.C.* 2 vols. London: Routledge, 1995.

Kuper, Adam. "Lineage Theory: A Critical Retrospect." *Annual Review of Anthropology* 11 (1982): 71–95.

LaBianca, Øystein S. "Excursus: Salient Features of Iron Age Tribal Kingdoms." In *Ancient Ammon,* edited by B. MacDonald and R. W. Younker. Studies in the History and Culture of the Ancient Near East 17. Leiden: E. J. Brill, 1999. 19–23.

LaBianca, Øystein S., and Randall W. Younker. "The Kingdoms of Ammon, Moab, and Edom: The Archaeology of Society in Late Bronze/Iron Age Transjordan (ca. 1400–500 B.C.E.)." In *The Archaeology of Society in the Holy Land.* Edited by T. E. Levy. New York: Facts on File, 1995. 399–415.

Lamberg-Karlovsky, C. C. "The Near Eastern 'Breakout' and the Mesopotamian Social Contract." *Symbols* (Spring 1985): 8–11, 23–24.

Lambert, Frith. "The Tribe/State Paradox in the Old Testament." *SJOT* 8 (1994): 20–44.

Lambert, W. G. "Kingship in Ancient Mesopotamia." In *King and Messiah in the Ancient Near East: Proceedings of the Oxford Old Testament Seminar.* Edited by J. Day. JSOTSup 270. Sheffield: Sheffield Academic Press, 1998. 54–70.

Leahy, Anthony. "Ethnic Diversity in Ancient Egypt." *CANE,* vol. 2. New York: Charles Scribner's Sons, 1995. 225–34.

Lemche, Niels Peter. *Ancient Israel: A New History of Israelite Society.* Sheffield: JSOT Press, 1988.

_____. *The Canaanites and Their Land: The Tradition of the Canaanites.* JSOTSup 110. Sheffield: JSOT Press, 1991.

_____. *Early Israel: Anthropological and Historical Studies on the Israelite Society before the Monarchy.* VTSup 37. Leiden: E. J. Brill, 1985.

_____. "From Patronage Society to Patronage Society." In *The Origins of the Ancient Israelite States.* Edited by V. Fritz and P. R. Davies. JSOTSup 228. Sheffield: Sheffield Academic Press, 1996. 106–20.

_____. *The Israelites in History and Tradition.* Louisville: Westminster John Knox, 1998.

_____. "Justice in Western Asia in Antiquity; Or: Why No Laws Were Needed!" *Kent Law Review* 70 (1995): 1695–716.

_____. "Kings and Clients: On Loyalty between the Ruler and the Ruled in Ancient 'Israel.'" *Semeia* 66 (1995): 119–32.

_____. "On the Use of 'System Theory,' 'Macro Theories,' and 'Evolutionistic Thinking' in Modern Old Testament Research and Biblical Archaeology." *SJOT* 4:2 (1990): 73–88.

_____. *Prelude to Israel's Past: Background and Beginnings of Israelite History and Identity*. Peabody, Mass.: Hendrickson Publishers, 1998.

Lenski, Gerhard E. *Power and Privilege: A Theory of Social Stratification*. Chapel Hill, N.C.: Univ. of North Carolina Press, 1984.

_____. Review of *The Tribes of Yahweh*, by Norman K. Gottwald. *RelSRev* 6 (1980): 275–78.

Lerner, Gerda. *The Creation of Patriarchy*. New York: Oxford Univ. Press, 1986.

Lesko, Barbara S., ed. *Women's Earliest Records from Ancient Egypt and Western Asia*. BJS 166. Atlanta: Scholars, 1989.

Levin, C. *Der Sturz der Königen Atalja: Ein Kapitel zur Geschichte Judas im 9. Jahrhundert v. Chr.* Stuttgart: Katholisches Bibelwerk, 1982.

Lewellen, Ted C. *Political Anthropology: An Introduction*. 2d ed. Westport: Bergin & Garvey, 1992.

Lighthouse, Jack N. *Society, the Sacred, and Scripture in Ancient Judaism: A Sociology of Knowledge*. Studies in Christianity and Judaism. 3. Waterloo, Canada: Wilfred Laurier Univ. Press, 1988.

Lind, Millard C. "The Concept of Political Power in Ancient Israel." *ASTI* 7 (1970): 4–24.

Linville, James R. *Israel in the Book of Kings: The Past as a Project of Social Identity*. JSOTSup 272. Sheffield: Sheffield Academic Press, 1998.

Liverani, Mario. "The Collapse of the Near Eastern Regional System at the End of the Bronze Age: The Case of Syria." In *Centre and Periphery in the Ancient World*. Edited by M. Rowlands, M. T. Larsen, and K. Kristiansen. Cambridge: Cambridge Univ. Press, 1987. 66–73.

_____. "The Ideology of the Assyrian Empire." In *Power and Propaganda: A Symposium on Ancient Empires*. Edited by M. T. Larsen. Copenhagen: Akademisk Forlag, 1979. 297–317.

_____. *Prestige and Interest: International Relations in the Near East ca. 1600–1100 B.C.* History of the Ancient Near East Studies 1. Padova: Sargon, 1990.

Lloyd, Christopher. *The Structures of History*. Oxford: Blackwell, 1993.

London, Gloria. "A Comparison of Two Contemporaneous Life-Styles of the Late Second Millennium B.C." *BASOR* 273 (1989): 37–55.

Long, Burke O. *I Kings with an Introduction to Historical Literature*. FOTL 9. Grand Rapids, Mich.: Eerdmans, 1984.

_____. "Social Dimensions of Prophetic Conflict." *Semeia* 21 (1981): 31–53.

Long, Burke O., and Simon B. Parker, eds. *SBL Writings from the Ancient World*. 9 vols. to date, Atlanta: Scholars, 1990–.

Lowery, Richard H. *The Reforming Kings: Cults and Society in First Temple Judah*. JSOTSup 120. Sheffield: JSOT Press, 1991.

MacDonald, Burton. "Edom." *ABD* 2: 287–301.

MacDonald, Burton, and Randall W. Younker, eds. *Ancient Ammon*. Studies in the History and Culture of the Ancient Near East 17. Leiden: E. J. Brill, 1999.

Machinist, Peter. "Palestine, Administration of Assyro-Babylonian." *ABD* 5: 69–76.

_____. "The Question of Distinctiveness in Ancient Israel." In *Essential Papers on*

Israel and the Ancient Near East. Edited by F. E. Greenspahn. New York: New York Univ. Press, 1991. 420–42.

Maisler (Mazar), Benjamin. "Ancient Israelite Historiography." *IEJ* 2 (1952): 82–88.

_____. "Two Hebrew Ostraca from Tell Qasile." *JNES* 10 (1951): 265–67.

Malamat, Abraham. "Organs of Statecraft in the Israelite Monarchy." *BARead* 3 (1970): 163–98.

Mann, Michael. *The Sources of Social Power.* Vol. 1, *A History of Power from the Beginning to A.D. 1760.* Cambridge: Cambridge Univ Press, 1986.

Mansueto, Anthony. "From Historical Criticism to Historical Materialism." Seminar paper, Graduate Theological Union, Berkeley, 1983.

Mazar, Amihai. *Archaeology of the Land of the Bible 10,000–586 B.C.E.* New York: Doubleday, 1990.

_____. "Jerusalem and Its Vicinity in Iron Age I." In *From Nomadism to Monarchy: Archaeological and Historical Aspects of Early Israel.* Edited by I. Finkelstein and N. Na'aman. Jerusalem: Israel Exploration Society: 1994. 70–91.

Mazar, Benjamin. "The Aramean Empire and Its Relations with Israel." *BA* 25 (1962): 98–120.

_____. "The Campaign of Pharaoh Shishak to Palestine." *Congress Volume, Strasbourg 1956.* VTSup 4. Leiden: E. J. Brill, 1957. 57–66.

_____. "King David's Scribe and the High Officialdom of the United Monarchy of Israel." In *The Early Biblical Period: Historical Studies.* Edited by S. Ahituv and B. Levine. Jerusalem: Israel Exploration Society, 1986. 126–38.

_____. "Kingship in Ancient Israel." In *Biblical Israel: State and People.* Ed. Shmuel Ahituv. Jerusalem: Magnes Press, Hebrew Univ., and Israel Exploration Society, 1992. 55–66.

McCarter, P. Kyle. *Ancient Inscriptions: Voices from the Biblical World.* Washington, D.C.: Biblical Archaeology Society, 1996.

McKay, John W. *Religion in Judah under the Assyrians.* London: SCM Press, 1973.

McKenzie, Steven L. *The Chronicler's Use of the Deuteronomistic History.* HSM 33. Atlanta: Scholars, 1984.

_____. "Deuteronomistic History." *ABD* 2: 160–68.

McNeill, William H. *The Rise of the West: A History of the Human Community with a Retrospective Essay.* Chicago: Univ. of Chicago Press, 1963. Reprint 1991.

McNutt, Paula M. *Reconstructing the Society of Ancient Israel.* Louisville: Westminster John Knox, 1999.

Meek, Theophile J., trans. "The Code of Hammurabi." In *ANET.* Edited by James B. Pritchard. 3d ed. Princeton: Princeton Univ. Press, 1969. 163–80.

Meeks, M. Douglas. *God the Economist: The Doctrine of God and Political Economy.* Minneapolis: Fortress, 1989.

Meier, Samuel A. "Hammurapi." *ABD* 3: 39–42.

Mendenhall, George E. "The Census Lists of Numbers 1 and 26." *JBL* 77 (1968): 52–66.

Mettinger, Tryggve N. D. *Solomonic State Officials: A Study of the Civil Government Officials of the Israelite Monarchy.* ConBOT 5. Lund: Gleerup, 1971.

Meyers, Carol. *Discovering Eve: Ancient Israelite Women in Context.* New York: Oxford Univ. Press, 1988.

_____. "Tribes and Tribulations: Retheorizing Earliest 'Israel.'" In *Tracking a*

Classic: The Tribes of Yahweh Twenty Years On. Edited by R. Boer. Sheffield: Sheffield Academic Press, forthcoming.

Meyers, Carol L., and Eric M. Meyers. *Haggai, Zechariah 1–8.* AB 25B. Garden City, N.Y.: Doubleday, 1987.

Meyers, Eric M., ed. *The Oxford Encyclopedia of Archaeology in the Ancient Near East.* 5 vols. New York: Oxford Univ. Press, 1997.

Michalowski, Piotr. "Charisma and Control: On Continuity and Change in Early Mesopotamian Bureaucratic Systems." In *The Organization of Power: Aspects of Bureaucracy in the Ancient Near East.* Edited by McGuire Gibson and Robert D. Biggs. 2d ed. SAOC 46. Chicago: Oriental Institute, 1991. 45–57.

Middleton, John, and David Tate, eds. *Tribes without Rulers: Studies in African Segmentary Systems.* London: Routledge & Kegan Paul, 1958. Reprint with new preface, 1970.

Millard, A. R. "Literacy [Israel]." *ABD* 4: 337–40.

Miller, Daniel. "The Limits of Dominance." In *Domination and Resistance.* Edited by D. Miller, M. Rowlands, and C. Tilley. London: Unwin Hyman, 1989. 63–79.

Miller, J. Maxwell. "Moab." *ABD* 4: 882–93.

Miller, J. Maxwell, and John H. Hayes. *A History of Ancient Israel and Judah.* Philadelphia: Westminster Press, 1986.

Miller, Patrick D., Jr., and J. J. M. Roberts. *The Hand of the Lord: A Reassessment of the 'Ark Narrative' of I Samuel.* JHNES. Baltimore: Johns Hopkins, 1977.

Miller, R. D., III. "A Social History of Highland Israel in the 12th and 11th Centuries B.C.E." Ph.D. diss., Univ. of Michigan, 1998.

Modrzejewski, Joseph M. *The Jews of Egypt: From Rameses II to Emperor Hadrian.* Princeton: Princeton Univ. Press, 1995.

Montgomery, James A. *A Critical and Exegetical Commentary on the Book of Kings.* Rev. ed. ICC. New York: Charles Scribner's Sons, 1951.

Morgan, Robert, and John Barton. *Biblical Interpretation.* Oxford: Oxford Univ. Press, 1988.

Morony, Michael G. "'In a City without Watchdogs the Fox is the Overseer': Issues and Problems in the Study of Bureaucracy." In *The Organization of Power: Aspects of Bureaucracy in the Ancient Near East.* Edited by McGuire Gibson and Robert D. Biggs. 2d ed. SAOC 46. Chicago: Oriental Institute, 1991. 5–14.

Muhly, James D. "The Crisis Years in the Mediterranean World: Transition or Cultural Disintegration?" In *The Crisis Years: The Twelfth Century B.C. from Beyond the Danube to the Tigris.* Edited by W. A. Ward and M. S. Joukowsky. Dubuque, Iowa: Kendall/Hunt Publishing Co., 1989. 10–26.

————. "Mining and Metalwork in Ancient Western Asia." *CANE,* vol. 3. New York: Charles Scribner's Sons, 1995. 1501–21.

Mullen, E. Theodore, Jr. *Narrative History and Ethnic Boundaries: The Deuteronomistic Historian and the Creation of Israelite National Identity.* SemeiaSt. Atlanta: Scholars, 1993.

Munn-Rankin, J. M. "Diplomacy in Western Asia in the Early Second Millennium B.C." *Iraq* 18 (1956): 68–110.

Murname, William J. "The History of Ancient Egypt: An Overview." In *CANE,* vol. 2. New York: Charles Scribner's Sons, 1995. 691–717.

Myers, Jacob M. *I Chronicles.* AB 12. Garden City, N.Y.: Doubleday, 1965.

Na'aman, Nadav. "The Contribution of Royal Inscriptions for a Re-Evaluation of the Book of Kings as a Historical Resource." *JSOT* 82 (1999): 3–17.

———. "Sources and Composition in the History of Solomon." In *The Age of Solomon: Scholarship at the Turn of the Millennium.* Edited by L. K. Handy. Leiden: E. J. Brill, 1997. 57–80.

———. "Two Notes on the Monolith Inscription of Shalmaneser III from Kurkh." *Tel Aviv* 3 (1974): 97–102.

Nakanose, Shigeyuki. *Josiah's Passover: Sociology and the Liberating Bible.* Maryknoll, N.Y.: Orbis, 1993.

Nelson, Richard D. "The Anatomy of Kings." *JSOT* 40 (1988): 39–48.

Neusner, Jacob. *A History of the Jews in Babylonia.* Vol. 1, *The Parthian Period.* South Florida Studies in the History of Judaism 217. Atlanta: Scholars, 1969. Reprint of rev. ed., 1999.

Newby, Gordon Darnell. *A History of the Jews in Arabia from Ancient Times to Their Eclipse under Islam.* Columbia: Univ. of South Carolina Press, 1988.

Newman, Katherine S. *Law and Economic Organization: A Comparative Study of Preindustrial Societies.* Cambridge: Cambridge Univ. Press, 1983.

Nickelsburg, George W. E. *Jewish Literature between the Bible and the Mishnah: A Historical and Literary Introduction.* Philadelphia: Fortress, 1981.

Nicholson, Ernest W. "The Meaning of the Expression 'am ha'arez in the Old Testament." *JSS* 10 (1965): 59–66.

Niditch, Susan. *Oral World and Written Word: Ancient Israelite Literature.* Louisville, Ky.: Westminster John Knox, 1996.

Niehr, Herbert. "The Rise of YHWH in Judahite and Israelite Religion: Methodological and Religio-Historical Aspects." In *The Triumph of Elohim: From Yahwisms to Judaisms.* Edited by D. V. Edelman. Grand Rapids, Mich.: Eerdmans, 1995. 45–72.

Niemann, Hermann M. "The Socio-Political Shadow Cast by the Biblical Solomon." In *The Age of Solomon: Scholarship at the Turn of the Millennium.* Edited by L. K. Handy. Leiden: E. J. Brill, 1997. 252–99.

———. *Herrschaft, Königtum und Staat: Skizzen zur soziokulturellen Entwicklung im monarchischen Israel.* FAT 9. Tübingen: J. C. B. Mohr, 1993.

Nissen, Hans J. *The Early History of the Ancient Near East 9000–2000 B.C.* Chicago: Univ. of Chicago Press, 1988.

North, Robert. "Palestine, Administration of [Judean Officials]." *ABD* 5: 86–90.

Nylander, Carl. "Achaemenid Imperial Art." In *Power and Propaganda: A Symposium on Ancient Empires.* Edited by M. T. Larsen. Mesopotamia 7. Copenhagen: Akademisk Forlag, 1979. 345–59.

Oded, Busteney. *Mass Deportation and Deportees in the Neo-Assyrian Empire.* Wiesbaden: Reichert, 1979.

Ofer, Avi. "'All the Hill Country of Judah': From a Settlement Fringe to a Prosperous Monarchy." In *From Nomadism to Monarchy: Archaeological and Historical Aspects of Early Israel.* Edited by I. Finkelstein and N. Na'aman. Jerusalem: Israel Exploration Society: 1994. 92–121.

Olmstead, A. T. *History of Assyria.* Chicago: Univ. of Chicago Press, 1923.

———. *The History of the Persian Empire.* Chicago: Univ. of Chicago Press, 1948.

Olson, Dennis T. "Pekah" and "Pekahiah." *ABD* 5: 214–16.

Olyan, Saul. *Asherah and the Cult of Yahweh in Israel*. SBLMS 34. Atlanta: Scholars, 1988.

Oppenheim, A. Leo. *Ancient Mesopotamia: Portrait of a Dead Civilization*. Rev. ed. Chicago: Univ. of Chicago Press, 1977.

Ottosson, Magnus. *Gilead: Tradition and History*. ConBOT 3. Lund: Gleerup, 1969.

Overholt, Thomas W. "The Ghost Dance of 1890 and the Nature of the Prophetic Process." *Ethnohistory* 21 (1974): 37–63.

Pardee, Dennis. *Handbook of Ancient Hebrew Letters*. SBLSBS 15. Atlanta: Scholars, 1982.

Parker, Kim Ian, ed. *Liberal Democracy and the Bible*. Lewiston, N.Y./Queenston/ Lampeter: Edwin Mellen Press, 1992.

Parpola, Simo, and Kazuko Watanabe, eds. *Neo-Assyrian Treaties and Loyalty Oaths*. SAAS 2. Helsinki: Helsinki Univ. Press, 1988.

Parsons, Talcott. *Societies: Evolutionary and Comparative Perspectives*. Englewood Cliffs, N.J.: Prentice-Hall, 1966.

Pasto, James. "When the End Is the Beginning? Or When the Biblical Past Is the Political Present: Some Thoughts on Ancient Israel, 'Post-Exilic Judaism,' and the Politics of Biblical Scholarship." *SJOT* 12:2 (1998): 157–202.

Patte, Daniel. *Ethics of Biblical Interpretation: A Reevaluation*. Louisville: Westminster John Knox, 1995.

Payne, Elizabeth J. "The Midianite Arc in Joshua and Judges." In *Midian, Moab, and Edom: The History and Archaeology of Late Bronze and Iron Age Jordan and North-West Arabia*. Edited by J. F. A. Sawyer and D. J. A. Clines. JSOTSup 24. Sheffield: JSOT Press, 1983. 163–72.

Peckham, Brian. "Phoenicia, History of." *ABD* 5: 349–57.

Perdue, Leo G. *The Collapse of History*. OBT. Minneapolis: Fortress, 1994.

Pestman, P. W., ed. *A Guide to the Zenon Archive*. Leiden: E. J. Brill, 1981.

Peters, F. E. *The Harvest of Hellenism: A History of the Near East from Alexander the Great to the Triumph of Christianity*. New York: Simon & Schuster, 1970.

Pitard, Wayne T. *Ancient Damascus: A Historical Study of the Syrian City-State from Earliest Times until Its Fall to the Assyrians in 732 B.C.E.* Winona Lake, Ind.: Eisenbrauns, 1987.

Polanyi, Karl, C. M. Arensberg, and H. W. Pearson, eds. *Trade and Market in the Early Empires: Economies in History and Theory*. New York: Free Press, 1957.

Porton, Bezalel. *Archives from Elephantine: The Life of an Ancient Jewish Military Colony*. Los Angeles: Univ. of California Press, 1968.

_____. "Elephantine Papyri." *ABD* 2: 445–55.

Portugali, Juval. "Theoretical Speculations on the Transition from Nomadism to Monarchy." In *From Nomadism to Monarchy: Archaeological and Historical Aspects of Early Israel*. Edited by I. Finkelstein and N. Na'aman. Jerusalem: Israel Exploration Society, Washington, D.C.: Biblical Archaeology Society, 1994. 203–17.

Postgate, J. Nicholas. *Early Mesopotamia: Society and Economy at the Dawn of History*. London: Routledge, 1992.

_____. "The Economic Structure of the Assyrian Empire." In *Power and Propaganda: A Symposium on Ancient Empires*. Edited by M. T. Larsen. Copenhagen: Akademisk Forlag, 1979. 193–221.

Potts, D. T. *Mesopotamian Civilization: The Material Foundations*. Ithaca: Cornell Univ. Press, 1997.

Pritchard, James B., ed. *Ancient Near Eastern Texts Relating to the Old Testament*. 3d ed. Princeton: Princeton Univ. Press, 1969.

Provan, Ian W. "Ideologies, Literary and Critical Reflections on Recent Writing on the History of Israel." *JBL* 114 (1995): 585–606.

Purvis, James D. "The Samaritans and Judaism." In *Early Judaism and Its Modern Interpreters*. Edited by Robert A. Kraft and George W. E. Nickelsburg. Atlanta: Scholars, 1986. 81–98.

de Pury, Albert. "Yahwist ['J'] Source." *ABD* 6: 1012–20.

von Rad, Gerhard. "The Royal Ritual in Judah." In *The Problem of the Hexateuch and Other Essays*. New York: McGraw-Hill, 1966. 222–31.

Reade, Julian. "Ideology and Propaganda in Assyrian Art." In *Power and Propaganda: A Symposium on Ancient Empires*. Edited by M. T. Larsen. Mesopotamia 7. Copenhagen: Akademisk Forlag, 1979. 329–43.

Redford, Donald B. "Akhenaton." *ABD* 1: 135–37.

———. "The Ashkelon Relief at Karnak and the Israel Stela." *IEJ* 36 (1986): 188–200.

Redford, Donald B., and James M. Weinstein. "Hyksos." *ABD* 3: 341–48.

Redman, Charles R. *The Rise of Civilization: From Early Farmers to Urban Society in the Ancient Near East*. San Francisco: W. H. Freeman & Co., 1978.

Rendsburg, Gary A. "Biblical Literature as Politics: The Case of Genesis." In *Religion and Politics in the Ancient Near East*. Edited by Adele Berlin. Studies and Texts in Jewish History and Culture. Bethesda, Md.: Univ. Press of Maryland, 1996. 47–70.

Rendtorff, Rolf. "The Paradigm Is Changing: Hopes—and Fears." *BibInt* 1 (1993): 34–53.

———. *The Problem of the Process of Transmission in the Pentateuch*. JSOTSup 89. Sheffield: JSOT Press, 1990.

Renger, Johannes. "Interaction of Temple, Palace, and 'Private Enterprise' in the Old Babylonian Economy." In *State and Temple Economy in the Ancient Near East*. Edited by E. Lipiński. OLA 5, vol. 1. Louvain: Departement Orientalistiek, 1979. 249–56.

Reviv, H. "On the Days of Athaliah and Joash." *Beth Mikra* 47 (1970/71): 541–49. [Heb.]

Riley, William. *King and Cultus in Chronicles: Worship and the Reinterpretation of History*. JSOTSup 160. Sheffield: JSOT Press, 1993.

Roaf, Michael. *Cultural Atlas of Mesopotamia and the Ancient Near East*. New York: Facts on File, 1990.

Rogerson, John W. "Was Early Israel a Segmentary Society?" *JSOT* 36 (1986): 17–26.

Rosaldo, Michelle, and Louise Lamphere, eds. *Women, Culture, and Society*. Stanford, Calif.: Stanford Univ. Press, 1974.

Rosenberg, Joel. *King and Kin: Political Allegory in the Hebrew Bible*. Bloomington, Ind.: Indiana Univ. Press, 1986.

Rosenbloom, Joseph R. "Social Science Concepts of Modernization and Biblical History: The Development of the Israelite Monarchy." *JAAR* 40 (1972): 437–44.

Roth, Martha T. *Law Collections from Mesopotamia and Asia Minor*. 2d ed. SBLWAW 6. Atlanta: Scholars, 1997.

Rowlands, M., M. T. Larsen, and K. Kristiansen, eds. *Centre and Periphery in the Ancient World*. Cambridge Univ. Press, 1987.

Rowton, M. B. "Dimorphic Structure and the Parasocial Element." *JNES* 36 (1977): 181–98.

_____. "The Topological Factor in the Hapiru Problem." In *Studies in Honor of Benno Landsberger on His Seventy-Fifth Birthday*. Assyriological Studies 16. Chicago: Oriental Institute, 1965. 375–87.

Rozenberg, Martin S. "The Šōfĕtīm in the Bible." *ErIsr* 12 (1975): 77*–86*.

Rüterswörden, Udo. *Die Beamten der israelitischen Königszeit*. BWA(N)T 117. Stuttgart: Kohlhammer, 1985.

Sack, Robert D. *Human Territoriality: Its Theory and History*. Cambridge: Cambridge Univ. Press, 1986.

Saggs, H. W. F. "Assyrian Warfare in the Sargonid Period." *Iraq* 25 (1963): 145–54.

_____. "The Divine in History." In *Essential Papers on Israel and the Ancient Near East*. Ed. Frederick E. Greenspahn. New York/London: New York Univ. Press, 1998. 17–48.

_____. *The Greatness That Was Babylon*. New York: Hawthorn Books, 1962.

_____. *The Might That Was Assyria*. London: Sidgwick & Jackson, 1984.

Sahlins, Marshall D. *Tribesmen*. Foundations of Modern Anthropology Series. Englewood Cliffs, N.J.: Prentice-Hall, 1968.

Said, Edward W. *Orientalism*. New York: Random House, 1978.

Sancisi-Weerdenburg, Heleen. "The Construction and the Distribution of an Ideology in the Achaemenid Empire." In *Pivot Politics: Changing Cultural Identities in Early State Formation Processes*. Edited by M. van Bakel, R. Hagesteijn, and P. van de Velde. Amsterdam: Het Spinhuis, 1994. 101–19.

_____. "The Quest for an Elusive Empire." In *Achaemenid History*. Vol. 4, *Centre and Periphery*. Edited by H. Sancisi-Weerdenburg and A. Kuhrt. Leiden: Netherlands Institute of the Near East, 1990. 263–74.

Sasson, Jack M. "King Hammurabi of Babylon." In *CANE*, vol. 2. New York: Charles Scribner's Sons, 1995. 701–15.

Sasson, Jack M., ed. *Civilizations of the Ancient Near East*. 4 vols. New York: Charles Scribner's Sons, 1995.

Schäfer, Peter. "The Hellenistic and Maccabaean Periods." In *Israelite and Judaean History*. Edited by John H. Hayes and J. Maxwell Miller. London: SCM Press, 1977. 576–611.

_____. "Palestine under Ptolemaic Rule." In *Israelite and Judaean History*. Edited by John H. Hayes and J. Maxwell Miller. London: SCM Press, 1977. 571–75.

Schäfer-Lichtenberger, Christa. "Sociological and Biblical Views of the Early State." In *The Origins of the Ancient Israelite States*. Edited by V. Fritz and P. R. Davies. JSOTSup 228. Sheffield: Sheffield Academic Press, 1991. 78–105.

Schearing, Linda S., and Steven L. McKenzie, eds. *Those Elusive Deuteronomists: The Phenomenon of Pan-Deuteronomism*. JSOTSup 268. Sheffield: Sheffield Academic Press, 1999.

Schloen, J. David. "Caravans, Kenites, and *Casus Belli*: Enmity and Alliance in the Song of Deborah." *CBQ* 55 (1993): 18–38.

Schniedewind, William M. *Society and the Promise to David: The Reception History of 2 Samuel 7:1–17*. Oxford: Oxford Univ. Press, 1999.

Schramm, Brooks. *The Opponents of Third Isaiah: Reconstructing the Cultic History of the Restoration*. JSOTSup 193. Sheffield: Sheffield Academic Press, 1995.

Schulte, Hannelis. "The End of the Omride Dynasty: Social-Ethical Observations on the Subject of Power and Violence." *Semeia* 66 (1995): 133–48.

Scott, James C. *Weapons of the Weak: Everyday Forms of Peasant Resistance.* New Haven, Conn.: Yale Univ. Press, 1985.

Seyrig, H. "Seleucus I and the Foundation of Hellenistic Syria." In *The Role of the Phoenicians in the Interaction of Mediterranean Civilizations.* Edited by William A. Ward. Beirut: American Univ. of Beirut, 1968. 53–63.

Sharkansky, Ira. *Ancient and Modern Israel: An Exploration of Political Parallels.* Albany, N.Y.: State Univ. of New York Press, 1991.

_____. *Israel and Its Bible: A Political Analysis.* New York: Garland Publishing, 1996.

Shiloh, Yigal. "Jerusalem: The Early Periods and the First Temple Period: Excavation Results." In *The New Encyclopedia of Archaeological Excavations in the Holy Land.* Edited by Ephraim Stern. Vol. 2. Jerusalem: Israel Exploration Society and Carta, 1993. 701–11.

_____. "The Population of Iron Age Palestine in the Light of a Sample Analysis of Urban Plans, Areas, and Population Density." *BASOR* 239 (1980): 25–35.

_____. *The Proto Aeolic Capital and Israelite Ashlar Masonry.* Qedem 11. Jerusalem: Institute of Archaeology, Hebrew Univ., 1979.

Sigrist, Christian. *Regulierte Anarchie: Untersuchungen zum Fehlen und zur Entstehung politischer Herrschaft in segmentaren Gesellschaften Afrikas.* Olten u. Freiburg im Breisgau: Walter, 1967.

Simkins, Ronald A. "Patronage and the Political Economy of Monarchic Israel." *Semeia.* Atlanta: Scholars, forthcoming.

Singer, Itamar. "Egyptians, Canaanites, and Philistines." In *From Nomadism to Monarchy: Archaeological and Historical Aspects of Early Israel.* Edited by I. Finkelstein and N. Na'aman. Jerusalem: Israel Exploration Society, 1994. 282–338.

Smelik, Klaas A. D. *Converting the Past: Studies in Ancient Israelite and Moabite Historiography.* Leiden: E. J. Brill, 1992.

_____. *Writings from Ancient Israel: A Handbook of Historical and Religious Documents.* Louisville: Westminster John Knox, 1991.

Smith, Anthony D. *The Ethnic Origins of Nations.* Oxford: Blackwell, 1986.

Smith, Carol. "'Queenship' in Israel? The Cases of Bathsheba, Jezebel, and Athaliah." In *King and Messiah in Israel and the Ancient Near East.* Edited by J. Day. JSOTSup 270. Sheffield: Sheffield Academic Press, 1998. 142–62.

Smith, Clyde Curry. "The Birth of Bureaucracy." *BA* 40 (1977): 24–28.

Smith, Daniel L. *The Religion of the Landless: The Social Context of the Babylonian Exile.* Bloomington, Ind.: Meyer-Stone Books, 1989.

Smith, Mark S. *The Early History of God: Yahweh and the Other Deities in Ancient Israel.* San Francisco: Harper & Row, 1990.

Snell, Daniel C. *Life in the Ancient Near East. 3100–332 B.C.* New Haven, Conn.: Yale Univ. Press, 1997.

von Soden, Wolfram. *The Ancient Orient: An Introduction to the Study of the Ancient Near East.* Grand Rapids, Mich.: Eerdmans, 1994.

Soggin, J. Alberto. "Compulsory Labor under David and Solomon." In *Studies in the Period of David and Solomon.* Edited by T. Ishida. Tokyo: Yamakawa-Shuppansha, 1982. 259–67.

Southall, Aiden. "Orientations in Political Anthropology." *Canadian Journal of African Studies* 3 (1969): 42–52.

van der Spek, R. J. "Assyriology and History: A Comparative Study of War and Empire in Assyria, Athens, and Rome." In *The Tablet and the Scroll: Near Eastern Studies in Honor of William W. Hallo.* Edited by M. E. Cohen, D. C. Snell, and D. B. Weisberg. Bethesda, Md.: CDL Press, 1993. 262–70.

Speiser, E. A. "Census and Ritual Expiation in Mari and Israel." *BASOR* 149 (1958): 17–25.

Speiser, E. A., trans. "The Creation Epic." In *ANET.* Edited by James B. Pritchard. 3d ed. Princeton: Princeton Univ. Press, 1969. 60–72.

Sperling, S. David. *The Original Torah: The Political Intent of the Bible's Writers.* New York: New York Univ. Press, 1998.

Stager, Lawrence E. "Archaeology, Ecology, and Social History: Background Themes to the Song of Deborah." In *Congress Volume: Jerusalem, 1986.* Edited by J. Emerton. VTSup 40. Leiden: E. J. Brill, 1988. 221–34.

Stein, Gil J. *Rethinking World-Systems: Diasporas, Colonies, and Interaction in Uruk Mesopotamia.* Tucson, Ariz.: Univ. of Arizona Press, 1999.

Steinberg, Naomi. "The Deuteronomic Law Code and the Politics of State Centralization." In *The Bible and the Politics of Exegesis: Essays in Honor of Norman K. Gottwald on His Sixty-Fifth Birthday.* Edited by D. Jobling et al. Cleveland: Pilgrim Press, 1991. 161–70.

Steindorff, Georg, and Keith C. Seele. *When Egypt Ruled the East.* Rev. ed. Chicago: Univ. of Chicago Press, 1957.

Stern, Ephraim. "Between Persia and Greece: Trade, Administration, and Warfare in the Persian and Hellenistic Periods (539–63 B.C.E.)." In *The Archaeology of Society in the Holy Land.* Edited by T. E. Levy. New York: Facts on File, 1995. 432–44.

Stern, Philip D. *The Biblical Ḥerem: A Window on Israel's Religious Experience.* BJS 211. Atlanta: Scholars, 1991.

Sternhall, Zeev. *The Founding Myths of Israel: Nationalism, Socialism, and the Making of the Jewish State.* Princeton: Princeton Univ. Press, 1998.

Steussy, Marti J. *David: Biblical Portraits of Power.* Columbia, S.C.: Univ. of South Carolina Press, 1999.

Stolper, Matthew W. "Murashu, Archive of." *ABD* 4: 927–28.

Strange, John. "Joram, King of Israel and Judah." *VT* 25 (1975): 191–201.

Swanson, Guy E. *The Birth of the Gods: The Origin of Primitive Beliefs.* Ann Arbor, Mich.: Univ. of Michigan Press, 1960.

Tadmor, Hayim. "Assyria and the West: The Ninth Century and Its Aftermath." In *Unity and Diversity: Essays in the History, Literature and Religion of the Ancient Near East.* Edited by H. Goedicke and J. J. M. Roberts. Baltimore: Johns Hopkins, 1975. 36–48.

———. "The Campaigns of Sargon II of Assur." *JCS* 12 (1958): 22–40, 77–100.

———. "'The People' and the Kingship in Ancient Israel: The Role of Political Institutions in the Biblical Period." *Journal of World History* 11 (1968): 3–23.

Tarn, W. W. *Hellenistic Civilisation.* 3d ed. New York: New American Library, 1952.

de Tarragon, Jean-Michel. "Ammon, Ammonite." *ABD* 1: 184–96.

Taylor, J. Glen. *Yahweh and the Sun: Biblical and Archaeological Evidence for Sun Worship in Ancient Israel.* JSOTSup 111. Sheffield: Sheffield Academic Press, 1993.

Tcherikover, Victor A. *Hellenistic Civilization and the Jews*. Philadelphia: Jewish Publication Society of America, 1961.

Tcherikover, Victor A., and A. Fuks, eds. *Corpus Papyrorum Judaicarum*. Vol. 1. Jerusalem: Magnes Press, 1957.

Thiel, Winfried. "Athaliah." *ABD* 1:511–12.

Thiele, Edwin R. "Coregencies and Overlapping Reigns." *JBL* 93 (1974): 176–89.

_____. *The Mysterious Numbers of the Hebrew Kings*. 3d ed. Grand Rapids, Mich.: Eerdmans, 1983.

Thompson, Thomas L. *Early History of the Israelite People: From the Written and Archaeological Sources*. Leiden: E. J. Brill, 1992.

_____. *The Mythic Past: Biblical Archaeology and the Myth of Israel*. New York: Basic Books, 1999.

Tigay, Jeffrey H., ed. *Empirical Models for Biblical Criticism*. Philadelphia: Univ. of Pennsylvania Press, 1985.

Toews, Wesley I. *Monarchy and Religious Institutions under Jeroboam*. SBLMS 47. Atlanta: Scholars, 1993.

Trigger, B. G., Barry J. Kemp, David O'Connor, and Alan B. Lloyd. *Ancient Egypt: A Social History*. Cambridge: Cambridge Univ. Press, 1983.

Tuplin, Christopher. "The Administration of the Achaemenid Empire." In *Coinage and Administration in the Athenian and Persian Empires*. Edited by Ian Carradice. Oxford: British Archaeological Reports, 1987. 109–66.

Van Seters, John. *Abraham in History and Tradition*. New Haven, Conn.: Yale Univ. Press, 1975.

Vanstiphout, Herman. "Memory and Literacy in Ancient Western Asia." In *CANE*, vol. 2. New York: Charles Scribner's Sons, 1995. 81–96.

Van Zyl, A. H. *The Moabites*. Pretoria Oriental Series 3. Leiden: E. J. Brill, 1960.

Vatikiotis, P. J. *The History of Egypt*. 3d ed. Baltimore: Johns Hopkins, 1986.

de Vaux, Roland. *The Early History of Israel*. Philadelphia: Westminster Press, 1978.

Wallace, Anthony F. C. *Religion: An Anthropological View*. New York: Random House, 1966.

Walsh, J. P. M. *The Mighty from Their Thrones: Power in the Biblical Tradition*. OBT 21. Philadelphia: Fortress, 1987.

Ward, William A., ed. *The Role of the Phoenicians in the Interaction of Mediterranean Civilizations*. Beirut: American Univ. of Beirut, 1968.

Warner, Sean. "The Alphabet: An Innovation and Its Diffusion." *VT* 30 (1980): 81–90.

Washington, Harold C. "Violence and the Construction of Gender in the Hebrew Bible: A New Historicist Approach." *BibInt* 5 (1997): 324–63.

Weber, Max. *Ancient Judaism*. Translated and edited by Hans H. Gerth and Don Martindale. Glencoe, Ill.: Free Press, 1952; originally published 1917–21.

_____. *Economy and Society: An Outline of Interpretive Sociology*. Berkeley, Calif.: Univ. of California Press, 1978.

Weinberg, Joel. *The Citizen-Temple Community*. JSOTSup 151. Sheffield: JSOT Press, 1992.

Weinfeld, Moshe. "Covenant Terminology in the Ancient Near East and Its Influence on the West." *JAOS* 93 (1973): 190–99.

Weitzman, Steven. *Song and Story in Biblical Narrative: The History of a Literary Convention in Ancient Israel*. Indiana Studies in Biblical Literature. Bloomington, Ind.: Indiana Univ. Press, 1997.

Welles, C. B. *Alexander and the Hellenistic World*. Toronto: A. M. Hakkert, 1970.

Wesselius, Jan-Wim. *The Origin of the History of Israel: Herodotus' Histories as Blueprint for the First Books of the Bible*. JSOTSup. Sheffield: Sheffield Academic Press, forthcoming.

Westbrook, Raymond. "Biblical and Cuneiform Lawcodes." *RB* 92 (1985): 247–65.

Westenholz, Aage. "The Old Akkadian Empire in Contemporary Opinion." In *Power and Propaganda: A Symposium on Ancient Empires*. Edited by M. T. Larsen. Copenhagen: Akademisk Forlag, 1979. 107–23.

Whitelam, Keith W. "Israel's Traditions of Origin: Reclaiming the Land." *JSOT* 44 (1989): 19–42.

_____. *The Just King: Monarchical Judicial Authority in Ancient Israel*. JSOTSup 12. Sheffield: Sheffield Academic Press, 1979.

_____. "King and Kingship." *ABD* 4: 40–48.

Whitt, William. "The Story of the Semitic Alphabet." In *CANE*, vol. 4. New York: Charles Scribner's Sons, 1995. 2379–97.

Wildavsky, Aaron. *The Nursing Father: Moses As a Political Leader*. Tuscaloosa, Ala.: Univ. of Alabama Press, 1984.

Williamson, H. G. M. *Israel in the Books of Chronicles*. Cambridge: Cambridge Univ. Press, 1977.

Wilson, John A. *The Burden of Egypt*. Chicago: Univ. of Chicago Press, 1951.

Wilson, John A., trans. "Hymn of Victory of Mer-ne-Ptah (The 'Israel Stela')." In *ANET*. 3d ed. Edited by J. B. Pritchard. Princeton: Princeton Univ. Press, 1969.

Wiseman, D. J. *Chronicles of Chaldean Kings (626–556 B.C.) in the British Museum*. London: Trustees of the British Museum, 1961.

_____. *Nebuchadrezzar and Babylon*. Oxford: Oxford Univ. Press, 1983.

Wittfogel, Karl A. *Oriental Despotism: A Comparative Study in Total Power*. New Haven, Conn.: Yale Univ. Press, 1957.

Wolf, Eric R. *Europe and the People without History*. Berkeley, Calif.: Univ. of California Press, 1982.

Wolin, Sheldon S. *Politics and Vision: Continuity and Innovation in Western Political Thought*. Boston: Little, Brown & Co., 1960.

Wright, Christopher J. H. *God's People in God's Land: Family, Land, and Property in the Old Testament*. Grand Rapids, Mich.: Eerdmans, 1990.

Wright, Henry T. "Recent Research on the Origin of the State." *Annual Review of Anthropology* 6 (1977): 379–97.

Würthwein, Ernst. *Der 'amm ha'arez im Alten Testament*. BWA(N)T 17. Stuttgart: Kohlhammer, 1936.

Yadin, Yigael. *The Art of Warfare in Biblical Lands*. 2 vols. New York: McGraw-Hill, 1963.

Yee, Gale A. "Ideological Criticism: Judges 17—21 and the Dismembered Body." In *Judges and Method: New Approaches in Biblical Studies*. Edited by G. A. Yee. Minneapolis: Fortress, 1995. 146–70.

Yeivin, Shmuel. "The Age of the Patriarchs." *RSO* 38 (1963): 277–302.

_____. "Families and Parties in the Kingdom of Judah." In *Studies in the History of Israel and Its Land*. Tel Aviv: M. Nvuman, 1959. [Heb.]

Yoffee, Norman. "The Economy of Ancient Western Asia." In *CANE*, vol. 3. New York: Charles Scribner's Sons, 1995. 1387–99.

_____. "The Late Great Tradition in Ancient Mesopotamia." In *The Tablet and the*

Scroll: Near Eastern Studies in Honor of William W. Hallo. Edited by M. E. Cohen, D. C. Snell, and D. B. Weisberg. Bethesda, Md.: CDL Press, 1993. 300–308.

————. "Mesopotamian Interaction Spheres." In *Early Stages in the Evolution of Mesopotamian Civilization.* Edited by N. Yoffee and J. J. Clark. Tucson, Ariz.: Univ. of Arizona Press, 1993. 257–69.

————. "Too Many Chiefs? (or, Safe Texts for the '90s)." In *Archaeological Theory: Who Sets the Agenda?* Edited by N. Yoffee and A. Sherratt. Cambridge: Cambridge Univ. Press, 1993. 114–42.

Younger, K. Lawson, Jr. "The Fall of Samaria in Light of Recent Research." *CBQ* 61 (1999): 461–82.

Yurco, Frank J. "Merneptah's Canaanite Campaign." *Journal of the American Research Center in Egypt* 23 (1986): 189–215.

Zeitlin, Solomon. *The Rise and Fall of the Judaean State: A Political, Social, and Religious History of the Second Commonwealth.* Vol. 1, *332–37 B.C.E.* Philadelphia: Jewish Publication Society of America, 1962.

Zertal, Adam. "'To the Land of the Perizzites and the Giants': On the Israelite Settlement in the Hill Country of Manasseh." In *From Nomadism to Monarchy: Archaeological and Historical Aspects of Early Israel.* Edited by I. Finkelstein and N. Na'aman. Jerusalem: Israel Exploration Society: 1994. 47–69.

Index of Biblical Passages and Ancient Sources

Old Testament

Genesis

12–50	36
14	37
14:1–16	36
15:18	19
29:1–30:24	18
29:21–30:24	35, 37
32:22–32	18, 37
34	37, 300 n.29
35:16–18	18
35:16–20	35, 37
38	300 n.29
46:26–27	36
48:8–49:28	35, 37

Exodus

1:1–4	35
6:14–25	35
12:38	37
15	167, 298 n.22
15:20–21	164
17:8–16	38
18:13–23	38
18:13–27	36
18:21	38
19–24	37
20:23–23:19	37
22:26–27	233
22:28	38
23:1–3, 6–8	36
23:31	19
24:1–11	35
32	82
35–40	37

Leviticus

19–26	37

Numbers

1	35, 36
1:16	38
1:46	37
11:4	37
12:1–2	164
14:20–38	39
20:2–13	39
21:6–9	68, 80
21:21–35	38
22–24	38, 191
26	35, 36, 38
26:51	37
31:1–12	38
32	41

Deuteronomy

1:7	19
1:26–40	39
3:23–29	39
11:24	19
12–26	37
16:18–20	38
17	313 n.111
17:8–13	233
17:14–20	46, 313 n.111
18:8–13	38
20:10–18	62
26:16–19	35
32:48–52	39
34:1–8	39

Joshua

1	40
1:1	41
1:4	19
1:10	40
2	39
2:1	40, 41
2:1–24	299 n.25
2:12–15	41
3–6	40
3:1	41
3:2	40
4:19	41
6–8	39
6:1	299 n.25
6:2–21	299 n.25
6:17b, 22–23, 25	299 n.25
6:22–25	39
7:16–18	40
8:10	40
8:32	40
8:33	40
9	39
9:6	41
9:15, 18–19	38, 40
9:21	40
10–11	39
10:24	40
10:43	41
11:16–12:24	39
13:1–6a	39
14:1	40
19:51	40
21:1	40
21:1–42	41
22:14, 30	40
23	39
23:2	40
24:1	40
24:1–28	36
24:31	40

Judges

1:1	41
1:1–3, 16, 17	41
1:1–3:6	39
1:5–7	43
1:16	38
1:22–26	39, 41
1:27–29	41
1:34–36	41
2:1	41
3:7–8:28	41
3:15–25	43
4–5	39
4:4–5	41, 44
4:4–10	164
5	42, 44, 298 n.22
5:1	164
5:6	299 n.24
5:10b	299 n.24
5:12	164
5:28–30	43
6:24–32	34
8:1–3	44
8:18–19	43
8:22–27	42
9	42
9:4	302 n.39
9:7–15	42
10:1–5	42
10:6–12:6	41
11	222
11:1–33	42
11:3	302 n.39
11:5–11	44

349

11:22–28	43
11:27	222
12:1–6	44
12:7–13	42
17:6	43
17:7–18:31	42
17:7–13	42
18:1	43
18:14–26	44
19:1	43
19:1–20:7	42
20	44
20:8–13	44
20:8–48	44
21	44
21:16	44
21:25	43

Ruth

4:1–12	44

1 Samuel

2:12–17	42, 46
4–5	45
4:1–11	42
7:5–11	41
7:5–14	45
7:15–17	41, 44
8:1–2	46
8:1–3	41
8:4–22	46
8:9–18	46
9:1–10:16	46
10:17–24	46
10:17–27	46
10:25	46
11	46
11:1–2	90
12	46
12:1–5	41
13:1	54
13:1–14:46	47
13:2–14:46	46
13:8–14	79
13:8–15	47
14:52	47
15	62, 79
16:1–13	47
17:25	92
21:1–9	47
21:7	46
21:10–15	47
22:1–2	47, 302 n.39
22:7–8a	92, 303 n.42
22:9–23	47
22:18–19	302 n.42
23–24	47
26	47
27	47
27:6	92
28–29	47
28:3–10	79
30	47
31	47

2 Samuel

2:1–11	47
3:1	47
3:17–18	44, 268 n.16
4:4	47, 268 n.15
4:4–11	177
5:1–3	269 n.26
5:1–5	47
5:3	44, 268 n.16
5:6–10	48
5:9, 11	91
5:11	88
5:11–16	48
5:17–25	48
6	48
6:12–19	79
7	48, 215
7:1–17	79, 314 n.114
8:1	48
8:1–14	89
8:2–14	48
8:2	219
8:6	268 n.15
8:14	220
8:15–18	48
8:18	49, 95
9	47, 49
9:7, 9–13	92
10	89
10:1–6	90
10:1–11:1	48
12:26–31	48
13–14	48
14:4–11	232
14:30	93
15–19	48
15:1–6	95, 232
15:2	177
15:12	49
15:37	49
16:1	268 n.15
16:16	49
17:27–29	92
19:24	268 n.15
19:31–40	92
19:42	92
20:1–22	48
20:23–26	48
20:24	49
20:26	49
21:1–6	303 n.42
21:1–14	49
21:3–6	177
21:6	268 n.15
24:1–17	49, 79
24:18–25	48, 79

1 Kings

1	49
1–2	48
2	49, 77
2:1	54
2:26	93
3:1	88
3:3–4	79
3:16–28	232
4:1–6	50
4:7–19	50, 93
4:19	50
4:22–28	50
4:22–29	93
5:1–12	50, 88, 93
5:13–18	50, 93
6:1–9:9	50
6	91
6–8	79
6:38	91
7:1–8	91
7:1	91
7:23–36	82
8:46–53	79
9:5–23	93
9:10–14	51, 93
9:15–22	50
9:15–24	50
9:15	91
9:15–17	91
9:26–28	50, 91
9:28	310 n.98
10:1–10	50, 88
10:11–12, 13	50
10:14–15	93
10:14, 22, 26	50
10:28–29	50, 93
11–14	319 n.6
11:1–13	79
11:9–13	34
11:14–22	51
11:23–24	51
11:26–40	52
11:26–14:20	59
11:29–39	34
11:41	71
11:42	54
11:43–12:24	60
12:1–16	52
12:5	34
12:16b–17	53
12:17, 20	52
12:24	34, 52
12:25–30	91
12:26–27	82
13	82
13:2	82
14:7–16	79
14:17	91
14:19	71
14:21–31	60
14:22–24	80
14:25–28	88, 192
14:29	72
15:1–8, 9–24	60
15:12	61, 63
15:13	271 n.40
15:16–22	88
15:16–20	65
15:18–19	94
15:24	63
15:25–27	94
15:25–32	59

15:27	221
15:33–16:7	60
16:6, 8–10, 14	60
16:9–13, 15–20	61
16:15	221
16:16–17, 21–26, 21–22	61
16:24	91
16:29–22:40, 51–53	61
16:31	88
16:31–33	80
16:32	61, 91
16:33	34
16:34	61–2
17	269 n.26
17:1	62
18–19	80
18:1–6	62
18:5–6	93
18:3b–4, 7–14, 18, 22, 40	62
19:1–3, 14	62
19:15	88
20:1–11, 20b–34	90
20:1–25	62
20:26–34	62
20:30b–34	88
20:34	93
20:35–42	62
21	62
21:5–14	233
21:20–24	62
22	88
22:1–36	63
22:1–37	62
22:13–28, 34	62
22:39	61–2, 91
22:41–50	63
22:49	310 n.98
22:51–53	61

2 Kings

1	61
1:1–16	80
1:17	61
3	61
3:4–5	63, 93
3:4–27	194
3:6–25, 6–27, 26–27	63
3:27	80
5	88
5:5–8	61, 63
6:8–8:6	61, 63
6:8–23	64
6:21–24	65
6:24–31	232
7:6	269 n.21
8:1–6	232
8:7–15	88
8:16–24	63
8:17	65
8:18	271 n.38
8:20	220
8:25–29	63
8:26	65, 271 n.38
9–10	64

9:14–26	61
9:21–24, 27–29	63
9:27–28	76
9:30–37	88
9:32	95, 276 n.75
10:12–14	76
10:13	271 n.40
10:18–28	34
10:18–31	80
10:29	82
11	76
11–12	65
11:1–16	65
11:17–18	80
11:18	80
12:4–5	94
12:17–18	88, 94
12:20–21	76
13:1–9	64
13:3–4	88
13:5	64, 88
13:7	88
13:10–25	64
13:10	58
13:14–19	64
13:14–25	88
13:20–21	219
13:23–29	64
14:1–14	65
14:5	76
14:7	220
14:13–14	94
14:15, 17–20	65
14:19–20	77
14:21–22	65
15:1–7	65
15:5	54
15:8–12, 10, 11, 13–15, 17–22	66
15:19–20	94
15:23–26	66
15:25, 27–31	67
15:32–38	68
16	68
16:3	80
16:5–9	67
16:6	220
16:7–9, 10–18	84
16:15	88–9
17	258 n.25
17:1–4	67
17:5–41	68
17:24	258 n.25
17:28	68
17:29	20
17:30	258 n.25
17:33, 41	68
18–20	68
18:1–6, 4	80
18:9–12	68
18:13–19:37	309 n.88
18:14–16	69
18:15–16	94
18:18	95
18:19–35	222

18:19–37	90
18:21	89
19:7	69
19:9	89
19:35–36	69
19:35, 36–37	196
19:37	69
20:12–15	94
20:12–19	69, 85
20:20	91
21:1–18	69
21:3, 5	80
21:19–26	69
21:23–24	77
21:24	69
22:1–23:30	69
22:3–4	95
22:47	220
23:1–25	80
23:15–20	82
23:24	59
23:29	70, 197
23:29–35	88
23:31–34	69
23:33–35	94
23:34–24:6	69
24:1–16	198
24:2	219
24:8–16	69
24:10–17	95
24:11–16	97
24:13	94
24:14	70
24:15	71
24:16	70
24:17–25:21	69
25:11	95
25:12	71
25:18–21	95, 99
25:22–24, 22, 25	98
25:26	97, 98
25:27–29	100
25:27–30	69, 71, 198

1 Chronicles

3:15	69
8:34	268 n.15
9:40	268 n.15
21:21–27	49
27:33	49

2 Chronicles

10–12	60
10:15	34
11:4	34
11:13–16, 13, 14	59
11:17	83
11:18–23	60
11:22–24	96
12:1, 2–12	83
12:1–12	192
12:4	60
13	59–60
13:13–20	60
14–16	60

14:6–14	60	36:22	111	45	313 n.113
14:6	91	39:20	97	72	156, 294 n.89,
16:7–10	61				313 n.113
16:7–12	84	**Ezra**		89	156
17–20	63	1:1–4	111	101	313 n.113
17:1–2	91	1:2–4	106	110	156, 215, 313 n.113
17:6	84	2	104, 237	132	313 n.113
17:11	63	2:1	104	144:1–11	313 n.113
18:1–2	61	2:59	99		
19:1–3	84	3:2	104	**Proverbs**	
19:4–8	233	3:8–13	106	25:1	68
19:8–11	63	4:1–2	16		
20:1–30	63	4:3	16, 104	**Isaiah**	
20:1, 10, 20, 22–23	220	4:6–23	17	1–6	67
20:33, 35–37	84	4:23	110	1–7	310 n.96
21	63	5:2	104	7	68
21:1–4	77	6:3–5	106	7:1	89
21:4	64	7:1–7, 25–26	102	7:1–6	67
21:10–15	70	7:28	109	7:3	91
21:16–22:1	64	8	104	7:5–6	67, 76
22:1–9	63	8:17	99	22:8b–11	90
22:3	77	9–10	103	22:15–19	190–1
22:10–23:15	65	10:7–8	105	36–38	309 n.88
23:26–27	70			36–39	68
24:1–27	65	**Nehemiah**		36:4–20	90
24:7	65, 77–8	2:1	102	37:8–13	90
24:17–27	66, 84	2:8	106	40–55	100
25	65	2:9	110	44:28	100
25:14–24	66	2:10	105	45:1	100
25:14–28	84	2:11–4:23	103	57–58	274 n.56
26	65	2:17–20	17	66:19	107
26:2	91	2:19	105		
26:4	76	2:20	16	**Jeremiah**	
26:6	66, 91	4:1–3	105	7	274 n.56
26:7	66	4:1–9	17	13:18	271 n.40
26:8	66, 220	4:7–23	110	22:11	69
26:9, 10	66, 91	5:1–13	105	22:13–16	91
26:11–15	66	5:4, 14–15	110	24	97
26:16–21	84	6:1	105	26	69
27	68	6:10–11	106	27:1–3	69, 71
27:3	91	6:15–19	104	27:1–7	99
27:5	68, 220	7	105	27:2, 3	219
28	68, 84	7:1–70	237	27:20–23	70
28:16–18	68	7:5, 6–73	104	29	97
28:22–24	84	8:1–10:39	102	29:1–2	69
29–32	68	8:9	102	29:1–3	99
30:1–11, 18	69	10:30–39	102	29:2	271 n.40
32	309 n.88	10:32–39	103	29:3	71
32:22–23	84	11	103	29:5	69
32:25	85	12	105	29:20–23, 24–26	99
32:30	91	12:1	104	32:1–5	69, 71
32:31	85	12:26	102	34	69, 71
33:1–20	69	13:6–7	102	34:8–22	71
33:3–7	70	13:10–13, 15–22, 23–28	103	36:1–2, 20–26	70
33:6	80	13:25–27	105	36:1–2, 20–32	69
33:10–17	70	14	105	37:1–39:10	69, 71
33:14	91	14:30–31	103	37:5–10	89
33:17	81			39:39	97
33:21–25	69	**Psalms**		40:5, 7–12	98
34–35	69	2	156, 215, 313 n.113	40:7	71
34:26–28	85	16:5–6	302 n.38	40:7–12	109
35:20–22	70, 197	18	156, 313 n.113	40:13–41:18	98
35:20–24	85	20	313 n.113	40:14	220
36:1–4, 4–8, 9–10	69	21	313 n.113	41:3	109

41:4–5	20	
41:11–43:13	98	
41:16–43:13	97	
44	274 n.56	
44:30	89	
50–51	111	
51:59	71	
51:59–60	69	
52:1–11	69	
52:15–16	71	
52:28	70	
52:29	71	
52:30	71, 98	
52:31–34	69, 100	

Lamentations
4:21–22	98
5:2, 4, 13	98

Ezekiel
1:1–3	97
3:15	97, 99
8	274 n.56
8:1	97
8:15–18	80
14:1–3	97, 99
17:1–21	222
18:1–2	97
19	97
20:1–3	97, 99
25	97
27:13	106
30–33	97
33:10	97
33:30–35	99
37:11	97
40–48	112

Daniel
1–5	100
1–6	88, 96
2–4	111
5	111
6	111
7–11	111
7:7–8, 19–27	107
8:5–12, 20–25	107
11:2–39	107

Hosea
10:5–6	222

Joel
3:6	106

Amos
1:1	65
2:8	233
7:10–17	64, 65

Jonah
1:1	65

Micah
2:5	302 n.38
6:16	61

Haggai
1:1	103
2:1, 4	104
2:21–23	111

Zechariah
3–4	104
3:1, 6, 8	277 n.83
4:6–10	277 n.83
6:11, 12, 14	277 n.83
9–14	107
9:13	107

Apocrypha and Pseudepigrapha

Ahikar, 259 n.27
Letter of Jeremiah, 259 n.27
1 and 2 Maccabees, 96, 108, 259 n.30, 260 n.31, 279 n.93
Tobit, 259 n.27
Wisdom of Ben Sira, 237–38, 317 n.140

Ancient Near Eastern Sources

Admonitions of Ipu-wer, 154
Annals of Tiglath-pileser III, 195, 309 n.86
Arad Letters, 191, 203, 208, 307 n.68
Assyrian Synchronistic History (Chronicle 21), 53, 269 n.27
Black Obelisk of Shalmaneser III, 193, 309 n.80
Calah Slab of Adad-nirari III, 195, 309 n.85
Campaign of Sheshonk I, 191, 308 n.76
Chronicles of Chaldean (Neo-Babylonian) Kings, 197–98, 310 nn.90–92
Code of Hammurabi, 122, 283 n.18
Creation Epic (Babylonian), 117, 124, 137, 283 n.19
Deir 'Alla Inscriptions, 191, 308 n.73
Display Inscriptions of Sargon II, 195, 309 n.87
el-Rimah Stela of Adad-nirari III, 195, 309 n.85
Epitaph of a Royal Steward, 190, 307 n.65

Gilgamesh Epic, 256 n.14, 313 n.107
Hymn of Victory of Mer-ne-Ptah (Israel Stela), 163–67, 257 n.18, 295 n.7, 296 n.8, 298 n.20
Khirbet el-Qom Inscriptions, 191, 208, 308 n.72
Kuntilleth 'Ajrud Inscriptions, 191, 201, 208, 308 n.71
Lachish Letters, 191, 203, 208, 307 n.66, 310 n.97
Letter from the Time of Josiah, 203, 233–34, 307 n.68
Letters of the Jews in Elephantine, 258 n.27, 317 n.134
Lists of Asiatic Countries under the Egyptian Empire, 192, 308 n.76
Moabite Stone (Mesha Stela), 194, 208, 219, 221, 309 nn.82–83
Monolith Inscription of Shalmaneser III, 192–93, 308 nn. 77–79
Murashu Business Archive, 237, 317 n.136
Nebi Yunus Slab of Sennacherib, 196–97, 309 n.88
Oriental Institute Prism of Sennacherib, 196–97, 309 nn.88–89, 310 n.96
Piye Stela, 298 n.22
Protests of the Eloquent Peasant, 234, 316 n.128
Ration List for Jehoiachin, 198, 310 n.93
Samarian Ostraca, 187–88, 190, 307 n.63
Samarian Papyri, 237, 317 n.135
Siloam Inscription, 190, 307 n.64
Sumerian King List, 295 n.5
Tel Dan Inscription, 182, 190, 199, 304 n.52
Tell Qasile Ostraca, 311 n.98
Zenon Papyri, 237, 317 n.139

Classical Sources

Herodotus, 256 n.14, 261 n.33, 272 n.44
Josephus, *Antiquities*, 219, 237, 317 n.137

Index of Authors

Ackerman, Susan, 274 n.56, 313 n.108
Adams, Robert McC., 280 n.5
Adcock, Frank E., 289 n.64
Ahlström, Gösta W., 273 n.53, 275 n.68, 289 n.61, 298 n.20
Aldred, Cyril, 288 n.56
Alt, Albrecht, 255 n.13, 313 n.109
Amin, Samir, 254 n.9
Amit, Yairah, 319–20 n.6
Anderson, Benedict, 257 n.24
Anderson, Gary A., 297 n.16
Anderson, Robert T., 258 n.25
Applebaum, S., 317 n.142
Aufrecht, Walter E., 314 n.120
Auld, A. Graeme, 267 n.13, 295 n.3
Avi-Yonah, Michael, 306 n.58
Avigad, Nahman, 307 nn.65, 69

Bader-Saye, Scott, 319 n.4
Bagnall, Roger S., 282 n.9, 289 n.66, 294 n.1
Bailey, Christine W., 279 n.3
Baines, John, 281 n.9, 286 nn.33, 34, 35; 288 n.55, 289 n.57, 290 n.71, 291 n.76
Barkay, Gabriel, 306 n.58, 316 nn.131, 132
Barnett, R. D., 314 n.122
Barstad, Hans M., 277 n.78
Bartlett, John R., 277 n.79, 314 n.121
Barton, John, 265 n.46
Beaulieu, P. A., 288 n.54
Beer, M., 317 n.142
Begrich, Joachim, 276 n.74
Bendix, Richard, 280 n.7
Bengston, Hermann, 289 n.62
Berlev, Oleg, 286 n.32
Berlinerblau, Jacques, 264 n.44, 313 n.108
Berquist, Jon L., 278 n.84
Bevin, Edwyn R., 282 n.9
Biale, David, 255 n.13, 318 n.145, 319 n.2
Bible and Culture Collective, The, 264 n.44
Bickerman, Elias J., 290 n.68
Bienkowski, Piotr, 314 n.121
Biggs, Robert D., 283 n.21
Bikai, Patricia M., 287 n.43
Biran, Avraham, 304 n.52

Bird, Phyllis, 276 n.73
Black, Jeremy A., 287 n.45
Bleiberg, Edward, 281 n.9
Blenkinsopp, Joseph, 278 n.92
Boer, Roland, 264 n.45, 265 nn.46, 3; 319–20 n.6
Borgen, P., 317 n.142
Boudon, Raymond, 253 n.1
Bourricaud, François, 253 n.1
Boyarin, Daniel, 256 n.14
Brettler, Marc Zvi, 260–1 n.31, 261 n.34
Briant, Pierre, 282 n.9
Bright, John, 269 n.24
Brinkman, J. A., 310 n.92
Briquel-Chatonnet, F., 314 n.118
Bronson, Bennett, 285 n.28
Brookman, W. R., 268 n.13
Broshi, Mogen, 307 n.61, 310 n.95
Brueggemann, Walter, 265 n.46
Buccellati, Giorgio, 313 n.109
Burns, John Barclay, 267 n.13

Carneiro, Robert L., 280 n.6, 302 n.41
Carney, T. R., 294 n.1, 316 n.130
Carroll, Robert P., 260 n.30, 277 n.78, 316 n.130
Carter, Charles E., 278 n.84, 279 n.92, 316–17 nn.132, 133
Cazelles, Henri, 255 n.13, 290 n.71
Chaney, Marvin L., 292 n.82, 293 n.85, 302 nn.38, 39, 40
Charpin, Dominique, 281 n.9
Chikafu, P. T., 265 n.46
Claburn, William E., 274 n.59
Claessen, Henri J. M., 254 n.9, 279 n.3, 304 n.47
Clastres, Pierre, 253 n.3
Clements, Ronald E., 265 n.3
Clines, David J. A., 264 n.44
Cogan, Mordechai, 55, 57, 58, 270 nn.28, 29, 31; 271 n.41, 275 n.66, 277 n.75, 308 n.75
Coggins, Richard J., 258 n.25, 274 n.61
Cohen, C., 275 n.66
Cohen, Martin A., 274 n.57

Cohen, Ronald, 253 n.4, 284 n.25
Collins, John J., 259 n.27
Coogan, Michael David, 297 n.12
Cook, J. M., 282 n.9, 289 n.60
Cook, Stephen L., 277 n.82, 315 n.124
Coote, Robert B., 295 n.4, 303 n.41
Cross, Frank M., 256 n.14, 257 n.20, 258 n.26, 259 n.28, 271 n.37, 278 nn.86, 87; 293 n.85, 298 n.22, 299 n.27, 308 n.70, 312 n.104, 317 nn.135, 143
Crown, A. D., 282 n.14
Crüsemann, Frank, 276 n.73, 294 n.88, 301 n.32
Cryer, Frederick H., 304 n.52
Curtis, Edward L., 271 n.43

Damrosch, David, 256 n.14
Dandamayev, Muhammad A., 269 n.23
Davies, Philip R., 256 n.16, 259–60 n.30, 261 n.32, 262 n.37, 263 n.40, 317 n.140
Dayagi-Mendels, Michal, 307 n.69
Dearman, J. Andrew, 309 n.82
Deutsch, Robert, 307 nn.69, 70
Dever, William G., 292 n. 82, 296 n.9, 297 n.12, 304 n.49, 306 nn.58, 59, 60; 307 n.61, 308 n.72, 315 n.125
DeVries, Simon J., 269 n.22, 270 nn.28, 29, 30
Di Lella, Alexander A., 317 n.140
Dietrich, Walter, 309 n.84
Diringer, David, 312 n.104
Dothan, Trude, 314–15 n.122
Dumbrell, William J., 299 n.24
Dutcher-Walls, Patricia, 273 n.50

Eagleton, Terry, 263 n.41
Earle, Timothy, 283 n.22
Eberhard, Wolfram, 254 n.11, 303 n.45
Eddy, Samuel K., 289 n.65
Edelman, Diana V., 268 n.15, 275 n.62, 314 n.121
Ehrlich, Carl S., 315 n.122
Eisenstadt, S. N., 263 n.39, 280 n.7
Eissfeldt, Otto, 299 n.24
Elazar, Daniel J., 293 n.83, 318 n.146
Endres, John C., 267 n.13
Engel, Donald W., 283 n.14, 289 n.64
Engelken, Karen, 303 n.45
Eph'al, Israel, 288 n.48
Eskenazi, Tamara C., 277 n.84
Evans, Carl D., 271 n.37

Fales, Frederick Mario, 268 n.20
Farb, Peter, 300 n.31
Feldman, Louis H., 317 n.137
Finkelstein, Israel, 296 n.9, 297 nn.15, 17; 304 n.49, 306 n.57, 307 n.61
Fischer, Thomas, 279 n.93
Flanagan, James W., 267 n.10, 301 n.33, 305 n.53
Frandsen, Paul J., 288 n.55

Frankel, Rafael, 297 n.18
Freedman, David N., 298 n.22, 299 n.27
Frick, Frank S., 262 n.37, 267 n.10, 297 n.16
Fried, Morton H., 253 n.4, 300 n.31
Friedman, Richard Elliott, 295 n.3, 320 n.6
Fritz, Volkmar, 306 n.58
Frye, Richard N., 282 n.9
Fuks, A., 317 n.139

Gal, Zvi, 297 n.18
Gibson, McGuire, 283 n.21
Gledhill, John, 254 n.11
Gnuse, Robert K., 275 n.62, 313 n.108
Goedicke, H., 286 n.39
Goldstein, Jonathan A., 279 n.93
Goodman, Martin, 317 n.142
Goody, Jack, 262 n.36
Gottwald, Norman K., 256 n.15, 257 n.20, 261 n.34, 262 nn.35, 37; 264 nn.43, 44, 45, 46; 265 n.1, 266 nn.4, 6, 8; 267 n.11, 270 n.29, 271 n.39, 275 n.71, 277 nn.76, 80, 81, 84; 278 nn.88, 90; 290 n.67, 291–2 nn.77, 80; 298 n.21, 299 nn.26, 27, 28; 300 nn.30, 31; 301 n.35, 302 nn.37, 40; 303 n.45, 309 n.84, 310 n.97, 311 n.100, 313 n.112, 315 n.125, 316 nn.129, 130; 319 nn.3, 5
Grabbe, Lester, 258 n.27, 277 n.84
Gray, John, 269 n.21, 270 nn.29, 32; 271 nn.41, 42; 310 n.89
Grayson, A. Kirk, 269–70 n.27, 282 n.9, 288 n.50, 308 n.77
Green, W. S., 317 n.142
Greengus, Samuel, 294 n.88
Gropp, Douglas M., 317 n.135
Gunkel, Hermann, 299–300 n.29, 313–14 n.113
Gurney, O. R., 282 n.9

Halbertal, Moshe, 318 n.2
Hallo, William W., 281 n.9, 282 n.10, 287 n.42, 312 nn.106, 107
Halpern, Baruch, 267 n.13, 268 n.17, 274 n.58, 275 n.65, 293 n.83, 303 n.46, 304 nn.50, 52
Hammond, N. G. L., 282 n.9
Handy, Lowell K., 304 n.49
Hanson, Paul D., 277 n.82
Harvey, Graham, 256 n.17
Hata, G., 317 n.137
Hauer, Chris Jr., 276 n.72
Hayes, John H., 255 n.13, 258 n.26, 268 n.17, 270 nn.28, 35, 308 n.79, 310 n.89
Healey, Joseph P., 313 n.110
Herm, Gerhard, 314 n.118
Herzog, Ze'ev, 306 n.58
Hestrin, Ruth, 307 n.69
Hjelm, Ingrid, 258 n.25
Hobbs, T. R., 265 n.2, 271 n.41, 272 n.45
Hoftijzer, J., 308 n.73
Holladay, John S. Jr., 292 n.82, 306 n.56

Holloway, Steven W., 271 n.42
Honeyman, A. M., 270 n.36
Hooker, P. K., 270 n.28
Hopkins, David C., 276 n.72, 292 n.82, 305 n.54, 311 n.102
Hornung, Erik, 273 n.51
Houston, Walter, 294 n.89
Hudson, Michael, 286 n.37
Hull, John H. Jr., 272 n.49
Hunt, Lynn, 264 n.42
Hunt, Robert C., 283 n.22, 292 n.82
Hurowitz, Victor (Avigdor), 273 n.52, 275 n.67

Ikeda, Yutaka, 269 n.21
Ishida, Tomoo, 266 n.7, 268 nn.14, 18; 269 n.25, 272 n.48, 294 n.86, 303 nn.43, 44; 313 n.109

Jacobsen, Thorkild, 282 n.12
Jamieson-Drake, David W., 304 n.50
Jankowska, N. B., 288 n.50
Janssen, Jac J., 286 nn.31, 32
Jenks, Alan W., 295 n.4
Jobling, David, 264 nn.44, 45; 294 n.89, 304 n.48
Johnson, Gregory A., 306 n.59
Joukowsky, Martha S., 314 n.118

Kamp, Kathryn A., 284 nn.24, 25
Kapelrud, Arvid S., 273 n.52
Katzenstein, H. J., 271 n.38, 314 n.122
Kaufman, Herbert, 254 n.7
Kautsky, John H., 280 n.7, 288 n.49
Kees, H., 281 n.9
Kemp, Barry J., 281–2 n.9, 285 n. 31, 286 n.37
Khazanov, Anatoly M., 284 n.25
King, Philip J., 310 n.94
Klein, Ralph W., 271 n.43, 299 n.26
Klengel, Horst, 314 n.117
Knauf, Ernst A., 299 n.24, 305 nn.53, 54
Knight, Douglas A., 315 n.125, 316 n.127
Knoppers, Gary N., 272 n.47
Kooij, G. van der, 308 n.73
Krader, Lawrence, 254 n.9
Kraeling, Emil G., 314 n.117
Kreissig, H., 279 n.92
Kuan, Jeffrey Kah-Jin, 308 nn.77, 78, 79; 309 nn.80, 81, 85, 86, 87
Kuhn, K. G., 256 n.17
Kuhrt, Amélie, 282 nn.9, 11, 13; 283 nn.16, 17; 286 nn.34, 35, 36; 288 nn.52, 53, 55, 57; 289 n.59, 291 n.78
Kuper, Adam, 288 n.9

LaBianca, Øystein S., 305 n.53
Lambert, Frith, 262 n.37, 300 n.29
Lambert, W. G., 290 n.71
Lamphere, Louise, 296 n.10
Leahy, Anthony, 284 n.26

Lederman, Zvi, 297 n.17
Lemche, Niels Peter, 254 nn.9, 10; 256 n.16, 262 n.37, 263 n.40, 266 nn.4, 9; 295 nn.2, 6; 296 n.9, 298 nn.20, 23; 302 n.39, 303 n.45
Lenski, Gerhard E., 254 n.9, 281 n.7, 300 n.30
Lerner, Gerda, 279 n.3, 296 n.11
Levin, C., 273 n.50
Levine, Baruch, 286 n.38
Levy, Thomas E., 306 n.57
Lewellen, Ted C., 254 n.8
Linville, James R., 256 nn.16, 17; 257 nn.22, 24; 260 n.30, 268 n.16, 272 n.47
Liverani, Mario, 263 n.41, 287 nn.42, 46; 288 n.52, 301–2 n.36
Lloyd, Alan B., 282 n.9
Lloyd, Christopher, 254 n.10
Lohfink, Norbert, 271 n.39, 274 n.61
London, Gloria, 311 n.101
Long, Burke O., 272 nn.44, 46; 310 n.97, 312 n.106
Lowery, Richard H., 273 n.53

MacDonald, Burton, 314 nn.120, 121
Machinist, Peter, 288 n.50, 311 n.100
Madsen, Albert A., 271 n.43
Maisler (Mazar), Benjamin, 271 n.43, 311 n.98
Malamat, Abraham, 269 n.24
Málek, Jaromír, 281 n.9, 286 nn.33, 34, 35; 288 n.55, 289 n.57, 291 n.76
Mandell, Sara R., 258 n.26
Mann, Michael, 253 n.2, 254–5 n.11, 255 n.12, 263 nn.38, 39; 279 nn.1, 2, 3; 280 nn.4, 5, 6, 7; 281 nn.7, 9; 283 n.14, 285 nn.27, 28, 29; 286 n.40, 287 n.47, 288 n.49, 289 n.62, 302–3 n.41
Mansueto, Anthony, 315 n.125
Margalit, Avishai, 318 n.2
Mazar, Amihai, 297 nn.13, 17; 306 n.58, 308 n.74, 310 n.94, 311 n.103, 312 n.105
Mazar, Benjamin, 269 n.24, 308 n.76, 314 n.117
McCarter, P. Kyle, 312 n.104
McKay, John W., 271 n.41
McKenzie, Steven L., 274 n.61, 275 n.63, 295 n.3
McNeill, William H., 263 nn.38, 39; 280 n.5, 281–2 nn.9, 12; 285 n.28, 287 n.46
McNutt, Paula M., 262 n.37, 266 nn.4, 9; 267 n.10
Meeks, M. Douglas, 319 n.5
Meier, Samuel A., 283 n.17
Mendenhall, George E., 299 n.26
Mettinger, Tryggve N. D., 268 n.19, 269 n.24, 275 n.70, 276 n.74, 292 n.81, 303 n.42
Meyers, Carol, 275 n.69, 276 n.73, 278 nn.86, 87; 296 n.10, 301 n.34
Meyers, Eric M., 278 nn.86, 87; 306 n.58

Michalowski, Piotr, 290 n.73
Middleton, John, 253 n.3, 254 n.8
Milbank, John, 277 n.81
Millar, William R., 267 n.13
Millard, A. R., 311 n.99
Miller, Daniel, 285 n.27
Miller, J. Maxwell, 255 n.13, 268 n.17, 270 n.35, 308 n.79, 310 n.89, 314 n.119
Miller, Patrick D. Jr., 315 n.123
Miller, R. D. III, 301 n.34
Modrzejewski, Joseph M., 289 n.58
Montgomery, James A., 271 n.42
Morgan, Robert, 265 n.46
Morony, Michael G., 290 n.70
Muhly, J. D., 287 nn.42, 44
Mullen, E. Theodore Jr., 256 n.16, 272–3 nn.47, 50
Murname, William J., 282 n.9
Myers, Jacob M., 271 n.43

Na'aman, Nadav, 269 n.21, 303 n.46, 306 n.57, 308 nn.75, 78
Nakanose, Shigeyuki, 274 n.59, 293 n.85
Naveh, Joseph, 304 n.52
Nelson, Richard D., 272 n.44
Neusner, Jacob, 258 n.27
Newby, Gordon Darnell, 259 n.27
Newman, Katherine S., 292 n.82
Newsom, Carol A., 277 n.81
Nickelsburg, George W. E., 258–9 n.27
Nicholson, Ernest W., 313 n.110
Niditch, Susan, 262 n.36, 311 n.99
Niehr, Herbert, 297 n.12
Niemann, Hermann M., 304 n.50, 305 n.54
Nissen, Hans J., 281 n.9
North, Robert, 265 n.2

O'Connor, David, 282 n.9, 288 n.55, 289 n.57
Oded, Busteney, 288 n.51
Ofer, Avi, 297 n.17
Olmstead, A. T., 282 n.9
Olson, Dennis T., 270 n.34
Olyan, Saul, 297 n.14
Oppenheim, A. Leo, 273 n.51, 281 n.9
Ottosson, Magnus, 298 n.19
Overholt, Thomas W., 301 n.31
Overman, J. A., 317 n.142

Pardee, Dennis, 307 nn.66, 67, 68
Park, Robert E., 318 n.1
Parker, Kim Ian, 318 n.146, 319 n.4
Parker, Simon B., 312 n.106
Parpola, Simo, 288 n.50
Parsons, Talcott, 263 n.39
Pasto, James, 260 n.31, 274 n.58, 278 n.91
Patte, Daniel, 264 n.45
Payne, Elizabeth J., 299 n.24
Peckham, Brian, 281 n.8
Perdue, Leo, 265 n.46
Pestman, P. W., 317 n.139

Peters, F. E., 289 n.65
Pfeiffer, Robert H., 267 n.13
Pippin, Tina, 264 n.44
Pitard, Wayne T., 314 n.117
Polanyi, Karl, 283 n.22
Porton, Bezalel, 317 n.134
Portugali, Juval, 305 n.55
Postgate, J. Nicholas, 281 n.9, 288 n.50
Potts, D. T., 283 n.15
Pritchard, James L., 312 n.106
Provan, Ian W., 263 n.40
Purvis, James D., 258 n.25
Pury, Albert de, 295 n.3

Rad, Gerhard von, 256 n.17, 259 n.29, 293 n.83
Reade, Julian, 275 n.69
Redford, Donald B., 286 n.36, 288 n.56, 296 n.8
Redman, Charles R., 279 n.2
Rendsburg, Gary A., 265 n.3
Rendtorff, Rolf, 295 n.3
Renger, Johannes, 283 n.23
Reviv, H., 273 n.50
Riley, William, 273 n.54
Roaf, Michael, 281 n.9, 282 n.11, 283 n.17, 286 n.41, 289 nn.59, 60
Roberts, J. J. M., 315 n.123
Rogerson, John W., 301 n.32
Rosaldo, Michelle, 296 n.10
Rosenberg, Joel, 265 n.3
Rosenbloom, Joseph R., 276 n.72
Roth, Martha T., 283 n.18
Rowlands, M., 290 n.69
Rowton, M. B., 302 n.36
Rozenberg, Martin S., 266 n.7
Rüterswörden, Udo, 276 n.74

Sack, Robert D., 285 n.27
Saggs, H. W. F., 282 n.9, 288 n.48
Sahlins, Marshall D., 300 n.31
Said, Edward W., 290 n.72
Sancisi-Weerdenburg, Heleen, 289 nn.60, 63
Sasson, Jack M., 281 n.9, 283 nn.17, 20
Schaefer, Peter, 289 n.66, 290 n.67, 317 n.141
Schaefer-Lichtenberger, Christa, 303 n.47, 304 nn.50, 51
Schloen, J. David, 299 n.24
Schniedewind, William M., 304 n.47, 314 n.114
Schramm, Brooks, 277 n.82
Scott, James C., 316 n.130
Seele, Keith C., 282 n.9, 288 n.55
Service, Elman R., 253 n.4
Seyrig, H., 282 n.9
Sharkansky, Ira, 293 n.83, 318 n.145, 319 n.2
Shiloh, Yigal, 307 n.61, 310 n.94, 311 n.103
Sigrist, Christian, 301 n.32
Simkins, Ronald A., 254 n.9, 315 n.125
Simpson, William K., 281 n.9

Singer, Itamar, 296 n.8
Skalnik, Peter, 254 n.9, 279 n.3, 304 n.47
Smelik, Klaas A. D., 307 nn.64, 66, 67, 68;
  308 nn.71, 72, 73; 309 n.82, 314 n.119
Smith, Anthony D., 257 n.24, 284 n.26, 286
  n.40, 288 n.52, 291 nn.77, 79
Smith, Carol, 271 n.40
Smith, Clyde Curry, 283 n.21
Smith, Daniel L., 278 n.92
Smith, Mark S., 274 n.56, 275 n.62, 297
  nn.12, 14; 313 n.108
Snell, Daniel C., 281 n.9, 283 n.22
Soden, Wolfram von, 281 n.9
Soggin, J. Alberto, 269 n.23
Southall, Aiden, 253 n.6
Speiser, E.A., 268 n.20
Spek, R. J. van der, 288 n.49, 291 n.74
Sperling, S. David, 265 n.3
Stager, Lawrence E., 299 n.27
Stein, Gil J., 285 n.28
Steinberg, Naomi, 274 n.60, 293 n.85
Steindorff, Georg, 282 n.9, 288 n.55
Stern, Ephraim, 306 n.58, 317 n.138
Stern, Philip D., 271 n.39
Sternhall, Zeev, 318 n.2
Steussy, Marti J., 273 n.54
Stolper, Matthew W., 317 n.136
Strange, John, 270 n.35
Swanson, Guy E., 291 n.80

Tadmor, Hayim, 275 n.66, 277 n.75, 293
  n.84, 308 n.77, 309 n.87
Tait, W. J., 287 n.45
Tarn, W. W., 289 n.65
Tarragon, Jean-Michel de, 314 n.120
Tate, David, 253 n.3, 254 n.8
Taylor, J. Glen, 273 n.55
Tcherikover, Victor A., 290 n.68, 317 nn.139,
  142
Thiele, Edwin R., 55, 57, 58, 270 nn.28, 29,
  32
Thompson, Thomas L., 261 nn.32, 33; 262
  n.37, 263 n.40, 286 n.36, 309 n.83
Tigay, Jeffrey H., 312–13 n.107
Toews, Wesley I., 270 n.37
Trigger, B. G., 282 n.9
Tuplin, Christopher, 278 n.89, 289 n.60

Van Seters, John, 295 n.3
Van Zyl, A. H., 314 n.119

Vanstiphout, Herman, 287 n.45
Vatikiotis, P. J., 282 n.9
Vaux, Roland de, 257 n.21
Velde, P. van de, 284 n.25

Wallace, Anthony F. C., 300 n.31
Walsh, J. P. M., 317–18 n.145
Ward, William A., 314 n.118
Warner, Sean, 311 n.99
Washington, Harold C., 297 n.11
Watanabe, Kazuko, 288 n.50
Watkins, Frederick M., 253 n.4
Weber, Max, 253 n.4, 254 n.9, 318 n.1
Weinberg, Joel, 278 n.92
Weinstein, James M., 286 n.36
Weitzman, Steven, 298 n.22
Welles, C. B., 282 n.9
Wesselius, Jan-Wim, 256 n.14
Westbrook, Raymond, 294 n.88
Westenholz, Aage, 282 n.13
Whitelam, Keith W., 266 n.7, 293 n.83, 294
  n.87, 298 n.21, 303 n.41
Whitt, William, 287 n.45
Widengren, Geo, 289 n.61
Wildavsky, Aaron, 266 n.5
Williamson, H. G. M., 256 nn.17, 23
Wilson, John A., 296 n.8
Wilson, Robert R., 274 n.61
Wiseman, Donald J., 288 n.53, 310 nn.90,
  91, 92
Wittfogel, Karl A., 290 n.72
Wolf, Eric R., 255 n.11
Wolin, Sheldon S., 253 n.5
Wright, Christopher J. H., 302 n.38
Wright, Henry T., 279 n.3
Würthwein, Ernst, 313 n.110

Yadin, Yigael, 275 n.64
Yee, Gale A., 267 n.12
Yeivin, Shmuel, 312 n.104, 315 n.126
Yoffee, Norman, 253 n.2, 267 n.10, 279 n.2,
  281 n.9, 284 nn.24, 25, 285 n.30, 291 n.75
Younger, K. Lawson Jr., 309 n.87, 312 n.106
Younker, Randall W., 305 n.53, 314 n.120
Yurco, Frank J., 296 n.8

Zeitlin, Solomon, 290 n.67
Zertal, Adam, 297 n.17
Zobel, Hans-Joachim, 256 n.17, 257 n.21

Index of Subjects

Aaron, 39, 40
Abda, 51
Abiathar, 49, 92
Abijam=Abijah, 55, 59, 60, 89, 96
Abimelech, 42, 43
Abner, 47
Absalom, 48, 49, 92–93, 95, 178
Achish, 48, 49, 92, 184
Acts of Solomon, 71
Adad-nirari III, 64, 195
Adonibezek, 43
Adonijah, 48
Adoniram (see Adoram)
Adoram, 49, 51, 52, 59
Adullam, 36
Agag, 62
Ahab, 34, 52, 54, 56, 61–62, 63, 64, 65, 78, 79,
    82, 84, 87, 88, 89, 90, 91, 93, 193, 194,
    222
Ahaz=Jehoahaz I (see also Jehoahaz)
    king of Judah, 57, 58, 67, 68, 76, 84, 87, 89,
    191, 195, 200, 213, 220, 224
Ahaziah
    king of Israel, 56, 62–633
    king of Judah (see Jehoahaz=Azaiah)
Ahijah
    of Shiloh, 34, 234
    son of Seraiah, 51
Ahilud, 49, 51
Ahishar, 51
Ahithophel, 49
Ahura Mazda, 142
Ai, 39
Akh-en-Aton, 139
Akkad, 122, 125, 126, 132, 284–285 n.277
Alexander, 107, 142–143
Amalekites, 38
Amaziah, 56, 65–66, 76, 77, 84, 87, 89, 213, 220
Ammon, 48, 66, 87, 90, 93, 98, 104, 133, 179,
    197, 200, 216, 219–221, 314 n.120
Ammonites, 43, 46, 68, 104, 110, 167–168,
    175, 193
Amnon, 48

Amon
    Egyptian god (see Amon-Ra)
    king of Judah, 57, 69–70, 77
Amon-Ra, 129, 139
Amorites, 38, 123, 125
Amos, 65, 234
Anatolia, 27, 36, 50, 93, 121, 124, 132, 134,
    138, 140, 141, 147, 172
ancient Near East (see also statehood in
    ancient Near East)
    as context for Israelite political history,
    2–3, 26–27, 111, 120, 151, 158, 172, 181,
    211–212, 246
    culture of, 133, 149, 204
    diversification of power in, 124
    and literacy, 133
    politics of, 13, 90, 113, 114, 126, 144–150
    records of, 192–198
    religion in, 78
    and technology, 133
    and trade, 133
Antiochus Epiphanes IV, 107, 144
Aphek, 62
apocalyptic, 107, 242
Apocrypha and Pseudepigrapha, 97, 259 n.27
Arad, 191–192, 203, 208
Aram-Damascus, 51, 61, 62, 63, 67, 83, 84, 87,
    88, 89, 90, 93, 94, 193, 195, 199 (see also
    Damascus)
Arameans, 125, 133, 134, 137
archaeology, 163, 164, 171, 279 n.2, 292–293
    n.82
    and biblical studies, 306 n.56
    "central place theory," 187–190, 306 n.59
    and colonialism, 236–237
    in Palestine, 185–192
    and political history, 1, 97, 128, 176,
    181–183, 198–199, 246, 296 n.9, 310 n.94
    and religion, 165, 208–209
    and warfare, 168
Artaxerxes I, 102
Artaxerxes II, 102, 107
arts and crafts, 205–206

Asa, 55, 60–61, 63, 65, 83, 91, 213, 217
Ashdod, 91, 104, 221
Asherah, 61, 80, 82, 165, 205, 208
Ashkelon, 221
Ashur, 136
Ashurbanipal, 136–137, 219, 220
assassination (*see* political power)
Assyria, 68, 69, 83, 84, 88, 89, 90, 94, 124, 132, 133, 134, 167, 223, 249, 282 n.9 (*see also* Neo-Assyrian empire)
Astarte, 208
Athaliah, 55, 56, 62, 63, 65, 76, 77, 78, 80, 82, 89, 213, 216, 271 nn. 38, 40; 272 n.50
Aton, 139
Azariah
    son of Nathan, 51
    son of Zadok, 51
Azariah=Uzziah, 54, 56, 65–66, 68, 73, 84, 91, 191, 214, 218, 220, 223, 230

Baal, 34, 61, 62, 64, 65, 77, 78, 80, 82, 83, 91, 165, 215, 216, 221–222, 226
Baalath, 91
Baalis, 98, 220
Baasha, 55, 58, 60, 62, 76, 88, 89
Babylon, 69, 97, 101, 123, 137, 198
Babylonia, 85, 97, 123, 133, 239
Balaam, 191
Barak, 41
"barbarism," 285 n.28
Barzillai, 92
Bathsheba, 48
Beersheba, 188
Belshazzar, 111
Benaiah, 48, 50
Ben-hadad, 61, 62, 88, 90
Benjamin
    territory of, 96, 236
    tribe of, 18, 46, 60, 176
Ben Sira, 237–238
Bethel, 39, 59, 67, 70, 78, 79, 82, 91, 215, 226
Beth-horon, 91
Bethlehem, 236
Beth-shemesh, 66, 213
Byblos, 218

Caleb, 39
Canaan, 37, 41, 62, 169, 175, 303 n.45
    city-states of, 36
    entry into, 39, 166–167
    settlement of, 39–40
Carchemish, battle of, 133, 140
centralized politics, Israelite (*see* statehood, Israelite; *see also* monarchy)
Chaldeans (*see* Neo-Babylonian empire)
Chemosh, 194, 221, 222
Cherethites, 50
Christianity, 251
Chronicles
    book of, 16, 19, 20, 34, 45, 53, 55, 59, 66, 69–70, 72, 74, 75, 77, 79, 81–87, 89, 97, 160, 197, 255 n.17, 267 n.13, 271–272 n.43
    of the Kings of Israel, 71
    of the Kings of Judah, 71
chronology, 262 n.35
    in colonial period, 102, 107
    of kings, 53–72, 74, 269 n.27, 270 nn.28–29
    parallel with ancient Near East, 53
    sources for reconstruction of, 54–55
colonial period, Israelite, 15–16, 24, 32, 96–112, 155–156, 235–245-245
    chronology of, 96, 108
    politics in, 108–112, 240
    sources for, 96, 236–238
coregencies, 54–55, 66, 68, 84, 227
covenant
    and politics, 209–210, 215, 247, 293 n.83, 313 n.111
    among tribes, 36, 210
    with Yahweh, 37
Cyrus, 88, 96, 100–101, 111, 138, 140–141

Damascus, 48, 64–65, 93, 133, 180, 193, 194, 202, 213, 214, 215, 217–218, 225, 314 n.117 ((*see also* Aram-Damascus)
Dan, 59, 78, 79, 82, 91, 182, 188, 190, 215, 226 (*see also* "House of David" inscription)
Daniel, 21, 107, 108, 111, 237
Darius, 111
David, 18, 25, 54, 72, 79, 87, 89, 90, 91, 92, 177–179, 183–184, 219, 221
    administration of, 48–49, 51, 94–95, 267 n.11
    House of, 53, 59, 74, 76, 80, 198, 215
    rebellions against, 49, 178
    rise of, 47–48, 173, 177, 210
Deborah, 41, 164
    Song of, 42
Deir 'Allah, 191
deportation (*see* Judah, deportations from)
Deuteronomy, 62, 70, 83, 85, 194
Diaspora, 21, 96, 97, 111–112, 140, 236, 239, 248, 249, 258 n.27, 317 nn.142, 144
Dibon, 194
dispersion (*see* Diaspora)
Doeg, 46
"dual causality principle," 252, 319–320 n.6

Ebla, 124
Ecclesiastes, 96, 107
Edom, 38, 48, 63, 64, 66, 68, 87, 93, 98, 133, 179, 180, 192, 197, 200, 213, 214, 219–221, 314 n.121
Edomites, 63, 66, 84, 99, 191
Eglon, 43, 51
Egypt, 27, 35, 36, 37, 38, 50, 51, 52, 67, 70–71, 88, 89, 90, 93, 94, 97, 98, 121, 133, 134, 137, 141, 144, 175, 221, 239, 281–282 n.9, 286 n.40

administration of, 128, 129, 131, 139, 143
bondage in, 38, 166–167, 298–299 n.23
Early Dynastic period, 129
economics in, 129, 131
First Intermediate period, 129, 131
Middle Kingdom, 129
migration from, 38–39, 166–167, 298 n.21
and multiculturalism, 139–140
New Kingdom, 129, 130, 138–139, 192, 288
   n.55
Old Kingdom, 129
politics in, 128, 130, 132, 144
religion in, 129, 131, 146–147
rulers of, 128, 131
Second Intermediate period, 129, 131
state formation in, 127–128, 150
trade in, 129, 192, 201
tribute in, 139, 201
urbanization of, 128
Ehud, 43
Ekron, 221
Elah, 56, 60
Elamites, 123
Elath, 87, 91, 220
Eleazar, 40
Elephantine, 237, 240, 258 n.27
Eliakim (see Jehoiakim)
Elihoreph, 51
Elijah, 33, 73, 80, 88, 215, 222, 234
Elisha, 33, 63, 64, 72–74, 80, 88, 234, 235
En-gedi, 63
Enuma Elish, 124
Ephraim
   territory of, 67, 68, 165
   tribe of, 41, 44, 176
Esarhaddon, 218, 221
Esther, 21, 88, 96, 111
Ethbaal, 61
ethics, 11
ethnicity, 125–126, 257 n.24, 284 nn.25–26,
   291 n.79
Evil-merodach, 71, 100
exile, 97, 99, 102, 109 (see also Judah, depor-
   tations from)
Exodus, book of, 167
Ezekiel, 80, 99, 222
   book of, 97, 109, 111, 208
Ezion-geber, 63, 91
Ezra, 16, 20, 96, 102–103, 107, 108, 109–110,
   238, 240
   book of, 97, 101, 102, 104, 106, 111, 237,
   277–278 n.84

Gad, tribe of, 41, 44
Galilee, 61, 67, 93, 165
Gath, 49, 65, 221
Gaza, 221
Geba, 61
Gedaliah, 97–98, 109, 220, 231
Gerar, 36
Gezer, 88, 91, 182, 187, 188

Gibbethon, 60, 89
Gibeah, 46, 92, 176
Gibeon, 39, 79, 192
Gibeonites, 40, 49
Gideon, 34, 42, 43
Gihon, 91
Gilead, 42, 44, 47, 67, 89, 165
Gilgal, 41
Greece, 106–107, 121, 140, 141, 142–143, 282
   n.9, 289 n.65
   and Persian empire, 141–142
Guti, 125

Hadad, 63
Haggai, 111–112
   book of, 97, 101, 109
Hamath, 48, 193, 194
Hammurabi, 123
Hanun, 90
Haran, 137, 197
Hasmoneans, 20, 96, 108, 144, 238, 242, 243,
   244, 249
Hatti, 132
Hazael, 63, 64, 65, 88, 193, 218
Hazor, 91, 182, 187, 188
Hebrew Bible
   and ancient Near Eastern literature,
   206–208
   ancient Near Eastern references in, 150
   canon of, 21, 96, 108, 259 n.28, 317 n.143
   colonial ideology of, 246
   composition of, 22, 96, 240–241
   compositors of, 2, 13, 97, 157
   historicity of, 2, 22–24, 28, 185, 261–262
   nn.33–34, 264 n.45
   and "legitimation crisis," 160–161
   as source of political information, 13,
   96–97, 185, 228, 238, 245, 246, 250
   as source for reconstructing history, 1, 252
   as source of religious authority, 30, 250
Hebron, 47, 48, 184, 191
Hellenistic kingdoms, 97, 107, 108, 111, 140,
   143–144, 148, 151, 167, 237, 238,
   242–243, 249, 282 n.9
Hezekiah, 57, 68–69, 74, 75, 80, 83, 84, 89,
   91, 94, 190, 191, 196, 200–201, 202, 210,
   221, 222, 226, 230
"high places," 33, 70, 80, 81, 82, 83, 84,
   226
Hiram, 93
historiography, 4, 24, 28–29, 246, 263 n.41
   "biblical," 13
   Hellenistic, 108
Hittites, 124, 132, 138, 282 n.9
Hosea, 222, 226, 234
Hoshea, 57, 67
"House of David" inscription, 182, 190, 193,
   199
Huldah, 85
Hushai, 49
Hyksos, 129–130, 132, 138

ideology
    and architecture, 92
    of author, 30–311
    and composition of Hebrew Bible, 2,
        22–23, 28, 246
    and history, 5–6, 29, 72, 263–264 n.41
    "holy war," 194
    and identity, 2
    of restoration, 98, 105, 239, 241
    and statehood, 156–157, 179–180, 184,
        211, 215, 221–222, 225, 244, 246
Imlah, Micaiah ben, 234
inscriptions, 190–198
Ira, 49
Iran, 121, 138, 140
Isaiah
    of the Exile, 88
    cc. 40–55, 97, 100, 111
    cc. 40–66, 109
    of Jerusalem, 74, 190, 191, 234
Ishbaal, 47
Ishmael, 98, 220
Isin, 123
Islam, 251
Israel
    as Assyrian province, 20, 67, 195
    fall of, 67, 68, 76, 90, 140, 153, 215, 244,
        248
    geography of, 151–152
    as inclusive community, 19–20, 52, 74–75,
        152, 217, 257 nn.23, 24
    multiple identities of, 17, 18, 21, 52–53,
        249, 255 n.16
    as northern kingdom, 16–17, 19, 34, 52–53,
        58, 61, 66, 76, 81, 83, 90, 93, 151, 152,
        161, 199, 204–210, 217–218, 223
    origins of, 36, 133, 138
    population of, 189–190
    relations with Judah, 89, 201, 212–216
    relations with other states, 216–227
    settlement patterns in, 187–190
"Israel/Israelite(s)," 17–18
Israel, state of, 250

Jabesh-gilead, 90
Jacob, as "Israel," 37
(Je)coniah (see Jehoiachin)
Jehoahaz (see also Ahaz)
    king of Israel, 56, 63, 64–65, 88
Jehoahaz=Ahaziah, 63, 64, 65, 76, 77, 89, 213,
        214, 217
Jehoahaz II=Shallum, 57, 69–70, 140
Jehoash (see also Joash)
    king of Israel, 56, 58, 64–65, 66, 84, 88, 89,
        213
Jehoiachin=(Je)coniah, 57, 69–70, 99–100, 198
Jehoiada, 48, 50, 65–66, 80, 84
Jehoiakim=Eliakim, 57, 59, 69–70, 91, 94, 140,
        219–220, 230
Jehoram, 56, 58, 63–64, 89, 213

Jehoshaphat, 49, 51, 52, 56, 62, 63, 84, 89, 91,
        214, 220, 233
Jehu, 56, 58, 63–65, 67, 73, 74, 77, 78, 80, 82,
        88, 89, 154, 193, 195, 202, 213, 214, 215,
        217–218
    House of, 76, 88, 90
Jehu ben Hanani, 234
Jephthah, 42, 43
Jeremiah, 70, 71, 98, 99, 234
    book of, 97, 109, 111, 191, 208
    Letter of, 259 n.27
Jericho, 39, 61, 168
Jeroboam I, 34, 51–52, 53, 55, 58, 59–60, 76,
        78, 79, 80, 82, 89, 91, 188, 209
Jeroboam II, 56, 58, 64–65,66, 67, 73, 191,
        202, 214, 218, 223, 230
Jerusalem, 36, 52, 59, 63, 65, 66, 68, 69, 75,
        77, 79, 83, 92, 93, 110, 182, 201,
        226–227, 241
    as David's capital, 48, 91, 177, 184
    resettlement of, 103
    sieges of, 89, 90, 190, 196, 197–198, 200,
        213, 220, 222, 224
    temple in, 70, 79, 81, 82, 84, 94, 111,
        179–180, 192, 208, 275 n.69
    and Zion tradition, 215
Jethro, 38
Jezebel, 61, 64, 77, 214, 215, 216, 217, 222
Jezreel, 62, 63, 233
Joab, 48, 49, 219, 228
Joash=Jehoash
    king of Judah, 56, 58, 65–66, 76, 77, 78, 84,
        88, 93, 195, 210, 218
Jonah, book of, 88
Jonah ben Amittai, 65
Jonathan, 46, 47
Joram, 56, 58, 62, 63–64, 76, 77, 78, 87, 89,
        96, 1944
Joseph, 36
    House of, 41
    tribe of, 44
Josephus, 237
Joshua, 39, 42, 43
    book of, 40, 41, 62, 194
    high priest, 102, 103, 104, 109
Josiah, 57, 69–70, 74, 77, 80, 82, 83, 85, 88,
        89, 91, 154, 197, 201, 202, 210, 223, 224,
        230, 233, 248
Jotham, 54, 57, 66, 68, 91, 220
Judah
    as Assyrian vassal, 197, 201, 215, 223
    deportations from, 71, 97, 98, 99–100, 104,
        138, 196, 310 n.89
    fall of, 71, 85, 90, 96, 97, 99, 140, 159–160,
        223, 238, 244
    in Hellenistic period, 21–22, 97, 104,
        106–108, 143, 151, 156, 238
    as Persian province, 16, 20, 97, 103, 104,
        107–110, 151, 154, 156, 236–239, 241,
        248

population of, 189–190, 237
relations with Israel, 89, 201, 212–216
relations with other states, 216–227
and religious legacy, 20, 21
restoration of, 21, 68, 97, 101–105, 109, 111–112, 141, 160, 239, 240–242, 249, 278–279 nn. 91–92
settlement patterns in, 187–190
as southern kingdom, 16, 19, 52, 58, 60, 61, 71, 80, 81, 93, 151, 161, 200, 201, 204–210
territory of, 95, 165
trade in, 201–202
tribe of, 41, 44, 47, 50
"Judah-ism(s)," 97, 240, 249, 252, 259–261, nn.30–31
"Judah/Judahite(s)," 17–18
"Judahite=Jew," 22
Judaism
contemporary, 251
rabbinic, 21, 251–252
judges, 38, 41–42, 44, 46, 63, 155 (*see also* kings, as judges)
Judges, book of, 40, 41, 42, 43, 64
justice, administration of, 232–235

Kassites, 124, 125, 132
Khirbet el-Qom inscriptions, 208
Kings
books of, 19, 34, 53, 54, 55, 59, 70, 72, 74, 79, 81–87, 95, 160, 191, 194, 196, 197, 198, 216, 217, 255 nn.16–17
kings
biblical presentation of, 73
building projects of, 78, 90–92, 137, 179, 186–187, 311 n.103
chronology of (*see* chronology)
economic policies of, 92–94, 202–203, 292 n.82, 294 n.89
as judges, 232–233
as reformers, 78, 154
sons of, 95
standards for, 74, 79, 80–82
Kirhareseth, 89
Kuntilleth 'Ajrud, 191, 201, 205, 208

Lachish, 66, 188, 191, 193, 196, 203, 208
Lamentations, 97, 98, 109, 111
Language (*see* statehood, language and)
Larsa, 123
law codes, 153–154, 155, 194, 233, 240, 289 n.611
Lebanon, 50
Levi, tribe of, 41, 44
Levitical priests, 41, 42, 103 (*see also* priest-hood)
Libnah, 64
"local-historical time," 11–12, 15, 27, 255 n.11

Maccabean revolt, 96, 109, 111, 242
Maccabees, books of, 96, 108, 237

Maacah, 61
Macedonian kingdom (*see* Greece)
Machir (*see* Manasseh, tribe of)
Malachi, 109
Manasseh
king of Judah, 57, 69–70, 73, 80, 81, 91
territory of, 67, 68, 165
tribe of, 41, 43, 44, 176
Marduk, 124, 137, 138
Mareshah, 60
Mari, 124
Mattaniah (*see* Zedekiah)
Medes, 137, 138
Megiddo, 70, 91, 182, 187, 188, 192, 197
Memphis, 128, 129
Menahem, 57, 58, 66–67, 70, 76, 94, 195, 224, 230
Mephibosheth=Meribaal, 47, 92
Meribaal (*see* Mephibosheth)
Merneptah stela, 163, 164, 166, 298 n.20
Merodach-baladan, 69, 94
Mesha
of Moab, 63, 87, 194, 219
stela, 194, 208, 221, 309 n.83
Mesopotamia, 27, 36, 67, 95, 121, 134, 140, 150, 172, 210, 281 n.9, 290 n.73
administration in, 123, 124
centralized power in, 130
decentralized power in, 133
diplomacy in, 133
economics in, 122, 123, 124, 283 n.22
ideology of, 123, 125
immigrants in, 125
influence of, 127, 128
literacy in, 122
religion in, 122, 123, 125, 147
trade in, 122, 124
tribute in, 122, 124, 127
methods in biblical studies
cultural criticism, 4
historical criticism, 1, 32, 159, 266 n.4
ideological criticism, 246, 264 n.44
literary criticism, 4, 5, 32
Micah, 61, 234
Middle Babylonian period, 124
Midian, 43
Midianites, 38, 167–168, 175, 299 n.24
Miriam, 164
Mitanni, 124, 132
Mizpah, 61, 98, 236
Moab, 48, 61, 80, 87, 89, 90, 93, 98, 133, 179, 194, 197, 200, 214, 216, 217, 219–221, 314 n.119
Moabites, 167–168, 175
monarchy, 2, 13, 15–16, 24, 42–43, 227, 243–245, 295 n.5
biblical critique of, 154
and continuity, 154–155, 178
divided, 18, 33, 52–71, 74, 95, 151, 152, 165, 198, 222

(monarchy *continued*)
  postexilic view of, 161–162
  traditions of, 85
  united, 17, 18, 47–52, 79, 151, 161,
    178–182, 198, 214, 244, 304 n.49
  and women, 164
monumental architecture, 182, 205 (*see also*
    kings, building projects of)
Moses, 37, 38, 39, 41, 42, 43, 68, 80
Mt. Ebal, 165
"myth of the empty land," 98, 104, 105
myths, 117

Naaman, 88
Nabonidus, 137, 138
Naboth, 62, 233
Nadab, 55, 59–60
Nahash, 90
Naram-Sin, 122
Nathan, 48, 51, 234
Nebuchadnezzar, 70, 71, 97, 99–100, 111,
    137, 198, 219, 220
Neco, 59, 70, 85, 88, 140, 197, 224
Nehemiah, 16, 20, 96, 102–103, 105, 107–110,
    238
  book of, 97, 101, 102, 104–106, 111, 237,
    277–278 n.84
Neo-Assyrian empire, 19, 67, 126, 134–137,
    138, 140, 148, 192–194, 197, 200–201,
    203, 215, 217–220, 224–226, 288
    nn.50–52 (*see also* Assyria)
Neo-Babylonian Chronicles, 197–198
Neo-Babylonian empire, 70, 88, 89, 90, 94,
    95, 97, 99, 137–138, 140, 167, 191, 197,
    217, 218–219, 223–224, 241, 249, 282
    n.9, 288 nn.53–54
Nineveh, 197
Nob, priests of, 47
northern kingdom (*see* Israel)
Nubia, 129

Og, 38
Old Babylonian period, 123–124, 126, 132,
    284–285 n.27
Omri, 55, 56, 58, 61, 65, 73, 91, 93, 199–200,
    215, 223, 231
  House of, 53, 63, 64, 76, 88, 89, 90, 93,
    184, 187, 194, 202, 213–214, 217, 219,
    230
Onias, Simon ben, 238
Ophir, 91

Palestine, 21, 70, 139, 150, 192, 194, 196, 219
    (*see also* Syro-Palestine)
Pekah, 57, 58, 67, 68, 87, 88, 89, 195, 213
Pekahiah, 57, 58, 66–67
Pelethites, 50
Pentateuch, 242
  composition of, 167, 295 n.3
  dating of, 295 n.2

Priestly source of, 97
Penuel, 59, 91
"people of the land," 71, 101, 104, 154, 210,
    228, 231
Persian empire, 97, 100–101, 148, 236, 249,
    282 n.9
  administration of, 140–142, 289 n.60
  biblical assessment of, 101–106, 111
  and Greece, 141–142
  and religion, 142
Philistia, 66, 93, 143, 184, 197, 201, 205, 214,
    218, 221, 314–315 n.122
Philistines, 41, 45, 47, 48, 63, 68, 69, 87,
    166–167, 168, 172, 175, 222
philosophy of history, 4
Phoenicia, 50, 77, 93, 106, 121, 133, 134, 141,
    143, 187, 193, 197, 205, 209, 219, 281
    n.8, 314 n.118
political history of ancient Israel, 6, 17, 255
    n.13
  in ancient Near Eastern context, 2,
    150–157, 192–198
  as "confusing montage," 71–74
  and contemporary politics, 250
  and power, 5, 317–318 n.145
  sources for, 71–72
  traditional approach to, 1, 24
political philosophy, 11
political power, 9
  assassination and, 76–78, 155, 213, 218,
    220, 225, 228–229, 231, 272 n.48
  and the state, 8, 9, 75–78
political theology, 225–227, 244
politics (*see also* ancient Near East; colonial
    period, Israelite; monarchy; statehood;
    tribal period)
  comparative, 12, 120–121, 203–210
  definition of, 7
  relationship to power, 7, 10, 211–212
  study of, 9, 10–11
Pompey, 243
positivism, 13–14
power
  definition of, 7
  relationship to politics, 7–8, 10, 211–212,
    254 n.9, 287 n.47
prestate traditions, Israelite, 158–172 (*see
    also* tribal period, tribes)
  reliability of, 160, 162–169
  survival of, 161, 168–169, 300 n.29
  theories about, 159–160
priesthood, 37, 38, 44, 46, 79, 103, 165, 243
    (*see also* Levitical priests)
prophets
  social location of, 234
  and state politics, 45, 231, 234–235
Proverbs, 45, 95
Psalms, 45, 97, 156, 225
Pseudepigrapha (*see* Apocrypha and
    Pseudepigrapha)
Ptolemies (*see* Hellenistic kingdoms)

Qarqar, battle of, 54, 192–193, 220
Qaus, 192
Qumran, 259 n.27

Ra (see Amon-Ra)
Rahab, 39
Ramah, 60–61
Ramoth-Gilead, 62, 63, 64, 89
Rehoboam, 52, 53, 55, 59, 60, 80, 82, 83, 88, 96, 192
religion, Israelite
  and identity, 247
  influence on history, 3
  and literature, 208
  reform of, 226–227, 230, 293–294 n.85
  relationship to politics, 3, 13–15, 34, 35, 156–157, 185, 191–192, 209, 225–227, 243–245, 246, 250, 250
Reuben, tribe of, 41
Rezin, 67, 68, 76, 87, 88, 213
Roman empire, 140, 144, 167, 243
Ruth, 40

Samaria, 16–17, 20, 21, 34, 54, 61, 62, 64, 67, 77, 78, 80, 82, 86, 89, 90–93, 103, 104, 110, 199, 200, 202, 215, 226
Samarian Ostraca, 190
Samarians=Samaritans, 104, 110, 258 n.25
Samson, 41
Samuel, 41, 42, 43, 46, 62, 72, 222, 235
  books of, 40, 46, 72, 194
Sanballat, 104, 237
Sargon, 122, 219
Sargon II, 195–196, 221
satraps, 141
Saul, 18, 25, 46–47, 49, 54, 62, 72, 79, 87, 92, 168, 172, 176–177
  House of, 74
Seleucids (see Hellenistic kingdoms)
Sennacherib, 69, 84, 90, 193, 196, 202, 221
Seraiah, 49
settlement (see Canaan, settlement of)
Shallum (see also Jehoahaz II)
  king of Israel, 57, 58, 66–67
  king of Judah, 57, 58
Shalmaneser III, 192–193, 195, 202, 220
Shalmaneser V, 67, 195, 218
Shaphan, 228
Sheba, 50, 178
  of Benjamin, 48, 49
  queen of, 88
Shebna, 190
Shechem, 34, 36, 42, 43, 52, 59, 91, 215
Shemaiah ben Nehelam, 99
Sheshbazzar, 102, 103, 109
Sheshonk I (see Shishak)
Sheva (see Seraiah)
Shiloh, 215
Shisha, 51
Shishak=Sheshonk I, 60, 83, 88, 192, 199, 200, 223

Sidon, 195, 216, 218
Sihon, 38
Simeon, tribe of, 41, 44
Sin, 137
Sinai, 38, 129
Sisera, 44
  mother of, 43
social sciences, 4, 158, 183, 262 n.37
Sodom, 36
Solomon, 18, 33–34, 48, 54, 59, 63, 75, 77, 79, 81, 83, 87, 91, 92, 93, 179–180, 183–184, 187, 202, 216, 218, 219, 235, 248
  Acts of (see Acts of Solomon)
  administration of, 49–52, 94–95, 267 n.11
  decline of, 51–52
  succession of, 49
southern kingdom (see Judah)
statehood, ancient Near Eastern
  administration, 114, 124, 145–146, 290 n.70
  economics in, 113, 124, 145
  Egyptian, 113, 114 (see also Egypt)
  formation of, 113–119, 279–280 nn.2–3, 305 n.53
  and imperialism, 147–148
  and language, 149
  legitimation of, 114
  Mesopotamian, 113, 114, 124–125 (see also Mesopotamia)
  opposition to, 117–119, 316 n.130
  religion and, 146–147
  social contexts of, 119, 148–149
  as social organization, 116–118
  and trade, 113
statehood, Israelite, 10, 32, 35, 37, 45, 71, 150–157, 225
  administration of, 94–96, 229, 276–277 nn. 74–75, 316 n.126
  definition of, 8, 9
  and diplomacy, 87–90, 180
  and economics (see kings, economic policies of)
  formation of, 25, 46, 150, 152, 161, 172–176, 181, 186, 223, 304 n.47
  and literacy, 203–204, 248, 311 n.99
  opposition to, 117–118
  political center of, 227–235
  and power, 150, 230
  and religion, 78–87, 157, 225–227, 248, 311 n.101 (see also political theology)
  and revenue, 276 n.73
  traditions about, 45, 152
  and warfare, 87–90
Syria, 50, 65, 70, 89, 92, 93, 123, 124, 133, 134, 138, 139, 150, 193, 210, 223
Syro-Palestine, 27, 67, 69, 88, 90, 103, 121, 129, 132, 134, 138–140, 147, 153, 172, 192, 195, 198, 209, 214, 223, 225, 239

Tabeel, son of, 213
Tamar, 48

Tamir, 91
Tammuz, 80
Tanis, 138
Tappuah, 67
tel, 99
Tel Dan stela (*see* "House of David" inscription)
Tell Beydar, 124
Tell en-Nasbeh (*see* Mizpah)
Tell Mozan, 124
Tel Qasile, 201
Thebes, 129, 138
Thebez, 42
Tibni, 55, 56, 58, 61, 231
Tiglath-pileser III, 67, 68, 134, 195, 218, 219, 220, 221, 223
Tirzah, 59, 91
Tobiah, 104–105
Tobit, 259 n.27
traditions (*see also* prestate traditions, Israelite)
  and archaeology, 23
  and cult, 85–86
  decline of, 97
  and history, 24
  and ideology, 22
  and political history, 26, 85
  in postexilic period, 23, 109, 241
  and religion, 33, 222
  tribal, 44–45, 75, 152
tribal confederacy, 18, 43, 151, 161, 173
  origins of, 35, 134, 223
tribal period, 15–16, 17, 24–25, 32, 117, 150, 205, 246
  decentralized politics in, 40, 43, 162–163, 170, 172
  theoretical models for, 170–1711
tribes, 40, 44, 164
  definition of, 35
  eponymous progenitors of, 37
  leadership of, 36, 38, 42, 43–44, 163, 267 n.10

and religion, 164–165, 169, 171, 247, 301 n.35
social organization of, 40, 44–45, 169, 253 n.1, 266 n.4, 300 n.31
tribute, 223–224, 309 nn.85–86
Tyre, 50, 51, 61, 88, 93, 106, 184, 195, 200, 202, 214, 217, 219, 314 n.118

Ugarit, 133
Ur III, 123, 126, 132, 284–285 n.27
Uriah, 70
Uzziah (*see* Azariah)

wisdom, 181, 242
women, status and role of, 164, 296–297 nn.10–11
"world-historical time," 11–12, 15, 27, 31, 113, 120, 171–172, 254–255 n.11, 280–281 n.7

Yavneh-Yam, 191, 203

Zabud, 51
Zadok, 51
Zalmunna, 43
Zeba, 43
Zechariah
  book of, 97, 101, 109
  king of Israel, 57, 66–67
  prophet, 111–112
  son of Jehoiada, 66, 84
Zedekiah=Mattaniah, 57, 69–71, 89, 99, 219, 225
Zenon papyri, 237
Zephaniah, 234
Zerah, 60
Zerubbabel, 101, 102, 103, 104, 109, 111
Zeruiah, 48
Ziba, 92
Ziklag, 92
Zimri, 56, 60, 61
Zobah, 48, 87
Zoroastrianism, 142